Consular Jurisdiction

Legal History Library

VOLUME 83

Studies in the History of International Law

VOLUME 30

The titles published in this series are listed at *brill.com/shil*

Consular Jurisdiction

On the History of the Judicial Functions of Consulates (12th–20th Centuries)

Edited by

Lars Regula and Jörg Ulbert

BRILL | NIJHOFF

LEIDEN | BOSTON

ISSN 1874-1793
ISBN 978-90-04-75518-5
ISBN 978-90-04-75519-2 (PDF)
DOI https://doi.org/10.1163/9789004755192

Library of Congress Control Number: 2026931259

Brill and Koninklijke Brill BV are part of De Gruyter Brill.
www.degruyterbrill.com

Questions about General Product Safety Regulation: productsafety@degruyterbrill.com.

Contents

PART 2
The Ottoman Empire and North Africa

PART 3
Asia and Africa

Acknowledgements

The present volume is based primarily on a conference held under the same name from 2 November to 4 November 2023, in Hamburg. Our thanks therefore go first and foremost to the organisations and institutions that contributed to the success of this event. This especially includes the *Université franco-allemande*, the *Deutsche Forschungsgemeinschaft* (DFG), the *Akademie der Wissenschaften in Hamburg*, and the *École française de Rome*.

We would also like to express our gratitude to the staff of Brill Publishers for kindly including this volume in their catalogue. Particular thanks are due to Mr. Maurits van den Boogert, who supported and welcomed the publication project from the very beginning. We would also like to thank Professor Randall C. H. Lesaffer for including the volume in the series.

On a personal note, I would like to thank my Ph.D. supervisor, Professor Tilman Repgen, without whose support this project would not have been successful. Finally, my personal thanks go to my co-organiser, Mr. Arnaud Bartolomei, and especially to my co-organiser and co-editor, Mr. Jörg Ulbert. As a young academic, it is by no means a given to be able to work so closely with the established scholars in one's field of interest. I am very grateful for the trust that particularly Jörg has been placed in me.

Lars Regula
Hamburg, 2025

Maps, Figures, and Tables

Maps

Figures

Tables

Notes on Contributors

Marcella Aglietti
is a full professor in the History of Political Institutions at the Department of Political Science, University of Pisa (Italy). Her research focuses on comparative history of political institutions and governmental practices, history of consular institutions, procedures for the recognition and naturalisation of citizenship, and history of ruling elites. Among her publications: *L'istituto consolare tra Sette e Ottocento* (Pisa, 2012); *In nome della neutralità. Storia politico-istituzionale di Spagna durante la prima guerra mondiale* (Rome, 2017); with Fabrice Jesné and Mathieu Grenet (ed.), *Consoli e consolati italiani dagli Stati preunitari al fascismo* (1802–1945) (Roma, 2020); and *Citizenship under pressure. Naturalisation policies from the late XIX century until the aftermath of World War I* (Rome, 2021).

Eleonora Angella
is a post-doctoral researcher at the Università per Stranieri in Siena. After completing a Ph.D. in International Studies at the University of Naples "L'Orientale," she held positions as a visiting scholar at the University of Bern (2021–2022) and as a post-doctoral researcher at the Università della Tuscia in Viterbo (2022–2023). Her research examines the lives of the Italians in Egypt during the late nineteenth century, with particular attention to the impact of extraterritoriality on social history, the agency of subalterns within the justice system, and the history of the Italian consulate in Cairo. She is the author of the monograph *Italiani al Cairo. Consoli, giurisdizione e società* (Palermo: New Digital Frontiers, 2023/2024).

Arnaud Bartolomei
Ancien membre de la Casa de Velázquez, Arnaud Bartolomei est actuellement professeur d'histoire moderne et contemporaine à l'Université Côte d'Azur et membre du Centre de la Méditerranée Moderne et Contemporaine. Il a co-dirigé trois publications consacrées à l'institution des consuls des étrangers (« La chancellerie consulaire française (XVIe–XXe siècle) : attributions, organisation, agents, usagers », *MEFRIM*, 2016, *De l'utilité commerciale des consuls. L'institution consulaire et les marchands dans le monde méditerranéen (XVIIe–XIXe siècle)*, 2018, « Stratégies identitaires et procédures d'identification des étrangers en Espagne, dans l'Amérique hispanique et en Méditerranée (XVIIe–XIXe siècle) », *Mélanges de la Casa de Velázquez*, 2021). Il travaille actuellement à l'édition d'un ouvrage dédié à l'ouverture commerciale du

Mexique au moment de son indépendance (*À l'aube de la mondialisation contemporaine. Exclusifs coloniaux et liberté du commerce dans l'Atlantique hispanique, 1750–1850*, en cours).

Thibault Bechini
Docteur en histoire de l'Université Paris 1 Panthéon-Sorbonne, Thibault Bechini a soutenu en 2020 une thèse intitulée *Des villes migrantes : Marseille, Buenos Aires. Construire et habiter les périphéries urbaines au temps des migrations italiennes (1860–1914)*, récompensée par le prix d'histoire sociale de la Fondation Mattei Dogan, le prix d'histoire de la Société française d'histoire urbaine et le prix du Comité des travaux historiques et scientifiques. Il est actuellement membre scientifique de l'École française de Rome.

Giorgio Ennas
is a Postdoctoral Fellow at the University of Utrecht (UU) and an affiliated scholar at Franklin University Switzerland (FUS). His fields of interest are the history of knowledge, diplomacy and health in the Mediterranean during the nineteenth and twentieth centuries, with particular reference to the relations between the Ottoman Empire and the European countries in the Balkan area and in North Africa, particularly with Italy and Switzerland. Between 2021 and 2023, he has worked as the Principal Investigator (PI) of a two-year project entitled *Pandemics and Borders* funded by the Swiss Network for International Studies (SNIS). Between 2023 and 2025, he worked as the PI and Research Associate (AR) of research projects funded by the Giunta Centrale per gli Studi Storici (GCSS) of Rome and the Laboratorio di Storia delle Alpi (LabisAlp) of the University of Italian Switzerland (USI). Since September 2024, he works as postdoctoral fellow at the University of Utrecht in the ERC project *Fighting Pandemics from Below* led by Ozan Ozavci (UU). In 2026, he published with Bloomsbury his first monograph entitled *Italo-Ottoman Relations in the Age of the Congress of Paris. Mirroring the 'Other', 1856–1871.*

Ana Belem Fernández Castro
is a postdoc researcher at the Scuola Superiore Meridionale in Naples. She got her Ph.D. in History and Civilization at the European University Institute in Florence. She is interested in commercial legal history, legal institutions, and the support of long-distance trade in early modern times. She is the author of the book *Justicia, Comercio e Instituciones en la Carrera de Indias. Siglo XVI* (Presses de l'Université de Toulouse Capitole, 2024).

Juliette Françoise
is completing a joint Ph.D. at the University of Geneva and the University Paris 1 Panthéon-Sorbonne. She is interested in the monetary history of the early modern French empire, with a particular focus on the French presence in Asia. Her thesis examines the nature and the effects of liquidity provision by the French State to finance trade and war overseas and govern and rule the settlements it conquered or acquired in Asia. Her research aims to redefine the workings of the French Empire through the lens of money.

Laura Galoppini
Ph.D. in medieval history at the University of Ghent, is Associate Professor of Medieval History at the University of Pisa. Her studies and main research topics concern the Tuscan mercantile presence in the Late Middle Ages, in the Mediterranean area (Sardinia, Catalonia), and north of the Alps with particular attention to the Lucca presence in Flanders. Among her main publications: *Mercanti toscani e Bruges nel tardo Medioevo* (Pisa: Edizioni Plus, Pisa University Press, 2009); *I Parlamenti dei viceré Angelo di Vilanova (1518–1523 e 1528) e Martino Cabrero (1530)*, 2 vol. (Cagliari: Consiglio Regionale della Sardegna, 2016).

Sacha Gauthier Olssy
est diplômé d'un master en Sciences historique obtenu à l'université Nice-Côte d'Azur en 2022. Durant ce master il a écrit un mémoire intitulé « La juridiction consulaire dans la concession française de Tianjin entre 1900 et 1943 ».

Thomas Gidney
is an international historian whose research focuses on the impact of colonial politics on international relations. His first book, *An International Anomaly: Colonial Accession to the League of Nations*, examines the British Empire's promotion of colonies to international organisations, and this reconceptualises perceptions of international recognition and inter-state sovereignty. He completed his Ph.D. at the Graduate Institute of Geneva and is currently a visiting fellow at the University of Geneva.

Berna Kamay Ulusay
is a lecturer at Sabancı University, Foundations Development Programme (FDP), where she offers courses on the Ottoman Empire, the Turkish Republic, and World History. She received her Ph.D. in History from Boğaziçi University in 2022 with a dissertation entitled "Extradition in the Ottoman International

Legal Practice of the Nineteenth Century." Her research focuses on legal history in the Ottoman Empire and Early Turkish Republic, international law, and the politics of legal belonging. She is particularly interested in diplolegal encounters and the ways in which property rights and nationality were negotiated across imperial and trans-imperial contexts. One of her recent publications, *The Ottoman Empire, the United States, and the Legal Battle over Extradition: The 'Kelly Affair,'* has been published in *New Perspectives on Turkey.*

Jessica Marglin
is Professor of Religion, Law, and History, and the Ruth Ziegler Chair in Jewish Studies at the University of Southern California. She earned her Ph.D. from Princeton and her BA and MA from Harvard. Her research focuses on the history of Jews and Muslims in North Africa and the Mediterranean, with a particular emphasis on law.

Cédric Quertier
Chargé de recherche au CNRS (LAMOP – UMR 8589), ancien membre de l'École Française de Rome et de la Villa i Tatti, Cédric Quertier coordonne le projet ANR ECOMED (Les économies méditerranéennes à la fin du Moyen Âge [1350–1500] : crises, reconstructions, restructurations). Spécialiste de la régulation judiciaire des conflits marchands, des nations marchandes et des migrations, il a notamment publié *Guerres et richesses d'une nation. Les Florentins à Pise au XIVe siècle* (Publication de l'École française de Rome, 2022) et, avec Marie Dejoux, Harmony Dewez et Emmanuel Huertas, *Les fruits de la terre. Études d'histoire médiévale offertes à Laurent Feller* (Éditions de la Sorbonne, 2023).

Lars Regula
studied law and Middle Eastern Studies at the University of Hamburg. His Ph.D. thesis deals with the German consular jurisdiction in the Ottoman Empire between 1761 and 1917.

Victor Simon
Agrégé des facultés de droit, Victor Simon est professeur d'Histoire du droit à l'Université de Lille et membre du Centre d'histoire judiciaire (UMR 8025). Il a notamment publié un ouvrage sur *Les échelles du Levant et de Barbarie : droit du commerce international entre la France et l'Empire ottoman (XVIe–XVIIIe siècle*). Ses recherches portent plus largement sur l'histoire du droit des affaires, l'histoire de la justice commerciale ou l'histoire du droit des sociétés.

Jörg Ulbert
est maître de conférences d'allemand à l'Université Bretagne Sud. Ses recherches portent essentiellement sur l'histoire des services consulaires français à l'époque moderne. Ses publications peuvent être consultées à l'adresse suivante : https://univ-ubs.academia.edu/JörgUlbert.

Dominique Valérian
Ancien membre de l'École française de Rome, Dominique Valérian est professeur d'histoire médiévale à l'Université Paris 1 Panthéon-Sorbonne et directeur de l'équipe Islam médiéval de l'UMR 8167 Orient et Méditerranée. Il est spécialiste de l'Islam et de la Méditerranée au Moyen Âge, notamment des relations entre chrétiens et musulmans. Il a publié notamment *Bougie, port maghrébin. 1067–1510* (Rome : EFR, 2006) et *Ports et réseaux d'échanges dans le Maghreb médiéval* (Madrid : Casa de Velázquez, 2019), et coédité *Le détroit de Gibraltar. À la croisée des mers et des continents (Antiquité – Moyen Âge)* (Toulouse, Madrid : Presses Universitaires du Midi, Casa de Velázquez, 2022).

Glossary

Actor sequitur forum rei Lat. "The plaintiff follows the court of the defendant" is a procedural legal principle whereby the lawsuit must be filed at the residence of the defendant.

ʿAhdnāme, imtiyāzāt Ott., Arab. "letter of promise," see "capitulation".

Amān Arab. "safety," protection letter that turns a *ḥarbī* (see below) in the *dār al-ʾIslam* (see below) into a *mustʾamīn* (see below)

Arbitration Private dispute resolution based on an arbitration agreement.

Assessor In France: An assistant judge.
In Common Law: Lay judge.
In Germany: A lawyer with the second bar exam.

Bureau Consultatif Department in the Ottoman Ministry of Foreign Affairs for international law issues.

Chargé d'affaires The lowest class of envoys.

Consolat de mar Cata. "Consulate of the Sea," quasi-judicial body of the Crown of Aragon for maritime and commercial affairs.

Consular handbooks Handbooks on consular law, diplomatic protocols, etc.

Dār al-Ḥarb Arab. "House of War," opposite of *dār al-ʾIslam* (see below).

Dār al-ʾIslam Arab. "House of Islam," region where *sharīʿa* (see below) applies.

Dhimmīs Arab. "Protected subjects," non-Muslims residing permanently in the *dār al-ʾIslam* (see above) and subject to the *ǧizya*.

English School of Thought Current within international relations that envisions a society of states based on values, norms, and institutions.

Equity From Lat. *aequitas* = "Justice of the individual case," in Common Law the counterpart to positive law.

Extraterritoriality The application of one's own law on foreign territory.

Forum shopping The opportune exploitation of different jurisdictions.

Ḥarbī From Arab. *ḥarb* = war, inhabitant of the *dār al-ḥarb.*

Hong Chinese merchant guild authorised to trade with foreigners.

Institut de Droit international Institute founded in Ghent in 1873 for the advancement of international law.

Juez conservador Judge in Spain dealing with foreign affairs.

Jus gentium Lat. "law of the people," opposite of Roman civil law, meaning the law common to all peoples and applicable to non-citizens.

League of Nations International organisation, predecessor organisation of the United Nations.

Locus regit actum Lat. "The place governs the action," legal principle.

Millet From Arab. “community,” non-Muslim community in the Ottoman Empire

Mixed Tribunal A court with international participation.

Must'amīn Holder of an *amān* (above), non-Muslim staying temporarily in *dār al-'Islam* and not subject to *ğizya.*

Nation Designation of a foreign community.

***Nizamiye* courts** Secular courts during the Tanzimat period.

Ordonnance Historically a general law for the entire kingdom as opposed to a specific edict.

Permanent Court of International Justice International court, predecessor court of the International Court of Justice.

Prises Part of the laws of war regulating measures against civilian ships.

Protégés, *Schutzgenossenschaft* Foreigners under the (international legal) protection of a state.

Qadi Designation of an Islamic judge.

Reichsgericht The highest German criminal and civil court until 1945.

Sharīʿa Islamic law.

Tanzimat Name of the reform period in the Ottoman Empire.

Introduction

Lars Regula

> Les attributions d'un consul sont variées à l'infini .... Les consuls sont dans le cas d'exercer dans l'étendue de leur arrondissement, vis-à-vis de leurs compatriotes, les fonctions de juges, d'arbitres, de conciliateurs; souvent, ils sont officiers de l'état-civil; ils remplissent l'emploi de notaires, quelquefois celui d'administrateurs de la marine; ils surveillent et constatent l'état sanitaire; ce sont eux qui, par leurs relations habituelles, peuvent donner une idée juste et complète de la situation du commerce, de la navigation et de l'industrie particulière au pays de leur résidence.
>
> CHARLES MAURICE DE TALLEYRAND-PÉRIGORD, *Éloge de M. le comte Reinhard* (Paris: Gabriel Warée, 1838), 15–6

Talleyrand knew how to flatter. On the occasion of the death of the Franco-German diplomat Count Karl Friedrich Reinhard, Talleyrand emphasised in his eulogy delivered before the *Académie des sciences morales et politiques* the breadth of the consular profession.[1] Indeed, the words of France's most famous foreign minister contained much truth. The scope of consuls' duties was immense.[2] Throughout their history, they served as community leaders, liaisons to the economy and navy, as well as notary officers. "A consul was," wrote the German consul Gustav Humbert, "in terms of work, a jack-of-all-trades."[3] Yet, one function has received particularly little attention in scholarly discourse: the legal one. Consular jurisdiction typically elicits shrugs even from

1 Charles-Maurice de Talleyrand, *Éloge de M. le Comte Reinhard* (Paris: Gabriel Warée, 1838), 15–16.

2 For the different aspects of consular work, cf. Jörg Ulbert, "La fonction consulaire à l'époque moderne: définition, état des connaissances et perspectives de recherche," in *La fonction consulaire à l'époque moderne: L'affirmation d'une institution économique et politique (1500–1800)*, eds. Jörg Ulbert and Gérard Le Bouëdec (Rennes: Presses universitaires de Rennes, 2006).

3 Gustav Humbert, *Konstantinopel, London, Smyrna*: *Skizzen aus dem Leben eines kaiserlich deutschen Auslandsbeamten* (Berlin: Hochschule und Ausland, 1927), Preface.

 | HTTPS://DOI.ORG/10.1163/9789004755192-002

specialised audiences. Jurists, whose training focuses on current law, have long forgotten it, and among historians, legal matters provoke bewilderment. Therefore, this volume aims to make an interdisciplinary contribution to this mysterious consular function.

1 What Were the "Juridical Functions" of Consulates?

When we speak of "juridical functions," we primarily mean three things: the function as a court (1.1), the role of consulates as arbitration tribunals (1.2), and their general administrative tasks (1.3).

1.1 *The Function of a Court*

One passage in Talleyrand's obituary may seem particularly strange to the modern reader: the function of a judge. Judges are called upon to administer justice. This usually takes place in an adversarial procedure, in which the will of the parties plays only a limited role. A decision can, of course, be rendered even if one party does not agree.[4] Generally, a distinction is made between civil, criminal, and administrative jurisdiction, although only the first two branches are relevant for consular jurisdiction. A defining characteristic of civil proceedings is that two legally equal parties are in dispute with one another. Criminal proceedings concern the prosecution of offenses, with consular criminal proceedings continuing to exhibit characteristics of a private action or a classic inquisitorial process even at a later time, since a public prosecuting authority never developed.[5]

Which law consuls, acting as judges, could apply naturally depends greatly on the respective legal-historical period and can only be briefly highlighted here. Until modern times, law was generally something highly local and shaped by regional customs.[6] Voltaire famously mocked this in his *Dictionnaire philosophique*, under the entry "des loix," where he ridiculed the 25 supposedly distinct customary laws in effect solely in Paris.[7] On this basis, establishing a uniform consular jurisdiction was naturally difficult. The hypothesis that at least a more uniform substantive commercial law may have developed through long-

---

4 In contrast to abitration, cf. below.

5 Cf. Johannes Berchtold, *Recht und Gerechtigkeit in der Konsulargerichtsbarkeit: Britische Exterritorialität im Osmanischen Reich 1825–1914* (Munich: Oldenbourg, 2009), 141–144.

6 Tilman Repgen, "Ius Commune," in *Usus modernus pandectarum: Römisches Recht, Deutsches Recht und Naturrecht in der Frühen Neuzeit*, eds. Hans-Peter Haferkamp and Tilman Repgen (Köln: Böhlau, 2007), 164–165.

7 Voltaire, *Dictionnaire philosophique, ou la raison par alphabet* (London: s.n., 1770), 2:19.

distance trade is certainly plausible. However, legal historical research has largely dispelled the enthusiasm for a universally valid *Lex mercatoria*.[8] It was only with the natural law codification efforts beginning in the eighteenth century that the normative framework was created to ensure a uniform national consular jurisdiction.[9]

As "exterritorial" courts of the home state, the consular courts were subject to the laws of their home countries in organisation and legal application.[10] From the eighteenth century onwards, various states began to put their courts on a legal basis. The most important ones are:

For France: The *Édit du Roi* from June 1778[11]
For England: The Foreign Jurisdiction Act from 1843 (6&7 Vict c 94)
For Austria: The *Kaiserliche Verordnung* from 29.01.1855
For Italy: The *Legge Consolare* from 28.01.1866
For Germany: The *Gesetz über die Konsulargerichtsbarkeit* from 1879.

---

8 Albrecht Cordes, "Auf der Suche nach der Rechtswirklichkeit der mittelalterlichen Lex mercatoria," *Zeitschrift der Savigny Stiftung für Rechtsgeschichte* (*Germanistische Abteilung*) 118 (2001): 168–184 = "The search for a medieval *Lex mercatoria*," in *From* lex mercatoria *to commercial law*, ed. Vito Piergiovanni (Berlin: Duncker & Humblot, 2005), 53–68 = "À la recherche d'une Lex mercatoria au Moyen Âge," in *Stadt und Recht im Mittelalter*, eds. Pierre Monnet and Otto Gerhard Oexle (Göttingen: Vandenhoeck & Ruprecht, 2003), 117–132; Albrecht Cordes, "Jenseits des Lex mercatoria-Mythos," in *100 Jahre Rechtswissenschaft in Frankfurt: Erfahrungen, Herausforderungen, Erwartungen*, ed. Fachbereich Rechtswissenschaft der Goethe-Universität Frankfurt am Main (Frankfurt: Vittorio Klostermann, 2014), 390; Éric Marquer, "Doux commerce et droit naturel: la fable de la lex mercatoria," *Astérion*, n° 20 (2019), https://doi.org/10.4000/asterion.3829.

9 For the fruits of this process, cf. Jessica Marglin, "Nationalizing Consular Jurisdiction in the Nineteenth-Century Middle East and North Africa," in *this volume*, 275–294.

10 In the course of this volume I follow a rather modern distinction between the terms "*ex*territoriality" and "*extra*territoriality." While the first one describes the concept that the law of the sending state is applied abroad, as it was the case with consular courts, the second one means that a state applies its law to matters that have no domestic connections whatsoever, as the United States do it, for example, with their Foreign Corrupt Practice Act of 1977 (15 U.S.C. §78dd-1 et seq.), cf. Claudia Kurkin, *Extraterritorialität: Eine Kategorie des transnationalen Rechts* (Tübingen: Mohr Siebeck, 2021), 46–48; Kevin Li, *Reconceiving Extraterritorial Jurisdiction: From Formality to Function* (Baden-Baden: Nomos, 2022), 22–24. This (modern) distinction is, however, not commonly made. Marglin, "Nationalizing Consular Jurisdiction," 275–294, for example, is using "*extra*territoriality."

11 The first legal foundation for the French consular jurisdiction was actually the Grande Ordonnance de la Marine from 31.07.1681. Unlike the Édit du Roi, the Ordonnance de la Marine presupposed consular jurisdiction without regulating any details. The Édit du Roi is thus more comparable to the other laws cited.

Thus, consulates functioned as "normal courts" for the longest time of their history. When contemporaries spoke of "consular jurisdiction," they primarily meant this judicial function.

Finally, courts are usually part of a hierarchy of instances, in which judgments are reviewed for legal errors. Here, too, it naturally depends on the particular legal-historical period. In general, however, a three-tiered system of appeals can be distinguished between appellation (second instance) and cassation (third instance). The appellate instance reviews the judgment both in terms of facts and law, which may require a completely new taking of evidence. Cassation, by contrast, examines a judgment solely for legal errors. Consular courts could – at least in theory – also assume the function of an appellate court.[12]

1.2 *Consulates as Arbitration Tribunals*

Arbitration refers to a dispute resolution mechanism based on an arbitration agreement. The parties are not bound by the law that state courts must apply, but can instead determine the applicable law themselves in their agreement. As it is a private form of dispute resolution, it is only natural that this discreet form leaves fewer traces. However, sources suggest that consuls also acted as arbitrators.

Before the *Édit du Roi* of June 1778 detailed the French consular jurisdiction, the older provision of Lib. I Tit. IX Art. XII of the *Grande Ordonnance de la Marine* of July 31, 1681, was interpreted by French commentators as opening up arbitration primarily to the French consuls.[13] However, even later, consuls were still readily granted the function of arbitrators. For example, the *Dictionnaire des chancelleries diplomatiques et consulaires* of the mid-nineteenth century spoke openly about how the consular arbitration office had the advantage that French citizens would not need to turn to local courts.[14] The German consular law even explicitly provided for the office of arbitrator.[15] The only disadvantage was that an arbitration award could not be enforced on-site, as

12 Berchtold, *Recht und Gerechtigkeit*, 95–100; Friedrich Martens, *Das Consularwesen und die Consularjurisdiction im Orient* (Berlin: Weidmannsche Buchhandlung, 1874), 290–315.

13 René-Josué Valin, *Nouveau commentaire sur l'ordonnance de la marine du mois d'aout 1681* (La Rochelle: J. Légier and P. Mesnier, 1760), 236; generalising this argument: Jessica Marglin, "Nationalizing Consular Jurisdiction in the Nineteenth-Century Middle East and North Africa," in *this volume*.

14 L.-J.-A. de Moreuil, *Dictionnaire des chancelleries diplomatiques et consulaires* (Paris: Jules Renouard, 1855), 133.

15 § 21 Gesetz, betreffend die Organisation der Bundeskonsulate, sowie die Amtsrechte und Pflichten der Bundeskonsuln, BGBl. Norddeutscher Bund 1867, No. 11, 137–156.

enforcement was a sovereign act that fell under the jurisdiction of the host state. However, domestic procedural laws provided for enforcement back home.[16]

1.3 *Administrative Functions*

In addition to their function as courts, consulates also had administrative and notarial tasks. When the consulate had its own office, a chancellor acted as court clerk and enforcement officer.[17] Additionally, the consulate authenticated documents, maintained registers, and issued passports. In this role, the consulate fulfilled its core responsibility of regulating life within the foreign community. In non-European consulates, this could even extend to police powers.[18] Through its notarial functions, the consulate legalised various documents, thus contributing to the usability of paperwork between domestic and foreign entities.[19]

In this area, the "juridical functions" of consulates can be traced to the present day. Most of the administrative tasks have remained unchanged in the consular laws of countries (British Consular Relations Act 1968, French Decree No. 76–548 of June 16, 1976, Konsulargerichtsgesetz of September 11, 1974 (Germany), Konsulargerichtsgesetz of May 23, 2019 (Austria), Russian Consular Law of July 18, 2010), as well as the Vienna Convention on Consular Relations of April 24, 1963.

2 State of Research

Throughout its existence, consular jurisdiction was primarily a popular dissertation topic among jurists.[20] The famous Russian international law scholar

16 Cf. for example §§ 851–872 of the German Civilprozessordnung or Art. 1024 of the French Code de procédure civile.

17 Jörg Ulbert, "Qu'est-ce qu'un chancelier de consulat? Une approche par les textes de droit français," *Mélanges de l'École de Rome. Italie et Méditerranée modernes et contemporaines* 128, n° 2 (2016).

18 Johannes Berchtold, *Recht und Gerechtigkeit in der Konsulargerichtsbarkeit: Britische Exterritorialität im Osmanischen Reich 1825–1914* (Munich: Oldenbourg, 2009), 161; cf. furthermore Victor Simon, "Juridiction ou police ?," in *this volume*.

19 Critical to the extent, however: Arnaud Bartolomei, "Actes notariés versus actes de chancellerie. Le rôle des chancelleries consulaires françaises dans la formalisation des actes commerciaux et civils (XVIIIᵉ–XIXᵉ siècle)," *Mélanges de l'École de Rome. Italie et Méditerranée modernes et contemporaines* 128, n° 2 (2016).

20 Cf. Lars Regula, "Consular Jurisdiction in 19th-Century Legal Thinking," in *this volume*; a collection of contemporary and modern literature can be found in: Hans Wehberg,

Fjodor Fjodorovič Martens, known for the Martens Clause in the Hague Conventions, earned his doctorate in 1873 with a 500-page dissertation on European consular jurisdiction.[21] The French standard work was written by the judge from Aix, Louis-Joseph Féraud-Giraud.[22] Naturally, French literature was particularly influential.

However, with its disappearance, the interest of legal practitioners naturally waned. From the 1970s onwards, Richard Chang revisited the issue of consular jurisdiction.[23] Guided by the question of whether the work of (British) consular courts in the East Asian region was truly as poor as remembered, Chang encountered moderate interest in this institution, as evidenced by some overview articles.[24] It wasn't until 2009 that Johannes Berchtold once again presented a more comprehensive monograph on British consular jurisdiction in the Ottoman Empire.[25] Unlike the studies of the nineteenth century, Chang and Berchtold work on the basis of court records. Their approach is case-oriented.

"Literatur über die Frage der Exterritorialität," *Weltwirtschaftliches Archiv* 28 (1928); Jörg Ulbert, Matthias Manke, and Gustaf Fryksén, "Bibliographie: L'histoire de la fonction consulaire jusqu'au début de la première guerre mondiale," *Cahiers de la Méditerranée* 93 (2016). With regard to the research situation, I make a conceptual break at the Second World War. When I speak of "contemporary literature," I mean literature that was produced before 1945. This is partly because consular jurisdiction was still so prominent at that time that authors understood the institution as a current, not necessarily historical, phenomenon. Unlike post-1945 literature, pre-war literature often holds the character of a source itself. Additionally, it was only after 1945 that diplomatic archives became sufficiently accessible to allow decent historical research.

21 Friedrich Martens, *O Konsulach i Konsul'koj Jurisdikcii na Vostoke* (Saint Petersburg: A. Benke, 1873); translated one year later and published again as Martens, *Das Consularwesen und die Consularjurisdiction im Orient.*

22 Louis Joseph Delphin Féraud-Giraud, *De la juridiction française dans les échelles du Levant et de Barbarie* (Paris: A. Durand, 1859).

23 Richard Chang, "The Chishima Case," *The Journal of Asian Studies* 34, n° 3 (1975); Richard Chang, "A British Trial in Japan. Regina V. Archibald King (1875)," *Journal for Asian History* 10, n° 2 (1976); Richard Chang, *The Justice of the Western Consular Courts in Nineteenth-Century Japan,* Contributions in intercultural and comparative studies n° 10 (Westport, CT: Greenwood Press, 1984).

24 Gerhard Rill, "Zur Geschichte der österreichischen Konsulargerichtsbarkeit in Bosnien," *Mitteilungen des österreichischen Staatsarchivs* 30 (1977); John Spagnolo, "Portents of Empire in Britian's Ottoman Extraterritorial Jurisdiction," *Middle Eastern Studies* 27, n° 2 (1991); C. R. Pennell, "The British Consular Courts and Moroccan Muslim Identity: 'Christian' Justice as a Tool," *The Journal of North African Studies* 1, n° 2 (1996); Horst Hammen, "Kolonialrecht und Kolonialgerichtsbarkeit in den ehemaligen deutschen Schutzgebieten: Ein Überblick," *Verfassung und Recht in Übersee*, n° 32 (1999).

25 Berchtold, *Recht und Gerechtigkeit in der Konsulargerichtsbarkeit.*

Since then, there has been a renewed growing interest in the subject. In 2012, Marcella Aglietti also dealt with the legal aspects of Tuscan consuls.[26] Under the editorship of Arnaud Bartolomei, Mathieu Grenet, Fabrice Jesné, and Jörg Ulbert, the administrative and notarial tasks of French consular offices were examined.[27]

Harald Fuess has conducted initial studies on German consular jurisdiction in Japan and Korea.[28] The most recent work on the topic, for now, comes from Gábor Teschmayer on Austro-Hungarian consular jurisdiction.[29]

Apart from the institution of the consulate, the impact of "exterritorial jurisdiction" has also attracted considerable attention. In 2010, Turan Kayaoğlu apodictically stated that great powers frequently used law as an imperial tool.[30] Kayaoğlu highlighted a school of thought focused on the relationship between law and imperialism.[31] Jessica Marglin, on the other hand, examined the interaction of various competing jurisdictions under the term "legal pluralism."[32] In this context, the relationship of Europeans from different eras

---

26 Marcella Aglietti, *L'istituto consulare tra sette e ottocento: Funzioni, profilo giuridico e percosi professionali nella Toscana Granducale* (Pisa: ETS, 2012).

27 *Mélanges de l'École de Rome. Italie et Méditerranée modernes et contemporaines* 128, n° 2 (2016).

28 Harald Fuess, "Selbstregulierung einer Fremdenkolonie: Deutsche Konsulargerichtsbarkeit in Japan und Korea, 1861–1913," *Zeitschrift für Japanisches Recht* 18, n° 36 (2013).

29 Gábor Teschmayer, "A magyar konzuli tevékenység és bíráskodás az Osztrák-Magyar Monarchia alatt: Szabályozás, szervezet és gyakorlat" (PhD diss., Károli Gáspár Református Egyetem, 2019).

30 Turan Kayaoğlu, *Legal Imperialism: Sovereignty and Extraterritoriality in Japan, the Ottoman Empire, and China* (New York: Cambridge University Press, 2010), 1.

31 Cf. Andrew Cobbing, "A Victorian Embarrassment. Consular Jurisdiction and the Evils of Extraterritoiality," *The International History Review* 40, n° 2 (2018); Wolfgang J. Mommsen and Johannes A. de Moor, eds., *European Expansion and Law: The Encounter of European and Indigenous Law in 19th and 20th-Century Africa and Asia* (Oxford: Berg, 1992); Teemu Ruskola, *Legal Imperialism: China, the United States, and Modern Law* (Cambridge, MA: Harvard University Press, 2013); Antony Anghie, "Imperialism and International Legal Theory," in *The Oxford Handbook of the Theory of International Law*, eds. Anne Orford, Florian Hoffmann and Martin Clark (Oxford: Oxford University Press, 2016); Donna Brunero and Brian Farrell, eds., *Empire in Asia: A New Global History* (London: Bloomsbury, 2018); Emily Whewell, *Law Across Imperial Borders: British Consuls and Colonial Connections on China's Western Frontiers, 1880–1943* (Manchester: Manchester University Press, 2020); Martti Koskenniemi, *To the Uttermost Parts of the Earth: Legal Imagination and International Power 1300–1870* (Cambridge: Cambridge University Press, 2021).

32 Jessica Marglin, *Across Legal Lines: Jews and Muslims in Mordern Morocco* (New Haven, London: Yale University Press, 2016); Jessica Marglin, "Extraterritoriality Meets Islamic Law: Legal Pluralism and Elements of Proof in the International Mixed Court of Morocco, 1871–1872," *Quaderni Storici*, n° 3 (2016).

with Islamic justice has been particularly examined.[33] Recently, Francisco Apellániz has revisited this relationship once again.[34] In this research perspective, consulates appear as a component of a diverse judicial and jurisdictional landscape. Related to the institution of consular courts are also works dealing with the international legal foundations of consulates. Victor Simon recently explored the French capitulation system in the Levant, while Maurits van den Boogert shed light on the subject from an Islamic legal perspective.[35]

3 Outlook on Research

The considerable amount of literature should not obscure the fact that many very fundamental questions about the structure and functioning of consular jurisdiction remain unanswered. General historical scholarship has so far found it easy to exclude the topic of consular jurisdiction.[36] Legal history, as studied in law faculties, often deals with broadly conceived topics when

---

33 Cf. only *Christians & Jews in the Ottoman Empire*, ed. Benjamin Braude (Boulder: Lynne Rienner, 2014); Dominique Valérian, "Conflits et résolution des conflits dans les communautés européennes au Maghreb (XIIe–XVe siècle)," *Mélanges de l'École Française de Rome* 115, n° 1 (2003); Philippe Gourdin, "Les marchands étrangers ont-ils un statut de dhimmi ?," in *Migrations et diasporas méditerranéennes (Xe–XVIe siècles)*, eds. Michel Balard and Alain Ducellier (Paris: Éditions de la Sorbonne, 2002); Karen Barkey, "Aspects of Legal Pluralism in the Ottoman Empire," in *Legal Pluralism and Empires, 1500–1850*, eds. Lauren Benton and Richard Ross (New York: New York University Press, 2013).

34 Francisco Apellániz, *Breaching the Bronze Wall: Franks at Mamluk and Ottoman Courts and Markets* (Leiden: Brill, 2020).

35 Victor Simon, *Les échelles du Levant et de Barbarie: Droit du commerce international entre la France et l'Empire Ottoman (XVIe–XVIIIe siècle)* (Paris: LGDJ, 2021); Maurits van den Boogert, *The Capitulations and the Ottoman Legal System: Qadis, Consuls and Beraltlis in the 18th Century* (Leiden: Brill, 2005); Maurits van den Boogert, "Consular Jurisdiction in the Ottoman Legal System in the Eighteenth Century," in *The Ottoman Capitulations: Text and Context*, eds. Maurits van den Boogert and Kate Fleet, *Oriente Moderno* 83 (Rome: Ist. per l'Oriente C.A. Nallino, 2003).

36 Vgl. Inge von Berg, "Die Entwicklung des Konsularwesens im Deutschen Reich von 1871–1914 unter besonderer Berücksichtigung der außenhandelsfördernden Funktionen dieses Dienstes" (PhD diss., Universität zu Köln, 1995); Desmond Platt, *The Cinderella Service: British Consuls since 1825* (London: Archon Books, 1971); Raoul Clément, *Les Français d'Égypte aux XVIIe et XVIIIe siècles* (Cairo: Institut Français d'Archéologie Orientale, 1960), which touch upon judicial powers but, due to their primary focus on non-legal topics, nonetheless relegate consular jurisdiction to a secondary matter.

addressing foreign contexts. Diplomatic institutions or consulates are considered too specific an interest in this regard.[37]

On the other hand, while contemporary literature is extensive, most authors lacked insight into the day-to-day legal operations on the ground or access to diplomatic archives. As a result, the analyses remain on a theoretical level, offering little realistic portrayal of the institution. For Great Britain, Berchtold and Chang have partially addressed this gap. However, for all other (great) powers, there are still no corresponding archival studies. This is partly because consular research, with the exception of France, has not yet advanced far.[38]

In part, the question already arises as to whether there were any proceedings led by consuls at all and what these were based on. French scholarship has repeatedly pointed out that there is insufficient source material available for the early modern period.[39] Harald Fuess has identified similar issues for the German consular jurisdiction in the nineteenth century.[40]

An imbalance in research can also be observed with regard to the regions where consular jurisdiction was exercised. The Ottoman Empire, China, and Japan are most frequently studied, while the Maghreb has already been overlooked. Siam and Persia, as far as can be seen, remain completely unstudied. This also applies, to a certain extent, to Europe. Sources like the trade treaty of June 20, 1766, between England and Russia suggest that forms of consular jurisdiction existed in Europe longer than is currently known. The disappearance of the institution, and the corresponding rise of the territoriality principle, has not yet been explored. It should be noted in passing that the same finding applies to forms of "legal pluralism." Interest has typically focused on competing legal systems in the Ottoman Empire or the Maghreb. Jewish *Bet Din* courts in Europe or Huguenot judicial privileges have remained largely overlooked. Furthermore, legal history has also contributed to the question of the competi-

37 Vgl. Thomas Duve and José Luis Egío, *Rechtsgeschichte des frühneuzeitlichen Hispanoamerika* (Berlin: De Gruyter, 2023) or Klaus Mühlmann, *Criminal Justice in China: A History* (Cambridge, MA: Harvard University Press, 2009), that deal with the entire legal system over several decades.

38 Ulbert, "La fonction consulaire à l'époque moderne: définition, état des connaissances et perspectives de recherche," 18–19; cf. furthermore the still relevant summary in: Mathieu Grenet, "Consuls et "nations" étrangères: État des lieux et perspectives de recherche," *Cahiers de la Méditerranée* 93 (2016).

39 Arnaud Bartolomei, "Juridiction contentieuse des étrangers et fonctions judiciaires des consuls français dans les mondes hispaniques (XVIIIe–XIXe siècle)," in *this volume;* concerning the uncertainties around the French capitulation of 1535, cf. Simon, *Les Échelles du Levant et de Barbarie*, 18–19; Gaston Zeller, "Une légende qui a la vie dure: Les capitulations de 1535," *Revue d'Histoire moderne et contemporaine* 2, n° 2 (1955).

40 Fuess, "Selbstregulierung einer Fremdenkolonie," 61.

tiveness of political and economical systems with regard to Ottoman legal pluralism. Timur Kuran has raised the controversially discussed "jurisprudential shift hypothesis," which still requires conclusive clarification.[41]

Thus, in many areas, it remains to be clarified what forms of consular jurisdiction were exercised and how they functioned. This applies to informal methods of dispute resolution as well as institutional forms. Likewise, the sources and content of formal and substantive consular law often remain to be reviewed. Sovereignty conflicts arising from the exercise of judicial functions abroad also require more in-depth research. This is related to the fact that consular jurisdiction, while not identical, was at least related to colonial jurisdiction in the nineteenth century. Finally, there is a great need for research to study consular jurisdiction from the perspective of host countries, that is, through non-European sources.

4 The Contributions

The present volume is mainly based on contributions presented at the conference of the same name held from November 2 to November 4, 2023, in Hamburg. The contributions are initially organised by geographical and then by chronological aspects. The central question of this volume is where consular jurisdiction originated and how it developed. We know that consular courts existed to a certain extent in Europe.[42] Likewise, we know that at some point the focus shifted to the Islamic regions of the Mediterranean and later to East Asia. Somewhere along the way, then, a turning point must have occurred – though the precise time frame remains unknown. The subject of examination is always the formal legal institution of the court. The study of substantive law played only a secondary role.

At the beginning, *Laura Galoppini* focuses on the Lucca merchant community in Bruges. Building on the *Libro della comunità,* Galoppini outlines the

---

41 Timur Kuran, *The Long Divergence: How Islamic Law Held Back the Middle East* (Princeton: Princeton University Press, 2011), 198–201; Timur Kuran, "The Islamic Commercial Crisis: Institutional Roots of Economic Underdevelopment in the Middle East," *The Journal of Economic History* 63, n° 2 (2003). Kuran's hypothesis was challenged by Maurits van den Boogert, "Legal Reflections on the "Jurisprudential Shift Hypothesis," *Turcica* 41 (2009); Francisco Apellániz, "Judging the Franks: Proof, Justice, and Diversity in Late Medieval Alexandria and Damascus," *Comparative Studies in Society and History* 58, n° 2 (2016).

42 Albrecht Cordes and Philipp Höhn, "Konfliktlösung im Fernhandel," in *Konfliktlösung im Mittelalter*, ed. David von Mayenburg (Wiesbaden: Springer, 2021), 283–284.

structures and competencies of the Luccan consuls as they existed at the end of the fourteenth century. *Cédric Quertier* continues this approach for the Florentine merchant communities in the thirteenth and fourteenth centuries, using the statutes of various merchant communities in Europe as his source. *Ana Belem Fernández Castro,* on the other hand, focuses on Valencia.

In her contribution on the sixteenth century, Fernández Castro examines a transitional period in which the medieval principle of personality disappeared in favour of modern judicial privileges. *Jörg Ulbert* illustrates, using the example of the French consular service, how the judicial powers of consuls in the Levant and Europe qualitatively differed during the ancien régime. *Arnaud Bartolomei* also turns to the Spanish-speaking world, showing that judicial functions could persist even after their formal legal abolition.

Marcella Aglietti traces consular jurisdiction in Europe into the eighteenth century. Using the example of Livorno, Aglietti demonstrates that the legal competencies of consuls primarily flourished in free ports. *Thibault Bechini* similarly shows that consular jurisdiction was mainly a stopgap when local jurisdiction was insufficient, focusing on inheritance law in his contribution about the Italian consulates in the USA in the early twentieth century.

Dominique Valérian makes an important contribution with his examination of consular jurisdiction among Latin merchant communities in the medieval Levantine ports. Valérian primarily situates consular jurisdiction within Islamic law. *Victor Simon* illustrates that the lines between judicial functions and police regulatory roles were sometimes not easy to separate, highlighting the discrepancy between domestic doctrine and local practice. *Eleonora Angella* lays the groundwork for further research on other powers with her contribution to Italian consular jurisdiction in the nineteenth century, a system that has received little attention. This is even more pronounced for Switzerland. *Giorgio Ennas,* in his contribution, examines a nation that benefited from consular judicial privileges for the longest time only indirectly, pointing out structural differences between the various consular systems observed from a third perspective.

The contributions by *Berna Kamay-Ulusay, Jessica Marglin,* and myself (*Lars Regula*) are guided by specific doctrinal questions. Kamay-Ulusay investigates from a Turkish perspective the extent to which consular jurisdiction impacted the creation of Ottoman criminal procedure law. I explore the significance of consular jurisdiction in nineteenth-century legal thought. Marglin, on the other hand, reflects on consular jurisdiction in the context of national legislative processes, demonstrating that it constituted a coherent (legal) system.

Juliette Françoise then addresses East Asia and consular arbitration. In her contribution, Françoise extracts French consular jurisdiction from its local context in Canton and instead situates it within the French legal system. *Sacha Gauthier Olssy* also deals with China. In his contribution, Gauthier examines how the Chinese leased territories led to a territorialisation of consular jurisdiction.

The volume concludes with *Thomas Gidney*'s investigation of the end of consular jurisdiction. Gidney shows how a changed understanding of the system of international order in the twentieth century gradually abolished consular jurisdiction.

5 Sketch of a Comprehensive Trajectory

Anyone who reads the collected contributions from beginning to end will probably come away with two main insights. First, there is the cross-epoch developmental trajectory. The position of the "consul" emerged in the medieval port cities as the head of a community of merchants.[43] Consuls first appear in 1063 in the *Ordinamenta et consuetudo maris* of the city of Trani. During the Middle Ages, consular jurisdiction was also firmly established in Western European trade metropolises.[44] The example of Bruges confirms that this was by no means a purely Mediterranean phenomenon. From the *funduqs* of the Levant to the Hanseatic kontors in the far north, it was rather the *zeitgeist* that granted long-distance merchants far-reaching jurisdictional powers.[45] The trend reversal posited at the beginning appears to set in within Europe starting in the sixteenth century. In Valencia, for instance, jurisdictional authority is limited

---

43 There are, however, terminological uncertainties. Particularly French literature makes a distinction between consuls *de la* mer, who reside at home, consuls *sur* mer, who held jurisdictional powers on a ship at sea, and consuls *d'outre* mer who preside a foreign community, Louis Blancard, "Du consul de mer et du consul sur mer," *Bibliothèque de l'École des chartes* 18 (1857): 427–438; Ulbert, "La fonction consulaire à l'époque moderne," 10.

44 Laura Galoppini, "The consuls of the Lucchese community in Bruges (1377–1404)," in *this volume*, 21–35; Cédric Quertier, "La justice des consuls d'après les statuts des nations Florentines (fin XIIIe–début XIVe siècle)," in *this volume*, 37–65.

45 Cf. for further examples, Cordes and Höhn, "Konfliktlösung im Fernhandel," 283–287 concerning the concept of *funduq*, cf. Olivia Constable, *Housing the Stranger in the Mediterranean World: Lodging, Trade, and Travel in Late Antiquity and the Middle Ages* (Cambridge: Cambridge University Press, 2003).

at least to arbitration.[46] By the eighteenth century, consular jurisdiction can no longer be found at all – at least in the Spanish-speaking world.[47] In between, a transitional phase can be observed, in which – using France as an example – the claim to a globally comprehensive court system is still articulated in normative texts, though in practice this system increasingly comes under pressure from territorial rulers.[48]

However, while the European states gradually began to cease renewing such privileges at the beginning of the modern era, thereby gaining control over foreign merchants, the Ottomans in the East did not touch the existing privileges.[49] As a result, the legal work of consulates in Europe and the Levant developed qualitatively in different directions.[50] While domestic consuls primarily became commercial judges, their colleagues abroad gradually came under the administrative control of the developing foreign services.[51] Since European states no longer recognised judicial privileges, consuls in European countries increasingly focused on notarial duties and voluntary jurisdiction.[52] In the Ottoman Empire, however, consulates remained courts with full jurisdiction over their own subjects.[53] In the nineteenth century, the consular

46 Ana Belem Fernández Castro, "Jurisdiction and Foreign Consuls in Sixteenth-Century Valencia," in *this volume,* 66–88.

47 Arnaud Bartolomei, "Juridiction contentieuse des étrangers et fonctions judiciaires des consuls français dans les mondes hispaniques (xviiie–xixe siècle)," in this *volume,* 137–148.

48 Ulbert, "Les fonctions judiciaires des consuls de France en pays de Chrétienté sous l'Ancien Régime," 89–108.

49 Guillaume Calafat, "La juridiction des consuls français en Méditerranée. Litiges marchands, arbitrages et circulations des procès (Livourne et Tunis au xviie siècle)," in *De l'utilité commerciale des consuls l'institution consulaire et les marchands dans le monde méditerranéen (xviie–xxe siècle)*, eds. Arnaud Bartolomei *et al.* (Rome: École française de Rome, 2017).

50 Jörg Ulbert, "Les fonctions judiciaires des consuls de France en pays de Chrétienté sous l'Ancien Régime," 89–108.

51 In French literature, "juridiction consulaire" usually refers to the French local commercial jurisdiction, cf. Ernest Genevois, *Histoire critique de la juridiction consulaire* (Paris: A. Durand, 1866); Guillaume Denière, *La juridiction consulaire de Paris 1563–1792* (Paris: Henri Plon, 1872). That French commercial judges are nowadays still called *juge consulaire* is thus not a coincidence.

52 Calafat, "La juridiction des consuls français en Méditerranée."

53 Dominique Valérian, "Les juridictions consulaires des nations latines dans les ports musulmans (xiiie–xve siècle): Droit musulman, traités bilatéraux et forum shopping," in *this volume,* 165–181; Victor Simon, "Juridiction ou police?: Les ambigüités de la distinction entre competence juridictionelle et pouvoirs de police du consul dans les échelles du Levant et de Barbarie (xvie – xviiie siècle," in *this volume,* 182–199; Eleonora Angella, "Italien Consular Jurisdiction: Theory, Practice, Effects," in *this volume,* 200–217.

court system was eventually expanded beyond the borders of the Islamic world. The legal and judicial reforms at home also led to the emergence of a coherent court system abroad.[54] In China, the lease agreements even reveal a trend from "exterritorial" to "innerterritorial" jurisdiction, as the Chinese leased territories increasingly developed into colonies.[55] In the final phase, it becomes evident that consular jurisdiction stood on increasingly shaky ground due to the steady reception of European legal thought.[56]

Finally – and this seems to me the second main insight of the overall picture – one can observe the same recurring dynamic in the final phase of consular jurisdiction: Extensive privileges gradually give way, through negotiations, to hybrid forms such as arbitration courts or mixed tribunals. Only afterwards does dissolution occur. Expansion of legal authority only takes place in cases where the host state has neither a vested interest nor superior competence in the matter.[57]

Bibliography

Aglietti, Marcella. *L'istituto consulare tra sette e ottocento: Funzioni, profilo giuridico e percosi professionali nella Toscana Granducale*. Pisa: ETS, 2012.

Anghie, Antony. "Imperialism and International Legal Theory." In *The Oxford Handbook of the Theory of International Law*, edited by Anne Orford, Florian Hoffmann and Martin Clark, 156–172. Oxford: Oxford University Press, 2016.

Apellániz, Francisco. "Judging the Franks: Proof, Justice, and Diversity in Late Medieval Alexandria and Damascus." *Comparative Studies in Society and History* 58, n° 2 (2016): 350–378.

Apellániz, Francisco. *Breaching the Bronze Wall: Franks at Mamluk and Ottoman Courts and Markets*. Leiden: Brill, 2020.

Barkey, Karen. "Aspects of Legal Pluralism in the Ottoman Empire." In *Legal Pluralism and Empires, 1500–1850*, edited by Lauren Benton and Richard Ross, 83–108. New York: New York University Press, 2013.

54 Marglin, "Nationalizing Consular Jurisdiction, 275–294.

55 Sacha Gauthier Olssy, "Une jurisdiction consulaire territoriale en Chine?," in *this volume*, 317–333.

56 Berna Kamay-Ulusay, "Capitulations 'in a box'," in *this volume*, 233–252; Regula, "Legal Thinking," 253–274; Thomas Gidney, "The End of Exterritoriality," in *this volume*, 334–352.

57 Thibault Bechini, "Les actions juidiciaires des consulats d'Italie aux États-Unis (1890–1915)," in this volume, 149–162.

Bartolomei, Arnaud. "Actes notariés versus actes de chancellerie: Le rôle des chancelleries consulaires françaises dans la formalisation des actes commerciaux et civils (XVIIIe–XIXe siècle)." *Mélanges de l'École de Rome. Italie et Méditerranée modernes et contemporaines* 128, n° 2 (2016).

Berchtold, Johannes. *Recht und Gerechtigkeit in der Konsulargerichtsbarkeit: Britische Exterritorialität im Osmanischen Reich 1825–1914*. Munich: Oldenbourg, 2009.

Berg, Inge von. "Die Entwicklung des Konsularwesens im Deutschen Reich von 1871–1914 unter besonderer Berücksichtigung der außenhandelsfördernden Funktionen dieses Dienstes." PhD diss., Universität zu Köln, 1995.

Blancard, Louis. "Du consul de mer et du consul sur mer." *Bibliothèque de l'École des chartes* 18 (1857): 427–438.

Braude, Benjamin, ed. *Christians and Jews in the Ottoman Empire*. Boulder, CO: Lynne Rienner, 2014.

Brunero, Donna, and Brian Farrell, eds. *Empire in Asia: A New Global History*. London: Bloomsbury, 2018.

Calafat, Guillaume. "La juridiction des consuls français en Méditerranée litiges marchands, arbitrages et circulations des procès (Livourne et Tunis au XVIIe siècle)." In De l'utilité commerciale des consuls: L'institution consulaire et les marchands dans le monde méditerranéen (XVIIe–XXe siècle), edited by Arnaud Bartolomei, Guillaume Calafat, Matthieu Grenet and Jörg Ulbert, 155–172. Rome: École française de Rome, 2017.

Chang, Richard. "The Chishima Case." *The Journal of Asian Studies* 34, n° 3 (1975): 593–612.

Chang, Richard. "A British Trial in Japan: Regina V. Archibald King (1875)." *Journal for Asian History* 10, n° 2 (1976): 134–150.

Chang, Richard. *The Justice of the Western Consular Courts in Nineteenth-Century Japan*. Westport, CT: Greenwood Press, 1984.

Clément, Raoul. *Les Français d'Égypte aux XVIIe et XVIIIe siècles*. Cairo: Institut français d'archéologie orientale, 1960.

Cobbing, Andrew. "A Victorian Embarrassment. Consular Jurisdiction and the Evils of Extraterritoriality." The International History Review 40, n° 2 (2018): 273–291.

Constable, Olivia. *Housing the Stranger in the Mediterranean World: Lodging, Trade, and Travel in Late Antiquity and the Middle Ages*. Cambridge: Cambridge University Press, 2003.

Cordes, Albrecht. "Auf der Suche nach der Rechtswirklichkeit der mittelalterlichen Lex mercatoria." *Zeitschrift der Savigny Stiftung für Rechtsgeschichte* (*Germanistische Abteilung*) 118 (2001): 167–184.

Cordes, Albrecht. "The Search for a Medieval Lex Mercatoria." In *From* Lex mercatoria *to commercial law*, edited by Vito Piergiovanni, 53–68. Berlin: Duncker & Humblot, 2005.

Cordes, Albrecht. "À la recherche d'une Lex mercatoria au Moyen Âge." In *Stadt und Recht im Mittelalter*, edited by Pierre Monnet and Otto Gerhard Oexle, 117–132. Göttingen: Vandenhoeck & Ruprecht, 2003.

Cordes, Albrecht. "Jenseits des Lex mercatoria-Mythos." In *100 Jahre Rechtswissenschaft in Frankfurt: Erfahrungen, Herausforderungen, Erwartungen*, edited by Fachbereich Rechtswissenschaft der Goethe-Universität Frankfurt am Main, 383–394. Frankurt: Vittorio Klostermann, 2014.

Cordes, Albrecht, and Philipp Höhn. "Konfliktlösung im Fernhandel." In *Konfliktlösung im Mittelalter*, edited by David von Mayenburg, 283–293. Berlin: Springer, 2021.

Denière, Guillaume. *La juridiction consulaire de Paris 1563–1792*. Paris: Henri Plon, 1872.

Duve, Thomas, and José Luis Egío. *Rechtsgeschichte des frühneuzeitlichen Hispanoamerika*. Berlin: De Gruyter, 2023.

Féraud-Giraud, Louis Joseph Delphin. *De la juridiction française dans les Échelles du Levant et de Barbarie*. Paris: A. Durand, 1859.

Fuess, Harald. "Selbstregulierung einer Fremdenkolonie: Deutsche Konsulargerichtsbarkeit in Japan und Korea, 1861–1913." *Zeitschrift für Japanisches Recht* 18, n° 36 (2013): 53–94.

Genevois, Ernest. *Histoire critique de la juridiction consulaire*. Paris: A. Durand, 1866.

Gourdin, Philippe. "Les marchands étrangers ont-ils un statut de dhimmi ?" In *Migrations et diasporas méditerranéennes (xe–xvie siècles)*, edited by Michel Balard and Alain Ducellier, 435–446. Paris: Éditions de la Sorbonne, 2002.

Grenet, Mathieu. "Consuls et 'nations' étrangères: État des lieux et perspectives de recherche." *Cahiers de la Méditerranée* 93 (2016): 25–34.

Hammen, Horst. "Kolonialrecht und Kolonialgerichtsbarkeit in den ehemaligen deutschen Schutzgebieten: Ein Überblick." *Verfassung und Recht in Übersee*, n° 32 (1999): 191–209.

Humbert, Gustav. *Konstantinopel, London, Smyrna: Skizzen aus dem Leben eines kaiserlich deutschen Auslandsbeamten*. Berlin: Hochschule und Ausland, 1927.

Kayaoğlu, Turan. *Legal Imperialism: Sovereignty and Extraterritoriality in Japan, the Ottoman Empire, and China*. New York: Cambridge University Press, 2010.

Koskenniemi, Martti. *To the Uttermost Parts of the Earth: Legal Imagination and International Power 1300–1870*. Cambridge, MA: Cambridge University Press, 2021.

Kuran, Timur. "The Islamic Commercial Crisis: Institutional Roots of Economic Underdevelopment in the Middle East." *The Journal of Economic History* 63, n° 2 (2003): 414–446.

Kuran, Timur. *The Long Divergence: How Islamic Law Held Back the Middle East*. Princeton: Princeton University Press, 2011.

Kurkin, Claudia. *Extraterritorialität: Eine Kategorie des transnationalen Rechts*. Tübingen: Mohr Siebeck, 2021.

Li, Kevin. *Reconceiving Extraterritorial Jurisdiction: From Formality to Function*. Baden-Baden: Nomos, 2022.

Marglin, Jessica. *Across Legal Lines: Jews and Muslims in Modern Morocco*. New Haven: Yale University Press, 2016.

Marglin, Jessica. "Extraterritoriality Meets Islamic Law: Legal Pluralism and Elements of Proof in the International Mixed Court of Morocco, 1871–1872." *Quaderni Storici*, n° 3 (2016): 673–700.

Marquer, Éric. "Doux commerce et droit naturel: la fable de la lex mercatoria." *Astérion* 20 (2019), https://doi.org/10.4000/asterion.3829.

Martens, Friedrich. *O Konsulach i konsul'koj Jurisdikcii na Vostoke*. Saint Petersburg: A. Benke, 1873.

Marglin, Jessica. *Das Consularwesen und die Consularjurisdiction im Orient*. Berlin: Weidmannsche Buchhandlung, 1874.

Mommsen, Wolfgang J., and Johannes A. de Moor, eds. *European Expansion and Law: The Encounter of European and Indigenous Law in 19th and 20th-Century Africa and Asia*. Oxford: Berg, 1992.

Moreuil, L.-J.-A. de. *Dictionnaire des chancelleries diplomatiques et consulaires*. Paris: Jules Renouard, 1855.

Mühlmann, Klaus. *Criminal justice in China: A History*. Cambridge, MA: Harvard University Press, 2009.

Pennell, C. R. "The British Consular Courts and Moroccan Muslim Identity: 'Christian' Justice as a Tool." *The Journal of North African Studies* 1, n° 2 (1996): 172–191.

Platt, Desmond. *The Cinderella Service: British Consuls since 1825*. London: Archon Books, 1971.

Repgen, Tilman. "Ius Commune." In Usus modernus pandectarum: Römisches Recht, Deutsches Recht und Naturrecht in der Frühen Neuzeit, edited by Hans-Peter Haferkamp and Tilman Repgen, 157–174. Köln: Böhlau, 2007.

Rill, Gerhard. "Zur Geschichte der österreichischen Konsulargerichtsbarkeit in Bosnien." *Mitteilungen des österreichischen Staatsarchivs* 30 (1977): 153–190.

Ruskola, Teemu. *Legal Imperialism: China, the United States, and Modern Law*. Cambridge, MA: Harvard University Press, 2013.

Simon, Victor. *Les échelles du Levant et de Barbarie: Droit du commerce international entre la France et l'Empire Ottoman (XVIe–XVIIIe siècle)*. Paris: LGDJ, 2021.

Spagnolo, John. "Portents of Empire in Britian's Ottoman Extraterritorial Jurisdiction." *Middle Eastern Studies* 27, n° 2 (1991): 256–282.

Talleyrand, Charles-Maurice de. *Éloge de M. le Comte Reinhard*. Paris: Gabriel Warée, 1838.

Teschmayer, Gábor. "A Magyar Konzuli Tevékenység És Bíráskodás Az Osztrák–Magyar Monarchia Alatt: Szabályozás, Szervezet És Gyakorlat." PhD diss., Károli Gáspár Református Egyetem, 2019. http://corvina.kre.hu:8080/phd/Teschmayer_ertekezes_10.24395_KRE.2020.001.pdf.

Ulbert, Jörg. "La fonction consulaire à l'époque moderne: Définition, état des connaissances et perspectives de recherche." In *La fonction consulaire à l'époque moderne: L'affirmation d'une institution économique et politique (1500–1700)*, edited by Jörg Ulbert and Gérard Le Bouëdec, 9–20. Rennes: Presses universitaires de Rennes, 2006.

Ulbert, Jörg. "Qu'est-ce qu'un chancelier de consulat? Une approche par les textes de droit français." *Mélanges de l'École de Rome. Italie et Méditerranée modernes et contemporaines* 128, n° 2 (2016).

Ulbert, Jörg, Matthias Manke, and Gustaf Fryksén. "Bibliographie: L'histoire de la fonction consulaire jusqu'au début de la première guerre mondiale." *Cahiers de la Méditerranée* 93 (2016): 79–336.

Valérian, Dominique. "Conflits et résolution des conflits dans les communautés européennes au Maghreb (XIIe–XVe siècle)." *Mélanges de l'École Française de Rome* 115, n° 1 (2003): 543–564.

Valin, René-Josué. *Nouveau commentaire sur l'ordonnance de la marine du mois d'aout 1681*. La Rochelle: J. Légier and P. Mesnier, 1760.

Van den Boogert, Maurits. "Consular Jurisdiction in the Ottoman Legal System in the Eighteenth Century." *Oriente Moderno*, NS 22 (83), n° 3 (2003): 613–634.

Van den Boogert, Maurits. *The Capitulations and the Ottoman Legal System: Qadis, Consuls and Beraltlis in the 18th Century*. Leiden: Brill, 2005.

Van den Boogert, Maurits. "Legal Reflections on the 'Jurisprudential Shift Hypothesis'." *Turcica* 41 (2009): 373–382.

Voltaire. *Dictionnaire philosophique, ou la raison par alphabet*. London: s.n., 1770.

Wehberg, Hans. "Literatur über die Frage der Exterritorialität." *Weltwirtschaftliches Archiv* 28 (1928): 170–184.

Whewell, Emily. *Law Across Imperial Borders: British Consuls and Colonial Connections on China's Western Frontiers, 1880–1943*. Manchester: Manchester University Press, 2020.

Zeller, Gaston. "Une légende qui a la vie dure: Les capitulations de 1535." *Revue d'histoire moderne et contemporaine* 2, n° 2 (1955): 127–132.

PART 1

In Christian Lands

1

The Consuls of the Lucchese Community in Bruges (1377–1404)

Laura Galoppini

> ... noi tutti ci tengnamo e ghoverniamo
> sotto l'ordine delli staduti
>
> LIBRO DELLA COMUNITÀ (1384)

This chapter investigates the role played by the consuls of the Lucchese merchant community in Bruges. The events and examples covered herein date back to 1377–1404. In fact, the *natio lucensis* had already been operating in Bruges since at least the mid-fourteenth century and continued to exist well beyond 1404. However, the direct source we have available, the *Libro della comunità dei mercanti lucchesi in Bruges*,[1] covers, in the extant part, the years 1377–1404.[2] From this *Libro*, we have also learned about the contents of the Charter of the Merchant Community in Bruges (the text of which has not sur-

1 *Libro della comunità dei mercanti lucchesi in Bruges*, ed. Eugenio Lazzareschi (Milan: R. Malfasi, 1947), with a *Prefazione* by Armando Sapori, hereinafter referred to as *Libro*. This source, preserved in the Archivio di Stato di Lucca (= ASLU), *Archivio Buonvisi* (part I), 40 bis, edited by Lazzareschi just after World War II (1947) is now being presented in a new, revised critical edition by myself and by Giancarlo De Fecondo, with a study by Christine Meek on the *La compagnia Guinigi*. Raymond de Roover, "La communauté des marchands lucquois à Bruges," *Annales de la Société d'Émulation de Bruges* 86 (1949): 23–89.

2 The community remained in Bruges until the early sixteenth century. In the last decades of the fifteenth century, Bruges had slipped into a slow, irreversible decline after the silting up of its harbour (Damme) and the canals of the Reie river. In addition, its trading privileges, which had been exclusive until then, had been extended to Brabant, thus 'punishing' Bruges for the active role it had played in the riots of 1482 and 1487. So, in the early sixteenth century, the trading centre of Antwerp, in the Brabant province, had overshadowed the Flemish one of Bruges and, with the other European merchant communities, the Lucchese *loggia* moved there; cf. Laura Galoppini, "'Retornare a quella antica usanza del consolato': uno statuto per i mercanti lucchesi in Anversa (metà XVI sec.)," *Bollettino Storico Pisano* 86 (2017): 131–146.

HTTPS://DOI.ORG/10.1163/9789004755192-003

vived), which was approved in 1369 and enforced in those years. Therefore, the only extant source of information about the business of the *loggia* – as the Lucchese community in Bruges was often called – is the *Libro*, a handwritten notebook kept by the incumbent consul. From this document, we have gathered almost all information about the life of the Lucchese merchant community, the problems and conflicts within, its relations with local authorities and merchants, as well as details regarding similar problems in the Lucchese communities of France and England.

1 The Consul of the *natio lucensis* in Bruges

The Lucchese community had been established as an oath-bound secular corporation sharing a devotion for the *Volto Santo* (Holy Face) of Lucca, which, as in their native country, served a purpose of social and civil cohesion.[3] Such purpose is quite apparent in Lucca, on the occasion of the procession and *luminaria della Santa Croce* on 14 September: a solemn celebration, regulated – since the time of the 1308 Charter – like a demonstration of unity among all the components of the city. It had to be compulsorily attended by the institutional bodies, the city quarters, all the Comuni of Lucca's dominion. The men, citizens aged 14 to 70, were all required to attend, on pain of a fine.[4]

In Bruges, the essential opportunities for socialisation in such secular religiosity were mass on the first Sunday of the month, officiated in the community's chapel (the chapel of the Holy Cross in the monastery of the Augustinians Fathers), and the yearly Feast of the Holy Cross (14 September). The consul was in charge of organising such events and making sure all the mer-

3 The *Volto Santo* (Holy Face) or the Holy Cross is a wooden crucifix, held in the Cathedral of San Martino in Lucca, which in the Middle Ages was an object of devotion that spread from Lucca all over Europe; *Lucca, il Volto Santo e la civiltà medioevale*, Proceedings of the International Study Conference (Lucca, Palazzo Pubblico 21–23 October 1982). Lucca: Maria Pacini Fazzi Editore, 1984; for its wide-ranging bibliography, ARVO-Archivio Digitale del Volto Santo (www.archiviovoltosanto.org/it/bibliografia).

4 It established that all men "masculi Lucane civitatis, burgorum et suburgorum, a XIIII usque in LXX, veniant ad predictum festum et luminariam Sancte Crucis in eius vigilia post lucanum Regimen et eius curiam et Capitaneum lucani Populi et dominum Maiorem Sindicum lucani Comunis et Collegia Anxianorum et Priorum … se debeant congregare in vigilia dicti festi et simul convenire in platea Sancti Fridiani, ante quam Potestas lucanus et alii suprascripti Officiales et Rectores se moveant," in *Statuto del Commune di Lucca dell'anno 1308 ora per la prima volta pubblicato*, eds. Salvatore Bongi and Leone Del Prete (Lucca: Tip. Giusti, 1867), 44.

chants of the *loggia* attended them, as they were required to do, wearing the *livery* of the *natio lucensis*.[5] Likewise, the consul was responsible for the upkeep of the Chapel of the Holy Cross in Bruges, using the tribute that all merchants were required to pay to the 2 *operai* (vestry members or trustees) of the chapel, who were also appointed once a year along with the consul and the councillors. The payment of the tribute was recorded in the *Libro*.[6]

The 1369 Charter (as well as the later one, enforced in 1478[7]) placed a consul, elected by all the merchants, in charge of the *loggia*, assisted by three councillors.[8] The names of the consuls and councillors elected in 1376–1403 can be inferred from the text of the *Libro*, shown in Table 1.1.

Consuls were appointed for a year and had different kinds of responsibilities in addition to the above, as discussed below.

---

5 The *livrea* or livery was a ceremonial robe, "usually decorated with coats of arms, or with exploits and motifs of great evocative, suggestive and symbolic value, an elegant attire that was extremely fashionable in the 15th century." Laura Galoppini, "Lucchesi e uomini di comunità a Bruges nel tardo Medioevo," in *"Mercatura è arte." Uomini d'affari toscani in Europa e nel Mediterraneo tardomedievale*, eds. Lorenzo Tanzini and Sergio Tognetti (Rome: Viella, 2012), 60–61.

6 The character of the *natio Lucensis*, which has been defined as a "oath-bound secular corporation" in which the binding element was the religious worship of the *Volto Santo* of Lucca, looks unchanged in the 1478 Charter. Conversely, in the Charter of the Antwerp community, drawn up in the mid-sixteenth century, the religious character of the secular community feels less emphasized, and the obligations to attend religious services (with milder fines for transgressors) seem less pressing. Note, in this respect, that the merchant *loggia* in Antwerp did not have a chapel of its own, as it had in Bruges. The Antwerp Charter was never formally ratified by the Elders of Lucca, Galoppini, "Retornare a quella antica usanza del consolato," 134–137.

7 Drawn up and issued in 1478, the Charter was approved by the Elders of Lucca on 3 April 1498; Laura Galoppini, "Lo statuto della nazione dei lucchesi di Bruges (1478–1498)," in *Honos alit artes. Studi per il settantesimo compleanno di Mario Ascheri*, vol. II, *Gli universi particolari. Città e territori dal medioevo all'età moderna*, eds. Paola Maffei and Gian Maria Varanini (Florence: Firenze University Press, 2014), 33–41.

8 As we do not have the text of the 1369 Charter, we do not know how the three councillors used to be appointed; however, based on the elections described in the *Libro*, we can see that in most cases one of the three councillors was the outgoing consul. On the contrary, the 1478 Charter established that the consul should be assisted by two councillors, one of whom had to be the outgoing consul and the other had to be chosen by the new consul, the outgoing consul and the outgoing councillor ("E li due consilieri si debbino eleggere in questo modo: cioè che il consolo vechio resti per uno de' consilieri nuovi e l'altro nuovo consilieri si debbia eleggere per lo consolo nuovo et consolo vechio e vechio consiglieri", Galoppini, "Lo statuto," 38).

TABLE 1.1 List of consuls and councillors in Bruges during 1376–1403

Date of appointment	Consul	Councillors
1376	Iacopo Fava	Piero Testa Orlandino Volpelli Forteguerra Forteguerra
1377, September 6	Orlandino Volpelli	Iacopo Fava Nicolao Guinigi Giannino Spada
1378, August 15	Lazzaro Guinigi	Orlandino Volpelli Francesco Sandei Giovanni Cristofani
1379, August 15	Piero Testa	Lazzaro Guinigi Giannino Spada Iacopo Fava
1380, August 15	Giannino Spada	Piero Testa Matteo Matafelloni Gallico da Piastra
1381, August 15	Giovanni Cristofani	Giannino Spada Giovanni Totti Pietro Brunelli
1382, August 15	Gallico da Piastra	Giovanni Cristofani Piero Testa Francesco Panichi
1384	Forteguerra Forteguerra *Remained in office in 1385*	Gallico da Piastra Aloisio Brunelli Paolo Domaschi
1386, August 15	Iacopo Fava	Piero Testa Francesco Totti Lorenzo Trenta
1387, August 15	Piero Testa *Elected by the Elders' Council of Lucca*	Iacopo Fava Francesco Totti Agostino da Massa
1388	Aloisio Brunelli	–

TABLE 1.1 List of consuls and councillors in Bruges during 1376–1403 (*cont.*)

Date of appointment	Consul	Councillors
1389, August 15	Gallico da Piastra	Aloisio Brunelli Aloisio dal Portico Lorenzo Trenta
1390, August 15	Francesco Totti	Gallico da Piastra Iacopo Orsi Francesco Vinciguerra
1391, August 15	Paolo Domaschi	Francesco Totti Piero Panichi Tomasino Brunelli
1392, August 15	Nicolao da Volterra	Paolo Domaschi Piero Orselli Cecio Cristofani
1393, August 15	Iacopo Orsi	Nicolao da Volterra Bartolomeo Moriconi Antonio Quarti
1394, August 15	Francesco Panichi	Iacopo Orsi Francesco Panichi Gallico da Piastra
1395, August 31	Gallico da Piastra	Filippo Rapondi Piero Orselli Davino Pagani
1396, August 20	Filippo Rapondi	Gallico da Piastra Paolo Domaschi Nicolao Guidiccioni
1397, September 3	Giacomello Fava	Filippo Rapondi Francesco Totti Nicolao da Volterra
1398, August 15	Davino Pagani	Giacomello Fava Giovanni Franchi Gallico da Piastra
1399, August 31	Paolo Domaschi	Davino Pagani Nicolao Ronghi Orlandino Benetti

TABLE 1.1 List of consuls and councillors in Bruges during 1376–1403 (*cont.*)

Date of appointment	Consul	Councillors
1401, August 19	Nicolao Ronghi	Piero Panichi Francesco Totti Paolo Domaschi
1402, August 15	Marco Guidiccioni	Nicolao Ronghi Davino Pagani Tommaso Fortebraccia
1403, August 15	Paolo Domaschi	Marco Guidiccioni Gallico da Piastra Nicolao ser Pauli

Note: ASLu, *Archivio Buonvisi* (part 1), 40 bis.

The incumbent consul, at the end of his appointment, had to organise the election of the new consul. As soon as the new consul was elected, all the merchants of the *loggia* took their oath before him, swearing they would comply with the Charter, and the names of all the merchants who had taken their oath were written in the *Libro*.

Finally, every year, after hearing the merchants' statements, the consul drew up a list of associations operating in Bruges, their membership – including the members' roles: *fattori, maestri, compagni, garzoni* – a list of any other place in which the association worked (Paris, London and elsewhere), and the designs of the merchants' marks, if they had any.

2 The Judicial Role of the Consul

All the formalities above were recorded year by year in the *Libro*, but they were not the only records there, just like the consul's responsibilities did not end here, as he basically played a judicial and political role. In terms of legal jurisdiction, he had to ensure compliance with the statutory rules that governed the life of the *loggia* in Bruges, and any infringement was sanctioned as laid down by the Charter itself. Of the very many cases recorded in the *Libro*, here we will mention just a few of the most relevant examples.

On 5 September 1377, the consul Iacopo Fava and the officials sentenced Giovanni Antelminelli to pay 5 gold florins because he had had Bruges authorities arrest another merchant from Lucca, Matteo Matafelloni, without asking the consul for permission first, thus breaching Chapter 8 of the Charter.[9] Such statutory rule aimed to encourage the merchants to settle their conflicts within the community: that's why it laid down that anyone who intended to bring their cases to Bruges authorities had to ask the consul for permission first. A few days later, on 24 September, some merchants were sentenced to pay 12 florins for failing to disclose information about their associations and the relevant membership.[10] On 4 October 1377, some merchants who had not shown up for Mass at Holy Cross[11] were sentenced to pay 3 *grossi* each. One month later, on 3 November, Tommaso ser Landi was sentenced by the consul (Orlandino Volpelli) to pay a fine of 5 gold florins, because he had had Nicolao Morla's horse seized without asking the consul for permission first.[12]

In some assumedly very serious cases, the penalty did not just consist of a fine but could go as far as to have a member expelled from the Lucchese community. The expulsion of a member meant that all the merchants of the *loggia*

9 "A dì XXXI agosto, anno ditto, Giovanni Interminelli fecie arestare chon un sergente Matheo Mathafeloni e volsello fare mantenere in pregione, e cioe fecie lo ditto Giovanni sensa lisensia dell'oficio del chonsolo nè de chonsiglieri, di che à misfato chontra li nostri ordini, sichome si chontiene in scritto a chapitoli VIII. A dì V setembre, anno ditto, noi oficiali cioè Iacopo Fava chonsolo, Piero Testa, Orlandino Volpelli e Forteguera de' Forteguera chonsiglieri d'achordio in la nostra loggia chondanamo per virtude e posansa del nostro oficio Giovanni Interminelli per lo misfato ditto di sopra di avere fatto prendere Matheo Mathafeloni sensa lisensia, chondanamolo fiorini cinque d'oro, li qualli debia avere paghato da questo dì a quindici giorni a li operari nostri della chapella a pena di fiorini dieci d'oro. E chosì fue nostra sentensia"; ASLu, *Archivio Buonvisi* (part I) 40 bis, c. 3–5 [19].

10 The merchants were: Dino Malapresa, Biagio Guiducci, Iacopo del Pellaio, Tommaso ser Landi, Bartolomeo Ramoli, Clais Barbagialla, Clais Borgognoni, Dino Sanocci, Giannino Guasconi, Andrea Ronsini, Nicolao Scandaleoni, Francesco Totti; ASLu, *Archivio Buonvisi* (part I) 40 bis, c. 7–9 [23].

11 They were Giovanni Antelminelli, Andrea Ronsini, Pietro Brunelli, Duccio Sandei, Giovanni Cristofani; ASLu, *Archivio Buonvisi* (part I), 40 bis, c. 8–10 [24].

12 "A dì III novembre anno MCCCLXXVII noi officiali, cioè Orlandino Volpelli consolo, Nicolao Guinigi, Iacopo Fava, e Giannino Spada consiglieri della comunitade de luchesi, abitanti in Brugia di concordia e volontà di tutti noi officiali condanamo Tomazo ser Landi in fiorini cinque d'oro, li quali dovesse pagare da questo die a XV giorni, a pena del quarto più; la quale condanagione fue fatto perchè fece arestare lo cavallo di Nicolao Morla; lo quale aresto fue fatto sensa volontà del consolo e sensa essere richiesto, e questo è contra li nostri capitoli e ordini; li quali denari li comandamo dovesse dare alli operari della capella della Santa Croce"; ASLu, *Archivio Buonvisi* (part I), 40 bis, c. 10–12 [26]v.

were forbidden from having any business relation with the expelled individual. For instance, Giovanni Scandaleoni[13] was expelled in January 1379. He had failed to attend Mass on the first Sunday of the month many times, and, though reprimanded by the consul, Lazzaro Guinigi, he had refused to obey, showing contempt for the community. It should be noted that not long afterwards, on 10 February, Scandaleoni went to the community to apologise and ask to be readmitted. After admonishing him not to behave like that ever again, his request was granted.[14]

Again, on 8 February the same year (1379), Giovanni Pilistri was fined to pay 2 florins for not having disclosed details of the membership of his association nor provided a guarantor, as he was required to do under the Charter.[15] On 3 March 1387, Simone Schiatta was sentenced to pay a fine of 4 *grossi* for not having worn his "ghona de la livrea."[16] A month earlier, he had been admonished for betting the "livrea di Santa Croce" on a dice game with Domenico Orsi, thus debasing the sacred and symbolic value the livery had for the Lucchese community.[17]

3 Ghoverno e pace della nostra communità

The most important task that the consul was responsible for was, however, the internal management of the *loggia* and its relationships with the host country and its merchant community. Elected by merchants "per ghoverno e pace della nostra communità"[18] (for the supervision and peace of our community),

13 ASLu, *Archivio Buonvisi* (part I), 40 bis, c. 17–19 [33]v.

14 ASLu, *Archivio Buonvisi* (part I), 40 bis, c. 18–20 [34]. The prohibition to trade with merchants expelled from the *loggia* was strictly adhered to: a short while after the expulsion of Scandaleoni, another merchant, Iacopo Maulini, accused by Piero Brunelli, was sentenced to pay the quite hefty fine of 10 florins for breaching the prohibition to do business with the expelled Scandaleoni.

15 «A dì VIII di ferraio 1379 lo consolo e consiglieri di choncordia fecieno fare comandamento a Iohanni Pilistri, nostro lucchese, che infra VIII dì dovesse avere pagato a Luizo Anguilla, operaio della chappella di Santa Croce nostra di Brugia, fiorini due d'oro, perchè non avea dato per scripto li compagni e fattori, nè dato pagaria, chome si contiene per li staduti della nostra comunità che ciascuno debbia fare; di che lo ditto, benchè grave li paresse, paghò al ditto Luizo li ditti II fiorini», ASLu, *Archivio Buonvisi* (part I), 40 bis, c. 18–20 [34] v.

16 ASLu, *Archivio Buonvisi* (part I), 40 bis, c. 53–55 [72] v.

17 ASLu, *Archivio Buonvisi* (part I), 40 bis, c. 52–54 [71] v.

18 This phrase comes from the 1478 Charter of the Bruges *loggia*, Galoppini, "Lo statuto," 38.

the consul was called to deal with and attempt to settle the problems and controversies that could arise within the community, usually trying to "sedare e pacificare"[19] (subdue and reconcile) to keep the community united.

This was not an easy feat, since the squabbles and controversies were not always for financial reasons, but sometimes they reflected conflicts between political factions that were taking place in Lucca.[20] In the intricate web of family and business relationships among merchants, which inevitably were influenced by the events unfolding in Lucca, the consul had to try to keep a neutral stance towards the Lucchese merchant community in a foreign land. We know that in 2 years (1387, 1400) the community failed to find agreement over the election of the consul. In 1387, it was the Elders of Lucca who elected the consul and the councillors, lacking a decision from the Bruges community. The latter opposed to the appointment made by the Elders, and fierce arguments burst out at the merchant assembly.[21] So, the Elders of Lucca had to reconfirm their decision in December of the same year and obliged the community to accept it. [22]

No election took place in 1400 either, due to internal strife: in this case, the consul does not seem to have been elected by Lucca.

Again, in 1401, internal strife, "dibatti e discordie" (arguments and disagreements) made the new election problematic. On this occasion, the merchants of Bruges decided to ask Paolo Domaschi, "ultimo consolo," the last consul elected in 1399, and a merchant, Clais Barbagialla, who had encouraged the community to overcome their disagreements,[23] to elect the new consul.

Quarrels within the Bruges community were certainly influenced by the faction fights between the Rapondi-Forteguerra and the Guinigi families and

19 "Però che la intensione di questo capitulo è … che tale questioni fusseno sedate e pacificate per gente della natione et intra lor medesimi che andando in altro luogo," Galoppini, "Lo statuto," 38.

20 Conflicts that quite often escalated into violent, bloody fights; let's mention the tragic demise of Forteguerra Forteguerra, who had been consul in Bruges in 1384–1385. A prominent supporter of the anti-Guinigi faction, because of this Forteguerra was killed in Lucca on 12 May 1392; Christine Meek, *The Commune of Lucca under Pisan Rule (1342–1369)* (Cambridge, MA: The Mediaeval Academy of America, 1980), 268.

21 "… una gran parte si opuoseno alla ditta electione del ditto consolo e consiglieri, per modo che grande discordia e disensione fue intra dicti raunati," ASLu, *Archivio Buonvisi* (part 1), 40 bis, c. 57–59 [76].

22 On 28 December 1387, the consul Piero Testa summoned the *loggia* to read out the order received from the Elders of Lucca, which confirmed the election, and then nobody objected "non vi fue niuno contradicesse," ibid.

23 ASLu, *Archivio Buonvisi* (part 1), 40 bis, c. 107–109 [128].

their *secta* in Lucca in those years. 1400, the year in which the community failed to elect a consul due to internal strife, was also the year in which, in October, Paolo Guinigi seized power and became the Lord of Lucca. [24]

Based on recurring examples from the *Libro,* when the consul had to deal with problems and controversies, he did not have the role of a monocratic authority that wielded exclusive power. The method we see constantly applied was referring the discussion of a problem to an ad hoc committee of merchants of the *loggia,* to which the consul and the councillors belonged. The committee decided by a majority rule. All this procedure too is written in the *Libro* each time, along with a list of the names of the merchants that served on the committee.

One of the many examples contained in the *Libro* is the controversy that arose in November 1393 between Carlo Ronghi and Luiso Brunelli, regarding a few financial liabilities from the Forteguerra's estate.[25] Brunelli wanted the consul to persuade Carlo Ronghi into referring the matter to the *loggia* and, if Ronghi brought the controversy to the court of Bruges instead, he wanted to be assisted by the community itself. A committee of eight merchants was set up to investigate such claim.[26] After a long discussion, the committee decided to assist neither party, which sparked Brunelli's harsh protests. [27]

It should be pointed out that in some circumstances the whole community was called to vote on individual decisions: for instance, in the case of Piero Graziani's expulsion from the merchant community (17 April 1379) and in the case of his readmission (7 July 1380), the decision was voted on by the entire assembly.

4 The Consul and Relations with the Host Cities

Even more complex than the internal management of the community and its conflicts and tensions was the consul's task of handling the relationships

24 *Paolo Guinigi e il suo tempo*, Proceedings of the Conference (Lucca, 24–25 May 2001), Quaderni lucchesi di Studi sul Medioevo e sul Rinascimento 4, n°1-2 (2003). Lucca: San Marco Litotipo. Franca Ragone, "Guinigi, Paolo," *Dizionario Biografico degli Italiani* 61 (2004), https://www.treccani.it/enciclopedia/paolo-guinigi_%28Dizionario-Biografico%29/.

25 Cf. nt. 20; ASLu, *Archivio Buonvisi* (part 1), 40 bis, c. 80–82 [100].

26 *Ibidem*: Gallico da Piastra, Paolo Domaschi, Betto Schiatta, Francesco Totti, Iacopo del Bello, Piero Panichi, Tommaso Fortebraccia and Orlandino Benetti.

27 About such controversy, see Laura Galoppini, "Il Libro della comunità dei Lucchesi a Bruges (1377–1404): i conflitti celati," *The Southern African Journal of Medieval and Renaissance Studies* 22/23 (2012/13), 63–90.

between the *natio lucensis* and the authorities of Bruges. Relations with the political authorities and the merchants of Flanders were one of the most awkward issues for the Lucchese community, which was also involved in those that concerned the *logge* in England, "nostri fratelli da Londra"[28] (our brothers from London), and in France, "nostri fratelli luchesi abitanti in Parigi"[29] (our Lucchese brothers living in Paris). Actually, the Bruges community was the vertex of an economic-mercantile triangle that included Paris and London, the cities in which many of the Lucchese communities in Bruges had their *fattori*, or agents. These relations clearly emerge from the records of the *Libro,* where at least a couple of times we see the Bruges *loggia* involved in the vicissitudes of the Lucchese community in London.

The first case arose in 1379 following a request made by the London's merchants to the *natio lucensis* in London, asking them to deal exclusively with their community, a request that the Lucchese merchants had turned down.[30] A merchant, Piero Graziani, was the only one who, in contrast with the decision of the *loggia,* signed a secret agreement with the London merchants, granting their requests, and for this reason he was expelled from the London community. At first, it seemed to be an internal matter, which the London consul informed the Bruges *loggia* about. Then, he asked those he considered his "elder brothers" to do the same, that is, to exclude Graziani from any business relationship with the *loggia*, which the Bruges community, as we mentioned before, did.

The case had serious consequences, because Piero Graziani reported some of his compatriots to the London authorities, accusing them of attempting to kill him. The London authorities arrested several merchants from Lucca, conducted searches of their homes and seized confidential letters and documents, as the consul of London reported to the consul of Bruges.[31]

This case, the conclusion of which is unknown to us,[32] is extremely significant in showing how serious tension within the community could escalate into a conflict with the local authorities. These were probably not completely

28 ASLu, *Archivio Buonvisi* (part 1), 40 bis, c. 19–21 [35]; Bart Lambert, "Nostri fratelli da Londra": the Lucchese community in Late medieval England," in *Anglo-Italian Cultural Relation in the Later Middle Ages*, eds. Helen Fulton and Michele Campopiano (York: York Medieval Press, 2018), 87–102.

29 ASLu, *Archivio Buonvisi* (part 1), 40 bis, c. 14–16 [30].

30 The "angiusta e dizordinata domanda che mercieri di questa villa fecieno alla nostra comunità, che voleano che noi ci legassimo di non vendere nessuna merchantia ad altri che solo a lloro, e a pezi del paeze," ASLu, *Archivio Buonvisi* (part 1), 40 bis, c. 18–20 [34] v.

31 ASLu, *Archivio Buonvisi* (part 1), 40 bis, c. 19–21 [35] v.

32 No additional mentions of this event can be found in the *Libro* nor have they been found in any other source.

disinterested nor impartial since the cause of it all was the request made by the London merchants, which the Lucchese merchants had rejected. This explains the cautious and confidential tone in which such events were discussed in Bruges later on, where it was decided that the matter should not be investigated within the entire community, but "molto meglio e più segretamente ... per poghi" (much better and more confidentially .... with few), namely by the consul, the three councillors and a selected group of four or six merchants.[33]

A second case was reported in 1387: Francesco Vinciguerra had been accused by the King of England (Richard II) of having left London with his family in secrecy for Flanders, carrying along some precious items he had in his safekeeping for the Bishop of Durham, to whom he also owed a large sum of money. So, the King asked the consul, as he had already asked the Elders of Lucca, to compel Vinciguerra to repay what he owed or go back to England and answer for the charges that had been brought against him, threatening him, if he did not, to take his revenge on all the Lucchese merchants in the country.[34] The matter was addressed by Iacopo Fava, consul of the *loggia* of Bruges, where Francesco Vinciguerra resided at that time. He had to be treated with the utmost caution, since he was not just a merchant of Lucca, he also was a citizen of Bruges, the "burgesia di Brugia." Therefore, the consul discussed the case with the burgomaster and the aldermen of Bruges – "ser Gianni Metenon burghimastro chon IIII schiavini" – showing them the letter of the King of England.[35] Even in this case, the situation was so delicate that they decided not to discuss the best course of action with the entire community but with a selected committee, that is, with the consul, Iacopo Fava, the three councillors (Piero Testa, Lorenzo Trenta, Francesco Totti) and four merchants.[36] Within the committee, the discussion about what should be done was very heated and became so fierce that it had consequences.[37] In conclusion, with a majority of five to

33 The six merchants were Giannino Spada, Iacopo Fava, Matteo Mattafelloni, Gallico da Piastra, Francesco Totti and Luiso Brunelli, ASLu, *Archivio Buonvisi* (part I), 40 bis, c. 20–22 [36] v.

34 The King's letter was delivered to consul Iacopo Fava of the Bruges *loggia* in Middelburg on 23 April 1387, ASLu, *Archivio Buonvisi* (part I) 40 bis, c. 54–56 [73] v.

35 Ibid.

36 Ibid. The four merchants were: Francesco Panichi, Gallico da Piastra, Luiso Brunelli and Paolo Domaschi.

37 Insults had flown during the discussion, and the consul threatened to directly summon the Elders of Lucca and punish the transgressors who at this point withdrew their statements (ASLu, *Archivio Buonvisi* (part I), 40 bis, c. 55–57 [74] v.), except for Dino Sanocci, who did not want to recant what he had said, namely that the consul and the

three, they decided to order Vinciguerra to go back to London and explain his position.

The decision to discuss the matters that were most sensible and complex for the Lucchese community within a much more restricted circle than the merchant assembly – as we saw in the two cases above – is part of a *modus operandi*, inspired by the will to protect the *natio* in a foreign land to the greatest extent, while keeping the community's own problems as secret as possible. In this respect, it might be useful to recall that Chapter 9 of the 1478 Charter set forth the obligation of secrecy over the matters that the consul considered to be confidential and particularly sensitive.[38] As the text of the 1369 Charter is missing, we do not know whether it contained any guidelines to such effect, but we can assume, however, that there must have been a similar concern about disclosing the most awkward matters of the community.[39]

Sometimes, there were problems and disagreements with the authorities of Bruges as well: sometimes, they arose from the fact that some Lucchese merchants were citizens of Bruges – as in the case of Francesco Vinciguerra – and they appealed to that when they found it most convenient.

A case in point is that of Caterina Rapondi, widow of Pietro Brunelli (July 1393). When her late husband's inheritance had to be shared, Caterina, who, like Brunelli and their children, was a citizen of Bruges, asked that the city's law be enforced, whereby she was owed three quarters of the inheritance, half of which to her and a quarter for her late children.[40] On the contrary, the Elders of

---

others had behaved worse than tyrants, "pegio che i tirani" – and for this he was eventually fined, ASLu, *Archivio Buonvisi* (part I), 40 bis, c. 56–58 [75].

38 "Item che quelle cose si praticheranno e delibereranno nella nostra natione, le quali il consolo amonisse doversi tenere secrete, che ciascuno sia tenuto tenerle segrete sensa parlarne a persona, salvo con quelli che a ditta deliberatione si sianno trovati, a pena di fiorini 4 d'oro," Galoppini, "Lo statuto," 39.

39 Laura Galoppini, "Mantenere il segreto: mercatura e politica per i lucchesi a Bruges nel tardo medioevo," in *La necessità del segreto. Indagini sullo spazio politico nell'Italia medievale ed oltre*, eds. Jacques Chiffoleau, Étienne Hubert and Roberta Mucciarelli (Rome: Viella, 2018), 323–335.

40 The request was submitted on 23 July by Clais Barbagialla, Caterina's new husband: "a dì 23 luglio Clais soprascritto fecie domanda ... in nome della donna di Clais dicto e donna in qua di rieto che fue di Petro Brunelli, di tre quarti dello avere ... apresso la morte del dicto Petro, cioè la metà apartenente a lei e il ¼ per la morte de' figli, sicome di ciòe che lli perviene per loia et borgesia, è uzansa della villa di Brugia, sicome burgiese ella e Petro e figli ch'erano di questa villa." On 26 July, the consul told the Elders of Lucca about Barbagialla's request, cf. ASLu, *Archivio Buonvisi* (part I), 40 bis, c. 74–76 [94]. Laura Galoppini, *Mercanti toscani e Bruges nel tardo Medioevo* (Pisa: Edizioni Plus, Pisa University Press, 2009), 105, 301–302; for all the merchants from Lucca mentioned in this article, refer to the index, *sub nomine*.

Lucca claimed that the laws of their city applied to the Brunelli estate because Caterina Rapondi was a native of Lucca, where, in addition, most of such property was located. The controversy dragged on for a long time, and the Flemish authorities threatened reprisals against the whole community in Bruges.

Some other times, problems could arise with the authorities of Bruges because of conflicts of interest with the local merchants, similar to what had happened in London in 1379.

In 1393, the authorities of Bruges, upon request of the city's Society of Apothecaries, ordered all foreign merchants to sell spices and other wares wholesale only, leaving the retail trade exclusively to the local merchants. The *loggia* informed the Elders of Lucca in a letter, a copy of which is in the community's *Libro,* dated 3 September 1393. In the letter, they complained that the merchants had to suffer all sorts of harassment from the local apothecaries, under the guise of supervising public order.[41]

5 Conclusions

From the records of the *Libro della comunità,* we can easily infer the duties that the 1369 Charter, the text of which is missing – assigned to the consul. These duties were the same as those of the 1478 Charter: organising the yearly election of the consul and the other officials; making all the members of the Lucchese community take an oath of loyalty to the Charter; recording the merchant communities operating in Bruges; demanding payment of the tributes from the merchants for the upkeep of the Chapel of the Holy Cross (*diritto di Santa Croce*); organising the yearly procession of the *Volto Santo*; enforcing attendance of the monthly Mass; trying to solve problems among merchants within the community; checking that no one infringed the Charters, and imposing sanctions on those who did.

The consul, a merchant elected by a community of merchants who were his equals, working in a foreign country, was essentially entrusted to maintain, partly through a strict adherence to all the religious rites, the unity and cohesion of the *natio Lucensis,* to ensure the commune of Lucca of the loyalty of these men, away from their motherland, and to defend and protect their business and interests by handling relations with the authorities of Bruges. This in a context in which they had to face lots of competitors from different Euro-

41 ASLu, *Archivio Buonvisi* (part 1), 40 bis, c. 78–80 [98].

pean nations and the mistrusting competition of the local merchants, to keep their community, as aptly said by one of these Lucchese merchants, as "la meglio unita e più pregiata comunità che fusse a Brugia"[42] (the closest and most esteemed community that ever was in Bruges).

Bibliography

Bongi, Salvatore and Del Prete, Leone, eds. *Statuto del Comune di Lucca dell'anno 1308 ora per la prima volta pubblicato*. Lucca: Tip. Giusti, 1867.

De Roover, Raymond. "La communauté des marchands lucquois à Bruges." *Annales de la Société d'Émulation de Bruges* 86 (1949): 23–89.

Galoppini, Laura. *Mercanti toscani e Bruges nel tardo Medioevo*. Pisa: Pisa University Press, 2009.

Galoppini, Laura. "Lucchesi e uomini di comunità a Bruges nel tardo Medioevo." In *'Mercatura è arte': Uomini d'affari toscani in Europa e nel Mediterraneo tardomedievale*, edited by Lorenzo Tanzini and Sergio Tognetti. Rome: Viella, 2012.: 45–79

Galoppini, Laura. "Il Libro della comunità dei Lucchesi a Bruges (1377–1404): i conflitti celati." *The Southern African Journal of Medieval and Renaissance Studies* 22/23, n° 13 (2012): 63–90.

Galoppini, Laura. "Lo statuto della nazione dei lucchesi di Bruges (1478–1498)." In *Honos alit artes. Studi per il settantesimo compleanno di Mario Ascheri, vol. II, Gli universi particolari: Città e territori dal medioevo all'età moderna*, edited by Paola Maffei and Gian Maria Varanini, 33–42. Florence: Firenze University Press, 2014.

Galoppini, Laura. "'Retornare a quella antica usanza del consolato': uno statuto per i mercanti lucchesi in Anversa (metà XVI sec.)." *Bollettino Storico Pisano* 86 (2017): 131–146.

Lambert, Bart. "'Nostri fratelli da Londra': the Lucchese community in Late Medieval England." In *Anglo-Italian Cultural Relation in the Later Middle Ages*, edited by Helen Fulton and Michele Campopiano. York: York Medieval Press, 2018: 87–102.

Lazzareschi, Eugenio, ed. *Libro della comunità dei mercanti lucchesi in Bruges*. Milan: R. Malfasi, 1947.

Lucca, il Volto Santo e la civiltà medioevale, Proceedings of the International Study Conference (Lucca, Palazzo Pubblico 21–23 October 1982). Lucca: Maria Pacini Fazzi Editore, 1984.

Meek, Christine, *The Commune of Lucca under Pisan Rule (1342–1369)*. Cambridge, MA: The Mediaeval Academy of America, 1980.

42 ASLu, *Archivio Buonvisi* (part I), 40 bis, c. 107–109 [128].

Paolo Guinigi e il suo tempo, Proceedings of the Conference (Lucca, 24–25 May 2001), *Quaderni lucchesi di Studi sul Medioevo e sul Rinascimento* 4, n 1-2 (2003). Lucca: San Marco Litotipo.

Ragone, Franca. "Guinigi, Paolo." *Dizionario Biografico degli Italiani*. Accessed November 05, 2024. https://www.treccani.it/enciclopedia/paolo-guinigi_(Dizionario-Biografico)/.

2

La justice des consuls florentins d'après les statuts des nations marchandes (fin XIIIe–début XVIe siècle)

Cédric Quertier

1 Introduction

Les nations marchandes florentines sont moins connues que leurs homologues vénitiennes, génoises, pisanes ou catalanes[1]. De même, l'historiographie récente de la justice marchande a rarement pris en compte les nations[2]. L'ana-

1 Les nations marchandes sont définies par Giovanna Petti Balbi comme « des associations privées et volontaires, constituées par des hommes d'affaires qui séjournent temporairement en terre étrangère. Ils s'y agglomèrent en fonction de leur origine géographique afin de poursuivre des objectifs et des intérêts communs, se proposent comme interlocuteurs directs des pouvoirs locaux, sans pourtant relâcher les liens avec la patrie ou chercher à s'établir dans une zone exclusive. […] Pour exister, une nation a aussi besoin de soutien externe, ainsi que de reconnaissance politique et juridique » (je traduis). Giovanna Petti Balbi, « Le *nationes* italiane all'estero », dans *Il Rinascimento italiano e l'Europa*. IV : *Commercio e cultura mercantile*, éd. Franco Franceschini, Richard A. Goldthwaite et Reinhold Ch. Mueller (Costabissara : Angelo Colla editore, 2007), 399.

2 Voir notamment Albrecht Cordes et Philipp Höhn, « Extra-Legal and Legal Conflict Management among Long Distance Traders (1250–1650) », dans *The Oxford Handbook of European Legal History*, éd. Heiki Pihlajamäki, Marcus D. Dubber, Mark Godfrey (Oxford : Oxford University Press, 2018), 511–512, https://doi.org/10.1093/oxfordhb/9780198785521.013.22; *Conflict Management in the Mediterranean and the Atlantic, 1000–1800 : Actors, Institutions and Strategies of Dispute Settlement*, éd. Louis Sicking et Alain Wijffels (Leyde : Brill, 2020). Sur la *lex mercatoria* et ses limites, voir : Albrecht Cordes, « À la recherche d'une *Lex mercatoria* au Moyen Âge », dans *Stadt und Recht im Mittelalter. La ville et le droit au Moyen Âge*, éd. Pierre Monnet et Otto Gerhard Oexle (Göttingen : Vandenhoeck & Ruprecht, 2003), 117–132 ; *id.*, « en italiques ? Local, Regional and Universal Maritime Law in the Middle Ages », dans *The Routledge Handbook of Maritime Trade around Europe 1300–1600*, éd. Willem Pieter Blockmans, Michail Marcovic Krom et Justyna Wubs-Mrozewicz (Londres etc. : Routledge, 2017), 69–85. Plus généralement Vito Piergiovanni, *Norme, scienza giuridica tra Genova e l'Occidente medievale e moderno* (Gênes : Società Ligure di Storia Patria, 2012) ; Stefania Gialdroni *et al.*, *Migrating Words, Migrating Merchants, Migrating Law : Trading Routes and the Development of Commercial Law* (Leyde : Brill, 2020) ; *From Lex Mercatoria to Commercial Law*, éd. Vito Piergiovanni (Berlin : Duncker & Humblot, 2005) ; *The Courts and the Development of Commercial Law*, éd. Vito Piergiovanni (Berlin : Duncker & Humblot, 1987).

 | HTTPS://DOI.ORG/10.1163/9789004755192-004

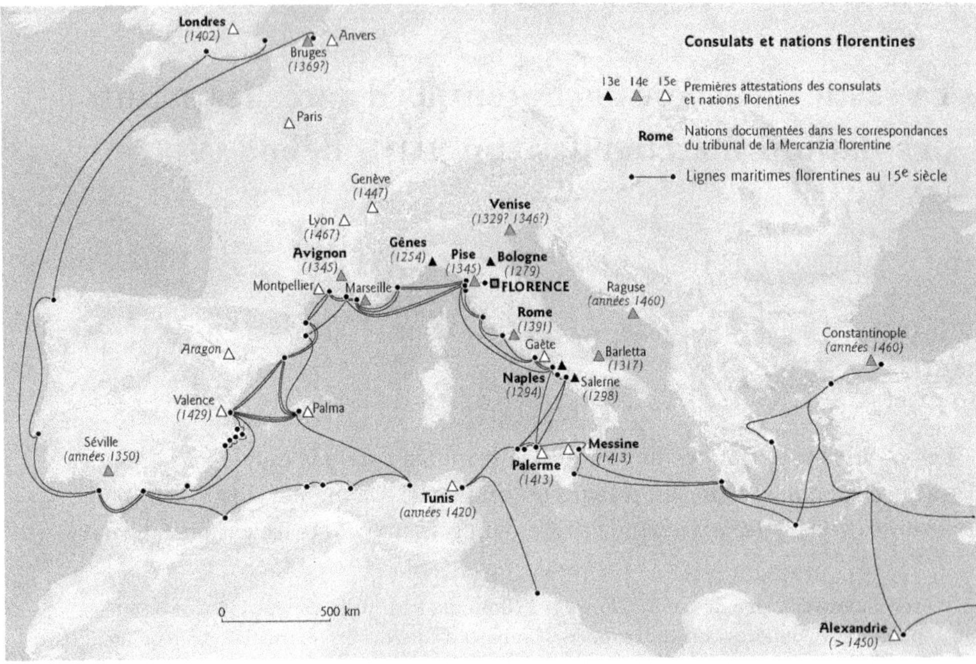

MAP 2.1 Premières attestations des consulats et nations florentines

SOURCE : CÉDRIC QUERTIER ET PATRICK PENTSCH, PRODUCTION PROPRE

lyse du rôle judiciaire des nations florentines du XIIIe siècle au début du XVIe siècle cherche donc à combler cette double lacune en examinant dix statuts. Or, l'institution de rattachement des nations, qui conserve leurs statuts, a varié dans le temps. Au XIIIe siècle, l'Art de la Calimala exerce cette tutelle et ne conserve que le statut de Bologne (1279–1289). Elle est ensuite récupérée par le tribunal de la *Mercanzia* en 1308, qui a enregistré le statut de Pise (1381) et des informations partielles pour Venise (1346), Rome (1391), la Sicile (1413) et Tunis (1421). Après les années 1420, le Consulat de la Mer prend le relais[3]: bien mieux conservées[4], ses archives ont permis à Gino Masi d'éditer une partie des sta-

3 ASFi, Consoli del mare, 3, fol. 4. Le Consulat de la Mer est une magistrature florentine instituée de manière stable à partir de 1421, chargée de développer le commerce, de surveiller et de développer la navigation, et d'entretenir des rapports commerciaux avec les autres États. Elle marque un tournant dans l'histoire de Florence, qui se dote alors d'une flotte d'État sur le modèle vénitien, et transfère la gestion des nations aux Consuls de la Mer. Voir la note 76 de cet article pour la bibliographie.

4 Notamment ASFi, Consoli del mare, 3, 8, 9, 15 et 17.

tuts du XVe et du XVe siècle[5]: ceux de Bruges (1427 et 1460), de Constantinople (1488 et 1492), de Lyon (1501), de Londres (1513) et de Rome (1515)[6], mais pas ceux de Raguse (1570), d'Ancône (1548), d'Anvers (qui reprend en réalité celui de Bruges) et de Venise (1540). Trop tardifs pour notre étude ou fragmentaires, ces derniers n'ont pas été pris en compte ici, contrairement à celui de Naples (1430) conservé à la Biblioteca Riccardiana de Florence[7]. En somme, plusieurs époques de compilation des statuts des nations se dégagent, lorsque Florence formalise l'extension de son réseau commercial avec des pouvoirs partenaires favorables : les années 1380 (Pise), autour de 1430 (Bruges et Naples), les années 1480 (Constantinople), 1500 (Lyon) et 1510 (Londres et Rome), avec par la suite d'autres phases dans les années 1540 et 1570.

Ces statuts précisent comment les nations constituaient et conservaient leurs archives par-delà la rotation des consuls. Ces derniers doivent ainsi tenir un registre chronologique contenant tous les décrets, délibérations, procès et traces écrites concernant la nation[8]. Il s'agit donc de livres-journaux et d'aide-mémoires mêlant des sujets divers, où le judiciaire côtoie le financier et le politique[9]. Tenus par les consuls, par un notaire-syndic (Pise 1381) ou parfois par le camerlingue (Constantinople 1488), ces registres sont hétérogènes : l'écriture et la conservation des registres de statuts doivent être soignés[10], mais l'enregistrement des procès peut devenir une annexe du livre de compte[11]. Que les actes soient compilés chronologiquement ou thématiquement, les registres judiciaires ne font pas l'objet d'une attention particulière. Le tout est conservé dans un petit coffre transmis de consul en consul, sans jamais faire l'objet de rapatriement à Florence[12]. Pour ces raisons, l'exi-

5 Pour la période postérieure, voir Marcella Aglietti, *L'istituto consolare tra Sette e Ottocento. Funzioni istituzionali, profilo giuridico e percorsi professionali nella Toscana granducale* (Pise : ETS, 2012).

6 Irene Polverini Fosi, « Il consolato fiorentino a Roma ed il progetto per la chiesa nazionale », *Studi Romani* 37 (1989) : 50–70. La copie florentine est conservée dans ASFi, Consolato del Mare, 9, fol. 39r–53r.

7 Naples 1430 ; Bruno Figliuolo, « L'organigramma della nazione fiorentina a Napoli dagli statuti del 1430 », dans *Comunità forestiere e « nationes » nell'Europa dei secoli XIII–XVI*, éd. Giovanna Petti Balbi (Naples : Liguori, 2001), 191–200.

8 Bruges 1461, rub. 35, 21 ; Londres 1513, rub. 22, 176.

9 Hermann U. Kantorowicz, *Albertus Gandinus und das Strafrecht der Scholastik, t. I : Die Praxis. Ausgewählte Strafprozessakten des dreizehnten Jahrhunderts nebts diplomatischer Einteilung* (Berlin : J. Guttentag, 1907), 72.

10 Constantinople 1488, rub. 36, 71–72.

11 Constantinople 1488, rub. 24, 60–63.

12 Bruges 1461, rub. 34, 20–21 ; Constantinople 1488, rub. 36, 71–72 ; Lyon 1501, rub. 30, 219–220 ; Londres 1513, rub. 22, 176.

TABLEAU 2.1 Liste simplifiée des statuts retenus pour cette étude

Ville d'accueil	Date
Bologne	1279–1289
Pise	1381
Bruges	1427
Naples	1430
Bruges	1461
Constantinople	1488
Constantinople	1492
Lyon	1501
Londres	1513
Rome	1515

SOURCE: L'ouvrage de Masi, *Statuti delle colonie* comporte l'édition de fragments de statuts pour Lyon (1487), Londres (1457 et 1505), et Constantinople (1500, 1503, 1505, 1507, 1511, 1528, 1531, 1534, 1544, 1546). On ne les a pas retenus ici car ils ne permettent pas de se faire une idée complète de l'activité d'une nation. Pour des raisons de concision, nous utiliserons les abréviations suivantes, mentionnant la ville du statut, son année de compilation, sa rubrique (rub.), et la page (pour une édition moderne) ou le folio (pour le manuscrit original) correspondant. Bologne 1279 = Augusto Gaudenzi, « Statuti dei mercanti fiorentini dimoranti in Bologna degli anni 1279–1289 », *Archivio storico italiano* 163, n° 1 (1888) : 1–19, la numérotation des rubriques est de notre fait ; Pise 1381 = Cédric Quertier, *Guerres et richesses d'une nation. Les Florentins à Pise au XIVe siècle* (Rome : École Française de Rome, 2022), 467–472 ; Bruges 1427 et 1461 = *Statuti delle colonie fiorentine all'estero* (*secc. XV–XVI*), éd. Gino Masi (Milan : Giuffrè, 1941), 3–33 ; Naples 1430 = *Statuti per il console della repubblica fiorentina in Sicilia* (Florence : Biblioteca Riccardiana, 1825), http://www.riccardiana.firenze.sbn.it/colorionLAB/page.php?segn=Ricc.1825 ; Constantinople 1488 = *Statuti delle colonie*, 37–78 ; Constantinople 1492 = *Statuti delle colonie*, 79–96 ; Lyon 1501 = *Statuti delle colonie*, 201–234 ; Londres 1513 = *Statuti delle colonie*, 165–189 ; Rome 1515 = ASFi, Consoli del mare, 9, fol. 39r–53r.

stence de registres judiciaires *ad hoc*, comme dans le cas des Lucquois de Bruges[13], est dans l'ensemble très rare.

Le statut de Naples (1430) explique comment ces écrits doivent être conservés : savoir clairement à quel stade se trouve chaque litige et garder en mémoire la procédure[14]. À Constantinople (1488)[15], les registres doivent conserver la trace dûment datée de toutes les transactions de la communauté

13 Voir les travaux de Laura Galoppini et son article dans ce volume.

14 Naples 1430, rub. 4, fol. 10 et rub. 22, fol. 30r–32r.

15 Constantinople 1488, rub. 25, p. 63.

et de tous les actes décisionnels (délibérations) et juridiques (pétitions et sentences, avec les demandes et les réponses apportées). À Rome (1515)[16], les compagnies doivent même fournir au consul un compte-rendu annuel de leurs activités. Cela suppose donc un enregistrement rapide et sans altération : à Lyon (1501), l'inscription être faite trois jours après le procès[17] et, à Londres (1513), il est interdit de canceller les condamnations sans l'autorisation du consul, des conseillers ou des trois quarts des chefs de compagnie[18]. Ces registres « nationaux » ont donc avant tout une fonction mémorielle. Mais dès la fin du XVe siècle, les consuls doivent pouvoir exhiber les preuves des transactions de toute la communauté : l'idée n'est pas de conserver les archives d'une hypothétique jurisprudence, mais plutôt d'être capable de prouver que les privilèges et les transactions sont légitimes.

On s'attachera donc ici à décrire l'importance et la conception de la justice consulaire dans l'organisation des nations florentines entre la fin du XIIIe siècle et le début du XVIe siècle. Pour cela, on analysera la figure du juge consulaire et des procédures, avant de circonscrire les pouvoirs judiciaires du consul. Enfin, la nécessaire confrontation avec les autres juridictions sera abordée.

2 Le consul et ses officiers : qui juge dans les nations ?

Le consul – sous ses diverses appellations – à la tête de la nation marchande possède le pouvoir de commander et de contraindre. Il dispose donc d'un pouvoir judiciaire, seul ou assisté d'officiers spécialisés.

Dans la première configuration, le consul est le seul détenteur de l'autorité judiciaire, à Bruges (1427)[19], à Naples (1430)[20], à Londres (1513)[21] et à Lyon (1501)[22]. C'est aussi le cas dans les anciens consulats pisans réorganisés par Florence : dès 1413[23], les Florentins s'approprient les consulats pisans de

16 Polverini Fosi, « Il consolato fiorentino a Roma », 60–61 ; rub. 31–32, confirmée en 1515 et en 1519.

17 Lyon 1501, rub. 50, 230–231.

18 Londres 1513, rub. 26, 177–178.

19 Bruges 1427, rub. 2–4, 7–8.

20 Naples 1430, rub. 13, fol. 20r–25r.

21 Londres 1513, rub. 10, 171.

22 Lyon 1501, rub. 40, 224–225 ; Michele Cassandro, « I forestieri a Lione nel '400 e '500 : la nazione fiorentina », dans *Dentro la città : stranieri e realtà urbane nell'Europa dei secoli XII–XVI*, éd. Gabriella Rossetti (Naples : Liguori, 1989), 155, note 20.

23 ASFi, Mercanzia, 11312, fol. 26r–v, 31 mai 1413. Le mouvement se renforce plus tard : Henri Bresc, *Un monde méditerranéen. Économie et société en Sicile 1300–1450* (Rome : École

Sicile[24], qui possédaient une compétence judiciaire arbitrale et, en 1421, de celui de Tunis[25], qui délègue le règlement des conflits entre chrétiens au consul de l'accusé et non plus aux seuls Pisans[26]. Dès 1513 enfin, le consul de Rome peut juger les conflits civils entre Florentins, traités par un notaire après 1519[27].

Dans une seconde configuration, le consul partage ses prérogatives judiciaires avec un officier. À Bologne (1279–1289), le consul doit ainsi faire élire un syndic et procurateur pour les conflits entre sociétés florentines, et un autre pour ceux déclenchés par des transactions avec d'autres sociétés non-florentines[28]. À Pise, la direction bicéphale se partage des attributions judiciaires dès 1345. Le notaire-syndic (florentin) s'occupe de la discipline interne, du rappel des normes par une lecture publique du statut tous les trois mois, de la correspondance avec la *Mercanzia* et de l'arbitrage des différends dans un délai de trente jours. De son côté, le consul (pisan) s'assure que les tribunaux locaux traitent favorablement les Florentins[29]. De même, à Venise vers 1346, si le consul et le *recollector* ont des fonctions judiciaires, un notaire exerçant les fonctions de procurateur, syndic et défenseur des Florentins commerçant à Venise et ses alentours apparaît. Procurateur officiel devant les tribunaux, il doit défendre les Florentins afin de prévenir toute injustice dans l'application des accords bilatéraux[30]. Au XVIe siècle, la Compagnia di San Giovanni Battista dei Fiorentini, confrérie fonctionnant en parallèle de la nation, voit son consul et ses deux conseillers chargés d'administrer « ragione et giustitia alli mercatanti et a tutta la natione fiorentina »[31]. De même, des années 1460 aux années 1530, le consul (puis l'*emin* après 1500)[32] des Floren-

---

française de Rome, 1986), 387, tableau n° 79 : à Palerme en 1445, 1455, 1458 et à Messine en 1445, 1454, 1455.

24 David Abulafia, « Pisan Commercial Colonies and Consulates in Twelfth-Century Sicily », *The English Historian Review* 93 (1978) : 75–78 : ils existaient à Messine depuis 1270, voire 1189, et à Palerme depuis 1308.

25 *I diplomi arabi del R. Archivio Fiorentino*, Michele Amari éd. (Florence : Le Monnier, 1863), série 2, n° 36, 326.

26 Ingrid Houssaye Michienzi, *Datini, Majorque et le Maghreb (14e–15e siècles) : réseaux, espaces méditerranéens et stratégies marchandes* (Leyde : Brill, 2013), 173–174, qui cite l'article 2 du traité.

27 Polverini Fosi, « Il consolato fiorentino a Roma », 62, rub. 12, confirmée en 1515 et 1519.

28 Gaudenzi, « Statuti dei mercanti fiorentini », 16–17, rub. *De electione syndici et procuratoris societatis*.

29 Quertier, *Guerres et richesses d'une nation*, 175–193.

30 ASFi, Mercanzia, 153, 15 décembre 1346.

31 Reinhold C. Mueller, « Mercanti e imprenditori fiorentini a Venezia nel tardo Medioevo », *Società e Storia* 55 (1992) : 32 ; Agostino Sagredo, « Statuti della fraternità e compagnia dei fiorentini in Venezia dell' anno MDLVI », *Archivio storico italiano* 9 (1853) : 441–492.

32 Ingrid Houssaye Michienzi, « Les milieux d'affaires florentins, le commerce des draps et les marchés ottomans à la fin du XVe et au début du XVIe siècle », *Mélanges de l'École*

tins de Romanie est assisté d'un *baylos* pour les affaires judiciaires, qui gère les conflits entre Florentins, et laisse les cadis juger les litiges avec les sujets ottomans[33]. À Rome (1515), le consul et les deux tiers des conseillers jugent les cas dont la valeur n'excède pas 100 ducats, tandis qu'un juge élu se réserve les litiges supérieurs[34].

3 Les procédures judiciaires : comment juge-t-on ?

Qu'il soit assisté ou non d'officiers judiciaires, la première préoccupation des statuts est d'affirmer la pleine autorité du consul, qui assure la cohésion et la réputation de la nation.

Pour renforcer son autorité, les membres d'une nation doivent jurer d'obéir à ses ordres, dès le statut de Bologne (1279–1289)[35]. Plus précis, le statut de Bruges (1427 et 1461), impose de respecter sa réglementation et les décisions des Consuls de la mer, sous peine d'exclusion, de boycott, d'une amende de 25 livres, d'être déclaré parjure et ne pouvoir recevoir ni aide de la nation ni logement d'un particulier. Pour que nul ne puisse l'ignorer, tout nouvel arrivant est informé par le consul, et doit prêter serment dans les deux mois suivant son arrivée[36]. Ces injonctions sont répétées à Constantinople (1488)[37], Lyon (1501)[38], Londres (1513)[39] et Rome (1515)[40].

La justice consulaire est donc d'abord la justice du consul. Son but est de préserver la concorde entre les membres de la nation et d'éviter les procès (Lyon 1501)[41]. En amont, les insultes, sources de rixes et de procès, sont sévèrement punies[42], de même que les jeux de hasard, qui ajoutent les risques de blasphème et de ruine familiale[43]. Lorsqu'un conflit survient, le consul doit

---

française de Rome – Moyen Âge 127, n° 2 (2015), https://doi.org/10.4000/mefrm.2753, § 26, tableau 3.

33 Houssaye Michienzi, « Les milieux d'affaires florentins », § 24.

34 Rome 1515, rub. 11, fol. 42r–v.

35 Bologne 1279, rub. 6, 7.

36 Bruges 1427, rub. 6, 11 et Bruges 1461, rub. 36, 45, respectivement 8, 10, 21, 25.

37 Constantinople 1488, rub. 2, 39–40.

38 Lyon 1501, rub. 6, 207.

39 Londres 1513, rub. 37, 183.

40 Rome 1515, rub. 16, fol. 44.

41 Lyon 1501, rub. 40, 209.

42 Bologne 1279, rub. 44–45 (additions de 1289), 18–19 ; Bruges 1427, rub. 8 et 10, 9 et 10 ; Naples 1430, rub. 13, § 14, fol. 24v–25r ; Londres 1513, rub. 7 et 9, 169 et 171 ; Rome 1515, rub. 18 (cas des étrangers) et 20 (concitoyens), fol. 44v et fol. 45r.

43 Constantinople 1488, rub. 15, 51–52.

pousser au compromis durant deux jours avant le dépôt d'une pétition (Constantinople 1488)[44]. En revanche, la logique des acteurs peut être inverse : déclencher un procès vise à faire le plus de dommages possibles à l'adversaire, et à procurer aux Florentins le plus de profits, à la fois en récupérant des créances et en éliminant un concurrent (confrérie saint Jean Baptiste d'Avignon, 1345)[45].

Pour discipliner le règlement des conflits, les consuls s'appuient sur une procédure judiciaire et de larges pouvoirs de sanction.

Les statuts de Naples (1430) sont ceux qui nous renseignent le mieux sur la procédure[46]. Un recours judiciaire suppose le dépôt d'une pétition et d'une caution, le paiement d'une taxe (*diritto ovvero tricesima*) et de fournir un garant florentin (y compris pour les étrangers)[47]. Ces conditions sont reprises à Constantinople (1488)[48], et en partie à Rome (1515)[49].

À Lyon (1501), le consul doit juger en première instance les causes civiles en convoquant les parties, en collectant les pétitions, les réponses, les justifications des deux parties, et en émettant une sentence qui doit être ratifiée[50]. Les attributions sont similaires à Londres (1513)[51]. Ces actions doivent reposer sur la « buona usanza di merchatantia », à savoir le jugement en équité et la procédure sommaire, qui se basent sur les écritures marchandes, repérables à la fois à Bologne (1279)[52], à Naples (1430)[53] et à Lyon (1501)[54]. Ces usages s'appliquent même quand il faut prouver l'absence du défendeur pour pouvoir le juger comme contumace ou exécuter une sentence des *Sei del ricorso* (Naples 1430)[55].

Les procédures doivent donc arriver rapidement à terme. Dans le cas général, le consul de Naples (1430) doit enquêter, questionner et confronter les

---

44 Constantinople 1488, rub. 18, p. 55–56.

45 ASFi, Mercanzia, 11303, fol. 35v–36v, 6 septembre 1345 : « [una] necessità per fare al[l]a parte aversaria più dampno e a fiorentini più profitto ».

46 Naples 1430, rub. 13, fol. 20r–25r. Celle de Constantinople 1488 (rub. 18, 22, 27, 32, 34, respectivement 55–56, 58–59, 65, 69, 70–71 ; corrections 77 *sqq.*) sont également développées.

47 Naples 1430, rub. 13, §1–3, fol. 20r–21r.

48 Constantinople 1488, rub. 32, p. 69. Le consul doit aussi appliquer la rub. 18.

49 Rome 1515, rub. 13–14, fol. 43v.

50 Lyon 1501, rub. 40, 224–225.

51 Londres 1513, rub. 2, 167.

52 Bologne 1279, rub. 5, 10 et rub. 25, 14.

53 Naples 1430, rub. 13, § 4, fol. 21r–v.

54 Lyon 1501, rub. 40, 224–225.

55 Naples 1430, rub. 13, § 4, 7, 13 et 16, fol. 21r–v, 22r–23r et 25r.

parties dans les cinq jours suivant le dépôt de pétition[56]. Ensuite, tout procès doit être conclu par une sentence prise en accord avec un ou deux conseillers, par une délibération ou par une *determinazione* dans les cinq mois après le dépôt de la pétition[57] – un délai réduit à quatre mois à Lyon (1501)[58] et à un mois à Rome (1515)[59]. S'il s'agit de faire exécuter les sentences des *Sei del ricorso* de la *Mercanzia*, le délai est de 15 à 30 jours[60]. Les délais sont même plus ténus dans certains cas : pour les litiges sur les objets laissés en gage, le consul doit laisser huit jours à l'endetté pour tenter de racheter ses biens (Naples 1430)[61]; pour les successions, les sentences ordinaires doivent être confirmées trois jours après leur rédaction et les sentences définitives doivent être rendues six jours après l'interjection en appel (Constantinople 1488)[62].

Une fois ces procédures respectées, le consul dispose d'une pleine autorité et de larges pouvoirs pour faire appliquer les sentences et les peines qu'il a prononcées. Le consul doit en effet appliquer rapidement et fermement les sentences, pourvues de son sceau (Bologne 1279–1289)[63] et récolter les amendes. À Naples (1430), les sentences inscrites dans le livre des condamnations doivent entraîner immédiatement le paiement d'amendes ou la privation d'office, même si un recours dans le mois devant le conseil de la nation reste possible. Si le consul peine à récolter les amendes, il peut solliciter les officiers du royaume de Naples, qui reçoivent alors la moitié des sommes perçues[64]. À Londres (1513), les amendes sont récoltées par le consul ou son commis, en Angleterre ou dans le territoire florentin (si le membre de la nation s'y rend par la suite) et, en cas d'impayés, elles peuvent être doublées[65]. Les Florentins de Lyon (1501) doivent aussi verser leurs amendes et une taxe de 0,5 % du montant de la condamnation au consulat[66].

La justice du consul sert donc à garder secrets les litiges internes qui pourraient ternir l'image des Florentins. L'objectif de cette garantie de « pureté » de la réputation communautaire autorise le consul à bannir les membres ne

56 Naples 1430, rub. 13, §1, fol. 20r–v.
57 Naples 1430, rub. 13, § 15–16, fol. 25r.
58 Lyon 1501, rub. 40, 224–225.
59 Rome 1515, rub. 12, fol. 42v–43v plus 15 jours pour les *Sei del ricorso*.
60 Naples 1430, rub. 13, § 12–13, fol. 24r–v.
61 Naples 1430, rub. 13, § 8, fol. 23r.
62 Constantinople 1488, 77, correction de la rub. 18 sur la justice du consul.
63 Bologne 1279, rub. 37 (correction de 1289), 18.
64 Naples 1430, rub. 22, fol. 30v–32r.
65 Londres 1513, rub. 39–40, 184–185.
66 Lyon 1501, rub. 10, 209.

respectant pas les statuts : à Bologne (1279)[67], à Rome (1391 et 1515)[68], à Pise (1381)[69], à Bruges (1427)[70], à Constantinople (1488)[71] et à Lyon (1501)[72]. Au XVᵉ siècle, ces bannissements sont préventivement appliqués aux vagabonds, marginaux susceptibles de ruiner la réputation collective et d'être impliqués dans de nombreux litiges[73]. Les pouvoirs judiciaires des consuls ne sont cependant pas sans borne.

4 Circonscrire le pouvoir judiciaire des consuls

4.1 *Quelle importance la thématique judiciaire revêt-elle dans les statuts ?*

Il importe tout d'abord d'évaluer l'importance de la justice parmi les autres thématiques abordées par les statuts, grâce à l'analyse des 363 rubriques des 10 statuts pris en compte. La justice est ainsi le deuxième sujet (17 % des rubriques), après les questions financières (20 %) mais avant l'autorité du consul (12 %), et « l'organigramme » de la nation (15 %). Dans le détail, l'importance de la justice varie entre 3 (Bruges 1461) et 44 % (Bruges 1427). Schématiquement, le sujet gagnerait en importance dans les années 1420–1430, au moment de la profonde réorganisation institutionnelle transformant Florence en seigneurie régionale[74], et redeviendrait ensuite moins prégnant, sauf dans le cas

67 Bologne 1279, rub. 13, 17 et 42, respectivement 9, 10 et 18.

68 ASFi, Mercanzia, 11310, fol. 47r, 30 mars 1391 ; Rome 1515, rub. 18 et rub. 21, fol 44v–45v.

69 Pise 1381, § 21–22, 471–472. Il s'agit davantage d'un boycott commercial plutôt qu'un bannissement physique.

70 Bruges 1427, rub. 8, 9–10 ; Armand Grunzweig, « Le fonds du consulat de la mer aux archives de l'État à Florence », *Bulletin de l'Institut historique belge de Rome* 10 (1930) : 106.

71 Constantinople 1488, rub. 27, 65.

72 Lyon 1501, rub. 34, 220–221 ; Michele Cassandro, « I forestieri a Lione nel '400 e '500 : la nazione fiorentina », dans *Dentro la città : stranieri e realtà urbane nell'Europa dei secoli XII–XVI*, éd. Gabriella Rossetti (Naples : Liguori, 1989), 155.

73 Bruges 1427, rub. 9, 9–10 ; Naples 1430, rub. 23–24, fol. 32rv et fol. 32v–33r ; Constantinople 1488, rub. 34, 70–71 ; Londres 1513, rub. 8, 170 ; Rome 1515, rub. 19, fol. 44v–45r. Cédric Quertier, « I vagabondi nel basso Medioevo (Francia, Italia) : verso la criminalizzazione della mobilità illegitima », dans *Il Medioevo degli esclusi e degli emarginati. Tra rifiuto e solidarietà*, éd. Isa Lori Sanfilippo et Giuliano Pinto (Rome : Istituto Storico Italiano per il Medioevo, 2020), 101–129.

74 Voir notamment Andrea Zorzi, *La trasformazione di un quadro politico. Ricerche su politica e giustizia a Firenze dal comune allo Stato territoriale* (Florence : Firenze University Press, 2008 [1995]) ; *id.*, « Aspetti e problemi dell'amministrazione della giustizia penale nella Repubblica fiorentina. I : La transizione dal XIV al XV secolo », *Archivio storico italiano* 145 (1987) : 391–453 ; *id.*, « Aspetti e problemi dell'amministrazione della

à part de Rome (1515 ; 24 %). En réalité, la prise en compte de la longueur des rubriques (exprimées en lignes) tend à prouver que cette préoccupation se renforce plus précocément, dès la seconde moitié du XIVe siècle : 19,3 % du contenu des statuts concerne la justice, une valeur dépassée à Pise en 1381 (20,6 %), à Bruges en 1427 (37,7 %), à Naples en 1430 (30,3 %) et à Rome en 1515 (25 %). La thématique judiciaire prendrait donc de l'importance dès la seconde moitié du XIVe siècle.

Cependant, associer la justice aux thèmes de l'autorité du consul et au contrôle social qu'il exerce donne une vision plus juste de ses capacités coercitives. Ce regroupement rassemble 33 % des rubriques (34,1 % de la longueur des statuts), toujours le deuxième sujet si on groupe les rubriques renvoyant à l'organisation de la nation (organigramme, finances et archives : 42 %). Une analyse pour chaque statut donne une idée plus précise. Le cas bolonais (1279, 21,2 % de la longueur du statut) montre d'abord que la thématique n'est pas importante avant la seconde moitié du XIVe siècle. En effet, la conflictualité est plus souvent abordée à Bruges en 1427 (53 % des rubriques ; 49,7 % de la longueur), à Constantinople en 1492 (46 % des rubriques ; 43,1 % de la longueur), à Pise en 1381 (48 % / 47,2 %), à Naples en 1430 (43 % / 44,4 %), voire à Rome en 1515 (38 % / 40,1 %) à Lyon en 1501 (34 % / 34,6 %), à Londres en 1513 (29 % / 29,5 %). Toutes ces destinations ont en commun d'être situées dans un royaume où l'autorité judiciaire du consul peut être contestée par les élites ayant accès au roi à la cour, et peut subir des remises en cause arbitraires. Pise n'entre pas dans ce schéma, mais la seigneurialisation de son gouvernement et l'hostilité d'une partie de la population gibeline envers l'ennemi guelfe (Florence) peut expliquer les similarités. Les nations florentines ont donc renforcé leurs attributions judiciaires à la fin du XIVe siècle, après une phase de concentration sur le contrôle social.

4.2 *Les thématiques privilégiées de la justice consulaire*

Tous les statuts ne sont cependant pas uniformes ; certains comportent une « spécialisation » thématique : souvent les finances de la nation, comme à Lyon (1501, 17 rub.), Bruges (1461, 16 rub.), Constantinople (1492, 12 rub.) et Rome (1515, 12 rub.) ; le transport des marchandises à Bologne (1279, 6 rub. dont 1 addition)[75], étape essentielle pour atteindre Venise, les galères d'État à Bruges (1427, 11 rub.) et en Angleterre (1513, 4 rub.), débouchés commerciaux aussi éloignés qu'essentiels pour Florence qui venait de mettre en place sa

giustizia penale nella Repubblica fiorentina. II : Gli aspetti quattrocenteschi e dell'ultimo periodo repubblicano », *Archivio storico italiano* 145 (1987) : 527–578.

75 Bologne 1279, rub. 33 (correction de 1287), 16.

flotte étatique dans les années 1420[76]; l'importance de l'église nationale à Bologne (1279, 6 rub.), Lyon (1501, 4 rub.)[77] et Constantinople (1488, 6 rub. et 1492, 4 rub.), rappelant ainsi l'importance des structures religieuses collectives[78]. Le secteur productif reste rare, dans la mesure où il s'agit bien de nations peuplées par les élites marchandes avec peu d'artisans : la production et la vente de draps florentins sont néanmoins abordés dans les statuts de Bologne (1279, 5 rub. dont 1 addition), Pise (1381, 1 rub.) et Constantinople (1488, 5 rub.).

Hormis les questions financières internes (amendes), la réglementation économique et commerciale est donc paradoxalement périphérique dans les statuts de ces nations marchandes, qu'elle soit abordée dans d'autres sources normatives (statuts de la commune, du Popolo et de la Mercanzia, traités internationaux) ou laissée aux procédures d'arbitrage. La régulation de certaines activités et conflits marchands est néanmoins abordée. Le statut de Naples (1430) mentionne ainsi : les conflits sur les objets laissés en gage pour une dette non remboursée ; les sentences pour établir la reconnaissance de dettes, faire saisir et redistribuer les biens de l'endetté ; la participation des filiales des compagnies au remboursement des dettes de leurs employés ou fournisseurs[79]. Mais les autres statuts ne sont pas aussi précis sur les types de conflits économiques. La question de la durée du remboursement des crédits est ainsi abordée à Bologne (1279)[80]. La réglementation des conflits avec les courtiers ne sont mentionnés qu'à Pise[81]: ailleurs, on se contente de mentionner leurs tarifs[82]. De même, dans les successions, on insiste sur le rôle du consul comme

76 Raúl González Arévalo, « Diplomacia y navegación : Florencia en el Mediterráneo aragonés (siglo XV) », dans *Diplomacia y desarrollo del Estado en la Corona de Aragón (siglos XIV–XVI)*, éd. Concepción Villanueva Morte (Gijon : Trea, 2020), 277–296 ; Eleonora Plebani, *I Consoli del Mare di Firenze nel Quattrocento* (Rome : Sapienza Università Editrice, 2019) ; Michael E. Mallett, *The Florentine Galleys in the Fifteenth Century* (New York : Oxford University Press, 1967).

77 Celle-ci est en plein réaménagement depuis les années 1460 : Federica Carta, « La Cappella Panciatichi in Notre-Dame de Confort a Lione », *Prospettiva* 159–160 (2015) : 163–173.

78 Déjà mis en évidence dans Cédric Quertier, « Les Florentins, étrangers privilégiés ou alliés encombrants ? Heurs et malheurs des nations florentines (Europe, Méditerranée, XIIIe–XVe siècles) », *Mélanges de l'École française de Rome – Moyen-Âge* 131, n° 2 (2019) : 461–472.

79 Naples 1430, rub. 13, § 8, 10–11, fol. 23r–24r.

80 Bologne 1279, rub. 17 et 24, 10 et 12.

81 Pise 1381, rub. 9 et 21, 469 et 471–472.

82 Bologne 1279, rub. 25–26, 12–13 ; Naples 1430, rub. 18, fol. 27v–28v ; Constantinople 1488, rub. 37, 72–73.

administrateur des biens du défunt[83], les conflits étant réglés par des arbitres et très rarement par le consul[84].

4.3 *Des limitations géographiques et thématiques*

La juridiction des consuls fait pourtant l'objet d'une limitation géographique et thématique, bien mise en évidence à Naples (1430). Le consul doit y traiter les conflits portant sur les échanges, contrats ou sentences au sein ou à destination du royaume de Naples impliquant des Florentins (présents ou qui feraient expédier de l'argent ou des marchandises depuis Florence, Gênes ou Venise après y avoir résidé), ou, inversement, appliquer la justice florentine à ses concitoyens présents[85]. Les personnes qui ne seraient pas florentines ou qui n'auraient pas de relations d'affaire avec le royaume de Naples ne relèvent donc pas de sa juridiction.

Celle-ci est également limitée à certains sujets. Elle est cantonnée aux causes civiles, les pénales restant la compétence du roi de Naples. Cela suppose de renoncer aux clauses pénales contenues dans les contrats notariés de dettes[86]. Cette limitation se retrouve pour le consul délégué des Florentins à Barletta (1317)[87], pour le consul pisan de Tunis (1358)[88], mais dans le contre-exemple romain (1515), la bulle papale de 1519 interdit l'arrestation des Florentins dans toutes les causes civiles et pénales[89]. Les limites sont aussi financières : en première instance, les consuls des Florentins ne peuvent juger que les litiges portant sur une somme inférieure à 5 livres de gros des Flandres à Bruges (1427)[90], à 25 ducats à Lyon (1501)[91], à 5 livres sterlings en Angleterre (1513)[92] et à 20 ducats d'or à Rome (1515)[93].

De plus, parmi les causes civiles, leurs compétences ne sont pas universelles. Ainsi à Naples (1430), le consul ne peut ni s'emparer des cas d'usure, réser-

---

83 Bruges 1427, rub. 17, 13 ; Naples 1430, rub. 26, fol. 33v–34v ; Constantinople 1488, rub. 22, 58–59 et correction de la rub. 18, 77–78 ; Constantinople 1492, rub. 17, 88–90. Le cas est différent à Bologne 1279, rub. 18, 10–11 : la communauté doit se rendre aux enterrements des leurs.

84 Constantinople 1488, rub. 22, 58–59 et correction de la rub. 18, 77–78 ; Constantinople 1492, rub. 17, 88–90.

85 Naples 1430, rub. 13, § 9 et 13, fol. 23v et 24v. Rome 1515, rub. 16, fol. 44r.

86 Naples 1430, rub. 13, § 5–6, fol. 21v–22r.

87 Robert Davidsohn, *Storia di Firenze* (Florence : Sansoni, 1977–1978), 5–266.

88 Houssaye Michienzi, *Datini, Majorque et le Maghreb*, 173.

89 Polverini Fosi, « Il consolato fiorentino a Roma », 62–63.

90 Bruges 1427, rub. 7, 9.

91 Lyon 1501, rub. 43, 227.

92 Londres 1513, rub. 4, 168.

93 Rome 1515, rub. 17, fol. 44v–45r.

vés aux tribunaux ecclésiastiques, ni des cas de faillite, prérogatives de la *Mercanzia* et des *Sei del ricorso*[94]. De même, dans un cas de vol de soie de Bursa en Serbie – qui dépend de la nation de Constantinople –, les Florentins s'appuient sur une lettre du sultan et non pas sur l'autorité du consul pour punir les voleurs[95]. La justice consulaire n'est donc pas omnipotente. Elle est amenée à composer avec les autres juridictions comme nous le verrons ci-dessous.

4.4 *Des limites fonctionnelles*

Les consuls ne peuvent pas davantage être juge et partie. Pour préserver la neutralité du consulat dans un procès concernant les intérêts de sa compagnie ou de sa famille[96], les statuts de Bruges (1427), Naples (1430), Lyon (1501), Londres (1513) et Rome (1515) préconisent qu'ils se déportent[97]. Sur pétition du demandeur, le conseil de la nation choisit un autre consul ou un arbitre (Naples 1430)[98] et de nouveaux conseillers temporaires (Lyon 1501)[99].

De plus, l'obligation d'être jugé par la nation n'implique pas nécessairement de l'être par le consul. L'autre possibilité est de recourir à l'arbitrage[100], qui sert même parfois à définir la justice consulaire, à Lyon (1501) et en Sicile

94 Naples 1430, rub. 13, § 1 et 12, fol. 20r et 24rv. Sur cette commission, voir Luca Boschetto, « L'ufficio del ricorso presso la Mercanzia fiorentina tra Quattro e Cinquecento », dans *Tribunali di mercanti e giustizia mercantile nel tardo Medioevo*, éd. Elena Maccioni et Sergio Tognetti (Florence : Leo S. Olschki, 2016), 183–205.

95 Ingrid Houssaye Michienzi, « The Silk Market in Bursa around 1500 as it Appears in the Florentine Business Archives », *Turcica* 50 (2019) : 77–78.

96 Naples 1430, rub. 16, fol. 26rv : « del detto chonsolo o di sua chompagnia o veramente al suo padre o suo figliuolo o suo fratello o suo zio o nipote charnale ».

97 Bruges 1427, rub. 13, 11 ; Naples 1430, rub. 16, fol. 26r–v ; Lyon 1501, rub. 42 et 43, 226–227 ; Londres 1513, rub. 6, 169 ; Rome 1515, rub. 23, fol. 45v–46r.

98 Naples 1430, rub. 16, fol. 26r.

99 Lyon 1501, rub. 42, 226.

100 La littérature à ce sujet est vaste. Parmi les parutions récentes, voir Albrecht Cordes, « La résolution juridique et extra-juridique des conflits en matière commerciale (1250–1650) », dans *Les chimères de l'alternativité ? Regards croisés sur les Modes alternatifs de règlement des conflits* (*Droit, Histoire, Anthropologie*), éd. Gilduin Davy *et al.* (Paris : Mare & Martin, 2018), 47–57. Sur ses origines doctrinales, voir Luciano Martone, *Arbiter-arbitrator : forme di giustizia privata nell'età del diritto comune* (Naples : Jovene, 1984). Pour des cas pratiques d'utilisation, voir les articles d'Elena Maccioni, « Justice pour les étrangers : stratégies de résolution des conflits internationaux dans la Gênes médiévale », et de Florent Garnier, « *Ad pacem et concordiam utriusque partis*. Les voies de règlement des différends commerciaux au XIIIe siècle », In *Villes, marchands et tribunaux : institutions judiciaires et gestion des conflits commerciaux* (*Europe occidentale, XIIIe–XVIe siècles*), éd. Cédric Quertier et Stefania Montemezzo, dossier dans *Histoire urbaine* 74 (2025-3), 5–96.

(1413) notamment[101]. À Bruges (1427), où plus des trois quarts des conflits sont résolus par cette voie[102], le recours à l'arbitrage (*arbitri et terzo*) se fait sur requête du demandeur ; les arbitres, membres de la nation, ont le pouvoir d'achever le procès – prolongeable une seule fois – et de prononcer une sentence[103]. Le consul doit forcer les défendeurs à accepter l'arbitrage, qui ne peut pas être utilisé si le procès devant le consul a déjà débuté[104]. À Naples (1430), la fonction d'arbitre n'apparaît qu'incidemment, pour remplacer un consul ou un conseiller devant se déporter dans un litige[105]. En revanche, le statut de Londres (1513)[106] reprend exactement les mêmes termes, la même procédure, et la même amende[107] que celles de Bruges (1427). La procédure est similaire à Lyon (1501) : des Florentins qui fréquenteraient les foires et y seraient arbitres sont mentionnés la même année[108]; d'ailleurs, la procédure du consul est équiparée à celle des arbitres et aimables compositeurs qui doivent recourir à la procédure sommaire[109]. Si les parties ne s'accordent pas, le consul et les conseillers choisissent les arbitres[110]. En somme, l'*arbitrator* médiéval choisi par les parties est plus souvent présent dans les statuts étudiés que l'*arbiter*, d'origine antique et désigné par le tribunal[111], bien que les termes *arbiter, arbitrator* et *amicabilis compositor* soient souvent employés ensemble depuis le XIIIe siècle[112].

101 Bresc, *Un monde méditerranéen*, 386–387 ; ASFi, Mercanzia, 11312, fol. 26r–v, 31 mai 1413.
102 Oscar Gelderblom, « The Resolution of Commercial Conflicts in Bruges, Antwerp, and Amsterdam (1250–1650) », dans *Law and Long-Term Economic Change : an Eurasian Perspective*, éd. Debin Ma et Jan Luiten van Zanden (Stanford : Stanford University Press, 2011), 247.
103 Bruges 1427, rub. 3, 7.
104 Bruges 1427, rub. 4, 8.
105 Naples 1430, rub. 16, fol. 26r.
106 Londres 1513, rub. 3, 167–168, qui fusionne les rub. 3 et 4 de Bruges 1427.
107 Le même chiffre, mais pas la même monnaie : 10 livres sterling au lieu de 10 gros des Flandres.
108 Lyon 1501, rub. 10, 209.
109 Lyon 1501, rub. 40, 225.
110 Lyon 1501, rub. 41, 225–226.
111 Sur cette distinction doctrinale, voir : Karl Siegfried Bader, « *Arbiter arbitrator seu amicabilis compositor*. Zur Verbreitung einer kanonistischen Formel in Gebieten nördlich der Alpen », *Zeitschrift der Savigny-Stiftung für Rechtsgeschichte, Kanonistische Abteilung* 61 (1960) : 239–276. Karl-Hans Ziegler, « *Arbiter, arbitrator und amicabilis compositor* », *Zeitschrift der Savigny-Stiftung, Romanistische Abteilung* 84 (1967) : 367–381.
112 Garnier, « *Ad pacem et concordiam utriusque partis* ».

5 L'impossible évitement des conflits de juridiction

Les compétences judiciaires des nations sont donc bien circonscrites, mais elles ne peuvent jamais rester isolées. Des conflits de juridiction peuvent donc survenir entre les tribunaux consulaires et locaux.

Par principe, les sentences du consul ne sont appelables (Londres 1513)[113]. Les demandeurs doivent jurer de ne pas les contester ou faire appel, sous peine de perdre leur caution (Naples 1430)[114]. À Constantinople (1488), aucune loi ou tribunal ne peut la casser, et même un étranger doit s'engager à ne pas faire appel[115]. Ce principe est repris à Venise par la Compagnia di San Giovanni Battista dei Fiorentini au milieu du XVIe siècle[116]. Rome (1515) est néanmoins à part, car après trois injonctions d'application infructueuses, on peut faire appel auprès d'une commission de six chefs de maisonnée tirés au sort dont les décisions ne sont contestables que par les conseils communaux[117].

En conséquence, il est souvent interdit de recourir à une autre juridiction civile : même si le conflit n'est pas réglé par le notaire-syndic dans les 30 jours impartis, il est interdit de s'adresser à un autre tribunal, sauf s'il s'agit d'un Florentin condamné et réfugié à Pise (1381)[118]. Ces interdictions, assorties de fortes amendes, sont répétées à Bruges (1427), à Naples (1430), à Londres (1513) et à Rome (1515)[119]. Mais le cas de Naples (1430) rappelle qu'elles ne concernent que le civil : être jugé par un tribunal pénal est permis si le consul l'autorise dans un acte notarié. Impossible toutefois de maquiller une cause civile en une cause criminelle afin de la présenter devant un autre tribunal, ce qui témoigne des manipulations par certains demandeurs[120].

Cependant, les modalités de collaboration avec les autres juridictions sont prévues, puisque les consuls doivent aussi assister les membres de la nation florentine mis en cause. Dans une ville comme Pise où l'opposition aux Florentins peut être forte, une des fonctions essentielles du consul est de défendre les Florentins devant les juges locaux afin qu'ils bénéficient d'un traitement bienveillant, ce qui passe par de nombreux échanges épistolaires et

113 Londres 1513, rub. 2, 167.

114 Naples 1430, rub. 13, § 1, fol. 20r–25r, ici fol. 20r.

115 Constantinople 1488, rub. 25 et 32, 63 et 69.

116 Mueller, « Mercanti e imprenditori fiorentini a Venezia », 32 ; Sagredo, « Statuti della fraternità e compagnia dei fiorentini in Venezia ».

117 Rome 1515, fol. 50 et 53, fol. 51v–52v.

118 Pise 1381, rub. 2 et 15, 468 et 470–471.

119 Bruges 1427, rub. 5, 8 : 25 livres de gros des Flandres ; Naples 1430, rub. 14, fol. 25rv : 10 carlini ; voir aussi Naples 1430, rub. 13, § 6, fol. 22r ; Londres 1513, rub. 5, 169 : 25 livres sterling ; Rome 1515, rub. 15, fol. 44r : 50 ducats.

120 Naples 1430, rub. 14, fol. 25r–v.

par une présence physique[121]. En 1375, dans un litige portant sur une transaction de peaux de cuirs, le consul est ainsi présent lors de la copie des livres de comptes et lors de l'interrogatoire de toutes les parties. Son rapport double même les lettres envoyées par les Pisans, comme le traité bilatéral le prévoit[122]. La représentation consulaire au tribunal et à la cour est aussi prévue dans les royaumes de Naples et de France. En effet, si un Florentin honorable avait un litige à la cour de Naples (1430), il peut demander aide et conseil au consul, tenu de l'accompagner avec un gonfalonier exhibant les armes de la Cité du Lys et avec des Florentins venus faire nombre ; inversement, il doit forcer un coupable à obéir[123]. La nation de Lyon (1501) confie cette tâche à un procureur de bonne réputation, ayant l'esprit pratique et au fait des coutumes locales, sans animosité ou attache à l'égard des parties, apte à faire le voyage et à représenter les Florentins à la cour du roi[124]. Les relations interpersonnelles comptent enfin pour beaucoup : le consul des Florentins doit être un allié politique du seigneur de Pise, et il est même parfois enjoint aux consuls de se jeter aux pieds du pape pour espérer obtenir le déplacement d'un procès de Rome à Venise[125].

6 Conclusion

Qu'il soit assisté ou non d'officiers judiciaires, la justice consulaire florentine est d'abord celle du consul, dont on affirme fermement l'autorité en lui permettant de rassembler les parties et les preuves, tout comme de rendre une sentence qu'il appliquera avec célérité. Il s'appuie sur la procédure sommaire pour juger les litiges civils, et détient l'exclusivité sur ceux portant sur de petites sommes. Mais il est concurrencé par les tribunaux locaux pour les procès au pénal, et sa juridiction est strictement limitée aux Florentins dans le territoire où est reconnue la nation qu'il dirige. Ainsi, il n'est pas possible pour un consul florentin d'être à la tête du tribunal de référence pour les autres communautés chrétiennes en terre d'Islam, comme ce fut le cas pour les

121 Quertier, *Guerres et richesses d'une nation*, 181–191 et 384–387.

122 Cédric Quertier, « Les tanneurs, le cordonnier et l'apothicaire : comment des artisans prouvent-ils leurs transactions ? (Pise-Florence, 1375) », dans *Transiger. Vers une ethnographie des transactions médiévales*, éd. Julie Claustre (Paris : Publications de la Sorbonne, 2019), 307–352.

123 Naples 1430, rub. 15 et 20, fol. 25v et fol. 30r ; Figliuolo, « L'organigramma della nazione fiorentina », 197.

124 Lyon 1501, rub. 39, 222–223.

125 ASFi, Mercanzia, 11311, fol. 73v–74r, 5 novembre 1395, ici fol. 74r.

consulats pisans, vénitiens (par exemple à Alexandrie) ou génois. En amont, cela l'incite à traquer les comportements causes de conflits (insultes, jeux de hasard, vagabondage, etc) et de ruine de la réputation collective et, en aval, à négocier la protection de la communauté. Au final, la justice – en général, car la typologie des conflits économiques est rarement abordée – est la deuxième thématique la plus souvent traitée dans les statuts.

Pour autant, si la présente étude se concentre sur les statuts des nations pour des raisons de concision, l'analyse devrait être approfondie par l'examen d'autres sources. Tout d'abord parce que les statuts comportent des limites structurelles. Ils expriment la vision idéale des autorités et représentent le produit final du processus de compilation normatif, alors que le flux documentaire d'une institution conserve les étapes antérieures de la réglementation, par exemple dans les délibérations et les lettres de la *Mercanzia* ou des Consuls de la Mer. De plus, ils ne sont pas la seule source de droit, et doivent être croisés avec la législation et les délibérations communales, mais surtout avec les traités de paix et de commerce, comme celui entre Pise et Florence (1369) qui définit les prérogatives du notaire-syndic et du consul, fixe la manière de réguler les représailles et recommande de traiter avec bienveillance les Florentins[126].

La correspondance de la *Mercanzia* donne enfin une vision plus dynamique des types de conflits. Elle précise le traitement judiciaire en définissant les contours de la nation, soit en certifiant la citoyenneté, soit en prononçant des boycotts ou des bannissements, mais aussi en demandant l'application de la procédure sommaire. Elle insiste sur la transmission des preuves marchandes, surreprésentée dans cette correspondance pratique. Elle démontre enfin l'importance diplomatique du consul, tenu de gérer les cas les plus graves, notamment la bonne application de la réglementation commerciale, des exemptions de taxes de douanes[127] et surtout du droit de représailles, une arme économico-juridique délicate à manier en fonction du rapport de forces. La reconstitution pratique des procès est donc un véritable travail de romain.

126 Pietro Silva, « L'ultimo trattato commerciale tra Pisa e Firenze », *Studi storici del prof. Crivellucci* 18 (1908) : respectivement rub. 8, 689–690, et rub. 12–14, 693–695.

127 Le sujet n'est abordé qu'à Constantinople 1488, rub. 23, 60.

Annexe

TABLEAU 2.2 Classement des thématiques des statuts[a]

	Bologne (1279–1289)	Pise (1381)	Bruges (1427)	Naples (1430)	Bruges (1461)
Crédit (n et %)	3 (7%)	0	0	0	0
Crédit (n° rub.)	13 ; 17 ; 24	NR	NR	NR	NR
Citoyenneté (n et %)	0	1 (4%)	0	0	0
Citoyenneté (n° rub.)	NR	18	NR	NR	NR
Courtiers (n et %)	4 (9%)	2 (9%)	0	1 (4%)	0
Courtiers (n° rub.)	14 ; 25–26 ; 41	9 ; 21	NR	18	0
Hérédité (n et %)	1 (2%)	0	0	0	0
Hérédité (n° rub.)	18	NR	NR	NR	NR
Bâtiments non religieux (l et %)	*18 (3,7%)*	*15 (8,3%)*	*0*	*16 (0,9%)*	*16 (4,6%)*
Bâtiments non religieux (n et %)	3 (7%)	2 (9%)	0	1 (4%)	2 (7%)
Bâtiments non religieux (n° rub.)	21 ; 27 ; 37	3 ; 23	NR	21	33 ; 37
Archives (l et %)	*0*	*0*	*0*	*28 (1,6%)*	*25 (7,2%)*
Archives (n et %)	0	0	0	2 (7%)	3 (10%)
Archives (n° rub.)	NR	NR	NR	27–28	34–35 ; 43
Galères (l et %)	*43 (8,8%)*	*0*	*167 (51,2%)*	*0*	*17 (4,9%)*
Galères (n et %)	5 (11%)	0	10 (43%)	0	1 (3%)
Galères (n° rub.)	19 ; 22 ; 30 ; 34 ; 36 ;	NR	14–23	NR	24
Production (l et %)	*41 (8,4%)*	*7 (3,9%)*	*0*	*0*	*0*
Production (n et %)	5 (11%)	1 (4%)	0	0	0

a Abréviations utilisées : (n° rub.) = numéro des rubriques du thème dans les statuts concernés ; (n et %) = nombre de rubriques d'un thème et pourcentage correspondant ; (l et %) = nombre de lignes d'un thème et pourcentage correspondant.

Constantinople (1488)	**Constantinople (1492)**	**Lyon (1501)**	**Londres (1513)**	**Rome (1515)**	**Totaux / % moyen**
0	0	0	0	0	3
NR	NR	NR	NR	NR	
0	0	1 (2%)	1 (2%)	1 (2%)	4
NR	NR	38	36	43	
1 (2%)	1 (4%)	1 (2%)	0	0	9
37	NR	NR	NR	0	
1 (2%)	1 (4%)	1 (2%)	1 (2%)	0	5
22	17	1	32	0	
40 (3%)	*0*	*0*	*0*	*13 (1,6%)*	*118 (1,6%)*
1 (2%)	0	0	0	1 (2%)	10
9	NR	NR	NR	33	
108 (8,2%)	*31 (5,6%)*	*47 (6%)*	*32 (5%)*	*52*	
3 (8%)	2 (8%)	5 (10%)	4 (10%)	5 (9%)	24
1 ; 36 ; 40	27 ; 30	1 ; 14 ; 28 ; 30 ; 45	22 ; 26–27 ; 42	34, 35, 37, 40, 49	
34 (2,6%)	*0*	*0*	*70 (10,9%)*	*0*	
1 (2%)	0	0	4 (10%)	0	21
26	NR	NR	29–31 ; 33	NR	
184 (13,9%)	*21 (3,8%)*	*0*	*0*	*0*	*253 (3,5%)*
5 (12%)	2 (8%)	0	0	0	13

TABLEAU 2.2 Classement des thématiques des statuts (*cont.*)

	Bologne (1279–1289)	**Pise (1381)**	**Bruges (1427)**	**Naples (1430)**	**Bruges (1461)**
Production (n° rub.)	20 ; 23 ; 29 ; 33 ; 42	4	NR	NR	NR
Finance (l et %)	0	*4 (2,2%)*	0	*134 (7,7%)*	*168 (48,3%)*
Finance (n et %)	0	1 (4%)	0	2 (7%)	16 (54%)
Finance (n° rub.)	NR	11	NR	11 ; 17	25–32 ; 38 ; 44 ; 46–49 ; 52–53
Somme justice +autorité ±contrôle social (l. %)	30,2 %	47,2%	49,7%	44,4%	12,9%
Contrôle social (l et %)	*25 (5,1%)*	0	0	*108 (6,2%)*	0
Contrôle social (n et %)	2 (4%)	0	0	3 (11%)	0
Contrôle social (n° rub.)	44–45	NR	NR	23 ; 25 ; 26	NR
Justice (*l et* %)	*95 (19,5%)*	*37 (20,6%)*	*123 (37,7%)*	*528 (30,3%)*	*25 (7,2%)*
Justice (n et %)	6 (13%)	4 (17%)	10 (44%)	7 (25%)	1 (3%)
Justice (n° rub.)	9 ; 15 ; 28 ; 31 ; 39 ; 43	2 ; 5 ; 15 ; 17	2–10 ; 13	13–16 ; 19–20 ; 24	45
Autorité (*l et* %)	*27 (5,6%)*	*48 (26,7%)*	*39 (5,8%)*	*139 (8%)*	*20 (5,7%)*
Autorité (n et %)	3 (7%)	7 (31%)	2 (9%)	2 (7%)	2 (7%)
Autorité (n° rub.)	6–8	1 ; 7–8 ; 16 ; 19–20 ; 22	11–12	12 ; 22	36 ; 40
Religion (*l et* %)	*53 (10,9%)*	0	0	*204 (11,7%)*	*10 (2,9%)*
Religion (n et %)	6 (13%)	0	0	2 (7%)	1 (3%)
Religion (n° rub.)	10–12 ; 16 ; 32 ; 35	NR	NR	9–10	41

Constantinople (1488)	Constantinople (1492)	Lyon (1501)	Londres (1513)	Rome (1515)	Totaux / % moyen
17 ; 28–31	19–20	NR	NR	NR	
351 (26,6%)	*24 (4,3%)*	*143 (18,2%)*	*216 (33,7%)*	*150*	*1190 (16,5%)*
10 (25%)	1 (4%)	12 (24%)	17 (40%)	12 (22%)	71
10 ; 13–14 ; 16 ; 19–21 ; 23–24 ; 33	26	7 ; 9 ; 11–13 ; 15–17 ; 21–22 ; 26 ; 29	13–21 ; 23–25 ; 28 ; 35 ; 39–41	25, 26, 27, 28, 29, 30, 31, 32, 42, 44, 45, 48	
16,2%	43,1%	34,6%	29,5%	40,1%	34,1%
0	*43 (7,8%)*	*30 (3,8%)*	*59 (9,2%)*	*35 (4,2%)*	*300 (4,1%)*
0	3 (12%)	2 (4%)	3 (7%)	2 (3%)	15
NR	16 ; 24–25	35–36	7–9	19, 21	
105 (8%)	*100 (18,1%)*	*83 (10,5%)*	*88 (13,7%)*	*209 (25%)*	*1393 (19,3%)*
5 (12%)	5 (19%)	5 (10%)	5 (12%)	13 (24%)	59
18 ; 25 ; 27 ; 32 ; 34	7 ; 18 ; 21–23	10 ; 40–43	2–6	11, 12, 13, 14, 15, 16, 17, 18, 20, 22, 23, 50, 53	
109 (8,3%)	*95 (17,2%)*	*159 (20,2%)*	*42 (6,6%)*	*91 (10,9%)*	*769 (10,7%)*
5 (12%)	4 (15%)	10 (20%)	4 (10%)	6 (11%)	45
2–3 ; 35 ; 38–39	12–15	5–6 ; 18 ; 20 ; 23–25 ; 47–48 ; 50	10–12 ; 37	4, 36, 38, 46, 54, 55	
184 (13,9%)	*71 (12,9%)*	*30 (3,8%)*	*13 (2%)*	*0*	*565 (7,8%)*
6 (15%)	4 (15%)	4 (8%)	1 (2%)	0	24
4–8 ; 15	9–11 ; 29	2–4 ; 44	38	NR	

TABLEAU 2.2 Classement des thématiques des statuts (*cont.*)

	Bologne (1279–1289)	**Pise (1381)**	**Bruges (1427)**	**Naples (1430)**	**Bruges (1461)**
Organigramme (l et %)	*80 (16,5%)*	*40 (22,2%)*	*27 (8,3%)*	*512 (29,3%)*	*32 (9,2%)*
Organigramme (n et %)	7 (16%)	5 (22%)	1 (4%)	8 (29%)	4 (13%)
Organigramme (n° rub.)	1–5 ; 38 ; 40	6 ; 10 ; 12–14	1	1–8	39 ; 42 ; 50–51
Total lignes	486	180	326	1745	348
Total rubriques (sans les additions)	45	23	23	29	30

Constantinople (1488)	Constantinople (1492)	Lyon (1501)	Londres (1513)	Rome (1515)	Totaux / % moyen
39 (3%)	*65 (11,8%)*	*99 (12,6%)*	*36 (5,6%)*	*204*	*1108 (15,3%)*
2 (7%)	3 (11%)	9 (18%)	2 (5%)	14 (25%)	53 (15%)
11–12	1–2 ; 8	19 ; 27; 31–34 ; 39 ; 46 ; 49	1 ; 34	1, 2, 3, 5, 6, 7, 8, 9, 10, 39, 41, 47, 51, 52	
1319	552	787	641	836	7220
40	26[b]	50	42	55	363

b Les rub. 3 à 6 manquent dans cette compilation.

SOURCE: VOIR NOTE 7 DE CET ARTICLE

Bibliographie

Abulafia, David. « Pisan Commercial Colonies and Consulates in Twelfth-Century Sicily ». *The English Historian Review* 93 (1978) : 68–81.

Aglietti, Marcella. *L'istituto consolare tra Sette e Ottocento : Funzioni istituzionali, profilo giuridico e percorsi professionali nella Toscana granducale*. Pise : ETS, 2012.

Amari, Michele, éd. *I diplomi arabi del R. Archivio Fiorentino*. Florence : Le Monnier, 1863.

Bader, Karl Siegfried. « *Arbiter arbitrator seu amicabilis compositor*. Zur Verbreitung einer kanonistischen Formel in Gebieten nördlich der Alpen ». *Zeitschrift der Savigny-Stiftung für Rechtsgeschichte, Kanonistische Abteilung* 61 (1960) : 239–276.

Boschetto, Luca. « L'ufficio del ricorso presso la Mercanzia fiorentina tra Quattro e Cinquecento ». Dans *Tribunali di mercanti e giustizia mercantile nel tardo Medioevo*, édité par Elena Maccioni et Sergio Tognetti, 183–205. Florence : Olschki, 2016.

Bresc, Henri. *Un monde méditerranéen : Économie et société en Sicile 1300–1450*. Rome : École française de Rome, 1986.

Carta, Federica. « La Cappella Panciatichi in Notre-Dame de Confort a Lione ». *Prospettiva* 159–160 (2015) : 163–173.

Cassandro, Michele. « I Forestieri a Lione nel '400 e '500 : la nazione fiorentina ». dans *Dentro la città : stranieri e realtà urbane nell'Europa dei secoli XII–XVI*, édité par Gabriella Rossetti, 151–162. Naples : Liguori, 1989.

Cordes, Albrecht et Philipp Höhn. « Extra-Legal and Legal Conflict Management among Long Distance Traders (1250–1650) ». Dans *The Oxford Handbook of European Legal History*, édité par Heiki Pihlajamäki, Marcus D. Dubber, et Mark Godfrey, 509–527. Oxford : Oxford University Press, 2018.

Cordes, Albrecht, « À la recherche d'une *Lex mercatoria* au Moyen Âge ». dans *Stadt und Recht in Mittelalter : La ville et le droit au Moyen Âge*, édité par Pierre Monnet et Otto Gerhard Oexle, 117–132. Göttingen : Vandenhoeck & Ruprecht, 2003.

Cordes, Albrecht, « Lex Maritima ? Local, Regional and Universal Maritime Law in the Middle Ages ». Dans *The Routledge Handbook of Maritime Trade Around Europe 1300–1600*, édité par Willem Pieter Blockmans, Michail Marcovic Krom et Justyna Wubs-Mrozewicz, 69–85. Londres : Routledge, 2017.

Cordes, Albrecht. « *Per amorem vel per iusticiam*. La résolution juridique et extra-juridique des conflits en matière commerciale (1250–1650) ». Dans *Les chimères de l'alternativité ? Regards croisés sur les modes alternatifs de règlement des conflits (droit, histoire, anthropologie)*, édité par Soraya Amrani-Mekki, Gilduin Davy, Soazick Kerneis et Marjolaine Roccati, 47–58. Paris : Mare & Martin, 2018.

Davidsohn, Robert. *Storia di Firenze*. Florence : Sansoni, 1977–1978.

Figliuolo, Bruno, « L'organigramma della nazione fiorentina a Napoli dagli statuti del 1430 ». Dans *Comunità forestiere e « nationes » nell'Europa dei secoli XIII–XVI*, édité par Giovanna Petti Balbi, 191–200. Naples : Liguori, 2001.

Garnier, Florent. « *Ad pacem et concordiam utriusque partis.* Les voies de règlement des différends commerciaux au XIIIe siècle ». Dans *Villes, marchands et tribunaux : institutions judiciaires et gestion des conflits commerciaux (Europe occidentale, XIIIe–XVIe siècles)*, édité par Cédric Quertier et Stefania Montemezzo Histoire urbaine 74 (2025), 5–96.

Gaudenzi, Augusto. « Statuti dei mercanti fiorentini dimoranti in Bologna degli anni 1279–1289 ». *Archivio storico italiano* 163, n° (1888) : 1–19.

Gelderblom, Oscar. « The Resolution of Commercial Conflicts in Bruges, Antwerp, and Amsterdam (1250–1650) ». Dans *Law and Long-Term Economic Change : an Eurasian Perspective*, édité par Debin Ma et Jan Luiten van Zanden, 244–276. Stanford : Stanford University Press, 2011.

González Arévalo, Raúl. « Diplomacia Y Navegación : Florencia En El Mediterráneo Aragonés (Siglo XV) ». Dans *Diplomacia y desarrollo del Estado en la Corona de Aragón (siglos XIV–XVI)*, édité par Concepción Villanueva Morte, 277–296. Gijon : Trea, 2020.

Grunzweig, Armand. « Le fonds du consulat de la mer aux archives de l'État à Florence ». *Bulletin de l'Institut historique Belge de Rome* 10 (1930) : 5–121.

Houssaye Michienzi, Ingrid. « The Silk Market in Bursa around 1500 as it Appears in the Florentine Business Archives ». *Turcica* 50 (2019) : 77–78.

Houssaye Michienzi, Ingrid. « Les milieux d'affaires florentins, le commerce des draps et les marchés ottomans à la fin du XVe et au début du XVIe siècle ». *Mélanges de l'École française de Rome – Moyen Âge* 127, n° 2 (2015) : 421–441.

Houssaye Michienzi, Ingrid. *Datini, Majorque et le Maghreb, 14e–15e siècles : réseaux, espaces méditerranéens et stratégies marchandes.* Leyde : Brill, 2013.

Kantorowicz, Ernst. *Albertus Gandinus und das Strafrecht der Scholastik, t. I : Die Praxis. Ausgewählte Strafprozessakten des 13. Jahrhunderts nebts diplomatischer Einteilung.* Berlin : J. Guttentag, 1907.

Maccioni, Elena. « justice pour les Étrangers : stratégies de résolution des conflits internationaux dans la Gênes médiévale ». Dans *Villes, marchands et tribunaux : institutions judiciaires et gestion des conflits commerciaux (Europe occidentale, XIIIe–XVIe siècles)*, édité par Cédric Quertier et Stefania Montemezzo Histoire urbaine 74, 67–80.

Mallett, Michael E. *The Florentine Galleys in the Fifteenth Century.* Oxford : Oxford University Press, 1967.

Martone, Luciano. *Arbiter-arbitrator : forme di giustizia privata nell'età del diritto comune.* Naples : Jovene, 1984.

Masi, Gino, éd. *Statuti delle colonie fiorentine all'estero (secc. XV–XVI)*. Milan : Giuffrè, 1941.

Mueller, Reinhold C. « Mercanti e imprenditori fiorentini a Venezia nel tardo Medioevo ». *Società e Storia* 55 (1992) : 29–60.

Petti Balbi, Giovanna, « Le *nationes* italiane all'estero ». Dans *Il Rinascimento italiano e l'Europa.* IV : *Commercio e cultura mercantile,* édité par Franco Franceschini, Richard A. Goldthwaite et Reinhold Ch. Mueller, 397–424. Costabissara : Angelo Colla, 2007.

Plebani, Eleonora. *I Consoli del Mare di Firenze nel Quattrocento.* Rome : Sapienza Università Editrice, 2019.

Polverini Fosi, Irene. « Il consolato fiorentino a Roma ed il progetto per la chiesa nazionale ». *Studi Romani* 37 (1989) : 50–70.

Quertier, Cédric. « I vagabondi nel basso Medioevo (Francia, Italia) : verso la criminalizzazione della mobilità illegitima ». Dans *Il Medioevo degli esclusi e degli emarginati : Tra rifiuto e solidarietà,* édité par Isa Lori Sanfilippo et Giuliano Pinto, 101–129. Rome : Istituto Storico Italiano per il Medioevo, 2020.

Quertier, Cédric. « Les Florentins, étrangers privilégiés ou alliés encombrants ? Heurs et malheurs des nations florentines (Europe, Méditerranée, XIIIe–XVe siècles) ». *Mélanges de l'École française de Rome – Moyen-Âge* 131, n° 2 (2019) : 461–472.

Quertier, Cédric. « Les tanneurs, le cordonnier et l'apothicaire : comment des artisans prouvent-ils leurs transactions ? (Pise-Florence, 1375) ». Dans *Transiger : Vers une ethnographie des transactions médiévales,* édité par Julie Claustre, 307–352. Paris : Publications de la Sorbonne, 2019.

Quertier, Cédric. *Guerres et richesses d'une nation : Les Florentins à Pise au XIVe siècle.* Rome : Publications de l'École Française de Rome, 2022.

Sagredo, Agostino. « Statuti della fraternità e compagnia dei fiorentini in Venezia dell' anno MDLVI ». *Archivio storico italiano* 9 (1853) : 441–492.

Sicking, Louis et Alain Wijffels, éd. *Conflict management in the Mediterranean and the Atlantic, 1000–1800 : actors, institutions and strategies of dispute settlement.* Leyde : Brill, 2020.

Seaford, Richard. *Dionysos.* London / New York, 2006.

Silva, Pietro. « L'ultimo trattato commerciale tra Pisa e Firenze ». *Studi storici del prof. Crivellucci* 18 (1908) : 627–702.

Stefania Gialdroni, Albrecht Cordes, Serge Dauchy, Dave De Ruysscher et Heikki Pihlajamäki. *Migrating Words, Migrating Merchants, Migrating Law : Trading Routes and the Development of Commercial Law.* Leyde : Brill, 2020.

Vito Piergiovanni, éd. *From lex mercatoria to commercial law.* Berlin : Duncker & Humblot, 2005.

Vito Piergiovanni, éd. *The Courts and the Development of Commercial Law.* Berlin : Duncker & Humblot, 1987.

Vito Piergiovanni. *Norme, scienza giuridica tra Genova e l'Occidente medievale e moderno*. Gênes : Società Ligure di Storia Patria, 2012.

Ziegler, Karl-Hans. « *Arbiter, arbitrator und amicabilis compositor* ». *Zeitschrift der Savigny-Stiftung für Rechtsgeschichte, Romanistische Abteilung* 84 (1967) : 367–381.

Zorzi, Andrea. « Aspetti e problemi dell'amministrazione della giustizia penale nella Repubblica fiorentina II : Gli aspetti quattrocenteschi e dell'ultimo periodo repubblicano ». *Archivio storico italiano* 145 (1987) : 527–578.

Zorzi, Andrea. « Aspetti e problemi dell'amministrazione della giustizia penale nella Repubblica fiorentina. I : La transizione dal XIV al XV secolo ». *Archivio storico italiano* 145 (1987) : 391–453.

Zorzi, Andrea. *La trasformazione di un quadro politico. Ricerche su politica e giustizia a Firenze dal comune allo Stato territoriale*. Florence : Firenze University Press, 2008 [1995].

3

Jurisdiction and Foreign Consuls in Sixteenth-Century Valencia

Ana Belem Fernández Castro

The economic growth experienced in Europe following the consolidation of the Atlantic trade routes was made possible by the involvement of institutions designed to govern and administer justice in the extensive colonial territories.[1] In the Hispanic world, the Crown provided numerous officials and judicial bodies responsible for organising trade,[2] and these were supplemented by other institutions created by the merchants themselves to support international business, such as guilds and commercial tribunals, known as consulates.[3] This institutional diversity led to the participation of multiple jurisdictions in the governance of long-distance trade, creating various regulatory spaces that had to coexist and contend with each other for control of trade. This institutional dynamic describes one of the inherent features of early modern societies: legal pluralism.[4]

1 Daniel Strum, "Institutional Choice in the Governance of the Early Atlantic Sugar Trade: Diasporas, Markets, and Courts," *The Economic History Review* 71, n° 4 (2019): 1–27. Regina Grafe, "Was There a Market for Institutions in Early Modern European Trade?," in *Union in Separation. Diasporic Groups and Identities in the Eastern Mediterranean, 1100–1800*, ed. Georg Christ (Rome: Viella, 2015), 593–609.

2 Carlos Álvarez Nogal, "Instituciones y desarrollo económico: la Casa de la Contratación y la Carrera de Indias (1503–1790)," in *La Casa de la Contratación y la Navegación entre España e Indias*, eds. Enriqueta Vila Vilar, Antonio Acosta Rodríguez and Adolfo Luis González Rodríguez (Sevilla: Universidad de Sevilla, 2003), 21–51. Ana Belem Fernández Castro, *Justicia, Comercio e Instituciones en la Carrera de Indias* (*siglo XVI*) (Toulouse: Presses de l'Université Toulouse Capitole, 2024).

3 Sheilagh Ogilvie, *The European Guilds: An Economic Analysis* (Princeton, NJ: Princeton University Press, 2019). *Idem, Institutions and European Trade. Merchant Guilds (1000–1800)* (Cambridge: Cambridge University Press, 2011). Regina Grafe and Oscar Gelderblom, "The Rise and Fall of the Merchant Guilds: Re-thinking the Comparative Study of Commercial Institutions in Premodern Europe," *Journal of Interdisciplinary History* 40, n° 4 (2010): 477–511.

4 Lauren Benton and Richard Ross, eds., *Legal Pluralism and Empires. 1500–1850* (New York: New York University Press, 2013). Sally Engle Merry, "Legal Pluralism," *Law & Society Review* 22, n° 5 (1988): 869–896. Guillaume Calafat, "Jurisdictional Pluralism in a Litigious Sea (1590–1630): Hard Cases, Multi-Sited Trials and Legal Enforcement between North Africa and Italy," *Past and Present* (2019): 142–178.

 | HTTPS://DOI.ORG/10.1163/9789004755192-005

In a plural regulatory context, the jurisdictional power of institutions to control and influence the behaviour[5] of those involved in trade is asymmetrical and depends on the dynamics of authority between institutions, characterised by constant negotiation.[6] The figure of the foreign consul is a good example. Together with the task of representing and defending the collective interests of the nation on foreign soil, consuls emerged essentially as magistrates to mediate in disputes between members of their community, although their jurisdictional powers depended on being recognised by the political authorities of the host territory.[7]

1 Jurisdictional Asymmetry: The Valencian Case

The composite nature of the Hispanic monarchy[8] meant that the jurisdictional capacity of foreign consuls was different in each territory until the Consular Regulations of 1765 permanently stripped consuls of any kind of jurisdictional prerogative.[9] In early modern Seville, for example, there were foreign magistracies with recognised but limited competence. One such case was the jurisdictional privilege granted to the Genoese, which consisted of the power to appoint two consuls with authority to settle disputes arising between members of their nation. The privileges were restricted, expressly stipulating that consuls could not adjudicate in criminal matters, nor in cases involving residents of the city. They were only empowered to resolve lawsuits of Genoese litigants who were not residents of Seville and their decision could be appealed

5 Benton and Ross, *Legal Pluralism*, 1–17.

6 Regina Grafe, *Entre el mundo ibérico y el atlántico: comercio y especialización regional, 1550–1650* (Bilbao: Diputación Foral de Bizkaia, 2005).

7 Jörg Ulbert, "Introduction. La fonction consulaire à l'époque moderne: définition, état de connaissances et perspectives de recherche," in *La fonction consulaire à l'époque moderne. L'Affirmation d'une institution économique et politique (1500–1800)*, eds. Jörg Ulbert and Gérard Le Bouëdec (Rennes: Presses universitaires de Rennes, 2006), 9–20. Marcella Aglietti, "El debate sobre la jurisdicción consular en la monarquía hispánica (1759–1769)," in *Los cónsules de extranjeros en la Edad Moderna y a principios de la Edad Contemporánea*, eds. Marcella Aglietti, Manuel Herrero Sánchez and Francisco Zamora Rodríguez (Madrid: Ediciones Doce Calles, 2013), 105–118.

8 John Elliot, "A Europe of Composite Monarchies," *Past and Present* 137 (1992): 48–71; *idem*, *Spain, Europe and the Wider World (1500–1800)* (New Haven, London: Yale University Press, 2009).

9 Aglietti, "El debate," 114–115.

before the local justices. Even Genoese who were residents of Seville were subject to the jurisdictions of the city.[10]

The jurisdiction of foreigners in northern Spain was much more limited. The French community in the Basque territories faced the opposition of local merchants to the presence of a consul for their nation throughout the early modern period. Basque traders were particularly resistant to granting foreigners any kind of jurisdictional authority, as well as to the power of consuls to collect debts by virtue of their position, considering it contrary to the *fueros* (customary laws and privileges) of the kingdom. In any case, consuls were able to represent and defend the interests of their community before Basque institutions and to act, even without jurisdiction, as mediators to reconcile merchants in dispute and help them choose counsel to institute legal proceedings in the local courts, if need be.[11]

Nor could foreign consuls act as judges in the Kingdom of Valencia. All merchants, both native and foreign, were subject to the courts of ordinary jurisdiction in civil and criminal matters, while mercantile jurisdiction was exercised by the Consulate of the Sea, competent in all matters of trade[12] in

10 Marco Fernández Gómez, *Libro de privilegios de la ciudad de Sevilla. Estudio Introductorio y transcripción* (Sevilla: Ayuntamiento de Sevilla, 1993), 401; José Damián González Arce, "El consulado genovés de Sevilla (siglos XIII–XV). Aspectos jurisdiccionales, comerciales y fiscales," *Studia historica. Historia medieval* 28 (2010): 179–206; Giovanna Petti Balbi, *Negoziare fuori patria. Nazioni e genovesi in età medievale* (Bologna: CLUEB, 2005).

11 Álvaro Aragón Ruano, "Entre el rechazo frontal y la aceptación con condiciones: cónsules extranjeros en los puertos vascos entre los siglos XVI y XVII," *Espacio, Tiempo y Forma* 27 (2014): 242–246.

12 The configuration of the Consulate of the Sea in the early modern period was determined by the privileged that the king Ferdinand the Catholic enacted on March 14, 1493. This privilege gave merchants the control of the Consulate, thus confirming the power local merchants acquired in Valencia. A former privilege (1360) granted by Peter the Ceremonious established that the jurisdiction of the Consulate of the Sea was in the hands of two consuls: a merchant and a seaman: Arcadi García Sanz, "La primera época del Consolat de Mar de València (1283–1362)," in *Primer Congreso de Historia del País Valenciano* (*Valencia, 14–18 de abril de 1971*) (Valencia: Universidad de Valencia, 1980), 511. From the privilege of the Catholic king onwards, the consuls appointed had to be a citizen (*ciudadano*) and a merchant, omitting seamen with the additional novelty of extending the competence of the Consulate to both maritime and land trade: Ricardo Franch Benavent, "El Consulado y los Cuerpos de Comercio," in *La ciudad de Valencia: historia, geografía y arte de la ciudad de Valencia*, ed. José Hermosilla Plá (Valencia: Universidad de Valencia, 2009), 307. Since 1284 in the Consulate of the Sea there was also an appeal judge who was directly appointed by the monarch: Arcadi García Sanz, "Las apelaciones en el Consulado," *Boletín de la Sociedad Castellonense de Cultura* 37 (1961): 17–25.

the kingdom since its foundation in 1283.[13] There is compelling evidence of the zeal with which the Valencian Consuls of the Sea defended their jurisdictional preserve, especially against two institutions that by the very nature of their functions posed a threat to their competence: the *Bailía General* (Royal Treasury) and foreign consuls.

The jurisdictional monopoly of the Valencian Consulate of the Sea extended, in practice, throughout the kingdom, giving rise to quite a number of conflicts with other institutions, especially in Alicante, a burgeoning commercial enclave. From 1550, Alicante became a vital economic hub for the kingdom thanks to the halving of customs duties, attracting many foreign merchants who established their business headquarters there.[14] The port was an important centre for redistribution of merchandise and the outlet for Castilian wool bound for Italian markets and was consequently an inevitable staging post on the sea route connecting the Mediterranean and the Atlantic.[15]

Despite the importance of Alicante to the economy of the kingdom, the consulate did not formally exist there as an autonomous institution until the eighteenth century,[16] owing to the opposition of the Consulate of the Sea in Valencia. However, the merchants of Alicante had other judicial bodies available through which to remedy the lack of specialised commercial courts. From the sixteenth century, the local merchants called for such courts to be established in Alicante, arguing that they had to travel to Valencia to litigate in the Consulate of the Sea, which was causing them severe financial losses. Philip II responded by granting a privilege ordering the creation of a credentiary judge empowered to adjudicate in commercial cases.[17]

---

13 The Consulate of the Sea emerges as a jurisdictional privilege granted by the king Peter the Great to the city of Valencia, through which seamen could appoint two consuls to settle the disputes arising from maritime trade. García Sanz, "La primera época," 501–505.

14 José Ignacio Martínez Ruíz and Perry Gauci, *Mercaderes ingleses en Alicante en el siglo XVII* (Alicante: Universidad de Alicante, 2008); Vicente Montojo Montojo, "Crecimiento mercantil y desarrollo corporativo en España: los consulados extraterritoriales extranjeros (ss. XVI–XVII)," *Anuario de Historia del Derecho Español* 62 (1992): 47–66.

15 Armando Alberola Romá, "Relacions econòmiques entre el país valencià i Europa durant l'edat moderna: aproximació al cas d'Alacant," *Pedralbes. Revista d'Història Moderna* 18 (1998): 15–19; Valentín Vázquez de Prada, "Consideraciones en torno al cambio estructural del comercio español en el siglo XVI," in *Las sociedades ibéricas y el mar a finales del siglo XVI*, eds. Luis Antonio Ribot García and Ernest Belenguer Cebrià (Lisbon: Sociedad Estatal Lisboa '98, 1998), 37–57.

16 Francisco Figueras Pacheco, *El Consulado Marítimo y Terrestre de Alicante y Pueblos del Obispado de Orihuela* (Alicante: Instituto de Estudios Alicantinos, 1957), 51–61; Montojo, "Crecimiento mercantil," 61.

17 Privilege of Madrid granted on December 21st, 1591. Figueras, *El Consulado*, 51.

Some years later, in 1636, the ordinances drawn up by Dr Martín de Funes, following a visit and *juicio de residencia* (appraisal of tenure) of the judges and officials of Alicante, were published. These ordinances legally recognised the *bailía general* as a court of the sea or consulate competent to pass summary judgment in commercial cases arising in the city, both at first instance and on appeal if the litigants so wished.[18] The opposition of the Valencian consuls to the new law was immediate but fruitless. Although the Valencian Consulate of the Sea considered that recognition of the new competence acquired by the *baile* of Orihuela was detrimental to its jurisdiction (since it could henceforth hear mercantile cases from Alicante only on appeal), the extension of the *bailía* court's jurisdiction and its equivalence to a consulate remained in force.[19]

Judicial sources show that in practice the merchants of Alicante had been using the jurisdiction of the *bailía general* as a consulate since well before it was officially recognised as such. In Aragonese regional law, the *bailía general* was the institution responsible for protecting crown property. It ensured that laws were complied with and taxes were collected, and it regulated maritime trade, making it an attractive jurisdiction for merchants. This is confirmed by a lawsuit in 1595 brought in the *Real Audiencia* (Royal Courts of Justice) by the Genoese merchant Pantaleón Tallacarne, appealing against a judgment by the *baile* of Alicante in favour of Benito Ganducio and others.[20]

The *baile*'s judgment awarded Ganducio ownership of 49 sacks of wool owed to him by Juan Francisco Palavecino, not present, of whose property Pantaleón Tallacarne was trustee. Tallacarne asked the judges of the *Real Audiencia* to set aside this judgment on the grounds of defects of jurisdiction. He argued that Palavecino was a foreigner and therefore could not be com-

18 James Casey, *The Kingdom of Valencia in the Seventeenth Century* (Cambridge: Cambridge University Press, 1979), 81; Vicente Montojo Montojo, "El comercio de Alicante en los reinados de Felipe II y Felipe III. Una construcción desde la cooperación," *Cuadernos de Historia Moderna* 32 (2007): 87–90. Montojo, "Crecimiento mercantil," 61.

19 The importance of the Southern *Bailía* for the commercial development of the kingdom is manifested in its move from Orihuela to Alicante in 1647; Figueras, *El Consulado*, 66–71; Franch, "El Consulado," 309.

20 Appeal of 13 January 1595 presented by Joan Vicent Palop, notary and legal representative of Pantaleón Tallacarne. Archivo del Reino de Valencia (ARV), Procesos de la Real Audiencia, Part II, Letter P, number 788. Pantaleón Tallacarne against Vicent and Benet Ganducio about certain wool. Year 1594. See also ARV, Procesos de Madrid, Letter P, number 486. Pantaleón Tallacarne on behalf of Juan Bautista Palavecino, absent, against Vicent and Benet Ganducio about some money. Year 1594.

pelled by the *baile* but only by a competent judge.[21] Benito Ganducio opposed the appeal and insisted that the *baile*'s judgment was valid. He stated that the *baile* had jurisdictional competence to resolve mercantile and maritime disputes in Alicante, as there was no consulate in the city with jurisdiction over trade matters. Ganducio also argued that the fact that Juan Francisco Palavecino was a foreigner did not prevent him from being bound by the *baile*'s jurisdiction, since despite being Genoese he was settled in Alicante, where he engaged in trade, and for this reason, he was immediately subject to the local courts, including the *bailía*.

Legally, the jurisdictional monopoly of the Consulate of the Sea over maritime and terrestrial mercantile disputes arising throughout the Kingdom of Valencia obliged the merchants of the kingdom, native and foreign, to travel to the city of Valencia[22] to litigate mercantile matters in the Consulate. But the fact is that merchants litigated in any jurisdiction that suited them. Traders went to pursue their lawsuits in the institutions of the capital – including the Consulate of the Sea – not because they were concerned to satisfy the legal criteria of institutional competence, but as a specific strategy that might consist, for example, in improving a judgment already passed by another judge by appealing against it to the supreme court of the kingdom, the *Real Audiencia*, putting pressure on one's opponent, gaining time, or simply discomfiting the other party. In practice, the jurisdictional monopoly of the Consulate of the Sea was a legal provision that guided merchants' choice of institution to settle their disputes, but without limiting it. This certainly did not mean that those in charge of the Consulate of the Sea did not fight to protect their jurisdictional privilege, the very privilege that gave them control of the Valencian trade.

We know that the Consuls of the Sea repeatedly asked the *Real Audiencia* of Valencia to intervene to ensure that the consuls of foreign nations respected its competence in matters of trade in the kingdom.[23] The invasions of competence annoyed not only the Consuls of the Sea but also some merchants, especially when the intrusion was inconvenient to their interests in a lawsuit. An example of this was the Milanese merchant Bernardino Canarisio, who in 1565, as evidence in litigation he was pursuing in the *Real Audiencia* against his compatriot and partner, Geroni de Vecchi, attached a series of documents

21 Writ of 6 April 1595 presented by Joan Linyana, legal representative of Benet Ganducio and others. ARV, Procesos de la Real Audiencia, Part II, Letter P, number 788. Pantaleón Tallacarne against Vicent and Benet Ganducio about certain wool. Year 1594.

22 Jurisdiction confirmed by Philip III in 1604 within the context of the ratification of the privileges of the Consulate of the Sea granted in 1493 by the Catholic King. Franch, "El Consulado," 307–309.

23 Franch, "El Consulado," 309.

containing copies of the exclusive privilege granted by Ferdinand the Catholic to the Consuls of the Sea of Valencia to decide all mercantile cases in the kingdom. Canarisio also presented a copy of an order from the *baile* of Valencia, issued on 9 April 1554, requiring Joan Batista Barzi, the Ragusan consul, to desist from any jurisdictional practice detrimental to the competence of the Consulate of the Sea.

The fact that Canarisio presented the *baile*'s order as evidence is significant for two reasons. First, it confirms the jurisdictional incapacity of foreign consuls in Valencian territory. Second, the lawsuit in question highlights the complexity of jurisdictional practice in the context of the legal and institutional pluralism of early modern societies, forcing us to reassess the position of institutions, in this case, foreign consuls, in the dynamics of power and conflict resolution in the Valencian commercial sphere.

Bernardino Canarisio's intention was to force Hieroni Vecchi to conduct his lawsuit before the Consuls of the Sea, a jurisdiction that Vecchi was trying to avoid by bringing proceedings in the *Real Audiencia*.[24] Essentially, Vecchi was seeking to evade arbitration on the accounts of the trading company he had with Canarisio, in which the award was disadvantageous to him as it left him owing large sums of money. The arbiters were the merchants Juan Pablo Dadda and Nicolas Olginat, but they lacked the material resources to enforce the award, which is why Canarisio asked the Consulate of the Sea to intervene to execute the judgment. The story ends with a ruling from the *Real Audiencia* which arrived two years after the initial arbitration, confirming the award that ordered Hieroni de Vecchi to pay what he owed to Canarisio.[25]

What was Canarisio's interest in showing the judges of the *Audiencia* the document from the *baile* denying consuls of foreign nations any kind of jurisdiction? Vecchi's evasion of the Consulate's jurisdiction was regarded by Canarisio as opportunistic: through multiple lawsuits Vecchi was aiming to wear down his creditor and thereby increase his own chances of renegotiating the debt by playing the game of forum shopping. In this case, the game involved the jurisdictions of the Consulate of the Sea, the *Audiencia Real* and arbitration. By presenting the *baile*'s order, Canarisio was seeking to protect the arbitral award that benefited him. On the one hand, he recognised the authority of the Consulate of the Sea to enforce it and documented that

24 ARV, Procesos de la Real Audiencia, Part II, Letter G, Appendix, number 219. Geroni de Vecchi, against Juan Pablo Dadda about the accounting of their partnership. Year 1565. Petition presented by Bernardino Canarisio on 9 June 1565.

25 Ibid. As it can be seen in the documents presented by Canarisio on 5 September 1567, asking the magistrate of the Royal Audience to confirm the judgment and condemn Vecchi to also pay the expenses of the lawsuit.

authority with the relevant legislation. On the other, he emphasised that the merchants who acted as judges were doing so in the capacity of arbiters (arbitrators-at-law), not foreign consuls since in the latter case Vecchi could have annulled the award in view of the prohibition against foreign consuls exercising jurisdiction in the kingdom.

The jurisdictional disqualification of foreign consuls in Valencia forced foreign merchants to use local courts or alternative mechanisms such as arbitration. Indeed, foreigners – whether consuls of their nations or not – could freely act as arbiters or intermediaries to resolve disputes involving other merchants and participate in lawsuits before the courts of ordinary jurisdiction of the kingdom as attorneys to represent the economic interests of other traders.

2 Foreign Consuls and Conflict Management

Arbitration was undoubtedly one of the options favoured by merchants to settle their disputes because it was quick and inexpensive.[26] It is reasonable to believe that foreign consuls were leading figures in the practice of arbitration in Valencia, though given the lack of sources to confirm it, this can be no more than a hypothesis. In any case, a study of arbitration both in Valencia and in Seville has enabled me to identify two essential features of this institution that necessarily have a bearing on the use that merchants made of the practice and consequently on their use of other jurisdictions: the professional prestige of the arbiters and the pre-existence of a socioeconomic link between the litigants.[27]

Foreign consuls were usually merchants with an impeccable reputation and plentiful social and economic resources. They were familiar with the

26 Ogilvie, *Institutions*, 297; Oscar Gelderblom, *Cities of Commerce. The Institutional Foundations of International Trade in the Low Countries, 1250–1650* (Princeton, Oxford: Princeton University Press, 2013), 104–105; Stuart Jenks, "Conclusion," in *The Hanse in Medieval and Early Modern Europe*, eds. Justyna Wubs-Mrozewicz and Stuart Jenks (Leiden, Boston: Brill, 2013), 265; Christian Burset, "Merchant Courts, Arbitration, and the Politics of Commercial Litigation in the Eighteenth-Century British Empire," *Law and History Review* 34, n° 3 (2016): 621.

27 Ana Belem Fernández Castro, "Handling Conflicts in Long-Distance Trade: A View of the Mediterranean through the Experience of Merchants Operating in the Kingdom of Valencia in the Late Sixteenth-Century," in *Conflict Management in the Mediterranean and the Atlantic, 1000–1800. Actors, Institutions and Strategies of Dispute Settlement*, eds. Louis Sicking and Alain Wijffels (Leiden, Boston: Brill, 2020), 248–252; *idem*, "¿Quitarse de pleitos? Litigiosidad mercantil y práctica arbitral en la Carrera de Indias a finales del siglo XVI," *Revista de Indias* 79, n° 275 (2019): 51–77.

local and international markets and with the laws and customs governing trade and they knew how to interact with local institutions. They were excellent agents, as they had access to reliable information on trade and on other merchants.[28] All these skills made them figures of choice for other traders, especially to mediate in resolving disputes.

Foreign consuls had a considerable presence in the kingdom as some historians have noted,[29] particularly in Valencia and Alicante. Many of them represented the interests of other merchants as private individuals: in other words, acting not as consuls but merely as businessmen. Their involvement was especially in demand in cases of shipwrecks, whose management required individuals familiar with the dynamics of local bureaucracy, and particularly of the law courts.

A case in point was Joan Andrea Ullio, a Milanese merchant resident in Alicante. We know that Ullio was Milanese consul from the end of the sixteenth century[30] and he is found as an agent of various Italian merchants involved in the shipwreck of the Marolina.[31] Indeed, Ullio administered Florestano Lodi's estate following his death in 1570.[32] Joan Andrea had a son with the same name and the two formed a company with another Milanese merchant resident in Alicante, Ambrosio Bosso, and with Mariano Casini, who was based in Valencia. Yet another Milanese, Hércules Dadda, acted as his legal representative in Valencia. The Ullios, father and son, were involved in the art trade. It was they who organised the transaction for the sculptures that the Grand Duke of Florence sent to the Duke of Lerma in 1604. They had business in Cadiz, where they sent luxury goods and mirrors.[33]

---

28 As it was the case of the consul of the French nation. Ana Belem Fernández Castro, "Redes Mercantiles y Soporte Institucional. La comunidad francesa de Valencia a finales del siglo XVI," in *La dynamique juridique des réseaux marchands: Hanses, nations, agences, filiales et comptoirs*, ed. Luisa Brunori (Toulouse: Presses de l'Université Toulouse Capitole, 2023), 173–206.

29 Montojo, "Crecimiento mercantil," 47–66.

30 Andrea Caracausi, "The Wool Trade, Venice and the Mediterranean Cities at the End of the Sixteenth Century," in *Commercial Networks and European Cities, 1400–1800*, eds. Andrea Caracaussi and Christof Jeggle (London: Pickering & Chatto, 2014), 219.

31 ARV, Maestre Racional, Shipwreck of the Marolina ship in 1572, number 9882.

32 ARV, Procesos de la Real Audiencia, Part II, Letter J, Appendix, number 570. Juan Andrea Ullio against Gaspar Pasqual about an appeal. Year 1572.

33 Edward Goldberg, "Artistic Relations between the Medici and the Spanish Courts, 1587–1621: Part II," *The Burlington Magazine* 138, n° 1121 (1996): 529; Suzanne Butters, "The Uses and Abuses of Gifts in the World of Ferdinando de' Medici (1549–1609)," *I Tatti Studies* 11 (2007): 352.

TABLE 3.1 Consuls of foreign nations active in the Kingdom of Valencia

Name	National origin	Nation of representation	Years of practice
Glaudo Martí	Dauphiné	French	1575–1585
Glaudo Matheu	Thizy	Marseille	1590
Pedro Moreno	Valencian?	Marseille	1593
Gabriel Avillon		Marseille	1600
Carlos Tirant	Valencian?	Marseille	
Joan Andrea Ullio	Milan	Milan	End of the sixteenth century
Joan Batista Imperial	Genoese	English	
Jacinto Boacio		Flemish	
Pablo Jeronimo Bergali	Genoese	Genoese	
Joan Batista Barzi		Ragusean	1554
Joan Vanovesquier	Flemish	Ingleses	
Miguel Juan Guesa		Flemish	Beginning of the seventeenth century
Benet Garibo	Saboyan	Saboyan	1597
Nicolas Ginoin/ Genovi		Saboyan	1603
Batista Spínola	Genoese	Genoese	1572

SOURCE: Montojo, "Crecimiento mercantil," 52–58. Álvaro Castillo Pintado, *Tráfico marítimo y comercio de importación en Valencia a comienzos del siglo XVII* (Madrid: Seminario de Historia Social y Económica, 1967), 58–74. Caracausi, "The wool trade," 219. Emilia Salvador Esteban, *La economía valenciana en el siglo XVI (Comercio de importación)* (Valencia: Universidad de Valencia, 1972), 64–75.

Foreign consuls could also act as arbiters and mediate other merchants' disputes, although their involvement did not guarantee that the conflict would be resolved. Indeed, the expertise of arbiters and their reputation were elements that were not sufficient on their own to effectively resolve a dispute through arbitration. It is possible that the participation of foreign consuls as arbiters was limited to very specific cases: firstly, to conflicts between merchants of their own nationality who were passing through the kingdom, that is, non-resident, provided that the object of the dispute did not involve significant sums of money. This hypothesis is based on the bond of nationality that linked the merchants and plausibly prompted them to seek the assistance of the consul of their nation, without excluding other available jurisdictional alternatives.

The complexity of the conflict influenced the types of institutions that merchants used to manage it. In matters where substantial amounts of capital were at stake, such as shipwrecks or bankruptcies, the effectiveness of arbitration was limited. In such cases, merchants preferred to turn to institutions that specialised in trade matters, such as the Consulate of the Sea or even the civil courts, where the administration of justice was in the hands of jurists who had the coercive resources necessary to oblige merchants to comply with their judgments and face the financial liability resulting from them. It is in these cases that we see foreign consuls acting as intermediaries between merchants and local institutions.[34]

In the case of foreign merchants who were totally disconnected from Valencian institutional life, the Consulate of the Sea emerged as the inevitable jurisdictional option merely for reasons of competence, and it certainly offered litigants a much more expeditious and inexpensive procedural route than the courts of ordinary jurisdiction. But the Consulate of the Sea was just another institution in the vast Valencian organisational structure, where even those passing through could obtain access to local judicial institutions, even though they lacked a social network to underpin their interaction with those institutions.

Secondly, foreign consuls could be called upon to act as judges by other merchants who were part of their business network, especially those who engaged in long-distance trade. It is a question that needs to be confirmed but that seems plausible, given the characteristics of arbitration practice in Valencia. Indeed, for arbitration to work, the merchants in dispute needed the incentive of a personal and business relationship that was important to safeguard in the future.

The jurisdictional advantages of arbitration were numerous and highly favourable, but its use can be regarded as a privilege reserved for those who had a solid record of trust prior to the dispute. The potential evasion of the arbitral judgment due to the arbiters' lack of coercive powers, however much support they received from the courts, which by law had to assist in enforcing awards,[35] was an unnecessary risk for merchants, to whom the jurisdictional

34 Fernández Castro, "Handling Conflicts," 244–248.

35 Ibid., *Justicia*, 140–175.

force of the local courts was directly available.[36] Judicial sources confirm this preference. In all the arbitrations studied, the opposing parties had a bond prior to the dispute, which could be of an economic, social, or family nature, and which they had an interest in preserving.

3 Arbitration and Its Peculiarities

In commercial arbitration the underlying relationship between the parties is economic. The pre-existence of a personal relationship between the parties can be assumed, given how often business led to friendship, and vice versa. Numerous studies on the mercantile bourgeoisie in the early modern era show the interdependence of the private and business spheres, the former being a strategy to preserve and enhance the latter.[37] Identifying the family relationships between the parties in an arbitration is easier since they themselves refer to this link. Of the thirty arbitrations studied, three involve members of the same family with business in common. Two of them concern the Valencian Salvador family,[38] while the third involves the Ariño family, another powerful lineage in the local bourgeoisie.[39]

---

36 The rise on litigation rates before civil courts all around Europe during the early modern era confirms the familiarity merchants had with courts: Richard Kagan, *Lawsuits and Litigants in Castile, 1500–1700* (North Carolina: University of North Carolina Press, 1981); Amalia Kessler, *A Revolution in Commerce: The Parisian Merchant Court and the Rise of Commercial Society in Eighteenth Century France* (New Haven: Yale University Press, 2007); Gelderblom, *Cities of Commerce.*

37 Xavier Lamikiz, *Trade and Trust in the Eighteenth-Century Atlantic World. Spanish Merchants and their Overseas Networks* (Great Britain: Boydell Press, 2010); Francesca Trivellato, *The Familiarity of Strangers. The Sephardic Diaspora, Livorno, and Cross-Cultural Trade in the Early Modern Period* (New Haven, London: Yale University Press, 2009); Tijl Vanneste, *Global Trade and Commercial Networks: Eighteenth-Century Diamond Merchants* (London: Pickering & Chatto, 2011).

38 The first arbitration took place in 1577 between Hieroni Salvador the elder and his brother-in-law Joan Colomer. They wanted to settle a dispute arising from the purchase of cattle. Archivo del Real Colegio Seminario de Corpus Christi (ARCSCC), Protocolos, file 1601. Arbitration agreement registered on 3 May 1577 before the Valencian notary, Antoni Joan Zamora. The second arbitration occurred in 1582 between Hieroni Salvador the younger and his creditors. Most of the creditors were Salvador's relatives: Francés and Hieroni Salvador the elder, his brothers, and Joseph Vallés, his brother-in-law, married to Esperanza Salvador y de Vallés. ARV, Procesos de la Real Audiencia, Part II, Letter F, number 651. Lawsuit of Francés Salvador against Hieroni Salvador about debts. Year 1593.

39 In 1595 Hieroni Ariño's heirs wanted to solve through arbitration a controversy they had with Vicent Ariño, Hieroni's brother who resided in Madrid, about the accounting of the

The existence of a prior economic and personal relationship between the parties submitting to arbitration remained a constant and almost intrinsic feature of the institution, a pattern unaffected by the differences in identity between those involved. Thus, Valencian sources show that arbitration was a dispute resolution mechanism used by both native and foreign merchants: in eleven arbitrations the parties were of Valencian origin, while in another sixteen at least one of the parties was foreign to the kingdom of Valencia.[40] Within the latter category, in eight cases the national origin of the parties was the same and in the other eight, they were of different nationalities.

What do these proportions tell us? Firstly, they show that arbitration was a practice used equally by native and foreign merchants to settle disputes, contrary to the assertion of A. M. Bernal, who argues that in the context of the *Carrera de Indias*, arbitration was a type of jurisdiction mainly requested by foreign merchants, due to their interest in preserving their autonomy and avoiding the use of local jurisdictions, even those that specialised in trade matters.[41] According to Bernal's proposal, the foreign consul, familiar with the law of his own nation, would have been the ideal judge-arbitrator to settle disputes between his compatriots. However, the patterns of behaviour of foreign merchants as litigants, in the cases of both Valencia and Seville, show that they frequently had recourse to the courts, apparently without any fear that the community they belonged to would lose autonomy by involving local judges. Indeed, in Valencia, they had no jurisdictional autonomy, and the judicial assistance of the courts of ordinary jurisdiction and the Consulate was necessary and even wished for by the foreigners themselves, who, after submitting to arbitration, applied to the courts to request their assistance in enforcing the arbitral award.

---

partnership they had together. ARCSCC, Protocolos, file 1832. Arbitration agreement registered on 23 May 1595 before the notary Jaume Fores.

40 In three cases it was not possible to confirm the national origin of the parties: First, Tomás Sagri, who probably had Genoese origins. ARCSCC, Protocolos, file 1611. Award enacted by Joan Bautista Sauli and Cosme Alexandre, merchants and arbiters appointed in the arbitration between Tomás Sagri and Nicolao Isola, Genoese merchant, about the accounting of the business they had together. The judgment was registered before the notary Antoni Joan Zamora on 5 December 1587. Second, the national origin of neither Hieroni Tinto nor Joan Martí has been confirmed, although they were presumably Valencians. ARV, Procesos de Madrid, Letter J, number 124. Juan Mercader against Hieroni Tinto about an arbitration award. Year 1561. Finally, in the arbitration between Hieroni Salvador the younger and Carles Gahi, the nation of the before mentioned remains unknown. ARCSCC, Protocolos, file 1598. Arbitration agreement registered on 29 October 1573.

41 Antonio Miguel Bernal, "La contabilidad como instrumento de conciliación y arbitraje en la Carrera de Indias (siglos XV–XVIII)," *Anuario de Estudios Atlánticos* 54 (2008): 518.

TABLE 3.2 Arbitrations in which the parties belonged to the same nation

Partie A	Partie B	Arbiters
Bastian de Antoni Parsiq Paniale (Corsican residing in Marseille)	Bartolomé Sernati French (Master of the ship Our Lady of Grace)	Joan Miquel Balaguer (Valencian) Glaudo Jarlade French?
Joan Batista y Joan Ángel Miquitin (Milan)	Jerónimo Biunto (Milan)	Jacobo Cerioto (Milan) Joan Antoni Bononi (Milan)
Joan Batista Sauli (Genoese) Domingo de San Remo (Genoese)	Benito Pito (Genoese)	Juan Vidania Jacobo Antonio Canale Baltasar Doria (All Genoese)
Hieroni de Vecchi (Milan)	Bernardino Canarisio (Milan)	Juan Pablo Dada Nicolao Olginat (Both from Milan)
Joseph Negrón (Genoese)	Francés Lomelin (Genoese)	Bernardo Calvo Pedro Gentil Third umpires: Esteban Lomelin y Bernabé Spinola (All from Genoa)
Joan Puig (French)	Jacques Serrut (French)	
Antoni Gedes (Marseille)	Guillem Manuel (French residing in Gandia)	Bernardino Costa de Olana (Valencian)
Joan Batista Sauli (Genoese)	Nicolao y Joan Maria Basi Bartolomé Nicolini Joan Negroto (All from Genoa)	Hieroni Delfino Marco Antonio Musefi (Both from Milan)

SOURCE: ARCSCC, Protocolos, file 22019. Register of 1 March 1580 made by notary Joan Nofre Masquefa. ARCSCC, Protocolos, file 1613. Register of 9 August 1589 made before notary Antoni Joan Zamora. ARCSCC, Protocolos, file 1597. Register of the notary Antoni Joan Zamora. Year 1572. ARV, Procesos de la Real Audiencia, Part II, Letter G, Appendix, number 219. Geroni de Vecchi, against Juan Pablo Dadda about accounting. Year 1565. ARV, Procesos de la Real Audiencia, Part II, Letter J, Appendix, number 806. Joseph Negrón against Francesc Lomelin about debts. Year 1589. ARV, Procesos de Madrid, Letter J, number 626. Juan Puig against Jaume Serrut and Frances Berrali about some grain. Year 1595. ARV, Procesos de la Real Audiencia, Part I, Letter A, number 539. Antoni Gedes against Guillén Manuel, about a debt. Year 1593. ARCSCC, Protocolos, file 1617. Agreement between Joan Batista Sauli, Nicolao y Joan María Basi, Bartolomé Nicolini and Joan Negroto, all Genoese and partners, made before Antoni Joan Zamora on 14 January 1592.

Moreover, to argue that arbitration was a practice used by foreign communities to preserve their autonomy would only make sense between parties from the same country in which all those involved shared the same national identity, which was frequently the case, but certainly not always. The proportion of arbitrations between members of the same community versus those of different nationalities in our sample was equal: eight of each. The relationship can be explained in the light of intercultural trade, in which negotiation between individuals of different nations or identities became normal practice, particularly in long-distance trade. Such interculturality transformed traditional structures of trust, which were now orientated towards professional, economic and social criteria, the first being related to knowledge of the market and business experience, the second to the material ability of the person concerned to meet the commitments acquired and cope with any hitch in the transaction, and the third associated with the availability of human capital to make the transaction possible de facto.

The reconfiguration of structures of trust is evident in the choice of arbitration panels, which perfectly fit the criteria described above. In twenty-seven cases it has been possible to determine the nationality of the arbiters. When this is correlated with the nation of origin of the parties involved in the arbitration, it turns out that in twelve cases the arbiters and the parties shared the same nationality, in ten cases the nationality of the arbiters and that of the parties were different, while in five cases the arbiter's nationality only coincided with that of one of the parties. Although nationality helps to strengthen the bonds between people, the fact is that in the sources studied the choice of arbiters seems to reflect more powerful criteria that have to do with the arbiters' knowledge and experience in situations the same as or similar to the one in dispute in the arbitration.

In the arbitration to which the citizen Pere Luis Almenara and the exchange broker Miquel Sanchis submitted in 1577 over an exchange dispute, the arbiters appointed by the parties to resolve the situation were the merchant Luis Núñez and the notary Luis Coscolla. All of them were natives of the Kingdom of Valencia, but that was not the reason why Almenara and Sanchis chose their judges. Luis Núñez was a well-known merchant in Valencian commercial circles, with experience in the exchange and insurance markets, as well as in import trade.[42] Luis Coscolla, in turn, was the notary who notarised the protest

42 A document of 1573 confirms the participation of Luis Núñez as insurer of a ship coming from Seville loaded with New World's merchandise. The ship sank in Gibraltar, fact that explains the nature of the document analyzed; that is, a power of attorney the insures granted to Martín Mahin to authorize him to act on their behalf in all the issues related to the shipwreck. ARCSCC, Protocolos, file 1598. Deed of 5 January 1573.

TABLE 3.3 Arbitration in which the nation of the parties was different

Partie A	Partie B	Arbiters
Joan Batista y Paolo Tridi (Milan)	Fernando García Valencian?	Joan Batista Sauli (Genoese) Gabriel Trobado (Valencian) Jon Pallares (Valencian and third arbiter)
Pedro Peralta Luis Camarena (Both from Valencia)	Bernardo Pascual (Venetian)	Joan Batista Assoris (Valencian)
Guillem Manuel (French)	Luch Monfort (Valencian)	Hieroni Delfino (Milan) Francisco Salón Valencian?
Hieroni Salvador mayor (Valencian)	Joan Colomer (Aragon)	Luis Núñez Luis Coscolla (Both from Valencia)
Joan Batista Sauli (Genoese)	Francés Farant (Nice)	Hieroni Delfino (Milan) Joan Porta (Valencian)
Benito Pito (Genoese)	Joseph Combo (Mallorca)	Sebastián Joan Xulbi Antonio Fornari (Both from Valencia)
Benito Pito (Genoese)	Pere Martí Esteve (Valencian)	Baltasar de Ros Joan Rodilla Francés Lois Martínez (All from Valencia)
Benito Pito (Genoese)	Berthomeu Vallés (Mallorca)	Melchor Soria Jordi García (Both from Valencia)

SOURCE: ARCSCC, Protocolos, file 1598. Register of 10 October 1573. Arbitration resolution of the dispute between Joan Batista and Paolo Tridi, from Milan, against Ferrando García. ARCSCC, Protocolos, file 1597. Register of 5 January 1572. Intima extrajudicial ordered by Benito Pito, Genoese. ARCSCC, Protocolos, file 1611. Arbitration judgement made by Melchor Soria and Jordi García, arbiters, on 27 February 1587. ARCSCC, Protocolos, file 1607. Arbitration judgement made by Joan Batista Assoris on 7 April 1582. ARCSCC, Protocolos, file 1610. Arbitration judgement published on 22 November 1586 before notary Antoni Joan Zamora. ARCSCC, Protocolos, file 1601. Register of 3 May 1577 made before the notary Antoni Joan Zamora. ARCSCC, Protocolos, file 1621. Arbitration judgement published on 2 February 1597 in the dispute between Joan Batista Sauli, and Frances Farant.

of the exchange at issue in the arbitration, non-payment of which gave rise to a debt of 200 *castellanos*.[43] The appointment of Coscolla to arbitrate the dispute between Sanchis and Almenara was based on his knowledge of the historical context of the situation and his profession. The *notariat* in Valencia has a very long historical tradition. Following the conquest of the kingdom, King James approved and institutionalised Valencian notarial practice on a customary basis.[44] Although they did not have the university training of jurists, notaries received technical training steeped in law, giving them a certain legal and juridical background that put them in a privileged position as legal intermediaries.[45] It was precisely this training and knowledge that may have motivated the choice of Coscolla as an arbiter.[46]

If there was a profession with authority recognised by the mercantile community, it was precisely that of merchants. The figures provided by the sources are conclusive; in twenty-two of the arbitrations analysed at least one of the arbiters was a merchant, and their selection as judges reflected their cognitive and practical skills as individuals that made them suitable for resolving the dispute. The arbitration between the Genoese Joan Batista Sauli and the shipmaster Francés Farant from Nice in 1597 is highly revealing. The parties – of different nationalities – chose the Valencian Joan Porta and the Milanese Hieroni Delfino as their arbiters, both of whom were merchants of renowned repute among the mercantile community. Joan Porta, on the one hand, was a merchant with great influence in the Consulate of the Sea, where he served as

43 ARCSCC, Protocolos, file 1601. Arbitration award of 29 August 1577.

44 José María Mengual, "El notariado en el derecho foral valenciano," *Revista Crítica de Derecho Inmobiliario* 107 (1933): 824.

45 José María Cruselles Gómez, *Els notaris de la Ciutat de València. Activitat professional i comportament social a la primera meitat del segle XV* (Barcelona: Pagès Editor, 1998), 27–58. Nigel Ramsay, "Scriveners and Notaries as Legal Intermediaries in Late Medieval England," in *Enterprise and Individuals in Fifteenth Century England*, ed. Jennifer Kermode (United Kingdom: Alan Sutton, 1991), 118–131.

46 Besides the before mentioned case, in other three arbitrations notaries appear as arbiters. First, in the arbitration between Benito Pito and Joseph Combo the arbiters appointed were the notary Sebastián Xulbi and the merchant Antonio Fornari. ARV, Procesos de la Real Audiencia, Part II, Letter B, number 324. Benito Pito and Joseph Combo about the agreement they made to rescue Hieroni Planelles. Year 1583. Second, in the arbitration that took place in 1562 between Francisco Senini and Batista Pavesi, the arbiters appointed were Luch Verger and the notary Baltasar Scuder. ARV, Procesos de la Real Audiencia, Part II, Letter F, number 151. Francisco Senini against Joseph Pavesi about an executive process, Year 1563. Finally, in the arbitration between Hieroni Salvador the elder and his brother-in-law, Joan Colomer, the arbiters were the notaries Gaspar Joan Mico and Antoni Balançat. ARCSCC, Protocolos, file 1601. Arbitration award registered on 3 May 1577 before the Valencian notary Antoni Joan Zamora.

a consul in 1589, 1594 and 1595, and in the *Taula de Canvis*, the local bank in which he worked as cashier between 1596 and 1597. Hieroni Delfino, on the other hand, was a Milanese living in Valencia who enjoyed great prestige as a merchant. He was well connected in local and international mercantile circles and the scope of his business was considerable, as evidenced by the company he had in 1581 with Salvi Xifre, a Valencian resident in Seville. This company had been in operation since 1575, and in 1581 it was extended for a further five years, counting from that year.[47] In addition, from 1583 to 1585 he leased the rights of the *generalitat* with Joan Mata.[48]

Evidence of merchants' concern to obtain expert and impartial judgments through arbitration is the figure of the *tercero en discordia*, a third arbiter to settle disagreement. The role of the *tercero en discordia* was to prevent deadlock in arbitration process if the arbiters could not reach an agreement on how to resolve it. The third arbiter took control of the arbitration, discussing the contentious points with the arbiters until a solution was arrived at, which was to be the definitive judgment.[49] In this sense, and bearing in mind that in arbitration, where each party appointed their own arbiter, the latter not only acted as a judge but also represented the interests of the party that appointed him, the intervention of a *tercero en discordia* proved essential to ensure the neutrality of the process and avoid it becoming deadlocked. The phenomenon is explicit in the arbitration between the brothers Joan Batista and Paolo Tridi and Ferrando García. In 1573, the parties appointed the merchants Joan Batista Sauli and Gabriel Trobado as arbiters. They also assigned the role of *tercero en discordia* to the merchant Joan Pallares. And, indeed, Pallares played an essential part in judging the case. It is clear from the arbitration that Joan Batista Sauli, a close associate of the Milanese Tridi brothers, for whom he acted as an agent in Valencia, intended to satisfy their claims at all costs. The arbitral

47 ARCSCC, Protocolos, file 1606. Power of attorney granted before the notary Antoni Joan Zamora on 17 January 1581. The agreement of the five years extension of the partnership Hieroni Delfino and Salvi Xifre had, was made on 17 February 1581.

48 ARV, Procesos de la Real Audiencia, Part I, Letter J, number 1130. Appeal submitted before the Royal Audience by Joan Mata, about a judgment of the *Justicia Civil* concerning the earnings of the leasing of the *Generalitat* during the triennial 1583–1585 in favour of Hieroni Delfino. 23 December 1589.

49 Vicent Royo Pérez, "El arbitraje en la documentación medieval valenciana. La caracterización de la institución arbitral en la práctica documental de las comarcas del Els Ports y El Maestrat entre 1232 y 1412," *Anuario de Historia del Derecho Español* 86 (2016): 157–159.

award resulted from the majority of votes formed by Pallares and Trobado, with Sauli expressly voting against it.[50]

4 Final Remarks

Joan Pallares was a member of the Consulate of the Sea. He was part of the Valencian merchant elite, competent in both the habits of commerce and mercantile laws. His expertise made him an excellent candidate to act as arbiter to settle disputes out of court, competences other professionals had, such as notaries, lawyers, and, certainly, merchants that could also represent and defend the interests of a nation. Consuls of foreign nations were key instruments in the protection of other merchants' wealth indeed. They were respectable authorities in the mercantile community since they had the material and human resources and the know-how to interact with the institutional system. All merchants identified as consuls of foreign nations in Valencia satisfied the profile, being ideal candidates to made up arbitration panels, especially considering the particularities of arbitration in the Hispanic kingdoms: it was a highly technical practice that followed the rules of local law.

Even if consuls of foreign nations did not have any kind of jurisdictional powers in the Kingdom of Valencia, consuls could participate in conflict settlement merely as merchants without interfering with the monopoly of the commercial jurisdiction of the Consulate of the Sea. Arbiters should administer justice according to the laws and privileges of the kingdom, discarding any possibility of applying foreign laws in the solution of commercial conflicts in Valencia.

Bibliography

Aglietti, Marcella. "El debate sobre la jurisdicción consular en la monarquía hispánica (1759–1769)." In *Los cónsules de extranjeros en la Edad Moderna y a principios de la Edad Contemporánea*, edited by Marcella Aglietti, Manuel Herrero Sánchez and Francisco Zamora Rodríguez, 105–118. Madrid: Ediciones Doce Calles, 2013.

Alberola Romá, Armando. "Relacions econòmiques entre el país valencià i Europa durant l'edat moderna: aproximació al cas d'Alacant." *Pedralbes. Revista d'Història Moderna* 18 (1998): 15–24.

50 ARCSCC, Protocolos, file 1598. Arbitration award published on 10 October 1573 to settle the lawsuit between Joan Batista and Paolo Tridi from Milan against Ferrando García.

Álvarez Nogal, Carlos. "Instituciones y desarrollo económico: la Casa de la Contratación y la Carrera de Indias (1503–1790)." In *La Casa de la Contratación y la Navegación entre España e Indias*, edited by Enriqueta Vila Vilar, Antonio Acosta Rodríguez and Adolfo Luis González Rodríguez, 21–51. Sevilla: Universidad de Sevilla, 2003.

Aragón Ruano, Álvaro. "Entre el rechazo frontal y la aceptación con condiciones: cónsules extranjeros en los puertos vascos entre los siglos XVI y XVII." *Espacio, Tiempo y Forma* 27 (2014): 239–264.

Benton, Lauren, and Richard Ross, eds. *Legal Pluralism and Empires*. 1500–1850. New York: New York University Press, 2013.

Bernal, Antonio Miguel. "La contabilidad como instrumento de conciliación y arbitraje en la Carrera de Indias (siglos XV–XVIII)." *Anuario de Estudios Atlánticos* 54 (2008): 513–540.

Burset, Christian. "Merchant Courts, Arbitration, and the Politics of Commercial Litigation in the Eighteenth-Century British Empire." *Law and History Review* 34, n° 3 (2016): 615–647.

Butters, Suzanne. "The uses and abuses of gifts in the world of Ferdinando de' Medici (1549–1609)." *I Tatti Studies* 11 (2007): 243–354.

Calafat, Guillaume. "Jurisdictional Pluralism in a Litigious Sea (1590–1630): Hard Cases, Multi-Sited Trials and Legal Enforcement Between North Africa and Italy." *Past and Present* (2019): 142–178.

Caracausi, Andrea. "The Wool Trade, Venice and the Mediterranean Cities at the End of the Sixteenth Century." In *Commercial Networks and European Cities, 1400–1800*, edited by Andrea Caracaussi and Christof Jeggle, 201–222. London: Pickering & Chatto, 2014.

Casey, James. *The Kingdom of Valencia in the Seventeenth Century*. Cambridge: Cambridge University Press, 1979.

Cruselles Gómez, José María. *Els notaris de la Ciutat de València: Activitat professional i comportament social a la primera meitat del segle XV*. Barcelona: Pagès Editor, 1998.

Elliot, John. "A Europe of Composite Monarchies." *Past and Present* 137 (1992): 48–71.

Elliot, John. *Spain, Europe and the Wider World (1500–1800)*. New Haven: Yale University Press, 2009.

Engle Merry, Sally. "Legal Pluralism." *Law & Society Review* 22, n° 5 (1988): 869–896.

Fernández Castro, Ana Belem. "¿Quitarse de pleitos? Litigiosidad mercantil y práctica arbitral en la Carrera de Indias a finales del siglo XVI." *Revista de Indias* 79, n° 275 (2019): 51–77.

Fernández Castro, Ana Belem. "Handling Conflicts in Long-Distance Trade: A View of the Mediterranean through the Experience of Merchants Operating in the Kingdom of Valencia in the Late Sixteenth-Century." In *Conflict Management in the*

Mediterranean and the Atlantic, 1000–1800. Actors, Institutions and Strategies of Dispute Settlement, edited by Louis Sicking and Alain Wijffels, 237–266. Leiden: Brill, 2020.

Fernández Castro, Ana Belem. "Redes Mercantiles Y Soporte Institucional: La comunidad francesa de Valencia a finales del siglo XVI." In *La Dynamique Juridique des Réseaux Marchands: Hanses, Nations, Agences, Filiales et Comptoirs*, edited by Luisa Brunori, 173–206. Toulouse: Presses de l'Université Toulouse Capitole, 2023.

Fernández Castro, Ana Belem. *Justicia, Comercio e Instituciones en la Carrera de Indias (siglo XVI)*. Toulouse: Presses de l'Université Toulouse Capitole, 2024.

Fernández Gómez, Marco. *Libro de privilegios de la ciudad de Sevilla: Estudio Introductorio y transcripción*. Sevilla: Ayuntamiento de Sevilla, 1993.

Figueras Pacheco, Francisco. *El Consulado Marítimo y Terrestre de Alicante y Pueblos del Obispado de Orihuela*. Alicante: Instituto de Estudios Alicantinos, 1957.

Franch Benavent, Ricardo. "El Consulado y los Cuerpos de Comercio." In *La ciudad de Valencia: historia, geografía y arte de la ciudad de Valencia*, edited by José Hermosilla Plá, 307–310. Valencia: Universidad de Valencia, 2009.

García Sanz, Arcadi. "La primera época del Consolat de Mar de València (1283–1362)." In *Primer Congreso de Historia del País Valenciano (Valencia, 14–18 de abril de 1971)*, 501–512. Valencia: Universidad de Valencia, 1980.

García Sanz, Arcadi. "Las apelaciones en el Consulado." *Boletín de la Sociedad Castellonense de Cultura* 37 (1961): 17–25.

Gelderblom, Oscar. *Cities of Commerce: The Institutional Foundations of International Trade in the Low Countries, 1250–1650*. Princeton: Princeton University Press, 2013.

Goldberg, Edward. "Artistic relations between the Medici and the Spanish courts, 1587–1621: Part II." *The Burlington Magazine* 138, n° 1121 (1996): 105–114.

González Arce, José Damián. "El consulado genovés de Sevilla (siglos XIII–XV): Aspectos jurisdiccionales, comerciales y fiscales." *Stud. Hist., Historia medieval* 28 (2010): 179–206.

Grafe, Regina and Oscar Gelderblom. "The Rise and Fall of the Merchant Guilds: Rethinking the Comparative Study of Commercial Institutions in Premodern Europe." *Journal of Interdisciplinary History* 40, n° 4 (2010): 477–511.

Grafe, Regina. "Was There a Market for Institutions in Early Modern European Trade?." In *Union in Separation: Diasporic Groups and Identities in the Eastern Mediterranean, 1100–1800*, edited by Georg Christ, 593–609. Rome: Viella, 2015.

Grafe, Regina. *Entre el mundo ibérico y el atlántico: comercio y especialización regional, 1550–1650*. Bilbao: Diputación Foral de Bizkaia, 2005.

Jenks, Stuart. "Conclusion." In *The Hanse in Medieval and Early Modern Europe*, edited by Justyna Wubs–Mrozewicz and Stuart Jenks, 255–281. Leiden: Brill, 2013.

Kagan, Richard. *Lawsuits and Litigants in Castile, 1500–1700*. North Carolina: University of North Carolina Press, 1981.

Kessler, Amalia. *A Revolution in Commerce: The Parisian Merchant Court and the Rise of Commercial Society in Eighteenth Century France*. New Haven: Yale University Press, 2007.

Lamikiz, Xavier. *Trade and Trust in the Eighteenth-Century Atlantic World: Spanish Merchants and their Overseas Networks*. Woodbridge: Boydell Press, 2010.

Martínez Ruíz, José Ignacio, and Perry Gauci. *Mercaderes ingleses en Alicante en el siglo XVII*. Alicante: Universidad de Alicante, 2008.

Mengual, José María. "El notariado en el derecho foral valenciano." *Revista Crítica de Derecho Inmobiliario* 107 (1933): 821–838.

Montojo Montojo, Vicente. "Crecimiento mercantil y desarrollo corporativo en España: los consulados extraterritoriales extranjeros (ss. XVI–XVII)." *Anuario de Historia del Derecho Español* 62 (1992): 47–66.

Montojo Montojo, Vicente. "El comercio de Alicante en los reinados de Felipe II y Felipe III: Una construcción desde la cooperación." *Cuadernos de Historia Moderna* 32 (2007): 87–111.

Ogilvie, Sheilagh. *Institutions and European Trade: Merchant Guilds (1000–1800)*. Cambridge: Cambridge University Press, 2011.

Ogilvie, Sheilagh. *The European Guilds: An Economic Analysis*. Princeton: Princeton University Press, 2019.

Petti Balbi, Giovanna. *Negoziare fuori patria: Nazioni e genovesi in età medievale*. Bologna: CLUEB, 2005.

Ramsay, Nigel. "Scriveners and Notaries as Legal Intermediaries in Late Medieval England." In *Enterprise and Individuals in Fifteenth-Century England*, edited by Jennifer Kermode, 118–131. Cheltenham: Alan Sutton, 1991.

Royo Pérez, Vicent. "El arbitraje en la documentación medieval valenciana. La caracterización de la institución arbitral en la práctica documental de las comarcas del Els Ports y El Maestrat entre 1232 y 1412." *Anuario de Historia del Derecho Español* 86 (2016): 141–195.

Strum, Daniel. "Institutional choice in the governance of the early Atlantic sugar trade: diasporas, markets, and courts." *The Economic History Review* 72, n° 4 (2019): 1202–1228.

Trivellato, Francesca. *The Familiarity of Strangers: The Sephardic Diaspora, Livorno, and Cross-Cultural Trade in the Early Modern Period*. New Haven: Yale University Press, 2009.

Ulbert, Jörg. "Introduction: La fonction consulaire à l'époque moderne: définition, état de connaissances et perspectives de recherche." In *La fonction consulaire à l'époque moderne: L'Affirmation d'une institution économique et politique (1500–1800)*, edited by Jörg Ulbert and Gérard Le Bouëdec, 9–20. Rennes: Presses universitaires de Rennes, 2006.

Vanneste, Tijl. *Global Trade and Commercial Networks: Eighteenth-Century Diamond Merchants*. London: Pickering & Chatto, 2011.

Vázquez de Prada, Valentín. "Consideraciones en torno al cambio estructural del comercio español en el siglo XVI." In *Las sociedades ibéricas y el mar a finales del siglo XVI*, edited by Luis Antonio Ribot García and Ernest Belenguer Cebrià, 37–57. Lisboa: Sociedad Estatal Lisboa '98, 1998.

4

Les fonctions judiciaires des consuls de France en pays de Chrétienté sous l'Ancien Régime

Jörg Ulbert

1 Introduction

Parmi les missions du consul moderne, celle de juge de la communauté à laquelle il préside est sans doute la plus ancienne. C'est aussi celle qui le caractérise le mieux. Ainsi Pierre Ariste affirme en 1667, dans son *Traité des consulats*, que les consuls étaient d'abord et avant tout à considérer comme des « juges des marchands »[1]. La doctrie postérieure ne varie guère sur le sujet. Encore au XVIIIe siècle, elle postule que le droit de dire la justice demeure « inséparable de la dignité consulaire »[2].

Les pouvoirs juridictionnels des consuls sont bornés par deux limites : celle fixée par le pays émissaire, et celle imposée par le pays d'accueil. En théorie, un consulat peut donc travailler efficacement lorsque ces deux bornes se recoupent suffisamment pour dégager une aire d'entente acceptable pour les deux parties. Or, même lorsque deux souverains se mettent d'accord sur l'étendue de la juridiction à accorder aux consuls, comme les rois de France et les sultans le font à partir de la mise en place du système capitulaire, l'exercice de la justice consulaire peut toujours se heurter à des résistances : celles manifestées par certains justiciables qui tentent de s'y soustraire, et celles opposées par des autorités subalternes (pachas, agas des douanes ou cadis ottomans) ou semi-souveraines (deys et beys d'Afrique du Nord) qui refusent d'appliquer les règles prévues par les capitulations. Aux deux premières limites théoriques déjà mentionnées, il faut donc ajouter une troisième, plus pratique : à savoir les moyens concrets dont dispose un consul pour faire respecter sa juridiction et faire exécuter ses sentences.

1 Pierre Ariste, *Traicté des consuls de la nation françoise aux pays estrangers concernant leur origine, leurs establissements, leurs fonctions, leurs droicts, esmolumens, & autres prerogatives* (s.l. : 1667, Paris : BnF, département des manuscrits, Français 18595), 8.

2 Yvan Debbasch, *La Nation française en Tunisie (1577–1835)* (Paris : Sirey, 1957), 195.

 HTTPS://DOI.ORG/10.1163/9789004755192-006

C'est sur les côtes de la Méditerranée musulmane que la juridiction consulaire française prend forme[3]. Elle peut s'y développer parce que les capitulations ottomanes et les traités bilatéraux conclus avec les régences d'Afrique du Nord en définissent les limites souhaitées par les pays d'accueil et parce que les résistances locales ne sont pas assez fortes pour la paralyser. Ce qui fonctionne dans l'Empire ottoman, ne se transpose pourtant pas automatiquement ailleurs. Notamment en Italie, au Portugal et en Espagne, où se situent la grande majorité des consulats que la France entretient en dehors de l'Empire ottoman, la juridiction consulaire est vigoureusement contestée. Elle l'est à tous les niveaux : aussi bien par les pouvoirs centraux et leurs émanations régionales et locales que par les justiciables eux-mêmes. Ici, les trois limites de la juridiction ne se recoupent par conséquent que très insuffisamment, et ne dégagent pas assez de terrain commun pour permettre aux consuls d'exercer efficacement leur juridiction. La pratique juridictionnelle diffère donc entre l'Empire ottoman (où, malgré quelques résistances locales, elle peut se déployer comme prévu par les ordonnances) et les pays de Chrétienté où elle très largement entravée. Cette disparité s'explique surtout par l'autorité du consul, dont le prestige et les prérogatives effectives ne sont pas les mêmes dans les différentes aires géographiques considérées.

Avant de se pencher sur les limites que le France souhaite donner à la juridiction de ses consuls en pays de Chrétienté, puis sur celles que les États d'admission sont prêts à accepter, il convient donc d'éclaircir les origines de ces dissemblances.

2 La prémisse : Une autorité à deux vitesses

Lorsque la France renoue au début du XVIe siècle avec la tradition d'entretenir des consulats, elle n'en commissionne dans un premier temps que dans l'Empire ottoman. Il faut attendre la fin du siècle pour en voir ailleurs. Tous ces consuls disposent du même statut : d'abord celui d'officier royal entre 1589 et 1681, puis celui de commissaire du roi. Tous sont, du moins initialement, dotés des mêmes prérogatives et missions. Les tutelles administratives tout comme les justiciables des consuls les traitent et les perçoivent néanmoins différemment. Cette séparation des consulats français en deux sous-entités n'a jamais

3 Un résumé de son fonctionnement voir dans : Victor Simon, *Les échelles du Levant et de Barbarie. Droit du commerce international entre la France et l'Empire ottoman* (*XVIe–XVIIIe siècle*) (Paris : LGDJ, 2021), 186–190.

été décidée explicitement. Aucun texte de loi ne l'ordonne en toutes lettres. Elle peut cependant être observée à plusieurs niveaux.

La chambre de Commerce de Marseille intervient ainsi uniquement, du moins après 1660, dans la gestion des consulats situés dans ce qu'on prend alors l'habitude de désigner par « échelles du Levant » ou, avec une attention particulière pour les régences d'Afrique du Nord et le Maroc, « Levant et Barbarie », ou encore, tout simplement, « le Levant ». Les postes établis en dehors des pays musulmans échappent en revanche à son emprise administrative. Le rôle prépondérant que joue le négoce marseillais dans le commerce méditerranéen français tout comme les privilèges commerciaux liés à l'Empire ottoman dont la ville jouit au moins depuis son rattachement au royaume[4], justifient sans doute que le roi lui confie « l'administration générale du commerce des Échelles du Levant et de Barbarie »[5]. En revanche, nous ne pouvons que présumer pour quelles raisons les autres consulats n'ont pas été inclus dans cette délégation administrative. L'importance économique de ces autres postes pour le commerce phocéen n'a en tout cas pas pu en être la cause : au cours de la seconde moitié du XVIIe siècle, lorsque Marseille se voit confirmer ses privilèges qui lui assurent le contrôle du commerce levantin, l'Italie et l'Espagne sont en effet plus importants pour son négoce que l'Empire ottoman[6].

À défaut de l'ordonner explicitement, l'administration royale entérine la particularisation du Levant. C'est elle qui octroie les privilèges à Marseille, et c'est elle qui décide de lui déléguer la gestion des échelles, ainsi que celle des consulats qui y exercent. La législation différencie également les consulats du Levant de ceux en pays de Chrétienté. Il existe ainsi des ordonnances royales qui concernent l'ensemble des consulats[7], d'autres qui ne portent que sur un

---

4 Sur l'évolution de ces privilèges, voir : Mireille Zarb, *Histoire d'une autonomie communale. Les privilèges de la ville de Marseille du Xe siècle à la Révolution* (Paris : Picard, 1961), 318–344.

5 Louis Bergasse, *Notice historique sur la Chambre de Commerce de Marseille (1599–1912)* (Marseille : Barlatier, 1913), 26.

6 C'est du moins ce qu'insinue la statistique des sorties de navires du port de Marseille pour les années 1680–1684 : *L'Intendance de Provence à la fin du XVIIe siècle. Édition critique des mémoires « pour l'instruction du duc de Bourgogne »*, éd. François-Xavier Emmanuelli (Paris : Bibliothèque nationale, 1980), 26. La chambre de Commerce de Marseille entretient d'ailleurs une correspondance soutenue avec les consuls qui exercent sur les côtes italiennes et espagnoles Pour des exemples, voir : Gaston Rambert, *Histoire du commerce de Marseille, t. IV : de 1660–1789* (Paris : Plon, 1954), 305–306 ; Guillaume Calafat, « Livourne et la Chambre de commerce de Marseille au XVIIe siècle. Consuls français, agents et perception du droit de *cottimo* », dans *La mer en partage. Sociétés littorales et économies maritimes (XVIe–XIXe siècle)*, éd. Xavier Daumalin *et al.* (Aix-en-Provence : Presses universitaires de Provence, 2016).

7 Par exemple : *Ordonnance de Louis XIV roy de France et de Navarre. Donnée à Fontainebleau au mois d'Aoust 1681. Touchant la Marine* (Paris : Thierry, Ballard, 1681).

seul poste[8], et il y a surtout celles, beaucoup plus nombreuses que toutes les autres, qui s'appliquent uniquement au Levant et à la Barbarie[9]. Que les consulats dans l'Empire ottoman et ceux dans des pays de Chrétienté soient alors considérés comme deux choses bien distinctes, se vérifie aussi dans l'organisation de leur principale tutelle administrative. Leur gestion revient en effet, entre 1687 et 1743, à deux bureaux séparés au sein du département de la Marine : un pour le Levant, et un autre pour tous les autres postes qu'on y résume alors par la formule « pays de Chrétienté »[10].

Cette partition géographique se double de ce qui ressemble à une différentiation *de facto* au sein du service consulaire français. Pierre Ariste précise ainsi en 1667 que les « consulz, particulierement ... ceux qui sont en Italie, en Espagne, en Portugal, en Hollande et dans les autres royaumes »[11] ont moins de collaborateurs et moins d'« esclat »[12] que leurs collègues dans l'Empire ottoman. Leurs « fonction » et leurs « pouvoirs ... ne sont pas si considerables ny si amples que ceux des consulz de Levant »[13]. Le contraste observé par Ariste est confirmé par le monde marchand. Dans un mémoire rédigé à la fin du XVIIe siècle, les membres de la nation française de Livourne exposent ainsi qu'un consul qui exerce dans un pays de Chrétienté « ne doit pas se regarder comme s'il était un consul des Échelles du Levant ou de la Barbarie ». C'est le topos de la cruauté arbitraire des potentats musulmans qui est invoquée pour expliquer cette disparité. La « domination » exercée par les autorités ottomanes serait « bien différente de celle des Chrétiens » : les « infidèles ... ne respirent qu'après les prétextes de faire des avanies sur le public pour les fautes des particuliers » nous disent encore les auteurs du mémoire. Pour éviter ce genre de punition collective[14], les expatriés doivent scrupuleusement s'en tenir aux

8 Par exemple : *Ordonnance du roy, Servant de Reglement pour le Consulat de la Nation Françoise à Cadiz, du 24. May 1728* (Paris : Imprimerie royale, 1728).

9 *Ordonnance du roi, Concernant les Consulats, la Résidence, le Commerce & la Navigation des Sujets du Roi, dans les Échelles du Levant & de Barbarie, du 3 Mars 1781* (Paris : Imprimerie royale, 1781). La liste des ordonnances, arrêts et règlements dressée par Victor Simon peut donner une idée du nombre considérable de texte législatifs uniquement destinés aux postes en Levant et Barbarie : Simon, *Les Échelles*, 245–247.

10 Jörg Ulbert, « L'administration des consulats au sein du secrétariat d'État de la Marine (1669–1715) », dans *La Liasse et la plume. Les bureaux du secrétariat d'État de la Marine (1669–1792)*, éd. Jörg Ulbert et Sylviane Llinares (Rennes : Presses universitaires de Rennes, 2017), 77.

11 Ariste, *Traicté des consuls*, 216–217.

12 Ibid., 223.

13 Ibid., 216–217.

14 Pour une comparaison entre la réalité des avanies et leur réception en Europe, voir : Merlijn Olnon, « Towards Classifying *Avanias :* A Study of Two Cases Involving the English and Dutch Nations in Seventeenth-Century Izmir », dans *Friends and Rivals in*

règles. C'est au consul d'y veiller. À cette fin, il doit faire preuve d'une « certaine autorité de distinction nécessaire pour contenir les Français dans une retenue convenable parmi des barbares & des infidèles »[15]. Son principal moyen de coercition découle des pouvoirs de police que les ordonnances royales lui confèrent : c'est le renvoi forcé des échelles. Cette autorité « presqu'absolu(e) » voire « despotique »[16] dont disposent alors les consuls français dans le Levant est d'ailleurs régulièrement dénoncée par les Français installés dans les échelles.

Une dernière caractéristique distingue les consuls au Levant et en Barbarie : leur rôle de négociateurs au nom du roi. La doctrine contemporaine du droit naturel s'accorde pour ne considérer les consuls que comme des marchands, et leur refuse par conséquent les privilèges et immunités propres aux diplomates. Or François de Callières, un des plus importants théoriciens de la diplomatie, concède dès 1716 que les consuls en poste à Alep, Smyrne, Alexandrie, au Caire, Tunis ou Alger « sont regardez comme Ministres » et peuvent donc être assimilés à des diplomates[17]. En effet, ce statut se vérifie en Syrie et en Égypte mamelouke, mais il est sans doute le plus manifeste dans les trois régences d'Afrique du Nord. En théorie, c'est l'ambassadeur français à Constantinople qui y devrait représenter le roi. Or, la souveraineté ottomane n'y est plus que nominale et ce sont par conséquent les consuls qui y négocient et qui y représentent le roi[18]. Au Maroc, où la France n'entretient pas d'ambassadeur permanent non plus, les consuls se substituent également à une représentation diplomatique.

Au cours du XVIIe siècle les consuls du Levant se singularisent donc. Cela se vérifie également en matière de justice. La large autorité dont jouissent les consuls en terre musulmane leur confère alors l'ascendant nécessaire sur

---

the East : Studies in Anglo-Dutch Relations in the Levant from the Seventeenth to the Early Nineteenth Century, éd. Alastair Hamilton *et al.* (Leyde : Brill, 2000), 159–186 ; Maurits H. van den Boogert, *The Capitulations and the Ottoman Legal System : Qadis, Consuls, and Beratlı in the Eighteenth Century* (Leyde, Boston : Brill, 2005), 117–157.

15 Cité d'après Guillaume Calafat, « Les juridictions du consul : une institution au service des marchands et du commerce ? Introduction », dans *De l'utilité commerciale des consuls. L'institution consulaire et les marchands dans le monde méditerranéen (XVIIe–XXe siècle)*, éd. Arnaud Bartolomei *et al.* (Rome : École française de Rome, 2018), 149.

16 Pour les références de ces deux citations, voir la contribution de Victor Simon, notes 7 et 8. Voir dans cet article également le détail de la fonction de police.

17 Géraud Poumarède, « Le consul dans les dictionnaires et le droit des gens : émergence et affirmation d'une institution nouvelle (XVIe–XVIIIe siècles) », dans *La fonction consulaire à l'époque moderne*, éd. Jörg Ulbert et Gérard Le Bouëdec (Rennes : Presses universitaires de Rennes, 2006), 29.

18 Voir entre autres à ce sujet : Christian Windler, *La Diplomatie comme expérience de l'autre. Consuls français au Maghreb (1700–1840)* (Genève : Droz, 2002).

leurs administrés pour imposer leur juridiction, autorité qui fait défaut à leurs collègues en poste dans les pays de Chrétienté. Leur juridiction en matière civile et criminelle constitue « une dérogation à la règle générale », constate L.-J.-A. Moreüil en 1850 dans son *Manuel des agents consulaires*, car ailleurs en Europe elle serait revenue dès le XVIIe siècle « aux autorités territoriales », c'est-à-dire aux gouvernements des pays hôtes.

> On ne laissa aux consuls, poursuit-il, dans la plupart des États, que la juridiction volontaire et contentieuse, et dans d'autres, toute espèce même de juridiction leur fut refusée. Les consuls perdirent ainsi la plus importante de leurs attributions, et avec elle la haute considération attachée à l'exercice de leurs fonctions.

Moreüil donne aussi la raison pour laquelle « les consuls du Levant formèrent ainsi une catégorie à part, entièrement différente de celle des consuls dans les pays chrétiens » : ce seraient les « différences caractéristiques entre l'état stationnaire des peuples musulmans et la civilisation progressive des nations chrétiennes »[19]. Plaquer ce discours colonialiste du milieu du XIXe sur le XVIIe siècle serait assurément anachronique. Sous Louis XIV, il n'est pas encore question, comme pendant le Congrès de Vienne, de refuser de négocier d'égal à égal avec les Ottomans parce que leurs normes différeraient trop de celles des puissances chrétiennes. Or l'altérité que constitue néanmoins le monde musulman est sans doute un des éléments déterminants pour expliquer les divergences entre les consulats au Levant et ceux dans les pays de Chrétienté.

3 La théorie : Les fonctions judiciaires octroyées par le roi

Le premier texte de loi qui mentionne la juridiction consulaire, sans pourtant entrer dans le détail, date de 1625. Or il n'est valable que pour le seul consulat d'Alep[20]. Il faut attendre 1681, et la promulgation de la grande ordonnance de

---

19 L.-J.-A. Moreüil, *Manuel des agents consulaires français et étrangers* (Paris : Videcocq, 1850), 2–3.

20 « S'il arrive quelq[u]e differens entre … neg[ociant]s qu'ils ne puissent avoir recours a la justice turque et que n'i a autre justice du pays, ains seulem[en]t aud[it] consul auquel elle attribüe meme juridiction qu'icelle des juges du commerce de la ville de Mars[eil]le, et telle qu'elle est portée par les statuts des consulats », Ordonnance du 26 novembre 1625 (Marseille, ACCIM, J 1557), non folioté. Je remercie vivement Victor Simon de m'avoir fourni les photos de cette ordonnance.

la Marine, pour voir apparaître des règles qui définissent l'étendue et les détails de la juridiction des consuls en Chrétienté. Avant, leur action s'y base sur le seul usage. En 1667, Pierre Ariste résume ce dernier de la manière suivante :

> Ilz ont pouvoir et autorité de composer, regler, juger et terminer souverainement tous leurs [les Français et ceux qui naviguent sous la bannière de française] procez et differendz, le plus sommairement toutefois que faire se peut[21].

Or, à cette époque, la juridiction des consuls souffre d'un certain nombre de faiblesses :

> La jurisdiction de ces Consuls s'etoit formée sur la déference des Parties qui se soumettoient volontairement au jugement de ces officiers, mais comme il n'en avoit aucun titre positif, leurs decisions ne passoient proprement que pour des arbitrages, et s'il survenoit quelque difficulté dans leur execution, les parties interessées, n'ayant pas de juges certains pour les regler, s'adressoient tantôt aux ambassadeurs plus prochains des lieux de la residence des Consuls, et tantôt au Conseil du Roy[22].

Avant 1681, les consuls ne disposent donc que d'une juridiction volontaire. Afin d'éviter que les justiciables, pour obtenir des jugements opposables, ne continuent de submerger les ambassades et le Conseil du roi de leurs litiges, la monarchie décide d'« illustrer » la charge de consul, et la munissent en outre d'« une espece de juridiction contentieuse »[23]. C'est l'ordonnance de la Marine de 1681 qui en définit les contours. Il ne convient pas ici d'énumérer le détail de ce qui est contenu au livre 1, titre IX, de ce texte[24]. Il est connu et a été amplement commenté dès le XVIIIe siècle.

À bien des égards, l'ordonnance de la Marine reste pourtant floue. Notamment en matière de juridiction civile, qui constitue sans doute l'essentiel du travail juridique, elle ne précise pas si le fait de s'adresser au consul des lieux reste une possibilité ou constitue une obligation[25]. Par conséquent elle est

---

21 Ariste, *Traicté des consuls*, 217.

22 « Mémoire sur l'etablissement des consuls de la nation françoise dans les pays etrangers » (anonyme, s.l.n.d. [vers 1700], AN, AE/B/III/244, pièce 77), non paginé.

23 Ibid.

24 *Ordonnance de 1681*, 40–49. Voir à ce sujet la contribution de Victor Simon dans ce même volume.

25 Voir à ce sujet : Debbasch, *Nation française*, 197–198.

amendée au cours des décennies par un certain nombre de textes complémentaires. L'ordonnance du 28 février 1687 défend ainsi aux « maîtres & les matelots [...] qui vont dans les pays étrangers » de « se pourvoir pour raison des différends qu'ils pourront avoir entre eux [...] pardevant les Juges des lieux, à peine de desobéissance : voulant qu'ils s'adressent aux Consuls de Nation Françoise »[26]. L'ordonnance pour les armées navales et arsenaux de la Marine du 15 avril 1689 reprend, dans son livre 8, titre I, art. 26 les mêmes interdictions, mais enjoint par ailleurs aux consuls de rendre la « plus prompte & sommaire justice qu'il se pourra, & sans frais »[27]. En 1713, une ordonnance entière réitère les mêmes interdictions. Sans surprise, la raison de ce rappel est la non-observance des dispositions précédentes :

> Sa Majesté estant informée que quelques Negocians François establis dans les Ports d'Espagne, d'Italie, & autres Pays estrangers, [...] s'adressent aux Juges ordinaires sur les differends, contestations, & procés qu'ils ont entre eux, & aux Notaires publics desdits lieux pour passer les Actes & Contracts[28].

Ce sont tantôt des frais de justice moins onéreux, tantôt l'espoir d'un jugement plus favorable (le *forum shopping*) qui conduisent certains Français expatriés à s'adresser plutôt à la justice locale qu'à celle du consul de leur nation. Ceux qui procèdent de la sorte n'y voient d'ailleurs aucun mal. Ainsi un Français de Livourne se justifie-t-il, en 1714, de la manière suivante d'avoir fait appel aux juges toscans :

> Il n'y a que les Consuls des Echelles de Levant qui aient naturellement droit de revendiquer les Français et d'empêcher qu'ils ne se plaindent [sic] par devant la justice des Turcs, par la raison que les chrétiens ne peuvent pas reconnoitre une telle justice, mais à l'égard de touttes les autres, il n'a jamais été deffendu de s'y pourvoir[29].

---

26 Ordonnance du 28 février 1687 reproduite dans : René-Josué Valin, *Nouveau commentaire sur l'ordonnance de la Marine du mois d'août 1681*, t. 1 (La Rochelle : Legier et Mesnier, 1760), 221–222.

27 Valin, *Nouveau commentaire*, 157–158.

28 *Ordonnance du Roy, Concernant la Jurisdiction des Consuls de la Nation Françoise establis dans les Ports Estrangers, du 4 janvier 1713* (AMAE, Personnel, édits, lois et ordonnances, vol. 44, pièce 34), 3–4. Je remercie vivement Mathieu Grenet de m'avoir fourni le contenu de cette source.

29 BNF, mss NAF 21394, fol. 150–151, cité d'après Debbasch, *Nation française*, 198.

Comme beaucoup d'autres, l'obligation de recourir en pays étranger au consul pour le règlement des différends, et au chancelier du consulat pour toute production ou authentification d'acte a dû être rappelée pendant près d'un siècle pour être respectée. Elle figure ainsi dans l'ordonnance du roi servant de règlement pour le consulat de Cadix, du 24 mai 1728[30], et à nouveau dans l'édit de juin 1778. Ce dernier ne se limite d'ailleurs pas à réitérer la seule interdiction faite aux Français à l'étranger de faire appel aux juges locaux (art. 2) : il définit aussi le détail des fonctions judiciaires des consuls. Là où les textes plus anciens avaient péché par leur concision, voire leur imprécision, l'édit de 1778 tente d'épuiser le sujet en y consacrant 85 articles[31]. Les consuls s'y voient confier l'instruction « en première instance des contestations, de quelque nature qu'elles soient, qui s'élèveront entre nos Sujets négocians, Navigateurs & autres », et « de rendre fidèlement justice » (art. 1). L'édit leur confirme donc les compétences juridictionnelles en matière civile et criminelle. Seules les accusations qui pourraient entraîner des condamnations à des peines afflictives ou infamantes leur échappent : ces dernières sont toujours du ressort des amirautés (art. 76). Afin de rendre leurs « sentences définitives », les consuls se font assister par deux notables choisis parmi la nation française de leur district consulaire. Ces assesseurs ont une « voix délibérative » (art. 6). L'édit décrit par le menu la façon dont les parties peuvent saisir le tribunal consulaire, comment doivent se dérouler les convocations des parties et des témoins, comment s'organisent les auditions, les interrogatoires, les confrontations, le dépôt des pièces à conviction, les appels ou les exécutions des peines. Ces dispositions de 1778 sont restées en vigueur jusqu'en 1836[32].

4 La pratique : Les limites imposées par les États d'accueil

Les compétences juridictionnelles des consuls ne se définissent pas seulement par la forme que le roi de France souhaite leur donner dans ses ordonnances et

30 Art. XXXI : Valin, *Nouveau commentaire*, 226. Sur cette ordonnance voir aussi : Olivier Le Gouic, « Les négociants dans les assemblées de la Nation française à Cadix : représentation, assiduité et implication du négoce dans les affaires du Consulat de France (1716–1728) », *Annales de Bretagne et des Pays de l'Ouest* 120, n° 1 (2013).

31 *Édit du roi, Portant règlement sur les fonctions Judiciaires & de Police, qu'exercent les Consuls de France en Pays étrangers, donné à Versailles au mois de Juin 1778* (Paris : Imprimerie royale, 1779). Les précisions contenues dans cet édit expliquent pourquoi la grande l'ordonnance de 1781 qui refonde le fonctionnement des consulats des échelles du Levant et de Barbarie ne contient plus aucune mention de la juridiction des consuls.

32 L.-J.-D. Féraud-Giraud, *Juridiction française dans les échelles du Levant et de Barbarie. Étude sur la condition légale des étrangers dans les pays hors Chrétienté*, 2e éd., t. 2 (Paris : Durand, 1866), 6.

édits. Elles doivent également être acceptées par l'État qui reçoit le consul sur son territoire. Il s'agit là, pour reprendre la formule de Jean Bouquin, d'« une concession toute gratuite de la part du pays étranger où se trouvait le consulat », faveur que « ce dernier était [...] libre d'étendre plus ou moins »[33]. La reconnaissance de la juridiction consulaire se fonde sur l'octroi ponctuel de privilèges ou, plus fréquemment, sur des traités bilatéraux, et à défaut sur le droit public ou l'usage. Et en effet, l'article de l'ordonnance de la Marine de 1681 qui attribue « la jurisdiction tant en matière civile que criminelle » aux consuls prévoit bien que ces derniers devaient se conformer « à l'usage, & aux capitulations faites avec les Souverains des lieux »[34].

Si le fonctionnement de la justice consulaire dans l'Empire ottoman, tel que garanti par les capitulations, ne semble pas avoir inquiété outre mesure le département de la Marine ou la chambre de Commerce de Marseille, il n'en allait pas de même pour les États de Chrétienté. Au cours du XVIIIe siècle sont produits une petite vingtaine de mémoires qui synthétisent et analysent la juridiction consulaire française en Chrétienté. Certains de ces mémoires sont rédigés par les consuls eux-mêmes, d'autres émanent des bureaux du département de la Marine, c'est-à-dire de l'administration tutélaire des consulats. Sauf une exception[35], ces textes se focalisent tous sur la situation des consuls dans un espace précis : un traite du Portugal[36], un autre de Livourne[37] et tous les autres portent sur l'Espagne. Cette répartition témoigne aussi bien de l'importance que les autorités françaises accordaient à l'Espagne, que du fait que c'était là que la contestation de la juridiction consulaire française était la plus vigoureuse.

Ce sont donc les obstructions espagnoles qui préoccupent le plus les autorités versaillaises sous Louis XIV et Louis XV. Dix-sept des vingt-deux instructions commerciales envoyées entre 1669 et 1756 à l'ambassadeur de France à Madrid traitent ainsi de la juridiction consulaire[38]. L'importance accordée à la

---

33 Jean Bouquin, *De la juridiction consulaire en droit maritime français. Compétence des consuls à l'égard des faits passés à bord des navires de commerce : répression des infractions, règlement des différends civils et commerciaux* (Lyon : Bosc, 1935), 11.

34 Livre I, titre IX, art. XII.

35 « Mémoire sur les prérogatives, les fonctions, attributions et juridiction des Consuls de la nation française dans les ports où ils sont établis » (s.l., 30 avril 1731, CADN, Livourne, série A, vol. 4), non paginé.

36 « Memoire sur l'etablissement d'un juge conservateur de la nation françoise à Lisbonne » (s.l., 22 mars 1717, AN/AE/B/III/385), non paginé.

37 « Mémoire des veritables moyens que l'on pourroit prendre pour soutenir la juridiction consulaire... » (AN/AE/B/III/409, s.l.n.d.), non paginé.

38 Sylvain Lloret, « Entre princes et marchands : les agents généraux de France à Madrid dans les interstices de la diplomatie (1702–1793) » (thèse de doctorat, Sorbonne Université, 2018), 131.

question ne saurait surprendre : la monarchie ibérique est alors le premier partenaire commercial de la France[39] et les attributions juridiques des consuls de France font partie d'un vaste ensemble de mesures qui visent à accompagner et à faciliter le commerce extérieur français.

En Espagne, la juridiction consulaire française est censée être couverte par les traités internationaux. C'est le traité des Pyrénées de 1659 qui en jette les bases. L'article 6 de ce texte garantit à la France de profiter « des mesmes privilèges, franchises, libertez et seuretez [...] dont les Anglois ont eu le droit de jouir »[40]. Cette disposition transforma de fait tous les privilèges concédés aux Anglais et ceux donnés au Français en un seul bloc. Les Provinces Unies disposaient déjà de leur propre clause de la nation la plus favorisée depuis 1648. L'Espagne, affirme Albert Girard, « perdit ainsi le contrôle des étrangers sur son territoire ». Les conséquences en auraient été, toujours d'après Girard, d'une part un « extraordinaire développement de la pénétration économique étrangère », de l'autre une difficulté accrue de l'Espagne « de réprimer la fraude et d'enrayer sa décadence économique »[41].

La juridiction consulaire telle que l'usage, les traités, puis les ordonnances de 1681 et 1687 la prévoient, sont, à croire Gaston Rambert « à peu près observés jusqu'à la guerre de Succession d'Espagne »[42]. Or à y regarder de près, ce n'est pas le cas pour toutes les facettes des compétences prévues par les textes. À cette époque, les consuls français en Espagne ne semblent avoir pu exercer qu'une partie de leur juridiction sans être gênés par les autorités espagnoles. Ainsi, ils dressent les inventaires des effets des Français décédés en Espagne et les préservent à leurs héritiers[43]. L'instruction des prises faites par les armateurs français et amenées dans les ports espagnols ne semble pas non plus leur être disputée. Ils conservent de même la partie dite « volontaire » de leur juri-

39 Sylvain Lloret, « Défendre le négoce français en Espagne : L'agent général de la Marine et du Commerce de France à Madrid et le Congrès d'Utrecht », dans *La Diplomatie-monde. Autour de la paix d'Utrecht (1713)*, éd. Lucien Bély *et al.* (Paris : Pedone, 2019), 379.

40 *Traitté de paix entre les covronnes de France et d'Espagne...* (Paris : Imprimerie royale, 1660), 7. Il ne s'agit donc pas d'une clause de la nation la plus favorisée comme on peut le lire ici et là. Elle ne garantissait que l'alignement sur les privilèges concédés aux seuls Anglais. Ce n'est qu'en matière de droits à payer par les marchands français que les Français obtenaient par le même article le traitement de la nation la plus favorisée.

41 Albert Girard, *Le commerce français à Séville et Cadix au temps des Habsbourg. Contribution à l'étude du commerce étranger en Espagne aux XVIe et XVIIe siècles* (Paris : Boccard, 1932), 109–110.

42 Gaston Rambert, « La France et la politique commerciale de l'Espagne au XVIIIe siècle », *Revue d'Histoire moderne et contemporaine* 6 (1959) : 271.

43 « Jurisdiction des consuls françois en Espagne » (15 février 1710, AN, AE/B/III/359, pièce 2), non paginé.

diction, c'est-à-dire la production et l'authentification d'actes au sein de la chancellerie consulaire.

La partie contentieuse, en revanche, leur échappe largement. Elle est déléguée depuis 1663 à un juge conservateur général à Madrid[44], flanqué d'homologues subalternes dans les provinces. Ce juge conservateur est, pour reprendre la définition proposée par Albert Girard, un magistrat espagnol désigné et payé par le Roi Très Catholique, lequel a seul le droit de juger les étrangers au civil et au criminel. Sa juridiction est « exceptionnelle et exclusive » : il est donc censé juger toutes les affaires qui impliquent des étrangers, même celles qui opposent deux d'entre eux issus de la même nation. À défaut d'avoir pu imposer la juridiction du consul, telle que prévue par l'ordonnance de la Marine de 1681, le « juge conservateur apparaît donc comme un moyen d'assurer [...] une justice plus rapide et aussi plus équitable que celle des tribunaux ordinaires »[45]. Cette forme de justice n'était certes pas celle qu'aurait pu exercer un consul sur ses nationaux, mais elle était toujours préférable à celle d'un juge local. Ainsi, lorsque le gouvernement espagnol tente, en 1679, de retirer la juridiction criminelle aux juges conservateurs pour forcer les Français à s'en remettre à la justice locale, la France intervient à plusieurs reprises et parvient finalement à faire annuler le projet[46].

En 1709, le gouvernement de Philippe V entreprend de s'attaquer aux privilèges restants. Porté par une vague gallophobe, cette charge coïncide avec le départ des troupes françaises de la péninsule. Là où les ambassadeurs français à Madrid avaient jusqu'alors pu défendre l'essentiel de ce qui demeurait encore de la juridiction consulaire, ils n'en sont plus capables pendant ces

44 Voir la liste des juges conservateurs généraux de la nation française dans : Lloret, *Princes et marchands*, 287. Sur l'institution des juges conservateurs, voir : Roberto Zaugg, « Judging Foreigners. Conflict Strategies, Consular Interventions and Institutional Changes in Eighteenth-Century Naples », *Journal of Modern Italian Studies* 13, n° 2 (2008) ; Roberto Zaugg, « Mercanti stranieri e giudici napoletani. La gestione dei conflitti in Antico Regime », *Quaderni Storici* 133, n° 1 (2010) ; Guillermo Pérez Sarrión, *La península comercial : mercado, redes sociales y Estado en España en el siglo XVIII* (Madrid : Marcial Pons, 2012) ; Ana Crespo Solana, « El juez conservador ¿ una alternativa al cónsul de la nación ? », dans *Los cónsules de extranjeros en la edad moderna y al principio de la edad contemporánea*, éd. Marcella Aglietti *et al.* (Madrid : Ediciones Doce Calles, 2013) ; Francisco Zamora Rodríguez, « 'Dar el cordero en guarda del lobo'. Control hispánico sobre los consulados extranjeros durante el siglo XVII e inicios del XVIII », *Tiempos Modernos* 30 (2015) ; Alejandro García Montón, « Corona, hombres de negocios y jueces conservatores. Un acercamiento en Escala transatlántica (s. XVII) », *Jerónimi Zurita* 90 (2015).

45 Girard, *Commerce français*, 103–105.

46 Ibid., 155–157.

« années noires de l'ambassade de Madrid »[47], pour reprendre la formule de Catherine Désos.

Le cédule du 1er décembre 1709 déclare que les consuls français ne disposeront plus d'aucune juridiction en Espagne[48]. Le gouvernement espagnol justifie cette mesure par la volonté de vouloir endiguer la contrebande[49]. Son angle d'attaque ne passe donc pas par la contestation du traité des Pyrénées et des privilèges qui en découlent. Il remet en cause le statut même des consuls français qu'il souhaite voir réinterprété pour le « réduire au simple titre d'*agent des gens de mer* »[50]. Cette charge s'engouffre dans la brèche que la délégation française avait laissée ouverte lors des négociations pour la paix des Pyrénées. Le projet initial d'y inclure, dans l'article XXVI, une phrase qui aurait assimilé les consuls aux agents diplomatiques, n'avait alors pas été finalisé par les négociateurs[51].

L'attaque amorcée en 1709 se dirige contre toute forme d'activité consulaire française qui pourrait s'apparenter aux codes de la diplomatie et en revendiquer les prérogatives. En Catalogne, l'intendant José Patiño y Rosales s'insurge contre l'accrochage des armes du roi de France dans la résidence du consul de France à Barcelone et se montre « outré de la juridiction consulaire »[52]. Dès juillet 1715, Patiño intente un procès au consul français, Simon Dupin, pour avoir « établi un tribunal et un juge dans la demeure qu'il a » à Barcelone[53]. Les autorités catalanes finissent par obtenir la destitution du consul qui, du point de vue français, n'a commis d'autre forfait que de défendre ses prérogatives garanties par les traités.

Au cours des décennies suivantes, les bureaux du ministère de la Marine produisent des dizaines de mémoires historiques et d'expertises juridiques pour prouver la validité des prétentions françaises. Rien n'y fait. En 1763, un mémoire résume la juridiction des consuls français en Espagne de la manière suivante :

---

47 Catherine Désos, *Les Français de Philippe V : Un modèle nouveau pour gouverner l'Espagne (1700–1724)* (Strasbourg : Presses universitaires de Strasbourg, 2009), 183.

48 « Mémoire touchant la jurisdiction des consuls de France en Espagne » (14 octobre 1715, AN, AE/B/III/359, pièce 3), non folioté.

49 Lloret, « Princes et marchands », 241.

50 « Mémoire sur le pacte de famille » (anonyme, s.l., juillet 1763, AN, AE/B/III/342), non paginé. Soulignement dans l'original. Voir d'autres références à ce sujet dans : Lloret, « Princes et marchands », 246, note 107.

51 Girard, *Commerce français*, 123.

52 Dupin à Pontchartrain (Barcelone, 20 juillet 1715, AN, AE/B/I/180, non fol.), cité d'après : Julien Sempéré, *S'informer pour s'enrichir. Le consul français à Barcelone et ses réseaux (1679–1716)* (Perpignan : Presses universitaires de Perpignan, 2018), 352.

53 Cité d'après : Sempéré, *S'informer*, 354.

> La jurisdiction des consuls, telle qu'elle etoit établie dans le principe par le traité [anglo-espagnol] de 1667 et par l'ordonnance de la Marine de France de 1681, est presque anéantie. [...] Dans le fait ils ont conservé plus ou moins le droit de décider par voye d'arbitrage [...] des différends des François [...] ; la police des équipages de leur nation ; la disposition et réclamation des matelots et autres pour les renvoyer en France ; la faculté de faire par eux mêmes le sauvetage des bâtimens naufragés[54].

La juridiction contentieuse du consul est donc réduite « plus ou moins » à un arbitrage[55], et il n'est plus en mesure de dresser les inventaires après décès de ceux de sa nation morts *ab intestat*. La partie volontaire de sa juridiction, c'est-à-dire la production et l'authentification des actes en chancellerie de consulat n'est en revanche pas remise en cause. Il n'y a guère qu'à Barcelone que même ce dernier volet semble également avoir été contesté :

> On a un avis [...] que les juges et autres ministres des tribunaux espagnols ne veulent point souffrir ny jurisdiction ny chancellerie dans le consulat de la nation françoise sous pretexte des ordres donnés par la cour d'Espagne depuis quelques années[56].

Il faut attendre la convention consulaire franco-espagnole du 13 mars 1769[57] pour voir les consuls français réinvestis dans certains des droits dont ils jouissaient avant 1709. Ce texte apporte quelques changements notoires par rapport aux règles en vigueur depuis la grande ordonnance de la Marine de 1681.

54 « Mémoire sur le pacte de famille » (anonyme, s.l., juillet 1763, AN, AE/B/III/342, non paginé).

55 Pour une typologie de l'arbitrage consulaire, voir : Guillaume Calafat, « La juridiction des consuls français en Méditerranée : litiges marchands, arbitrages et circulations des procès (Livourne et Tunis au XVIIe siècle) », dans *De l'utilité commerciale des consuls. L'institution consulaire et les marchands dans le monde méditerranéen (XVII*e*–XX*e* siècle)*, éd. Arnaud Bartolomei *et al.* (Rome : École française de Rome, 2017).

56 « Mémoire touchant la jurisdiction et la chancellerie des consulats de la nation françoise en Espagne » (sans date [début 1722], AN/AE/B/III/364, pièce 59), non folioté.

57 Voir le texte bilingue dans : BnF, mss, Fr. 10766, fol. 545r–554v. Le texte français a été publié dans : Friedrich August Wilhelm Wenck, *Codex iuris gentivm recentissimi, e tabvlariorvm exemplorvmqve fide dignorvm monvmentis compositvs*, t. 3 (Leipzig : Haer. Weidmann et Reich, 1795), 746–752 ; ainsi que dans : Jules de Clercq, *Recueil des traités de la France*, t. 1 : 1713–1802 (Paris : A. Durand et Pedone-Lauriel, 1880), 106–111. Pour une analyse succincte et de la convention et de la version espagnole de son texte, voir : Calixto Alfredo Armas Barea, « La convención consular hispano-francesa de 1769 », *Revista de Derecho Internacional y Ciencias Diplomáticas* (Rosario, Argentine), n° 15/16 (1959).

Ainsi les consuls se voient bien attribuer le droit d'arbitrer « les différens qui peuvent survenir entre les capitaines et équipages, relativement au temps de leur service, fret et salaires » ainsi que ceux qui opposeraient entr'eux « leurs nationaux *transeuntes* ». Par *transeuntes*, les autorités espagnoles entendent depuis le décret du 8 mars 1716, les étrangers qui séjournent depuis moins de dix ans en Espagne[58]. Or, à la différence de tout ce que cherchaient à imposer les règlements du XVIIe siècle, les consuls ou vice-consuls n'interviendront que lorsque les capitaines, matelots ou *transeuntes* « voudront se soumettre volontairement à l'arbitrage ». Il n'est donc plus question de les contraindre de s'adresser au consulat pour faire juger les différends qui les opposeraient à des compatriotes. La convention leur attribue même explicitement « le droit d'avoir recours à la justice du pays, lorsqu'ils se sentiront préjudiciés ou opprimés par le Consul ou Vice-Consul » (art. 5). Les grands absents du texte sont les *domiciliados*, ces Français expatriés depuis plus de dix ans. Le fait que la convention n'en fasse pas mention montre bien que, dans l'espoir de redonner une base juridique stable à l'action de ses consuls en Espagne, le gouvernement français a fini par accepter le point de vue défendu depuis des décennies par la doctrine espagnole. Celle-ci avait théorisé, puis formalisé dès 1716, une distinction fondamentale entre les *extranjeros transeuntes*, arrivés depuis moins de dix ans, et les sujets étrangers intégrés (*extranjeros avecindados y arraigados*) dont les droits et devoirs étaient les mêmes que ceux des régnicoles espagnols[59]. Par conséquent, les *domiciliados* relevaient dorénavant des autorités espagnoles, et non plus des consuls français, y compris pour tout ce qui relevait du judiciaire. Par conséquent, le droit de procéder à la liquidation des successions des Français morts *ab intestat*, que les consuls se voient enfin garantir, ne porte lui aussi plus que sur les étrangers *transeuntes* (art. 8).

La convention consulaire franco-espagnole de 1769 est importante à plusieurs titres. Elle institue un nouveau type de traités bilatéraux dont le contenu est exclusivement consacré aux relations consulaires. Ce texte a en effet servi de matrice pour bon nombre de conventions consulaires ultérieures[60]. Il a également un effet immédiat, car il permet de rétablir les relations consulaires entre la France et l'un de ses plus gros partenaires commerciaux. Or la convention de 1769 permet avant tout de fournir, du moins pour le cas de l'Espagne, un début de réponse à la question centrale qui occupe la recherche sur l'histoire

58 Ce délai passé, les *transeuntes* deviennent, aux yeux des Espagnols, des *domiciliados*. Lloret, « Princes et marchands », 101.

59 Tamar Herzog, *Defining Nations. Immigrants and Citizens in Early Modern Spain and Spanish America* (New Haven et Londres : Yale University Press, 2003), 83–84.

60 Armas Barea, « La convención consular », 143–144.

de la juridiction consulaire française : compte tenu de l'importance accordée par le gouvernement français à la question de la juridiction consulaire, pourquoi les archives ne regorgent-elles pas de documents liés aux procédures[61] ?

Pour la période d'avant l'expulsion des consuls français en 1635, cette question est condamnée à rester une aporie : les archives des chancelleries consulaires en Espagne sont perdues, et les correspondances avec les tutelles ministérielles n'ont été conservées que par bribes. Il nous est par conséquent impossible de vérifier dans quelle mesure les consuls y exerçaient effectivement une juridiction sur leurs compatriotes, et si de véritables tribunaux y tranchaient des procès. Lorsque les consulats français en Espagne rouvrent peu à peu après la paix des Pyrénées, la question de la juridiction civile et criminelle des consuls, français ou autres, ne se pose plus. Elle est dorénavant assurée par les juges conservateurs. Dans le but de soustraire les Français installés ou de passage en Espagne à la justice ordinaire, réputée « lente, coûteuse, avide et hostile »[62], l'ambassadeur de France à Madrid était davantage occupé à influer sur le choix des juges conservateurs et à définir leur périmètre d'intervention aussi large que possible, que de réclamer une extension des compétences juridictionnelles des consuls français. Bien que l'indignation française soit palpable – les nombreux mémoires produits après 1709 par les bureaux du département de la Marine en témoignent – rien n'y fait. Or, la convention de 1769 n'apporte peut-être pas autant de nouveautés qu'il y paraît. Vraisemblablement elle n'entérine qu'une situation qui existait au moins depuis 1709, voire depuis la paix des Pyrénées.

5 Conclusion

L'affirmation d'Yvan Debbasch, selon laquelle « il n'est pas d'exemple, aussi loin que l'on remonte, de consul à qui soit refusé compétence au civil sur ses nationaux »[63], est de toute évidence à nuancer. Si elle peut à la limite être considérée valable pour le Levant et la Barbarie, elle ne l'est assurément pas pour les pays de Chrétienté. Certes, les autorités françaises ont tenté de calquer le modèle juridictionnel hérité du Moyen-Âge levantin et de l'étendre à d'autres régions – l'ordonnance de Marine de 1681 en témoigne – mais n'y sont parvenues que très insuffisamment. En Espagne, du moins après la Guerre de

61 Pour une analyse plus profonde de ce phénomène, voir les contributions d'Arnaud Bartolomei et de Victor Simon dans ce même volume.

62 Girard, *Commerce français*, 150.

63 Debbasch, *Nation française*, 197.

Trente Ans, les autorités locales ont largement réussi à faire obstruction à la juridiction consulaire. Au Portugal, où la juridiction civile et criminelle avait aussi été transférée à un juge conservateur[64], il en a été de même. À Livourne et à Gênes, la juridiction des consuls français était également contestée[65]. Dans les deux péninsules, où « la juridiction consulaire est d'abord un excellent révélateur des contextes et des rapports de force politiques et diplomatiques »[66], la France a tout au plus réussi à conserver la juridiction volontaire. Or le réseau consulaire français des XVIIe et XVIIIe siècles ne se limite pas aux postes ibériques, à Livourne et à Gênes, bien qu'il s'agisse là sans doute des plus importants. Il y en a des dizaines d'autres, aussi bien en Italie que dans le Nord. Ici, les pouvoirs locaux ne semblent pas avoir disputé les pouvoirs juridictionnels aux consuls français. Du moins les archives n'en gardent-elles pas la trace.

Bibliographie

Barea, Calixto Alfredo Armas. « La convención consular hispano-francesa de 1769 ». *Revista de Derecho Internacional y Ciencias Diplomáticas* (Rosario, Argentine), n° 15/16 (1959) : 143–158.

Bergasse, Louis. *Notice historique sur la Chambre de Commerce de Marseille (1599–1912)*. Marseille : Barlatier, 1913.

Bouquin, Jean. *De la juridiction consulaire en droit maritime français : Compétence des consuls à l'égard des faits passés à bord des navires de commerce : répression des infractions, règlement des différends civils et commerciaux.* Lyon : Bosc, 1935.

Calafat, Guillaume. « Livourne et la Chambre de commerce de Marseille au XVIIe siècle : Consuls français, agents et perception du droit de *cottimo* ». Dans *La mer en partage : Sociétés littorales et économies maritimes (XVIe–XIXe siècle)*, édité par Xavier Daumalin, Daniel Faget et Olivier Raveux, 209–226. Aix-en-Provence : Presses universitaires de Provence, 2016.

64 Andréa Slemian, « Les territoires des corporations : l'administration et la justice dans les places commerciales de l'Empire portugais (v. 1750–1820) », dans *Raison administrative et logiques d'empire (XVIe–XIXe siècle)*, éd. François Godicheau et Mathieu Grenet (Rome : École française de Rome, 2021) ; Évelyne Oliel-Grausz, « La surveillance des négociants de passage : les juifs de signal à Lisbonne au XVIIIe siècle », dans *Étrangers et sociétés*, éd. Pilar González-Bernaldo *et al.* (Rennes : Presses universitaires de Rennes, 2009).

65 Pour une analyse approfondie de la situation livournaise, voir : Calafat, « La juridiction des consuls français en Méditerranée ».

66 Calafat, « Les juridictions du consul », 145.

Calafat, Guillaume. « Les juridictions du consul : une institution au service des marchands et du commerce ? Introduction ». Dans *De l'utilité commerciale des consuls : L'institution consulaire et les marchands dans le monde méditerranéen (XVIIe–XXe siècle)*, édité par Arnaud Bartolomei, Guillaume Calafat, Mathieu Grenet et Jörg Ulbert, 143–153. Rome : École française de Rome, 2017.

Calafat, Guillaume. « La juridiction des consuls français en Méditerranée : litiges marchands, arbitrages et circulations des procès (Livourne et Tunis au XVIIe siècle) ». Dans *De l'utilité commerciale des consuls : L'institution consulaire et les marchands dans le monde méditerranéen (XVIIe–XXe siècle)*, édité par Arnaud Bartolomei, Guillaume Calafat, Mathieu Grenet et Jörg Ulbert, 155–172. Rome : École française de Rome, 2017.

Clercq, Jules de. *Recueil des traités de la France*, t. 1 : 1713–1802. Paris : A. Durand et Pedone-Lauriel, 1880.

Crespo Solana, An. « El juez conservador ¿ una alternativa al cónsul de la nación ? ». Dans *Los cónsules de extranjeros en la edad moderna y al principio de la edad contemporánea*, édité par Marcella Aglietti, Manuel Herrero Sánchez et Francisco Javier Zamora Rodriguez, 23–33. Madrid : Ediciones Doce Calles, 2013.

Debbasch, Yvan. *La Nation française en Tunisie (1577–1835)*. Paris : Sirey, 1957.

L'Intendance de Provence à la fin du XVIIe siècle : Édition critique des mémoires « pour l'instruction du duc de Bourgogne », édité par François-Xavier Emmanuelli. Paris : Bibliothèque nationale, 1980.

Désos, Catherine. *Les Français de Philippe V : Un modèle nouveau pour gouverner l'Espagne (1700–1724)*. Strasbourg : Presses universitaires de Strasbourg, 2009.

Féraud-Giraud, Louis-Joseph-Delphin. *Juridiction française dans les échelles du Levant et de Barbarie : Étude sur la condition légale des étrangers dans les pays hors Chrétienté*. Paris : Durand, 1866.

Girard, Albert. *Le Commerce français à Séville et Cadix au temps des Habsbourg : Contribution à l'étude du commerce étranger en Espagne aux XVIe et XVIIe siècles*. Paris : Boccard, 1932.

Le Gouic, Olivier. « Les négociants dans les assemblées de la Nation française à Cadix : représentation, assiduité et implication du négoce dans les affaires du Consulat de France (1716–1728) ». *Annales de Bretagne et des Pays de l'Ouest* 120, n° 1 (2013) : 97–127.

Lloret, Sylvain. *Entre princes et marchands : les agents généraux de France à Madrid dans les interstices de la diplomatie (1702–1793)*. thèse de doctorat, Sorbonne Université, 2018.

Lloret, Sylvain. « Défendre le négoce français en Espagne : L'agent général de la Marine et du Commerce de France à Madrid et le Congrès d'Utrecht ». Dans *La Diplomatie-monde : Autour de la paix d'Utrecht – 1713*, édité par Lucien Bély, Géraud Poumarède, Guillaume Hanotin, 379–390. Paris : Pedone, 2019.

Montón, Alejandro García. « Corona, hombres de negocios y jueces conservatores : Un acercamiento en Escala transatlántica (s. XVII) ». *Jerónimi Zurita* 90 (2015) : 75–112.

Moreüil, L.-J.-A. *Manuel des agents consulaires français et étrangers*. Paris : Videcocq, 1850.

Oliel-Grausz, Évelyne. « La surveillance des négociants de passage : les juifs de signal à Lisbonne au XVIIIe siècle ». Dans *Étrangers et sociétés*, édité par Pilar González-Bernaldo, Manuela Martini et Marie-Louise Pelus-Kaplan, 103–113. Rennes : Presses universitaires de Rennes, 2009.

Olnon, Merlijn. « Towards Classifying *Avanias* : a Study of Two Cases Involving the English and Dutch Nations in Seventeenth-Century Izmir ». Dans *Friends and Rivals in the East : Studies in Anglo–Dutch Relations in the Levant from the Seventeenth to the Early Nineteenth Century*, édité par Alastair Hamilton, Alexander Hendrik de Groot et Maurits van den Boogert, 159–186. Leyde : Brill, 2000.

Pérez Sarrión, Guillermo. *La península comercial : mercado, redes sociales y Estado en España en el siglo XVIII*. Madrid : Marcial Pons, 2012.

Poumarède, Géraud. « Le consul dans les dictionnaires et le droit des gens : émergence et affirmation d'une institution nouvelle (XVIe–XVIIIe siècles) ». Dans *La fonction consulaire à l'époque moderne*, édité par Jörg Ulbert et Gérard Le Bouëdec, 23–36. Rennes : Presses universitaires de Rennes, 2006.

Rambert, Gaston. *Histoire du commerce de Marseille*, t. IV : *De 1660–1789*. Paris : Plon, 1954.

Rambert, Gaston. « La France et la politique commerciale de l'Espagne au XVIIIe siècle », *Revue d'Histoire moderne et contemporaine* 6 (1959) : 269–288.

Sempéré, Julien. *S'informer pour s'enrichir : Le consul français à Barcelone et ses réseaux (1679–1716)*. Perpignan : Presses universitaires de Perpignan, 2018.

Simon, Victor. *Les échelles du Levant et de Barbarie : Droit du commerce international entre la France et l'Empire ottoman (XVIe–XVIIIe siècle)*. Paris : LGDJ, 2021.

Slemian, Andréa. « Les territoires des corporations : l'administration et la justice dans les places commerciales de l'empire portugais (v. 1750–1820) ». Dans *Raison administrative et logiques d'empire (XVIe–XIXe siècle)*, édité par François Godicheau et Mathieu Grenet, 237–252. Rome : École française de Rome, 2021.

Ulbert, Jörg. « L'administration des consulats au sein du secrétariat d'état de la Marine (1669–1715) ». Dans *La Liasse et la plume : Les bureaux du secrétariat d'État de la Marine (1669–1792)*, édité par Jörg Ulbert et Sylviane Llinares, 73–86. Rennes : Presses universitaires de Rennes, 2017.

Valin, René-Josué. *Nouveau commentaire sur l'ordonnance de la Marine du mois d'août 1681*. La Rochelle : Legier et Mesnier, 1760.

Van den Boogert, Maurits H. *The Capitulations and the Ottoman Legal System : Qadis, Consuls, and Beratlı in the Eighteenth Century*. Leyde et Boston : Brill, 2005.

Wenck, Friedrich August Wilhelm. *Codex iuris gentivm recentissimi, e tabvlariorvm exemplorvmqve fide dignorvm monvmentis compositvs*. Leipzig : Haer. Weidmann et Reich, 1795.

Windler, Christian. *La Diplomatie comme expérience de l'autre : Consuls français au Maghreb (1700–1840)*. Genève : Droz, 2002.

Zamora Rodríguez, Francisco. « 'Dar el cordero en guarda del lobo' : Control hispánico sobre los consulados extranjeros durante el siglo XVII e inicios del XVIII ». *Tiempos Modernos* 30 (2015) : 1–20.

Zarb, Mireille. *Histoire d'une autonomie communale : Les privilèges de la ville de Marseille du Xe siècle à la Révolution*. Paris : A. et J. Picard, 1961.

Zaugg, Roberto. « Judging Foreigners : Conflict Strategies, Consular Interventions and Institutional Changes in Eighteenth-Century Naples ». *Journal of Modern Italian Studies* 13, n° 2 (2008) : 171–195.

Zaugg, Roberto. « Mercanti stranieri e giudici napoletani. La gestione dei conflitti in Antico Regime ». *Quaderni Storici* 133, n° 1 (2010) : 139–169.

5

The Consular Jurisdiction in the Eighteenth Century

A Trade Commodity for Free Ports?

Marcella Aglietti

1 The Consular Jurisdiction in the Eighteenth Century: An Anachronistic Prerogative or a Temporary Exception?

Consular jurisdiction of the modern period consisted of a series of varying prerogatives aimed at resolving conflicts and exercising justice, proving useful to the different actors – mainly the trading community, sending, and receiving States and the myriad of individual and collective, local and international interests that were occasionally involved.[1] It was, therefore, subject to variations and redefinitions based on the opposing and conflicting dialectics, presenting itself as a fluctuating, potential, temporary, or occasional jurisdiction, that fell completely under the umbrella of *juridictions liquides* typical of the Mediterranean, as clearly highlighted by recent research.[2]

---

1 For a historiographical outline, see *La fonction consulaire à l'époque moderne. L'affirmation d'une institution économique et politique (1500–1800)*, eds. Jörg Ulbert and Gérard Le Bouëdec (Rennes: Presses Universitaires de Rennes, 2006). See also Marcella Aglietti, *L'istituto consolare tra Sette e Ottocento: funzioni istituzionali, profilo giuridico e percorsi professionali nella Toscana granducale* (Pisa: ETS, 2017); Guillaume Calafat, "La juridiction des consuls français en Méditerranée: litiges marchands, arbitrages et circulations des procès (Livourne et Tunis au XVIIe siècle)," in *De l'utilité commerciale des consuls. L'institution consulaire et les marchands dans le monde méditerranéen (XVIIe–XIXe siècle)*, eds. Arnaud Bartolomei *et al.* (Rome: École française de Rome, 2018), 155–171; David Do Paço, "Une collaboration économique et sociale: consuls et protecteurs des marchands ottomans à Vienne et à Trieste au XVIIIe siècle," *Cahiers de la Méditerranée* 98 (2019): 57–74; Manuel-Reyes García Hurtado, "Jean-Baptiste Dauvergne, cónsul de Francia en Galicia (1721–1735). Los trabajos y los días en defensa de los intereses de su nación," *Tiempos Modernos. Revista Electrónica de Historia Moderna* 11, n° 43 (2021): 166–187; Marcella Aglietti, "Lo Stato oltreconfine. L'intermediazione dei consoli all'estero tra rappresentanza e amministrazione," in *Intermediari. Modi, figure e istituti del collegamento tra autorità centrale e comunità locali*, eds. Livio Antonielli and Alessandro Buono (Soveria Mannelli: Rubbettino, on press).

2 Roberto Zaugg, "Mercanti stranieri e giudici napoletani. La gestione dei conflitti in Antico Regime," *Quaderni Storici* 133, n° 1 (April 2010): 139–169; Guillaume Calafat, *Une mer jalousée.*

 HTTPS://DOI.ORG/10.1163/9789004755192-007

Taking Friederich F. Martens' work,[3] an initial element of classification can be found in the nature of the state in which it is practised, differentiating European countries from all others. The specificity of the jurisdiction of European consuls stationed in the ports of the Levant and the Ottoman Empire appeared to be well-defined during the eighteenth century, thanks to the spread of their own regulations, rules, and tariffs.[4] An entirely different story is how consular jurisdiction was exercised in Mediterranean Europe. Through the affirmation during the century of the sovereignty of the territorial state, and then of state law, this prerogative clashed with the consolidation of the hierarchy of individual state laws. Consuls increasingly relied on the sending state, and far less on the respective local community. Consequently, in this scenario, allowing foreign consuls to exercise jurisdiction in the host territory became tantamount to legitimising an asymmetry of power and sovereignty between the receiving and sending states and, as such, unacceptable, even in a system of reciprocity.

Nevertheless, this theoretical interpretation was forced to acknowledge an established practice, and, for much of the eighteenth century, consular jurisdiction was widely exercised for the convenient and rapid solution of disputes. Although not formally recognised, special jurisdictional powers were tolerated or, at least, went unopposed by the authorities of the receiving state, and had consolidated to the point of becoming mandatory rules that were difficult to circumvent.[5] The jurisdictional powers of the consuls, which could no longer be ascribed *sic et simpliciter* to a legacy remaining from medieval consular jurisdiction, instead gained a new foothold in the regime of free ports.

In Genoa, Venice, Livorno, Trieste, Civitavecchia, Ancona, and Messina, but even Villefranche, Marseilles, Cádiz, and Marstrand, the development of free

---

Contribution à l'histoire de la souveraineté (*Méditerranée*, XVIIe *siècle*) (Paris: Le Seuil, 2019): 4–8.

3 Andreas T. Müller, "Friedrich F. Martens on 'The Office of Consul and Consular Jurisdiction in the East'," *The European Journal of International Law* 25, n° 3 (2014), 871–891 and in particular 876.

4 Géraud Poumarède, "Le consul dans les dictionnaires et le droit des gens: émergence et affirmation d'une institution nouvelle (XVIe–XVIIIe siècles)," in *La fonction consulaire à l'époque moderne. L'affirmation d'une institution économique et politique* (1500–1800), eds. Jörg Ulbert and Gérard Le Bouëdec (Rennes: Presses Universitaires de Rennes, 2006), 23–36; Umberto Signori, "Supplier pour le consulat. Entre défense des intérêts personnels et service fidèle des consuls vénitiens dans le Levant ottoman (1670–1703)," *Cahiers de la Méditerranée* 98 (2019): 29–44.

5 Cf. Roberto Zaugg, "*La mediazione contestata.* Notes on the French Consuls in 18th-Century Naples," in *Lo spazio tirrenico nella 'grande trasformazione'. Merci, uomini e istituzioni nel Settecento e nel primo Ottocento,* ed. Biagio Salvemini (Bari: Edipuglia, 2009), 441–454.

ports represented a mainly European phenomenon that took hold between the end of the seventeenth and the eighteenth century, with the specific goal of developing trade.[6] Here, alongside the great systems of national diplomacy based on complete juridical structures of reference, it became compulsory for the republics and small states of Italy to react quickly to specific requirements in line with strategies prompted by political opportunism.[7] Based on this new combination, consular jurisdictions represented a strategic factor in attracting foreign merchant communities, a commodity to be granted to their stakeholders that was also useful in boosting local trade over other competing trading centres.

An analysis based on a simple state-building approach appears far less conclusive, and a more flexible interpretative framework is, therefore, required to weigh up the logic of balances of power, economic interests, and cultural dynamics. It is also a question of investigating an empirical dimension that cannot be identified in official sources, where it was often rendered invisible, or presented to us with apparently contradictory accounts, which change depending on the authority producing the information. "Grey documentation" was, therefore, mainly used, produced by administrative local offices, for internal use only, inspired by a conscious desire to act in the name of a more streamlined principle of expediency and mutual interest. In order to look at and understand their characteristics, it was essential to resort to a vast array of testimonies, including economic and property disputes, commercial, tax and customs litigations, smuggling and corruption cases, extradition proceedings, debt collection, and even broken marriage vows. This required restricting the investigation to a specific territorial area, while not excluding a comparative approach, and to the epistemological category of microhistory, which proved to be a useful tool for observing "anomalies" that do not fit into

6 Corey Tazzara, "Ports and free ports in the Old World. Political economy in the Mediterranean and the Indian Ocean (1500–1750)," in *Free Trade and Free Ports in the Mediterranean*, eds. Giulia Delogu, Koen Stapelbroek, and Antonio Trampus (London, New York: Routledge, 2025), 23–40. See also Antonio Iodice, "L'istituzione del porto franco in un Mediterraneo senza frontiere," *Politics, Rivista di studi politici* 5, n° 1 (2016): 19–33.

7 Free ports have long been interpreted as *une arme pour les faibles*, see Paul Masson, *Ports francs d'autrefois et d'aujourd'hui* (Paris: Hachette, 1904), 201. For a more detailed commentary, see: Koen Stapelbroek and Corey Tazzara, "The Global History of the Free Port," *Global Intellectual History* 8, n° 6 (2023), 666–667; Koen Stapelbroek and Antonio Trampus, "The History of Mediterranean Free Ports as the Invention of Free Trade?," in *Free Trade and Free Ports in the Mediterranean*, eds. Giulia Delogu, Koen Stapelbroek and Antonio Trampus (London: Routledge, 2024), 1–23.

broader generalisations.[8] Admittedly, this increases the distortion of the local standpoint but in an era in which legal particularism was still widespread, I believe it must remain a fundamental methodology.

2 Ports and "Free-Port" Cities: A Natural Consular Jurisdiction Habitat?

During the eighteenth century, the question of the foreign consuls' possible jurisdictional power entered fully into the ongoing dialectic between territorial sovereignty and free trade.[9] On the one hand, the state authority denied its legitimacy while, on the other, it had to recognise its existence and find forms of compatibility. A French memorandum of 1731 about the French consuls residing in Italy and Spain confirmed the "pleine 'possession' d'un pouvoir de juridiction consulaire" throughout the Mediterranean.[10] The *junta de comercio y de dependencias de extranjeros* of the Kingdom of Spain produced documentation that also firmly rejected such an eventuality on its territory but was then forced to come to terms with the widespread practices contrary to this prohibition. In May 1759, the *junta* requested its governors and intendants in the port cities of Spain to carry out an investigation, which was to last several years.[11] This inquiry confirmed that it was common practice for some foreign consuls to "exercise jurisdiction in the disputes of their countrymen," despite

8 On the epistemological value of microhistory, see Francesca Trivellato, "Microstoria, storia del mondo e storia globale," in *Microstoria. A venticinque anni da "L'eredità immateriale,"* ed. Paola Lanaro (Milan: FrancoAngeli, 2011) 119–132. In this perspective, also Guillaume Calafat, "Jurisdictional Pluralism in a Litigious Sea (1590–1630): Hard Cases, Multi-Sited Trials and Legal Enforcement between North Africa and Italy," *Past & Present* 242, supplement 14 (November 2019), 142–178.

9 Marcella Aglietti, "Nuove prerogative di Stato e conflitti giurisdizionali dalle carte di Giuseppe Bonechi, console toscano a Napoli (1764–1796)," in *Napoli e il Mediterraneo nel Settecento. Scambi, immagini, istituzioni*, ed. Anna Maria Rao (Naples: Edipuglia, 2017), 75–92.

10 Guillaume Calafat, "La juridiction du consul: une institution au service des marchands et du commerce? Introduction," in *De l'utilité commerciale des consuls. L'institution consulaire et les marchands dans le monde méditerranéen (XVIIe–XXe siècle)*, eds. Arnaud Bartolomei *et al.* (Rome: École française de Rome, 2018), 143–153.

11 The investigation was concluded in 1763; see preliminary report of the Junta in Archivo Histórico Nacional (Madrid, Spain) (hereafter referred to as AHN), Estado, folder 647, insert 25, 30 July 1763. Marcella Aglietti, "El debate sobre la jurisdicción consular en la Monarquía hispánica (1759–1769)," in *Los cónsules de extranjeros en la Edad Moderna y principios de la Edad Contemporanea*, eds. Marcella Aglietti, Manuel Herrero and Francisco Javier Zamora (Madrid: Doce Calles, 2013), 105–118.

the measures taken to counter these practices (such as suspensions, fines or even the removal of the most disruptive individuals).[12] Not long after, a similar inquiry was carried out among Spanish consuls stationed abroad, who confirmed the exercise of jurisdiction not only in Genoa and Trieste, but also in other places,[13] revealing a reality that was far more consolidated and widespread than imagined. The existence of these consular jurisdictions emerged, above all, when the balance between social groups and international power relations changed, or when the anomaly no longer served its purpose and was subsequently deemed inadmissible and opposed by local authorities.

In Nice in 1713, after the Duke of Savoy had been crowned King of Sicily and had become even more determined to fulfil his ambition of achieving autonomy, he grasped the opportunity of the investiture of a new French consul in the free port of Villefranche to devolve all jurisdiction over disputes there to the local Consulate of the Sea. A decision that interrupted the connivance with the local authorities on the pretext introduced at the time of the *Grande ordonnance de la Marine* in 1681, with which the King of France claimed a monopoly in jurisdiction over his subjects abroad, leaving the settlement of disputes to the consuls and their respective chancelleries.[14]

In the same year, the governor of the free port of Livorno formally raised the question of legitimacy when faced with another French sovereign decree on 4 January 1713, in which the jurisdictional power of consuls over their compatriots was reiterated. On the diplomatic front, the Tuscan Minister Plenipotentiary to Paris and the Secretary of War in Florence signalled that "no visible sign of jurisdiction" would be tolerated by the consuls "and especially the one from France." Then, however, in the instructions to the governor of Livorno, he was told to 'ignore' the well-known consular chancelleries that were regularly involved in issuing contracts, notarial deeds, and settling maritime claims, and to be careful not to admit such deeds to the Tuscan courts.[15] A comprom-

12 AHN, Estado, folder 608, ins. 19, *Breve notizia de las controversias que hasta aquì se han ofrezido y visto en la Junta de dependenzias y negozios de Estrangeros en punto de consules de las Naziones. Resoluziones de Su Majestad en esta razon, y fundamentos de ellas*, 1730.

13 AHN, Estado, folder 647, ins. 25, preliminary report of the Junta, 30 July 1763 and Consulta de la Junta de comercio y de dependencias de extranjeros to the king, 30 July 1763 and resolution of royal assent the following autumn.

14 Françoise Hildesheimer, "Les difficultés du consulat de France à Nice (1713–1720)," in *1388, La Dédition de Nice à la Savoie*, eds. Rosine Cleyet-Michaud *et al.* (Paris: Éditions de la Sorbonne, 1990).

15 Memoir dating back to the beginning of the century and transmitted by the government of Livorno to Senator Piccolomini in Florence on 12 December 1770, State Archives of Florence (Italy) (hereafter referred to as ASFi), Secretariat and Foreign Ministry, folder 1083, ins. 7. On consular chancelleries, see Arnaud Bartolomei and Anne Brogini, "De la

ise not without consequences. A century later, the Tuscan "merchants" of Livorno "rebelled" against the renewed demands of the consuls of England and France to issue "acts of authority" on the insurance of goods damaged during maritime transport. The Foreign Secretary of Florence thus found himself in extreme difficulty in retracting a privilege that had become standard practice in the meantime. It fell to the president of the Civil and Consular Magistrate of Livorno to clarify how this commonplace practice in foreign ports of allowing consuls to intervene in areas far beyond mere amicable settlements, was neither based "on the universal laws of all peoples" nor belonged to "ordinary attributions," but depended on an "express convention and the mutual will of the contracting powers."[16] In short, it was founded on reciprocal convenience and, only for as long as it was recognised and tolerated.

Hence, in the port cities smouldered a "permanent conflict" surrounding the question of foreign consuls' jurisdiction. While the latter were constantly trying to expand their jurisdiction, the local authorities were busy trying to "shrink" it. Since another government official from Livorno would later point out in 1815, "nothing is positive or decided," i.e. there were no positive laws or unequivocal regulatory provisions, the jurisdiction of the consuls was "more or less extensive in each port, according to the use that has authorised the privileges, exemptions, and distinctions in their regard to a greater or lesser extent." Incidentally, the Tuscan official also added that Livorno was reputed to be one of the ports where there was less jurisdictional freedom than elsewhere, especially compared to Genoa or many other trading centres where, he added, consuls were known to enjoy "much greater consideration" and freedom.[17]

---

réglementation aux pratiques marchandes: l'enregistrement des actes dans les chancelleries consulaires françaises (XVIIe–XIXe siècles)," in *De l'utilité commerciale des consuls. L'institution consulaire et les marchands dans le monde méditerranéen (XVIIe–XXe siècle)*, eds. Arnaud Bartolomei *et al.* (Rome: École française de Rome, 2018), 173–198; Jörg Ulbert, "Qu'est-ce qu'un chancelier de consulat? Une approche par les textes de droit français," *Mélanges de l'École française de Rome – Italie et Méditerranée modernes et contemporaines* 128, n° 2 (2016), https://doi.org/10.4000/mefrim.2892.

16 See the correspondence between various Livorno government authorities and the foreign secretariat in Florence, November 1817, in ASFi, Secretariat and Foreign Ministry, folder 1083, ins. 7.

17 "Affare relativo alla giurisdizione, immunità ed altro di cui godono i consoli esteri," letter from Governor Spannocchi to the Secretary of State Councillor Fossombroni in Florence, from Livorno, 13 February 1815, ASFi, Secretariat and Foreign Ministry, folder 2997, n.p.

3 Free Ports with Multiple Jurisdictions: Strictly Confidential Documents in Livorno

The claim that Livorno was one of the ports with the greatest restrictions on consular jurisdiction remains to be verified. Undoubtedly, the trading nations that settled there during the seventeenth century were unable to benefit from the presumed medieval privileges because it was a "new city," as the officials of the Venetian Republic wrote when formally installing their own consul in 1680,[18] that "it only started to be known under Ferdinand I de Medici."[19] And it is undoubtedly true that Livorno, "the main port of call in the Mediterranean" and the most widely copied free port model during the eighteenth century,[20] differed from all the other free ports of the time.[21] It had been founded with a special regime aimed at favouring trade and guaranteeing coexistence between communities with different origins, religions, and economic interests, thanks to the establishment of more extensive exemptions than elsewhere.[22] It had thus succeeded in ensuring the installation of a significant number of resident foreign consuls.[23] Moreover, the regime of neutrality that had contributed to its success had been formalised in 1691, thanks to the con-

18 Relazione ai Cinque Savi della mercanzia di Venezia sul consolato della Repubblica di Venezia a Livorno, anon., 1682, State Archives of Venice (Italy) (hereafter cited as ASVe), Cinque Savi della Mercanzia, Series II, 34, n.p.

19 Letter from the Venetian ambassador Antonio de' Negri from Milan to the Cinque Savi della mercanzia in Venice, 1 September 1688, ASVe, Cinque Savi della Mercanzia, Serie II, 34, n.p.

20 Tazzara, "Ports and free ports," 26.

21 "Livorno è formato e si regge con delle regole e dei principi diversi affatto da quelli che militano per tutti gli altri Paesi della Toscana non solo, ma anco per tutti gli altri Porti di mare e per le altre piazze di commercio, e sarebbe soggetto ad ingannarsi chi giudicasse di Livorno come di qualunque altro Paese" in "Massime di Governo ed altre istruzioni per l'uso," 1789, in State Archives of Livorno (Italy) (hereafter cited as ASLi), Governo of Livorno papers (hereafter Gov.), folder 958, fol. 2r–2v.

22 The free port of Livorno was based on a stratification of privileges granted to people and goods from 1591 until the law instituting the free port proper, of 11 March 1676. Lucia Frattarelli Fischer, "Livorno 1676: la città e il porto franco," in *La Toscana nell'età di Cosimo III*, eds. Franco Angiolini, Vieri Becagli and Marcello Verga (Florence: Edifir, 1993), 45–66; Guillaume Calafat, "Être étranger dans un port franc. Droits, privilèges et accès au travail à Livourne (1590–1715)," *Cahiers de la Méditerranée* 84 (2012), 102–122; Corey Tazzara, *The Free Port of Livorno and the Transformation of the Mediterranean World* (Oxford: Oxford University Press, 2017).

23 In 1765, there were 12 (for Denmark, England, France, Genoa, Naples, the Netherlands, Malta, Ragusa, Spain, Sardinia, Sweden and Venice), in Massimo Sanacore, "La relazione del governatore Filippo Bourbon del Monte del 1765," in *Fonti per la storia di Livorno. Fra Seicento e Settecento*, eds. Lucia Frattarelli Fischer and Carlo Mangio (Livorno: 2006),

suls in the city, who had acted as diplomatic agents for their respective Crowns.[24] An entirely inappropriate role that could, in part, reinforce what Luigi Spagnolini, consul of the Kingdom of Sardinia, wrote in 1815. In his opinion, the "many abusive privileges granted out of habit in various foreign powers" were explained by the fact that "in those States, the foreign power did not have a resident diplomatic minister"; therefore, the consul was invested with a power of *iurisdictio* resulting in "abuses, usurpation and privileges which, although not sanctioned by law, nor by the Courts, are tolerated, and have become the norm."[25]

How the jurisdictional confrontation between local authorities and foreign consuls worked was explained more clearly, as early as 1765, by the governor of Livorno, Filippo Bourbon del Monte, to the newly appointed Pietro Leopoldo Habsburg-Lorraine, who had just become Grand Duke in Florence. "Generally speaking," the consuls, and above all the ones representing the major powers, had *claimed jurisdiction* over their compatriots, on land and on board the ships, working hard to obtain this privilege. The local authority had continually opposed, or, to be more exact, had never allowed them to take possession of it "on a permanent basis."

References to this constant redefinition of the sovereign spaces can be found in an extensive collection of records for internal use of the Livorno administration, which gathered information for much of the eighteenth century and included numerous later annotations.[26] One of the most commonly repeated statements was that all communication between the governor and consuls, concerning any "business," including declarations of "anything even notorious," was to be made "exclusively by word of mouth" and never in writ-

---

53–71, 62. They became 18 in 1789 (with the addition of Hamburg, Austria, Massa, Prussia, the Papal States and Russia), in ASLi, Gov., folder 958, fol. 204v.

24 The first treaty of neutrality, of 9 October 1691, ratified "the observance of neutrality and security of all those in the port and on the shores of Livorno" and was concluded by the governor Alessandro Del Borro with the consuls of Spain, England, France and the United Provinces. Marcella Aglietti, *I governatori di Livorno dai Medici all'Unità d'Italia. Gli uomini, le istituzioni, la città* (Pisa: ETS, 2009), 80–82.

25 Luigi Spagnolini, from Livorno, to the Secretary of State for Foreign Affairs in Turin, the count of Vallesa, 24 October 1815, State Archives of Turin (Italy) (hereafter cited as ASTo), Political matters for foreign relations, National Consulates, Livorno, folder 1, n.p.

26 The main author of these records was Giuseppe Francesco Pierallini (1721–1793), an official with extensive legal and legislative knowledge. In his role as civil court registrar and later, hearing officer, he worked alongside three successive governors in Livorno in the second half of the eighteenth century, whilst also filling in as governor in the interim years between appointments. On Pierallini, see Aglietti, *I Governatori di Livorno*, 81–82.

ing.[27] Thus, this body of information was intended to remain strictly confidential, and ample space was given to relations with the *nations* and foreign consuls, including a comprehensive collection of letters exchanged between Livorno and Florence that marked the beginning of a modus operandi and provided precedents to which to refer at a later date.

It is clear from these reports that the point of friction lies in the interpretation of the exemption system. The free exercise of the government's jurisdiction on people and foreign ships had always been "one of the most controversial articles by the consuls residing in Livorno." In fact, they claimed to interpret and extend the port exemption to the point of not granting the government any jurisdictional authority.[28] On the Tuscan side, only the right to enjoy "those conveniences and privileges contained in the chapters of the free port," limited to customs matters and not involving jurisdiction, was recognised. However, "the prudential approach" adopted by the governor and "prescribed by several sovereign orders" had always favoured "silencing [grand ducal] jurisdictional rights, and dissimulating them, when resorting to them might lead to inconvenient consequences."[29]

The nature of the regime that prevailed in a freeport city was linked to a complicated balance of opposing jurisdictions, as expressed in another governor's memorial, dated 1758:

> In short, we have always endeavoured to combine, on the one hand, the privileges and exemptions, and on the other, sovereignty, jurisdiction and the interest of maintaining a fair balance in Livorno so that foreigners are reined in, without resenting not being free.
>
> The matter itself is of the utmost delicacy because any decision in favour of foreigners, who have always made up the most respectable part of Livorno's population, may result in total independence, if not disguised under some pretext.
>
> And even though these pretexts have been carefully designed, given that a repeated series of actions contrary to the sovereign's jurisdiction could have led to its demise, those rights, which had sometimes been suppressed in the past, were reinstated when circumstances permitted.

27 Letters from Governor Filippo Bourbon del Monte dated 17 March 1758, 5 March 1764, 2 April 1781, in ASLi, Gov., folder 958, fol. 241r; Letters from Governor to the Secretary Pandolfini, Florence, 5 December 1759, in ASFi, Reggenza, folder 649, ins. 11, n.p.

28 Report on the Jurisdiction of the Government over foreign persons and vessels, Memoir of 9 January 1762, ASLi, Gov., folder 958, fol. 24.

29 Government Letters of 14 and 22 March 1759, 22 May 1771 and 14 June 1780, in ASLi, Gov., folder 958, fol. 24.

> Hence, the system by which Livorno is governed is very complicated. Many aspects must be factored into the resolutions to be taken; no general rules have been established, and we have *often followed precedent which with the most important rules regarding the system to be observed are only found in the correspondence that the Grand Duke's secretaries maintained with the Governor.*[30]

Even sovereign edicts, especially if affecting trade, had to be approved by the governor as "suited to the system and to the respect owed to Livorno" before they could be enacted in the city.[31] And to be enacted, the governor should have consulted the "merchants"[tradesmen] of foreign nations represented by the consuls.[32] In this framework, the consuls "were always viewed in their true role as leaders and defenders of their countries' merchants" and, as such and only as such, endowed with wide-ranging privileges. The government had always *formally* rejected their demand to "unduly claim [the status] of public ministers for themselves," even though they were the only ones recognised "in the service of foreign powers."[33] When faced with their "claims" of jurisdiction "over their countrymen and ships and on different occasions," the governor "has always opposed them, nor has he ever tolerated their taking possession of them";[34] they were only granted "the jurisdiction that the sovereign of Tuscany wishes to allow them."[35]

Here the paradox arose: consular jurisdiction existed because that was the Grand Duke's wish, preserving his sovereignty while securing the coveted autonomy of Livorno at one stroke. This resulted in a continuous negotiation, according to a policy of "national interest" and opportunity, adjusted on a case-by-case basis. In most circumstances, the governor did not intervene either in the conscription[36] or recruitment of soldiers or sailors for foreign sovereigns, as this was an infringement of the basic rule underlying the functioning of Livorno's system of neutrality, assuming that the consul would always act "in a discreet and appropriate manner."[37] Because of this closeness

30 Report of the Governor dated 17 March 1758, ASLi, Gov., folder 958, fols. 6r–7v. Underlined in the original text.

31 ASLi, Gov., folder 958, fol. 140r.

32 ASLi, Gov., folder 958, fol. 141v.

33 ASLi, Gov., folder 958, fols. 205r–v.

34 ASLi, Gov., folder 958, fol. 206r.

35 Ibid., fol. 205v.

36 Report of the Regency Council to the sovereign, 16 June 1744, ASFi, Reggenza, folder 48, ins. 6.

37 Letters from the governor dated 17 March 1758, 5 March 1764, 2 April 1781, in ASLi, Gov., folder 958, fol. 241v.

to arbitrariness, there was no shortage of occasions on which unpleasant incidents arose, especially in times of major changes when the memory of the practices in use was lost or challenged, or priorities shifted. One of the most conflictual and contradictory periods was the one of reform in the mid-eighteenth century, which in Tuscany coincided with the dynastic change from the Medici family to the House of Habsburg-Lorraine, starting in 1737.[38]

4 Consular Jurisdiction in the Name of Mutual Benefit

One of the most widely debated jurisdictional powers of foreign consuls was undoubtedly the matter of settling disputes, and especially the power to arrest and hand over offenders.

On these fronts, Livorno enjoyed a series of brazen immunities and exemptions, both civil and criminal, revived and extended by the more famous "Livornine" laws of 1592 and 1593, which were never expressly repealed until the nineteenth century, and which became opportunities that the consuls were quick to exploit.

Ensuring "public peace" still remained a priority for the governor,[39] respecting privileges and exemptions, with care taken over maintaining good relations with foreign nations, while also making "a distinction between the royal flags and others of inferior rank," affording greater regard for the former, for obvious reasons of expediency.[40]

The governor was legitimised "to have jurisdiction or to proceed on one's own authority over persons and vessels of foreign nations" solely for civil affairs, for criminal cases, for economic interests of customs, and for the Grand Duke's tenders.[41] In particular, the governor's intervention was expected in the event of criminal cases that risked putting the local authority "at loggerheads with foreign nations" or, more generically, if there was any "relation to the rights, claims and peaceful residence of foreign nations in Livorno."[42] The governor was thus constantly vigilant in limiting jurisdictional conflicts and, in order to

38 Marcella Aglietti, "Giuliano Capponi governatore di Livorno tra Medici e Lorena," *Nuovi Studi Livornesi* 16 (2009): 33–63.

39 ASLi, Gov., folder 958, fol. 91r.

40 "Memoria de' signori segretario Pierallini e avvocato Baldasseroni sopra il Portofranco di Livorno," 30 January 1762, ASFi, Reggenza, folder 741, ins. 18, n.p.

41 Memorandum of the governor of Livorno, Giuliano Capponi, a Florence, 1739, in ASFi, Reggenza, folder 644, ins. 5.

42 ASLi, Gov., folder 958, fols. 100v–101r.

prevent possible friction, he had the power to suspend the local competent courts of ordinary jurisdiction and proceed "at his own discretion."[43]

Two events, that took place in 1738, within a short distance of each other, clearly show how important it was to proceed according to a principle of cautious flexibility. In the first episode, Collen Campbell, shipmaster of an English vessel anchored in the port of Livorno, had been sentenced by the magistrates of the Consulates of the Sea in Pisa[44] to hand over approximately 3,000 gold "pieces" (*pezze*) to a merchant named Huigens of Livorno. Consuls were generally entrusted with the task of monitoring troublemakers on board ships docked in the harbour, provided they were not allowed to disembark. The shipmaster, however, refused to return the ill-gotten gains, claiming that he had lost the gold during a storm and, after taking refuge on his ship to avoid arrest, threatened to set the ship on fire with the gunpowder stored on board. The English consul, therefore, together with various fellow countrymen, including the British minister to Florence, Lord Charles Fane, decided to resolve the matter by force, requesting the intervention of the governor of Livorno, Marquis Giuliano Capponi. The marquis duly assessed the options available with the Council of Regency in Florence. Having reiterated the right of the Tuscan authorities to intervene, they nevertheless deemed it appropriate to install safeguards "in order to guarantee the legitimacy of the actions taken" and thus avoid subsequent complaints. A special document to be signed by the consul was, therefore, drawn up by the Secretary of War and reviewed by the governor, with the express declaration that any use of military force by the local authority was at the repeated request, and full consent, of the consul, the nation, and the plenipotentiary himself. The consul agreed to the commitment, refused "all protection" to the shipmaster and referred the matter back to local justice system, hoping that it would serve as an example for the future.[45] A different case, this time involving the French consul occurred in September of the same year. The Court of Livorno had put out a warrant for the arrest of the shipmaster of a French merchant ship, accused of failing to honour a debt of 100 francs to one of his sailors, a Maltese national, who had then taken him to court. The Court had acted in accordance with "all civil enforcements that are permitted against foreign debtors,"

43 Ibid.

44 Alessandro Lo Bartolo, "The Consoli del Mare of Pisa, 1550–1750: an institutional and social profile," in *Un mare connesso. Europa e mondo islamico nel Mediterraneo (secoli XV–XIX)*, eds. Jake Dyble, Alessandro Lo Bartolo and Elia Morelli (Rome: Carocci, 2024), 177–200.

45 Report of Marquis Capponi, Governor of Livorno, 22 April 1738, ASFi, Reggenza, folder 41, n° 1, 1.

but before the shipmaster was taken into custody, the French consul appealed to the governor, complaining of the illegitimacy of interference in a case between French sailors, which he claimed fell under his jurisdiction. To avoid trouble, Capponi immediately ordered the shipmaster's release. The Council of Regency applauded the intervention of the governor, with the recommendation, however, "not to show any approval of the jurisdictional rights that the Consul of France claims to have in Livorno, which have never been granted to him by this government."[46]

In 1779 again, when the Spanish consul, Manuel de Silva, sent a request to the governor of Livorno for the arrest of three Neapolitan sailors, he did not make any secret of the fact that he had, in the meantime, questioned them to ascertain their guilt. The consul's request was, nevertheless, granted, except to reiterate that only the Grand Duke's ministers were authorised to interrogate foreign individuals within the state borders.[47] Especially since, at least until the second half of the eighteenth century,[48] it was not customary to respond to requests for extradition of individuals found guilty of crimes in the Tuscan port. If the request for detention was made by a foreign State, it would be accepted by the governor only on the basis of an order that had to come expressly from Florence. If the request was made by a consul, the governor formally complied with the consul's request, but more often than not, would "secretly" warn the suspect and facilitate his escape, or even spring him from the city's prisons.[49] Resorting to consular jurisdiction became a solution to solve possible disruptions for the governor in cases where he could not intervene directly because of Livorno's privileges, but the consuls could, within their own *nation*, with mutual benefit and advantage of local security. So, even though consuls had no formal permission, the governor "benevolently" granted it or simply refrained from objecting to the guilty party being handed over to his homeland by the respective consul.[50]

Such complicity on the part of the local authorities was also evidenced by the ban on consuls producing legal documents and keeping chancelleries

46 Minute of letter sent to the Grand Duke, 16 September 1738, ASFi, Reggenza, 41, n° 1, insert 2.

47 ASLi, Gov., folder 970, fols. 218r–v, letter of 6 August 1779 from the governor of Livorno to Count Alberti.

48 Daniele Edigati, "Aspetti giuridici delle franchigie di Livorno: l'immunità personale in criminalibus ed il problema dell'estradizione (secoli XVI–XVIII)," *Nuovi Studi Livornesi* 17 (2010): 17–41.

49 ASLi, Gov., folder 958, fols. 176r–178r.

50 Report of the Livorno Bargello of 28 June 1788, ASLI, Governor and Auditor, folder 3265, n.p.

open,[51] as was commonly known to be the case, with chancellors formally invested and the issuance of deeds and documents by them holding different legal value. In the midst of widespread irregularities and the active operation of consular chancelleries, the governor did not issue any punitive measures, following the rule of avoiding any engagement or cause for dispute with consuls, and indeed never taking part in disputes between them, or between them and other individuals.[52] The only caveat remained that no document signed by an *ex officio* consul should be accepted in local court, nor should any petition or plea submitted in the name of a resident foreign *nation* be accepted, to prevent *nations* from asserting acquired rights in jurisdictional matters or claiming the status of a political body as a recognised institution.[53] Those same documents would, however, have also been accepted in court if the consul had signed them as a mere private individual.[54]

5 Conclusions

The special statute of the city of Livorno, as in the cases of Trieste or Genoa, as free ports, substantiated the exception that justified the system of privilege from which consuls benefited, granted not because of their "special status" resulting from their title, but solely because they were the "heads of the merchants of their respective nation."[55]

This compromise of granting a certain flexibility in administrative and governing matters to the representatives of foreign communities, clearly depended on the cooperation of the consuls, thus refraining from overdoing their activities and seeking definitive recognition of their privileges. Otherwise, the governor of Livorno had no choice but to intervene to regain control of the situation. Although cases of conflict of jurisdiction between governors and consuls frequently occurred, sometimes even daily, they rarely, if ever, escalated to a higher level, as it was in everyone's interest to avoid clashes, that would later

51 "The consuls have certainly never been allowed to exercise any overt sign of jurisdiction, and although they, and especially the French consul, keep a chancellery on their own premises and dispatch certain documents from there, such as testimonies in cases of accidents at sea, the government is unaware of all this, and similar documents are certainly never admitted in the courts of Tuscany." Extract of a memorandum transmitted by the Government of Livorno to His Excellency Senator Piccolomini by letter dated 12/12/1770, excerpt, ASFI, Secretariat and Foreign Ministry, folder 1803, ins. 7, n.p.

52 ASLi, Gov., folder 958, fol. 140r.

53 ASLi, Gov., folder 958, fol. 120r–121r.

54 ASLi, Gov., folder 958, fol. 207v–208r.

55 ASLi, Gov., folder 958, fol. 228r–v.

prove difficult to rectify, or unpleasant diplomatic incidents between the Grand Duke and the foreign court in question. In addition, the high degree of social integration that Livorno guaranteed, and the fact that the consular post was almost never held by "transient" foreigners, but rather by permanent residents eager to integrate into the city's elite circles, provided a compelling reason for cooperation, perhaps even more so than with the authorities of the country of origin. The shared desire for the smooth running of Livorno was a mutual priority.

The documentation in Livorno, although not without inaccuracies, however, allows us to reconsider the interpretation that saw only a conflict between consular jurisdictions and local authorities. Instead of a simple competition, a practice based on the principle of responsibility emerges, with a dialogue between the parties that, although at times harsh and at other times compromising, was always mediated. Administrative sources shed light on the nature of these immunities and the jurisdictional autonomy of the consuls and how they were to be considered "merely voluntary" concessions by the Tuscan authority, thus not binding, and subject to revocation at any time. As also demonstrated by the case in Genoa, where the jurisdiction exercised by the consuls, of Spain in particular, was considered "una costumbre," "una condescendencia personal," and never a right.[56] From this perspective, the full right to wield sovereign power, in its various forms of expression of judicial, fiscal, and administrative authority, remained the exclusive prerogative of the state, which it granted and revoked at its discretion. This took the form of jurisdiction that was somehow delegated to others and not formally recognised as independent, but instrumental to the preservation of the free port system and the interests of the parties concerned.

Bibliography

Aglietti, Marcella. "El debate sobre la jurisdicción consular en la Monarquía hispánica (1759–1769)." In *Los cónsules de extranjeros en la Edad Moderna y principios de la Edad Contemporanea*, edited by Marcella Aglietti, Manuel Herrero and Francisco Javier Zamora, 105–118. Madrid: Doce Calles, 2013.

Aglietti, Marcella. *L'istituto consolare tra Sette e Ottocento: funzioni istituzionali, profilo giuridico e percorsi professionali nella Toscana granducale*. Pisa: ETS, 2017.

56 Agustín de Letamendi, *Tratado de jurisprudencia diplomático-consular y manual práctico para la Carrera de Estado* (Madrid: Repullés, 1843), 52.

Aglietti, Marcella. "Giuliano Capponi governatore di Livorno tra Medici e Lorena." *Nuovi Studi Livornesi* 16 (2009): 33–63.

Aglietti, Marcella. "Lo Stato oltreconfine: l'intermediazione dei consoli all'estero tra rappresentanza e amministrazione." In *Intermediari. Modi, figure e istituti del collegamento tra autorità centrale e comunità locali*, edited by Livio Antonielli and Alessandro Buono (unpublished manuscript, 2024).

Aglietti, Marcella. "Nuove prerogative di Stato e conflitti giurisdizionali dalle carte di Giuseppe Bonechi, console toscano a Napoli (1764–1796)." In *Napoli e il Mediterraneo nel Settecento: Scambi, immagini, istituzioni*, edited by Anna Maria Rao, 75–92. Naples: Edipuglia, 2017.

Aglietti, Marcella. *I governatori di Livorno dai Medici all'Unità d'Italia: Gli uomini, le istituzioni, la città*. Pisa: ETS 2009.

Bartolomei, Arnaud and Anne Brogini. "De la réglementation aux pratiques marchandes: l'enregistrement des actes dans les chancelleries consulaires françaises (XVIIe–XIXe siècles)." In *De l'utilité commerciale des consuls: L'institution consulaire et les marchands dans le monde méditerranéen (XVIIe–XXe siècle)*, edited by Arnaud Bartolomei, Guillaume Calafat, Mathieu Grenet and Jörg Ulbert, 173–198. Rome: École française de Rome, 2017.

Calafat, Guillaume. "Être étranger dans un port franc: Droits, privilèges et accès au travail à Livourne (1590–1715)." *Cahiers de la Méditerranée* 84 (2012): 102–122.

Calafat, Guillaume. "Jurisdictional Pluralism in a Litigious Sea (1590–1630): Hard Cases, Multi-Sited Trials and Legal Enforcement between North Africa and Italy." *Past & Present* 242, Supplement 14 (November 2019): 142–178.

Calafat, Guillaume. "La juridiction des consuls français en Méditerranée: litiges marchands, arbitrages et circulations des procès (Livourne et Tunis au XVIIe siècle)." In De l'utilité commerciale des consuls: L'institution consulaire et les marchands dans le monde méditerranéen (XVIIe–XXe siècle), edited by Arnaud Bartolomei, Guillaume Calafat, Mathieu Grenet and Jörg Ulbert, 155–172. Rome: École française de Rome, 2017.

Calafat, Guillaume. "La juridiction du consul: une institution au service des marchands et du commerce? Introduction." In *De l'utilité commerciale des consuls: L'institution consulaire et les marchands dans le monde méditerranéen (XVIIe–XXe siècle)*, edited by Arnaud Bartolomei, Guillaume Calafat, Mathieu Grenet and Jörg Ulbert, 143–153. Rome: École française de Rome, 2017.

Calafat, Guillaume. *Une mer jalousée. Contribution à l'histoire de la souveraineté (Méditerranée, XVIIe siècle)*. Paris: Le Seuil, 2019.

Do Paço, David. "Une collaboration économique et sociale: consuls et protecteurs des marchands ottomans à Vienne et à Trieste au XVIIIe siècle." *Cahiers de la Méditerranée* 98 (2019): 57–74.

Edigati, Daniele. “Aspetti giuridici delle franchigie di Livorno: l’immunità personale in criminalibus ed il problema dell’estradizione (secoli XVI–XVIII).” *Nuovi Studi Livornesi*, XVII (2010): 17–41.

Frattarelli Fischer, Lucia. “Livorno 1676: la città e il porto franco.” In *La Toscana nell’età di Cosimo III*, edited by Franco Angiolini, Vieri Becagli and Marcello Verga, 45–66. Florence: Edifir, 1993.

García Hurtado, Manuel-Reyes. “Jean-Baptiste Dauvergne, cónsul de Francia en Galicia (1721–1735): Los trabajos y los días en defensa de los intereses de su nación.” *Tiempos Modernos. Revista Electrónica de Historia Moderna* 11, n° 43 (2021): 166–187.

Hildesheimer, Françoise. “Les difficultés du consulat de France à Nice (1713–1720).” In *1388, La Dédition de Nice à la Savoie*, edited by Rosine Cleyet-Michaud, 425–441. Paris: Éditions de la Sorbonne, 1990.

Iodice, Antonio. “L’istituzione del porto franco in un Mediterraneo senza frontiere.” *Politics. Rivista di studi politici* 5, n° 1 (2016): 19–33.

Letamendi, Agustín de. *Tratado de jurisprudencia diplomático – consular y manual práctico para la Carrera de Estado*. Madrid: Repullés, 1843.

Lo Bartolo, Alessandro. “The Consoli del Mare of Pisa, 1550–1750: an Institutional and Social Profile.” In *Un mare connesso: Europa e mondo islamico nel Mediterraneo (secoli XV–XIX)*, edited by Jake Dyble, Alessandro Lo Bartolo and Elia Morelli, 175–198. Rome: Carocci, 2024.

Masson, Paul. *Ports francs d’autrefois et d’aujourd’hui*. Paris: Hachette, 1904.

Müller, Andreas T. “Friedrich F. Martens on ‘The Office of Consul and Consular Jurisdiction in the East’.” *The European Journal of International Law* 25, n° 3 (2014): 871–891.

Poumarède, Géraud. “Le consul dans les dictionnaires et le droit des gens: émergence et affirmation d’une institution nouvelle (XVIe–XVIIIe siècles).” In *La fonction consulaire à l’époque moderne: L’Affirmation d’une institution économique et politique (1500–1800)*, edited by Jörg Ulbert and Gérard Le Bouëdec, 23–36. Rennes: Presses universitaires de Rennes, 2006.

Sanacore, Massimo. “La relazione del governatore Filippo Bourbon del Monte del 1765.” In *Fonti per la storia di Livorno: Fra Seicento e Settecento*, edited by Lucia Frattarelli Fischer and Carlo Mangio, 45–71. Livorno: Benvenuti & Cavaciocchi, 2006.

Signori, Umberto. “Supplier pour le consulat: Entre défense des intérêts personnels et service fidèle des consuls vénitiens dans le Levant ottoman (1670–1703).” *Cahiers de la Méditerranée* 98 (2019): 29–44.

Stapelbroek, Koen and Antonio Trampus. “The history of Mediterranean free ports as the invention of free trade?” In *Free Trade and Free Ports in the Mediterranean*, edited by Giulia Delogu, Koen Stapelbroek and Antonio Trampus, 1–23. London: Routledge, 2024.

Stapelbroek, Koen and Corey Tazzara. "The Global History of the Free Port." *Global Intellectual History* 8, n° 6 (2023): 661–699.

Tazzara, Corey. *The Free Port of Livorno and the Transformation of the Mediterranean World.* Oxford: Oxford University Press, 2017.

Tazzara, Corey. "Ports and Free ports in the Old World: Political Economy in the Mediterranean and the Indian Ocean (1500–1750)." In *Free Trade and Free Ports in the Mediterranean*, edited by Giulia Delogu, Koen Stapelbroek and Antonio Trampus, 214–234. London: Routledge, 2025.

Trivellato, Francesca. "Microstoria, storia del mondo e storia globale." In *Microstoria: A venticinque anni da 'L'eredità immateriale'*, edited by Paola Lanaro, 119–131. Milan: FrancoAngeli, 2011.

Ulbert, Jörg and Gérard Le Bouëdec, eds. *La fonction consulaire à l'époque moderne: L'affirmation d'une institution économique et politique (1500–1800)*. Rennes: Presses Universitaires de Rennes, 2006.

Ulbert, Jörg. "Qu'est-ce qu'un chancelier de consulat? Une approche par les textes de droit français." *Mélanges de l'École française de Rome – Italie et Méditerranée modernes et contemporaines* 128, n° 2 (2016), https://doi.org/10.4000/mefrim.2892.

Zaugg, Roberto. "La mediazione contestata: Appunti sui consoli francesi nella Napoli del Settecento." In *Lo spazio tirrenico nella 'grande trasformazione': Merci, uomini e istituzioni nel Settecento e nel primo Ottocento*, edited by Biagio Salvemini, 441–454. Bari: Edipuglia, 2009.

Zaugg, Roberto. "Mercanti stranieri e giudici napoletani: La gestione dei conflitti in Antico Regime." *Quaderni Storici* 133, n° 1 (April 2010): 139–169.

6

Juridiction contentieuse des étrangers et fonctions judiciaires des consuls français dans les mondes hispaniques (XVIIIe–XIXe siècle)

Arnaud Bartolomei

1 Introduction

Dans l'Europe chrétienne, les juridictions consulaires contentieuses n'existèrent que de façon très résiduelle au cours de la période concernée. Là où elles furent établies, elles étaient en outre le plus souvent contestées, tantôt par les ressortissants desdits consuls, tantôt par les autorités des pays d'accueil. En revanche, presque tous les consulats exerçaient une juridiction dite « volontaire » sur leurs ressortissants (exercée par l'intermédiaire de leur chancellerie) – même si l'activité de certaines chancelleries put être aussi l'objet de contestations de la part des autorités d'accueil[1]. Un tel constat n'est cependant pas sans soulever un certain nombre de problèmes : pourquoi les juridictions consulaires contentieuses n'existaient-elles à peu près nulle part, alors même que leur installation était le plus souvent prévue et revendiquée dans les textes normatifs des pays émetteurs de consuls ? Et, plus encore, pourquoi les sources se font-elles l'écho des incessantes contestations auxquelles elles donnaient lieu de la part des autorités des pays d'accueil, jalouses de défendre leur souveraineté et leur exclusivisme juridictionnel, si elles n'avaient jamais réellement existé ? Pour lever ces ambiguïtés, nous proposons l'enquête suivante que nous avons menée de façon systématique à l'intérieur des fonds de divers consulats de France que nous avons eu l'occasion de consulter assidument au cours de la décennie écoulée : d'abord, ceux établis dans l'Espagne des XVIIIe et XIXe siècles (à Cadix et à Madrid en premier lieu) ; puis, ceux créés dans la jeune république indépendante du Mexique à partir des années 1820.

La présente contribution a pour objet de présenter les résultats de cette enquête, que nous pouvons résumer à travers les deux assertions suivantes. Nulle part, ni à Cadix, ni à Madrid, ni à Mexico, ni a priori dans aucun des

1 Sur la contestation de l'exercice de la juridiction volontaire du consulat de France à Barcelone, voir Julien Sempéré, *S'informer pour s'enrichir : Le consul de France à Barcelone et ses réseaux (1679–1716)*, Perpignan : Presses universitaires de Perpignan, 2018.

 HTTPS://DOI.ORG/10.1163/9789004755192-008

autres postes consulaires français ouverts en Espagne ou au Mexique, nous n'avons trouvé la moindre trace de tribunaux consulaires chargés de l'instruction ordinaire des contentieux civils ou pénaux impliquant les ressortissants français. En revanche, nous avons trouvé à chaque fois, dans ces différents endroits, des formes juridictionnelles qui s'approchent de celles des tribunaux consulaires proprement dits ou qui en avaient les mêmes attributions. À Cadix, par exemple, et ailleurs en Espagne, les consuls français ont présidé pendant toute la période des guerres révolutionnaires et napoléoniennes des tribunaux « extraordinaires » destinés à juger les prises faites par les corsaires français. Dans l'Espagne moderne, par ailleurs, il existait bien une juridiction contentieuse spécifique pour les étrangers (mais qui n'était pas exercé par leurs consuls). Enfin, à peu près partout, les consuls français exerçaient toute une pluralité de fonctions judiciaires au service de leurs ressortissants, aussi bien lorsque ces derniers avaient à faire à la justice locale que lorsqu'ils étaient convoqués devant les juridictions de leur pays d'origine. Ainsi, même si nous n'avons pas identifié de tribunaux consulaires ordinaires dans les mondes hispaniques, semblables à ceux qui ont pu exister à la même époque dans l'empire Ottoman ou, à partir du XIXe siècle, en Asie, il apparaît comme une évidence que les consuls de France n'en exerçaient pas moins de nombreuses fonctions judiciaires, qui étaient importantes aussi bien pour la protection des ressortissants placés sous leur juridiction que pour celle des Français qui résidaient sur le territoire national et qui possédaient des intérêts à l'étranger.

Pour exposer les résultats de notre enquête, nous procéderons en quatre temps. Nous reviendrons d'abord sur le constat, encore ambiguë et difficile à établir définitivement, de la quasi-absence de tribunaux consulaires formels au sein de l'Europe chrétienne. Puis, nous reviendrons sur l'évolution de la juridiction particulière qui existait dans la monarchie hispanique pour assurer la gestion du contentieux impliquant les étrangers séjournant dans la Péninsule (le *fuero de extranjería*). Enfin, nous décrirons la diversité des fonctions judiciaires qu'exerçaient les consuls de France établis dans les postes en Espagne et au Mexique dont nous avons consultés les fonds.

2 Des tribunaux consulaires dans l'Europe chrétienne ?

À l'échelle de l'Europe chrétienne, le premier constat qui se dégage de la masse des informations disponibles relève d'un évident paradoxe : alors que les souverains européens affirmaient généralement que leurs consuls à l'étranger devaient bénéficier de compétences juridictionnelles en matière contentieuse, très peu parmi eux étaient prêts à tolérer l'existence de telles juridictions sur leur territoire. Derrière l'énonciation de cette règle générale, on trouve cependant une très grande variété de cas ambigus, ce qui est source de confusion et complique l'appréhension que les historiens et les historiennes peuvent avoir du sujet. Ce constat est valable aussi bien lorsque l'on se place du côté des pays émetteurs que de celui des pays d'accueil des consuls des étrangers.

De ce point de vue, l'ordonnance de la Marine, émise par le gouvernement français en 1681 est parfaitement significative de telles ambiguïtés. Si elle envisage bien de façon explicite l'institution de juridictions consulaires françaises « en matière civile et criminelle », elle le fait de façon très imprécise et s'en remet « à l'usage et aux Capitulations faites avec les Souverains des lieux de leur établissement ». Cette phrase fait évidemment référence aux traités signés depuis le XVIe siècle avec la Sublime Porte (les « Capitulations »), lesquels prévoyaient bien l'exercice de telles prérogatives de la part des consuls étrangers. Mais, elle suggère que les consuls pouvaient également exercer les fonctions de juge, selon « l'usage des lieux de leur établissement », en dehors de l'empire Ottoman – ce qui, compte tenu des réalités géopolitiques de l'époque, renvoie inévitablement à des territoires situés dans l'Europe chrétienne[2]. Or, une telle interprétation a été confirmée par des textes normatifs postérieurs comme l'*Édit du Roi portant règlement sur les fonctions judiciaires et de police qu'exercent les consuls de France en pays étrangers* de 1778, qui se réfère lui-aussi aux « fonctions que remplissent nos consuls dans les pays étrangers, et particulièrement dans les Échelles du Levant et de Barbarie » et qui stipule, dans son article XXXVII, que les appels des sentences rendues par les consuls établis « tant aux Échelles du Levant qu'aux côtes d'Afrique » ressortiront du Parlement d'Aix alors que ceux des « autres consulats » ressortiront du Parlement « le plus proche du lieu où la sentence aura été rendue[3] », ce qui là-encore renvoie inévitablement à des postes situés en Europe.

---

2 Cette interprétation est confirmée par les commentaires ajoutés à la réédition du texte en 1714, lesquels précisent qu'il faut bien lire, d'une part, « à l'usage des lieux de leur établissement » et, d'autre part, « aux Capitulations faites avec les Souverains des lieux de leur établissement ». Il y aurait donc bien deux cas de figure envisagés : les pays capitulaires (où s'appliquerait ce que les traités prescrivent) et les autres pays, chrétiens, où c'est l'usage qui dicterait les contours de cette juridiction consulaire, *Ordonnance de la marine, du mois d'aoust 1681. Commentée & conférée avec les anciennes ordonnances, & le droit écrit, avec les nouveaux règlemens concernans la marine* (Paris : Guillaume Cavelier, 1714), livre premier, titre IX, article XII, 76.

3 *Édit... portant règlement sur les fonctions judiciaires et de police qu'exercent les consuls de France en pays étrangers... Registré au Parlement d'Aix le 15 mai 1779* (Paris : Imprimerie royale, 1779), 1, 11.

Si l'on se place maintenant du côté des pays récepteurs des consuls étrangers, la situation est tout aussi confuse. À première vue, l'exclusivisme juridictionnel ne souffre pas la moindre exception ni en France, ni en Angleterre, ni en Espagne – pour ne retenir que ces trois exemples. Marcella Aglietti, qui a compulsé d'importants pans de la littérature juridique de l'époque, a pourtant relevé des exceptions à cette règle générale. Ainsi, la convention du Pardo signée en 1769 entre la France et l'Espagne reconnaît une compétence juridictionnelle aux consuls des deux nations dans les affaires maritimes et commerciales impliquant leurs ressortissants à l'étranger[4]. La chose est cependant énoncée en des termes très vagues et, a priori, une telle juridiction ne concernait que les conflits pouvant survenir entre les capitaines de navires et leurs marins. La situation était encore plus confuse au sein des États italiens, où s'appliquaient une grande variété de règles contradictoires. Dans le royaume de Naples, la situation semble claire puisqu'il y existait une juridiction particulière pour juger les litiges impliquant des ressortissants étrangers : les *giudicci delegati*[5]. Mais, ce n'est pas le cas dans la Sicile voisine où siégea, dans les années 1720, une *judicature court* présidée par le consul britannique de Messine, avant d'être supprimée à la demande des marchands britanniques eux-mêmes[6]. À Livourne, la création d'un tribunal consulaire français fut prévue par le traité signé entre les deux pays en 1713 et son existence est attestée par différents témoignages de la première moitié du XVIIIe siècle[7]. Mais son activité n'a laissé aucune trace archivistique et on ne le connaît finalement que par les contestations dont il fut l'objet dans la seconde moitié du siècle, au moment de l'offensive dirigée par la nouvelle dynastie des Lorraine contre toute forme d'atteinte à la souveraineté du grand-duché[8]. À Gênes, Marcella

4 Marcella Aglietti, « El debate sobre la jurisdicción consular en la Monarquía hispánica (1759–1769) », dans *Los cónsules de extranjeros en la Edad Moderna y a principios de la Edad Contemporánea*, éd. Marcella Aglietti *et al.* (Madrid : Ediciones Doce Calle, 2013), 116.

5 Roberto Zaugg, « Entre diplomatie et pratiques judiciaires : la condition des étrangers sous l'Ancien Régime napolitain », *Revue d'histoire maritime* 17 (2013) : 321–333.

6 Salvatore Bottari, « Consoli inglesi nella Sicilia del Settecento : funzioni istituzionali e attività informali », dans *De l'utilité commerciale des consuls. L'institution consulaire et les marchands dans le monde méditerranéen (XVIIe–XXe siècle)*, éd. Arnaud Bartolomei *et al.* (Rome : École française de Rome, 2018), 215–216.

7 Guillaume Calafat, « Les juridictions du consul : une institution au service des marchands et du commerce ? Introduction », dans *De l'utilité commerciale des consuls. L'institution consulaire et les marchands dans le monde méditerranéen (XVIIe–XXe siècle)*, éd. Arnaud Bartolomei *et al.* (Rome : École française de Rome, 2018), 143–153.

8 Marcella Aglietti, *L'istituto consolare tra Sette e Ottocento. Funzioni istituzionali, profilo giuridico e percorsi professionali nella Toscana granducale* (Pise : ETS, 2012), 46–47.

Aglietti mentionne également l'existence de fonctions judiciaires des consuls espagnols, lesquels étaient autorisés à présider un « tribunal » qui siégeait dans leur « maison »[9]. Mais, là encore, ces tribunaux n'ont laissé aucun fonds d'archive significatif qui permettrait d'attester qu'ils ont bien fonctionné à un moment donné – alors même que le fonctionnement ordinaire d'une juridiction est supposé produire une masse documentaire qui laisse nécessairement des traces (procédures d'instruction, ordonnances de juge, expéditions des sentences rendues, recours en appel, etc.).

Ce déficit d'archives constitue finalement une énigme, qui laisse planer un sérieux doute sur le fait que de tels tribunaux consulaires aient réellement pu avoir une activité dans l'Europe moderne. De ce point de vue, les archives du consulat de France à Cadix, que nous avons assidument fréquentées pendant une vingtaine d'années, sont tout à fait conforme à l'impression générale qui se dégage d'autres postes consulaires. Si elles n'apportent aucun témoignage sur l'existence d'un tribunal consulaire à Cadix, elles recèlent en revanche une très riche documentation sur trois formes institutionnelles qui s'en rapprochent : elles contiennent d'importantes séries documentaires émanant de la chancellerie du consulat de France à Cadix, ce qui ne laisse aucun doute possible sur le fait que les consuls étrangers en Espagne disposait du droit d'exercer une juridiction volontaire, notamment vis-à-vis de leurs ressortissants ; elles contiennent par ailleurs des traces assez rares et dispersées, mais suffisamment significatives pour nous informer sur l'évolution de la juridiction spécifique dont bénéficiaient les étrangers dans l'Espagne moderne (l'institution des juges-conservateurs) ; elles contiennent enfin d'importantes séries illustrant les diverses fonctions judiciaires que pouvaient être amenés à exercer les consuls français en Espagne en dehors du cadre formel d'un tribunal consulaire. Dans la mesure où nous avons déjà eu l'occasion de consacrer divers travaux au fonctionnement de la chancellerie consulaire[10], nous nous concentrerons ici sur ces deux derniers points.

---

9 Aglietti, « El debate sobre la jurisdicción consular », 111.

10 Arnaud Bartolomei, « Actes notariés *versus* actes de chancellerie. Le rôle des chancelleries consulaires françaises dans la formalisation des actes commerciaux et civils (XVIIIe–XIXe siècle) », *Mélanges de l'École française de Rome, Italie et Méditerranée modernes et contemporaines* 128, n° 2, mis en ligne le 23 novembre 2016, consulté le 16 septembre 2024. URL : http://journals.openedition.org/mefrim/2801; DOI : https://doi.org/10.4000/mefrim.2801. Arnaud Bartolomei et Anne Brogini, « De la réglementation aux pratiques marchandes. L'enregistrement des actes commerciaux à la chancellerie consulaire à Cadix et à Tunis (XVIIIe et XIXe siècles) », dans *De l'utilité commerciale des consuls. L'institution consulaire et les marchands dans le monde méditerranéen (XVIIe–XXe siècle)*, éd. Arnaud Bartolomei *et al.* (Rome : École française de Rome, 2018), 173–198.

3 L'exercice de la juridiction contentieuse des étrangers dans l'Espagne moderne : la juridiction des juges-conservateurs

La littérature sur l'institution des juges-conservateurs dans l'Espagne moderne demeure assez lacunaire, malgré l'existence de quelques travaux anciens et d'apports plus récents qui sont utiles pour préciser les contours de cette juridiction singulière[11]. Il convient en premier lieu de rappeler le caractère tout à fait ordinaire d'une telle juridiction parmi les institutions de la monarchie hispanique. Au XVIIe siècle, notamment, la couronne a de plus en plus systématiquement doté des corps particuliers de sa population de « protecteurs », lesquels étaient chargés en premier lieu de fonctions de représentations auprès de la cour. Cela fut d'abord le cas pour les populations amérindiennes qui furent dotées d'un protecteur (« protector de indios »), puis la pratique s'étendit à bien d'autres catégories de la population[12]. C'est dans ce même contexte et avec des attributions assez similaires que fut créé le premier juge-conservateur des étrangers lors de la signature du traité de 1607 entre les royaumes de Castille et d'Aragon et la Hanse. L'institution fut ensuite ouverte à d'autres nations à l'occasion de la signature du traité de 1648, avant d'être étendue à la France lorsque le traité des Pyrénées de 1659 lui concéda la clause de la nation la plus favorisée[13]. Elle aurait ensuite fonctionné pendant plusieurs décennies, avant d'être l'objet de remises en cause et de contestations de plus en plus systématiques dans la seconde moitié du XVIIIe siècle.

Bien que l'existence d'une telle juridiction n'ait jamais été mise en doute, les modalités de son exercice demeurent assez floues. Quelques grands traits peuvent cependant être dégagés. La juridiction des juges-conservateurs s'exerçaient en premier lieu dans des litiges mixtes impliquant des étrangers. Selon les auteurs et les sources, il est dit qu'elle s'appliquait à tout le contentieux civil et criminel, ou seulement au civil, et qu'elle s'étendait aussi bien aux litiges dans lesquels les étrangers étaient demandeurs que ceux dans lesquels ils étaient défendeurs, ou seulement lorsqu'ils étaient défendeurs[14]. Comme l'a parfaitement exposé Albert Girard, cette imprécision dans la définition du

11 Sur le sujet, la référence demeure : Albert Girard, *Le commerce français à Séville et à Cadix au temps des Habsbourg. Contribution à l'étude du commerce des étrangers en Espagne aux XVIe–XVIIe siècles* (Paris : E. de Boccard, 1932). Plus récemment, voir : Ana Crespo Solana, « El juez conservador ¿ Una alternativa al cónsul de la nación ? », dans *Los cónsules de extranjeros en la Edad Moderna y a principios de la Edad Contemporánea*, éd. Marcella Aglietti *et al.* (Madrid : Ediciones Doce Calle, 2013), 23–33.

12 Óscar Recio Morales, « Gobernar la alteridad. El 'Protector de Extranjeros' en España (siglos XVI–XVIII) », *Mélanges de la Casa de Velázquez* 51, n° 1 (2021), 15–38.

13 Girard, *Le commerce français à Séville*, 149–150.

14 Cette dernière option est celle soutenue par Ana Crespo Solana dans « El juez conservador », 31.

ressort des juges-conservateurs tient pour l'essentiel à la confusion juridique qui caractérisait le déploiement de cette institution dès son origine. Une même confusion règne au sujet du profil des magistrats de cette juridiction. En effet, si ces fonctions étaient généralement attribuées à des agents des couronnes de Castille ou d'Aragon – typiquement des juges des *audiencias*, les plus hautes cours de justice espagnoles –, il semblerait qu'elles aient aussi pu être exercées par des consuls étrangers, ce qui est plus surprenant[15]. Cependant, même dans ce dernier cas et même si les juges-conservateurs étaient désignés par les communautés étrangères sur lesquelles ils exerceraient ensuite leur autorité, cette institution ne peut en aucune manière être considérée comme une juridiction étrangère ou extra-territoriale : c'est bien le souverain espagnol qui nommait, en dernier ressort, les juges-conservateurs, et ces derniers évoluaient dans le cadre juridictionnel des royaumes espagnols (leurs décisions pouvant par exemple faire l'objet d'appels devant les conseils de Castille ou de Guerre, selon les contextes). Il faut enfin remarquer que ces juges-conservateurs sont unanimement décrits dans la littérature administrative et diplomatique de l'époque comme un « privilège » pour les étrangers, leur permettant d'accéder à une justice plus rapide, moins coûteuse et moins partiale que celle dispensée par les juridictions civiles ordinaires et que c'est précisément pour cette raison qu'ils furent l'objet d'une vaste entreprise de remise en cause au cours de la seconde moitié du XVIIIe siècle. Les sources que nous avons pu consulter ne permettent pas réellement de déterminer qui se trouvait effectivement à l'origine de cette remise en cause de l'institution des juges-conservateurs. Elle a pu s'inscrire dans le mouvement plus large des réformes bourboniennes qui visaient à restaurer la souveraineté de l'État et à rationaliser son fonctionnement. Mais, il n'est pas impossible non plus qu'elle ait été le fait de corps sociaux qui, à l'image des juges des tribunaux de commerce (les *consulados*) ou même des juges ordinaires, étaient intéressés par la suppression de cette institution qui empiétait sur leurs propres prérogatives juridictionnelles et les privait d'une partie de leurs revenus. Si nos données ne nous autorisent pas à trancher ce dernier point, elles permettent en revanche de préciser la chronologie des décisions qui conduisirent finalement à la suppression progressive des juges-conservateurs.

Une première mesure adoptée en 1758 consista à confier la juridiction des juges conservateurs aux gouverneurs militaires des provinces d'Espagne, ce qui revenait de facto à faire bénéficier les étrangers du « for militaire », à savoir des

---

15 Le cas du consul anglais à Malaga, qui exerçait les fonctions de juge-conservateur de sa nation au XVIIe siècle est évoqué dans Olivier Caporossi, « Le statut des Anglais dans l'Espagne de Philippe IV (1621–1665) ou la construction d'une nation par la monarchie catholique », *Anglophonia/Caliban* 17 (2005), 170.

privilèges juridictionnels dont bénéficiaient habituellement les militaires. Ce changement fut largement dénoncé par la communauté française de Malaga, par exemple, ou dans d'autres communautés nationales, mais concrètement il n'impliqua aucun bouleversement d'ensemble de l'institution (plutôt un transfert de compétences d'un fonctionnaire vers un autre). À Cadix, le juge-conservateur était d'ailleurs déjà auparavant le gouverneur militaire de la place[16]. L'offensive suivante, qui eut lieu en 1764, eut un plus large retentissement puisqu'elle visait cette fois-ci à mieux distinguer les étrangers *transeuntes*, qui devaient continuer à jouir du « for militaire », des *domiciliados* qui seraient pour leur part placés dans le ressort des juridictions ordinaires[17]. Un bras de fer opposa alors les représentants diplomatiques et consulaires habilités en Espagne au gouvernement pour limiter au maximum le nombre de *domiciliados* et obtenir que tous les négociants (habituellement considérés comme les seuls sujets réellement « utiles ») soient inclus dans la catégorie des *transeuntes*. Enfin, à Cadix, la troisième manche de cet affrontement eut lieu en 1780, lorsque le Consulado de la ville exigea l'application d'une mesure datant de 1767 qui lui attribuait la gestion de la totalité du contentieux commercial local, celui concernant les Espagnols aussi bien que celui concernant les étrangers[18]. Cette décision souleva évidemment un tonnerre de protestations parmi le personnel diplomatique et consulaire du port andalou, français en premier lieu[19], sans que l'on puisse déterminer avec certitude qui sortit gagnant de l'affrontement. Ainsi, en 1786 par exemple, le Consulado réaffirma sans la moindre ambiguïté sa juridiction sur les commerçants français dans un courrier échangé avec le consul de France, lequel avait essayé de lui contester ce

16 Sur le cas de Malaga, voir Ahmed Farouk, « La dégradation du commerce français vue de Malaga dans la seconde moitié du XVIIIe siècle », *Mélanges de la Casa de Velázquez* 25 (1989), 227.

17 Óscar Recio Morales, « Las reformas carolinas y los comerciantes extranjeros en España : actitudes y respuestas de las ‹ naciones › a la ofensiva regalista, 1759–1793 », *Hispania. Revista española de historia* 72, n° 240 (2012), 75.

18 Centre des Archives diplomatiques de Nantes (dorénavant CADN), Cadix, 136PO/260, courrier des députés de la nation française de Cadix à l'ambassadeur de France à Madrid, 9 juin 1780.

19 Archives nationales (dorénavant AN), AE/B/III/343, mémoire non daté, intitulé « Précis des traités de commerce de l'Espagne avec la France et les autres nations d'Europe, et privilèges accordés à leurs sujets ». AN, AE/B/III/334, mémoire E, intitulé « Observations sur l'affaire de la juridiction militaire », non daté, et mémoire C, intitulé « Exposition des titres sur lesquels les français faisant le commerce en Espagne sont fondés à jouir du for militaire et la relation de ce qui a été pratiqué à cet égard dans ce royaume depuis 1648, date du traité de Munster, avec les villes hanséatiques, jusqu'au 28 juin de l'année 1764 », non daté.

droit[20]. Pourtant, vingt ans plus tard, le gouverneur militaire de la ville semblait également avoir conservé certaines de ses attributions en matière de juridiction commerciale. En 1804, le Conseil des Indes rejeta ainsi l'instruction d'un dossier impliquant une compagnie étrangère de Cadix (Martens y Von Lengerk) au prétexte que Nicolas Martens était un étranger *transeunte*, qu'à ce titre, il devait bénéficier du « fuero de extranjería » et que l'affaire relevait donc du ressort du gouverneur militaire de Cadix et du Conseil de Guerre et non de celui du Consulado et du Conseil des Indes[21]. Or, les sources de la pratique judiciaire disponibles ne permettent pas pour l'heure de lever cette incertitude. A priori, les archives des gouverneurs militaires comme celles du Conseil de Guerre n'ont pas été conservées. Celles émanant de la justice rendue par le Consulado ne l'ont pas été non plus. Seules les procédures d'appel élevées contre les décisions de ce dernier, qui étaient traitées par le Conseil des Indes, ont donc été conservées (dans la série « Consejo de Indias » de l'Archivo Histórico Nacional). Or, si cette série contient un certain nombre d'affaires concernant des étrangers, à l'image de celle impliquant Nicolas Martens, il s'avère cependant difficile de déterminer si tout le contentieux commercial relevait de la juridiction de ces deux institutions, ou seulement une partie de celui-ci (le contentieux mixte ? les affaires concernant le seul commerce des Indes ?). Enfin, nous sommes encore plus mal informés au sujet du contentieux non commercial impliquant les étrangers, même si l'affaire Jean-Pierre Priou, sur laquelle nous reviendrons plus loin, suggère que les gouverneurs de la ville avaient conservé dans les années 1790 une très large juridiction sur les affaires criminelles les concernant.

Si nos recherches, en l'état, soulèvent donc plus de questions sur le fonctionnement effectif de la juridiction des étrangers dans la seconde moitié du XVIIIe siècle qu'elles n'en résolvent, elles se révèlent en revanche du plus grand intérêt pour appréhender les enjeux réels que recouvraient ces luttes d'influence. Ainsi, les motivations du Consulado de Cadix auraient été claire-

---

20 Le Consulado rappelait au consul de France à Cadix, qui contestait la juridiction commerciale exercée sur les affaires des Français, que « Este Consulado está autorizado por Real Orden de SM de 21 de octubre del año proximo pasado para conocer en las primeras instancias de los negocios de comercio y demás de su inspección, en que sean reconvenidos extranjeros transeuntes, y adornado con al Juridicción militar, para determinar conforme a su instituto y ordenanzas en sus causas, como lo hace respecto de los españoles ; y el cumplimiento exacto con que observa y observará esta regia resolución le priva de todo arbitrio para admitir la protesta ». CADN, Cadix, 136PO/363, courrier du Consulado et de la Junta de Comercio, 28 mars 1786.

21 Archivo Histórico Nacional, Consejos, leg. 21448, « Instancia de Francisco de Pastor y Calle, sindico de la quiebra de Juan Ferrando del comercio de Cádiz contra Nicolas Martens Von Lengerk y Cía del comercio de Cádiz sobre paga de 54 000 pesos » (1804).

ment intéressées si l'on en croit les protestations que soulevèrent ses prétentions. La revendication de la juridiction sur les faillites et le contentieux commercial impliquant des étrangers, comme l'obligation qu'il tenta de leur imposer de tenir leurs livres de compte en castillan ou de déposer les actes de leurs sociétés auprès de son greffe, témoigneraient d'une même volonté de la part du Consulado, de limiter la participation illégale des marchands étrangers de Cadix à la Carrera de Indias – ou, du moins, d'empêcher qu'ils puissent y participer sans passer par l'intermédiaire des négociants espagnols immatriculés auprès du Consulado (les *cargadores*). Face aux risques d'une justice partiale rendue par des membres du Consulado « qui n'ont d'autre but et d'autre principe que l'exclusif » et qui « voudraient se défaire de la concurrence des étrangers et surtout des Français », les officiels français opposaient « la justice militaire [qui] est rendue par les gouverneurs, officiers de grade, ordinairement gens de mérite et justes, contenus d'ailleurs par la crainte des plaintes que peut porter contre eux un ambassadeur qui peuvent leur faire beaucoup de tort »[22]. Le propos révèle d'ailleurs le véritable intérêt du for militaire : il s'agissait d'une justice moins indépendante du pouvoir central et dans l'exercice de laquelle les diplomates étrangers pouvaient donc plus facilement s'ingérer.

De tels arguments mettant en avant la bienveillance dont bénéficiaient les étrangers devant la justice militaire et l'acharnement dont ils auraient été l'objet devant les juridictions ordinaires sont récurrents dans la littérature administrative et polémique de l'époque. Mais, faute de pouvoir réaliser un véritable travail d'évaluation de la qualité de la justice rendue par les différentes juridictions, on ne pourra malheureusement pas trancher ce point, ni faire la part des choses entre ce qui relève de simples préjugés, voire de lieux communs discursifs, et ce qui relèverait des réelles iniquités systémiques des institutions judiciaires espagnoles.

4 Les fonctions judiciaires du consul de France à Cadix

Peu explicites sur le fonctionnement du système juridictionnel auquel étaient effectivement intégrés les étrangers en Espagne, les archives du consulat de France à Cadix sont en revanche beaucoup plus riches et utiles pour préciser les différentes fonctions judiciaires que les consuls étaient amenés à exercer auprès de leurs ressortissants. Nous en distinguerons plus précisément trois.

22 AN, AE/B/III/334, mémoire E, intitulé « Observations sur l'affaire de la juridiction militaire », non daté.

4.1 *Le consulat de France à Cadix, antichambre des juridictions françaises*

Une première fonction judiciaire des consuls nous est révélée par la consultation de deux liasses apparaissant dans l'inventaire du fonds sous le titre « Affaires judiciaires et contentieuses », ainsi que par celle des registres de chancellerie du consulat. Il s'agit de la fonction de greffier que le consul, ou son chancelier, était amenée à exercer dans des contentieux judiciaires instruits en France, par des juridictions françaises. Les consuls français devaient par exemple veiller à remettre à leurs administrés les assignations judiciaires qui leur étaient transmises par les juridictions françaises. Ils pouvaient également effectuer, à la demande de ces dernières, certains actes procéduraux. Dans l'affaire opposant les sieurs Couchet et Guibaud de Bordeaux au sieur Delicterie, « la bourse consulaire de Bordeaux » a ainsi mandaté le consul de France à Cadix pour qu'il procède, à l'occasion d'une escale de ce dernier dans la baie de Cadix, à la saisie du montant d'une créance qu'il devait aux deux négociants bordelais[23]. Dans une autre affaire, impliquant Jacques Dubois et Cie de Lyon aux sieurs Mahiet Lemoine frères et Cie de Cadix, c'est du « tribunal de la Conservation des foires de Lyon » qu'émane l'ordonnance que le consul doit faire exécuter par son prévôt, laquelle prescrit une fois encore de saisir des marchandises faisant l'objet d'un contentieux chez un négociant français établi à Cadix[24]. On retrouve également le témoignage de procédures similaires dans les registres d'actes de chancellerie. Ainsi, en 1819, le tribunal civil des Basses-Pyrénées mandata le consul de France à Cadix pour qu'il fasse effectuer par son chancelier un « compulsoire » des livres de la compagnie Hedembaig Lapadu frères et Cie, afin de pouvoir statuer sur un contentieux opposant ces derniers à l'un de leurs associés, domicilié à Bayonne[25]. Pendant plusieurs jours, le chancelier consulta donc les livres de comptes de la société, consigna dans des procès-verbaux les informations extraites et transmit ensuite ces procès-verbaux au tribunal du demandeur. D'une manière générale, et sur la base du dépouillement de tous les registres de chancellerie de l'année 1820, nous pouvons estimer que près du tiers des actes enregistrés cette année-là relevaient de cette fonction de greffe des tribunaux français[26].

---

23 CADN, Cadix, 136PO/398, requête des sieurs Rey et Brandembourg, Cadix, 2 novembre 1784.

24 CADN, Cadix, 136PO/398, requête du sieur Guillaume Delotz, Cadix, 20 mars 1767.

25 CADN, Cadix, 136PO/251, fol. 77 et suivants, compulsoire des livres de la compagnie Hedembaig Lapadu frères et Cie, Cadix, 21 septembre au 10 décembre 1819.

26 Parmi ces actes, on relève notamment la remise de 16 significations judiciaires émanant de tribunaux français, qui représentent à elles seules le cinquième des 80 actes enregistrés cette année-là (CADN, Cadix, 136PO/251).

Quoique généralement négligée dans la littérature scientifique, cette mission dévolue aux consuls n'est pas inintéressante car elle révèle une facette méconnue de la fonction consulaire : dans ce cas, en effet, le consul n'apparait pas tant comme le « protecteur » de ses ressortissants expatriés vis-à-vis d'une une justice locale supposée hostile, mais plutôt comme celui des intérêts des justiciables résidant en France vis-à-vis de leurs partenaires résidant à l'étranger : le protecteur des intérêts des Français « absents », en quelque sorte.

4.2 *Le consulat de France à Cadix, chambre de justice*

La seconde fonction judiciaire que pouvaient être amenés à exercer les consuls est celle de juge. Deux cas de figure se présentent alors. Dans le premier cas, nous disposons d'abondants témoignages documentaires sur l'existence et le fonctionnement de tribunaux consulaires formels, mais il s'agit alors de tribunaux extraordinaires (les tribunaux de jugement des prises corsaires), qui ne siégeaient que dans des contextes particuliers (en temps de guerre). Dans le second cas de figure, les affaires traités sont beaucoup plus ordinaires (conflits entre gens de mer, arbitrages commerciaux), mais nous ne disposons alors que de preuves documentaires très ténues et nous n'avons aucune certitude que les décisions rendues par les consuls l'aient été devant des « tribunaux » formellement constitués, ni même qu'elles relèvent effectivement du champ de la justice.

Il n'est pas lieu de documenter précisément ici le fonctionnement des tribunaux chargés de juger des prises corsaires, lesquels étaient présidés par les consuls français établis dans les ports étrangers, puis par les « commissaires de la république » à partir de la Révolution et jusqu'à la fin de l'Empire[27]. Nous rappellerons donc seulement que, jusqu'au printemps 1796, c'étaient les consuls qui étaient chargés de l'instruction et du jugement en première instance des prises conduites par des corsaires français dans les ports étrangers[28]. Puis, ces fonctions furent attribuées aux chanceliers des consulats entre 1796 et 1800, avant d'être restituées aux « commissaires de la République » à partir de mars 1800[29]. Les décisions pouvaient être contestées, d'abord en appel, devant

---

27 Nous renvoyons pour cela à Florence Le Guellaf, *Armements en course et droit des prises maritimes 1792–1856* (Nancy : Presses universitaires de Nancy, 1990).

28 Voir le *Règlement concernant les prises qui seront conduites dans les ports étrangers et les formalités que doivent remplir les consuls de Sa Majesté qui y sont établis,* Paris, le 8 novembre 1779, art. 4 et 5 (cité dans Le Guellaf, *Armements en course*, 535).

29 L'arrêté du 6 germinal an VIII prévoit que les commissaires de la république soient assistés par deux assesseurs choisis « parmi les citoyens français immatriculés et établis dans le lieu de leur résidence » (Florence Le Guellaf, *Armements en course*, 536).

les tribunaux civils les plus proches (celui de la Loire-Inférieure, pour Cadix), puis à Paris, devant le Tribunal des prises (devenu le Conseil des prises à partir de 1800). La procédure suivie par ces deux dernières instances, qui sont l'objet de la thèse de Florence Le Guellaf, est bien connue. Mais il n'en est pas de même pour celle appliquée dans les consulats des ports étrangers. Il faudrait pour pallier cette lacune exploiter systématiquement les très riches fonds des consulats de France conservés dans les Archives diplomatiques de Nantes. Mais la tâche est immense. Les archives du seul consulat de France à Cadix comprennent des milliers de documents relatifs au jugement des quelques 200 prises conduites par des corsaires français dans les ports du ressort du consulat pendant la période des guerres révolutionnaires et impériales. Nous avons eu l'occasion de publier par ailleurs un premier travail réalisé à partir de ces documents, portant sur les aspects économiques de la course française gaditane à cette époque[30]. Nous nous contenterons donc de rappeler ici qu'il existe dans ces fonds des preuves indiscutables de l'existence et du fonctionnement régulier d'un tribunal ayant pour siège le consulat de France pendant toute la période allant de 1797 à 1808 (date où le consulat fut fermé, du fait de l'intervention napoléonienne en Espagne). En atteste, parmi beaucoup d'autres, le jugement que nous avons intégralement reproduit en annexe[31], qui montre que chaque prise faisait d'abord l'objet d'une instruction minutieuse, diligentée par le consul (pose de scellés, nomination d'experts, recueil de témoignages, examen de pièces, etc.), puis qu'un jugement explicite se référant précisément à des lois françaises, avant que ne soient précisées, une fois la sentence prononcée, les mesures exécutoires prévues et les possibilités de recours offertes aux justiciables. Notons que, dans ce cas, le jugement était rendu au consulat sous le « seing » du consul et le « contreseing » du chancelier. Tous les éléments constitutifs d'un tribunal siégeant en bonne et due forme sont donc bien réunis dans ce cas.

S'il ne fait aucun doute qu'un tribunal siégeait régulièrement au sein du consulat de France à Cadix en temps de guerre pour juger les prises réalisées par les corsaires français, nous ne disposons pas des mêmes certitudes documentaires dans les autres domaines où une telle juridiction est supposée avoir pu s'exercer ordinairement (contentieux commercial ou civil, litiges entre gens de mer). Un examen attentif des deux liasses « affaires judiciaires et contentieuses » conservées parmi les archives rapatriées prouve cependant qu'il arrivait au consul de France à Cadix de rendre des décisions de justice

30 Arnaud Bartolomei, *Les marchands français de Cadix et la crise de la Carrera de Indias (1778–1828)* (Madrid : Casa de Velázquez, 2017), chapitre 4, 201 et suivantes.

31 Voir annexe n° 1.

dans des contentieux opposant des Français établis à Cadix ou encore, entre ces derniers et leurs partenaires établis en France. Ces derniers attendaient en effet du consul établi par la France dans la ville qu'il veille à ce que les agents auxquels ils avaient confié leurs affaires se comportent comme ils étaient en droit de l'attendre. Le 18 octobre 1763, par exemple, le consul de France à Cadix convoqua le sieur François Maguet à la chancellerie du consulat, à la demande de son associé, Julien Cossé, qui résidait en France. Le plaignant reprochait à son associé de ne pas lui avoir procuré « des comptes en règle tels qu'il doit les donner » et de s'être « contenté après bien des sollicitations réitérées de la part du suppliant de lui présenter des brouillons de notes sur lesquels il est impossible de constater la nature des marchandises, ni la vente d'icelles ». Il demandait donc au consul d'exiger de François Maguet qu'il présente des comptes en bonne et due forme, ce que fit le consul dans son ordonnance. Cette dernière fut notifiée par le prévôt du consulat audit Maguet, lequel déclara s'en remettre volontairement à la « justice de M. le Consul ». Une note ajoutée en marge du document précise que « cette affaire a été renvoyée [?] au moyen de 25 piastres que le sieur Maguet doit payer au sieur Cossé »[32]. Dans une autre affaire, le consul est requis pour faire constater l'absence de la signature d'un concordat par le fondé de pouvoir des créanciers français intéressés dans la faillite de la société Gilly frères, ce qui donne également lieu à la prise d'une ordonnance[33]. D'autres cas évoquent la convocation « extra-judiciairement » de deux négociants français de Cadix (François Allègre et David Rivet), intéressés dans la faillite d'une société lyonnaise[34] ou encore des actes de saisie de marchandises ou de créances entre les mains de marchands français de Cadix dans des litiges les opposants à leurs partenaires établis en France (de même nature que celle concernant Guillaume Delotz, déjà mentionnée). Il n'est cependant pas toujours aisé de distinguer parmi ces affaires, les cas dans lesquels le consul se limite à être un greffier au service d'autres juridictions de ceux dans lesquels il rend explicitement des décisions de justice. Ni d'ailleurs de déterminer, dans ces derniers cas, s'il agit « extrajudiciairement », dans un rôle qui relèverait de l'arbitrage, ou dans le cadre d'une procédure civile clairement définie (impliquant par exemple la possibilité de recours). En outre, la matérialité même des jugements rendus nous échappe complètement : le consul dispose-t-il d'assesseurs ? une audience a-t-

32 CADN, Cadix, 136PO/398, ordonnance rendue à la requête de Julien Cossé, Cadix, 14 octobre 1763.

33 CADN, Cadix, 136PO/398, ordonnance rendue à la requête de Quentin frères, Cadix, 15 septembre 1768.

34 CADN, Cadix, 136PO/398, ordonnance rendue à la requête de Jean-Marie Madinier, Cadix, 15 décembre 1768.

elle eu lieu ? dans une salle dédiée au consulat ? En l'état de l'enquête, toutes ces questions demeurent sans réponse.

4.3 *Le consulat de France à Cadix, intercesseur auprès des juridictions autochtones*

La fonction judiciaire des consuls finalement la mieux établie d'un point de vue documentaire relève de la mission de protection que les consuls devaient à leurs ressortissants, notamment devant les juridictions autochtones. L'affaire suivante, qui impliqua deux des commis du négociant français Jean-Pierre Priou, accusés de propagande révolutionnaire, est de ce point de vue assez emblématique des ingérences diplomatiques auxquelles pouvait donner lieu l'inculpation de ressortissants français à Cadix, ainsi que des acteurs composant la chaîne de protection qui était activée dans ce genre d'affaire. L'alerte sur le cas de Jean-Pierre Priou fut donnée le 25 mai 1791 par les deux députés de la nation française de Cadix à l'ambassadeur de France à Madrid pour dénoncer la visite « illégale » dont fut l'objet son domicile et obtenir « la levée des arrêts qui ont été ordonnés »[35]. Le 14 juin 1791, l'ambassadeur de France à Madrid en donnait un récit circonstancié au ministre des Affaires étrangères : le 10 mai, un juge ordinaire espagnol (*alcalde*) s'était rendu au domicile de Jean-Pierre Priou « pour y reconnaître ses papiers » et le lendemain, il décida de « l'assigner à résidence » ; le 9 juin, il revint pour écouter les témoignages des deux commis et décida de les mettre aux arrêts. Cette décision suscita immédiatement une première représentation du consul auprès du gouverneur de la ville (Quevedo), pour lui réclamer « la juridiction et les privilèges pour [les] deux nationaux détenus dans la prison royale de cette ville ». Le 14 juin 1791, Quevedo répondit au consul en lui affirmant avoir transmis sa réclamation à l'*alcalde mayor* de la ville (Don Jospeh Miret) et en l'assurant que, « en sa qualité de juge conservateur des étrangers », il se chargerait « de faire observer les privilèges dont doivent jouir les individus de votre nation, toutefois qu'il ne s'y rencontrera pas d'inconvénient aussi puissant que ceux dont il s'agit dans la circonstance présente ». L'affaire évolua peu par la suite, jusqu'à ce qu'elle soit enterrée lors de la rupture de 1793 entre la France et l'Espagne, mais le consul souligna cependant que l'intervention de l'ambassadeur de France à Madrid (M. d'Urtebise) auprès du secrétaire d'État espagnol Floridablanca avait permis que les pièces de l'accusation soient communiquées à la défense. On apprenait encore par un courrier suivant, daté du 10 février 1792, que d'Urtebise avait aussi obtenu la levée de l'assignation à résidence sous réserve du versement d'un cautionnement.

35 AN, AE/B/III/362, Français arrêtés et expulsés d'Espagne (1790–1797), dossier « Jean-Pierre Priou ».

Le cas ne manque pas donc d'intérêt puisqu'il confirme tout autant l'enchevêtrement juridictionnel au sein duquel se trouvaient les étrangers (le gouverneur militaire n'ayant autorité que sur une partie des affaires les concernant) et la multiplicité des acteurs que la diplomatie française était susceptible de mobiliser pour s'ingérer dans le cours de la justice espagnole (depuis les « députés de la Nation » à Cadix jusqu'au ministre des Affaires étrangères à Paris, en passant par le consul de France à Cadix et l'ambassadeur à Madrid). D'une manière générale, il ne fait cependant aucun doute que l'assistance judiciaire apportée aux ressortissants français en Espagne, y compris sous la forme d'ingérences diplomatique, faisait pleinement partie des tâches auxquelles les consuls en poste consacraient une part significative de leur temps. Il s'agit d'ailleurs là d'un constat que nous pouvons aisément généraliser dans le temps et dans l'espace puisque les observations faites ans les fonds des consuls français au Mexique nous ont conduit à des conclusions tout à fait similaires.

5 Protection et assistance judiciaire des ressortissants français dans le Mexique indépendant (1821–1840)

Le contexte juridictionnel présenté par le Mexique indépendant n'a naturellement plus le moindre rapport avec celui de l'Espagne d'Ancien Régime : dans cette république fédérale, il n'existe aucune institution similaire à celle des juges-conservateurs et la seule juridiction reconnue pour les consuls étrangers est la juridiction « volontaire », à savoir le droit de disposer d'une chancellerie pour enregistrer les actes de leurs ressortissants. Du fait de la rapide suppression des *consulados* dans les années 1820 et jusqu'au rétablissement des tribunaux de commerce dans les années 1840, il n'existe plus non plus de juridiction spécifique pour les commerçants. Ainsi, tous les étrangers, qu'ils soient commerçants ou non, relevaient des tribunaux civils et criminels ordinaires. Cependant, l'action des autorités diplomatiques et consulaires françaises établies dans le pays prenait des formes d'assistance et d'ingérence assez similaires à celles que nous avons documentées pour l'Espagne des années 1790. Les deux cas que nous rapportons ici en témoignent.

Le premier, l'affaire Labourdive, concerne un modeste boutiquier français de Veracruz, qui louait depuis 1837 une boutique (*pulpería*) auprès d'un riche négociant de la ville (Troncoso), moyennant le paiement d'un loyer mensuel et le versement initial d'un *traspaso* (sorte de droit de bail) de 300 pesos[36]. Or,

36 CADN, Mexico, 432PO/181, dossier 83, « Pierre Labourdive. Son procès contre le sieur Troncoso », courrier du consul de France à Veracruz à l'ambassadeur de France à Mexico, 14 décembre 1840.

en décembre 1838, Étienne Labourdive fut expulsé de Veracruz, comme tous les ressortissants français du Mexique, à l'occasion de la guerre des Pâtisseries qui opposa la France de la monarchie de Juillet au Mexique pendant les quelques mois de l'hiver 1838–1839. Il revint aussitôt la paix signée, mais il découvrit à son retour que son propriétaire avait cédé le fonds de commerce à un tiers et qu'il refusait de lui verser la moindre somme pour l'indemniser de la perte de son *traspaso*. Labourdive fit alors appel au consul de France à Veracruz qui lui conseilla de se porter en justice. Il eut la satisfaction d'obtenir un jugement favorable en première instance à Veracruz (après, cependant, qu'un premier juge, intimidé par l'influence de Troncoso, se fut désisté de l'affaire, si l'on en croit le récit que fit le consul du déroulement des faits). Troncoso fit cependant appel de la décision devant le tribunal supérieur de Jalapa, où il obtint gain de cause en raison, toujours d'après le consul, de la collusion existante entre le juge et l'avocat commis d'office (qui n'était autre que le neveu de Troncoso). Au moment où le consul rapporta ces faits à l'ambassadeur de France à Mexico, l'affaire devait dorénavant être examinée en dernière instance par la « haute cour de Mexico ».

Cette affaire nous livre au moins trois éclairages intéressants sur la condition juridique des étrangers dans le Mexique indépendant. Elle apporte un énième exemple des dénonciations de partialité et de vénalité dont étaient habituellement l'objet les juridictions autochtones de la part des étrangers et de leurs représentants. Ainsi, le consul français remarquait à propos tribunal de Jalapa, que « sept ans passés de résidence ici m'ont appris [que ses] dispositions [sont] toujours hostiles aux étrangers » avant de constater, désabusé, que « dans ce malheureux pays, les plus sages et les plus justes prévisions, sont presque toujours en défaut et se tournent en folles illusions »[37]. Derrière ces habituels lieux communs discursifs, transparait cependant le fonctionnement d'un système judiciaire mexicain probablement moins déficient que ne le prétend le consul français. Ainsi l'existence de trois niveaux de juridiction tout autant que celle d'une procédure d'avocat commis d'office témoignent de la relative modernité et rationalité du système juridictionnel mexicain, y compris pour le traitement d'un contentieux civil assez modeste. De même, le jugement rendu en première instance par le magistrat de Veracruz et l'éloge que rendit à ce dernier le consul français prouvent que la corruption de la justice mexicaine n'était pas généralisée[38]. Enfin, l'affaire révèle le type d'assistance

37 *Ibidem.*

38 « Honneur au magistrat qui, appelé à juger entre le pauvre et le riche, entre le plébéien et le patricien, entre l'étranger et le naturel du pays, a rendu un jugement si remarquable par son impartialité, se montrant ainsi l'écho fidèle et énergique de la loi ! Honneur à Monsieur Lebrija ! », *ibidem.*

que l'institution consulaire française pouvait apporter à ses ressortissants : outre les conseils dispensés à Labourdive pour qu'il porte plainte devant les tribunaux et sollicite un avocat commis d'office, le consul de France à Veracruz aura finalement adressé deux courriers au juge de première instance pour exposer le cas du boutiquier français et le défendre, puis il en fit de même vis-à-vis du juge d'appel – lequel se serait cependant contenté de répondre, comme le faisait souvent l'administration mexicaine en pareil cas, que « le tribunal procéderait dans cette affaire conformément aux lois et sans autre considération que celle de la justice ». Il octroya également un soutien financier significatif à Labourdive tout au long de la procédure puisque, par deux fois il lui avança 25 pesos – mais il ne l'assista en revanche pas directement devant les tribunaux et ne lui proposa pas de lui servir d'interprète. Enfin, il recommanda ce dernier à l'attention de l'ambassadeur lorsque l'affaire fut transférée à Mexico, persuadé par le juge de première instance que l'influence de ce dernier, « comme ministre de France, [pouvait] beaucoup dans cette affaire et que c'[était] d'elle principalement qu'il [fallait] en espérer le succès »[39].

Le second cas que nous avons étudié, l'affaire Abello, a pour sa part fait l'objet d'un long courrier circonstancié adressé par l'ambassadeur de France (Deffaudis) au ministre mexicain des relations extérieures (Cuevas) et il présente de nombreux points communs avec le premier[40]. On retrouve en effet dans cette affaire une très classique dénonciation de la « sauvagerie » et de la gallophobie avec laquelle aurait été traitée une justiciable française (Madame Abello) par les autorités locales de la province de Zacatecas[41]. Les iniquités subies seraient notamment liées à la collusion et à la vénalité de ces mêmes autorités, puisque la modeste ressortissante française se serait trouvée en conflit avec un *alcade* comptant dans sa famille Joaquín de Llaguna à savoir « l'Espagnol le plus influent ici » et le « roi de Zacatecas » – ce qui expliquerait notamment les tentatives d'intimidation dont auraient été l'objet les témoins sollicités et finalement les lenteurs éprouvées par l'affaire. Mais, là encore, en dépit de la modestie des acteurs et des sommes en jeu, la chaîne de protection offerte par la diplomatie française fut activée jusqu'à son sommet comme en témoigne précisément ce courrier, directement adressé par le ministre de France au gouvernement central mexicain. On ne peut cependant déterminer, une fois de plus, si la conclusion extrêmement désabusée de Deffaudis (« de

39 *Ibidem.*

40 CADN, Mexico, 432PO/223, minute d'un courrier de Deffaudis à Cuevas, supprimer, 13 juin 1837.

41 « Le soussigné, ministre ..., a eu l'honneur de rendre compte à son Ex. M. le Ministre des Relations Extérieures, le 5 du mois du sauvage abus de pouvoir commis contre Mme Abello, sujette de sa Majesté, par le sr. A. Hoyo, sr Alcalde du Fresnillo », *ibidem.*

nombreux français [sic] qui ont eu à se plaindre des autorités du pays, n'ont obtenu d'autres résultats que de payer des frais de justice ») relève d'un constat objectif ou d'un simple lieu commun discursif. Il fait en revanche peu de doutes que c'est la réitération *ad nauseam* de tels propos dans les correspondances consulaires et diplomatiques qui finit par convaincre les autorités françaises, d'abord, qu'il fallait impérativement prévoir, dans le traité que la France négociait alors avec le gouvernement mexicain, la « création d'une juridiction consulaire sur les nationaux pour les soustraire à la vénalité des juges »[42], puis, dans un second temps, de la nécessité d'une intervention militaire destinée à obtenir le respect dû au « pavillon national » – ce qui finit par se produire, à l'occasion de la guerre des Pâtisseries en 1838.

6 Conclusion

En dépit de ses limites et de ses lacunes, notre enquête permet donc de dégager deux conclusions qui semblent assez solidement établies et qui pourront servir à la réflexion plus générale portée par le présent ouvrage. La première vient très largement confirmer l'inexistence dans les pays dits « de Chrétienté » (aussi bien dans l'Espagne d'Ancien Régime que dans le Mexique indépendant), de tribunaux consulaires français ordinaires – le cas du tribunal des prises de Cadix faisant exception. Les consuls de France étaient certes amenés à prendre des décisions de nature judiciaire, à effectuer des actes de procédures ou à intervenir dans des affaires judiciaires en cours, mais aucun des documents que nous avons consultés ne suggère l'existence d'une juridiction formelle et souveraine, similaire à celles qui fonctionnaient, dans ces mêmes années, dans les pays capitulaires ou en Asie orientale. En revanche, la diversité et la pluralité des fonctions judiciaires assumées par les consuls renvoient inévitablement à une même mission dévolue à l'institution consulaire que ces tribunaux ayant opéré en Asie ou en Afrique du Nord, celle de « protection » des ressortissants français. Dans un cas comme dans l'autre en effet, c'est la nécessaire protection de sujets (ou de citoyens français) vis-à-vis de justices autochtones toujours considérées a priori comme, au mieux « vénales »et « partiales », au pire, « barbares » et « sauvages », qui a justifié le déploiement de la protection offerte par l'institution consulaire.

42 Centre des Archives diplomatiques de La Courneuve, Correspondance Consulaire et Commerciale, Mexico, reg. 3, fol. 210, courrier du consul général de France au ministre des Affaires étrangères, Mexico, 12 décembre 1830.

Annexe : Jugement d'une prise corsaire rendu le 28 brumaire an VII par le consul de France à Cadix (CADN, Cadix, 136/PO/195, Registre des sentences et des condamnations de prises, folios 35 et 36)

R. Roquesante, consul général de la République française en Andalousie, résident à Cadix, ayant vu et examiné les différents papiers et documents qui m'ont été présentés et remis dans un paquet fermé par trois différents cachets et que concernent le navire suédois le Jean du port d'environ cent soixante tonneaux et commandé par le capitaine Jean Frédéric Swinhufurd venant du port de Liverpool avec destination pour Livourne où il portait une cargaison de porcelaine et autres fayences [*sic*], esprit de vitriol, harengs fumés et quelque mercerie pour compte et risque d'un négociant anglais de Londres par qui ledit navire fut fretté pour se rendre à Liverpool et y prendre la susdite cargaison pour Livourne, lequel a été capturé et pris dans le détroit de Gibraltar le dix-sept du présent mois de Brumaire par les corsaires français l'Affrique, capitaine Richelme, le Furet, capitaine Fouet, le Démocrate, capitaine Garnier, et la Couleuvre, capitaine Nicolas, qui après s'être emparé de ses papiers de mer, l'ont amariné et conduit à Algésiras, ainsi qu'il conste par le procès-verbal dressé à bord des susdits corsaires le dit jour dix-sept brumaire.

Par les déclarations prises à Algésiras par le tribunal militaire de ce lieu au capitaine Swinhufurd à son pilote et à deux hommes de son bord, il résulte que le navire suédois le Jean se trouvant à Londres a été fretté par un négociant anglais de ce lieu, pour se rendre à Liverpool à l'effet d'y prendre la cargaison ci-devant. […].

Considérant que tout démontre de la manière la plus évidente que les diverses marchandises composant la cargaison du navire le Jean sont du cru et de fabriques anglaises et qu'elles appartiennent à des sujets du Roy d'Angleterre, ce qui est en contravention aux articles III, IV et V du Règlement du 21 octobre 1744, qui ordonne que les marchandises du cru et fabrique des ennemis et celles appartenant à des sujets également ennemis qui seront trouvées à bord des bâtiments neutres seront déclarées de bonne prise.

Considérant également que la loi du vingt-neuf nivôse an 6e porte par l'article premier l'état des navires en ce qui concerne leur qualité de neutre ou d'ennemi sera déterminé par leur cargaison, en conséquence tout bâtiment trouvé en mer chargé en tout ou en partie de marchandises provenant d'Angleterre ou de ses possessions sera déclaré de bonne prise quelque soit le propriétaire de ces denrées ou marchandises.

J'ai en vertu des susdits règlements et loi et des pouvoirs et facultés qui me sont attribués par la Loi, jugé et déclaré de bonne prise, le navire le Jean et son entier chargement en faveur des corsaires l'Affrique, le Furet, le Démocrate et la Couleuvre, permis en conséquences aux capteurs d'en disposer de la manière la plus avantageuse à leurs intérêts, à charge pour eux d'en effectuer la vente dans la chancellerie de ce consulat et d'acquitter sur le montant d'icelle les droits dus aux Invalides de la marine en se conformant pour le surplus aux lois et règlements concernant les prises.

À charge également par eux de déposer le produit de ladite vente dans la caisse d'une maison solvable autorisée par moi et à la satisfaction des intéressés jusqu'à l'expiration du délai prescrit par la loi pour l'appellation du présent jugement ou, en cas d'appel, jusqu'au jugement définitif du tribunal du Département de la Loire-Inférieure.

Donné au Consulat Général de la République Française en Andalousie sous mon seing sous le Sceau de ce consulat et le contreseing du Chancelier par intérim d'icelui, Cadix le vingt-huit brumaire an septième de la République française une et indivisible [signatures] Roquesante, Sicard, chan. par intérim.

Bibliographie

Aglietti, Marcella. *L'istituto consolare tra Sette e Ottocento : Funzioni istituzionali, profilo giuridico e percorsi professionali nella Toscana granducale.* Pise : ETS, 2012.

Aglietti, Marcella. « El debate sobre la jurisdicción consular en la Monarquía hispánica (1759–1769) ». Dans *Los cónsules de extranjeros en la Edad Moderna y a principios de la Edad Contemporánea*, édité par Marcella Aglietti, Manuel Herrero Sánchez et Francisco Zamora Rodríguez, 105–118. Madrid : Ediciones Doce Calle, 2013.

Bartolomei, Arnaud. « Actes notariés versus actes de chancellerie : Le rôle des chancelleries consulaires françaises dans la formalisation des actes commerciaux et civils (XVIIIe–XIXe siècle). » *Mélanges de l'École française de Rome, Italie et Méditerranée modernes et contemporaines* 128, n° 2 (2016).

Bartolomei, Arnaud. *Les marchands français de Cadix et la crise de la Carrera de Indias (1778–1828)*. Madrid : Casa de Velázquez, 2018.

Bartolomei, Arnaud and Anne Brogini. « De la réglementation aux pratiques marchandes : l'enregistrement des actes commerciaux à la chancellerie consulaire à Cadix et à Tunis (XVIIIe et XIXe siècles) ». Dans *De l'utilité commerciale des consuls : L'institution consulaire et les marchands dans le monde méditerranéen (XVIIe–XXe siècle)*, édité par Arnaud Bartolomei, Guillaume Calafat, Mathieu Grenet et Jörg Ulbert, 173–198. Rome : École française de Rome, 2018.

Bottari, Salvatore. « Consoli inglesi nella Sicilia del settecento : funzioni istituzionali e attività informali ». Dans *De l'utilité commerciale des consuls : L'institution consu-

laire et les marchands dans le monde méditerranéen (*XVIIe–XXe siècle*), édité par Arnaud Bartolomei, Guillaume Calafat, Mathieu Grenet et Jörg Ulbert, 211–222. Rome : École française de Rome, 2018.

Calafat, Guillaume. « Les juridictions du consul : une institution au service des marchands et du commerce ? Introduction ». Dans *De l'utilité commerciale des consuls : L'institution consulaire et les marchands dans le monde méditerranéen* (*XVIIe–XXe siècle*), édité par Arnaud Bartolomei, Guillaume Calafat, Mathieu Grenet et Jörg Ulbert, 143–153. Rome : École française de Rome, 2018.

Caporossi, Olivier. « Le statut des Anglais dans l'Espagne de Philippe IV (1621–1665) ou la construction d'une nation par la monarchie catholique ». *Anglophonia/Caliban*, n° 17 (2005) : 163–173.

Crespo Solana, Ana. « El juez conservador ¿ Una alternativa al cónsul de la nación ? » Dans *Los cónsules de extranjeros en la Edad Moderna y a principios de la Edad Contemporánea*, édité par Marcella Aglietti, Manuel Herrero Sánchez et Francisco Zamora Rodríguez. Madrid : Ediciones Doce Calle, 2013.

Farouk, Ahmed. « La dégradation du commerce français vue de Malaga dans la seconde moitié du XVIIIe siècle ». *Mélanges de la Casa de Velázquez* 25, n° 1 (1989) : 221–237.

Girard, Albert. *Le commerce français à Séville et à Cadix au temps des Habsbourg : Contribution à l'étude du commerce des étrangers en Espagne aux XVIe–XVIIe siècles*. Paris : E. de Boccard, 1932.

Le Guellaf, Florence. *Armements en course et droit des prises maritimes 1792–1856*. Nancy : Presses universitaires de Nancy, 1990.

Recio Morales, Óscar. « Las reformas carolinas y los comerciantes extranjeros en España : actitudes y respuestas de las « naciones » a la ofensiva regalista, 1759–1793 ». *Hispania. Revista española de historia* 72, n° 240 (2012) : 67–94.

Recio Morales, Óscar. « Gobernar la alteridad. El "Protector de Extranjeros" en España (siglos XVI–XVIII) ». *Mélanges de la Casa de Velázquez* 51, n° 1 (2021) : 15–38.

7

Les actions judiciaires des consulats d'Italie aux États-Unis (1890–1915)

Thibault Bechini

1 Introduction

En juin 1912, faisant état des entraves que posent les tribunaux californiens à la liquidation des successions des Italiens de son ressort, Ferdinando Daneo, tout récemment nommé consul général d'Italie à San Francisco, déclare que « dans cette partie, au moins, de l'Amérique, il est nécessaire de mettre de côté les principes de droit international que nous sommes habitués à regarder comme indiscutables en Europe »[1]. Si pareille affirmation souligne indubitablement la manière dont les débats et les propositions relatifs au droit international irriguent la pensée des représentants des puissances occidentales au tournant des XIXe et XXe siècles, elle renvoie également aux nombreuses actions judiciaires intentées à la même époque par les consulats d'Italie aux États-Unis afin de faire valoir les droits de leurs compatriotes – y compris ceux qui résident dans la péninsule – dans les successions italiennes ouvertes sur le sol américain.

L'invocation des principes du droit international ne surprend guère sous la plume d'un fonctionnaire du Royaume d'Italie, diplômé de l'Institut « Cesare Alfieri » de Florence, où il s'est formé au cours des années 1890[2]. Le droit international moderne, « science et technique des transactions économiques et

1 Archivio storico diplomatico del Ministero degli Affari Esteri (désormais ASDMAE), Commissariato Generale dell'Emigrazione (désormais CGE), b. 17, chemise « Norme per liquidazione di successioni e infortuni », r. 228/2712, de Daneo (consul général d'Italie à San Francisco) au CGE, San Francisco, 7 juin 1912.

2 Fondé en 1875 sur le modèle de l'École libre des sciences politiques de Paris, l'*Istituto Cesare Alfieri* dispense à ses étudiants une solide formation en droit ; Giovanni Spadolini, *Il « Cesare Alfieri » nella Storia d'Italia. Nascita e primi passi della scuola fiorentina di Scienze sociali* (Florence : Le Monnier, 1975). On trouvera une notice biographique de Ferdinando Daneo dans AA. VV., *La formazione della diplomazia nazionale (1861–1915). Repertorio bio-bibliografico dei funzionari del Ministero degli Affari Esteri* (Rome : Istituto Poligrafico e Zecca dello Stato, 1987), 231.

 | HTTPS://DOI.ORG/10.1163/9789004755192-009

relations politiques qui enjambent les frontières »[3], se constitue comme discipline à la fin du XIXe siècle. Socle de la définition et de la défense des droits des individus, les principes du droit international sont promus par l'Institut de Droit international, fondé en 1873 à l'initiative d'un aréopage de juristes libéraux qui se réunissent annuellement en congrès et dont on peut considérer, avec Philippe Rygiel, qu'ils représentent « une notable partie des premiers experts de l'immigration »[4]. Conscients de l'interdépendance des différentes parties du monde, ces juristes examinent, entre autres questions qui ont trait aux migrations internationales, tout ce qui touche aux droits civils et privés des étrangers ; leurs propositions et leurs idées sont largement diffusées au sein des classes politiques et des appareils d'État des puissances occidentales[5]. À l'institutionnalisation progressive de ce nouveau champ de la pensée juridique répondent quelques grands procès successoraux qui, au cours des années 1880, soulèvent des problèmes de droit international. Tel est le cas de l'affaire « Samana contre Samana », étudiée par Jessica M. Marglin, qui, bien qu'elle concerne d'importantes sommes d'argent et implique des juristes de réputation internationale, met en lumière des questions qui n'ont rien d'exceptionnel et que l'on ne saurait cantonner aux seules mobilités d'élites[6].

En effet, de manière plus ordinaire, la mobilisation des principes du droit international, telle qu'elle apparaît dans la correspondance du consul général d'Italie à San Francisco, fait écho au vaste travail jurisprudentiel entrepris par les consulats d'Italie aux États-Unis depuis le milieu des années 1890, à l'occasion d'affaires successorales parfois très modestes. Ces actions judiciaires qui visent, dans un premier temps, à défendre le droit des sujets italiens à succéder et posséder aux États-Unis même s'ils n'y demeurent pas, dans un second temps, à réaffirmer la tutelle consulaire sur les successions italiennes ouvertes sur le sol américain, s'accompagnent d'une abondante production administrative de la part des services consulaires concernés. Dans la seconde moitié des années 1900, le travail bureaucratique réalisé quotidiennement dans les consulats d'Italie traduit tout autant la recrudescence des affaires d'héritage litigieu-

3 Philippe Rygiel, « De savants juristes au service de la France. Les experts du droit international auprès du Quai d'Orsay, 1874–1918 », dans *Experts et expertises en diplomatie. La mobilisation des compétences dans les relations internationales du congrès de Westphalie à la naissance de l'ONU*, éd. Stanislas Jeannesson, Fabrice Jesné, Éric Schnakenbourg (Rennes : Presses universitaires de Rennes, 2018), 221.

4 Philippe Rygiel, *L'ordre des circulations ? L'Institut de Droit international et la régulation des migrations (1870–1920)* (Paris : Éditions de la Sorbonne, 2021), 21.

5 Ibid., 10.

6 Jessica M. Marglin, « La nationalité en procès : droit international privé et monde méditerranéen », *Annales. Histoire, Sciences Sociales* 73, n° 1 (janvier 2018) : 116–117.

ses que le souhait de faciliter, par la standardisation des procédures, l'exercice des fonctions judiciaires des consuls comme administrateurs des successions de leurs nationaux – les liquidation successorales nécessitant, aux États-Unis, l'intervention des tribunaux locaux.

On doit signaler ici ce que ce travail bureaucratique à finalité judiciaire doit à la création par le Royaume d'Italie, au cours des années 1900, de services d'assistance juridico-légale spécialement destinés aux migrants italiens et à leurs familles. Ces services, connus sous le nom d'*uffici legali* et rattachés à quelques consulats italiens aux États-Unis, bénéficient du soutien financier du *Commissariato Generale dell'Emigrazione*, fondé dans le sillage de la grande loi sur l'émigration dont se dote l'Italie en 1901[7]. Apparus entre 1906 et 1911, les *uffici legali* viennent appuyer les actions judiciaires en matière successorale des consulats de New York (1906), Philadelphie (1907), Chicago (1908), Denver (1909), San Francisco (1909) et Boston (1911). Ils font appel à l'expertise d'avocats américains, à la fois avocats-conseils des consulats concernés et directeurs de ces nouveaux services d'assistance légale ; seul le bureau de Boston est placé sous la supervision directe du consul[8]. Si l'activité juridique, définie comme « le traitement des affaires qui supposent la mise en œuvre de catégories de droit[9] », est au cœur du travail réalisé au sein des *uffici legali*, elle ne saurait se comprendre sans les instances judiciaires intentées devant les cours de justice américaines au nom de sujets italiens et avec l'appui des services consulaires. En outre, la mise en place des *uffici legali* favorise la multiplication des collaborateurs permanents affiliés à l'appareil juridique dont dispose le ministère italien des Affaires étrangères et dont les bureaux d'assistance légale institués aux États-Unis sont les prolongements à l'étranger[10]. Le recrutement de ces collaborateurs se fait dans le milieu des avocats qui gravitent autour des consulats, hommes de loi qui, antérieurement à la création des *uffici legali*, avaient l'habitude de conseiller les consuls lorsqu'une affaire épineuse se présentait. À l'instar des juristes à l'expertise desquels l'administration centrale française fait appel à la même époque, les avocats liés aux consulats italiens prennent

7 Pour un aperçu synthétique de la genèse et des dispositions contenues dans cette loi, voir Dolores Freda, *Governare i migranti. La legge sull'emigrazione del 1901 e la giurisprudenza del Tribunale di Napoli* (Turin : G. Giappichelli, 2017), 56–74.

8 Sur la naissance des *uffici legali* aux États-Unis, nous nous permettons de renvoyer à Thibault Bechini, « Les successions des Italiens morts aux États-Unis, entre assistance légale et acculturation administrative des familles transnationales (années 1900–Première Guerre mondiale) », Mélanges de l'École française de Rome. Italie et Méditerranée modernes et contemporaines 136, n°1 (janvier 2024) : 147–168.

9 Rygiel, « De savants juristes », 205.

10 Exception faite du Canada, où un bureau d'assistance légale est fondé en 1911, les *uffici legali* n'existent nulle part ailleurs qu'aux États-Unis.

part à l'élaboration de la doctrine juridique du Royaume d'Italie dans le contexte de « juridicisation des rapports internationaux » qui accompagne la mondialisation accélérée des échanges au cours des trois décennies qui précèdent la Première Guerre mondiale[11].

Le passage des principes juridiques à leur mise en œuvre judiciaire s'observe, précisément, à l'occasion des liquidations successorales dans lesquelles sont impliquées les services consulaires italiens. De fait, les successions, problème classique de l'histoire économique et sociale, fournissent une entrée possible pour l'étude des appareils consulaires, de leur construction, de leur développement et de leurs rapports avec les juridictions locales[12]. Aussi le problème des successions italiennes liquidées aux États-Unis au tournant des années 1890 et 1900 permet-il de s'interroger sur la manière dont ces affaires privées, portées en justice, concourent à la réaffirmation des prérogatives consulaires au nom des principes du droit international.

2 Penser par cas

Les années 1880–1890 correspondent à un moment d'épanouissement conjoint des phénomènes d'ouverture mondiale et de nationalisation des sociétés, de globalisation des échanges et de renouveau des politiques protectionnistes[13]. C'est dans ce contexte que s'enracinent différentes mesures prises aux États-Unis afin de restreindre les droits des étrangers en matière de possession et de transmission des biens fonciers détenus dans l'Union, qui est pourtant une des destinations privilégiées des migrants européens et, en particulier, des

11 Philippe Rygiel a montré comment l'administration centrale du Quai d'Orsay recourait, dans le dernier tiers du XIXe siècle, aux services de juristes, toujours plus nombreux, collaborateurs permanents du ministère des Affaires étrangères, sans en être fonctionnaires ; il a souligné le rôle décisif qu'ils jouèrent dans la définition d'une doctrine juridique française en matière de politique extérieure. Rygiel, « De savants juristes », 221.

12 La tutelle consulaire sur les successions *ab intestat* est, par exemple, un enjeu de l'affirmation de la présence consulaire italienne en Argentine au lendemain de la proclamation du Royaume d'Italie. Alors que le gouvernement argentin a concédé aux consuls italiens la faculté d'administrer les successions de leurs ressortissants morts sans avoir fait de testament, l'application de la loi est entravée par les autorités argentines elles-mêmes, probablement afin d'éviter que les capitaux accumulés dans le pays par les migrants italiens n'en sortent. Catia Brilli, « Una nación en camino. La migración genovesa y la afiliación consular en las costas atlánticas (1770–1865) », *Mélanges de la Casa de Velázquez* 51, n° 1 (janvier 2021) : 110–112.

13 Nicolas Delalande, *La lutte et l'entraide. L'âge des solidarités ouvrières* (Paris : Éditions du Seuil, 2019), 195.

migrants italiens[14]. Les dispositions adoptées par plusieurs États fédérés sont amplement commentées par les consuls des puissances européennes qui s'y trouvent en poste et qui ne manquent pas d'en référer à la représentation diplomatique dont ils dépendent. Parfois même, un travail de synthèse, qui repose sur l'analyse approfondie des législations des différents États relativement aux droits civils et privés des étrangers, est entrepris, tel celui auquel se livre Charles-Adolphe de Chambrun, conseiller judiciaire de l'ambassade de France aux États-Unis. Chargé de remettre au ministère français des Affaires étrangères un mémoire « au sujet des droits conférés aux étrangers en matière immobilière par la législation des différents États de l'Union », le conseiller judiciaire ne peut que constater la différence de traitement qui, du fait des lois de certains États et malgré l'existence de traités, existe entre les étrangers résidant aux États-Unis et les citoyens américains établis en Europe[15]. Et de se permettre quelques réflexions personnelles que lui inspire son long séjour outre-Atlantique :

> Depuis mon arrivée aux États-Unis, l'esprit public s'est considérablement rétréci. En 1870 ou en 1871, les idées de réciprocité de traitement étaient acceptées par presque tous les hommes éclairés. Aujourd'hui, c'est à peine si elles trouveraient appui dans une minorité[16].

Les autorités consulaires italiennes se trouvent confrontées à cette problématique lorsque la Louisiane établit, en 1894, une taxe de 10 % au profit du *Charity Hospital* de La Nouvelle-Orléans sur les successions des étrangers qui détiennent des biens immobiliers dans l'État[17]. Le cas se présente d'une ressortissante

14 Entre 1880 et 1900, près d'un million d'Italiens entrent aux États-Unis ; au cours des vingt années suivantes, ce sont plus de trois millions de migrants italiens qui foulent le sol américain. Matteo Pretelli, *L'emigrazione italiana negli Stati Uniti* (Bologne : Il Mulino, 2011), 36.

15 Centre des archives diplomatiques de La Courneuve (désormais CADLC), 426/QO/443, Direction commerciale, Sous-direction consulaire, Conventions consulaires, Droits des étrangers en matière immobilière aux États-Unis, r. 134, de Roustan (ambassadeur de France aux États-Unis) à Ribot (ministre des Affaires Étrangères), Washington, 18 juin 1891.

16 Ibid., copie de la lettre de Chambrun (conseiller judiciaire près l'ambassade de France aux États-Unis) à Roustan (ambassadeur de France aux États-Unis), New York, 16 juin 1891.

17 Les consulats de La Nouvelle-Orléans semblent avoir été avisés de l'entrée en vigueur de cette disposition au moyen d'une lettre-circulaire envoyée en novembre 1894 ; on trouve un exemplaire de cette lettre au Centre des archives diplomatiques de Nantes (désormais CADN), 340PO/A/474, chemise « Successions des Français : règles et réactions françaises à la nouvelle taxe de 10 % établie au profit de l'hôpital de la Charité sur les

italienne, Amélie Rixner, épouse du comte Giuseppe de Sarzana, décédée en Sicile au début de l'année 1895 mais possédant des biens en Lousiane, hérités de ses parents. Dès leurs prémices, les développements judiciaires de cette liquidation successorale retiennent l'attention du régent du consulat d'Italie à La Nouvelle-Orléans ; ils constituent, selon lui, « un cas d'intérêt non seulement pour l'Italie, mais encore pour les autres puissances[18] ». Aussi s'empresse-t-il de consulter ses collègues qui représentent les autres États étrangers en Louisiane. Les réponses qu'il obtient sont unanimes : de l'avis des différents consuls, la taxe adoptée par la Louisiane ne peut être appliquée sur les successions des ressortissants de puissances qui ont signé des traités de réciprocité avec les États-Unis. Le régent du consulat d'Italie, après s'être entretenu avec le chancelier de la *Civil District Court* devant laquelle la succession est appelée, préfère s'abstenir de toute démarche officielle et entre en relations avec un certain Jules Andrieu, agent d'affaires de la défunte, lequel a d'ores et déjà embauché un homme de loi, l'avocat Claiborne, pour défendre les intérêts des ayants droit qui demeurent en Sicile[19]. Bien qu'il ne se fasse pas représenter devant les tribunaux locaux, le régent du consulat suit de près l'affaire par l'entremise de Claiborne.

L'affaire Rixner est l'occasion d'échanger des renseignements avec les autres consulats en vue de dégager, à partir des suites judiciaires de cette liquidation successorale, des principes irréfutables du point de vue du droit international. Comme « question posée à la pratique »[20], le cas Rixner passionne les consuls des différentes puissances représentées à La Nouvelle-Orléans[21]. Il ressort des

successions vacantes en Louisiane », lettre-circulaire du *Board of Administrators* (*Charity Hospital*) à Bosseront d'Anglade (consul de France à La Nouvelle-Orléans), La Nouvelle-Orléans, 21 novembre 1894.

18 ASDMAE, Rappresentanze diplomatiche negli USA (1848–1901), b. 46, fasc. 354 (pos. 3, fasc. 74), « Legge della Louisiane relativa alle successione di cittadini esteri. Successione di Rixner Amelia, 1895 », r. 327, de Naselli (régent du consulat d'Italie à La Nouvelle-Orléans) à Fava (ambassadeur d'Italie aux États-Unis), La Nouvelle-Orléans, 6 mai 1895.

19 Ibid.

20 Ainsi que le soulignent Jean-Claude Passeron et Jacques Revel, « avant de devenir des exemples cités et invoqués, les cas sont d'abord des questions posées à la pratique » ; les cas font problème et appellent « l'instauration d'un cadre nouveau de raisonnement », qui passe par la mise en relation du cas considéré avec d'autres cas, afin de parvenir à « une autre formulation de la normalité et de ses exceptions ». Jean-Claude Passeron, Jacques Revel, « Penser par cas. Raisonner à partir de singularités », dans *Penser par cas*, éd. Jean-Claude Passeron et Jacques Revel (Paris : EHESS, 2005), 10–11.

21 Voir, par exemple, la correspondance échangée par le consul de France avec ses collègues à La Nouvelle-Orléans dans CADN, 340PO/A/474, chemise « Successions des Français : règles et réactions françaises à la nouvelle taxe de 10 % établie au profit de l'hôpital de la Charité sur les successions vacantes en Louisiane ».

échanges entre le consul d'Italie et le consul de France que le précédent judiciaire créé par la succession d'un citoyen français, dont les héritiers ont été défendus devant les tribunaux louisianais par l'avocat du consulat, est de peu de portée pour les cas à venir, la sentence rendue se fondant exclusivement sur le principe de la non-rétroactivité des lois contenu dans le traité conclu entre la France et les États-Unis : le défunt était, de fait, décédé avant l'entrée en vigueur de la taxe instaurée au profit du *Charity Hospital*[22]. Aussi le régent du consulat d'Italie se réjouit-il que l'affaire Rixner soit « le premier cas pratique d'application de la loi en question, [grâce auquel] on verrait poser un précédent pour les cas futurs, une maxime de grande utilité pour les petites successions dans lesquelles les héritiers n'auraient pas les moyens d'ester en justice »[23]. Conscient de l'importance que revêt l'issue de l'affaire Rixner, l'avocat du consulat d'Angleterre demande à Claiborne « la permission de s'unir à lui dans la défense du principe en débat : » la proposition est favorablement accueillie par l'avocat des héritiers italiens[24]. En fin de compte, une sentence rendue en appel par la Cour suprême de la Louisiane au début de l'année 1896 établit que, Amélie Rixner étant sujette du Royaume d'Italie au moment de son décès, la clause de la nation la plus favorisée s'applique en faveur de sa succession, en vertu du traité signé en 1871 entre le Royaume d'Italie et les États-Unis ; à ce titre, ses héritiers sont exemptés du paiement de la taxe instaurée en 1894[25].

Le cas Rixner permet au consulat d'Italie de disposer d'une jurisprudence qui pose le principe de la nation la plus favorisée pour la liquidation des successions de ses ressortissants en Louisiane ; cette jurisprudence est obtenue à moindres frais, grâce aux dépenses engagées par les héritiers eux-mêmes qui, il est vrai, recueillent des biens évalués à près de 70 000 dollars. Le régent du consulat a très bien perçu, dès le début de l'affaire, tout le profit qu'il pouvait tirer de ce cas judiciaire pour l'exercice à venir de ses prérogatives en matière successorale. Ainsi qu'il l'écrit lui-même, tandis que l'avocat Claiborne se

---

22 ASDMAE, Rappresentanze diplomatiche negli USA (1848–1901), b. 46, fasc. 354 (pos. 3, fasc. 74), « Legge della Louisiane relativa alle successione di cittadini esteri. Successione di Rixner Amelia, 1895 », r. 327, de Naselli (régent du consulat d'Italie à La Nouvelle-Orléans) à Fava (ambassadeur d'Italie aux États-Unis), La Nouvelle-Orléans, 6 mai 1895.

23 Ibid.

24 ASDMAE, Rappresentanze diplomatiche negli USA (1848–1901), b. 46, fasc. 354 (pos. 3, fasc. 74), « Legge della Louisiane relativa alle successione di cittadini esteri. Successione di Rixner Amelia, 1895 », r. 327, de Naselli (régent du consulat d'Italie à La Nouvelle-Orléans) à Fava (ambassadeur d'Italie aux États-Unis), La Nouvelle-Orléans, 16 mai 1895.

25 Le texte intégral de cette sentence se trouve dans « Succession of Amelie Rixner, Wife of Count Joseph de Sarzana », *Reports of Cases Argued and Determined in the Supreme Court of Louisiana* 48, n° 1 (1897) : 552–564.

montre pleinement dévoué à la cause de ses clients, lui est surtout intéressée par le « principe général »[26] que le procès met en jeu. De fait, ce qui importe au régent du consulat, c'est de pouvoir liquider de petites successions italiennes de manière avantageuse pour leurs ayants droit sans avoir à faire les frais d'un procès.

3 Multiplier les actions judiciaires ?

Au tournant des années 1890 et 1900, la multiplication des petites successions qui impliquent des défunts étrangers dont les héritiers ne résident pas aux États-Unis soulève de nouvelles questions. Aussi le règlement des successions italiennes sur le sol américain au début du XXᵉ siècle requiert-il, bien souvent, l'assistance juridico-légale des services consulaires du Royaume d'Italie, qui s'engagent dans des instances judiciaires qui visent, elles aussi, à créer une jurisprudence assise sur les principes du droit international.

L'action des *uffici legali*, créés dans la seconde moitié des années 1900, est ici déterminante. À la fin des années 1900, le cas Ghio est très discuté dans les milieux consulaires et diplomatiques italiens ; il suscite également l'intérêt des autres puissances représentées aux États-Unis. L'affaire concerne la succession d'un ouvrier italien, Giuseppe Ghio, mort en Californie en avril 1908, à la suite d'un accident du travail. Elle pose la question de la procédure à suivre pour que les ayants droit du défunt, qui demeurent en Italie, puissent toucher les indemnités qui leur sont dues par la compagnie qui employait Giuseppe Ghio. En effet, dans de nombreux États américains, seul l'administrateur de la succession, judiciairement désigné, a la faculté d'intenter un procès pour obtenir ces indemnités. L'administrateur peut être choisi dans la parentèle du défunt, mais lorsque celui-ci n'a pas de famille aux États-Unis, les tribunaux locaux désignent des administrateurs d'office qui ne mettent pas toujours beaucoup de zèle à réclamer l'indemnisation des accidents du travail, notamment lorsqu'il s'agit d'administrateurs nommés à la demande des compagnies employeuses. Aussi l'affaire Ghio, portée en justice à l'initiative de l'avocat Gherini, avocat-conseil du consulat d'Italie à San Francisco, tend-elle à faire reconnaître les prérogatives des consuls en matière successorale et à leur accorder l'administration d'office des successions de leurs ressortissants. Elle

---

26 ASDMAE, Rappresentanze diplomatiche negli USA (1848–1901), b. 46, fasc. 354 (pos. 3, fasc. 74), « Legge della Louisiane relativa alle successione di cittadini esteri. Successione di Rixner Amelia, 1895 », r. 327, de Naselli (régent du consulat d'Italie à La Nouvelle-Orléans) à Fava (ambassadeur d'Italie aux États-Unis), La Nouvelle-Orléans, 6 mai 1895.

constitue la matière contentieuse à partir de laquelle est organisé, en 1909, l'*ufficio legale* rattaché au consulat d'Italie à San Francisco, bureau dont la direction est aussitôt confiée à l'avocat Gherini[27].

L'affaire, d'abord jugée par les tribunaux californiens, fait l'objet de différents appels, jusque devant la Cour suprême des États-Unis. Elle suscite une certaine émulation au sein de la nébuleuse d'hommes de loi qui conseillent les consulats d'Italie et dirigent leurs actions judiciaires. Il faut dire que le cas Ghio fait écho à bien d'autres cas portés, dans les mêmes années, devant les tribunaux d'autres États fédérés avec le soutien des services consulaires italiens. La similitude des affaires conduit notamment le consul d'Italie à Chicago à proposer que le cas Ghio soit rapproché d'une succession litigieuse ouverte dans l'Illinois, le cas Cariota[28]. Alors que la Cour Suprême s'apprête à juger le cas Ghio, le consul suggère à l'ambassadeur d'Italie que le directeur de l'*ufficio legale* de Chicago, l'avocat Hyde, plutôt que d'employer son énergie à faire appel de la sentence contraire aux intérêts italiens qu'a rendu la *Probate Court* du comté de Cook (Illinois) dans l'affaire Cariota, joigne ses efforts à ceux de l'avocat Gherini afin d'obtenir une sentence favorable au niveau fédéral[29]. À l'appui de cette proposition, le consul rappelle les résultats obtenus par l'avocat Hyde au cours des quatre années précédentes afin que soient reconnues les prérogatives consulaires en matière d'administration des successions italiennes ou, à tout le moins, que le consul ait la faculté de nommer comme administrateur des successions, au cas par cas, des citoyens américains ayant sa confiance – par exemple, l'avocat-conseil du consulat – et procédant à la liquidation sous le contrôle des tribunaux locaux[30]. Sur les conseils de l'avocat Viti, ancien directeur de l'*ufficio legale* de Philadelphie récemment promu avocat-conseil de l'ambassade d'Italie, l'ambassadeur refuse la proposition du consul de Chicago, de même qu'il finit par écarter l'avocat Gherini – dont il dénonce la « rapacité ». La défense du cas Ghio est finalement confiée au seul avocat Coudert, mandaté par l'ambassade et qui n'est lié à aucun consulat italien[31]. L'affaire Ghio et, plus largement, les actions judiciaires intentées avec le soutien financier des consulats d'Italie, crée en quelque

27 ASDMAE, CGE, b. 21, Assistenza legale, San Francisco, fasc. 73, « Affare Ghio (1909–1912) ».

28 ASDMAE, CGE, b. 18, Assistenza legale, Chicago, fasc. 64, « Affare Cariota (1911) ».

29 Ibid., r. 12155/2001, de Sabetta (consul d'Italie à Chicago) au CGE, Chicago, 3 octobre 1910.

30 Au sein de la circonscription consulaire de Chicago, de tels résultats ont été obtenus dans les États du Michigan, du Missouri, du Minnesota et de l'Ohio. Ibid., copie d'un rapport de Sabetta (consul d'Italie à Chicago) à Cusani (ambassadeur d'Italie aux États-Unis), Chicago, 10 janvier 1911.

31 Ibid., n° 137, de Cusani (ambassadeur d'Italie aux États-Unis) au CGE, Washington, 21 janvier 1911.

sorte un marché pour les avocats américains ; c'est aussi parce que de telles instances sont susceptibles de faire avancer leurs carrières qu'ils défendent avec passion les principes du droit international. L'émulation, pour ne pas dire la rivalité, qui existe entre les directeurs des différents *uffici legali* alimente l'abondante correspondance échangée autour du cas Ghio, tout en conduisant, *in fine*, à ce que soient écartés les avocats Gherini et Hyde à la demande de leur collègue Viti. Avant même qu'elle ne soit définitivement jugée, l'agitation autour de l'affaire Ghio engage l'ambassadeur d'Italie à proposer une réorganisation complète des services d'assistance juridico-légale[32].

La sentence rendue en février 1912 par la Cour suprême des États-Unis, qui repose sur une argumentation particulièrement touffue, est défavorable aux intérêts italiens. L'avocat-conseil de l'ambassade, Marcel A. Viti, l'analyse non seulement comme un « coup désastreux » porté aux fonctions consulaires en matière d'administration des successions, mais encore comme une remise en cause radicale de toutes les décisions de justice qui avaient pu être rendues favorablement aux intérêts italiens dans d'autres États que la Californie[33]. La multiplication des instances judiciaires a fini par desservir les objectifs poursuivis par les consuls italiens. Aussi n'est-on pas surpris de lire, en décembre 1913, dans la correspondance du consul d'Italie à Denver, qu'il est temps d'abandonner « le doctrinarisme juridique » et de s'intéresser à la manière dont on peut, dans la pratique, « encaisser le plus d'argent possible dû aux Italiens ». À cette fin, le consul recommande que les *uffici legali* soient placés sous la direction exclusive des consuls et non sous la supervision de leurs avocats-conseils[34].

4 Faciliter la pratique

La nécessité d'ester devant les tribunaux américains pour régler la moindre succession conduit à ce que soit envisagée, dans un certain nombre de configurations, la possibilité que les consuls interviennent dans la liquidation judiciaire des héritages comme mandataires des ayants droit qui ne résident pas aux États-Unis. Recourir à la médiation consulaire pour régler des affaires successorales, en particulier pour faire franchir des frontières à des capitaux,

32 Ibid.

33 ASDMAE, CGE, b. 21, Assistenza legale, San Francisco, fasc. 73, « Affare Ghio (1909–1912) », lettre de Viti (avocat-conseil de l'ambassade d'Italie aux États-Unis) à Cusani (ambassadeur d'Italie aux États-Unis), Washington, 1er mars 1912.

34 ASDMAE, Ambasciata d'Italia a Washington (1910–1925), b. 47, fasc. 249, copie d'un rapport du consul d'Italie à Denver au CGE, Denver, 29 décembre 1913.

n'est pas une nouveauté et la pratique est même ancienne dans la liquidation des successions négociantes[35]. Dans cette optique, les procurations apparaissent comme des actes pivots des pratiques successorales transnationales et font partie des « technologies de l'écrit » que les chancelleries consulaires ont l'habitude de manier[36].

Les procurations en bonne et due forme, que les familles doivent adresser aux services consulaires afin que les successions soient promptement liquidées, sont au nombre des questions que traite, en 1912, une circulaire du ministère italien des Affaires étrangères consacrée aux successions. Quand une procuration est nécessaire, les agents diplomatiques et consulaires doivent en informer les autorités locales péninsulaires dont relèvent les ayants droit et leur remettre, dans le même temps, le formulaire idoine[37]. Pareille insistance sur l'importance de fournir aux héritiers des modèles de procuration découle des difficultés que rencontrent fréquemment les consuls d'Italie aux États-Unis pour faire accepter par les cours de justice locales des pouvoirs rédigés selon des normes italiennes. En effet, dans certains États fédérés, non seulement le consul n'est pas reconnu comme administrateur de droit des successions laissées par ses ressortissants, mais en outre, quand bien même les héritiers qui résident en Italie l'auraient désigné comme leur mandataire à titre particulier, les procurations envoyées peuvent être déclarées irrecevables, soit qu'elles n'aient pas été rédigées selon les canons des tribunaux américains, soit que l'on dénie purement et simplement aux héritiers absents la possibilité d'être représentés par un mandataire. Ce dernier cas de figure se rencontre dans le Colorado, où le consul d'Italie à Denver signale, en 1908, l'impossibilité pour ses services de s'occuper des affaires successorales qui résultent d'accidents du travail. D'une part, une compagnie employeuse conteste le droit des héritiers absents à se faire représenter devant les tribunaux du Colorado ;

---

35 Un exemple pour le début du XIXe siècle : dans son article sur les successions des marchands tyroliens et lombards à Cadix, Klemens Kaps signale le testament de Pietro Rocco, rédigé en novembre 1810, dans lequel le testateur, originaire de Milan, prie ses exécuteurs testamentaires de s'entendre avec le consul d'Autriche à Cadix afin d'organiser le transfert de son héritage en Lombardie. Klemens Kaps, « Kinship, Trade, and Inheritance Strategies Between Generations and Space. Tyrolean and Lombard Merchants in Eighteenth-Century Cádiz », *Quaderni Storici* 58, n° 1 (avril 2023) : 75.

36 Arnaud Bartolomei *et al.*, « Introduction », dans *La chancellerie consulaire française (XVIe–XXe siècle) : attributions, organisation, agents, usagers*, éd. Arnaud Bartolomei *et al.* (Rome : École française de Rome, 2016), 313–319.

37 ASDMAE, Ambasciata d'Italia in Washington (1910–1925), b. 82, fasc. « Legislazione statale in materia di successioni », circ. n° 12 « Nuove norme per il servizio delle successioni dei connazionali morti all'estero », Antonino di San Giuliano (MAE) aux agents diplomatiques et consulaires à l'étranger, Rome, 23 mars 1912.

d'autre part, les administrateurs désignés par les tribunaux locaux pour veiller aux liquidations successorales refusent de reconnaître le consul comme mandataire des héritiers et se réservent le droit d'entrer directement en contact avec les familles des défunts[38].

La remise en ordre des *uffici legali* voulue par l'ambassadeur d'Italie à l'époque de l'affaire Ghio s'accompagne d'une réflexion sur les formulaires de procuration qui pourraient être fournis aux héritiers afin qu'ils soient correctement représentés devant les tribunaux américains. La mise au point d'un formulaire unique occupe quelque temps l'avocat-conseil de l'ambassade d'Italie à Washington, Marcel A. Viti, mais les différentes tentatives faites en ce sens semblent vouées à l'échec, tant les normes divergent d'un État fédéré à l'autre[39]. L'étude des dossiers individuels conservés pour l'année 1915 et qui concernent les successions ouvertes dans les circonscriptions consulaires de San Francisco et de Denver confirme la difficulté de disposer d'un modèle de procuration unique qui permettrait aux consuls d'Italie ou à leurs avocats-conseils de représenter les héritiers devant n'importe quelle juridiction américaine. La correspondance contenue dans ces dossiers souligne néanmoins l'attention que les services consulaires prêtent aux chaînes de certification, qu'ils décrivent précisément aux familles des défunts, afin de leur épargner des démarches inutiles[40]. Ainsi, tandis que les procurations rédigées dans la péninsule italienne et destinées aux tribunaux californiens doivent être légalisées par un consul des États-Unis en Italie, l'authentification de la signature des ayants droit par le maire de leur commune suffit pour que leur procuration soit valable dans les États du Colorado et de l'Utah[41].

À la fin du XIXe siècle, les consuls d'Italie aux États-Unis tentent de tirer parti des procès successoraux pour consolider les principes de droit international auxquels ils sont attachés et en vertu desquels ils entendent administrer les successions de leurs ressortissants. L'implication des consulats d'Italie dans

38 ASDMAE, Ambasciata d'Italia in Washington (1901–1909), b. 144, fasc. 3170.

39 ASDMAE, CGE, b. 17, fasc. 59, « Norme per la liquidazione di successioni e infortuni. Progetto di circolare per l'invio di procure agli uffici legali (1907–1912) ».

40 Sur la fonction des procédures de légalisation dans un monde juridique fragmenté, en particulier en ce qui concerne les procurations, voir la mise au point très utile d'Arnaud Bartolomei, « Actes notariés *versus* actes de chancellerie. Le rôle des chancelleries consulaires françaises dans la formalisation des actes commerciaux et civils (XVIIIe–XIXe) », dans *La chancellerie consulaire française (XVIe–XXe siècle) : attributions, organisation, agents, usagers*, eds. Arnaud Bartolomei *et al.* (Rome : École française de Rome, 2016), 385–397.

41 ASDMAE, CGE, b. 88, fasc. 917, « Ufficio di Denver », et fasc. 922, « Ufficio di San Francisco ».

la liquidation judiciaire des successions fait émerger, à la fin des années 1900, plusieurs affaires qui visent à fonder en droit l'action des *uffici legali*, bureaux d'assistance juridico-légale au service des migrants et de leurs familles. Parallèlement, une réflexion est engagée afin de faciliter, au quotidien, le bon exercice des fonctions judiciaires des consuls. La place que tiennent les procurations dans cette réflexion rappelle que les « technologies de l'écrit » peuvent aussi être des leviers de protection sociale : quand le bon formulaire de procuration est adressé aux ayants droit et qu'il est retourné dûment complété aux services consulaires – plutôt que remis aux intermédiaires douteux qui proposent parfois aux héritiers de s'occuper de leurs intérêts aux États-Unis –, il est possible de rapatrier en Italie, en toute sécurité, les petits héritages qui échoient aux familles des migrants.

Bibliographie

AA. VV. *La formazione della diplomazia nazionale (1861–1915) : Repertorio bio-bibliografico dei funzionari del Ministero degli Affari Esteri*. Rome : Istituto Poligrafico e Zecca dello Stato, 1987.

Bartolomei, Arnaud, Mathieu Grenet, Fabrice Jesné et Jörg Ulbert. « Introduction ». *Mélanges de l'École française de Rome : Italie et Méditerranée modernes et contemporaines* 128, n° 2 (2016).

Bartolomei, Arnaud. « Actes notariés *versus* actes de chancellerie : Le rôle des chancelleries consulaires françaises dans la formalisation des actes commerciaux et civils (XVIIIe–XIXe) ». *Mélanges de l'École française de Rome : Italie et Méditerranée modernes et contemporaines* 128, n° 2 (2016).

Bechini, Thibault. « Les successions des Italiens morts aux États-Unis, entre assistance légale et acculturation administrative des familles transnationales (années 1900–Première Guerre mondiale) ». *Mélanges de l'École française de Rome : Italie et Méditerranée modernes et* 136, n°1 (janvier 2024) : 147-168.

Brilli, Catia. « Una nación en camino : La migración genovesa y la afiliación consular en las costas atlánticas (1770–1865) ». *Mélanges de la Casa de Velázquez* 51, n° 1 (January 2021) : 95–116.

Delalande, Nicolas. *La lutte et l'entraide : L'âge des solidarités ouvrières*. Paris : Seuil, 2019.

Freda, Dolores. *Governare i migranti : La legge sull'emigrazione del 1901 e la giurisprudenza del Tribunale di Napoli*. Turin : G. Giappichelli, 2017.

Kaps, Klemens. « Kinship, Trade, and Inheritance Strategies between Generations and Space : Tyrolean and Lombard Merchants in Eighteenth-Century Cádiz ». *Quaderni Storici* 58, n° 1 (April 2023) : 51–92.

Marglin, Jessica M. « La nationalité en procès : droit international privé et monde méditerranéen ». *Annales. Histoire, Sciences Sociales* 73, n° 1 (January 2018) : 83–117.

Passeron, Jean-Claude, Jacques Revel, « Penser par cas. Raisonner à partir de singularités ». Dans *Penser par cas*, éd. Jean-Claude Passeron et Jacques Revel, 9–44. Paris : EHESS, 2005.

Pretelli, Matteo. *L'emigrazione italiana negli Stati Uniti.* Bologne : Il Mulino, 2011.

Rygiel, Philippe. « De savants juristes au service de la France : Les experts du droit international auprès du Quai d'Orsay, 1874–1918 ». Dans *Experts et expertises en diplomatie. La mobilisation des compétences dans les relations internationales du congrès de Westphalie à la naissance de l'ONU*, édité par Stanislas Jeannesson, Fabrice Jesné et Éric Schnakenbourg, 205–222. Rennes : Presses universitaires de Rennes, 2018.

Rygiel, Philippe. *L'ordre des circulations ? L'Institut de Droit international et la régulation des migrations (1870–1920).* Paris : Éditions de la Sorbonne, 2021.

Spadolini, Giovanni. *Il « Cesare Alfieri » nella Storia d'Italia. Nascita e primi passi della scuola fiorentina di Scienze sociali.* Florence : Le Monnier, 1975.

« Succession of Amelie Rixner, Wife of Count Joseph de Sarzana ». *Reports of Cases Argued and Determined in the Supreme Court of Louisiana* 48, n° 1 (1897) : 552–564.

PART 2

The Ottoman Empire and North Africa

8

Les juridictions consulaires des nations latines dans les ports musulmans (XIIIe–XVe siècle)

Droit musulman, traités bilatéraux et forum shopping

Dominique Valérian

L'essor du commerce méditerranéen des marchands latins à partir du XIe siècle, et leur fréquentation de plus en plus régulière et parfois pérenne des ports musulmans, ont conduit à une définition juridique du statut de ces marchands chrétiens étrangers au *dār al-islam* et des communautés qu'ils constituent. Le droit musulman, tel qu'il apparaît dans les premiers grands traités du IXe–Xe siècle, aborde bien la question des non-musulmans vivant en terre d'Islam, à travers le statut de *dhimmīs* qui définit leur place dans la société islamique comme l'organisation des communautés minoritaires et leurs relations avec le pouvoir musulman[1]. Ils bénéficient à la fois d'une protection, de certaines libertés dont celle du culte et de la possibilité d'organiser leurs communautés avec leurs propres élites. Ces juifs et chrétiens sont cependant sujets du souverain musulman, et soumis au droit musulman, sauf pour certaines affaires internes ou de nature strictement religieuses gérées par leurs propres élites[2]. Ces textes juridiques traitent aussi, de manière moins détaillée, du statut des étrangers extérieurs à l'empire musulman qui y pénètrent voire viennent y résider. Originaires du domaine de la guerre ou *dār al-ḥarb*, ils sont qualifiés de *ḥarbīs*, donc d'ennemis de l'Islam, mais peuvent bénéficier d'une sauvegarde provisoire, l'*amān*, qui leur confère un nouveau statut, celui de *musta'min* qui les place sous la sauvegarde du pouvoir musulman tout en continuant à relever de la souveraineté de leur pays d'origine[3]. Ce statut ne peut cepen-

1 Antoine Fattal, *Le Statut légal des non-musulmans en pays d'Islam* (Beyrouth : Imprimerie catholique, 1958) ; Anver M. Emon, *Religious Pluralism and Islamic Law : Dhimmīs and Others in the Empire of Law* (Oxford : Oxford University Press, 2012) ; Nora Berend, Youna Masset, Capucine Nemo-Pekelman et John Tolan, éd., *Religious Minorities in Christian, Jewish and Muslim Law (5th–15th Centuries)* (Turnhout : Brepols, 2017).

2 Mathieu Tillier, *L'Invention du cadi : la justice des musulmans, des Juifs et des chrétiens aux premiers siècles de l'Islam* (Paris : Publications de la Sorbonne, 2017), 547–572.

3 John Wansbrough, « The Safe-Conduct in Muslim Chancery Practice », *Bulletin of the School of Oriental and African Studies* 34, n° 1 (1971) : 20–35.

 | HTTPS://DOI.ORG/10.1163/9789004755192-010

dant en principe pas dépasser une durée d'un an. Au-delà, ils rejoignent la catégorie des *dhimmīs*, donc deviennent sujets du souverain musulman[4].

Ces textes ont cependant été pour la plupart rédigés dans un contexte particulier, au IXe–Xe siècle, caractérisé par une faible présence étrangère, et notamment chrétienne occidentale, en terre d'Islam, laquelle se limite bien souvent à quelques pèlerins venant à Jérusalem, mais encore peu nombreux avant le XIe siècle[5]. Par ailleurs cette période est marquée par une nette domination de l'Islam en Méditerranée et par un rapport de forces très défavorable aux Latins qui permet aux pouvoirs musulmans d'imposer de manière unilatérale le droit en vigueur dans les pays qu'ils gouvernent. Il n'en est plus de même à partir du XIIe siècle, avec à la fois un retournement des forces en Méditerranée, sur le plan militaire et commercial, et par la venue en nombre de marchands italiens, puis également catalans et provençaux dans les ports musulmans. Dès lors, le droit musulman, qui jusque-là réglementait la présence de rares étrangers en terre d'Islam est confronté à de nouvelles réalités.

À la même époque du côté chrétien, la question du statut des minorités religieuses se pose avec l'expansion territoriale du monde latin, en Sicile, en péninsule Ibérique ou en Syrie-Palestine[6], et celui des étrangers de passage fait l'objet de réflexions, notamment en lien avec l'essor du commerce à longue distance et l'émergence de nations marchandes à l'étranger[7], avec la création de la fonction de consul d'outre-mer[8]. S'il est difficile à l'heure actuelle d'établir un lien précis entre ces réflexions juridiques, qui répondent à des contextes particuliers très différents, il est probable qu'elles ont toutes contribué à repenser le statut des marchands latins et le fonctionnement des communautés qu'ils constituent dans le monde islamique. Les derniers siècles du Moyen Âge correspondent donc à une phase d'expérimentation, de tâtonnements, dans la définition du statut des marchands étrangers et l'organisation de

4 Majid Khadduri, *War and Peace in the Law of Islam* (Clark, NJ : Lawbook Exchange, 2006), 162–168, 225.

5 Le récit du pèlerinage de saint Willibald au début du VIIIe siècle fait référence à une taxe, dont il est exempté, et à un document (*epistola*) accordé par un gouverneur musulman. Michael McCormick, *Origins of the European Economy : Communications and Commerce, A.D. 300–900* (Cambridge : Cambridge University Press, 2001), 131–133.

6 Brian Catlos, *Muslims of Medieval Latin Christendom : c.1050–1614* (Cambridge : Cambridge University Press, 2014).

7 Giovanna Petti Balbi, *Comunità forestiere e « nationes » nell'Europa dei secoli XIII–XVI* (Naples : Liguori Editore, 2001).

8 Maria Teresa Ferrer i Mallol, « El consolat de Mar i els consolats d'Ultramar, instrument i manifestació de l'expansió del comerç català », dans *L'expansió catalana a la Mediterrània a la baixa edat mitjana*, éd. Damien Coulon et Maria Teresa Ferrer i Mallol (Barcelone : CSIC, 1999), 53–79.

leurs nations. Ce statut a été réglementé principalement par les traités bilatéraux, et non dans des textes juridiques musulmans, qui continuent globalement à raisonner sur les bases des normes fixées au IXe–Xe siècle, et ce malgré l'opposition des oulémas, exprimée notamment dans des fatwas émises à l'époque mamelouke[9]. Il résulte donc à la fois d'une réflexion des juristes et de négociations politiques dans lesquelles l'équilibre des forces du moment, qu'il soit militaire ou économique, a pu jouer un rôle important, contribuant notamment à s'éloigner plus ou moins des normes d'inspiration religieuses en vigueur. Mais on constate aussi la construction d'un certain nombre de règles qui, progressivement, se retrouvent dans de nombreux accords, quel qu'en soit le contexte d'élaboration, et constituent la base de normes partagées, tout en laissant dans la pratique une certaine souplesse dans la résolution des conflits, marquée par un grand pragmatisme des différents acteurs.

Ces traités diplomatiques ne visent pas en soi à organiser le fonctionnement de ces nations latines[10], mais avant tout à fixer les droits et devoirs des souverains ou des cités signataires, représentés par leurs consuls respectifs. La question de la souveraineté sur les marchands latins est essentielle, et pose donc celle des limites de juridiction entre l'autorité musulmane et les consuls des nations latines. Or, sa résolution entre très vite en contradiction avec le droit musulman. L'accord de paix octroie un *amān* collectif ou général (*'āmm*) à tous les marchands de la nation concernée[11] – parfois étendu à ceux qui viendraient à bord de leurs navires. Mais aucun traité, à ma connaissance, ne fixe une durée de validité de cet *amān* qui ferait basculer au bout d'un an le marchand latin du statut de *musta'min* à celui de *dhimmī*, comme le prévoit le droit musulman[12]. En effet si la question a pu être posée, notamment par Philippe Gourdin[13], pour des marchands demeurant pour de

9 Pierre Moukarzel, « La législation des autorités religieuses et politiques sur les marchands européens dans le sultanat mamelouk (1250–1517) », dans *La cohabitation religieuse dans les villes européennes, Xe–XVe siècles*, éd. Stéphane Boissellier et John Tolan (Turnhout : Brepols, 2014), 125–129.

10 Ce fonctionnement est davantage réglementé par les statuts des villes maritimes, comme par exemple ceux de Marseille au XIIIe siècle pour les consulats de Ceuta et Bougie. Dominique Valérian, « Les archives de Marseille, sources de l'histoire du Maghreb médiéval : le cas du port de Bougie (XIIIe–XVe siècles) », *Annales du Midi* 233 (2001) : 14.

11 Wansbrough, « The Safe-Conduct », 29–30.

12 Et comme le rappellent certains juristes à l'époque mamelouke : Moukarzel, « La législation », 124.

13 Philippe Gourdin, « Les marchands étrangers ont-ils un statut de dhimmi ? À propos de quelques statuts de marchands étrangers dans les pays chrétiens et musulmans de Méditerranée occidentale au XIIIe siècle », dans *Migrations et diasporas méditerranéennes*

longues durées[14], les preuves manquent à l'heure actuelle pour affirmer qu'ils passaient au bout d'un an sous souveraineté musulmane[15]. Il paraît en outre difficilement concevable, dans les rapports de forces politiques et économiques de l'époque, que les monarchies ou les cités aient accepté que leurs marchands, et à plus forte raison leurs consuls, renoncent à reconnaitre la souveraineté de leur métropole. Dans ce cas, comme dans d'autres[16], une hiérarchie des normes établit, dans les faits sinon dans les théories juridiques, la primauté des traités bilatéraux entre États sur la loi d'inspiration religieuse.

L'apparition des consuls chrétiens dans les ports musulmans est progressive, et suit une phase d'expérimentation avec des communautés sans doute peu structurées et dirigées par des personnages aux fonctions assez imprécises, comme le *scriba* des Pisans présent à Bougie un peu avant 1200, et père du mathématicien Fibonacci[17]. À la même époque à Tunis un conflit avec les Pisans, bien documenté par un dossier de lettres à la fois privées et officielles, suggère qu'il n'existe aucune autorité pisane reconnue dans le port, même si certains marchands, par les liens privilégiés qu'ils entretiennent avec le milieu local, jouent un rôle prééminent[18]. Les premiers consulats outre-mer semblent d'abord émerger, mais assez tardivement dans le XIIe siècle, dans les ports des

---

(*Xe–XVIe siècles*), éd. Michel Balard et Alain Ducellier (Paris : Publications de la Sorbonne, 2002), 435–446.

14 C'est le cas notamment des facteurs des grandes compagnies marchandes, mais aussi du personnel permanent des fondouks (consuls, artisans, chapelains), voire des mercenaires chrétiens qui parfois faisaient souche en terre d'Islam.

15 Wansbrough, « The Safe-Conduct », 31–32.

16 La fiscalité appliquée aux marchands chrétiens s'écarte ainsi des normes générales du droit musulman, qui prévoit un taux de taxation différencié pour les musulmans, les *dhimmīs* et les *ḥarbīs*, voir : Claude Cahen, « Douanes et Commerce dans les Ports méditerranéens de l'Égypte médiévale d'après le *Minhādj* d'al-Makhzūmī », *Journal of the Economic and Social History of the Orient* 7, n° 3 (1964) : 267–271. Il en est de même du droit de la paix, les traités ne faisant pas référence le plus souvent aux distinctions religieuses : Dominique Valérian, « Traités de paix et normes juridico-religieuses en Méditerranée à la fin du Moyen Âge. Entre pluralisme normatif et hiérarchie des normes », dans *Avant l'État. Droit international et pluralisme politico-juridique en Europe,* XIIe–XVIIe *siècle*, éd. Dante Fedele, Randall Lesaffer et Pierre Savy (Rome : Historia et ius, 2024), 251–268 .

17 Djamil Aissani et Dominique Valérian, « Mathématiques, commerce et société à Béjaïa (Bugia) au moment de séjour de Leonardo Fibonacci (XIIe–XIIe siècle) », *Bollettino di storia delle scienze matematiche* 23, n° 2 (2003) : 9–10.

18 Travis Bruce, « Commercial Conflict Resolution across the Religious Divide in the Thirteenth-Century Mediterranean », *Mediterranean Historical Review* 30, n° 1 (2015) : 19–38; Romain Rousseau, *L'Affaire de Tunis. Commerce et politique en Ifrīqiya almohade (596–598/1200–1202)* (Paris : L'Harmattan, 2025), 113-116.

États latins de Syrie dans le contexte des croisades[19] ou en Sicile normande[20], et leur fonctionnement reste mal connu. C'est surtout à partir du XIIIe siècle que les consuls apparaissent, sous ce nom ou sous celui de bayle pour les Vénitiens, mais avec des fonctions comparables[21]. Au Maghreb comme en Orient ils figurent dans les traités des années 1230, avec Venise ou Pise[22], alors que les accords précédents se contentent d'accorder une protection (*amān*) aux marchands et de fixer quelques règles, et cette apparition des consuls est contemporaine de l'institutionnalisation des fondouks dans lesquels les marchands sont accueillis[23]. Dès les premiers traités du XIIIe siècle les limites de leur juridiction commencent à être définies, et par la suite elles sont précisées selon des modalités variables, qui montrent des formes d'expérimentation mais aussi une adaptation au contexte de rapport de forces entre puissances.

Le cas le plus simple est celui des affaires internes à une nation donnée. Suivant le principe, largement admis, de la personnalité des lois, ces questions sont traitées uniquement par le consul, sauf en cas d'arbitrage non contesté entre marchands[24]. En ce sens, cela s'inscrit facilement dans le cadre des normes qui régissent le statut de *dhimmīs*, qui prévoient le règlement des affaires

19 C'est le cas par exemple pour les Catalans à Tyr en 1187. Damien Coulon, « Los consulados catalanes en Siria (1187–1400). Algunos datos de historia e historiografía », dans *XVIII Congrés Internacional d'Història de la Corona d'Aragó, La Mediterrània de la Corona d'Aragó, segles XIII–XVI & VII centenari de la Sentència arbitral de Torrellas, 1304–2004*, 1, éd. Rafael Narbona Vizcaíno (Valence : Universitat de Valencia – Fundació Jaume II el Just, 2005), 180.

20 Un consulat pisan est attesté à Messine en 1189. David Abulafia, « Pisan Commercial Colonies and Consulates in Twelfth-Century Sicily », *The English Historical Review* 93 (1978) : 75–76.

21 David Abulafia, « Las redes consulares del Mediterráneo : Función, orígenes y desarrollo », dans *Mediterraneum : el esplendor del Mediterráneo medieval s. XIII–XV* (Barcelone : Lunwerg Editores, 2004), 339–351 ; Daniel Durán Duelt, « La red consular catalana : Origen y desarrollo », dans ibid., 353–361.

22 *Traités de paix et de commerce et documents divers concernant les relations des chrétiens avec les Arabes de l'Afrique septentrionale au moyen âge*, éd. Louis de Mas Latrie (Paris : H. Plon, 1865), 31–35, 196–199.

23 Ils apparaissent vers le milieu du XIIe et se développent largement au XIIIe siècle, Olivia Remie Constable, *Housing the Stranger in the Mediterranean World : Lodging, Trade, and Travel in Late Antiquity and the Middle Ages* (Cambridge : Cambridge University Press, 2009), 107–133.

24 En 1458 le marchand génois Giovanni da Pontremoli écrit à son facteur à Constantine, Giovanni Battista Mirono, à propos de la dette d'un autre Génois, Oliverio de Nigro : il lui recommande, si l'affaire ne se règle pas à l'amiable, de se retourner vers le consul du lieu. Domenico Gioffrè, éd. *Lettere di Giovanni da Pontremoli mercante genovese, 1453–1459* (Gênes : Istituto di paleografia e storia medievale – Università di Genova, 1982), 208.

internes de chaque communauté par ses propres cadres. Le consul suit alors, en matière civile et parfois aussi criminelle[25], les lois de la métropole, précisées parfois dans des codes spécifiques aux affaires maritimes ou commerciales, comme le *Breve dell'Ordine del Mare* de Pise (fin XIIIe–XIVe siècle)[26], voire des règlements propres à des communautés outre-mer, comme ceux qui régissent le consulat catalan à Alexandrie ou Damas à la fin du XIVe siècle[27]. La *promissio* du consul vénitien d'Alexandrie en 1284, éditée et analysée par David Jacoby, précise les règles auxquelles il s'engage avant de partir, et aborde la question de sa juridiction, en accord avec les traités signés par Venise avec les souverains égyptiens depuis le début du siècle[28]. Il devra juger en matière civile entre les Vénitiens, dont les sujets coloniaux de la Sérénissime, selon la coutume (*secundum usum*), que Jacoby interprète comme les règles édictées par le doge Jacopo Tiepolo dans les *statuti venetis*[29] et, si celle-ci fait défaut, il devra agir en conscience (*secundum conscienciam meam sine fraude*)[30].

Les peines pouvaient cependant être appliquées par la métropole, au moins lorsque le marchand n'était plus dans le port musulman. En 1451 c'est l'*Ufficio Gazariae* qui condamne le Génois Gaspare Doria à payer le nolis de marchan-

---

25 « Faciant et reddant jus et justiciam inter gentes vestras ibidem existentes, tam criminaliter quam civiliter ». Traité de 1312 entre Majorque et Bougie (art. 3), éd. Estanislao de Kostka Aguiló, « Tractat de pau entre el Rey de Mallorca Don Sanxo y el de Bugia Boyhahia Abubechre, firmat a Mallorca pels seus representants Gregori Sallambé de una part y Mahomat Abdellá Ben Acet de l'altra, dia 23 de novembre de 1312 », *Bolletí de la Societat Arqueológica Luliana* 15 (1915) : 217–226. Il est précisé que ni le *mushrif* (directeur de la douane), ni un autre officier du sultan ne pourra intervenir. Le traité de 1229 entre Venise et le sultan ayyūbide d'Alep prévoit également que « s'il advient qu'un litige oppose des Vénitiens ou qu'entre eux ils se blessent ou se tuent, leur baile et lui seul doit avoir le pouvoir de juger » (« si infra dictos Venetos evenerit discordia aliqua, aut se ad invicem verberarent vel occiderent, super hoc baiulus eorum potestatem habere debet »), éd. Marco Pozza, *I trattati con Aleppo : 1207–1254* (Venise : Cardo, 1990), 53.

26 Bonaini, Francesco, éd., *Statuti inediti della citta di Pisa : dal XII al XIV secolo raccolti* (Florence : G. P. Vieusseux, 1857), vol. 3.

27 Amada López de Meneses, « Los consulados catalanes de Alejandría, y Damasco en el reinado de Pedro el Ceremonioso », *Estudios de edad media de la Corona de Aragón* 6 (1956) : 83–183.

28 David Jacoby, « Le consulat vénitien d'Alexandrie d'après un document inédit de 1284 », dans *Chemins d'outre-mer. Études d'histoire sur la Méditerranée médiévale offertes à Michel Balard*, éd. Damien Coulon, Catherine Otten-Froux, Paule Pagès et Dominique Valérian (Paris : Publications de la Sorbonne, 2004), 461–474.

29 Georg Christ considère pour sa part que cela renvoie à la coutume locale : Georg Christ, *Trading Conflicts : Venetian Merchants and Mamluk Officials in Late Medieval Alexandria* (Leyde : Brill, 2012), 68–69.

30 Jacoby, « Le consulat vénitien », 466–467, 471.

dises à la suite d'une sentence prononcée par le consul génois de Tunis[31]. Mais cette juridiction du consul peut aussi être contestée, localement ou dans la métropole. Certains, contestant l'objectivité du consul, en appellent à l'arbitrage des marchands[32]. Ces derniers peuvent surtout se tourner d'eux-mêmes vers la justice de leur cité, qui agit en appel. Dans une affaire opposant en 1289 deux Génois de Tunis, le jugement du consul ayant été contesté, il est décidé de s'en remettre aux autorités génoises de métropole compétentes, à savoir le capitaine du peuple, le *podestà* ou un juge[33]. Par ailleurs la métropole, qui garde un œil attentif sur ses ressortissants outre-mer, peut intervenir comme en 1306 lorsque le consul des Catalans de Bougie reçoit une lettre du roi à propos d'un procès opposant deux de ses sujets à la suite d'une commande non honorée[34].

Les cas d'affaires mixtes sont plus complexes et donnent lieu à des règles qui ne sont pas homogènes, et qui montrent à la fois des formes d'expérimentation mais aussi l'influence des rapports de force à l'œuvre lors de la signature du traité[35]. Deux modalités principales se rencontrent pour les affaires impliquant des chrétiens latins et des musulmans[36].

---

31 Rossana Urbani, « Genova e il Maghrib tra il '400 e '500 (nuovi documenti archivistici) », dans *Genova, la Liguria e l'Oltremare tra medioevo ed età moderna : studi e ricerche d'Archivio*, vol. 2 (Gênes : Bozzi, 1976), 205.

32 Giovanna Petti Balbi, « Il consolato genovese di Tunisi nel Quattrocento », *Archivio Storico Italiano* 156, n° 2 (1998) : 244–245.

33 Geo Pistarino, éd., *Notai genovesi in Oltremare : Atti rogati a Tunisi da Pietro Battifoglio (1288–1289)* (Gênes : Istituto di Medievistica, 1986), 80–83.

34 Archivo de la Corona de Aragón, *Cancillería*, Reg. 139, fol. 78 (7 janvier 1306).

35 Francisco Apellaniz conteste ce rôle des rapports de forces dans la négociation des règles définissant le fonctionnement de la justice. Francisco Javier Apellániz Ruiz de Galarreta, *Breaching the Bronze Wall : Franks at Mamluk and Ottoman Courts and Markets* (Leyde : Brill, 2020), 29, 170. Mais il ne prend en compte que le contexte militaire, auquel ne se résument pas les relations entre puissances chrétiennes et musulmanes. La diversité des solutions adoptées montre par exemple des règles bien plus souples et favorables aux chrétiens au Maghreb qu'en Égypte. Dominique Valérian, « Conflits et résolution des conflits dans les communautés européennes au Maghreb (XIIe–XVe siècle) », *Mélanges de l'École française de Rome* 115, n° 1 (2003) : 543–564.

36 Un cas particulier concerne les musulmans sujets d'un roi chrétien se rendant en terre d'Islam, ou les chrétiens convertis à l'islam. Il a été parfois abordé dans les traités entre la couronne d'Aragon et le Maghreb, avec des solutions variables qui montrent la complexité des questions de souveraineté dans ces contextes de mobilités marchandes. Ibid., 547–549. À l'inverse le traité entre les Mamelouks et le roi d'Aragon de 1290 met les chrétiens et les *dhimmīs* sujets du sultan (qu'il distingue) sous la protection de ce dernier. *Early Mamluk Diplomacy (1260–1290) : Treaties of Baybars and Qalāwūn with Christian Rulers*, éd. Peter Malcolm Holt (Leyde : Brill, 1995), 135.

La première suit le principe du droit romain *actor sequitur forum rei*, qui confie le règlement de l'affaire à l'autorité judiciaire dont relève l'accusé. Au-delà du raisonnement juridique et des précédents qui ont pu éventuellement être pris en considération par les négociateurs, mais qui nous restent inconnus, ce choix résulte aussi et surtout d'une volonté politique d'éviter une contestation de la sentence par l'accusé, qui pouvait entraîner un cycle de représailles et donc menacer la paix. Dans une Méditerranée instable sur le plan géopolitique, tout est fait pour qu'un incident isolé ne vienne pas rompre la paix, d'où la nécessité de lui trouver une issue judiciaire qui ne puisse pas être contestée[37]. Ce principe est appliqué de manière assez générale pour les conflits entre chrétiens de différentes nations[38], mais aussi parfois pour ceux impliquant des chrétiens et des musulmans. C'est le cas par exemple dans l'accord de 1343 entre Tunis et Gênes[39], qui stipule que si un musulman a une plainte contre un Génois, il doit la porter au consul qui doit faire justice – et c'est seulement s'il ne le fait pas que le musulman pourra se tourner vers la douane. Si à l'inverse c'est un Génois qui est le plaignant et l'accusé un musulman ou un autre chrétien en paix avec le sultan, l'affaire doit être portée devant la douane[40]. Dans ces cas les consuls sont donc compétents pour juger des membres d'autres nations, mais aussi potentiellement des musulmans[41]. Dans l'autre sens, quand les textes le précisent, ce sont rarement les

37 C'est également ce principe qui conduit à exiger que, dans les affaires de piraterie, la puissance dont relève le pirate se charge de le poursuivre et de faire justice. Cela a conduit notamment la république de Gênes à mettre en place un tribunal spécial chargé de juger ses ressortissants accusés d'actes de piraterie. Benjamin Z. Kedar, « L'Officium Robarie di Genova : un tentativo di coesistere con la violenza », *Archivio Storico Italiano* 143, n° 3 (1985) : 331–372.

38 Par exemple dans le traité de 1231 entre Tunis et Venise, voir : *Venezia e il regno di Tunisi : gli accordi diplomatici conclusi fra il 1231 e il 1456*, éd. Francesca Girardi (Rome : Viella, 2006), 15 (art. 7).

39 Giovanna Petti Balbi, « Il trattato del 1343 tra Genova e Tunisi », dans *Saggi e documenti*, vol. 1 (Gênes : Civico istituto colombiano, 1978), 297–322 (art. 5).

40 C'est aussi la solution adoptée par le traité de 1290 entre les Mamlouks et Gênes, *I libri iurium della Repubblica di Genova*, éd. Eleonora Pallavicino (Gênes : Regione Liguria, 2001), 79.

41 Le traité de 1358 entre les Mérinides et Pise prévoit cependant que pour les cas graves l'affaire doit être traitée par le cadi. *I diplomi arabi del R. Archivio Fiorentino*, éd. Michele Amari (Florence : F. Le Monnier, 1863), 311. En l'absence de consul, on devra se tourner vers le gouverneur (*aveli de la terra*) ou le gouverneur de la citadelle (*signore del catello*). Le recours à une autorité judiciaire musulmane peut aussi être prévue dans le cas de défaillance du consul, comme par exemple dans le traité de 1433 entre Gênes et les Hafsides qui envisage alors la possibilité de se tourner vers la douane (*Traités*, éd. Mas Latrie, 135).

cadis[42] qui jugent, mais plutôt des autorités en lien avec le pouvoir, notamment au Maghreb le chef de la douane. On ne sait pas précisément quel droit était appliqué – mais le fait qu'aucune réclamation, dans la correspondance diplomatique, porte sur le choix de ces normes, laisse penser que cela ne constituait pas un problème majeur mais aussi que le droit islamique, suivi par les cadis, n'était pas forcément systématiquement privilégié.

La deuxième modalité consister à renvoyer vers une autorité musulmane tous les litiges qui concernaient un sujet du sultan. On la trouve très tôt, par exemple dans le traité de 1234 entre Pise et les Hafsides qui confie cette tâche au drogman[43], ou dans celui de 1238 entre Venise et les Ayyūbides, qui renvoie ces cas à la *justitiam terre*, sans plus de précision[44]. C'est aussi cette modalité qui est choisie systématiquement par les traités signés avec les Mamlouks après le milieu du XIVe siècle, qui confient les jugements au *ḥājib* (chambellan) à Damas ou au vice-roi (*nā'ib*) à Alexandrie[45], donc à une autorité civile et militaire. Francisco Apellaniz a bien montré que ce recours à une juridiction distincte de celle des cadis, relevant de la *siyāsa* ou art de gouverner, et de la cour des *maẓālim* distincte de celle des cadis[46], permettait de s'affranchir d'un certain nombre de règles du droit musulman qui pouvaient poser problème, notamment sur la validité des contrats écrits ou sur l'inégalité de valeur du témoignage et du serment entre croyants et non-croyants, facilitant ainsi le règlement des conflits commerciaux[47]. Les traités bilatéraux ne se réfèrent en effet jamais à la loi religieuse comme fondement juridique, et celle-ci reposait, pour les relations entre croyants et non-croyants, sur un principe d'inégalité difficilement compatible avec les relations partenaires commerciaux. Le recours à une autorité civile, qui pouvait en partie s'écarter des textes produits

---

42 Traité de 1358 entre les Mérinides et Pise (*I diplomi arabi*, éd. Amari, 311). Le traité de 1290 entre les Mamlouks et Gênes stipule qu'un défaut de paiement d'une dette résultant d'une vente faite sans témoins ou courtiers (*sensariis*) de la douane doit être porté devant le cadi (*archadi*), *I libri iurium*, éd. Pallavicino, 80–81. Voir également : Apellániz Ruiz de Galarreta, *Breaching the Bronze Wall*, 180.

43 *Traités*, éd. Mas Latrie, 33. Il devra juger selon la coutume (*consuetum*).

44 *Urkunden zur älteren Handels- und Staatsgeschichte der Republik Venedig*, éd. Georg Martin Thomas et Gottlieb Lukas Friedrich Tafel, vol. 2 (Vienne : Kaiserlich-königliche Hof- und Staatsdruckerei, 1856), 338.

45 Apellániz Ruiz de Galarreta, *Breaching the Bronze Wall*, 187.

46 Jørgen S Nielsen, *Secular Justice in an Islamic State : Maẓālim under the Baḥrī Mamlūks, 662/1264–789/1387* (Leyde : Instituut voor het Nabije Oosten, 1985) ; Christ, *Trading conflicts*, 45–47.

47 Apellániz Ruiz de Galarreta, *Breaching the Bronze Wall*, 196–203. Francisco Apellániz, « Judging the Franks : Proof, Justice, and Diversity in Late Medieval Alexandria and Damascus », *Comparative Studies in Society and History* 58, n° 2 (2016) : 350–378.

par les *fuqahā'*, était donc un moyen de limiter les problèmes induits par le pluralisme normatif entre mondes chrétiens et musulmans. En 1415 cependant, le Sénat de Venise envoie une ambassade au Caire, qui doit rappeler au sultan que les litiges entre ses sujets et les Vénitiens ne devaient pas être portés devant les cadis mais devant une justice séculière[48], ce qui suggère que ce principe n'était pas toujours respecté et pouvait être contesté, notamment par les élites religieuses[49].

Cette distinction générale n'exclut cependant pas de nombreuses exceptions qui montrent à la fois que les règles sont loin d'être fixées et qu'elles laissent place à des solutions qui tiennent compte aussi des rapports de force du moment, avec le souverain musulman ou entre puissances chrétiennes rivales. Elles peuvent ainsi parfois privilégier le représentant d'une nation donnée, en charge de tous les conflits entre chrétiens, comme dans le cas de Tlemcen et ses avant-ports dans le traité passé avec la couronne d'Aragon en 1286, alors que les Catalans dominent largement le commerce dans ces ports : l'accord prévoit que tous les chrétiens, quelle que soit leur condition ou leur seigneurie, seront jugés selon le *fuero* d'Aragon par le caïd de la milice catalane que le roi d'Aragon enverra dans le sultanat[50]. De même, dans certains accords du début du XVe siècle avec Tunis, alors que l'autorité des sultans s'est notablement renforcée, les affaires visant des chrétiens d'une autre nation sont renvoyées systématiquement devant la douane, et non pas devant le consul de l'accusé[51]. Le choix peut parfois être laissé aux parties, comme dans le traité de 1430 entre la couronne d'Aragon et les Mamlouks qui prévoit que, dans les conflits entre Catalans et sujets du sultan et si les deux parties sont d'accord, le consul des Catalans pourra juger, mais qu'en cas de désaccord l'instance légale de recours sera l'émir (*malik al-umarā'*) et l'inspecteur du port d'Alexandrie (*nāẓir al-thaghr*)[52]. On peut trouver aussi, de manière exceptionnelle des cas

48 Eliyahu Ashtor, *Levant Trade in the Later Middle Ages* (Princeton : Princeton University Press, 1983), 249.

49 Moukarzel, « La législation », 125–129.

50 *Die äussere Politik Alphonsos III. von Aragonien (1285–1291 : Beiträge zur Geschichte der inneren Politik Alfonsos*, éd. Ludwig Klüpfel (Berlin : W. Rothschild, 1911), 171. Dans ce cas très particulier cependant, en l'absence de consul, c'est le chef de la milice chrétienne du sultan qui agit comme représentant du roi d'Aragon.

51 Estanislao de Kostka Aguiló, « Pau feta entre els reys de Aragó y de Sicilia de una part y el rey de Tunis de l'altre (1403) », *Boletín de la Sociedad Arqueológica Luliana* 9 (1902) : 350–355 ; Petti Balbi, « Il trattato del 1343 », 315 ; *Traités*, éd. Mas Latrie, 356 (traité entre Florence et Tunis de 1445).

52 Mercè Viladrich, « L'extraterritorialitat del dret : una concessio atorgada al consol dels catalans a Alexandria el 1430 », dans *La Corona d'Aragona ai tempi di Alfonso il Magna-*

de tribunaux mixtes, comme dans le projet de traité de 1444 entre la couronne d'Aragon et les Hafsides – mais qui ne fut jamais ratifié[53].

Ces règles sont surtout diversement appliquées en raison d'une tendance des parties à parfois recourir à l'instance judiciaire qui leur semble la plus favorable, soit parce qu'elle est considérée comme plus rapide ou moins coûteuse, soit parce que le jugement qu'on peut en attendre est préféré par l'une des parties. Ce que les juristes appellent le *forum shopping* était déjà très tôt pratiqué dans le monde islamique, marqué par un pluralisme normatif, entre musulmans et non-musulmans mais aussi entre les différentes écoles juridiques de l'Islam[54]. Les *dhimmīs* en particulier n'hésitaient pas à s'adresser à la justice des cadis pour des affaires les opposant à des musulmans mais aussi pour des affaires internes à leur communauté, parfois en absence de solution satisfaisante donnée par leur propre justice, mais pas seulement[55]. Dans le contexte de la Geniza, au XIe–XIIe siècle, Jessica Goldberg constate cependant que le recours aux tribunaux musulmans par les marchands juifs de Fusṭāṭ apparaît peu, les affaires étant prioritairement traitées par les cours rabbiniques et le pouvoir musulman n'intervenant que lorsque l'usage de la force était requis pour appliquer la sentence, notamment en cas d'emprisonnement[56].

Cette possibilité n'est pas envisagée par les traités, sauf en cas d'absence d'un consul, comme dans le traité de 1358 entre Pise et les Mérinides qui prévoit que la plainte sera alors traitée par le gouverneur ou le seigneur de la citadelle[57]. Mais cette absence n'a rien de surprenant, car cela contrevient au partage de juridiction et donc de souveraineté qu'établit l'accord de paix. En revanche on trouve, notamment dans la correspondance diplomatique ou

---

nimo. XVI Congresso internazionale di storia della corona d'Aragon, Napoli, 1997, éd. Guido d'Agostino et Giulia Buffardi, vol. 1 (Naples : Paparo, 2000), 811.

53 L'affaire devra être traitée par le « seigneur de la douane » *et* le consul du roi d'Aragon : Francesco Cerone, « Alfonso il Magnanimo ed Abu 'Omar Othmân, Trattative e negoziati tra il Regno di Sicilia di qua e di là dal Faro ed il Regno di Tunisi (1432–1457) », *Archivio storico per la Sicilia Orientale* 10 (1913) : 25–33 (art. 25).

54 Mathieu Tillier, « Introduction. Le pluralisme judiciaire en Islam, ses dynamiques et ses enjeux », *Bulletin d'études orientales* 63 (2015) : 23–40.

55 Tillier, *L'Invention du cadi*, 555 ; Delfina Serrano, « Forum Shopping in al-Andalus (II) : Discussing Coran V, 42 and 49 (Ibn Hazm, Ibn Rushd al-Jadd, Abû Bakr Ibn al-'Arabî and al-Qurtubî) », in *Law and Religious Minorities in Medieval Societies : Between Theory and Praxis*, éd. Ana Echevarría, Juan Pedro Monferrer Sala et John Tolan (Turnhout : Brepols, 2016), 173–196.

56 Jessica Goldberg, « The Courts, the Qadi, and the 'People' : Resolving Mercantile Disputes in the Medieval Islamic Mediterranean », dans *Conflict Management in the Mediterranean and the Atlantic, 1000–1800: Actors, Institutions and Strategies of Dispute Settlement*, éd. Louis Sicking, Alain Wijffels (Leyde : Brill, 2020), 19–42.

57 Cf. note 41 supra.

avec les consuls, de nombreuses plaintes des États chrétiens contre cette pratique, surtout au XVe siècle quand la documentation devient plus abondante. Cela montre à la fois qu'elle n'était pas absente mais aussi qu'elles contrevenaient aux normes admises et défendues par les consuls ou les pouvoirs qu'ils représentaient. Ainsi, en 1449 Gênes se plaint de l'intervention du sultan de Tunis dans un procès et même contre la délivrance d'un Génois arrêté par le consul[58]. Mais il n'est pas sûr dans cette affaire que les plaignants se soient spontanément tournés vers la justice du sultan. Plus explicite est la lettre adressée en 1470 par les autorités génoises à leur consul de Tunis, lui demandant de faire « justice sommaire et expéditive » pour éviter que les Génois ne se tournent vers la justice locale[59] – ce qui suggère que la lenteur des procédures suivies par les consuls a pu être une des raisons de ces choix. Francisco Apellaniz note que les cours civiles, voire celles des cadis, pouvaient avoir la préférence des marchands latins, y compris pour des litiges survenant entre eux[60], ce qui n'allait pas sans contestation de la compétence de ces juridictions. En 1460 à Damas, un Vénitien accuse ainsi un de ses compatriotes devant les autorités musulmanes de certains délits, dont un trafic d'esclaves, ce que dénie l'accusé, sur la base des preuves apportées mais surtout en contestant la légitimité de cette cour : « Cela est contre nos lois et coutumes et contre les devoirs du consul de porter devant les autorités musulmanes nos différents entre Francs et notamment entre Vénitiens »[61]. Ces plaintes, du moins celles que conserve la documentation, montrent toutes une préférence pour les cours musulmanes et non pour celles des consuls, et surtout montrent que, du point de vue des consuls et des métropoles, il s'agissait clairement d'une violation des règles fixées par les traités. Au-delà des pertes financières pour les consuls, qui prélevaient des droits sur ces jugements, la contestation de leur juridiction posait en effet un problème plus large de souveraineté qui explique les protestations diplomatiques.

Ce bref panorama, qui est loin d'être exhaustif et mériterait une enquête plus systématique des normes et des pratiques, montre la grande diversité des solutions adoptées et un certain tâtonnement marqué par des expérimentations. On voit bien émerger assez tôt quelques modèles définissant les limites

58 Nicolas Jorga, « Notes et extraits pour servir à l'histoire des croisades au XVe siècle », *Revue de l'Orient Latin* 8 (1901) : 62 (1er décembre 1449).

59 « Summarie et expedite iusticiam », Petti Balbi, « Il consolato genovese », 243.

60 Apellániz Ruiz de Galarreta, *Breaching the Bronze Wall*, 195 ; Apellániz. « Judging the Franks », 371–376.

61 Apellániz Ruiz de Galarreta, *Breaching the Bronze Wall*, 199.

de la juridiction des consuls, et qui s'écartent en partie des principes du droit musulman en vue de faciliter la résolution par la voie judiciaire des conflits impliquant ces Latins, en confiant notamment ces affaires aux consuls chrétiens ou à des juridictions islamiques mais que l'on pourrait qualifier de civiles. Mais il est difficile pour autant de déceler une évolution linéaire vers une solution qui ferait consensus à la fin du Moyen Âge dans l'ensemble des ports musulmans. Au contraire, les normes produites par les traités résultent de négociations dans lesquelles entrent en jeu les rapports de forces à la fois politiques et économiques. Par ailleurs l'application de ces normes se heurte à une pratique des acteurs qui laisse une place importante à la fois à l'arbitrage entre marchands, mais aussi à un *forum shopping* qui retire aux consuls une partie de leurs prérogatives judiciaires, malgré leurs protestations et celles des États impliqués. Il n'en demeure pas moins que le règlement de la question dans la plupart des traités à partir du XIIIe siècle, mais aussi les protestations diplomatiques rappelant les droits et devoirs des consuls, montrent qu'il y a là des enjeux importants de souveraineté, qui expliquent sans doute l'impossibilité de voir émerger, avant la fin du Moyen Âge, une solution faisant l'objet d'un consensus entre toutes les puissances chrétiennes et musulmanes.

Bibliographie

Abulafia, David. « Pisan Commercial Colonies and Consulates in Twelfth-Century Sicily ». *The English Historical Review* 93 (1978) : 68–81.

Abulafia, David. « Las redes consulares del Mediterráneo : Función, orígenes y desarrollo ». Dans *Mediterraneum : el esplendor del Mediterráneo medieval s. XIII–XV*, édité par Joan Alemany et Xabier Barral i Altet, 338–351. Barcelone : Lunwerg Editores, 2004.

Aguiló, Estanislao de Kostka, « Pau feta entre els reys de Aragó y de Sicilia de una part y el rey de Tunis de l'altre (1403) », *Boletín de la Sociedad Arqueológica Luliana* 9 (1902) : 350–355.

Aguiló, Estanislao de Kostka. « Tractat de pau entre el Rey de Mallorca Don Sanxo y el de Bugia Boyhahia Abubechre, firmat a Mallorca pels seus representants Gregori Sallambé de una part y Mahomat Abdellá Ben Acet de l'altra, dia 23 de novembre de 1312 ». *Bolletí de la Societat Arqueológica Luliana* 15 (1915) : 217–226.

Aissani, Djamil et Dominique Valérian. « Mathématiques, commerce et société à Béjaïa (Bugia) au moment de séjour de Leonardo Fibonacci (XIIe–XIIe siècle) ». *Bollettino di storia delle scienze matematiche* 23, n° 2 (2003) : 9–31.

Amari, Michele, éd. *I diplomi arabi del R. Archivio Fiorentino*. Florence : F. Le Monnier, 1863.

Apellániz, Francisco. « Judging the Franks : Proof, Justice, and Diversity in Late Medieval Alexandria and Damascus ». *Comparative Studies in Society and History* 58, n° 2 (2016) : 350–378.

Apellániz Ruiz de Galarreta, Francisco Javier. *Breaching the Bronze Wall : Franks at Mamluk and Ottoman Courts and Markets*. Leyde : Brill, 2020.

Ashtor, Eliyahu. *Levant Trade in the Later Middle Ages*. Princeton : Princeton University Press, 1983.

Berend, Nora, Masset, Youna Nemo-Pekelman, Capucine et Tolan, John, éd. *Religious Minorities in Christian, Jewish and Muslim Law (5th–15th Centuries)*. Turnhout : Brepols, 2017.

Bonaini, Francesco, éd. *Statuti inediti della citta di Pisa : dal* XII *al* XIV *secolo raccolti*. Florence : G. P. Vieusseux, 1857.

Bruce, Travis. « Commercial Conflict Resolution across the Religious Divide in the Thirteenth-Century Mediterranean ». *Mediterranean Historical Review* 30, n° 1 (2015) : 19–38, https://doi.org/10.1080/09518967.2015.1044825.

Cahen, Claude. « Douanes et commerce dans les ports méditerranéens de l'Égypte médiévale d'après le *Minhādj* d'al-Makhzūmī ». *Journal of the Economic and Social History of the Orient* 7, n° 3 (1964) : 217–314, https://doi.org/10.2307/3596111.

Catlos, Brian. *Muslims of Medieval Latin Christendom : c.1050–1614*. Cambridge : Cambridge University Press, 2014.

Cerone, Francesco. « Alfonso il Magnanimo ed Abu 'Omar Othmân, Trattative e negoziati tra il Regno di Sicilia di qua e di là dal Faro ed il Regno di Tunisi (1432–1457) ». *Archivio storico per la Sicilia Orientale* 10 (1913) : 22–78.

Christ, Georg. *Trading Conflicts : Venetian Merchants and Mamluk Officials in Late Medieval Alexandria*. Leyde : Brill, 2012.

Constable, Olivia Remie. *Housing the Stranger in the Mediterranean World : Lodging, Trade, and Travel in Late Antiquity and the Middle Ages*. Cambridge : Cambridge University Press, 2009.

Coulon, Damien. « Los consulados catalanes en Siria (1187–1400) : Algunos datos de historia e historiografía ». Dans *La Mediterrània de la Corona d'Aragó, segles* XIII–XVI *& VII centenari de la Sentència arbitral de Torrellas, 1304–2004*. XVIII *Congrés Internacional d'Història de la Corona d'Aragó*, édité par Rafael Narbona Vizcaíno, 179–188. Valence : Universitat de Valencia – Fundació Jaume II el Just, 2005.

Durán Duelt, Daniel. « La red consular catalana : Origen y desarrollo ». Dans *Mediterraneum : el esplendor del Mediterráneo medieval s.* XIII–XV, édité par Joan Alemany et Xabier Barral i Altet, 352–361. Barcelone : Lunwerg Editores, 2004.

Emon, Anver M. *Religious Pluralism and Islamic Law : Dhimmīs and Others in the Empire of Law*. Oxford : Oxford University Press, 2012.

Fattal, Antoine. *Le statut légal des non-musulmans en pays d'Islam*. Beyrouth : Imprimerie catholique, 1958.

Ferrer Mallol, Maria Teresa. « El Consolat de Mar i els consolats d'Ultramar, instrument i manifestació de l'expansió del comerç català ». Dans *L'expansió catalana a la Mediterrània a la baixa edat mitjana*, édité par Damien Coulon et Maria Teresa Ferrer i Mallol, 53–80. Barcelone : CSIC, 1999.

Gioffrè, Domenico, éd. *Lettere di Giovanni da Pontremoli mercante genovese, 1453–1459*. Gênes : Istituto di paleografia e storia medievale – Università di Genova, 1982.

Girardi, Francesca, éd. *Venezia e il regno di Tunisi : gli accordi diplomatici conclusi fra il 1231 e il 1456*. Rome : Viella, 2006.

Goldberg, Jessica. « The Courts, the Qadi, and the « People » : Resolving Mercantile Disputes in the Medieval Islamic Mediterranean ». Dans *Conflict Management in the Mediterranean and the Atlantic, 1000–1800: Actors, Institutions and Strategies of Dispute Settlement*, édité par Louis Sicking et Alain Wijffels, 19–42. Leyde : Brill, 2020.

Gourdin, Philippe. « Les marchands étrangers ont-ils un statut de dhimmi ? : À propos de quelques statuts de marchands étrangers dans les pays chrétiens et musulmans de Méditerranée occidentale au XIIIe siècle ». Dans *Migrations et diasporas méditerranéennes (X^e^–XVIe siècles)*, édité par Michel Balard et Alain Ducellier, 436–446. Paris : Publications de la Sorbonne, 2002.

Holt, Peter Malcolm, éd. *Early Mamluk Diplomacy (1260–1290) : Treaties of Baybars and Qalāwūn with Christian Rulers*. Leyde : Brill, 1995.

Jacoby, David. « Le consulat vénitien d'alexandrie d'après un document inédit de 1284 ». Dans *Chemins d'outre-mer: Études d'histoire sur la Méditerranée médiévale offertes à Michel Balard*, édité par Damien Coulon, Catherine Otten-Froux, Paule Pagès et Dominique Valérian, 461–474. Paris : Publications de la Sorbonne, 2004.

Jorga, Nicolas. « Notes et extraits pour servir à l'histoire des croisades au XVe siècle ». *Revue de l'Orient Latin* 8 (1901) : 1–115.

Kedar, Benjamin Z. « L'Officium Robarie di Genova : un tentativo di coesistere con la violenza ». *Archivio Storico Italiano* 143, n° 3 (525) (1985) : 331–372.

Khadduri, Majid. *War and Peace in the Law of Islam*. Clark : Lawbook Exchange, 2006.

Klüpfel, Ludwig. *Die äussere Politik Alphonsos III : Beiträge zur Geschichte der inneren Politik Alfonsos*. Berlin : W. Rothschild, 1911.

López de Meneses, Amada. « Los consulados catalanes de Alejandría, y Damasco en el reinado de Pedro el Ceremonioso ». *Estudios de edad media de la Corona de Aragón* 6 (1956) : 83–183.

Mas Latrie, Louis de, éd. *Traités de paix et de commerce et documents divers concernant les relations des chrétiens avec les Arabes de l'Afrique septentrionale au moyen âge*. Paris : H. Plon, 1865.

McCormick, Michael. *Origins of the European Economy : Communications and Commerce, A.D. 300–900*. Cambridge : Cambridge University Press, 2001.

Moukarzel, Pierre. « La législation des autorités religieuses et politiques sur les marchands européens dans le sultanat mamelouk (1250–1517) ». Dans *La cohabitation religieuse dans les villes européennes, X^e–XVe siècles*, édité par Stéphane Boissellier et John Tolan, 121–139. Turnhout : Brepols, 2014.

Nielsen, Jørgen S. *Secular justice in an Islamic state : Maẓālim under the Baḥrī Mamlūks, 662/1264–789/1387*. Leyde : Instituut voor het Nabije Oosten, 1985.

Pallavicino, Eleonora, éd. *I libri iurium della Repubblica di Genova*. Gênes : Regione Liguria, 2001.

Petti Balbi, Giovanna. « Il consolato genovese di Tunisi nel Quattrocento ». *Archivio Storico Italiano* 156, n° 2 (576) (1998) : 227–256.

Petti Balbi, Giovanna. *Comunità forestiere e « nationes » nell'Europa dei secoli XIII–XVI*. Naples : Liguori Editore, 2001.

Petti Balbi, Giovanna, éd. *Saggi e documenti*. Gênes : Civico istituto colombiano, 1978.

Pistarino, Geo, éd. *Notai genovesi in Oltremare : Atti rogati a Tunisi da Pietro Battifoglio (1288–1289)*. Gênes : Istituto di Medievistica, 1986.

Pozza, Marco, éd. *I trattati con Aleppo : 1207–1254*. Venise : Cardo, 1990.

Rousseau, Romain. *L'affaire de Tunis. Commerce et politique en Ifrīqiya almohade (596–598/1200–1202)*. Paris : L'Harmattan, 2025.

Serrano, Delfina. « Forum Shopping in al-Andalus (II) : Discussing Coran V, 42 and 49 (Ibn Hazm, Ibn Rushd al-Jadd, Abû Bakr Ibn al-'Arabî and al-Qurtubî) ». Dans *Law and Religious Minorities in Medieval Societies : Between Theory and Praxis*, édité par Ana Echevarría, Juan Pedro Monferrer Sala et John Tolan, 173–196. Turnhout : Brepols, 2016.

Thomas, Georg Martin, et Lukas Friedrich Tafel, Gottlieb éd. *Urkunden zur älteren Handels- und Staatsgeschichte der Republik Venedig*. Vienne : Hof- und Staatsdruckerei, 1856.

Tillier, Mathieu. « Introduction : Le pluralisme judiciaire en Islam, ses dynamiques et ses enjeux ». *Bulletin d'études orientales* 63 (2015) : 23–40.

Tillier, Mathieu. *L'invention du cadi : la justice des musulmans, des Juifs et des chrétiens aux premiers siècles de l'Islam*. Paris : Publications de la Sorbonne, 2017.

Urbani, Rossana. « Genova e il Maghrib tra il '400 e '500 (nuovi documenti archivistici) ». Dans *Genova, la Liguria e l'Oltremare tra medioevo ed età moderna : studi e ricerche d'archivio*, édité par Raffaele Belvederi, 185–206. Gênes : Bozzi, 1976.

Valérian, Dominique. « Les archives de Marseille, sources de l'histoire du Maghreb médiéval : le cas du port de Bougie (XIIIe–XVe siècles) ». *Annales du Midi* 113, n° 233 (2001) : 5–26, https://doi.org/10.3406/anami.2001.2688.

Valérian, Dominique. « Conflits et résolution des conflits dans les communautés européennes au Maghreb (XIIe–XVe siècle) ». *Communautés et pouvoirs en Italie et au Maghreb au Moyen Âge et à l'époque moderne : Actes du séminaire de Rome, 26–27 octobre 2001, Mélanges de l'école française de Rome* 115, n° 1 (2003) : 543–564.

Valérian, Dominique. « Traités de paix et normes juridico-religieuses en Méditerranée à la fin du Moyen Âge. Entre pluralisme normatif et hiérarchie des normes ».

Dans *Avant l'État : Droit international et pluralisme politico-juridique en Europe, XIIe–XVIIe siècle*, édité par Dante Fedele, Randall Lesaffer et Pierre Savy, 251–268. Rome : Historia et ius, 2024.

Viladrich i Grau, Mercè. « L'extraterritorialitat del dret : una concessio atorgada al consol dels catalans a Alexandria el 1430 ». Dans *La Corona d'Aragona ai tempi di Alfonso il Magnanimo. XVI Congreso de Historia de la Corona de Aragón (Napoli, Caserta et Ischia, 18–24 settembre 1997)*, édité par Guido d'Agostino et Giulia Buffardi, t. 1, 807–829. Naples : Paparo, 2000.

Wansbrough, John. « The Safe-Conduct in Muslim Chancery Practice ». *Bulletin of the School of Oriental and African Studies* 34, n° 1 (1971) : 20–35.

9

Juridiction ou police ?

Les ambigüités de la distinction entre compétence juridictionnelle et pouvoirs de police du consul dans les échelles du Levant et de Barbarie (XVIe–XVIIIe siècle)

Victor Simon

Dans un mémoire adressé au comte de Castellane, ambassadeur à la Porte entre 1741 et 1747, la Chambre de commerce de Marseille insiste tout particulièrement sur le rôle des consuls dans le maintien de l'ordre public parmi les communautés françaises installées au Levant et en Barbarie. Selon elle, le « bon ordre et l'union parmy la nation, dans chaque échelle, étant absolument nécessaires pour la tranquilité des résidens et conséquemment pour le bien du commerce, il est essentiel que M. l'ambassadeur recommande aux consuls d'y entretenir la paix, de rompre les partis et les intrigues qui peuvent l'altérer et de luy rendre compte de tout ce qui peut troubler la tranquilité publique » et « s'il se remontroit des sujets scandaleux et de mauvaise vie et mœurs, il faudroit en délivrer les échelles »[1].

Les consuls français établis dans l'Empire ottoman jouissent du statut d'officiers royaux[2]. Cet office est notamment défini par Charles Loyseau dans ses *Cinq livres du droict des offices* publiés en 1610. Dans cet ouvrage, il l'envisage comme une « dignité avec function ordinaire en l'Estat »[3]. Dans son *Dictionnaire de droit et de pratique*, Claude-Joseph de Ferrière le définit lui aussi comme « une dignité ou fonction publique »[4]. À l'étranger, le consul est par

1 *Mémoire de la Chambre de commerce de Marseille à M. le comte de Castelanne, nommé par le roi son ambassadeur à la Porte ottomane*, s. d. (Paris : AN, AE/B/III/237, pièce 3, fol. 4).

2 Sur le statut d'officier, voir : Roland Mousnier, *La vénalité des offices sous Henri IV et Louis XIII* (Paris : PUF, 1971).

3 Charles Loyseau, *Cinq livres du droict des offices* (Paris : L'Angelier, 1610), 15. Loyseau (1564–1627) est avocat au Parlement de Paris puis magistrat. Il est l'auteur de plusieurs monographies consacrées aux rentes, à la justice, aux seigneuries ou aux offices. Sur cet auteur, voir Brigitte Basdevant-Gaudemet, *Charles Loyseau (1564–1627) : théoricien de la puissance publique* (Paris : Economica, 1976).

4 Claude-Joseph de Ferrière, *Dictionnaire de droit et de pratique*, t. 2 (Paris : Bauche, 1771), 287. D'abord avocat au Parlement de Paris, Ferrière (1666–1747) est nommé en 1703 professeur de droit civil à la faculté de droit de Paris où il finit sa carrière comme doyen. Sur cet auteur, voir Jacqueline Moreau-David, « Claude-Joseph de Ferrière », dans *Dictionnaire historique*

 | HTTPS://DOI.ORG/10.1163/9789004755192-011

conséquent chargé de représenter le roi et d'exercer une autorité sur ses sujets, afin de maintenir la discipline parmi les régnicoles[5]. En vertu de ses lettres de provision[6], il bénéficie d'une délégation de pouvoir de la part du roi qui lui confère de larges prérogatives sur les sujets français résidant dans le ressort de leur consulat. D'aucuns reprochent d'ailleurs aux consuls du Levant de jouir d'un pouvoir « presqu'absolu »[7], voire de se comporter en « petits despotes »[8] vis-à-vis de leurs nationaux. Dans un mémoire de 1688, des marchands établis à Smyrne se plaignent par exemple que le consul de l'échelle les « traite indignement … et avec des emportemens de mespris qui sont extraordinaires, et dez qu'on n'opine pas à son gré, il menace aussy tost de faire embarquer »[9].

Quoi qu'il en soit, le statut et les prérogatives des consuls dans les échelles du Levant et de Barbarie sont fixés conjointement par les capitulations ottomanes et la législation royale française. Ces capitulations promulguées par le sultan turc sont une concession de privilèges destinés aux sujets du roi de France[10]. Elles reposent sur le concept d'*amān* qui exprime la protection qui peut être accordée par n'importe quel musulman à un étranger présent sur le *dār al-'islām*[11]. En droit ottoman, ces textes sont d'ailleurs désignés par le terme turc-ottoman d'*'adhname* qui dérive de l'arabe *'ahd*, la promesse, et *'amān*, le

des juristes français (XIIe–XXe siècle), éd. Patrick Arabeyre, Jean-Louis Halpérin et Jacques Krynen (Paris : PUF, 2015), 424–425.

5 Sur cette volonté d'exercer un contrôle sur les sujets français établis en Orient, voir Victor Simon, « Légiférer contre l'acculturation des marchands français dans l'espace ottoman (XVIIe–XVIIIe siècle) : l'appréhension par le droit d'un entre-deux contraint », dans *L'expérience de la mobilité de l'Antiquité à nos jours, entre précarité et confiance*, éd. Claudia Moatti et Emmanuelle Chevreau (Bordeaux : Ausonius, 2021), 141–154.

6 Pour un exemple, voir la « Lettre de provision pour Raphaël Labia », 24 octobre 1532, dans *Ordonnances des rois de France. Règne de François Ier*, t. 6/1 (Paris : Imprimerie nationale, 1940), 289.

7 Charles de Peyssonnel, *Examen du livre intitulé Considérations sur la guerre actuelle des Turcs, par Monsieur de Volney* (Amsterdam : s. e., 1788), 227.

8 Constantin-François Chassebœuf de La Giraudais, *Considérations sur la guerre actuelle des Turcs* (Londres : s. e., 1788), 87.

9 « Mémoire concernant l'eschelle de Smyrne », 20 mai 1688 (Paris : AN, AE/B/III/235, pièce 18, fol. 2v).

10 Victor Simon, *Les échelles du Levant et de Barbarie. Droit du commerce international entre la France et l'Empire ottoman (XVIe–XVIIIe siècle)* (Paris : LGDJ, 2021), 13–73.

11 Suraiya Faroqhi, « Before 1600 : Ottoman Attitudes towards Merchants from Latin Christendom », *Turcica* 34 (2002), 75 Edhem Eldem, « Foreigners at the Threshold of Felicity : the Reception of Foreigners in Ottoman Istanbul », dans *Cultural Exchange in Early Modern Europe*, éd. Donatella Calabi et Stephen Christensen, t. 2, *Cities and Cultural Exchange in Europe* (Cambridge : Cambridge University Press, 2007), 117.

sauf-conduit[12]. Bien qu'elles soient souvent assimilées à des traités internationaux, les capitulations prennent la forme d'actes unilatéraux, comparables à des lettres patentes fondées sur le pouvoir législatif séculier du sultan[13]. En l'espèce, le sultan accorde donc une protection générale à l'ensemble des sujets français, leur permettant d'aller et venir sur le territoire turc, tout en consacrant la libre circulation de leurs marchandises. De plus, les capitulations autorisent le roi de France à établir des consulats dans les principales places commerciales de l'Empire ottoman, afin de représenter les intérêts commerciaux des marchands et de trancher, sur place, les litiges qui opposeraient deux ressortissants français[14].

Afin de préciser le statut et les compétences des consuls, la monarchie développe en outre une abondante législation. En la matière, l'inflation législative s'avère particulièrement significative et témoigne de l'emprise croissante de la monarchie sur cette institution. Seules trois ordonnances ayant directement trait aux consulats sont promulguées entre 1551 et 1625. Leur nombre se porte à dix-sept entre 1626 et 1699, auquel s'ajoutent dix-neuf arrêts du Conseil du roi. Au cours du XVIIIe siècle, trente-quatre ordonnances et vingt arrêts supplémentaires sont promulgués[15]. La plupart de ces dispositions sont finalement reprises par la grande *Ordonnance sur les consulats, la résidence, le commerce et la navigation des sujets du roi dans les échelles du Levant et de Barbarie* du 3 mars 1781, qui comporte plus de trois cents articles répartis en quatre titres[16].

En vertu de ces différents textes, les consuls disposent de trois attributions principales : le renseignement, la police de l'échelle et une compétence juridictionnelle. En effet, les consuls entretiennent d'abord une correspondance

12 Viorel Panaite, « Being a Western Merchant in the Ottoman Mediterranean », dans *Isam Konuşmalari. Osmanli Düşüncesi, Ahlâk, Huruk, Felsefe-Kelâm*, éd. Seyfi Kenan (Istanbul : ISAM, 2013), 92–94.

13 Cette unilatéralité repose d'ailleurs sur une conception asymétrique des relations internationales partagée par les princes musulmans qui leur interdit de traiter d'égal à égal avec des souverains chrétiens. Sur ce point, voir Mohammad Talaat Al-Ghunaimi, *The Muslim Conception of International Law and the Western Approach* (La Haye : Martinus Nijhoff, 1968) Viorel Panaite, « Islamic Tradition and Ottoman Law of Nations », dans *The Turks*, éd. Hasan Güzel, Cem Oğuz et Osman Karatay (Ankara : Yeni Türkiye, 2002), 5 : 597–604.

14 Géraud Poumarède, « Naissance d'une institution royale : les consuls de la nation française en Levant et en Barbarie aux XVIe et XVIIe siècles », *Annuaire-bulletin de la Société de l'histoire de France* (2001), 65–128.

15 Pour le détail de ces textes, voir Simon, *Les échelles du Levant*, 255–261.

16 « Ordonnance concernant les consulats, la résidence, le commerce et la navigation des sujets du roi, dans les échelles du Levant et de Barbarie », 3 mars 1781, dans Johann Christoph Wilhelm von Steck, *Essai sur les consuls* (Berlin : Frederic Nicolai, 1790), 71–172.

soutenue avec les secrétaires d'État de la Marine et des Affaires étrangères[17]. Ils y rapportent régulièrement à l'administration royale les principaux évènements qui ont eu lieu dans le ressort de leur consulat. Le domaine de cette mission de renseignement est précisé, au XVIIe siècle, par des instructions de Colbert expédiées le 16 mars 1669 à l'ensemble des consuls établis dans les pays étrangers. Ceux-ci doivent notamment informer le gouvernement des éventuelles évolutions de la politique locale et des mouvements de troupes, mais également des importations et des exportations réalisées par les marchands français, des types de marchandises transitant par l'échelle, de la production locale, des taux de changes pratiqués et plus généralement de l'ensemble des informations susceptibles d'affecter le commerce[18]. Ces prescriptions poursuivent la finalité d'informer précisément le gouvernement royal sur la situation locale, tant sur le plan politique et militaire que commercial, grâce au maillage de consulats français présents sur le territoire turc. Les consuls établis dans l'Empire ottoman disposent ensuite de compétences en matière de police, afin de maintenir l'ordre au sein des nationaux. À ce titre, ils peuvent promulguer des règlements applicables aux régnicoles ou encore ordonner l'expulsion des fauteurs de troubles. Les consuls sont enfin compétents pour trancher, dans les échelles, les litiges qui pourraient survenir entre les sujets du roi de France. En principe, ils font ainsi office de juges ordinaires des Français établis dans les échelles du Levant et de Barbarie. Si ces deux dernières compétences – police et juridiction – sont bien distinguées par la législation royale et la doctrine (1), elles semblent néanmoins faire l'objet d'une certaine confusion dans la pratique consulaire (2).

1 La double compétence théorique des consuls

Les capitulations octroyées par Sélim II en 1569 prévoient que « si les dicts François ont desbat et differend l'un avec l'autre, leurs ambassadeurs et consuls, selon leur conscience, decideront les differens sans que nul aye à les empescher »[19]. Les capitulations de 1581 promulguées par Mourad III

---

17 Jörg Ulbert, « La dépêche consulaire française et son acheminement en Méditerranée sous Louis XIV (1661–1715) », dans *Les consuls en Méditerranée, agents d'information*, éd. Silvia Marzagalli (Paris : Classiques Garnier, 2015), 31–57.

18 « Instruction pour les consuls de France à l'étranger », 16 mars 1669, dans Pierre Clément, *Lettres, instructions et mémoires de Colbert* (Paris : Imprimerie impériale, 1863), 2 : 453–455.

19 « Capitulations de Sélim II », 18 octobre 1569, art. 12, dans François-Emmanuel Guignard de Saint-Priest, *Mémoires sur l'ambassade de France en Turquie et sur le commerce des Français dans le Levant* (Paris : Ernest Leroux, 1877), 372.

renouvellent ce principe en prévoyant que « si les Français ont l'un avec l'autre quelque procès et différend, leurs ambassadeurs et consuls voient et décident, selon leurs usages, leurs procès et différends »[20]. Des dispositions analogues figurent par ailleurs dans toutes les capitulations postérieures[21]. Jusqu'à la fin du XVIIe siècle, aucune ordonnance royale française ne précise l'étendue de la compétence juridictionnelle des consuls. Le droit capitulaire fixe ainsi un cadre très souple, en laissant la plus grande latitude possible aux consuls pour trancher les litiges qui opposent leurs régnicoles. En leur laissant le soin des procès entre sujets du roi de France, les capitulations se bornent ainsi à proclamer un principe d'extraterritorialité, sans toutefois en fixer les contours.

Cette juridiction présente d'ailleurs des traits particulièrement originaux. Localement, le consul est en effet le juge de quelques dizaines de ressortissants français qu'il côtoie quotidiennement, pour la plupart des marchands marseillais[22]. Selon la lettre des capitulations, les consuls jouissent en principe d'une compétence universelle dans le ressort de leur échelle, tant dans les domaines civil, commercial que pénal. Dans un mémoire rédigé en 1665, les responsables de la Chambre de commerce de Marseille relèvent néanmoins qu'en cas de crime grave, le consul se limite le plus souvent à instruire l'affaire, avant de la déférer aux juridictions ordinaires du royaume[23].

Cet usage est d'ailleurs partiellement consacré par l'ordonnance sur la marine de 1681. Ce texte confirme en effet la pleine compétence du consul en matière civile et commerciale. Il établit néanmoins une limite à sa compétence en matière pénale. Selon l'ordonnance, les consuls rendent désormais leurs jugements en premier et dernier ressort lorsque l'auteur des faits n'encourt aucune peine afflictive[24], c'est-à-dire aucune peine portant atteinte à

20 « Capitulations de Mourad III », 15 juillet 1581, dans Guignard de Saint-Priest, *Mémoires*, 389.

21 « Capitulations de Mehmed III », 25 février 1597, dans Guignard de Saint-Priest, *Mémoires*, 404 « Capitulations d'Ahmed Ier », 20 mai 1604, art. 48, dans Guignard de Saint-Priest, *Mémoires*, 428 « Capitulations de Mehmed IV », 5 juin 1673, dans Guignard de Saint-Priest, *Mémoires*, 464 « Capitulations de Mahmud Ier », 30 mai 1740, art. 15, dans Guignard de Saint-Priest, *Mémoires*, 486.

22 Par exemple, voir le recensement des marchands résidant à Chypres réalisé en 1698 par le consul de Larnaca, François Luce, « Mémoire concernant les marchands françois résidans en l'isle de Chipres », dans Anna Pouradier Duteil-Loizidou, *Consulat de France à Larnaca (1696–1699). Documents inédits pour servir à l'histoire de Chypre* (Nicosie : CRS, 1995), 2 : 133–137.

23 *Responce aux articles de l'instruction généralle des affaires du commerce de Marseille au Levant et terres du grand seigneur*, 1665 (Paris : AN, AE/B/III/234, pièce 15, fol. 5v).

24 *Ordonnance de la marine*, août 1681, livre I, titre IX, art. 13 (Paris : Thierry, 1687), 47.

l'intégrité corporelle ou à la liberté du condamné[25]. Dans le cas contraire, le consul se limite à mener l'instruction et transmet ensuite les pièces du dossier aux juridictions de l'amirauté[26]. Ces dispositions ont notamment été analysées par René-Josué Valin, dans son célèbre commentaire sur l'ordonnance de 1681[27]. Selon lui, cette distinction repose sur le principe de collégialité imposé par l'ordonnance criminelle de 1670[28]. En vertu de ce texte, dans tous les procès susceptibles d'aboutir à une condamnation à une peine afflictive, il est nécessaire que le jugement soit rendu par au moins trois juges gradués en droit ou ayant la qualité d'officiers royaux[29]. Dès lors, cette disposition censée garantir la compétence des juges rend impossible toute condamnation à une peine afflictive dans les échelles. Seul le consul bénéficie en effet du statut d'officier royal et l'écrasante majorité des marchands français qui pourraient faire office d'assesseurs, n'ont le plus souvent collationné aucun grade universitaire.

S'il jouit d'une très large compétence pour juger les différends survenus entre régnicoles, le consul ne peut enfin pas connaître des litiges mixtes qui impliquent un sujet français et un sujet du sultan. En vertu des capitulations, ceux-ci relèvent en effet du juge ordinaire ottoman : le cadi[30]. Lors de l'instance, le consul peut simplement apporter son assistance et ses conseils à ses nationaux, assisté du drogman qui fait office de traducteur[31].

---

25 Sur les peines afflictives voir Jean-Marie Carbasse, *Histoire du droit pénal et de la justice criminelle* (Paris : PUF, 2014), 294–295.

26 *Ordonnance de la marine*, août 1681, livre I, titre IX, art. 14 (Paris : Thierry, 1687), 47.

27 Avocat au présidial de La Rochelle, Valin (1695–1765) est l'auteur de plusieurs ouvrages consacrés au droit maritime et à la coutume de La Rochelle. Sur cet auteur, voir Solange Ségala-de-Carbonnières, « René-Josué Valin », dans *Dictionnaire historique des juristes*, 994–995.

28 *Ordonnance criminelle*, août 1670, titre XXV, art. 10 (Paris : Les Associez, 1670), 145.

29 René-Josué Valin, *Nouveau commentaire sur l'ordonnance de la marine du mois d'août 1681*, t. 1 (La Rochelle : Legier, 1766), 257.

30 « Capitulations de Sélim II », 18 octobre 1569, art. 11, dans Guignard de Saint-Priest, *Mémoires*, 372 « Capitulations de Mourad III », 15 juillet 1581, dans Guignard de Saint-Priest, *Mémoires*, 389 « Capitulations de Mehmed III », 25 février 1597, dans Guignard de Saint-Priest, *Mémoires*, 408 « Capitulations d'Ahmed Ier », 20 mai 1604, art. 47, dans Guignard de Saint-Priest, *Mémoires*, 428 « Capitulations de Mehmed IV », 5 juin 1673, dans Guignard de Saint-Priest, *Mémoires*, 468 « Capitulations de Mahmud Ier », 30 mai 1740, art. 26, dans Guignard de Saint-Priest, *Mémoires*, 490–491.

31 Cette pratique est notamment décrite par Pierre Ariste : « Il est de leur devoir de protéger et soustenir les intérestz des marchandz françois et autres trafiquans soubz la bannière de France, de porter leurs plaintes et de deffendre leur cause devant les visirs, pachas, cadis et autres officiers de justice et de police, des vexations et avanies qui leurs sont faictes par les sujetz du grand seigneur et d'employer leur autorité a leur faire rendre la justice qui leur est deue ». *Traicté des consuls de la nation françoise aux pays*

Les lettres de provision qui fondent les offices consulaires au Proche Orient et en Afrique du Nord confèrent en outre des pouvoirs de police aux consuls. Elles leur assignent en effet la responsabilité de maintenir l'ordre entre les sujets du roi de France établis sur le territoire ottoman au moyen de pouvoirs de police. La lettre de provision délivrée par Henri III au consul de Tunis Louis de La Motte Dariès, le 28 mai 1577, dispose par exemple que ce consul est « créé et autorisé de nous pour avoir l'œil et intendance sur toutes les affaires qui peuvent concerner notre service et nos dits sujets, même pour y tenir un ordre politique »[32]. Elle ordonne également aux marchands présents dans le ressort du consulat qu'« ils obéissent et entendent diligemment ès choses touchant et concernant la dite charge »[33]. En vertu de leur statut d'officier royal, les consuls sont dès lors dépositaires d'une parcelle de l'autorité publique et représentent localement le roi.

Les pouvoirs de police dont sont pourvus les consuls sont précisés par la doctrine d'Ancien Régime qui les associent à une compétence réglementaire. Dans son *Traité des seigneuries*, Charles Loyseau les définit comme la capacité de « pouvoir faire des règlemens particuliers, pour tous les citoyens de son distroit et territoire »[34]. De manière générale, ces règlements de police ont pour objectif de maintenir l'ordre et la prospérité du royaume. À partir du XVIIe siècle, des auteurs commencent d'ailleurs à dresser des listes de domaines visés par les pouvoirs de police. Dans son ouvrage sur *La souveraineté du roy*, Cardin le Bret estime que ces règlements de police peuvent ainsi servir à orienter l'économie publique, à interdire les monopoles, à empêcher la corruption des mœurs, à adopter des mesures somptuaires, ou à lutter contre les jeux de hasard[35]. Cette liste est complétée par Nicolas Delamare qui fait paraître en 1705 un *Traité de la police*[36] et par Claude Fleury dans son *Droit public*

---

estrangers concernant leur origine, leurs establissements, leurs fonctions, leurs droicts, esmolumens, & autres prerogatives (s.l. : 1667, Paris : BnF, département des manuscrits, Français 18595), 190–191.

32 « Lettre patente d'Henri III », 28 mai 1577, dans Pierre Grandchamp, *La France en Tunisie* (Tunis : Imprimerie nationale, 1920), 1 : IX.

33 « Lettre patente d'Henri III », 28 mai 1577, dans Grandchamp, *La France en Tunisie*, 1 : X.

34 Charles Loyseau, *Traicté des seigneuries* (Paris : L'Angelier, 1609), 210.

35 Cardin Le Bret, *De la souveraineté du roy* (Paris : Toussaincts Du Bray, 1632), 683. Cardin Le Bret (1558–1655) occupe des fonctions de conseillers d'État et est l'auteur de plusieurs ouvrages sur le droit public et les parlements. Sur cet auteur, voir Gilbert Picot, *Cardin Le Bret (1558–1655) et la doctrine de la souveraineté* (Nancy : SIT, 1948).

36 Nicolas Delamare, *Traité de la Police* (Paris : Michel Brunet, 1722) 4. Procureur du roi puis commissaire au Châtelet, Delamare (1639–1723) n'a publié que cet unique ouvrage qui fait pourtant référence sous l'Ancien Régime. Sur cet auteur, voir Benoît Plessix, « Nicolas Delamare ou les fondations du droit administratif français », *Droits* 38 (2003), 113–133.

de France publié à titre posthume en 1769[37]. Ces deux auteurs y ajoutent un long catalogue de matières relevant de la police, comme la religion, la sûreté, la tranquillité publique, la voirie, le commerce, les manufactures, l'approvisionnement en nourriture, le logement, le chauffage, la santé publique, les poids et mesures, les monnaies ou la navigation.

Dans le Levant et en Barbarie, les pouvoirs de police du consul entrent néanmoins en concurrence avec ceux d'autres autorités. L'ambassadeur à Constantinople promulgue en effet ponctuellement des règlements de police applicables à certains consulats, et exerce ainsi une forme de tutelle hiérarchique sur les consuls. Le 25 septembre 1674, l'ambassadeur à la Porte, le marquis de Nointel, promulgue par exemple une ordonnance de police servant de règlement à l'échelle d'Alep. Il enjoint au consul de « bonifier le commerce », avant d'ajouter qu'« il est impossible d'y réussir si les marchands de chaque échelle négligent de vivre dans l'ordre, et si le consul manque à l'application qu'il y doit par son exemple, à la protection dont il est redevable à tous les marchands et à la juste autorité qui luy est due »[38]. Dans la suite du règlement, il impose une série de dispositions pour restaurer cet ordre, en fixant des règles sur la tenue des réunions de marchands, sur l'assistance aux offices religieux ou encore sur les politiques commerciales mises en œuvre dans le ressort de l'échelle. Une ordonnance du 26 novembre 1688 prévoit d'ailleurs qu'en cas de conflit entre le consul et les marchands de son échelle, l'affaire doit être portée devant l'ambassadeur[39].

Le roi dépêche également, à intervalle régulier, des inspecteurs des échelles dotés de commissions royales et chargés d'effectuer des tournées au Levant et en Barbarie afin d'y entendre les marchands et de remédier aux abus qui seraient portés à leur connaissance[40]. Ces inspecteurs promulguent eux aussi des règlements de police, dans lesquels ils encadrent le logement des mar-

37 Claude Fleury, *Droit public de France*, éd. J.-B. Daragon (Paris : Pierres, 1769) t. I, 135–136. Après avoir embrassé la carrière ecclésiastique, Claude Fleury (1640–1723) se voit confier l'abbaye du Loc-Dieu. Proche de la Cour, il est notamment nommé sous-précepteur des fils du roi, puis confesseur de Louis XV. Il est l'auteur de plusieurs traités juridiques publiés après sa mort, comme l'*Institution au droit françois*, ou le *Droit public de la France*. Sur cet auteur, voir Fabrice Hoarau, Claude Fleury (1640–1723) : *la raison et l'histoire* (Dijon : thèse dactyl., 2003).

38 « Ordonnance [du marquis de Nointel] servant de règlement à l'échelle d'Alep », 25 septembre 1674 (Paris : AN, Mar/B/7/205, fol. 141v).

39 Cette ordonnance du 26 novembre 1688 a été lue à l'assemblée du corps de la nation à La Canée et reproduite dans le *Procès-verbal de l'assemblée de la nation à La Canée*, 1er septembre 1710 (Nantes : CADN, 328 PO, série 1, 190).

40 À propos des inspecteurs, voir Bernard Barbiche, *Les institutions de la monarchie française à l'époque moderne* (XVIe–XVIIIe *siècle*) (Paris : PUF, 2001), 86–87.

chands, imposent le respect des fêtes religieuses, interdisent les jeux de hasard ou réglementent l'ouverture des auberges et des tavernes[41]. Enfin, la Chambre de commerce de Marseille délibère parfois elle aussi pour chercher à imposer des mesures de police destinées aux négociants installés dans les échelles. Dans une lettre du 16 août 1773 adressée à la Chambre, le secrétaire d'État de la Marine, le marquis de Boynes, censure toutefois cette pratique en rappelant qu'à l'étranger, les marchands français sont « entièrement sous la police des consuls », sans que la Chambre puisse s'« en mêler en aucune manière »[42].

En vertu des capitulations et de la législation des rois de France, les consuls sont donc pourvus d'une double compétence. Dans le ressort de leur consulat, ils disposent d'une compétence juridictionnelle pour trancher les litiges qui surviendraient entre régnicoles et de pouvoirs de police qui leurs permettent de promulguer des règlements pour maintenir l'ordre entre les sujets du roi de France établis sur le territoire ottoman. Toutefois, dans la pratique, on relève une certaine confusion entre l'emploi de ces deux compétences qui semblent souvent se confondre dans les échelles.

2 La confusion entre les deux compétences dans la pratique consulaire

La distinction fonctionnelle entre pouvoirs de police et compétence juridictionnelle est établie, semble-t-il pour la première fois[43], par Jean Bacquet dans son *Traicté des droictz de iustice* publié en 1587[44]. Dans cet ouvrage, l'avocat

---

41 Pour des exemples, voir *Règlement fait par Monsieur d'Ortières, envoyé de sa majesté pour la visite des échelles du Levant*, 8 octobre 1687 (Marseille : ACCIM, J 1573) *Idem*, 26 juin 1706 (Marseille : ACCIM, J 1575) *Idem*, 17 juillet 1706 (Paris : AN, AE/B/III/192, pièce 33) *Idem*, 25 septembre 1706 (Marseille : ACCIM, Ajout d'un espace insécable entre "J" et "1575") *Idem*, 29 septembre 1706 (Marseille : ACCIM, J 1575) *Idem*, 9 décembre 1706 (Marseille : ACCIM, J 1575) *Idem le corps de la nation françoise établie à Smirne à la teneur de leurs assemblées*, 20 mars 1778 (Marseille : ACCIM, J 1577).

42 *Lettre du marquis de Boynes à la Chambre de commerce de Marseille*, 16 août 1773 (Marseille : ACCIM, J 20), fol. 1v.

43 Des ordonnances de police sont promulguées dès l'époque médiévale, mais celles-ci ne font encore l'objet d'aucune analyse théorique en doctrine. Sur ce point, voir Albert Rigaudière, « Les ordonnances de police en France à la fin du Moyen Âge », dans *Policey im Europa der Frühen Neuzeit*, éd. Michael Stolleis, Karl Härter et Lothar Schilling (Frankfurt am Main : Klostermann, 1996), 97–162.

44 Jean Bacquet (1520–1597) est avocat au parlement de Paris, avant d'être nommé avocat du roi à la chambre des trésoriers de France en 1570. Il est notamment l'auteur de plusieurs traités sur le domaine de la couronne, ainsi que d'écrits consacrés au droit

parisien affirme en effet que « le droict de iustice ne contient en soy le droict de police, ains sont droictz distinctz et séparez », ou encore que le « droit de iustice et de police n'ont rien de commun l'un avec l'autre »[45]. Cette différence essentielle est approfondie au début du XVIIe siècle par Charles Loyseau, pour qui « il faut soigneusement distinguer le droict de faire les réglemens politiques, enquoy consiste le vray droict de police, d'avec l'exécution et cognoissance des contraventions à ce réglement qui dépend sans doute de la simple et ordinaire iustice »[46]. Cette définition est encore reprise au milieu du XVIIe siècle par l'abbé Fleury, selon qui il convient de séparer « le pouvoir de faire réglemens et ordonnances de police, qui est une espèce de législation, de la simple exécution de ces règlemens qui est acte de juridiction ordinaire »[47]. Un consensus semble dès lors se dégager dans la doctrine d'Ancien Régime, pour considérer que les pouvoirs de police et la compétence juridictionnelle relèvent bien de deux notions distinctes sur le plan du droit[48].

Cette distinction échappe néanmoins très vraisemblablement à l'immense majorité des consuls français établis au Proche Orient et en Afrique du Nord. Ceux-ci sont en effet majoritairement issus de la bourgeoisie d'affaires ou de la petite noblesse et ont rarement suivi une formation juridique[49]. En outre, leur éloignement géographique rend difficile l'accès aux ouvrages de doctrine, qu'ils méconnaissent probablement très largement.

De plus, les subtilités de la législation royale entretiennent cette confusion, notamment en matière pénale. Une ordonnance du 26 novembre 1625 autorise par exemple les consuls à prononcer des mesures de police individuelles. Ce texte leur permet en effet de faire embarquer, sans jugement et sur le premier navire en partance pour le royaume, les « vagabons, insolens, séditieux

---

privé. Sur cet auteur, voir Guillaume Leyte, « Jean Bacquet », dans *Dictionnaire historique des juristes*, 41.

45 Jean Bacquet, *Traité des droits de iustice, haute, moyenne et basse* (Paris : Du Mesnil, 1664), 254.

46 Loyseau, *Traicté des seigneuries*, 210.

47 Fleury, *Droit public de France*, 1 : 217.

48 Paolo Napoli, « Police : la conceptualisation d'un modèle juridico-politique sous l'Ancien Régime », *Droits* 9, n° 20 (1994), 183–196, et 10, n° 21 (1995), 151–160 Bernard Durand, « La notion de police en France du XVIe au XVIIIe siècle », dans *Policey im Europa der Frühen Neuzeit*, éd. Michael Stolleis, Karl Härter et Lothar Schilling (Francfort sur le Main : Klostermann, 1996), 163–211 Marguerite Boulet-Sautel, « Police et administration en France à la fin de l'Ancien Régime. Observations terminologiques », dans *Vivre au royaume de France* (Paris : PUF, 2010), 209–213.

49 Anne Mézin, *Les consuls de France au siècle des Lumières (1715–1792)* (Paris : Ministère des Affaires étrangères, 1997), 73–77. Voir également Jörg Ulbert, « L'origine géographique des consuls français sous Louis XIV », *Cahiers de la Méditerranée*, n° 98 (2019), 11–27.

ou réfractaires au contenu des arrêts du Conseil de sa majesté et de son Parlement »[50]. Ceux-ci seront remis entravés au capitaine du navire, avec un procès-verbal dans lequel le consul consigne les raisons du renvoi des échelles, afin qu'à son retour, ils soient déférés au Parlement de Provence qui décidera des suites à donner. Dans cette hypothèse, le consul est donc invité à user de ses pouvoirs de police pour expulser un fauteur de troubles des échelles, sans pour autant trancher l'affaire au fond. La correspondance des consuls avec le secrétariat d'État de la Marine témoigne d'ailleurs du fréquent recours à ces mesures. Voici par exemple ce qu'écrit, en 1758, le vice-consul d'Alexandrie au secrétaire d'État Nicolas-René Berryer, après avoir ordonné l'expulsion des échelles d'un marchand nommé d'Étienne Sauvaire :

> Je fus obligé, le 3 juillet dernier, de le faire arrêter et constituer prisonnier pour empêcher qu'il ne se perdît entièrement, qu'il ne ruinât [...] les intérêts d'un magazin dont il vendoit les effets en sous-main, qu'il ne se fit Turc avec une jeune grecque qu'il entretenait et chez qui il avoit été menacé plusieurs fois d'être assassiné, et finalement qu'il ne plongeât la nation dans quelque mauvaise affaire. [...] Il joignoit à son goût des femmes, la passion du jeu, et malgré toutes mes précautions, il trouvoit le moyen de courir pendant la nuit les tavernes grecques et autres lieux, et j'ay scu de luy, pendant sa détention, qu'il y avoit fait des pertes considérables. Livré à ses débauches, il négligeait entièrement les affaires de son magazin, s'en raportant entièrement au sieur Martin Charpentier [avec] qui il s'était associé et qui seul faisait toute la besogne[51].

Un édit de juin 1778 généralise d'ailleurs cette pratique en imposant à l'ensemble des consuls d'exposer au secrétaire d'État de la Marine les motifs qui les auront conduits à adopter une mesure de police pour ordonner le renvoi d'un sujet français dans le royaume[52].

---

50 « Ordonnance sur les consulats du Levant », 26 novembre 1625 (Marseille : ACCIM, J 1557), fol. 1v–2r.

51 *Copie d'une lettre écritte à M. Berryer par M. Vallière, vice consul à Alexandrie*, 27 octobre 1758 (Marseille : ACCIM, J 97).

52 « Édit portant règlement sur les fonctions judiciaires et de police qu'exercent les consuls de France en pays étrangers », juin 1778, art. 81, dans François-André Isambert, Decrusy et Alphonse-Honoré Taillandier, *Recueil général des anciennes lois françaises, depuis d'an 420 jusqu'à la Révolution de 1789*, t. 25 (Paris : Belin-Prieur, 1821), 347.

L'ordonnance sur la marine de 1681 impose par ailleurs au consul de consulter les députés du corps de la nation[53], avant de rendre une ordonnance de police prononçant l'expulsion des échelles[54]. Cette disposition est à l'origine d'une certaine confusion entre les pouvoirs de police et la compétence juridictionnelle du consul qui impose, elle aussi, une consultation des députés. Dès l'époque médiévale, les statuts de la ville de Marseille défendent en effet aux *consules extra Massiliam* de prononcer un jugement *sine consilio et assensu consiliariorum*[55]. Au début du XVIIe siècle, l'usage semble s'être maintenu puisqu'on trouve mention, dans les registres de chancelleries[56], de jugements consulaires pris en « rode » ou en « roue »[57]. Ces termes qui dérivent probablement de la rote, renvoient à des assemblées de marchands qui assistent le consul dans sa prise de décision. Lorsqu'ils sont appelés à juger une affaire, les consuls développent ainsi la pratique de consulter plusieurs marchands de leur échelle pour recueillir leurs avis. L'ordonnance de 1681 consacre cet usage, en prévoyant que les jugements consulaires seront rendus après consultation des deux députés du corps de la nation et de quatre négociants notables de l'échelle[58]. Dans les plus petites échelles, il s'avère néanmoins parfois impossible de réunir six marchands français. Pour remédier à cette difficulté, une déclaration de 25 mai 1722 autorise les consuls à prononcer leurs jugements, après avoir recueilli l'avis des deux seuls députés, ou, à défaut, des deux principaux négociants résidant dans le ressort du consulat[59]. La majorité

53 Dans chaque consulat, les marchands forment un corps qui s'assemble notamment pour élire deux députés chargés de les représenter. Sur le statut et les fonctions de ces députés, voir Simon, *Les échelles du Levant*, 126–132.

54 *Ordonnance de la marine*, août 1681, livre I, titre IX, art. 15 (Paris : Thierry, 1687), 48.

55 « Statuts municipaux de Marseille », titre XVIII, art. 3, dans Monique Pernoud, *Les statuts municipaux de Marseille* (Monaco : Archives du Palais, 1949), 30.

56 Sur ces registres, voir Jérôme Cras, « Une approche archivistique des consulats de la Nation française : les actes de chancellerie consulaire sous l'Ancien Régime », dans *La fonction consulaire à l'époque moderne. L'affirmation d'une institution économique et politique (1500–1800)*, éd. Jörg Ulbert et Gérard Le Bouëdec (Rennes : Presses universitaires de Rennes, 2006), 51–84. Sur la chancellerie, voir également Jörg Ulbert, « Qu'est-ce qu'un chancelier de consulat ? Une approche par les textes de droit français », *MEFRIM*, 128, n° 2 (2016).

57 Guillaume Calafat, « La juridiction des consuls français en Méditerranée. Litiges marchands, arbitrages et circulation des procès (Livourne et Tunis au XVIIe siècle », dans *De l'utilité commerciale des consuls. L'institution consulaire et les marchands dans le monde méditerranéen (XVIIe–XXe siècle)*, éd. Arnaud Bartolomei *et al.* (Rome : École française de Rome, 2018), 168.

58 *Ordonnance de la marine*, août 1681, livre I, titre IX, art. 13 (Paris : Thierry, 1687), 47.

59 *Déclaration du roy pour authoriser les consuls de la nation françoise à rendre leurs sentences en appellant à leurs jugemens deux des deputez ou principaux négocians de la nation*, 25 mai 1722 (Paris : Imprimerie royale, 1722) [Paris, AN, AE/B/III/192, fol. 62].

de la doctrine s'accorde pourtant à considérer que l'avis rendu par les députés ou les marchands n'est qu'un avis consultatif que le consul n'est pas obligé de suivre[60]. Ce dernier point est finalement clarifié par un édit de 1778 qui prévoit que les marchands qui assistent le consul auront désormais voix délibérative, après avoir prêté serment[61].

Quoi qu'il en soit, la procédure pour promulguer une ordonnance de police s'avère proche de celle suivie dans le cadre processuel, puisque dans les deux hypothèses, les députés de la nation doivent être consultés. Cette confusion se retrouve d'ailleurs au sein même de la doctrine qui analyse ces dispositions. Dans son commentaire de l'ordonnance de 1681, Pierre Biarnoy de Merville estime en effet que les consuls qui promulguent une ordonnance de police agissent comme « juges de police, justice et finance » et que leurs décisions, qu'il qualifie de « jugements », « s'exécutent nonobstant toutes oppositions ou appellations quelconques, s'agissant d'un fait de police et de vuider les lieux de personnes d'une vie et conduite scandaleuse »[62]. À l'inverse, Valin relève que la conduite d'un régnicole menant à son expulsion des échelles par ordonnance du consul, ne constitue pas nécessairement une infraction pénale. Selon lui, cette simple mesure individuelle de police est prononcée contre un sujet menant une « vie et conduite scandaleuse », or ces termes sont « applicables à ceux dont l'humeur fâcheuse trouble la société par des querelles et des insultes fréquentes que les punitions ordinaires ne peuvent réprimer, aussi bien qu'à ceux dont la conduite licentieuse et débauchée est un sujet de scandale continuel »[63]. Il en conclut que l'expulsion n'est dès lors qu'un « fait de police » et ne saurait être assimilé à un jugement[64].

Y compris lorsque les faits commis relèvent d'une qualification pénale, les consuls semblent le plus souvent recourir à leurs pouvoirs de police pour renvoyer immédiatement un régnicole dans le royaume afin qu'il soit remis aux

---

60 Pierre Biarnoy de Merville, *Ordonnance de la marine du mois d'aoust 1681 commentée et conferée sur les anciennes ordonnances, le droit romain et les nouveaux règlemens* (Paris : Osmont, 1714), 77; Valin, *Nouveau commentaire*, t. 1, 254.

61 *« Édit portant règlement sur les fonctions judiciaires et de police qu'exercent les consuls de France en pays étrangers »*, juin 1778, art. 6, dans Isambert, Decrusy et Taillandier, *Recueil général des anciennes lois françaises*, t. 25, 335.

62 Biarnoy de Merville, *Ordonnance de la marine*, 78. Avocat aux parlements de Normandie et de Paris, cet auteur a notamment commenté les coutumes de Normandie et de Chartres, ainsi que les ordonnances civile et de la marine. Sur cet auteur, voir Virginie Lemonnier-Lesage, « Pierre Biarnoy de Merville », dans *Dictionnaire historique des juristes*, 109–110.

63 Valin, *Nouveau commentaire*, t. 1, 258.

64 Ibid.

juridictions ordinaires, sans le juger sur place. Par exemple, en 1662, deux artisans français, Denis Aigneau et Antoine Bleau, établis à Seyde sont surpris en train de commettre des « sallettés impudiques » avec une « fame more de ce pays de mauvaise vie »[65]. Le consul ordonne alors leur renvoi en France, pour qu'ils soient jugés par le lieutenant de l'amirauté[66]. Une affaire similaire survient encore à Seyde, en 1697. Là encore, un garçon boulanger français est arrêté par la garde de la ville « dans une grotte avec une fame turque de mauvaise vie »[67], avant d'être remis au consul. Celui-ci prononce sur le champ une ordonnance de renvoi des échelles, afin qu'il soit jugé dans le royaume[68]. De la même manière, en 1736, un artisan tailleur nommé Blaise de Prague et accusé d'ivrognerie fait l'objet d'une ordonnance d'expulsion du consul de La Canée[69]. On pourrait ainsi multiplier les exemples, car les archives regorgent d'exemples d'ordonnances d'expulsion des échelles de sujets s'étant livrés à de petites infractions.

Pourtant, dans les dépouillements opérés aux Archives nationales, aux Archives de la Chambre de commerce de Marseille et au Centre des archives diplomatiques de Nantes, nous n'avons jamais trouvé aucun jugement consulaire portant sur la matière pénale[70]. Il semble dès lors que les consuls du Levant et de Barbarie n'aient jamais opéré de véritable distinction entre ce qui pouvait relever de leurs pouvoirs de police et de leur compétence juridic-

---

65 *Verbal faict par le consul de Seyde et la nattion françoise*, 14 octobre 1662 (Marseille : ACCIM, J 96), fol. 4v.

66 *Concluzions civilles des sieurs eschevins et députés du comerce contre Antoine Bleau et Denis Vigneau*, 1662 (Marseille : ACCIM, J 96). L'affaire a ensuite fait l'objet d'un appel devant le parlement de Provence, voir l'*Extrait des registres du Parlement*, 7 décembre 1662 (Marseille : ACCIM, J 96) et l'*Extrait des registres du Parlement*, 11 janvier 1663 (s. l. : s. e., 1663 [Marseille : ACCIM, J 96]).

67 *Extrait des registres de la chancellerie de Saïde et ses dépendences*, 23 septembre 1697 (Marseille : ACCIM, J 96), fol. 1.

68 *Ordonnance du M. Lempereur, consul, portant injonction au capitaine Louis Bruc d'embarquer le nommé Maire de la Ciotat, surpris avec une femme turque de mauvaise vie*, 26 septembre 1697 (Marseille : ACCIM, J 96) *Lettre des Sieurs maire, eschevins et députez du commerce de la ville de Marseille à M. le premier président et intendant*, 1698 (Marseille : ACCIM, J 96).

69 *Procès-verbal de l'assemblée de la nation à La Canée*, 15 mars 1736 (Nantes : CADN, 328 PO, série 1, 191).

70 Ces dépouillements sont loin d'être exhaustifs, puisqu'ils ont porté sur les registres d'Alep, de La Canée, de Saint Jean d'Acre, de Tripoli du Barbarie et de Tripoli de Syrie conservés au CADN, auxquels viennent s'ajouter les registres de Larnaca publiés par Duteil-Loizidou, *Consulat de France à Larnaca*. Toutefois, l'ensemble représente tout de même un volume substantiel de documents, dans lesquels figurent en revanche de nombreuses ordonnances de police.

tionnelle. De plus, dans la position du consul, il était probablement préférable de faire immédiatement expulser un sujet turbulent des échelles, plutôt que de prendre le risque de le voir récidiver, en entraînant ainsi le discrédit de l'ensemble des marchands français établis dans la ville. Cette manière de procéder avait d'ailleurs déjà été relevée au milieu du XVIIe siècle par Pierre Ariste dans son *Traicté des consuls*. Il relate en effet que « pour ce qui est des marchandz françois et autres négocians soubs la bannière de France, s'ilz sont accusés de quelque crime », le consul « en faict seulement informer, et les renvoye avec l'information en leur pays pour leur estre le procez faict et parfaict par les juges ordinaires des lieux »[71]. Enfin, la proximité quotidienne entre le consul et ses administrés créait sans doute une situation délicate pour le consul qui aurait eu à rendre un jugement pénal à l'encontre d'un compatriote qu'il fréquentait au quotidien. Pour toutes ces raisons, il semble que les consuls du Levant et de Barbarie n'aient pratiquement jamais rendus de jugements en matière pénale à l'encontre de leurs compatriotes, préférant bien souvent les faire expulser de l'échelle afin qu'ils soient remis aux juridictions du royaume.

De manière plus surprenante, si l'on retrouve bien des jugements consulaires portant sur le domaine civil ou commercial dans les registres de chancellerie jusqu'au milieu du XVIIe siècle[72], ceux-ci semblent disparaître des registres plus tardifs, au moment même où les ordonnances encadrant la compétence juridictionnelle des consuls se multiplient. De plus, à partir de cette période, on ne trouve aucune mention indirecte de procès qui auraient eu lieu dans les échelles, dans la correspondance des consuls ou les mémoires relatifs aux échelles. Les dépouillements opérés s'avèrent sans doute insuffisants pour en tirer des conclusions définitives, mais il conviendrait de les poursuivre pour expliquer cette absence, ou l'infirmer[73].

71 Pierre Ariste, *Traicté des consuls de la nation françoise aux pays estrangers* (Paris : BNF, ms. fr. 18595, 1667), 184.

72 Pour des exemples, voir *Registre de la chancellerie de Tripoli de Syrie* (Nantes, CADN, 708PO, série A, 1), fol. 241r–241v, 246, 253–253v *Registre de la chancellerie de Tripoli de Syrie* (Nantes, CADN, 708PO, série A, 7), fol. 141r–142v.

73 Deux pistes pourraient être explorées : un dépouillement plus systématique des registres de chancellerie pour rechercher d'éventuels jugements consulaires qui auraient échappé à nos dépouillements ; des recherches dans les archives du Parlement de Provence qui permettraient de trouver d'éventuels traces d'appels contre des jugements rendus par les consuls.

Bibliographie

Al-Ghunaimi, Mohammad Talaat. *The Muslim conception of international law and the Western approach.* La Haye : Martinus Nijhoff, 1968.

Arabeyre, Patrick, Jean-Louis Halpérin, et Jacques Krynen. *Dictionnaire historique des juristes français (XIIe–XXe siècle).* Paris : Presses universitaires de France, 2015.

Bacquet, Jean. *Traité des droits de iustice, haute, moyenne et basse.* Paris : Du Mesnil, 1664.

Barbiche, Bernard. *Les institutions de la monarchie française à l'époque moderne (XVIe–XVIIIe siècle).* Paris : Presses universitaires de France, 2001.

Basdevant-Gaudemet, Brigitte. *Charles Loyseau (1564–1627) : théoricien de la puissance publique.* Paris : Economica, 1976.

Biarnoy de Merville, Pierre. *Ordonnance de la marine du mois d'aoust 1681 commentée et conferée sur les anciennes ordonnances, le droit romain et les nouveaux réglemens.* Paris : Osmont, 1714.

Boulet-Sautel, Marguerite. *Vivre au royaume de France.* Paris : Presses universitaires de France, 2010.

Calafat, Guillaume. « La juridiction des consuls français en Méditerranée : Litiges marchands, arbitrages et circulation des procès (Livourne et Tunis au XVIIe siècle) ». Dans *De l'utilité commerciale des consuls. : L'institution consulaire et les marchands dans le monde méditerranéen (XVIIe–XXe siècle)*, édité par Arnaud Bartolomei, Guillaume Calafat, Mathieu Grenet et Jörg Ulbert, 155–172. Rome : École française de Rome, 2018.

Carbasse, Jean-Marie. *Histoire du droit pénal et de la justice criminelle.* Paris : Presses universitaires de France, 2014.

Chassebœuf de La Giraudais, Constantin-François. *Considérations sur la guerre actuelle des Turcs.* Londres : s.e., 1788.

Clément, Pierre, éd. *Lettres, instructions et mémoires de Colbert,* t. 2, Paris : Imprimerie impériale, 1863.

Cras, Jérôme. « Une approche archivistique des consulats de La Nation Française : Les Actes de Chancellerie Consulaire Sous L'Ancien Régime ». Dans *La fonction consulaire à l'époque moderne : L'affirmation d'une institution économique et politique (1500–1800)*, édité par Jörg Ulbert et Gérard Le Bouëdec, 51–84. Rennes : Presses universitaires de Rennes, 2006.

Delamare, Nicolas. *Traité de la Police.* Paris : Michel Brunet, 1722.

Durand, Bernard. « La notion de police en France du XVIe au XVIIIe siècle ». Dans *Policey im Europa der Frühen Neuzeit,* édité par Michael Stolleis, Karl Härter et Lothar Schilling, 163–211. Francfort-sur-le-Main : Klostermann, 1996.

Eldem, Edhem. « Foreigners at the Threshold of Felicity : the Reception of Foreigners in Ottoman Istanbul ». Dans *Cultural Exchange in Early Modern Europe,* édité par

Donatella Calabi et Stephen Christensen, 114–131. Cambridge : Cambridge University Press, 2007.

Faroqhi, Suraiya. « Before 1600 : Ottoman Attitudes towards Merchants from Latin Christendom ». *Turcica* 35 (2002) : 69–104.

Ferrière, Claude-Joseph de. *Dictionnaire de droit et de pratique*. Paris : Bauche, 1771.

Fleury, Claude. *Droit public de France*. Paris : Pierres, 1769.

Guignard de Saint-Priest, François-Emmanuel. *Mémoires sur l'ambassade de France en Turquie et sur le commerce des Français dans le Levant*. Paris : Ernest Leroux, 1877.

Hoarau, Fabrice. « Claude Fleury (1640–1723) : la raison et l'histoire ». Dijon : thèse dactyl., 2003.

Le Bret, Cardin. *De la souveraineté du roy*. Paris : Toussaincts Du Bray, 1632.

Loyseau, Charles. *Cinq livres du droict des offices*. Paris : L'Angelier, 1610.

Loyseau, Charles. *Traicté des seigneuries*. Paris : L'Angelier, 1609.

Mézin, Anne. *Les consuls de France au siècle des Lumières (1715–1792)*. Paris : Ministère des affaires étrangères, 1997.

Mousnier, Roland. *La vénalité des offices sous Henri IV et Louis XIII*. Paris : Presses universitaires de France, 1971.

Napoli, Paolo. « Police : la conceptualisation d'un modèle juridico-politique sous l'Ancien Régime ». *Droits* 9, n° 20 (1994) : 151–160.

Panaite, Viorel. « Being a Western Merchant in the Ottoman Mediterranean ». Dans *Isam Konuşmalari. Osmanli Düşüncesi, Ahlâk, Huruk, Felsefe-Kelâm*, édité par Seyfi Kenan, 91–135. Istanbul : ISAM, 2013.

Panaite, Viorel. « Islamic Tradition and Ottoman Law of Nations ». Dans *The Turks*, édité par Hasan Güzel, Cem Oğuz et Osman Karatay, 261–268. Ankara : Yeni Türkiye, 2002.

Pernoud, Monique. *Les statuts municipaux de Marseille*. Monaco : Archives du Palais, 1949.

Peyssonnel, Charles de. *Examen du livre intitulé Considérations sur la guerre actuelle des Turcs, par Monsieur de Volney*. Amsterdam : s. e., 1788.

Picot, Gilbert. *Cardin Le Bret (1558–1655) et la doctrine de la souveraineté*. Nancy : SIT, 1948.

Plessix, Benoît. « Nicolas Delamare ou les fondations du droit administratif français ». Dans *Droits* 38 (2003) : 113–133.

Poumarède, Géraud. « Naissance d'une institution royale : les consuls de la nation française en Levant et en Barbarie aux XVIe et XVIIe siècles ». *Annuaire-bulletin de la Société de l'histoire de France* (2001) : 65–128.

Pouradier Duteil-Loizidou, Anna. *Consulat de France à Larnaca : Documents inédits pour servir à l'histoire de Chypre*. Nicosie : CRS, 1995.

Rigaudière, Albert. « Les ordonnances de police en France à la fin du Moyen Âge ». Dans *Policey im Europa der Frühen Neuzeit*, édité par Michael Stolleis, Karl Härter et Lothar Schilling, 97–162. Francfort-sur-le-Main : Klostermann, 1996.

Simon, Victor. « Légiférer contre l'acculturation des marchands français dans l'espace ottoman (XVIIe–XVIIIe siècle) : l'appréhension par le droit d'un entre-deux contraint ». Dans *L'expérience de la mobilité de l'Antiquité à nos jours, entre précarité et confiance*, édité par Claudia Moatti et Emmanuelle Chevreau, 141–154. Bordeaux : Ausonius, 2021.

Simon, Victor. *Les échelles du Levant et de Barbarie. Droit du commerce international entre la France et l'Empire ottoman (XVIe–XVIIIe siècle)*. Paris : LGDJ, 2021.

Ulbert, Jörg. « La dépêche consulaire française et son acheminement en méditerranée sous Louis XIV (1661–1715) ». Dans *Les consuls en Méditerranée, agents d'information*, édité par Silvia Marzagalli, 31–57. Paris : Classiques Garnier, 2015.

Ulbert, Jörg. « Qu'est-ce qu'un chancelier de consulat ? Une approche par les textes de droit français ». *Mélanges de l'École française de Rome, Italie et Méditerranée modernes et contemporaines* 128, n° 2 (2016).

Ulbert, Jörg. « L'origine géographique des consuls français sous Louis XIV ». *Cahiers de la Méditerranée*, n° 98 (2019) : 11–27.

Valin, René-Josué. *Nouveau commentaire sur l'ordonnance de la marine du mois d'août 1681*. La Rochelle : Legier, 1766.

10

Italian Consular Jurisdiction

Theory, Practice, Effects

Eleonora Angella

1 Introduction

In 1899 a book was published in Italy with the title *I consoli e le colonie europee nei possedimenti ottomani* (The European Colonies in Ottoman Territories and their Consuls).[1] The name of the writer listed on the title page – *Anatolio Latino* – was a clever, if fairly transparent, pseudonym; the real author was in fact a former Italian consul, Enrico Vitto, who had lived for many years in Egypt.[2] On page forty-six of the book, Vitto writes: "With the capitulations in place, Europeans continue to live in foreign territories almost entirely under the protection of their own national law; in such contexts, the consul represents the State in miniature, and he exercises all the principal functions of the State in relation to his fellow nationals within his jurisdiction. Such consulates could be called 'microcracies'."[3] Vitto then proceeds to present a long list of the various functions exercised by consuls in such contexts, and he illustrates the list with a pictorial caricature designed by the Florentine painter Corrado Sarri, in which we see a consul with an enormous head, completely submerged by documents regarding some of the most common requests made of consuls by members of the colony, such as inquiries, criminal charges, complaints, petitions, advertisements of musical events, and so forth (Figure 10.1).

A little further on, Anatolio Latino a.k.a. Enrico Vitto moves to describing the specifically judicial functions required of the consul, apropos of which he adds: "The consul prefers to dedicate himself entirely to the law. He delegates every other branch of the consular service to his vice-consul, and constantly

1 Anatolio Latino, *I consoli e le colonie europee nei possedimenti ottomani* (Florence: Bernardo Seeber, 1899).

2 Enrico Vitto (1844–1914) was consul in Egypt and several other countries in the Middle East. Under the pseudonym Anatolio Latino he was also the author of the book *Gli Armeni e la mia missione a Zeitun* (Florence: R. Bemporard, 1897). See Mariella Vitto Massei, "Un console abruzzese in Egitto e nel Medio Oriente (1869–1896)," *Bullettino della deputazione abruzzese di storia patria* 84 (1994), 235–255.

3 Latino, *I consoli*, 46. All translations of primary sources from Italian to English have been made by Gregory Mellen.

 | HTTPS://DOI.ORG/10.1163/9789004755192-012

FIGURE 10.1 Illustration of a consul surrounded by documents representing his various functions
SOURCE: ANATOLIO LATINO, I CONSOLI E LE COLONIE EUROPEE NEI POSSEDIMENTI OTTOMANI (FIRENZE: BERNARDO SEEBER, 1899), P. 47.

mumbles the phrase '*de minimis non curat praetor*' (Figure 10.2)."[4] Once again, the verbal description is accompanied by an image, this time showing the consul in his role as president of the consular court: an elderly consul, wearing a frock coat and holding a heavy book in his right hand.

In this chapter, I will analyze Italian consular jurisdiction in Egypt in the late nineteenth and early twentieth centuries with particular reference to

4 Latino, *I consoli*, 95.

FIGURE 10.2 Illustration of a consul in his role as president of the consular court
SOURCE: ANATOLIO LATINO, I CONSOLI E LE COLONIE EUROPEE NEI POSSEDIMENTI OTTOMANI (FIRENZE: BERNARDO SEEBER, 1899), P. 47.

Cairo. I have divided my essay into three parts respectively related to the theory (2), practice (3), and effects (4) of consular jurisdictions.

First (Part 2), I will describe the place and function of Italian consular jurisdiction within the Egyptian context. My description will be largely based upon the Italian Consular Law of 1866 and its regulations, but I will also make use of contemporary *manuali consolari* (consular handbooks), which were an indispensable tool for new consuls, who, as we will see, were not always fully prepared to handle all the tasks required of them in their office.[5]

Next (Part 3), I will show how justice was administered at a practical level, day-to-day, within the Italian chancery in Cairo, and in particular I will analyze the consul's role in said administration of justice. Specifically, by examining the archival materials of the Italian consulate, I will attempt to provide some answers to the following questions: what was the relative importance of "the administration of justice" within the set of duties required of the consul? How did the consuls themselves perceive and understand their judicial functions? And what sort of relationships existed between the Italian consuls in Egypt and their collaborators in the field of law, especially as regards the so-called *console-giudici* or consul-judges?

Finally (Part 4), I want to suggest that we must also consider the impact that consular jurisdiction (as described in Parts 2 and 3) had upon the lives of the members of the Italian colony. Of course, consular archives generated by chancelleries located in countries where consuls exercised contentious jurisdiction contain a wide variety of heterogeneous sources – citizen census records, civil status and citizenship records, lists of *protégés*, passports, notarial acts, dossiers of criminal and civil trials, etc. – which can be a precious tool for analyzing the economic, social, and cultural history of expatriate communities.[6] But such documents do not only permit us to catch glimpses of certain

5 On the use of consular handbooks for the study of consular history between 1744 and 1914, see Jörg Ulbert, "Les manuels consulaires français d'avant 1914 comme sources des études consulaires," in *De l'utilité commerciale des consuls. L'institution consulaire et les marchands dans le monde méditerranéen (XVIIe–XXe siècle)*, eds. Arnaud Bartolomei *et al.* (Rome: École française de Rome, 2017), 104–122. Nineteenth- and twentieth-century Italian consular handbooks not only often contained a section devoted to consular jurisdiction (like the French ones analyzed by Ulbert at p. 104 of the introduction cited above); in presenting consular functions they also introduced a clear distinction between consulates with jurisdiction and those without jurisdiction, and in some cases the handbooks dealt with only one type of consulate. For instance, the handbook written by Tito Chiovenda (*Manuale di pratica consolare. Ad uso dei regi consoli e degli studi legali* (Roma: Foro Italiano, 1931) does not treat contentious jurisdiction.

6 While the practice of using court or notarial archives to study European or Middle Eastern societies in modern and contemporary times has a long and well-established history, that of using consular archives to study the lives of men and women outside their national borders is comparatively new and under-exploited. In this regard, see the call for papers written by Arnaud Bartolomei *et al.*, in which they consider consular archives as "des sources pour écrire une histoire sociale de l'expatriation," see "Les sources consulaires Pour une histoire sociale et globale des relations internationales," École Française de Rome, accessed April 27, 2024, https://www.efrome.it/actualite/default-2249027350. In a purely contemporary perspective with a focus on the political history of institutions, see also the recent volume edited by Vintila and Lafleur, which proposes to examine the (rather limited) assistance

aspects of the public and private lives of many Italians living in Egypt; they also contain traces of the concrete and direct effects that the capitulations, legal pluralism, and the consular institution itself had upon the lives of the Italians of Egypt and their consuls, to the extent that they played no small part in what it meant to be "Italian" in such a context.[7]

2 Theory

Late-nineteenth-century Cairo possessed a flourishing community of Italians who had come to Egypt to build new lives for themselves in the 1800s, along with a substantial group of Levantines of Italian origin, many of whom had been living in Egypt for centuries already.[8] Both of these groups – along with *protégés* of the Italian consulate – were to a large extent exempt from local jurisdiction, thanks to the phenomenon of *extraterritoriality*, which of course had its roots in the capitulations.[9] This did not mean that such individuals were completely isolated from the various spheres of legal influence present

functions exercised by modern-day consuls with a view to investigating the policies of various European states toward their citizens abroad (*Migration and Social Protection in Europe and Beyond*, eds. Daniela Vintila and Jean-Michel Lafleur, vol. 2: *Comparing Consular Services and Diaspora Policies* [Liège: Springer Nature, 2020]).

7 I develop this perspective in greater depth in Eleonora Angella, *Italiani al Cairo. Consoli, giurisdizioni, società (1861–1911)* (Palermo: New Digital Frontiers, 2024/2023).

8 Among the growing literature on the Italians of Egypt, see at least Angella, *Italiani al Cairo*; Lucia Carminati, *Seeking Bread and Fortune in Port Said: Labor Migration and the Making of the Suez Canal, 1859–1906* (Oakland: University of California Press, 2023); *Italian Subalterns in Egypt between Emigration and Colonialism (1861–1937)*, ed. Costantino Paonessa (Louvain: Louvain University Press, 2021); Joseph Viscomi, *Migration at the End of Empire: Time and the Politics of Departure between Italy and Egypt* (Cambridge: Cambridge University Press, forthcoming), along with the additional bibliography which can found in these works. On Italian Levantines see Elisabeth Shlala, *The Late Ottoman Empire and Egypt: Hybridity, Law and Gender* (London, New York: Routledge, 2018).

9 For a general discussion of the problem see Daniel S. Margolies *et al.*, eds., *The Extraterritoriality of Law: History, Theory, Politics* (London, New York: Routledge, 2019). Essential for our understanding of how extraterritoriality concretely took shape in eighteenth-century Ottoman society is Maurits H. van den Boogert, *The Capitulations and the Ottoman Legal System: Qadis, Consuls, and Beratlıs in the 18th Century* (Leiden: Brill, 2005). For nineteenth- and twentieth-century Egypt see especially David Todd, "Beneath Sovereignty: Extraterritoriality and Imperial Internationalism in Nineteenth-Century Egypt," *Law and History Review* 36, n° 1 (2018): 105–137; Ziad Fahmy, "Jurisdictional Borderlands: Extraterritoriality and 'Legal Chameleons' in Pre-colonial Alexandria, 1840–1870," *Comparative Studies in Society and History* 55, n° 2 (April 2013): 305–329. Jessica Marglin strikes a more critical tone in her contribution to this volume (Chapter #), "Nationalizing Consular Jurisdiction in the Nineteenth-Century Middle East and North Africa." (NB: the correct chapter number must be inserted for cross-reference.)

within Egypt at the time. To the contrary, after the judicial reforms of 1875–1876 and 1883–1884, Egypt was characterized by the coexistence, and in some cases the overlap, of numerous different types of jurisdiction, which were enforced simultaneously in a range of different courts: consular, mixed, and native courts.[10] In such a context, we find the Italians of Egypt engaged in phenomena like the forum shopping which other historians have analyzed for North Africa and the Middle East.[11] As a result, it was not at all rare for an Italian to be involved in lawsuits in courthouses which applied the law of other states; conversely, it was not at all rare for other Europeans, or local subjects, to have legal affairs within the Italian consular court.

Within a system such as this, what was the role and function of the Italian consular court? Like other European consular courts in Egypt, up until 1876 the Italian consular court had jurisdiction over criminal and civil cases according to the principle of *actor sequitur forum rei*, whereby trials fell under the jurisdiction of the national court of the defendant. Two examples may serve to illustrate how this worked: in 1861 a Greek shopkeeper named Socrate Tracca sued Luciano Chiappa, an Italian construction worker, for having insulted him in public (the Italian term is *ingiuria*), and so the case was tried in the Italian consular court;[12] vice versa, when the Italian doctor Giovanni Salemi brought the same charges against a local coachman by the name of Hassan, the case was tried in the native court.[13] And this principle was valid not only for criminal trials but also for civil cases as well. After the judicial reforms of 1875–1876, the principle of *actor sequitur forum rei* continued to be valid for criminal cases, but civil cases were now only tried by the Italian consular court when both parties were legally considered to be Italians or *protégés* of the Italian

10 On this last point, see Will Hanley's research on Alexandria in his work *Identifying with Nationality: Europeans, Ottomans, and Egyptians in Alexandria* (New York: Columbia University Press, 2017) which at p. 15 also contains a table that powerfully exemplifies jurisdiction ranges for British, French, and Egyptian subjects.

11 See Jessica Marglin, *Across Legal Lines: Jews and Muslims in Modern Marocco* (New Haven and London: Yale University Press, 2016); Ido Shahar, *Legal Pluralism in the Holy City: Competing Courts, Forum Shopping, and Institutional Dynamics in Jerusalem* (Farnham: Ashgate, 2015); and Julia Clancy-Smith, *Mediterraneans: North Africa and Europe in the Age of Migration, c. 1800–1900* (Berkeley, Los Angeles, London: University of California Press, 2010).

12 ASDMAE (= Archivio Storico Diplomatico Ministero degli Esteri), CC (= Consolato del Cairo), TC (= Tribunale Penale), 1861, n° 3, Socrate Tracca *vs* Luciano Chiappa.

13 ASDMAE, CC, TC, 1862, n° 2, Giovanni Salemi *vs* Hassan.

consulate; other case-configurations now fell within the jurisdiction of the newly instituted mixed courts in Egypt.[14]

However, Italian consular jurisdiction was not exercised exclusively in the consular court. The consul himself had the authority to directly adjudicate certain cases among the members of the Italian colony. In virtue of the Italian consular law of 1866, the consul had the authority to issue sentences without possibility of appeal when it came to disputes regarding navigation; disputes in which the monetary value at stake did not exceed 500 liras; and criminal charges for which the penalty was a monetary fine.[15] On the other hand, lawsuits whose value exceeded 500 liras, as well as trials regarding crimes subject to correctional punishment, went to the consular court, which was presided by the consul along with two other judges selected by the consul. Just like decisions of the consul himself, decisions of the consular court were unappealable, provided that the value at stake did not exceed 1500 liras; if it did, and an appeal was made, the relevant court of appeal was located not in Cairo, and not even in Egypt, but in Italy, at Ancona.[16]

It is also important to emphasize the fact that if the consular court was not able to meet, the consul had the power to assume its functions himself. In such cases, Italian law required him merely to make a record of this in the proceedings.[17] In other words, if there was an acceptable justification, the consul was not obliged to convene the court but could himself render decisions which normally fell within the court's purview. Moreover, when it came to criminal cases, the consul not only oversaw the preliminary or investigation phase of the trial but was also responsible for issuing verdicts. A limit was placed on this last power, however, insofar as the most serious crimes fell within the

14 An excellent reconstruction of how consular jurisdiction was narrowed through the introduction of mixed jurisdictions, with discussion of the ability of Egyptian authorities to deal at the same time with major European chanceries and Ottoman officials, may be found in Luigi Nuzzo, *Origini di una scienza. Diritto internazionale e colonialismo nel XIX secolo* (Frankfurt am Main: Klostermann, 2012), 169–201.

15 See *Legge consolare per il Regno d'Italia 28 gennaio 1866* (Milan, Florence: Sonzogno, 1866), art. 76–77 and *Regolamento per l'esecuzione della Legge 28 gennaio 1866* (Florence: Stamperia Reale, 1866).

16 See *Legge consolare* art. 68–70, 78, 105. According to Contuzzi – the author of a treatise that represented a key reference-point in the debate regarding consular law in Italy at the beginning of the twentieth century – the only reason behind this choice was geographical: the court in Ancona had jurisdiction over Italians in Egypt; the court in Genoa, on the other hand, had jurisdiction over all other sentences issued by consular courts located in Africa. See Francesco Paolo Contuzzi, *Trattato teorico-pratico di diritto consolare e diplomatico nei raffronti coi codici (civile, commerciale, penale e giudiziario) e con le convenzioni internazionali in vigore*, 2 vols. (Turin: UTET, 1910), 858–859.

17 See *Legge consolare* art. 71.

jurisdiction of the Court of Assizes at Ancona. For instance, if the investigation phase resulted in sufficient grounds to accuse an individual of homicide, then that individual was sent to be tried in the city of Ancona. The Court of Ancona thus served as both court of assizes and appellate court for cases originating in Egypt.

From what we have seen so far, it should be clear that Italian consular law granted extensive powers to the consul operating in Egypt under the capitulations. These powers in fact were not infrequently described as "excessive" or "exorbitant" by contemporary actors and observers. From the authors of consular handbooks[18] to the members of the commissions tasked with modifying the Italian consular law,[19] from European legal scholars to the Egyptian and European diplomats who took part in the debate over the reduction of consular jurisdiction – practically everyone agreed that the judicial powers granted to consuls were simply too vast.[20] Even as late as 1936, Francesco Ferrara wrote that "il console ha poteri amplissimi, e si può dire che fa tutto da sé."[21] In short, there can be no doubt that consuls potentially enjoyed enormous leeway in the exercise of their authority – at least, according to the letter of the law, and according to a generous interpretation of the capitulations. But, to what extent the consul *truly* "acted single-handedly" in the course of his daily work – *that* is a more complex question and deserves a closer look.

3 Practice

First, it is essential to understand the relative importance held by the administration of justice within the consuls' overall activities. As is well-known, the consul's tasks were not only judicial but also administrative and even political – and yet not all of these activities took up an equal portion of his time and

18 See Marcello Arduino, *Consoli, consolati e diritto consolare* (Milan: Hoepli, 1909); Chiovenda, *Manuale di;* Francesco Ferrara, *Manuale di diritto consolare* (Padova: Cedam, 1936).

19 In the 1880s, the Italian parliament discussed the possibility of amending the country's consular law by also addressing the issue of the excessive powers granted to consuls in countries where they exercised contentious jurisdiction. The debate did not lead to any real change, as can be seen from the reconstruction carried out by Manuela Cacioli, *La rete consolare nel periodo crispino (1886–1891)* (Roma: Istituto Poligrafico e Zecca dello Stato, 1988): 24–31 (esp. 29).

20 Part of this debate emerges in Nuzzo, *Origini di*, 172–176.

21 Ferrara, *Manuale di*, 280. "The consul has very extensive powers; one might even say he acts single-handedly."

TABLE 10.1 Criminal and civil cases and sentences for the period 1880–1883

	1880	1881	1882	1883
Criminal trials	ff. 41	ff. 37	ff. 27	ff. 27 (39)
Civil trials	ff. 44	ff. 76	ff. 54	ff. 66 (81)
	1861–1880		1882–1883	
Civil Sentences	14 record books		1 record book	
Criminal Sentences	2 record books		1 record book	

NB. "ff" = *files* (each file contains documents regarding one court case)
SOURCE: ASDMAE, CC, AN 1883, pp. 118–121

effort. For example, let us have a look at the inventory of the consular office of Cairo drawn up in 1883 by consul Perolari Malmignati (Table 10.1).[22]

If we compare the quantity of files regarding judicial activity listed in Table 10.1 with the number of files related to civil functions found in Table 10.2, it becomes quite clear just how much the consul must have been absorbed by his judicial tasks.

To give an idea, in the period of 1881–1883 there were 399 files regarding court cases, a total which significantly outnumbers the files concerning all of the civil functions combined for the same period. Although less striking, similar numbers emerge if one looks at the files regarding inheritances and notary deeds (Table 10.3). These last two categories represent the largest groupings of acts inventoried apart from those found in the two preceding tables; once again, the number of files is less than those relating to court cases.

In short, these numbers clearly suggest that the amount of time the consul dedicated to judicial tasks greatly outweighed that dedicated to administrative

22 *Inventario dell'ufficio*, ASDMAE, CC, AN (= Atti Notarili) 1883, 118–121. (NB. For the year 1883, the first number derives from the inventory compiled by Perolari Malmignati before he left office, whereas the one between parentheses represents the total number of files I found in the archives for that year.) Pietro Perolari Malmignati (18481866) was one of the most prolific writers of consular memoirs. See: *Alcune occhiate a Malta* (Padova: Sacchetto, 1870); *Su e giù per la Siria. Note e schizzi* (Milan: Treves, 1878); *Il Perù e i suoi tremendi giorni (1878–1881): pagine di uno spettatore* (Milan: F.lli Treves, 1882); *L'Egitto senza egiziani* (Milan: Fratelli Treves, 1886). He committed suicide while serving as vice-consul in Toulon. See ASDMAE; PI (Personale-serie I, diplomatici e consoli); Pietro Perolari Malmignati.

TABLE 10.2 Civil functions for the period 1881–1883

	1881	1882	1883
Marriages	ff. 13	ff. 17	ff. 28
Births	ff. 8		
Deaths	ff. 3		
Citizenship conferrals	ff. 9		—

SOURCE: ASDMAE, CC, AN 1883, pp. 118–121

TABLE 10.3 Inheritances and notary deeds for the period 1881–1883

	1881	1882	1883
Inheritances	ff. 17	ff. 9	ff. 13
Notary Deeds	ff. 76	ff. 59	ff. 58

SOURCE: ASDMAE, CC, AN, 1883, pp. 118–121

tasks (especially if one keeps in mind the differing time commitments required for the various functions). But the consul's judicial activities were not only the most prevalent ones in terms of *time*; the application of the law also greatly preoccupied the consul in terms of the effort he had to employ in acquiring the knowledge and competence needed for the successful performance of the relevant judicial tasks. In this regard, one may cite the following passage from a letter written in 1856 by the consul Licurgo Macciò to his brother Didaco:

> When you print some legal work or other, obtain a copy for me as well, since it is always useful … to see how questions of jurisprudence are discussed and resolved. Please also do not forget to respond to the next issue I'm about to mention. While we were in Europe, the consular chancellor acted as director of the consulate. When it came time to decide a certain case, he presided over the consular court, but he neglected to engage a second chancellor alongside himself. The losing party appealed on procedural grounds, and the royal court confirmed that the decision was invalid due to the absence of the second chancellor; and the parties

> were directed to arrange for proceedings 'where and as appropriate.' Now, it seems to me that 'where and as appropriate' would amount to conducting a re-trial during a new session of the same court, provided a sufficient number of judges are present. In this case, it seems logical to me that the consul, who did not decide the case initially, ought to preside over the new session of the court, alongside judges different from those who pronounced on the case previously. Does that seem correct, or not? Please do instruct me on this issue, as I would prefer there not to be any more gaffes of this sort, and tell me too where exactly one can inform oneself regarding these types of procedures.[23]

The consul Macciò had to learn about "questions of jurisprudence" on the job, and in order to do so he wrote for help from his brother, who was a lawyer by profession. Indeed, even though Italian consuls often had a university degree in law, it appears that they generally had no prior experience working in the courtroom, neither as judges nor as lawyers, before they began their terms of office in the consulate.[24] In any case, Macciò's successors in the Italian consulate in Cairo must have often had doubts quite similar to his, if we can judge from the number of letters containing legal advice addressed to the consul found in the proceedings of various trials.

In many respects, then, it seems that consuls felt a certain frustration with regard to their judicial duties, which proved to be a complicated subject requiring many hours of work. Indeed, this sense of frustration is almost palpable in the numerous letters sent by Italian consuls in Egypt to the Foreign Ministry in Rome. In these letters, the consuls often requested specifically that the Ministry send them help in the form of the so-called "consul-judges"

---

23 Letter of Licurgo Macciò to Didaco Macciò, Alexandria, 17 August 1856, in BCF (=Biblioteca Comunale Forteguerriana-Pistoia), MD (=Macciò Didaco), 54, III. Licurgo Macciò (1826–1905) spent a great part of his consular career in Egypt, where his presence spanned the transitional period of Italian unification, serving first as vice–consul of Tuscany at Alexandria (ca. 1850–1860), then as Italian vice-consul with consular authority at Cairo (from the annexation of Tuscany by the Kingdom of Sardinia on August 11, 1860, until 1866), and finally returning to Cairo to serve as the Italian General Consul from 1889 to 1894. See Pellegrino Gerardo Nicolosi, "Licurgo Macciò," in *Dizionario Biografico degli Italiani*, (Roma: Istituto della Enciclopedia Italiana 2006), https://www.treccani.it/enciclopedia/licurgo–maccio_(Dizionario–Biografico)/?search=MACCI%C3%92%2C%20Licurgo.

24 On the professionalization of consuls (with reference, however, to the period before Italian unification) see Marcella Aglietti, *L'istituto consolare tra Sette e Ottocento. Funzioni istituzionali, profilo giuridico e percorsi professionali nella Toscana granducale* (Pisa: ETS, 2012), especially chapters 5–7.

(*console-giudici*), magistrates whose principal task was to assist the consul in the administration of justice.[25] But should we understand this to mean that the Italian consuls in Egypt would have preferred to entirely relinquish the judicial functions they were tasked with, if this were possible?

Far from it. What we have seen so far suggests rather the contrary; and further evidence confirms that consuls were eager to maintain their judicial role. For instance, during the debate regarding the form of the first consular law to be adopted by the newly born Kingdom of Italy, some believed that the powers of consuls and those of consul-judges ought to be kept rigorously distinct and that the latter alone should be entrusted with the administration of the law.[26] Such an idea had been proposed specifically by Giovanni Giaccone, who at the time was acting as a magistrate in the service of the consul of Alexandria. But a vigorous opposition to this proposal was mounted by the consul Giovanni Bruno, and at the end of the day the first Italian consular law decreed that consul-judges were to assist consuls in the administration of the law while remaining explicitly subordinate to them.[27] In this instance, then, consuls seem to have desired to maintain their judicial prerogatives in those countries where these existed, since – as Bruno pointed out in a letter to the Foreign Ministry – the delegation of all judicial administration to the consul-judges "would harm the position of the consul, insofar as it would reduce his preeminence and authority."[28]

Many years later, a consul and a consul-judge would find themselves once again on two opposing sides of a heated debate. In 1914 an intense conflict

---

25 See *Legge consolare* art. 16. Some information on consul-judges (including those active in China and Japan) may be found in Fabrice Jesné, "Administrer la diaspora. L'institution consulaire italienne du fascisme à la démocratie (1943–1957)," (unpublished manuscript, June 2022).

26 See ASDMAE, CC, Consoli-giudici, pos. XII, C2/1, Giaccone Giovanni. On the Italian consular law see Fabrice Jesné, "La transition unitaire des services consulaires italiennes (1858–1870)," in *Consoli e consolati dagli Stati preunitari al fascismo (1802–1945)*, eds. Marcella Aglietti, Mathieu Grenet and Fabrice Jesné (Rome: École Française de Rome, 2020), 37–38.

27 *Legge consolare*, art 16. Giovanni Giaccone was in Egypt from 1861 to 1867 and cooperated with the Italian Ministry of Foreign Affairs, which at that time was working to give united Italy its first consular law, whose regulations were to determine the position of those magistrates sent to countries where consuls exercised consular jurisdiction. On Giaccone and his position see ASDMAE, CC, Consoli-giudici, pos. XII, C2/1 and Giaccone Giovanni and ACS (= Archivio Centrale di Stato, Roma), Ministero di grazia e giustizia, magistrati, I versamento, busta 220.

28 Letter of the general consul Giovanni Bruno to the minister of Foreign Affairs Visconti-Venosta, 19 February 1864, ASDMAE, CC, Consoli-giudici, pos. XII, C2/2, Consoli-giudici.

arose between Girolamo Naselli, the Italian consul in Alexandria, and Alessandro Libonati, his consul-judge, and ultimately led to the suspension of the latter from his duties as assistant in the administration of justice.[29] Naselli had in fact already made numerous requests that his inferior colleague be removed from office, on the grounds that his extensive personal debts were undermining his own position of influence as consul within the colony. Libonati, on the other hand, maintained that his superior was actually jealous of the prestige that he (i.e. Libonati) had managed to acquire among the Italians in Alexandria thanks precisely to the duties he was carrying out in his role as consul-judge. In other words, the idea we saw expressed above by the consul Giovanni Bruno shortly after the creation of the Italian state was reiterated, in this instance, by the consul-judge of Alexandria, Alessandro Libonati. In short, although Italian consuls may well have been frustrated by the excessive burden represented by their judicial role (both in terms of the time spent on court cases in the chancellery and, as we saw in the case of Macciò, in terms of the difficulties inherent in correctly administering such cases), nonetheless they did not want to yield this role over to the consul-judges entirely, since they considered it to be an important instrument of power within the life of the Italian colony abroad.[30]

Of course, it would be an oversimplification simply to assert – as the consuls and consul-judges themselves sometimes did – that the administration of justice served as a way to win over the goodwill of the persons falling under one's jurisdiction. Above all, such an idea obscures the many differences actually existing within the Italian colony in Egypt; it reduces the community to a single monolithic group and deprives its various individual members of any particular agency. And in any case, such an idea is not borne out by the actual effects consular jurisdiction had upon the members of the colony, as we may observe in our sources – and as we shall see in the next section.

---

29 For more details see Angella, *Italiani in*, 85–102.

30 Since the administration of justice in the Egyptian context has largely been viewed as the purview of the consul, the figure of the consul-judge has been left to a great extent unexplored. More research is needed, for instance, into the reasons motivating some consul-judges to abandon their role within consular courts so as to take up a position on the bench of the Egyptian mixed courts or else to occupy positions (sometimes very prestigious ones) within the local government. In any case, in light of the dispute between Libonati and Naselli discussed above, it seems clear that further study into the role of the consul-judges (and especially into the relationships between the latter and the consuls they were subordinate to) would help us to better understand what it meant to administer the law in areas characterized by extraterritoriality.

4 Effects

Up to this point, we have examined consular jurisdiction in Egypt only from the point of view of those who exercised it, i.e., consuls and consul-judges. But a thorough study of the phenomenon would also need to take into account the point of view of those who were subject to said jurisdiction, whether as defendants or plaintiffs. In recent years the utility of such an approach has been emphasized by numerous scholars working on consular history, especially in order to better define the exact functions carried out by consuls and to identify their sphere of action as accurately as possible.[31] My main objective here, however, is not to further examine the role of the consul, but rather to suggest how the study of consular jurisdiction – and especially the analysis of the effects of said jurisdiction upon those who were its subjects and/or beneficiaries – may allow us to better understand the social history of the Italians living in Egypt.

By now it is clear that in nineteenth-century Egypt it was not merely a limited segment of the expatriate community which was able to benefit from Italian consular jurisdiction (as was in fact the case in most of the European cities where Italian consuls were active in the same period).[32] The civil and criminal jurisdiction of the Italian consul – regulated and enacted in the forms we have seen above – concerned a vast quantity of women, men, and children who belonged legally to the category of "Italian" (whether they were Levantines, protégés, or had only recently moved to Egypt).[33] As a result, the

31 See especially Bartolomei, "*Introduction*," 14–15; and Arnaud Bartolomei *et al.*, "Introduction," *Mélanges de l'École française de Rome–Italie et Méditerranée modernes et contemporaines* 128, n° 2 (2016), https://doi.org/10.4000/mefrim.3047. In these studies, the authors use the terms "usagers" or "bénéficiaires" to describe the point of view of those who interacted with consular authority. Whereas the first term suggests an individual who actively attempts to make use of consular services, the second seems rather to indicate any individual who benefits from such services, whether they have sought such benefits or not. While building upon the analyses offered in these works, my own emphasis is not upon those who benefitted from consular authority (intentionally or not) but rather upon all individuals who were potentially subject to such authority and whose lives were impacted by it.

32 In consulates without jurisdiction the judicial functions carried out by Italian consuls were very limited and generally involved only the arbitration of settlements between Italian nationals or between the latter and citizens or subjects of the local government.

33 In this regard, I am in agreement with Marglin's suggestion that we ought to prefer the category of "legal belonging" over other categories based upon nationality or citizenship, since the latter, although more familiar and perhaps therefore more concrete at first glance, tend to obscure the variety and complexity of questions of identity in a country such as Egypt in the nineteenth century. See Jessica Marglin, "Extraterritoriality and

documents produced by the Italian consulate in Cairo, and especially by the consular court, are extremely rich in information which can help us not only to reconstruct the relationships – familial or matrimonial, of employment or vicinity – that Italian men and women established in the Egyptian context, but also to understand the way such individuals belonged to various different groups, whether on the basis of ethnicity, class, nationality, gender, generation, or (and especially in our case) legal jurisdiction.[34] Indeed, as some scholars have rightly pointed out, a schematic view of the capitulations – and of the related forms of consular jurisdiction – tends to envisage an opposition between Italians and other foreigners, on the one hand, and the local population, on the other hand; but this oversimplifies the complexities of social existence and distorts our view of the interpersonal relationships established by the Italians of Egypt. In contrast, a careful examination of the documents produced by the consular courts can permit us to comprehend the varied articulations of social belonging, based upon a multiplicity of categories, experienced by the Italians living in the Egyptian context.[35] Building upon the lesson of many social historians (especially those working on the Early Modern period), we may say that such documents offer a window onto the lives of the men and women of Cairo, often glimpsed in the most humble and intimate moments of their day-to-day lives.[36]

And yet, we must also realize that the very institution which provides us with this precious window also had its own effects on the lives of the Italians in Egypt. Thankfully, the archive of the consular court retains numerous traces of precisely these effects. For instance, trial documents tell us a great deal about the ways in which the Italians of Egypt reacted to the fact of living under consular jurisdiction by "exploiting" this system as best they could. In other words, consuls and consul-judges did not simply administer justice to an inert and powerless populace; rather, we find that the Italians of Egypt adopted various different strategies designed to navigate and employ the judicial system they found themselves in to their greatest advantage. One familiar

Legal Belonging in the Nineteenth-Century Mediterranean," *Law and History Review* 39, n° 4 (November 2021): 679–706.

34 On the differences between relational and categorical modes of identification see Roger Brubaker and Frederick Cooper, "Beyond 'Identity'," *Theory and Society* 29, n° 1 (February 2000): 1–47.

35 For this idea see the work of Anthony Gorman, especially "The Italians of Egypt: Return to Diaspora," in *Diasporas of the Modern Middle East: Contextualising Community*, eds. Anthony Gorman and Sossie Kasbarian (Edinburgh: Edinburgh University Press 2015), 142.

36 Among the many scholars one could cite, I would single out the names of Arlette Farge, Natalie Zemon Davies, and Carlo Ginzburg.

example is the well-known phenomenon of "forum shopping"; but another rather different example is the insistent assertion of being subject specifically to Italian consular jurisdiction, especially when this seemed to be the only way to avoid a particularly dangerous or negative outcome: we often find cases of men and women who, when faced with the threat of arrest, invoked what they viewed as their "right" to be tried only by their own consular authority – thanks to the capitulations, and thanks to the fact of their being "Italian."[37] In short, the Italians present in Egypt – of whatever sex, age, class, or background – were fully aware that they were living in a space characterized by extraterritorial jurisdiction (though few will have had an accurate understanding of the technical details of the legal regime), and they tended to interpret this fact as a safeguard against what they viewed as abuses, at times going so far as to think of themselves as possessing the right to a kind of immunity.[38] Living under consular jurisdiction thus concretely influenced the daily lives of the Italians in Egypt, producing certain effects which they were eager to retain – just as the consuls themselves (as we have seen above) were eager to maintain their own judicial authority.

Acknowledgement

I would like to thank Gregory Mellen for the translation of the text and sources from Italian.

Bibliography

Aglietti, Marcella. *L'istituto consolare tra Sette e Ottocento. Funzioni istituzionali, profilo giuridico e percorsi professionali nella Toscana granducale.* Pisa: ETS, 2012.

Angella, Eleonora. *Italiani al Cairo: Consoli, giurisdizioni, società (1861–1911)*. Palermo: New Digital Frontiers, 2024/2023.

Angella, Eleonora. "Italiens au Caire à la fin du XIXe siècle: quelques notes sur les subalternes et la justice." In *Italian Subalterns in Egypt Between Emigration and Colonialism (1861–1937)*, edited by Costantino Paonessa. Leuven: Presses universitaires de Louvain, 2021.

37 On forum shopping, see fn. 12 above. On the appropriation of consular jurisdiction by the Italians of Egypt, see Angella, *Italiani al*, 116–125.

38 Eleonora Angella, "Italiens au Caire à la fin du XIXe siècle: quelques notes sur les subalternes et la justice," in *Italian Subalterns in Egypt between Emigration and Colonialism (1861–1937)*, ed. Costantino Paonessa (Leuven: Presses universitaires de Louvain, 2021).

Arduino, Marcello. *Consoli, consolati e diritto consolare.* Milan: Hoepli, 1909.

Bartolomei, Arnaud, Mathieu Grenet, Fabrice Jesné, and Jörg Ulbert. "Introduction." *Mélanges de l'École française de Rome–Italie et Méditerranée modernes et contemporaines* 128, n° 2 (2016), https://doi.org/10.4000/mefrim.3047.

Brubaker, Roger, and Frederick Cooper. "Beyond 'Identity'." *Theory and Society* 29, n° 1 (February 2000): 1–47.

Cacioli, Manuela. *La rete consolare nel periodo crispino (1886–1891).* Rome: Istituto Poligrafico e Zecca dello Stato, 1988.

Carminati, Lucia. *Seeking Bread and Fortune in Port Said: Labor Migration and the Making of the Suez Canal, 1859–1906.* Oakland: University of California Press, 2023.

Chiovenda, Tito. *Manuale di pratica consolare: Ad uso dei regi consoli e degli studi legali.* Rome: Società editrice del "Foro Italiano," 1931.

Clancy-Smith, Julia. *Mediterraneans: North Africa and Europe in the Age of Migration, c. 1800– 1900.* Berkeley: University of California Press, 2010.

Contuzzi, Francesco Paolo. *Trattato teorico-pratico di diritto consolare e diplomatico nei raffronti coi codici (civile, commerciale, penale e giudiziario) e con le convenzioni internazionali in vigore.* Turin: UTET 1910.

École Française de Rome. "Les sources consulaires: Pour une histoire sociale et globale des relations internationales." Accessed April 27, 2024. https://www.efrome.it/actualite/default-2249027350.

Ferrara, Francesco. *Manuale di diritto consolare.* Padova: Cedam, 1936.

Hanley, Will. *Identifying with Nationality: Europeans, Ottomans, and Egyptians in Alexandria.* New York: Columbia University Press, 2017.

Jesné, Fabrice. "Administrer la diaspora: L'institution consulaire italienne du fascisme à la démocratie (1943–1957)." Unpublished manuscript, June 2022.

Jesné, Fabrice. "La transition unitaire des services consulaires italiens (1858–1870)." In *Consoli e consolati dagli Stati preunitari al fascismo (1802–1945)*, edited by Marcella Aglietti, Mathieu Grenet and Fabrice Jesné, 29–67. Rome: École française de Rome, 2020.

Latino, Anatolio. *Gli Armeni e la mia missione a Zeitun.* Florence: R. Bemporard, 1897.

Latino, Anatolio. *I consoli e le colonie europee nei possedimenti ottomani. Florence: Bernardo Seeber, 1899.*

Legge consolare per il Regno d'Italia 28 gennaio 1866. Milan: Sonzogno, 1866.

Marglin, Jessica. *Across Legal Lines: Jews and Muslim in Modern Marocco.* New Haven: Yale University Press, 2016.

Marglin, Jessica. "Extraterritoriality and Legal Belonging in the Nineteenth-Century Mediterranean." *Law and History Review* 39, n° 4 (November 2021): 679–706.

Margolies, Daniel S., Umut Özsu, Maïa Pal, and Ntina Tzouvala. *The Extraterritoriality of Law: History, Theory, Politics.* London: Routledge, 2019.

Nuzzo, Luigi. *Origini di una scienza: Diritto internazionale e colonialismo nel XIX secolo*. Frankfurt am Main: Klostermann, 2012.

Paonessa, Costantino, ed. *Italian Subaltern in Egypt: Between Emigration and Colonialism (1861–1937)*. Leuven: Louvain University Press, 2021.

Perolari Malmignati, Pietro. *Alcune occhiate a Malta*. Padua: Sacchetto, 1870.

Perolari Malmignati. *Il Perù e I suoi tremendi giorni (1878–1881): pagine di uno spettatore*. Milan: Fratelli Treves, 1882.

Perolari Malmignati. *L'Egitto senza egiziani*. Milan: Fratelli Treves, 1886.

Perolari Malmignati. *Su e giù per la Siria: Note e schizzi*. Milan: Treves, 1878.

Regolamento per l'esecuzione della Legge 28 gennaio 1866. Florence: Stamperia Reale, 1866.

Shahar, Ido. *Legal Pluralism in the Holy City: Competing Courts, Forum Shopping, and Institutional Dynamics in Jerusalem*. Farnham: Ashgate, 2015.

Shlala, Elisabeth. *The Late Ottoman Empire and Egypt: Hybridity, Law and Gender*. London: Routledge, 2018.

Todd, David. "Beneath Sovereignty: Extraterritoriality and Imperial Internationalism in Nineteenth- Century Egypt." *Law and History Review* 36, n° 1 (2018): 105–137.

Ulbert, Jörg. "Les manuels consulaires français d'avant 1914 comme sources des études consulaires." In *De l'utilité commerciale des consuls: L'institution consulaire et les marchands dans le monde méditerranéen (XVIIe–XXe siècle)*, edited by Arnaud Bartolomei, Guillaume Calafat, Mathieu Grenet and Jörg Ulbert, 117–140. Rome: Publications de l'École française de Rome, 2017.

Van den Boogert, Maurits H. *The Capitulations and the Ottoman Legal System: Qadis, Consuls, and Beratlıs in the 18th Century*. Leiden: Brill, 2005.

Vintila, Daniela, and Jean-Michel Lafleur, eds. *Migration and Social Protection in Europe and Beyond: Comparing Consular Services and Diaspora Policies*. Liège: Springer Nature, 2020.

Viscomi, Joseph. *Migration at the End of Empire: Time and the Politics of Departure between Italy and Egypt*. Cambridge: Cambridge University Press, forthcoming.

Vitto Massei, Mariella. "Un console abruzzese in Egitto e nel Medio Oriente (1869–1896)." *Bullettino della deputazione abruzzese di storia patria* 84 (1994): 235–255.

Ziad, Fahmy. "Jurisdictional Borderlands: Extraterritoriality and 'Legal Chameleons' in Pre-colonial Alexandria, 1840–1870." *Comparative Studies in Society and History* 55, n° 2 (April 2013): 305–329.

11

Protecting the Swiss

The Protection of the Swiss Citizens in the Ottoman Empire between Schutzgenossenschaft *and National Consuls in the 1870s*

Giorgio Ennas

1 Introduction

As highlighted by historians of Ottoman–Swiss relations like Stefan Sigerist, Beat Witschi, and Yiğit Topkaya, the presence of Swiss diasporas in the Ottoman Empire since the fifteenth and sixteenth centuries created the necessity for the Old Swiss Confederacy (1291–1798) to guarantee the security and properties of its members.[1] But, until the nineteenth century, the federal government avoided sending autonomous consular representatives to Constantinople or other imperial centres.[2]

Therefore, until the First World War the absence of Swiss representatives in the main centres of the Empire was generally compensated through the mediation of the Ottoman–Levantine networks, which, especially between the eighteenth and the nineteenth century, favoured and protected the interests of important Swiss firms and entrepreneurs,[3] and the *schutzgenossenschaft*, or "protective association," that placed Swiss migrants in the Empire under the protection of those European powers which had capitulation privileges with the Porte.[4] In particular, the French state played the role of protector of the

1 Beat Witschi, *Schweizer auf Imperialistischen Pfaden: Die Schweizerischen Handelsbeziehungen mit der Levante 1848 bis 1914* (Stuttgart: Steiner, 1987); Stefan Sigerist, *Schweizer im Orient* (Schaffhausen: self-published, 2004); Yiğit Topkaya, *Seidener Handel. Basel und das Osmanische Reich im 19. Jahrhundert* (Basel: Christoph Merian Verlag, 2023).

2 Sigerist, *Schweizer im Orient*, 25–26.

3 Topkaya, *Seidener Handel*, 26.

4 In an article published in 2022 with the peer-reviewed journal *Comparativ*, the author investigated the transition of the protection of the Swiss citizens in the Ottoman Empire between the 1850s and the 1910s, with a particular attention to the First World War as the moment of transition from the diplomatic Frenchsphere to the Germansphere. Instead, the present contribution aims to deepen the jurisdictional struggle for the protection of the Swiss citizens in the Ottoman Empire between the 1870s and 1880s. Giorgio Ennas, "Negotiating Protection. The Inclusion of Ottoman-Swiss Relations in the Diplomatic Germansphere during the First World War," in *The Ottoman Empire and the 'Germansphere' in the*

© 2026 THE AUTHOR(S) | HTTPS://DOI.ORG/10.1163/9789004755192-013

Swiss living in the Empire until the Congress of Vienna of 1814–1815. After the Congress, the Swiss had the possibility to extend the "protective association" toward other powers, like the Habsburg Empire, the Kingdom of Sardinia, or Prussia.

However, the privileged relationship with France continued undisputed until the second half of the nineteenth century, despite the claims of part of the Swiss communities residing in the Empire and the fact that the *schutzgenossenschaft* guaranteed to the Swiss the privilege of deciding under the protection of which Great Power to place themselves. The situation partially changed only with the Franco-Prussian War of 1870–1871, that compromised French international prestige and military primacy in Europe, and the unification of the German *Kaiserreich*, that offered to a part of the Swiss migrants in the Ottoman Empire an alternative to the French protection.

This flexibility was considered particularly useful by the federal government, as the latter was sometimes perceived as alien to the interests of Swiss citizens or detrimental to their national honour. Due to this situation, in the early 1870s the jurisdiction on the protection of the Swiss in the Ottoman Empire and the consular courts became a battlefield between those powers competing for hegemony over continental Europe and the Sublime Porte. Moreover, it produced a new internal discussion within the federal government on whether it should create its own consular system in the Ottoman Levant. This competition increased particularly during periods of major international crisis such as the Ottoman–Russian War of 1877–1878, with consequences that would last until the end of the First World War. Therefore, focusing on the transition period of the 1870s, the present contribution aims to highlight the immediately post-Franco-Prussian conflict period as the beginning of an effective jurisdictional struggle between European powers and the Ottoman Empire for the inclusion of Swiss citizens within the boundaries of their respective consular or legal jurisdictions in the 1870s. This could not be considered a conflict between equal opponents, but it was instead characterised by an asymmetric balance of power due to the international situation that placed the Ottoman Empire in a more difficult position than the Great Powers of Europe. However, it shows how, despite Swiss and Ottoman ambitions for emancipation, in this decade international events persuaded the Federal Council that the flexibility of the *schutzgenossenschaft* was the best guarantee of security for Swiss citizens living in the Empire.

Age of Imperialism, eds. Elife Biçer-Deveci and Ulrich Brandenburg (Leipzig: Comparativ, 2022), 349–363.

By analysing Swiss diplomatic documents, this article investigates if conflicts such as the Franco-Prussian War and the Ottoman–Russian War can be considered turning points for the Swiss protection system in the Empire. Moreover, it analyses how it was reflected in the different practices of the consular courts and how this sovereignty conflict between European powers and the Ottomans over the protection of the Swiss played out. Finally, it aims to reconstruct what the consequences of this consular clash were for the Swiss residing in the territories under the protection of the Sublime Porte.

2 The Franco-Prussian Turning Point

Swiss communities existed in the Ottoman Empire since the fifteenth century. Like other European communities, their members generally lived in the main trade centres along the coasts of the Empire, like Constantinople, İzmir, and Bursa, and worked in different sectors, such as watchmakers, goldsmiths, or textile merchants.[5] These communities were generally characterized by a relatively small number of members, the absence of a national colonial project, and the lack of proper diplomatic or consular representatives. For this reason, for the protection of its own citizens, for centuries the Swiss state had to turn to powers like the Kingdom of France, which were linked with the imperial government by capitulation rights, putting federal citizens under the peculiar system of the *schutzgenossenschaft*, or "protective association."

In the first half of the nineteenth century, this system allowed Swiss citizens to choose, according to their situation and personal preference, the protection of a particular European power bound by treaties with the Sublime Porte, but without being strictly controlled by any one of them. Despite the fact that from the nineteenth century onwards the capitulations were seen by the Ottomans as interventions by the Powers on imperial sovereignty, they ensured considerable mobility and fluidity of protection for the Swiss, and companies and firms residing in the Empire. Simultaneously, it avoided the federal government spending vital economic resources on maintaining national diplomatic and consular networks for communication with the Porte.

The situation began to change already in the 1850s, when the effects of the Ottoman *Tanzimat*, or reforms, persuaded part of the Swiss communities residing in the Empire of the opportunities which were opening up with individuals from Europe with knowledge deemed useful by the Sublime Porte, such

5 David Auberson, *Josef Koetschet (1830–1898): Un Suisse dans l'Empire ottoman* (Delémont: Société jurassienne d'émulation, 2008), 219.

as the Swiss physicians Josef Koetschet and Josephine Fallscheer-Zürcher.[6] The claiming for the continuation of negotiations and for the establishment of permanent diplomatic and consular relations went on throughout the 1850s and 1860s,[7] also under the impetus of European emigration produced by the events of the Crimean War of 1853–1856 and the Treaty of Paris of 1856, which brought the Ottoman Empire into the system of the Concert of the Great Powers.[8]

However, due to the high costs involved in setting up widespread diplomatic and consular networks in the Ottoman Empire and the Swiss impossibility of guaranteeing reciprocity to the Ottomans for the settlement of Muslims in several cantons, in 1861 the Federal Council signed the French-Ottoman Commercial Treaty. Once more, the Treaty linked Swiss activities in the Ottoman territories to the protection guaranteed by the French diplomatic and consular systems.[9] This French-Swiss system began to suffer a severe blow in the early 1870s, due to the modifications and upheavals in the international balance caused by the humiliating French defeat in the Franco-Prussian War of 1870–1871.

Since the 1860s, European and Ottoman representatives registered a generic increasing anxiety in Europe due to the nationalist policies pursued by the French Emperor Napoleon III and the Prussian Chancellor Otto von Bismarck. These diplomatic activities risked compromising the international order sanctioned with the Treaty of Paris of 1856.[10] For them, the risk was not only of a localised conflict between a waning Napoleonic regime and a rampant Prussian monarchy, that, after the Austro-Prussian War of 1866, aspired to the creation of a new national German Empire alternative to that of the Habsburgs, but of a global conflict leading to the annihilation of both the European Concert system and the Ottoman Empire.

Despite the Austro-Hungarian and French efforts to involve in different ways the Sublime Porte in the conflict, the Ottomans preserved their neutral-

---

6 Urs Boschung, "Josef Koetschet," *Historisches Lexikon der Schweiz* (HLS), *(23.08.2007):* accessed 16 February 2023, https://hls-dhs-dss.ch/de/articles/046486/2007-08-23/; Hans L. Kieser, "Josephine Fallscheer-Zürcher," in *Historisches Lexikon der Schweiz* (HLS), (15.11.2004): accessed 19 March 2023, https://hls-dhs-dss.ch/de/articles/014351/2004-11-15/.

7 Ennas, "Negotiating Protection," 353.

8 Ozan Ozavci, *Dangerous Gifts. Imperialism, Security, and Civil Wars in the Levant, 1798–1864* (Oxford: Oxford University Press, 2021), 285.

9 Ennas, "Negotiating Protection," 354.

10 *L'Empire Ottoman et l'Europe, I, Documents diplomatiques ottomans sur la Guerre franco-prussienne, la Commune de Paris et l'Internationale socialiste*, ed. Sinan Kuneralp (Istanbul: Isis, 2008), 7.

ity, thanks to the prudence of the Grand Vizier and Foreign Minister Emin Âli Pasha. During the war, he systematically ignored the sirens of intervention, linking the Empire to the group of the neutral powers which aimed to achieve peace without modification of the equilibrium.[11] Nevertheless, after the military conflict ended with the Prussian victory of Sedan, the humiliation of the French army, and the bloody repression of the Paris Commune in 1871, the Ottoman and European observers had to admit that the European equilibrium had been irrevocably modified.

The Second French Empire dissolved and its army downsized, while a new German Empire rose in the hearth of Europe, unifying the majority of the central European German-speaking states into a single national state entity. From that moment, the European balance began to dip to the German side and for a re-negotiation of international equilibrium. For the Ottomans as for other Europeans, from that moment the diplomatic efforts needed to focus on "cultivating friendship with the court and cabinet of Berlin."[12]

3 The 1870s–1880s and the Ottoman–Swiss Consular Issue

As underscored by Roland Ruffieux, the beginning of the 1870s represented a general turning point for Europe, and in particular for Switzerland.[13] Due to the downsizing of French hegemony in Europe and the rise of the German *Kaiserreich*, the international system was modified, and the federal government had to find its place in the new system that was being formed. The equilibrium system of Vienna and Paris that aimed for "universalism" was definitively abandoned, in favour of a new nationalist-imperialist system dominated by *realpolitik*.[14] The downsizing of French hegemony in Europe limited its "domination" over the federal government as well.[15] The new power relations led Bern to an internal strengthening of the national bonds, emphasising the concept of Swiss neutrality among federal public opinion. From a diplomatic point of view, the conflict produced a new activism with the inauguration of new diplomatic missions in Berlin and Rome, and consular seats in London, Washington, and Madrid.

---

11 Ibid., 108–109.

12 Ibid., 338–339.

13 *Diplomatische Dokumente der Schweiz* (from now onwards DDS) II (Bern: 1985), XIII.

14 Giorgio Ennas, *The Mediterranean Mirror. Italo-Ottoman Relations in an Age of Transition, 1856–1871* (Fiesole: European University Institute (unpublished thesis), 2021), 223–280.

15 DDS II (1985, XIII).

Following also internal strengthening after the constitutional reform of 1872–1874 led by the federal counsellor Emil Welti, the federal government began to re-consider establishing official autonomous relations with the Sublime Porte and creating its own consular legal space. In doing so, it would have gone against what were French diplomatic and economic interests in the Empire, opening up a season of confrontation between the actors involved.

For this reason, the naturalist and physician Johan Jakob von Tschudi, already in 1861 Swiss extraordinary minister for Brazil, where he negotiated a consular convention "to improve the life conditions of Swiss settlers,"[16] was appointed as *chargé d'affaires* in Vienna. During his long mission between 1868 and 1882, Tschudi negotiated with the Ottoman ambassadors İbrahim Haydar Efendi and Halil Şerif Pasha the autonomous inclusion of the Swiss in the Treaty of 18 June 1867, which permitted foreigners "to acquire real estate" in the Empire, guaranteeing them the same privileges as other Europeans under the regime of the capitulations.[17]

As reported by Tschudi, Swiss citizens under French protection claimed not only for the absence of their own representatives, but for the discrimination that they suffered in French consular courts:

> As you may know, apart from Constantinople, very few Swiss in the Orient are under French protection; a very large number, however, are under German protection. While the French consular courts are almost always composed of Frenchmen only, the Germans also include Swiss as assessors. As I have been assured, and with striking examples, the chancery fees at the French consulates are also disproportionately high. In the same case, for example, the French chancellery always charged 200 francs, but the German one only one Prussian thaler. The great wish of the Porte is that the Swiss in the Turkish states should simply be subject to the laws of the country.[18]

---

16 Veronika Feller-Vest, "Johann Jakob von Tschudi," *Historisches Lexikon der Schweiz* (HLS) (05.11.2013): accessed 1 November 2022, https://hls-dhs-dss.ch/it/articles/014903/2024-11-13/. See also André Holenstein, Patrick Kury and Kristina Schulz, *Storia svizzera delle migrazioni. Dagli albori ai giorni nostri* (Locarno: Armando Dadò Editore, 2022), 285–286.

17 Emil Welti to the Federal Council, 3 February 1872, Bern, DDS II, 395, E 13 (B) 271, 614.

18 French and German quotes have been translated into English by the author. For those in English, the author respected the original text as much as possible. Johann Jakob von Tschudi to A. Heer, 15 October 1873, Vienna, DDS III (Bern: Benteli Verlag, 1986), 27, Annex, E 2200 Wien 1/54, 71.

Apparently, although the French government had pledged to guarantee the safety and property of the Swiss living in the Empire, they did not have access to all the privileges of French citizens, such as being summoned to the consular courts as "assessors." On the contrary, Swiss citizens who placed themselves under Austro-Hungarian or German protection seemed to enjoy also this privilege and lighter fees.[19] Animated by this situation and by the increasing importance of trades with the Porte, Swiss diplomacy acted in search of a more advantageous proposal from the partners at stake, namely the German and Ottoman empires, and the Third French Republic.

During his mission, Tschudi tried to emancipate Swiss communities in the Ottoman Empire from French protection, rejecting the capitulations and trying to establish new official relations on a relatively egalitarian basis.[20] Despite French attempts to keep Swiss citizens under protection, Tschudi continued to negotiate with the Porte avoiding their mediation. On the other side, the Porte offered to the federal government the possibility to develop stable relations based on the principles of international law, and not anymore on the basis of capitulations. From this point of view, the Sublime Porte hoped that the Swiss precedent could create a virtuous circle, also preparing other international actors to abandon the asymmetrical system of the capitulations, so detrimental to the Ottoman economy and sovereignty.

Even if in this way Swiss citizens would become "objects of evidence for the [Ottoman] judicial system," they would avoid both foreign influences, and become one of the first communities to interact with the Ottomans on an effective level of reciprocity, probably obtaining a privileged status in front of imperial authorities. Tschudi underscored how, in his opinion, the Swiss:[21]

> In the Ottoman states should certainly not complain about the [Ottoman] courts, and that in any case that might arise, the [Ottoman] courts would certainly be more inclined to give justice to a Swiss than to a native, since a good administration of justice by the [Ottoman] authorities would contribute more to a favourable solution of the question of the abolition of the capitulations.[22]

The rejection of foreign protection and the consequent signature of a separate Ottoman–Swiss protocol would require: first of all, the formal acceptance of

19 Ennas, "Negotiating Protection," 355.

20 DDS III (1986, 71).

21 Ibid.

22 Ibid.

the capitulations by the federal government; the establishment of an official diplomatic representation in Constantinople; and, finally, the creation of an autonomous consular network.[23]

However, despite Tschudi's efforts and the desire of part of the Swiss government and diplomacy to emancipate themselves from foreign protection, especially of France, during the summer of 1875 the federal government, under the influence of the commercial chambers of Glarus, "whose companies have their houses and branches in the East or do business in there," decided to renovate French trade protection.[24] Once more, the possible costs of an effective consular network and the impossibility of the Swiss government to militarily impose its needs on the Porte played a key role in the decision to maintain the status quo and renew the agreement with France. Simultaneously, it was necessary to maintain and implement the *schutzgenossenschaft*, especially in cases of disputes with French nationals, or in case of international conflicts between powers appointed to the protection of Swiss citizens or with the Ottoman Empire, like in the case of the Ottoman–Russian War of 1877–1878.[25]

4 The Protection of the Swiss during the Ottoman–Russian War of 1877–1878

Despite some ambiguities in the relationship with the Great Powers, the Ottoman–Russian conflict of 1877–1878 proved to the federal government that it was right about maintaining the flexible system of the *schutzgenossenschaft* for its citizens in the Levant. The Herzegovinian Uprising of 1875 against the Ottoman tax collectors rapidly extended to the entire *vilayet-i Bosna*, or Ottoman province of Bosnia, territory.[26] The autonomous principalities of Serbia and Montenegro sustained the insurrection also thanks to the support of Russia and Austria-Hungary. In April 1877, the Ottoman rejection of the Serbian–Montenegrin peace proposal and the victories of the imperial army produced the Russian intervention, supporting its Balkan allies. The new Ottoman–Russian confrontation was destined to produce important modifications in the Balkans and in Ottoman society.

---

23 Ibid.

24 Minutes of the Federal Council meeting of 20 August 1875, Bern, DDS III (1986), 76, E 1004 1/102, 166; J. Heer to J. J. Scherer, 25 March 1875, Glarus, DDS III (1986), Annex, E 13 (B)/271, 167.

25 DDS III (1986, 166–167).

26 Caroline Finkel, *Osman's Dream. The History of the Ottoman Empire* (New York: Basic Books, 2005), 484–485.

Observing the progress of the conflict, in May 1877 the Political Department of the federal government reported that:

> The war ... is probably destined to arouse Muslim fanatism to a high degree, so that the situation of Christians living in Ottoman countries may become extremely critical depending on the course of the events.[27]

Therefore, for the Political Department the Swiss residents in the imperial territories needed the "efficacious protection of consuls" to effectively protect them and their properties. Due to the absence of Swiss national diplomatic and consular networks in the Ottoman Levant, the Department underscored the temporary necessity to put them under the protection of one of those European powers not involved in the conflict and "which are represented in the Orient by numerous agents who enjoyed an efficacious authority and power."[28]

From this perspective, they proposed the reinforcement of the traditional *schutzgenossenschaft*, particularly toward French, Habsburg, and Italian consuls, whose protection the Swiss found themselves under in the last decades.[29] Moreover, they proposed to contact the German and U.S. governments as well, through their representatives in Washington and Berlin in an attempt to optimise the result. On 29 May 1877, the head of the Political Department reported that Tschudi already obtained guarantees from the imperial–royal government of Vienna, putting the Swiss residents under Austro-Hungarian protections.[30] But Swiss consular activism did not finish here.

After contact through diplomatic and consular representatives, the German and Italian governments also promised to guarantee the protection of the Swiss citizens. As reported by the Swiss plenipotentiary minister in Rome, Giovan Battista Pioda, the Italian Minister of Foreign Affairs Luigi Amedeo Melegari answered the Swiss request writing that:

> The Federal Council cannot doubt that the King's agents will always look after the interests of Swiss nationals as well as those of Italian nationals, since it is the wish of the King's government that there should

27 Report of the Political Department for the Federal Council, 8 May 1877, Bern, Schweizerisches Bundesarchiv (from now onwards BAR), 1000/00044, E2#1000–44#173_3458275.

28 Report of the Political Department for the Federal Council, 8 May 1877, Bern, BAR, 1000/00044, E2#1000–44#173_3458275.

29 Ibid.

30 Johan Jakob von Tschudi to the Federal Council, 29 May 1877, Bern, BAR, 1000/00044, E2#1000–44#173_3458275.

> be no difference in treatment in this respect. As for the Swiss citizens who have not hesitated, until now, to be formally admitted to the protection of any other foreign consulate, the Federal Council can also be assured that the support of His Majesty's agents would not fail them, should the need arise. Although the King's consuls already have instructions to this effect, conceived in a largely humanitarian and liberal spirit, special instructions will still be addressed to them.[31]

In August 1877, the government of the United States also accepted to appoint its own consuls "to continue the exercise of their good offices on behalf of Swiss citizens," answering to the request of the Federal Council through the consul general at Washington.[32]

However, from the documents analysed so far it also emerges also how the peculiarity of the *schutzgenossenschaft* could potentially create compatibility problems with other national diplomatic and consular systems. For example, in the British case the Swiss government apparently found a compatibility problem between the *schutzgenossenschaft* and consular law concerning the protection of Swiss citizens residing in the territories administered by the Sublime Porte. Through the consulate general of London, between May and June 1877 the Federal Council required the assistance of the Foreign Office regarding the protection of Swiss in the Empire:

> My Lord. The breaking out of war in the East has naturally caused to my government some apprehension respecting the position of Swiss citizens residing in the various provinces of the [Ottoman] Empire where the Swiss Confederation has no diplomatic or consular representatives. In ordinary times Swiss citizens have claimed the protection of the representatives of the various powers with whom Switzerland entertains friendly relations, especially of those of Great Britain and I am instructed to convey to your lordship the thanks of my government for the protection hitherto accorded in cases of difficulty. My government further desires me to express the hope that in the present critical state of affairs in [the Ottoman Empire], it may still rely upon the powerful influence of

31 Giovan Battista Pioda to the Federal Council, 30 May 1877, Bern, BAR, 1000/00044, E2#1000–44#173_3458275.

32 The government of the United States to the Federal Council, summer of 1877, Bern, BAR, 1000/00044, E2#1000–44#173_3458275.

> English diplomatic and consular representatives in the East for the protection of Swiss citizens residing in the [Ottoman] Empire.[33]

Nevertheless, the co-existence of simultaneous kinds of protections risked to complicate the issue. In its reply, the Foreign Office observed how:

> In reply to the request of the Swiss government that the protection, which on previous occasions has been afforded to Swiss citizens by the representatives of this country, may now be continued to them. I am to state to you that the instructions issued to Her Majesty's Representatives in 1863 will still remain in force but that Her Majesty's government have been given to understand that Swiss citizens had been taken under German protection.[34]

As it emerges from the diplomatic correspondence, the jurisdictional issue was not clear for the Swiss government. Therefore, the Federal Council requested an investigation. A note from the British legation dated 31 July 1863 concerning the protection of two Swiss commercial houses in Syria was found in the archives. It reported that the British government was very happy to "render all such assistance as they can" offer to Swiss citizens, but that "they cannot give official 'protection' as it is understood in the East."[35] Then, the following question for Swiss government was: What difference was there between the protection granted by British agents to the Swiss and the official protection as it was understood in the Ottoman provinces, which cannot be granted to them?

At the end of July 1877, the issue was finally clarified by a document written by the Political Department and addressed to the Federal Council:

> That the precise nature of the protection referred to in the note addressed by Admiral Harris to the [Swiss] President in July 1863 is explained by a former note from the Admiral Harris to the President, dated 16 September 1859 and that, as in the East Her Majesty's diplomatic Representatives and Consuls exercise powers of jurisdiction as of protection, Her Majesty's government cannot extend protection to foreigners beyond the scope indicated in the note above referred to and that this

33 The British government to the Federal Council, summer of 1877, Bern, BAR, 1000/00044, E2#1000-44#173_3458275.

34 Ibid.

35 Ibid.

> reserve is shown to be more specially required in the case of Swiss citizens who are left the option of placing themselves under any flag to which they may give the preference; the instructions to British agents in 1863, referred to in the letter to Monsieur Verner of the last 18 are those mentioned in the note from Admiral Harris of 31 July 1863.[36]

Therefore, the British diplomacy and consular network can assist the Swiss citizens but cannot extend proper protection to them, not having the possibility to extend its jurisdiction as well, due to the flexibility of the *schutzgenossenschaft*. In its analysis for the Federal Council, the Political Department considered "neither necessary nor appropriate" to press the royal government any further, simply taking note of the issue.[37] The *schutzgenossenschaft* represented a very useful resource for Swiss citizens abroad due to its flexibility and its low cost for the Helvetic state. But, while normally its flexibility allowed Swiss citizens to always enjoy protection wherever they were, in other cases, such as in the British, it could potentially create jurisdictional issues or risks comparable to having a national consular system.

Nevertheless, if before the Ottoman–Russian War of 1877–1878 the Federal Council had looked with great interest at the possibility of establishing direct relations with the Sublime Porte through the creation of its own consular network outside the system of capitulations, during the conflict, which was to deeply change the balance in the Balkans by greatly reducing the dominions of the Ottoman Empire, the Swiss government and diplomacy found in the maintenance of the *schutzgenossenschaft* system an ideal guarantee of success for the protection of its own citizens even in such a difficult period of crisis.

5 Conclusion

The conclusion of the Ottoman–Russian War of 1877–1878 deeply re-shaped the status quo in the Balkans, in the rest of the Ottoman Empire, and in Europe. On the one hand, the Ottoman humiliation with the Treaty of San Stefano and the Congress of Berlin of 1878 downsized the international status of the Sublime Porte and reduced Ottoman territories through the emancipation of Balkan principalities. On the other hand, the predominant interpretation of inter-

---

36 Report of the Political Department to the Federal Council, 24 July 1877, Bern, BAR, 1000/00044, E2#1000–44#173_3458275.

37 Ibid.

national law became that of *realpolitik* advocated by Bismarck and the diplomacy of the age of imperialism. The Ottoman Empire overcame the crisis, however, being deeply transformed by it. Under the sultanate of Abdülhamid II, a profound process of reform in diplomacy and society was carried out to avoid partition by the government of the Great Powers. On the diplomatic front, it adopted *realpolitik*, but, simultaneously, adopted a defensive attitude in order to contain potential damages caused by the aggressive "gunboat diplomacy."[38]

Also, the relations with Switzerland changed. While the latter still tried to obtain the same privileges by avoiding the capitulations and without entering direct relations with the Porte, the Ottoman government tried to resist such attempts, in the effort towards a general downsizing of foreign influence. At the beginning of the 1880s, while maintaining the *schutzgenossenschaft* system and itself within the French diplomatic and trade system, the Federal Council and the Swiss commercial chambers were interested in re-opening the negotiations with the Porte concerning the adherence to the Protocol of 9 June 1867, which sanctioned the protection of foreign persons and properties in the Empire to the citizens of those Great Powers linked to the imperial government through capitulations. Although the French did not allow access to the Swiss under their protection, in 1883 the German-speaking powers still continued to allow protected people "as well as their own citizens, to benefit from the protocol" and be involved in consular courts.[39] Therefore, in the summer of 1883 Bern requested to also include its own citizens under French protection with the support of the government of Paris. Nevertheless, the Porte rejected the Swiss proposal. Apparently, its rejection by the government of the sultan and the continuous competition with the German-speaking consulates, persuaded Paris of the opportunity to send instructions to its diplomats and consuls in the Levant and also include the Swiss on an equal footing with the French citizens, preserving its protection toward the members of its communities in the Ottoman Empire.

In conclusion, the present article highlights the jurisdictional competition between European Great Powers and the Ottoman Empire to include Swiss

38 Giorgio Ennas, "Connecting the two seas. Italian and Ottoman diplomacies in the Suez-Red Sea area," in *Italy and the Suez Canal. A Mediterranean History, from the Mid-Nineteenth Century to the Cold War*, ed. Barbara Curli (London: Palgrave Macmillan, 2022), 253. See also Giorgio Ennas, "The Franco-Prussian War and the Ottoman Adoption of Realpolitik," in *The Franco-Prussian War. Turning-Points in European Experiences and Perceptions of Military Conflict*, ed. Karine Varley (London-New York: Routledge, 2024), 40–53.

39 Minutes of the Federal Council of 28 September 1883, DDS III (1986), 247, E 1004 1/134, 526–527.

citizens within the borders of their own jurisdictions in the 1870s. Moreover, it emphasised the federal government's oscillation between the system of *schutzgenossenschaft* and the development of autonomous diplomatic and consular systems in the Levant in the same decade. From a preliminary analysis of Swiss diplomatic documents, this article seems that the Franco-Prussian War did play a role in the Swiss effort to find possible alternatives to French protection. In contrast to the French republican government, other states such as the rampant German Empire seemed to offer new and more stable prospects of protection. In any case, a few years later the Russian–Ottoman conflict clearly showed that the *schutzgenossenschaft* still represented the best guarantee of security for Swiss citizens living in the Empire and for the state's finances.

A difference in treatment between the *protégés* of the various powers also clearly emerges. Although the French government obtained international prestige from extending its protection to citizens of other states, in the 1860s and 1870s its protection seemed less attractive to the latter due to the high costs of its consular services and the privilege of French citizens in the composition of consular courts. At the same time, German protection appeared less expensive and more egalitarian and, therefore, more attractive. This paved the way for the German and Ottoman proposals regarding possible alternatives, or even the development of their own consular network. Finally, it seems that the main consequences of this consular confrontation for the protection of Swiss citizens was basically a strengthening of the economic ties with France, especially for the Swiss chambers of commerce, and a strengthening of the confidence the Swiss government had in the *schutzgenossenschaft*, especially in times of great uncertainty and crisis in the Ottoman territories, despite the possible risks of incompatibility, as in the British case.

Bibliography

Auberson, David. "Josef Koetschet (1830–1898): Un Suisse dans l'Empire ottoman." *Actes de la Société jurassienne d'émulation* 111 (2008): 219–236.

Augusti, Eliana. "Storie e Storiografie dei Consolati in Oriente tra Otto e Novecento." *Historia e ius. Rivista di Storia Giuridica dell'Età Medievale e Moderna*, 11 (2017): 1–17.

Boschung, Urs. "Josef Koetschet." *Historisches Lexikon der Schweiz* (HLS), (*23.08.2007*). Accessed 16 February 2023. https://hls-dhs-dss.ch/de/articles/046486/2007-08-23/.

Ennas, Giorgio. "Connecting the Two Seas: Italian and Ottoman Diplomacies in the Suez-Red Sea Area." In *Italy and the Suez Canal: A Mediterranean history, from the mid-Nineteenth century to the Cold War*, edited by Barbara Curli, 247–260. London: Palgrave Macmillan, 2022.

Ennas, Giorgio. The Franco-Prussian War and the Ottoman Adoption of Realpolitik. In "*The Franco-Prussian War. Turning-Points in European Experiences and Perceptions of Military Conflict*," edited by Karine Varley, 40–53. London-New York: Routledge, 2024.

Ennas, Giorgio. "*The Mediterranean Mirror: Italo-Ottoman Relations in an Age of Transition, 1856–1871*." Fiesole: European University Institute (unpublished thesis), 2021.

Ennas, Giorgio. "Negotiating Protection: The Inclusion of Ottoman-Swiss Relations in the Diplomatic Germansphere during the First World War." In *The Ottoman Empire and the 'Germansphere' in the Age of Imperialism*, edited by Elife Biçer-Deveci and Ulrich Brandenburg, 349–363. Leipzig: Leipziger Universitätsverlag, 2022.

Feller-Vest, Veronika. "Johann Jakob von Tschudi." *Historisches Lexikon der Schweiz* (HLS), (05.11.2013). Accessed 1 November 2022. https://hls-dhs-dss.ch/it/articles/014903/2024-11-13/.

Finkel, Caroline. *Osman's Dream: The History of the Ottoman Empire*. New York: Basic Books, 2005.

Fischer, Harald, and Patricia Tiné-Purtschert. *Colonial Switzerland: Rethinking Colonialism from the Margins*. London: Palgrave Macmillan, 2015.

Holenstein, André, Patrick Kury, and Kristina Schulz. *Storia svizzera delle migrazioni: Dagli albori ai giorni nostri*. Locarno: Armando Dadò Editore, 2022.

Kieser, L. Hans. "Josephine Fallscheer-Zürcher." *Historisches Lexikon der Schweiz* (HLS), (*23.08.2007*). Accessed 19 March 2023. https://hls-dhs-dss.ch/de/articles/014351/2004-11-15/.

Kieser, L. Hans. *Vorkämpfer der "Neuen Türkei": Revolutionäre Bildungseliten am Genfersee (1870–1939)*. Zurich: Chronos, 2005.

Kuneralp, Sinan, ed. *L'Empire Ottoman et l'Europe, 1, Documents diplomatiques ottomans sur la Guerre franco-prussienne, la Commune de Paris et l'Internationale socialiste*. Istanbul: Les Editions Isis, 2008.

Maissen, Thomas. *Svizzera: Storia di una Federazione*. Trieste: Beit Storia, 2015.

Ozavci, Ozan. *Dangerous Gifts: Imperialism, Security, and Civil Wars in the Levant, 1798–1864*. Oxford: Oxford University Press, 2021.

Sigerist, Stefan. *Schweizer im Orient*. Schaffhausen: self published, 2004.

Topkaya, Yiğit. *Seidener Handel: Basel und das Osmanische Reich im 19. Jahrhundert*. Basel: Christoph Merian Verlag, 2023.

Windler, Christian. *La diplomatie comme expérience de l'autre: consuls français au Maghreb (1700–1840)*. Geneva: Librairie Droz, 2002.

Witschi, Beat. *Schweizer auf Imperialistischen Pfaden: Die Schweizerischen Handelsbeziehungen mit der Levante 1848 bis 1914*. Stuttgart: Steiner, 1987.

12

Capitulations "in a Box"

The Power of Ottoman Procedural Codes

Berna Kamay-Ulusay

It is difficult in a short time to do justice to justice.[1]

ROBERT MUSIL, *The Man without Qualities*

∵

1 Introduction

Robert Musil's unfinished novel, which is set in the final years of the Austria-Hungarian Empire, describes a legal commission's diligent efforts to revise the old laws and improve jurisdictional operation over many years. This task is not isolated, as the assigned committee had to address "a very long-lasting state of affairs" while falling behind "all the leaps of thought of the intellectual fashion prevailing."[2] As if echoing that story, this study examines another imperial episode from the same period in which the Ottoman Empire underwent a long-winded transformation to advance the legal system in its last century. By examining the jurisdictional authority of the 1879 Ottoman Procedural Codes, which have not been exhaustively studied in terms of their impact on courtroom culture and capitulations, this study situates the evolution of legal formalism within a broader historical context. The role of procedural codes is central to the operation of justice, showcasing the integrity of the judicial body. In other respects, the courtroom realm provides a lens to reflect on how competence in jurisdiction is displayed and advocated.[3]

1 Robert Musil, *The Man Without Qualities*, vol. 1 (New York: Vintage International, 1996), 585.

2 Ibid.

3 In the British Empire, in comparison, procedural codes were seen as protecting the dignity of royal justice. The courtrooms became the scene where people could observe the legal system of the Victorian Age. See Tamar Herzog, *A Short History of European Law: the Last Two and Half Millenia* (Cambridge: Harvard University Press, 2018), 103; and Sascha Auerbach, *Armed with Sword and Scales: Law, Culture, and Local Courtrooms in London, 1860–1913* (Cambridge: Cambridge University Press, 2021), 14 and 20.

 | HTTPS://DOI.ORG/10.1163/9789004755192-014

The Ottoman Empire stands out among other non-European states considering its centuries-old capitulation tradition in its interplay of diplomacy with Europe. Capitulations were always present and remained binding until the end of the empire. This study argues, however, that the treaty system gradually lost its sanction of jurisdictional power as legislative efforts gained pace at home. It also shows that the increasing prominence of the rule of law should not be taken for granted as the new procedural codes soon played a pivotal role in steering the Ottoman foreign policy against the backdrop of capitulations. When the competence of the judiciary was redefined, now rooted in a more substantive and self-reliant approach to adjudication, the capitulatory states had to find new legal outlets for their jurisdictional claims.

2 An Overview of Ottoman Jurisdiction and Capitulations

The nature and significance of the capitulations in the Ottoman legal system deserve in-depth analysis. *İmtiyâzât,* an umbrella term encompassing special rights and privileges granted to foreign residents, including capitulations, refers to a broad set of pact and treaties that regulated their legal status within the Ottoman Empire.[4] As a form of *jus gentium* in Roman law, the capitulations protected the legal status of these individuals since the sixteenth century. The capitulations were not confined to providing economic privileges to foreign merchants, as usually portrayed. They also prepared the groundwork for a separate legal framework in times of necessity. They were sometimes enforced by the Ottoman state as if they were an official legal ordinance.[5]

By the seventeenth century, the conventional conduct of Ottoman diplomacy in international relations was eclipsed by the increasingly dominant law

4 These pact and treaties, referred to in Ottoman Turkish as *ahdname* or capitulations, were granted bilaterally in the early centuries and took different forms depending on the legal status of foreign residents or the purpose of their stay within the Ottoman Empire. For instance, these included *hüccet,* a document used in judicial proceedings or *eman,* a document issued to ensure safe travel and temporal residence in the empire. These concessions were typically formalized in a *berat,* an official document bearing the sultan's signature which signified that a specific privilege or exemption had been conferred. See Halil İnalcık, "İmtiyâzât," in *Encylopedia of Islam,* Volume III (Leiden: Brill, 1986), 1179–1189.

5 Edhem Eldem, "Foreigners at the Threshold of Felicity: The Reception of Foreigners in Ottoman Istanbul," in *Cultural Exchange in Early Modern Europe: Cities and Cultural Exchange in Europe, 1400–1700,* eds. Donatella Calabi, Stephen Turk Christensen (Cambridge: Cambridge University Press, 2007), 117; and Edhem Eldem, "Capitulations and Western Trade," in *Cambridge History of Turkey,* ed. Suraiya Faroqhi, vol. 3: *The Latter Ottoman Empire* (Cambridge: Cambridge University Press, 2006), 292–293.

of nations. It was around this time that diplomatic negotiations that had previously been maintained on equal footing between the worlds began to change.[6] Many Europeans attributed this to the Ottoman Empire's insistence on conventional diplomacy or disregard for the law of nations, which was perceived as arrogance.[7]

However, this assumption cannot be solely attributed to the Ottoman Empire's incompetence in the art of diplomacy. The conduct of Ottoman diplomacy moved beyond the scope of treaty-making and court ceremony. Since the late eighteenth century, the Ottoman Empire already used the terminology as equivalents of a later phrase *hukuk-u düvel* (law of nations) in their diplomatic correspondences. In 1837, the work of Emer de Vattel, the *Law of Nations* was translated.[8]

In this respect, the motive behind the consular system also appeared to be less about territorial sovereignty than about the strong dichotomy Europeans put forward when appraising the Christian and Muslim worlds. Even as it voiced its reservations, the Foreign Office stated its intention to take full advantage of the privileges granted to it in a dispatch to the British Consulate in Istanbul in 1857 as follows:

> This state of things in Turkey is an exception to the system universally observed among Christian nations. But the Ottoman Emperors having waived in favor of Christian Powers' rights inherent in territorial sovereignty, such Christian Powers, in taking advantage of this concession are bound to provide as far as possible against any injurious effects resulting from it to the territorial Sovereign.[9]

---

6 Alexander H. de Groot, "The Historical Development of the Capitulatory Regime in the Ottoman Middle East from the Fifteenth to the Nineteenth Centuries," *Oriento Moderno* n.s. 22 (83), n° 3 (2003): 577.

7 The British Ambassador to Istanbul, Sir James Porter expressed similar ideas as follows: "The Turks has no idea of the law of nations, they consider themselves as the only nation on earth, and regulate their own conduct towards others on positive compact, spontaneous concessions, or usage or customs." Sir James Porter, *Turkey, Its History and Progress, Vol. 1* (London: Hurst and Blackett, 1854), 284.

8 The phrases *hukuk-u nas, hukuk-u ümem* and *hukuk-u milel* – all of which can be translated as "law of nations" – were employed intercheangeably, each denoting the concept of international law within their historical context in the earlier centuries. Mustafa Serdar Palabıyık, "The Emergence of the Idea of 'International Law' in the Ottoman Empire before the Treaty of Paris (1856)," *Middle Eastern Studies* 50, n° 2 (2014): 239–2340.

9 Sir George Cornewall Lewis, *On Foreign Jurisdiction and the Extradition of the Criminals* (London: J.W. Parker and Son, 1859), 16.

The ideas of French politician Auguste Champetier de Ribes (1882–1947) strikingly resemble the arguments of the Foreign Office:

> It is fair to recognize that it is exorbitant in law to ask a Turkish subject to renounce at home the benefit of his own jurisdiction because it is a trial with a foreigner, and it must also be admitted that the text of no capitulation authorizes in formal and explicit terms such a derogation from the rules of territorial justice. But, in fact, it may seem harsh and far too perilous for the interests of nationals, in the still persistent state of hostility that exists between the Muslim civilization and our Christian civilization to submit to the Muslim Courts the judgment of such a conflict.[10]

As such, the shifting power balance in favor of Europe crystallized the prejudices of European superiority. The new diplomatic discourse provides a clear example of this change of attitude. Terms such as *en ziyade müsaadeye mahzar memleket* (most favored nation) and *hâriç ez-memleket* (extraterritoriality), which were already in use, appeared more frequently in nineteenth-century diplomatic correspondences, distinguishing it from the official rhetoric of early centuries which often used words like *dostluk* (amity), *muhabbet* (affinity), and *müsâvat* (equality).[11]

On the other hand, the jurisdictional course of court trials further proved a more powerful consensus on the capitulations by the nineteenth century. The nineteenth century was a period when the Ottoman Empire underwent legal transformation as part of a larger reform program known as *Tanzimat*. The scope of these reforms was grounded in a judicial framework upon which the empire had relied for centuries. The first was the Islamic Sharia law, the principles of which were applied by the *kadı* (qadi) courts. Sharia served as public law for centuries. Qadi courts had jurisdiction over conflicts among Ottoman and non-Ottoman subjects. Criminal cases including the foreign nationals and the Ottoman subjects also fell under the jurisdiction of qadi courts.[12]

10 A. Champetier de Ribes, "Les capitulations ou la réforme dans les échelles du Levant," *Le Droit: Journal des Tribunaux* (4 May 1870): 2.

11 Gilles Veinstein, "Les fondements juridiques de la diplomatie ottomane en Europe," *Oriente Moderno* NS 88, n° 2 (2008): 520.

12 Antonis Anastasopoulos, "Non-Muslims and Ottoman Justice(s)?," in *In Law and Empire: Ideas, Practices, Actors*, eds. Jeroen Duindam, Jill Harries, Caroline Humfress and Nimrod Hurvitz (Leiden: Brill, 2013), 275–291; and Najwa al-Qattan, "*Dhimmis* in the Muslim

As a second legal venue, the consular courts retained the right to try their nationals or oversee their disputes with other foreigners.[13] However, under the spell of "customary usage" the capitulations served beyond the treaty clauses. They stood as an exception to the rule and territoriality of law and functioned to the detriment of imperial sovereignty. By the nineteenth century, each European consul claimed the right to apply its legislation to all their nationals and objected to the punishment and trial of their nationals by the Ottoman courts in the mixed criminal lawsuits.

The Ottoman state had to make significant efforts to ward off the jurisdictional claims of consular authorities through diverse avenues. After the Crimean War in 1856, international law stood more prominent in diplomacy. Ottoman participation in the Paris Peace Conference redefined the position of the Ottoman state on the global stage. The empire's well-trained officials, diplomats, and newly emerging group of legal advisors engaged in debates on international law.[14] The burgeoning awareness of legal sovereignty was reflected in the statements made by Ottoman officials. For example, the legal advisor Parnis Efendi quoted Grotius during an extradition negotiation with Austria-Hungary in 1864. He underscored that Grotius did champion the idea that the nations stand on equal footing. In this way, Parnis Efendi desired to frame a treaty of extradition on the basis of equality for the right of territorial jurisdiction. In his report, he also added the notion of punishment by the famous jurist Beccaria who stated that "the persuasion of finding no point on the earth where the crime go unpunished would be an effective means of preventing it."[15]

Notwithstanding the power of official rhetoric embedded in international law, procedural measures were needed in the jurisdictional realm. The 1858 Ottoman Penal Code, remodeled after the 1832 French Penal Code, was comprehensive in terms of legislative power, but it still coexisted with the Sharia law. The Qadi courts continued functioning alongside the newly founded

---

Court: Legal Autonomy and Religious Discrimination," *International Journal of Middle Eastern Studies* 31 (1999): 429–444.

13 A. Heidborn, *Manuel de droit public et administratif de l'Empire ottoman* (Leipzig: C.W. Stern, 1908), 202.

14 During the Paris Peace Conference, Ali Pasha underscored the importance of territorial sovereignty by criticizing the treaty system that created as "a multiplicity of governments within the government." See Mariya Tait Slys, *Exporting Legality: The Rise and Fall of Extraterritorial Jurisdiction in the Ottoman Empire and China* (Geneva: Graduate Institute Publications, 2014), 51.

15 BOA (Ottoman Archives, Istanbul; henceforth BOA) HR.H. 212/5, 24.09.1864.

Nizâmiye courts.[16] These fluid judicial bodies blurred the tangible limits of their legal boundaries and the scope of their authority to enforce penalties. Yet, the key issue of the 1858 Penal Code lies in the lack of regulations concerning criminal prosecution.[17]

The criminal lawsuits involving foreign nationals in the Ottoman court could not start without the presence of a consular dragoman. The consular dragomans in the Ottoman Empire were more than translators of official documents or court interpreters. These officials had a rich knowledge of the law and diplomacy, which was manifest in the art of their assigned translations. They were active participants in judicial procedures who claimed the right to confirm the court decisions and initiate prosecutions when conflicts arose among their consular agents.[18] In the absence of procedural law, the Ottoman justice perforce had to oversee the tribunal hearings with their presence.

As an initial step, the Ottoman government introduced measures in judicial policing to address this legal loophole. In December 1857, a commission established in Istanbul to improve the operation of police forces also examined regulations pertaining to foreigners. One of the topics was police investigation – without consular assistance – of public places that were reportedly harboring foreign fugitives. They proposed if any protest or resistance was encountered, police forces were obliged to take coercive measures. The commission also proposed to deport foreign criminals whom the Ottoman police had detained but who were not protected by their consular legations. They could be taken out of the empire by their own legations provided that they would never return. The same procedure was to be applied to foreigners with criminal records who had been previously released but still posed a threat to security in the empire. The consulates approved the proposals ensuring they did not contradict the spirit of the treaty agreements.[19]

A decade later, more measures in prosecution were foisted on a law that permitted foreign nationals to own real estate in the Ottoman Empire. The 1867 Property Law for Foreigners, *İstimlâk Nizamnâmesi,* granted this right as

16 Avi Rubin, *Ottoman Nizamiye Courts: Law and Modernity* (New York: Palgrave Macmillan, 2011).

17 Tobias Heinzelman, "The Ruler's Monologue: The Rhetoric of the Ottoman Penal Code of 1858," *Die Welt des Islams* 54, n° 3–4 (2014): 318; and Gabriel Baer, "The Transition from Traditional to Western Criminal Law," *Studia Islamica* 45 (1977): 146, 158.

18 Zülâl Muslu, "Language and Power: The Dragoman as a Link in the Chain Between the Law of Nations and the Ottoman Empire," *Journal of History of International Law* 22 (June 2020): 56.

19 BOA HR.MKT. 235/51, December 1857. The consulates of Netherlands, Greece, Belgium, the Hanseatic States, Spain, Sweden, Norway, France, Napoli, Sardines, and Russia attended this commission. Only Russia and Napoli demanded some modifications.

long as these foreigners complied with Ottoman laws in all situations. A protocol was added to this legal decree, which allowed the Ottoman police to issue search warrants for foreign properties. The protocol also authorized local courts to hold trials without consular assistance if the crime scene was more than 9 hours away from any consular institutions.[20] The consuls faced their first major hurdles in legal disputes with this protocol, but it was still far from establishing a standard for jurisdictional autonomy. In 1879, a set of judicial reforms introduced in the Ottoman Empire ultimately reached this goal.

3 Ottoman Procedural Codes

Since the onset of Tanzimat, the 1879 judicial reforms stand out as one of the most significant legal reforms in scope. Initially, the implementation of these reforms proved to be difficult due to the prolonged economic struggles as the Ottoman Empire had just emerged from The Russo-Turkish War (1877–1878) defeated with territorial loss and substantial war debt.[21] Despite the lack of official staff and financial deficits, the power of these codes is self-evident in function as they were in force until the first years of the Turkish Republic and in the way how they largely contributed to the growing legal formalism at home. To improve the operation of the judicial system and further elaborate on the evolution of Ottoman *Nizâmiye* Courts empire-wide, the courts were restructured into three branches: *bidâyet* (the court of first instance), *istînaf* (the court of appeal), and *temyiz* (the court of cassation). New bureaucratic posts were created to support the smooth operation of the justice system and detailed job descriptions were outlined. The defining feature of the 1879 judicial reforms was the introduction of civil and criminal procedural codes, as they regulated the operations of the entire court system. *Müdde-i umûmi* (public prosecutor) and *müstantik* (investigating magistrate) emerged as two distinct professions.[22]

---

20 On 1867 Property Law, see Berna Kamay-Ulusay, "Osmanlı'da 'Yabancının' Mülkiyet Hakkı Üzerine Bir Değerlendirme: 1867 İstimlâk-ı Emlâk Nizamnâmesi" (An Overview of Property Rights of 'the Foreigner' in the Ottoman Empire: the 1867 Property Law for Foreigners), in *Osmanlı Tarihçiliğinde Yeni Çalışmalar: Kaynak, Bağlam, Yöntem* (New Studies in the Ottoman Historiography: Source, Context, Method), eds. Fatma Öncel and Sinem Erdoğan İşkorkutan (Istanbul: Vakıfbank Kültür Yayınları, 2023), 129–160.

21 M. Hakan Yavuz and Peter Sluglett, eds., *War and Diplomacy: The Russo-Turkish War of 1877–1878 and the Treaty of Berlin* (Salt Lake City: University of Utah Press, 2011).

22 For further information on the 1879 judicial reforms, see Fatmagül Demirel, *Adliye Nezareti Kuruluşu ve Faaliyetleri (1876–1914)* (Istanbul: Boğaziçi Üniversitesi Yayınları, 2008).

While the Ottoman Code of Criminal Procedure entered into force on 26 June 1879, the Ottoman Code of Civil Procedure was enacted a year later, on 10 June 1880.[23] Avi Rubin defines the function and scope of the procedural codes as follows:

> These codes prescribed hundreds of procedural motions, from the very initial stage of submitting a civil lawsuit or criminal bill of indictment to the last stages of execution of rulings in both the civil and criminal courts. They ushered in functions hitherto unknown in Islamic law, such as the investigating magistrate (*müstantik*) and the public prosecutor (*müddei-i umûmi*). The latter carried out duties in both the criminal and the civil domains. The meticulous codes allowed the judges who worked in the courts no leeway as far as the procedure was concerned.[24]

This study focuses on the Ottoman Code of Criminal Procedure, as it particularly examines issues pertaining to criminal jurisdiction. The Ottoman Code of Criminal Procedure was largely remodeled after the 1808 French Code of Criminal Procedure, but it also relied on an accumulation of precedents in Ottoman penal codes. The legal text was composed of 487 articles, in this way serving as an exhaustively detailed legal guide to the procedures of the court.[25]

Due to the comprehensive regulations in every step of prosecution, the consular presence in court hearings among the Ottoman and foreign subjects was no longer deemed necessary as the public prosecutors brought the eyewitnesses to the tribunals. Lawyers were assigned from among the court members for the defendant, and the chief justice of the court-appointed interpreters. Therefore, the signature of dragomans under the verdict was automatically unauthorized. Another regulation was on provisory detention, which was a judicial precaution taken to prevent the accused from escaping until a bill of indictment was issued. *Kabl-el-hükm habs* (provisory detention) in Ottoman jails for 24 hours rendered it mandatory for the police forces prior to a court trial. Unlike the regular practice, the criminals stayed under Otto-

23 For the legal code, see George Young, *Corps de Droit Ottoman*, (Oxford: Clarendon Press, 1906), 2:226–300.

24 Avi Rubin, "Legal Borrowing and its impact on Ottoman legal culture in the late nineteenth century," *Continuity and Change* 22, n° 2 (August 2007): 284.

25 Young, *Corps de Droit Ottoman*, 226–300.

man custody rather than being surrendered to their consulates until the day of prosecution.[26]

These adjustments bypassed the established privileges of the consulates in the penal proceedings. In 1881, an official decree was issued further limiting the competency of consular jurisdiction. According to the decree, the Ottoman tribunals held the ultimate judicial authority over criminal suits involving different foreign nations that had been heard by consulates up until then. The Ottoman government asserted their claim to the new policy by referring to the capitulations which enabled consulates to oversee only *niza'* (the disputes) among the European nationals that pertained to civil affairs. Offenses of a criminal nature, on the other hand, were subject to Ottoman justice from the very outset.[27]

The new ordinances drew a rebuff from the consulates. They immediately made a request for a meeting with consular authorities and state officials to address the procedural codes. In a meeting held in April 1881, the consular dragomans presented their proposals to the Ministry of Justice. These proposals addressed both the civil and criminal procedural codes as well as the precepts of criminal sentencing. During the meeting, the dragomans objected to certain provisions of the procedural codes that stated the signatures of the public prosecutor and the investigative magistrates were sufficient to finalize the verdict. They reclaimed their right to be present during court hearings and have their signatures on judgments as before. Otherwise, they warned that the prosecution would be considered *keenlemyekûn* (null and void) in their eyes.[28]

The consular authorities further insisted that foreign suspects could be released on bail procured by another foreigner. Ultimately, they demanded that the official summons to court be delivered to indicted individuals by consul authorities and that the official waiting period be predicated on the time of this summons.[29]

These protests did not go unnoticed by the Ottoman government. Meanwhile, various state departments exchanged ideas on the issues propounded by the consulates. The discussions held illustrated how the Ottoman authorities reckoned critical matters that touched on the capitulations and territorial

26 Articles 71, 224, 250, and 286 of the Ottoman Code of Criminal Procedure elaborate on these regulations.

27 Philip Marshall Brown, *Foreigners in Turkey: Their Juridical Status* (Princeton University, 1914), 68.

28 BOA HR. HMŞ.IŞO 166/36, September 10, 1881; the report of the Ministry of Justice on this meeting.

29 BOA HR. HMŞ.IŞO 166/36, September 10, 1881; the report of the Ministry of Justice on this meeting.

sovereignty. The opinions proffered by each office also reveal a noticeable clash of ideas.

In his report, Grand Vizier Mehmed Said Pasha[30] reacted strongly to the consular demands by stating that customary practices encroached on territorial and jurisdictional autonomy. In his view, these demands could not be justified by the capitulations, but they carried the risk of bringing multiheaded legal procedures contrary to the nature of jurisdictional autonomy. He brushed off the points regarding bail and the summons to court for future discussion. Despite his critical stance, Mehmed Said Pasha refrained from making rash judgments that could incite a reaction from the European powers. He believed that a compromise that did not completely abandon customary practices or sacrifice legal sovereignty could be the most effective approach. The Grand Vizier sought advice from the Minister of Justice and Minister of Interior Affairs.[31]

The Minister of Justice, the famous Ahmed Cevdet Pasha,[32] was more familiar with the subject as he presided over that meeting with the dragomans. According to him, their meeting was an informal gathering, where the dragomans were the only ones to approve the proposal they submitted initially. Regarding the signatures in question, Ahmed Cevdet Pasha maintained that the dragomans did never have the right to sign under the verdict to approve the decision but only to confirm their presence at the trials. Before making a final decision, he recommended consulting legal experts and passed the discussion on to the Ministry of Foreign Affairs.

On the other hand, the Minister of Interior Affairs, Mahmud Nedim Pasha, remarked that they had attempted to abolish these procedures a few years before but had shelved the plans in the face of the consular pushback. The idea had actually been on the agenda ever since the establishment of *Nizâmiye* courts (1864), a time when the judicial system in Istanbul and the provinces was chaotic. However, they had decided to step back to maintain the status quo considering that the backlash could interrupt the administration of justice.[33]

30 Mehmed Said Pasha, also known as *Küçük* Said Pasha, served as grand vizier several times at intervals, during 1879–1912.

31 BOA HR. HMŞ.IŞO 166/36, 29.08.1881.

32 Ahmed Cevdet Pasha played a leading role behind the formulation of *Mecelle* (the Ottoman Civil Code) and authored twelve volumes of Ottoman history well-known as *Tarih-i Cevdet*.

33 Mahmud Nedim Pasha served as grand vizier several times in the last quarter of the nineteenth century. Due to his strong ties with Russian diplomats in Istanbul, he notoriously earned the nickname "Nedimof." BOA HR. HMŞ.IŞO 166/36, 06.09.1881.

Whereas the Minister of Interior openly confessed to the shortcomings of the judicial system in his report, the other ministries subtly indicated their reservations about taking action against practices that have been in place for years. This is also because the state officials were often in a quandary regarding their own judicial system. Rightly so, as the Ottoman legal transformation underwent a painstaking and slow process, which followed an erratic course of progress. The Ottoman intelligentsia often held similar opinions, as well. The renowned Ottoman intellectual Namık Kemal, for example, expressed his reservations about abolishing capitulations with a strong reasoning behind his arguments:

> To be honest, I hesitate to confront a foreign power just because of the ongoing presence of capitulations, as I fear the severe consequences. It is not just about the capitulations but our own legal system that deeply concerns me. The abundance of false witnesses in the Sharia courts on one side, what truly upsets me is the lack of accountability in the civil courts. The power of existing laws that millions depend on to safeguard their rights is undermined by a mindset that dismisses responsibility with the statement, "I am a Janissary, I act as a Janissary." Given this situation, there is no additional security provided other than relying on the trust that people have in the law.[34]

When the reports reached to the Ministry of Foreign Affairs as a final resort for discussion, the legal advisors proffered their opinions, which departed from the views articulated by the ministries. The Ottoman Office of Legal Counsel (*Hukuk Müşavirliği İstişâre Odası*), which was established in 1883 in the Department of Foreign Ministry, institutionalized this profession by providing counsel to the Ottoman state in an assortment of state affairs.[35] The occupation and task of the office were not limited to select political matters but soon covered diverse legal subjects and state affairs, most of which in large part related to diplomacy. Within a decade, the number of staff increased two-fold, and most were graduates of well-known schools that offered modern curricula.[36]

The Office of Legal Counsel agreed that there is a reasoning to hesitate and pointed out the problems that could emerge if customary practices were

34 Namık Kemal, "Kapitülasyonlar," *Diyojen* (1871).

35 *Chambre des conseillers légistes de la Sublime Porte: Rapports, avis et consultations sur la condition juridique des ressortissants étrangers, le statut des communautés non musulmanes et les relations internationales de l'Empire Ottoman,* eds. Sinan Kuneralp and öktem (Istanbul: Isis, 2012), 10.

36 BOA HR. HMŞ.IŞO. 188/49, 24.02.1901; and BOA Y.PRK. HR. 30/35, 19.04.1901.

quickly waved off. They acknowledged that consular privileges could no longer claim jurisdictional privileges under the new procedural codes. However, the legal advisors feared that any radical stance on the part of the Ottomans could result in the forfeit of the right to try foreign nationals altogether. The jurisdictional claims of the United States and Belgium, which relied on the conflicting interpretations of their capitulations, could serve as a model for other consulates. They suggested patiently preparing the groundwork for these procedures to be implemented. Whereas it was a matter of pride to refute the capitulations in the eyes of the ministries, the legal experts were discrete as they examined assorted foreign affairs and they were personally acquainted with the behavior of the consular authorities.[37]

In 1883, the embassies of Britain, Italy, Germany, Russia, and Iran reworded their earlier requests to the Ministry of Foreign Affairs, seeking a response to the proposals to procedural codes that had been discussed two years before. The consular authorities coordinated their efforts in unison, as their official correspondence echoed identical demands. This was actually their third appeal since the meeting, and they did not hear back from their calls in October 1881 and June 1882.[38]

However, the ministries were unable to reach a consensus whereas the procedural codes were already applied in full force. Over the next ten years, reports from every corner of the empire revealed how the consular reactions were hampering the smooth operation of the courts under the enforcement of procedural codes. There were ongoing protests regarding provisory detention which were ignored by the judicial authorities with the excuse that customary usage did not constitute a rule. The legations responded by refusing to send dragoman to the trials, to nullify the decisions of the tribunal. However, the courts assigned deputies of their own choosing who were considered sufficient for the prosecution to proceed.[39]

In order to address the ongoing problems, *Meclis-i Vükelâ* (the Council of Ministers) was called to convene. The Council of Ministers was an important state body in operation since the Tanzimat. Vested with administrative and judicial functions, this executive body was directly responsible to the Sultan.

---

37 BOA HR. HMŞ.IŞO 166/36, 04.03.1882. Both Article 4 of the 1830 Ottoman–US Treaty of Commerce and Article 9 of the 1838 Ottoman–Belgian Treaty assert the consular courts' jurisdictional rights. Regarding the diplomatic challenges posed by Article 4 of the Ottoman–US Treaty, see Berna Kamay, "The Ottoman Empire, the United States, and the legal battle over extradition: the 'Kelly Affair,'" *New Perspectives on Turkey* 65 (November 2021).

38 BOA HR. HMŞ.IŞO. 165/54, February 3, 1883.

39 BOA HR. HMŞ.IŞO. 174/20, September and April 1890.

The Grand Vizier presided over the meetings that the highest echelons of Ottoman bureaucracy such as the Shayk al Islam, the General of the Ottoman Army, the Grand Admiral and others attended.[40]

In 1893, the Council of Ministers addressed the subject of provisory detention at their initial meeting. The heated debate on this practice resulted in the unanimous decision among council members not to violate the procedural rules.[41] In 1895, the Council of Ministers came together one more time to review another set of protests sent to the Foreign Ministry. The legations insistently protested the validity of foreign testimony in the Ottoman courts without the presence of dragomans since the new proceeding nullified their authority in the verdict. However, the members of the council were determined to preserve the power of the procedural codes. Rather than annulling the practice of dragomans' presence, they advised Ottoman judicial authorities to respectfully seek the consent of the consular legations in the final judgments made by the court.[42] The efforts to convince the legations to cooperate remained abortive in all circumstances over the years. Therefore, in 1907, the Ministry of Justice officially announced that the regulations as prescribed by the procedural codes had been already in force and would remain so without any further discussion.[43]

4 Lasting Legacy of Capitulations?

The 1879 procedural codes brought radical prescriptions to the Ottoman courtroom culture, signaling growing legal autonomy in jurisdictional prosecution. In the meantime, the increasing complaints filed in the courts show that the Ottoman struggle to keep its legislative power in force against the grain of capitulations lasted forever. However, the reliance of the new Ottoman legal stance on the procedural codes stood in firm opposition to earlier practices that were shielded by the capitulatory system. There were setbacks and achievements that ruled out a single holistic approach to the operation of Ottoman justice.

The role of 1879 jurisdictional reorganization and legislative actions in this process aligns with the evolving state discourse in law and Ottoman claims

40 Stanford J. Shaw, *History of the Ottoman Empire and Modern Turkey*, vol. 2 (Cambridge: Cambridge University Press, 1977), 81–82.

41 BOA Y.PRK.AZN.7/8, 07.09.1893.

42 BOA BEO. 593/44469, 04.04.1895.

43 BOA HR.ID. 2037/71, 26 April 1907.

to sovereignty. Martin Koskenniemi argues that legally speaking, "an important part of the way power is exercised internationally depends on notions whose primary reference is at home."[44] This study shares Koskenniemi's view in the way that the Ottoman legal transformation created its own agency that involved state actors, legal scholars and diplomatic missions who pioneered the advancement of legal knowledge. They developed a legal strategy unique to the Ottoman state rather than completely modelled on a European pattern. Since professionalization of law was still underway, most legal scholars were also state officials who held various official posts during their careers. On account of their backgrounds, such figures were adept at applying the theory of law to everyday state politics during their long and varied careers.

In October 1914, the Ottoman Empire joined the Central Powers in the Great War. In the same month, the government ruled by the Committee of Union and Progress issued a memorandum to the consulates stating their intention to unilaterally abrogate the capitulations. The consulates immediately renounced it asserting that they were not consulted before dismantling the centuries-old system built on mutual grounds(!).[45] As a response, the Office of Legal Counsel crafted an official report upholding their rights to denounce such a "menace" to their system. The report sent to the Grand Vizier Said Halim Pasha laid stress on the exceptional nature of capitulations as standing in stark contrast to the notion of territorial sovereignty. In their view, the denial of the consulates to respect the Ottoman state's resolution on this occasion portrayed the empire as a power that did not hold the same rights as the others to abolish international acts on their own initiative.[46] They established a commission at the Sublime Porte to address how to regulate the judicial rights of the foreign nationals in accordance with international law.[47] In February 1915, a statement was drafted to be published in official newspapers declaring that "with the abrogation of capitulations, any foreigner who did not apply to the competent Ottoman courts in criminal, civil or commercial trials involving Ottomans, or their own nationals or other foreign nationals, would face administrative consequences

44 Koskenniemi focuses his research on mainly Europe, stating that "*bricolage* begins at European locations and then extends to 'the uttermost parts of the earth." An in-depth study of the evolution of Ottoman legal system shows that similar patterns may exist in other regions particularly those historically viewed as 'semi-civilized.' See Martin Koskenniemi, *To the Uttermost Parts of the Earth: Legal Imagination and International Power 1300–1870* (Cambridge: Cambridge University Press, 2021), 9 and 958.

45 BOA HR. HMŞ.İŞO. 72/11, 06.03.1916; HR.SYS. 2276/50, 30.09.1914.

46 BOA HR. SYS. 2276/22, 11.09.1914.

47 BOA HR. HMŞ. IŞO. 73/7, 10.10.1914.

for violating of the application of sovereign 'territorial rights'."[48] Only a month later, this statement received official recognition when the Council of Ministers approved the enactment of the "The Provisional Law Concerning the Rights and Obligations of Foreigners in the Ottoman Empire."[49]

Great War ended with the defeat of the Central Powers. The Ottoman government was put into a vulnerable position in the aftermath of the war, with European plans to partition the Empire's territories. Istanbul remained under Allied occupation until 1923.[50] During the occupation, the Allied powers reopened the consular courts. Under pressure, the Ottoman government had to temporarily establish *Muvakkat Muhtelit Encümen-i Adliye* (a Mixed Council of Justice). At first, this development could be seen as a bounce back from a century-long Ottoman struggle against jurisdictional constraints. However, this process was not a complete success for the occupying powers. The new legal structure in operation was a combination of "a sophisticated Ottoman legal system combining continental and Islamic law."[51]

In the post-Ottoman world, the political strategies that were played over non-Muslim Ottoman communities continued, albeit in a distinct form of capitulations. The phrasing of minority rights was the legacy of the 1919 Paris Peace Conference organized to settle disputes in the aftermath of the Great War. The dialogues started completely bona fide to prevent rage and bias toward religious denominations and ethnic communities in the post-war nation-states that were carved out of the old imperial powers.[52]

However, the political agenda of the League of Nations, which was founded after the Paris Peace Treaty, was transmuted into a similar course to the capitulatory system soon. The new dynamics of intervention worked for the remapped Anatolia and Eastern Europe under the pretext of minority protection. This stance, especially the policies adopted by British and French states, resembled the capitulatory system in the application with the slight difference that "the capitulations had operated in a context of potential (and often actual) military action" whereas "the minority treaties could normally

48 BOA HR. HMŞ. IŞO. 75/24, 07.02.1915.

49 All foreign residents of the empire became subject to Ottoman laws, with the exception of family law, which required the application of European laws due to the shortcomings of Ottoman legislation in this field regarding foreigners. BOA HR. HMŞ. IŞO. 72/7, 08.03.1915.

50 Erik-Jan Zürcher, "The Ottoman Empire and the Armistice of Moudros," in *At the Eleventh Hour: Reflections, Hopes, and Anxieties at the Closing of the Great War, 1918*, eds. Hugh Cecil and Peter H. Liddle (London: Leo Cooper, 1998), 266–275.

51 Daniel Joseph MacArthur-Seal, "Resurrecting Legal Extraterritoriality in Occupied Istanbul, 1918–1929," *Middle Eastern Studies* 54, n° 5 (2018): 777.

52 Laura Robson, "Capitulations Redux: The Imperial Genealogy of the Post-World War I 'Minority' Regimes," *American Historical Review* 126, n° 3 (November 2021): 979–980.

threaten little more than a strongly worded letter."[53] The goal of the League of Nations was fulfilled only with some variations in policy. The minority regime of the 1920s encapsulated diverse Muslim and non-Muslim groups alike, which were classified according to their numbers in the territories they settled and their political status in the eyes of the Turkish state. As such, the minority regime was as much the outcome of the local dynamics as it also pertained to foreign considerations.[54]

The Treaty of Lausanne, which was signed in July 1923 after the Lausanne Conference (1922–1923), officially resolved the conflicts between the Ottoman Empire and the Allied powers while also abolishing the capitulations.[55] The tact and diplomacy of İsmet İnönü, who was sent as a delegate of the Grand National Assembly of Turkey, was crucial in achieving this goal. During the initial session of the conference held on November 20, 1922, İnönü made the following statement:

> The Turkish nation, continually deprived of the benefits of peace, realized the inadequacy and fruitlessness of its ceaseless peaceful efforts to obtain equity and justice, and understanding that no other hope of salvation remained to it, it has succeeded in defending its existence by its own moral and material resources. In this course it has endured sufferings and has made innumerable sacrifices which have been sympathetically witnessed by free nations.[56]

We can quickly realize that the tone of remonstration in İnönü's statement was still intrinsic to the Ottoman experience. It is highly reminiscent of the Ottoman state's constant struggles against capitulations and what they cost the empire in its sovereign rights and unequal relations. In his following statement a month later, İnönü directly aimed at the capitulatory system by underlining the problems encountered in commercial relations and the legal cases

53 Ibid., 996.

54 Heather Sharkey, "History Rymes? Late Ottoman Millets and Post-Ottoman Minorities in the Middle East," *International Journal of Middle East Studies* 50 (November 2018): 761–764.

55 This conference was organized to outplace and reformulate the heavy sanctions imposed on the Ottoman Empire by the Treaty of Sèvres in August 1920, which the Grand National Assembly of Turkey renounced. The Grand National Assembly of Turkey was founded in April 1920 in Ankara; later on, the Turkish Republic was established in October 1923. For further information, see Umut Özsu, *Formalizing Displacement: International Law and Population Transfers* (Oxford: Oxford University Press, 2015).

56 *Lausanne Conference on Near Eastern Affairs 1922-1923: Records of proceedings and draft terms of peace* (London: h.m.s.o, 1923), 4.

pending with the impunity of criminals because of the interference in territorial jurisdiction. He elaborated on this observation by claiming that the capitulations were, "far from assuring any advantage to foreign nationals, gi(a)ve rise to innumerable difficulties in business and prejudice the interests of Turks and foreigners alike."[57]

During the Lausanne Conference, İsmet İnönü also withstood the call of delegates to appoint foreign representatives to protect the rights of minorities in Turkey. He opposed all forms of foreign intervention and instead supported the reciprocal exchange of minorities and civil prisoners, which prompted the population exchange between Turkey and Greece a year later.[58] This being the case, the Turkish government had to consent to allow foreign legal advisors to supervise the legal disputes that arose from the arrest and detention of foreign nationals in its initial years.[59]

As evident, the cumbersome weight of the capitulations lasted into the Turkish Republic.[60] They were always present, frequently as an obstacle to Ottoman legal autonomy. However, the gains and achievements in legislative efforts and diplomatic missions were a long way off from undervaluing them. As this study examines, the power of capitulations was as much embedded in such daily practices as diplomatic practices, which demonstrate a more significant change in the Ottoman legal system if taken as a cumulation.[61] In this legal system, the concept of legal sovereignty had a firm foothold in the Ottoman procedural codes since the restructured court system and the new operation of courtroom culture resonated profoundly in Ottoman foreign and domestic politics, and jurisdictional rights.

57 Ibid., 474–475.

58 Ibid., 204.

59 This statement was officially inserted in Article 1 of the Treaty of Commerce signed at Lausanne with the United States, July 24, 1923. See Leland J. Gordon, "Turkish-American Treaty Relations, " *American Political Science Review* 22, n°3 (August 1928): 715.

60 Umut Özsu argues that the Turkish nationalists felt an urge to fill the vacuum the capitulations left. The Turkish Civil Code of 1926, in this respect, was formulated to fill this vacuum of legal recognition by the European audience. See Umut Özsu, "'Receiving' the Civil Code: Translating Authority in Early Republican Turkey," *International Journal of Law in Context* 6, n° 1 (2010): 76.

61 By following a similar argument, Turan Kayaoğlu explains this as a historical process to end extraterritoriality, from the Treaty of Paris (1856) to the Treaty of Lausanne (1923), which mainly relied on "a legal-institutional logic." See, Turan Kayaoğlu, *Legal Imperialism: Sovereignty and Extraterritoriality in Japan, the Ottoman Empire, and China* (Cambridge: Cambridge University Press, 2014), 15.

Bibliography

Al-Qattan, Najwa. "*Dhimmis* in the Muslim Court: Legal Autonomy and Religious Discrimination." *International Journal of Middle Eastern Studies* 31 (1999): 429–444.

Anastasopoulos, Antonis. "Non-Muslims and Ottoman Justice(S)?" In *In Law and Empire: Ideas, Practices, Actors*, edited by Jeroen Duindam, Jill Harries, Caroline Humfress and Nimrod Hurvitz, 275–292. Leiden: Brill, 2013.

Auerbach, Sascha. *Armed with Sword and Scales: Law, Culture, and Local Courtrooms in London, 1860–1913*. Cambridge: Cambridge University Press, 2021.

Baer, Gabriel. "The Transition from Traditional to Western Criminal Law." *Studia Islamica*, n° 45 (1977): 139–158.

Brown, Philip Marshal. *Foreigners in Turkey: Their Juridical Status*. Princeton: Princeton University Press, 1914.

Cornewall Lewis, Sir George. *On Foreign Jurisdiction and the Extradition of the Criminals*. London: J.W. Parker and Son, 1859.

De Groot, Alexander H. "The Historical Development of the Capitulatory Regime in the Ottoman Middle East from the Fifteenth to the Nineteenth Centuries." *Oriento Moderno* 83, n° 3 (2003): 575–604.

Demirel, Fatmagül. *Adliye Nezareti Kuruluşu ve Faaliyetleri (1876–1914)*. Istanbul: Boğaziçi Üniversitesi Yayınları, 2008.

De Ribes, A.C. "Les capitulations ou La réforme dans les échelles du Levant." *Le Droit: Journal des Tribunaux* (4 Mai 1870).

Eldem, Edhem. "Capitulations and Western Trade." In *The Cambridge History of Turkey: The Latter Ottoman Empire*, edited by Suraiya Faroqhi, 281–335. Cambridge: Cambridge University Press, 2006.

Eldem, Edhem. "Foreigners at the Threshold of Felicity: the Reception of Foreigners in Ottoman Istanbul." In *Cultural Exchange in Early Modern Europe: Cities and Cultural Exchange in Europe, 1400–1700*, edited by Donatella Calabi, and Stephen Turk Christensen, 114–131. Cambridge: Cambridge University Press, 2007.

George Young, *Corps de Droit Ottoman, Vol. ii* (Oxford: Clarendon Press, 1906), 226–300.

Heidborn, A. *Manuel de Droit Public et Administratif de l'Empire Ottoman*. Leipzig: C.W. Stern, 1908.

Heinzelman, Tobias. "The Ruler's Monologue: The Rhetoric of the Ottoman Penal Code of 1858." *Die Welt des Islams* 54, n° 3–4 (2014): 292–321.

Herzog, Tamar. *A Short History of European Law: the Last Two and Half Millenia*. Cambridge, MA: Harvard University Press, 2018.

İnalcık, Halil. "İmtiyâzât." In *Encylopedia of Islam*, Volume III. Leiden: Brill, 1986: 1179–1189.

Kamay, Berna. "The Ottoman Empire, the United States, and the legal battle over extradition: the 'Kelly Affair'." *New Perspectives on Turkey* 65 (November 2021): 78–99.

Kamay-Ulusay, Berna. "Osmanlı'da 'Yabancının' Mülkiyet Hakkı Üzerine Bir Değerlendirme: 1867 İstimlâk–i Emlâk Nizamnâmesi." In *Osmanlı Tarihçiliğinde Yeni Çalışmalar: Kaynak, Bağlam, Yöntem*, edited by Fatma Öncel and Sinem Erdoğan İşkorkutan, 129–160. Istanbul: Vakıfbank Kültür Yayınları, 2023.

Kayaoğlu, Turan. *Legal Imperialism: Sovereignty and Extraterritoriality in Japan, the Ottoman Empire, and China*. Cambridge: Cambridge University Press, 2014.

Kemal, Namık. "Kapitülasyonlar." *Diyojen* (1871).

Koskenniemi, Martin. *To the Uttermost Parts of the Earth: Legal Imagination and International Power 1300–1870*. Cambridge: Cambridge University Press, 2021.

Kuneralp, Sinan, and Emre Öktem, eds. *Chambre des conseillers légistes de la Sublime Porte: Rapports, avis et consultations sur la condition juridique des ressortissants étrangers, le statut des communautés non musulmanes et les relations internationales de l'Empire Ottoman*. Istanbul: Isis, 2012.

Lausanne Conference on Near Eastern Affairs 1922–1923: records of proceedings and draft terms of peace (London: h.m.s.o, 1923), 4.

Leland J. Gordon, "Turkish-American Treaty Relations," American Political Science Review 22, n° 3 (August 1928): 715.

MacArthur-Seal, Daniel Joseph. "Resurrecting Legal Extraterritoriality in Occupied Istanbul, 1918–1929." *Middle Eastern Studies* 54, n° 5 (2018): 769–787.

Musil, Robert. *The Man Without Qualities*. New York: Vintage International, 1996.

Muslu, Zülâl. "Language and Power: The Dragoman as a Link in the Chain Between the Law of Nations and the Ottoman Empire." *Journal of History of International Law* 22 (June 2020): 50–74.

Özsu, Umut. "'Receiving' the Civil Code: Translating Authority in Early Republican Turkey." *International Journal of Law in Context* 6, n° 1 (2010): 63–89.

Formalizing Displacement: International Law and Population Transfers. Oxford: Oxford University Press, 2015.

Palabıyık, Mustafa Serdar. "The Emergence of the Idea of 'International Law' in the Ottoman Empire before the Treaty of Paris (1856)." *Middle Eastern Studies* 50, n° 2 (2014): 233–251.

Porter, Sir James. *Turkey, Its History and Progress*. London: Hurst and Blackett Publishers, 1854.

Robson, Laura."Capitulations Redux: The Imperial Genealogy of the Post-World War I 'Minority' Regimes" *The American Historical Review* 126, n° 3 (November 2021): 978–1000.

Rubin, Avi. "Legal Borrowing and its Impact on Ottoman Legal Culture in the Late Nineteenth Century." *Continuity and Change* 22, n° 2 (August 2007): 279–303.

Sharkey, Heather. "History Rymes? Late Ottoman Millets and Post-Ottoman Minorities in the Middle East." *International Journal of Middle East Studies* 50 (November 2018): 760–764.

Shaw, Stanford J. *History of the Ottoman Empire and Modern Turkey*. Cambridge: Cambridge University Press, 1977.

Slys, Mariya Tait. *Exporting Legality: The Rise and Fall of Extraterritorial Jurisdiction in the Ottoman Empire and China*. Geneva: Graduate Institute Publications, 2014.

Veinstein, Gilles. "Les fondements juridiques de la diplomatie ottomane en Europe." *Oriente Moderno* 88, n° 2 (2008): 509–552.

War and Diplomacy: The Russo-Turkish War of 1877–1878 and the Treaty of Berlin, eds. M.Hakan Yavuz and Peter Sluglett (Salt Lake City: University of Utah Press, 2011).

Zürcher, Erik Jan. "The Ottoman Empire and the Armistice of Moudros." In *At the Eleventh Hour: Reflections, Hopes, and Anxieties at the Closing of the Great War, 1918*, edited by Hugh Cecil and Peter H. Liddle, 266–275. London: Leo Cooper, 1998.

13

Consular Jurisdiction in Nineteenth-Century Legal Thinking

Lars Regula

1 Introduction

Anyone who enrolled at Hamburg's "Colonial Institute" (*Kolonialinstitut*) – the predecessor of today's university – at the beginning of the twentieth century had a good chance of encountering consular jurisdiction in the lectures of the jurist Kurt Perels or the sinologist Otto Franke.[1] But those who visited the library to expand upon their knowledge would find a certain irreverence regarding the phenomenon in the legal literature. For example, it was described there as "an abnormality of international and governmental law."[2] The literature referred to "grievances" and "monstrous jurisdictional complications."[3] Consular jurisdiction evidently did not enjoy the approval of contemporary jurists.

But what was consular jurisdiction? The "consul" originated in the Mediterranean as a representative and judge of a merchant community. Their jurisdiction can be found in the prominent *Llibre del Consulat de Mar*, which was ubiquitous in the whole Mediterranean region, as well as in the French Edict of King Charles IX. of 1563.[4] Foreign consuls were no exception to the jurisdictional powers, as Article 28 of the Spanish-Austrian Commercial Treaty of 1725 clearly shows.[5] However, while the domestic consuls remained judges, the

1 For the history of the University of Hamburg, see Tilman Repgen, "Eine kurze Geschichte der Fakultät anstelle eines Vorworts," in *100 Jahre Rechtswissenschaft an der Universität Hamburg*, eds. Tilman Repgen, Florian Jeßberger and Markus Kotzur (Tübingen: Mohr Siebeck, 2019).

2 Arthur von Brauer, *Deutsche Justizgesetze in ihrer Anwendung auf die amtliche Tätigkeit der Konsuln und diplomatischen Agenten und die Konsulargerichtsbarkeit* (Berlin: Carl Heymann, 1879), 67.

3 Karl Lippmann, *Die Konsularjurisdiktion im Orient: Ihre historische Entwicklung von den frühesten Zeiten bis zur Gegenwart* (Leipzig, 1898), 185; Jacob Simon Jacobovits, *Die Consulate als Gerichtsbarkeiten im Osmanischen Reiche* (Vienna: Wilhelm Braumüller, 1865), 4.

4 In France, commercial judges are in fact still non-professionals called *judge consulaire.*

5 "Spanish-Austrian Treaty of Commerce of 1725,") in *Recueil historique d'actes, négociations, mémoires et traitez*, ed. Jean Rousset De Missy (Amsterdam: Meynard Uytwerf, 1728), vol. 2.

 | HTTPS://DOI.ORG/10.1163/9789004755192-015

consuls of communities abroad came under the influence of the evolving foreign services. In the latter sense, the "consul" entered the international diplomatic vocabulary. Hence, consular jurisdiction, as it presented itself in the nineteenth century, was mostly understood as the exercise of jurisdiction over one nation's subjects abroad through the respective consulates. This exterritorial jurisdiction flourished in the nineteenth century. Although its origins were in the Mediterranean and in particular the Ottoman Empire, the "unequal treaties" also introduced consular jurisdiction in the Far East. As such, there is an obvious assumption of its use as an "imperialistic tool," and some discussion about the actual nature of the institution has arisen among scholars.[6] Surprisingly, however, the legal perspective has been ignored so far.[7] In the course of this paper, an overview shall be provided of the position of consular jurisdiction in nineteenth-century legal thinking. The argument shall be posited that consular jurisdiction, at least in its "diplomatic" form, was indeed an abnormality and that the universalisation of European international law actually promoted its abolition.

2 Western Jurisprudence

As part of the national court system, consular jurisdiction predominantly caught the interest of European lawyers. The most influential were the French lawyers, especially Louis Féraud-Giraud, a judge at the Appellation Court in Aix-en-Provence, who was cited repeatedly. The Russian professor Friedrich Fromholm Martens, known for the creation of "Marten's clause" during the Hague Peace Conferences, also contributed to the subject in the form of his doctoral thesis, which was published in Russian and German. Altogether, three main topics can be identified in this context. First, the problem of justification occupied the lawyers. Secondly, the legal nature of "exterritoriality" was explored and lastly, procedural problems were analysed.

6 See Turan Kayaoğlu, *Legal Imperialism: Sovereignty and Extraterritoriality in Japan, the Ottoman Empire, and China* (New York: Cambridge University Press, 2010), 1, who is criticised by Johannes Berchtold, "Schattenboxen: Rezension zu Turan Kayaoğlu, Legal Imperialsim. Sovereignty and Extraterritoriality in Japan, the Ottoman Empire, and China, New York: 2010," *Rechtsgeschichte* 18 (2011). Concerning the "nature" of consular jurisdiction, see furthermore Johannes Berchtold, *Recht und Gerechtigkeit in der Konsulargerichtsbarkeit: Britische Exterritorialität im Osmanischen Reich 1825–1914* (München: Oldenbourg, 2009); Richard Chang, *The Justice of the Western Consular Courts in Nineteenth-Century Japan* (Westport, CT: Greenwood Press, 1984).

7 Explicitly Berchtold, *Recht und Gerechtigkeit in der Konsulargerichtsbarkeit*, 54.

2.1 *The raison d'être: Civilisation and Global Order*

Originally, consular jurisdiction was merely a result of commercial self-administration. In fact, the 1790 *Essai sur les consuls* by the German Johann von Steck did not yet see anything unusual in consular jurisdiction.[8] Indeed, the eighteenth-century European legal topology was still confusingly diverse, and consular jurisdiction was neither special nor particularly notable. Article 17 of the British-Russian Treaty of Commerce of 20 June 1766 shows, however, that the European states had evidently begun to reject exterritorial jurisdiction on their own territory.[9] Furthermore, the nineteenth century was characterised by efforts to harmonise and centralise law.[10] The French *cinq codes* are one example of this. The British Judicature Acts and the German *Reichsjustizgesetze* from the 1870s are another. Against this background, the consular courts in the Levant became remarkable. Indeed, one of Steck's contemporaries, Franz Borel, had already emphasised that these consular courts were special since the consuls in the Ottoman Empire possessed incomparably broader jurisdictional powers.[11]

At first, there was little resonance. In 1836, the American Henry Wheaton published his famous *Elements of International Law*. Consular jurisdiction, Wheaton argued, was in fact simply a product of intergovernmental agreements.[12] He made reference to Steck's *Essai*. But another topic proved constructive. International law doctrine of the nineteenth century was fully aware that "international law," as it was taught in Europe, did not apply globally, and that some legal cultures even confronted it with their own concepts. Furthermore, legal positivism took international contracts as the source of law which, with the exception of the Ottoman Empire, did not exist *de facto* with non-European states. Hence, "international law" was not even conceptually a universal law. In this context, Wheaton detached "international law" from its European foundation and declared it to be a common law of all "civilised, Christian nations of Europe and America."[13] This step was as subtle as it was conse-

8 Johann von Steck, *Essai sur les consuls* (Berlin: Friedrich Nicolovius, 1790), 5–7.

9 "British-Russian Treaty of Commerce of 20.06.1766,") in *A Collection of all the Treaties of Peace, Alliance, and Commerce*, ed. Charles Jenkinson (London: J. Debret, 1785), 3:215–217.

10 Peter Collin, "Europäische Entwicklungslinien gerichtlicher und außergerichtlicher Konfliktlösung im 19. und 20. Jahrhundert," in *Konfliktlösung im 19. und 20. Jahrhundert*, ed. Peter Collin (Wiesbaden: Springer, 2021).

11 Franz Franzewitsch Borel, *De l'origine et des fonctions des consuls* (Saint Petersburg: A. Pluchart, 1807), 49–51.

12 Henry Wheaton, *Elements of International Law* (London: B. Fellows, 1836), 1:156.

13 Wheaton, *Elements of International Law*, 1:36.

quential, for Wheaton not only sharply demarcated non-European legal cultures, but also devalued them as "uncivilised" and thus *per se* irrelevant.

This corresponded with the zeitgeist at the time. Experiences like the "Lady Hughes incident,"[14] cultural misunderstanding and selective knowledge discredited non-European legal cultures in the eyes of Western jurists as being capricious and hostile.[15] Thus, Western jurists reinterpreted the institution such that the *raison d'être* was to protect Europeans from these arbitrary legal systems. This line of argumentation is highlighted in Martens' work, who saw the task of protection, and not customary law, as the sole reason for existence.[16] In the course of the nineteenth century, one can observe a remarkable convergence among the sources. Treaties, such as the above-mentioned between Spain and Austria, seem to have been forgotten. Beginning with Féraud-Giraud's influential study *De la juridiction française dans les échelles du Levant et de Barbarie* of 1859, the jurists' gaze focused exclusively on the Orient.[17] Geopolitical events, the opening of China and Japan in 1843 and 1853 respectively, and the Peace of Paris in 1856 fuelled interest in the subject. Consular jurisdiction became an exotic stigma related to foreign legal systems.

2.2 *Exterritoriality*

The understanding of sovereignty only strengthened this impression. A state was considered sovereign when it exercised sole power over the people within

14 In 1784, a gunner of the British vessel *Lady Hughes* killed two Chinese boatmen with a salute shot in the harbour of Canton. Under pressure from the Chinese authorities, the gunman was extradited and eventually hanged. *Li Chen* has provided comparative legal evidence that the negative image that was subsequently established in the West was primarily the result of British "litigation PR," Li Chen, "Law, Empire, and Historiography of Modern Sino-Western Relations: A Case Study of the *Lady Hughes* Controversy in 1784," *Law and History Review* 27, n° 1 (2009); comparable studies also in Mauritis van den Boogert, *The Capitulations and the Ottoman Legal System: Qadis, Consuls and Beraltlis in the 18th Century* (Leiden: Brill, 2005).

15 See Friedrich Martens, *Das Consularwesen und die Consularjurisdiction im Orient* (Berlin: Weidmannsche Buchhandlung, 1874), 104; Leo Strisower, *Konsular-Gerichtsbarkeit* (Vienna: Alfred Hölder, 1895), 1; Eduard Brücklmeier, *Die geschichtliche Entwicklung der Konsulargerichtsbarkeit und ihre Rechtsgestaltung für Deutschland im Anschluß an den Weltkrieg* (Leipzig: Mäser, 1927), 10.

16 Martens, *Das Consularwesen und die Consularjurisdiction im Orient*, 319–321.

17 At least the literature that focused on "diplomatic" consular jurisdiction. Studies like Ernest Genevois, *Histoire critique de la juridiction consulaire* (Paris: A. Durand, 1866) or Guillaume Denière, *La juridiction consulaire de Paris 1563–1792* (Paris: Henri Plon, 1872) had, of course, the French commercial jurisdiction in mind.

its territory.[18] For Georg Jellinek, territory and power were even prerequisites for the quality of a state.[19] The "long" nineteenth century gave validity to this principle by successively abolishing older privileges and integrating foreigners into national (private) law.[20] In Spain, the *juez conservador*, a special judge for foreigners, was abolished in 1868.[21] The German, Austrian and French codifications granted legal personality to foreigners, although not unconditionally.[22] The envoy, according to the supporters of the "fiction theory," was thus put in a position as if he had never left his home state. For the lawyers of the nineteenth century, this fiction aptly described the legal situation in the Middle East and later in the Far East.[23] The "fiction theory" produced an

18 Daniel Lee, *The Right of Sovereignty: Jean Bodin on the Sovereign State and the Law of Nations* (Oxford: Oxford University Press, 2021), 4–6.

19 Georg Jellinek, *Allgemeine Staatslehre* (Berlin: O. Haering, 1905), 381–383.

20 See Beate Althammer, "Verfassungsstaat und Bürgerliches Recht: Die Stellung von Fremden im Europa des langen 19. Jahrhunderts (1789–1914)," in *Fremd und Rechtlos? Zugehörigkeitsrechte Fremder von der Antike bis zur Gegenwart. Ein Handbuch*, eds. Altay Coşkun and Lutz Raphael (Cologne: Böhlau, 2014), 301–303.

21 Francisca Hernanz Sanchez, *Das Kollision-, Zuständigkeits- und Anerkennungsrecht der internationalen Ehescheidung in Spanien* (Berlin: Duncker & Humblot, 1987), 26–27; Volker Manz, *Fremde und Gemeinwohl: Integration und Ausgrenzung in Spanien im Übergang vom Ancien Régime zum Frühen Nationalstaat* (Stuttgart: Franz Steiner, 2006), 119–120.

22 Section 34, Introduction of the General State Laws for the Prussian States (ALR) as well as section 33, clause 1 of the Austrian General Civil Code (ABGB) conferred full legal personality under the reservation of retorsion and, therefore, the equal treatment of Prussian and Austrian subjects abroad. Conversely, art. 11 of the Code Civil conferred legal personality only based on international treaties. Section 1 of the "(German) Civil Code" finally conferred legal personality unconditionally; see also Althammer, "Verfassungsstaat und bürgerliches Recht," 311.

23 Louis Jospeh Delphin Féraud-Giraud, *De la juridiction française dans les Échelles du Levant et de Barbarie*, 1st edition (Paris: A. Durand, 1859), 1:7; Georg Friedrich Martens and Charles-Henri Vergé, *Précis du droit des gens moderne de l'Europe*, 2 vols. (Paris, 1838), 2:10; A. Miruss, *Das Europäische Gesandtschaftsrecht* (Leipzig: Wilhelm Engelmann, 1847), 407–409; Robert Philimore, *Commentaries upon International Law* (London: William G. Benning and Co., 1855), 192–194; Travers Twiss, *The Law of Nations: On the Rights and Duties of Nations in Time of Peace* (Oxford, London: Oxford University Press, 1861), 304–308; Henry Wheaton and Richard Henry Dana, *Elements of International Law*, 8th edition (London: Sampson Low, Son and Co., 1866), § 244; Martens, *Das Consularwesen und die Consularjurisdiction im Orient*, 319; Johannes Gottschalk, *Die Exterritorialität der Gesandten* (Berlin: Gustav Schade, 1878), 23–25; Stamatios Antonopoulos, *Über die Exterritorialität der Ausländer in der Türkei mit Rücksicht in Civil- und Strafprozessen* (Berlin: Hermann Bahr, 1895), 2; Franz von Liszt, *Das Völkerrecht*, 2nd edition (Berlin: O. Haering, 1902), 113–115; Raphael Caleb, *Die Konsulargerichtsbarkeit in Bulgarien* (Straßburg: Goeller, 1903), 85; from case law ROHG 22,398; RGSt 17,51,56; *Abdul Messih vs. Farrah* [1887] Privy Council 13 APPCAS 431.

appearance not only of immunity from a foreign legal system but also of the application of a state's law beyond its borders.[24] It also emphasised that there was indeed a qualitative difference compared to the jurisdiction that consuls in the West either exercised on a very limited group of people (e.g. sailors) or where the host state had little interest in exercising jurisdiction itself (e.g. inheritance cases). The jurisdictional competencies in the East were necessarily comprehensive – both *per definitionem* and against the background of their justification.

In the second half of the nineteenth century, however, doubts were increasingly raised about the practicability of this fiction, which ultimately led to the "exemption theory," which bound the envoy to the law of the host state and only prevented his execution.[25] This discussion took place in the literature on international law using the example of envoys. Jurists who wrote particularly on consular jurisdiction mostly adopted one view without further justification.[26] Indeed, the consular courts discovered the practical impact of this dispute. In 1891, the German *Reichsgericht* posed the question of whether a marriage that had been performed in Jerusalem without the presence of a registrar could be valid.[27] If the spouses had been exterritorial in terms of the "fiction

---

24 In this respect, there is a qualitative difference compared to modern developments, in which a state applies its domestic law to a foreign case, see *Morrison vs. National Australia Bank*, 561 U.S. 247 (2010); EGMR, Urt. v. 18.12.1996, 15318/89 – *Loizidou v. Turkey*; BVerfGE 154, 152; this phenomenon is discussed as "*extra*territoriality," see Claudia Kurkin, *Extraterritorialität: Eine Kategorie des transnationalen Rechts* (Tübingen: Mohr Siebeck, 2021), 48.

25 August Wilhelm Heffter, *Das europäische Völkerrecht der Gegenwart*, 3rd edition (Berlin: E.H. Schroeder, 1855), 78, especially footnote 2; Philipp Zorn, "Das Deutsche Gesandtschafts-, Konsular- und Seerecht," *Annalen des Deutschen Reichs* 15 (1882): 110–112; William Hall, *A Treatise on International Law* (Oxford: Clarendon Press, 1884), 147–149; August von Bulmerincq, *Das Völkerrecht* (Freiburg i.B.: Mohr, 1889), 319; Bernhard Hübler, *Die Magistraturen des völkerrechtlichen Verkehrs* (Berlin: Puttkammer & Mühlbrecht, 1900), 84; Georg Paul Müller, *Die Stellung des Reichsgerichts zur völkerrechtlichen Lehre von der Exterritorialität* (Stettin: Fischer & Schmidt, 1904), 14–16; Hans von Frisch, *Der völkerrechtliche Begriff der Exterritorialität* (Brünn: Alfred Hölder, 1917), 23; probably also Francis Taylor Piggot, *Exterritoriality: The Law relating to Consular Jurisdiction and to Residence on Oriental Countries* (London: William Clowes, 1892), 18–19; see furthermore RGZ 27,102; *Casgali v Casgali* [1919] House of Lords AC 145, 35.

26 Karl Falter, *Konsulargerichtsbarkeit in Strafsachen* (Nürnberg: Hilz, 1909), 8; Walther Weiser, *Die deutsche Konsulargerichtsbarkeit oder die Tätigkeit der Deutschen Konsulargerichte in Bürgerlichen Rechtsstreitigkeiten* (Dessau, 1912), 2; Hans Reder, *Das deutsche Konsularwesen in Aegypten* (Würzburg: Richard Mayr, 1931), 53.

27 See § 41 *Gesetz über die Beurkundung des Personenstandes und die Eheschließung* (RGBl. 1875, n° 4, 23): "Within the territory of the *Reich*, a marriage can only legally be performed before a registrar."

theory," they legally would have been married on German soil and thus, the marriage would not be valid due to the lack of a registrar. The *Reichsgericht*, however, referred to the "new theory" and hence opened German law for the principle "*locus regit actum*" and the application of Ottoman marriage law.[28] The ruling had an impact on German literature, where it was cited.[29]

A comparable case was presented to the House of Lords in 1918. A woman had filed a case for divorce before in England, since British consular courts lacked jurisdiction in this regard. If the spouses had been exterritorial in terms of the "fiction theory" – which was how the British case law saw the matter since the ruling in *Abdul Messih vs. Farrah* in 1887 – they would have been legally in England all that time and thus, English courts would have had jurisdiction in the case. Here, the House of Lords also referred to the "exemption theory," stating that since the creation of the mixed courts in Egypt, no complete exterritoriality could be assumed in any case.[30]

2.3 *Structural Deficits*

Furthermore, consular jurisdiction is interesting due to its multifaceted structural deficits, which did not go unnoticed by contemporary jurists. In 1865, Jakob Simon Jacobovits launched a sweeping blow in the form of an essay. First and foremost, there were "monstrous jurisdictional issues."[31] While consular courts in the Far East also had jurisdiction in cases involving a Chinese or Japanese party, the early capitulations had referred disputes with an Ottoman subject to the Ottoman courts. This was generally accepted.[32] In 1830, however, a formulation entered the French version of the American capitulation, which provided for the sole jurisdiction of consular courts in criminal matters.[33] That consular courts could indeed exercise jurisdiction was the prevail-

28 RGZ 27,102; unfortunately, the files of the cases are lost. The oldest files of the fourth senate in the *Bundesarchiv* start in 1899; see Bundesarchiv, R 3002. That the "fiction theory" stood in conflict with the principle of *locus regit actum* was already criticised by Heffter, *Das europäische Völkerrecht*, 78, footnote 2.

29 See Weiser, *Die deutsche Konsulargerichtsbarkeit*, 2.

30 *Casgali vs. Casgali* [1919] House of Lords AC 145, 35; see especially the opinion of Lord Finlay, who decided later on the famous "Lotus Case" at the Permanent Court of Justice, *Lotus Case* 1927 PCIJ series A n° 9.

31 Jacobovits, *Die Consulate als Gerichtsbarkeiten*, 4.

32 Stanislas Genton, *Les Capitulations* (Lyon: Imprimerie du Salut Public, 1873), 14; Martens, *Das Consularwesen*, 389; Brauer, *Deutsche Justizgesetze*, 124; Gérard Pélissié du Rausas, *Le régime des capitulations dans l'Empire Ottoman* (Paris: Arthur Rousseau, 1902), 435.

33 For background information, see Frank Erastus Hinckley, *American Consular Jurisdiction in the Orient* (Washington: W.H. Lowdermilk, 1906), 23–25; William Eleroy Curtis, *The United States and Foreign Powers* (Meadville: Flood and Vincent, 1892), 240.

ing opinion among contemporary jurists who, of course, only applied the French version.[34]

Equally problematic were legal disputes between Europeans. Although Western collision law received important impulses from the works of Joseph Story and Friedrich Carl von Savigny, exterritoriality prevented a (legal) crossing of the border and, therefore, did not differ from the old principle of personality.[35] Thus, these impulses were fruitless. In the Ottoman Empire, a diplomatic gentlemen's agreement to appoint mixed commissions was allegedly reached in 1820.[36] In 1859, however, the British Court of Admiralty and in 1864 the Court of Appeal in Aix rejected this procedure for lack of legal basis.[37] Literature and case law availed themselves of the principle of *actor sequitur forum rei*.[38] Noting that jurisdiction in the East was bound to the person, court practice additionally demanded an explicit submission to the court's own jurisdiction.[39]

However, this did not solve problems such as the impossibility of passive joinder of parties.[40] Furthermore, the courts had to deal with the question of whether they accepted the verdicts of foreign consular courts as binding and

---

34 Domenico Gatteschi, *Manuale di diritto pubblico e privato ottomano* (Alexandria: V. Minasi, 1865), 26; Martens, *Das Consularwesen*, 647; Hinckley, *American Consular Jurisdiction*, 23–25; Albéric Rolin, "L'affaire Joris: Étude sur la capitulation," *Revue de droit international et législation comparée* (1906): 372–374; Nikolaos Politis, "Les capitulations et la justice répressive ottomane a propos de l'affaire Joris," *Revue de droit international privé et de droit pénal international*, n° 2 (1906): 665–667.

35 Joseph Story, *Commentaries on the conflict of laws* (Boston: Billard, Gray, and Co., 1834); Friedrich Carl von Savigny, *System des heutigen römischen Rechts* (Berlin: Veit, 1849), 8.

36 Feliciano Orlando, *Della commissione mista e della competenza sulle domande riconvenionali in Levante* (Konstantinopel: Besantino, 1847); Alexandre de Clercq and Charles de Vallat, *Guide pratique des Consulats* (Paris: Guillaumin et Cie, 1851), 700; Féraud-Giraud, *De la juridiction française dans les Échelles du Levant et de Barbarie*, 230; Pélissié du Rausas, *Le régime des capitulations dans l'Empire Ottoman*, 144–146; an archival record of the agreement has not yet been found.

37 The "Griefswald" [1859] High Court of Admiralty, 166 E.R. 1200; Cour d'Appel d'Aix, Verdict of 28.11.1864, *Bulletin judiciare d'Aix* 2 (1865): 119.

38 Genton, *Les capitulations*, 14; Martens, *Das Consularwesen und die Consularjurisdiction im Orient*, 340; E. R. Salem, "Étrangers devant les tribunaux consularies et nationaux en Turquie," *Clunet* 18, n° 5 (1891): 420.

39 The "Griefswald" [1859] High Court of Admiralty, 166 E.R. 1200; Papayani vs. The Russian Trading Company [1863] Privy Council, UKPC 8; ROHGE 14, 423 (424); RGZ 34, 107 (109).

40 Jacobovits, *Die Consulate als Gerichtsbarkeiten im Osmanischen Reiche*, 4–6; Zorn, "Das Deutsche Gesandtschafts-, Konsular- und Seerecht," 186. In the case of joinder, two parties cooperate in their litigation. A joinder can either be "active" on the plaintiff's side or "passive" on the defendant's side. In terms of consular jurisdiction, a passive

enforceable.[41] Martens' proposition to establish mixed tribunals at a conference of the "Institute de Droit International" in 1881 in Wiesbaden garnered little attention.[42]

Lastly, the consul's person was a problem in itself. The exercise of jurisdiction by a civil servant bound by instructions flagrantly violated the achievement of the separation of powers. The question was particularly disputed in Germany. With the creation of the "Arnim Paragraph" (§ 353a StGB), Bismarck had impressively demonstrated that he did not tolerate dissenters in the foreign service.[43] Most jurists rushed, however, to emphasise that the consuls were independent in their judicial functions, and internal papers show that Bismarck did not hold a different opinion.[44] On the other side, Karl Goes supported an intervention competence on the part of the Reichskanzler, justifying it with the consuls' lack of legal education.[45] This was a sore point, although it did not carry equal weight in all services. France had already made legal education a prerequisite for consular service at an early stage and placed all *agents consulaire*, who did not necessarily have legal education,

joinder of two parties with different nationality was not possible since two different consular courts had jurisdiction over the case.

41 Dent vs. Smith [1869] L.R. 4 Q.B. 414; Messina v Petrocchino [1872] L.R. 4 P.C. 144.

42 Friedrich Martens, "Premier rapport de M. de Martens," *Annuaire de l'institut de droit international* 6 (1883): 228–230.

43 According to German criminal law, diplomats (and only diplomats) who contravene official instructions or file untrue reports can be punished with a fine or imprisonment for up to five years. In 1871, the German ambassador to France, Count Harry von Arnim-Suckow, ignored Bismarck's instructions and partied with the royalists against the official German line, which was to support Adolphe Thiers. Arnim was prosecuted and fled to France. The creation of the "Arnim Paragraph" was a direct reaction to contravening members of the Foreign Service.

44 Clercq and Vallat, *Guide pratique des consulats*, 30; Brauer, *Deutsche Justizgesetze*, 71; Caleb, *Die Konsulargerichtsbarkeit in Bulgarien*, 77; A. F. Vorwerk, *Konsulargerichtsbarkeit* (Berlin: Guttentag'sche Sammlung Deutscher Reichsgesetze, 1908), 36, 67; Weiser, *Die deutsche Konsulargerichtsbarkeit*, 27–29; Georg Gundermann, *Die völkerrechtlichen Grundlagen der Konsulargerichtsbarkeit* (Berlin: Juristische Verlagsbuchhandlung Dr. jur. Frensdorf, 1913), 65; letter from Bismarck to Brassier de St. Simon of 07.07.1865, in: Geheimes Staatsarchiv Preußischer Kulturbesitz, I. HA Rep. 81 Konstantinopel nach 1807, VI n° 271.

45 Karl Goes, "Das Reichsgesetz über die Konsulargerichtsbarkeit vom 10. Juli 1879: Unter Berücksichtigung seiner Anwendung in den deutschen Schutzgebieten," in *Annalen des Deutschen Reichs für Gesetzgebung, Verwaltung und Statistik: Staatswissenschaftliche Zeitschrift und Materaliensammlung*, eds. Georg Hirth and Max von Seydel (Munich, Leipzig: W. Hirth, 1897), 527.

under the jurisdiction of a consul.[46] The British judicial system, on the other hand, was generally more liberal with respect to (academic) legal education.[47] However in Great Britain, too, quality concerns were taken seriously; this finally led to the creation of professional Supreme Consular Courts throughout the empire.[48]

3 Eastern Jurisprudence

Naturally, consular jurisdiction was no monopoly of Western jurists. Ottoman, Chinese, and Japanese jurists contributed to the topic as well. To uncover the full dimension of this contribution, much work has yet to be done. Not least due to the language barrier, Eastern legal thinking also remains as obscure for Western scholars today as it was for the contemporaries in the nineteenth century. Unfortunately, a further investigation of this area lies beyond the purview of this paper. However, since a considerable number of sources in Western languages exist, these contributions should not be ignored in this context.

3.1 *Ottoman Empire*

What is most interesting about the Ottoman literature is that it was very reserved with respect to consular jurisdiction. Authors were preoccupied with other topics. Moulavi Ali, for example, tried to correct the Western image of the *ǧihād*.[49] Moreover, the officers Rustem Effendi and Seid Bey complained about the unfair portrayal of their home country, which was actually

46 Clercq and Vallat, *Guide pratique des consulats*, 62–64; Louis Jospeh Delphin Féraud-Giraud, *De la juridiction française dans les Échelles du Levant et du Barbarie: Étude sur la condition légale des étrangers dans les pays hors chrétienté*, 2nd edition (Paris: A. Durand, 1866), 2:46.

47 Until 1820, there was no possibility to study law at a university and in the middle of the nineteenth century, most British judges of higher courts had still studied mathematics, Patrick Polden and Michael Lobban, "The Education of Lawyers," in *The Oxford History of the Laws of England*, eds. William Cornish *et al.* (Oxford: Oxford University Press, 2010), 1175–1177; see furthermore the biography of *Edmund Hornby*, judge at the Supreme Consular Court, who had studied medicine, Edmund Hornby, *An Autobiography* (Boston: Houghzon Mifflin, 1928), 44.

48 Berchtold, *Recht und Gerechtigkeit in der Konsulargerichtsbarkeit*, 95–97.

49 Moulavi Cheragh Ali, *A critical exposition of the popular "Jihad"* (Calcutta: Thacker, Spink and Co., 1885).

much more tolerant than other European states.[50] Indeed, they had a point; tolerance and autonomy were among the characteristics of Islamic statecraft. In Sura 5:44–47, the Qur'an prescribes that Jews and Christians should be judged according to their (religious) law. The "people of the book" were organised under the Millet system, which granted the Jewish and Christian communities a far-reaching degree of self-government.[51] The Ottoman sultans, therefore, took little offence to a limited number of Christian merchants under self-administration. Even Nubar Pasha, the great reformer of the Egyptian consular system, did not fundamentally oppose commercial self-administration.[52]

The point of criticism was rather that the system became difficult to control in the nineteenth century. For example, Nubar Pasha criticised the custom in Egypt of being able to suit locals, contrary to the capitulations, before consular courts.[53] Furthermore, the Western states seemed to abuse their privileges by bringing Ottomans under their protection. The Arab historian Kāmil Ibn Ḥusain al-Ġazzī, who still had lived to see the capitulations, quantifies their number in Aleppo at 1,500 at the end of the eighteenth century.[54] The Ottoman problem was, of course, not the jurisdiction, which was not exercised in any case, but the loss of tax subjects and thus money. The impression of an abusive overstretch in the capitulations' wording intensified when the Western states started to refer to the unfortunate formulation concerning criminal jurisdiction in the American Capitulation of 1830. This concerned a diplomatic dispute behind closed doors.[55] However, it reached the legal community when Gabriel Noradounghian defended the arrest and conviction of the Belgian

50 Rustem Effendi and Seid Bey, *Réponse a quelques journaux aux affaires de Turquie* (Brussels: F. Michel, 1853), 3.

51 However, this undeniable tolerance also had its limits in terms of other religions. On the persecution of the Yazidi, see i.e. Majid H. Ali, "Genocidal Campaigns during the Ottoman Era: The Firman of Mir-I-Kura against the Yazidi religious minority in 1832–1834," *Genocide Studies International* 13, n° 2 (2019): 77–79.

52 Boghos Nubar Pascha, *Mémoires de Nubar Pascha: Introduction et notes de Mirrit Boutros Ghali* (Beirut, 1983), 146.

53 Nubar Pascha, *Mémoires de Nubar Pascha*, 147.

54 Kāmil Ibn-Ḥusain Al-Ġazzī, *Kitāb Nahr aḏ-ḏahab fī Tārīḫ Ḥalab* (Aleppo: al-Maṭbaʿa al-Mārūniyya, 1923), III, 311; modern research has rejected this number, see van den Boogert, *The Capitulations and the Ottoman Legal System*, 85–87. The relevant point here is that al-Ġazzī considered this number plausible.

55 "The exchange of letters between Foreign Secretary Frederick Frelinghuysen and the Ottoman envoy Hussein Tevfik Pasha," in *Papers Relating to the Foreign Relations of the United States*, ed. Department of States (Washington: United States Government Printing Office, 1886), 890.

Edward Joris in the "Joris affair."[56] Based on systematic arguments, and therefore perfectly reasonable for lawyers of the Western tradition, Noradounghian pleaded for a restrictive interpretation. As a legal advisor, Noradounghian worked from 1883 to 1908 in the *bureau consultatif* of the Ottoman Foreign Office.[57] Since the 1860s, predominantly European lawyers worked in the *Bureau* to advise the Ottoman government on questions concerning international law.[58] In doing so, the imported lawyers applied their European methodology and provided arguments that sought to strengthen the sovereignty of their employer. Arguments that Noradounghian used in the "Joris affair" can be found in the opinions of the *bureau*.[59]

Nevertheless, the conservative jurists of the Ottoman *ancien régime* did not break with the traditional understanding of the state, in which consular jurisdiction certainly had its place. The system was overgrown, but not *per se* illegitimate. Therefore, as a matter, of course, the late-nineteenth-century modernist Ǧamāl al-Qāsimī still advocated legal self-autonomy as a divine order in his commentary on the Qur'an.[60] In fact, it is even questionable if Ali Pasha meant a total abolition of legal self-administration in his "fiery" speech against the capitulations at the Paris Peace Conference in 1856.[61] The fundamental criticism came from the nationalist Young Turks, who saw multi-

---

56 Gabriel E. Noradounghian, "Le traité turco-belge de 1838: La compétence en matière pénale des autorités ottomanes envers les étrangers," *Revue de droit international et législation comparée* 38 (1906); for the "Joris affair," see *To Kill a Sultan: A Transnational History of the Attempt on Abdülhamid II. (1905)*, eds. Houssine Alloul, Edhem Eldem and Henk de Smaele (London: Palgrave Macmillan, 2018). Noradounghian's text was particularly criticised by Rolin, "L'Affaire Joris."

57 Sinan Kuneralp and Emre Öktem, eds., *Chambre des conseillers légistes de la Sublime Porte: Rapports, avis et consulations sur la condition juridique des ressortissants étrangers, le statut des communautés non Musulmanes et les Relations internaionales de l'Empire Ottoman (1864–1912)* (Istanbul: Aygaz, 2012), 9.

58 Kuneralp and Öktem, *Chambre des conseillers légistes de la Sublime Porte*, 9; at least one biography, that of the German councillor *Alfred von Gescher*, has survived. *Gescher* was a prosecutor from the Rhine province which was at that time still under French law and therefore by no means an expert in international law; see Alfred Gescher, *Loose Blätter: Erinnerungen aus meinem Leben* (Münster: C.J. Fahle, 1926).

59 I.e. the argument that a waiver of the originally privileged should also apply to the most favoured states, "Report n° 2728" in Kuneralp and Öktem, *Chambre des conseillers légistes de la Sublime Porte*, 251.

60 Ǧamāl-ad-Dīn Al-Qāsimī, *Tafsīr al-Qāsimī al-Musammā Maḥāsin at-Taʾwīl* (Kairo: Dār Iḥyāʾ al-Kutub al-ʿArabīya, 1970), 6:2014–2016.

61 See "Protocol n° 14 of 25.03.1856" in *Protocols of Conferences held at Paris relative to the general Treaty of Peace* (London: Harrison, 1856), 59.

culturalism as a threat to the existence of the state and who ruled from 1908 onwards.[62]

3.2 *China and Japan*

The situation in China and Japan was very different. It had always been important for these countries to keep contact with Europeans to a minimum and, unlike in the Ottoman Empire, legal autonomy was not embedded in the Japanese and Chinese state system. It is no wonder that the consular courts were met with distrust in East Asian societies. One of the first who expressed his discontent was the Japanese Tatsui Baba. In 1876, he published a harsh criticism of the British treaty with Japan. Consular courts, Baba wrote, would rather protect their subjects than convict them.[63] At that time, a British court had only recently sentenced an Englishman who raped a thirteen-year-old girl with an extremely lenient punishment.[64] The case in question was *Regina vs. Archibald King* in which the British consular court in Yedo had sentenced King to six months of imprisonment.[65] The outrage is clearly reflected in Baba's criticism.

In 1897, Tsurutarō Senga added a detailed critique of the state of consular jurisdiction in Japan. At least in German literature, the book became a standard reference. In particular, the lack of separation of powers met with Senga's disapproval, as the danger of political interference was obvious.[66] How, Senga asked, could the Japanese trust such an institution?[67] Senga's argumentation as well as the literature he cited shows that he knew the European perspective well and which arguments would convince European readers. However, Senga already eliminated the question of the *raison d'être* in the preface because of his fundamentally different view on it.[68] The European topos of the uncultured nature of non-Europeans must have offended the Japanese sense of honour.

---

62 Aygul Ashirova, "Die politische Ideologie der Jungtürken: Osmanismus oder Panturkismus," *Forum für osteuropäische Ideen- und Zeitgeschichte* 13, n° 1 (2009): 73.

63 Tatsui Baba, *The Treaty between Japan and England* (London: Trübner, 1876), 7.

64 Baba, *The Treaty between Japan and England*, 7.

65 Concerning the case, see Chang, *The Justice of the Western Consular Courts*, 27–29; Richard Chang, "A British Trial in Japan. Regina v. Archibald King (1875)," *Journal for Asian History* 10, n° 2 (1976).

66 Tsurutaro Senga, *Gestaltung und Kritik der heutigen Konsulargerichtsbarkeit in Japan* (Berlin: R. L. Prager, 1897), 142–144.

67 Senga, *Gestaltung und Kritik*, 158.

68 Ibid., preface.

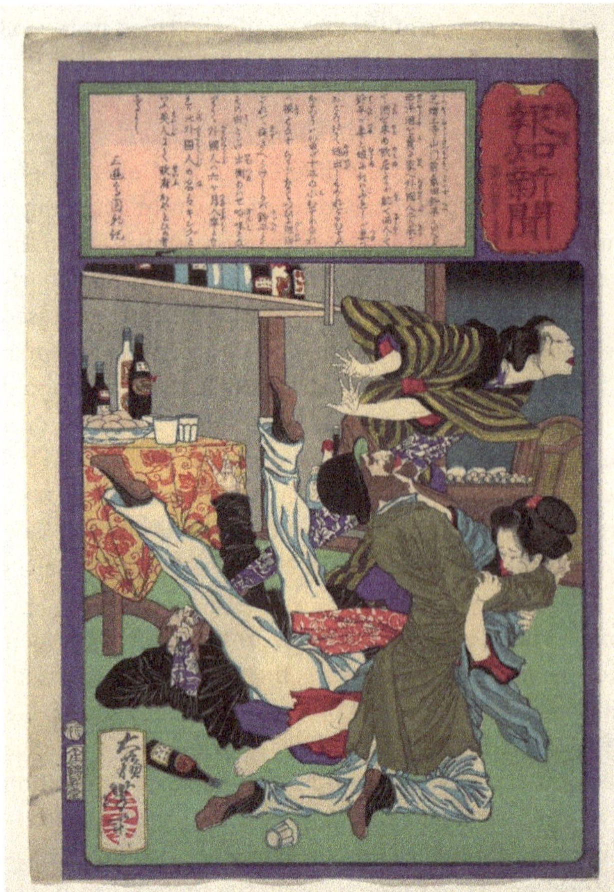

FIGURE 13.1 Woodcut Postal Hōchi, newspaper n° 645, Englishman raping a wine shopkeeper's daughter (Yūbin Hōchi shinbun, roppyaku yonjū gogō)
SOURCE: HTTPS://WWW.METMUSEUM.ORG/ART/COLLECTION/SEARCH/73624

But there were appeasing voices as well. Senga's compatriot Yorikadzu Matsudaira was more understanding.[69] The treatment of the Dutch was, according to Matsudaira, "almost humiliating."[70] Kazuo Hatoyama, on the other hand, referred to the low number of foreigners and concluded that the system did

69 Yorikadzu Matsudaira, *Die völkerrechtlichen Verträge des Kaisertums Japan in wirthschaftlicher, rechtlicher und politischer Bedeutung* (Stuttgart: Deutsche Verlags-Anstalt, 1890), 291.

70 Matsudaira, *Die Völkerrechtlichen Verträge*, 22.

not cause "any serious harm."[71] Nevertheless, the Japanese authors could not have failed to notice that while the European line of argument was that non-European legal systems were not "cultivated" enough, Western jurists actually had very little knowledge about the systems. Kaneko Kentarō, for example, who had studied law at Harvard, listed in the *Revue de droit international* all the legal institutions that Japan had already introduced in order to satisfy the European experts' questions about the state of Japanese reforms.[72]

The Chinese debate, on the other hand, began relatively late, as the jurist Wing Mah noted in 1924.[73] In terms of argumentation, it was the Japanese model that could be copied. In 1901, Wu Ting-Fang emphasised the deficiencies of the consular court system as well, but also admitted that some Chinese practices, such as locking up witnesses for the duration of the trial, must seem strange to Europeans and was, moreover, inconducive for the trial.[74] Wellington Koo, who earned a PhD in law at Columbia University, published an in-depth study of the exterritorial situation in his home country.[75] However, the more it became obvious that China was lagging behind, the harsher the criticism became. Chang Chung Tao advocated abolition on the basis of the *clausula rebus sic stantibus*.[76] The analysis of Tseng Yu-Hao on the background of Bolshevism shows, furthermore, that the face of the ongoing twentieth century had changed drastically.[77]

4 Theory and Practice

After examining mostly theoretical sources, the question remains if theory mirrors practice. Were consular courts indeed dysfunctional? Were they even political? It is possible to answer these questions based on nineteenth-century literature? Only very few authors knew consular jurisdiction first-hand. Fér-

71 Kazuo Hatoyama, "The Civil Code of Japan Compared with the French Civil Code," *The Yale Law Review* 11, n° 6 (June 1902): 298.

72 Kentaro Kaneko, "Les institutions judiciares du Japon," *Revue de droit international et législation comparée* (1893): 338–3340.

73 Wing Mah, "Foreign Jurisdiction in China," *The American Journal of International Law* 18, n° 4 (1924): 677.

74 Wu T.-F. Fang, "Chinese Jurisprudence," *The American Law Review* 35 (1901): 358.

75 Vi Kyuin Wellington Koo, *The Status of Aliens in China* (London: Longmans, Green, 1912).

76 Chang Chung Tao, *Les traités inégaux de la Chine et l'attitude des Puissances* (Paris: Librairie des Sciences Politiques et Sociales, 1929), 172; see also Wu Chiu Sheng, *La juridiction consulaire en Chine* (Toulouse: Imprimerie Régionale, 1936), 134–136.

77 Tseng Yu-Hao, *The Termination of Unequal Treaties in International Law* (Shanghai: The Commercial Press, 1933), 51–53.

aud-Giraud might have come into contact with it at the Appellation Court in Aix. The German PhD candidate Fritz Padel was at least the son of a dragoman in Saloniki.[78] Furthermore, actual court decisions were not available to the authors, and decisions of higher courts were cited very rarely.

However, the files of the Foreign Offices suggest that consular jurisdiction worked better than its reputation. Richard Chang was the first to take this view after studying the decisions of Western consular courts in Japan.[79] Johannes Berchtold confirmed this in his study on British consular courts in the Ottoman Empire.[80] Concerning German consular courts in the Ottoman Empire, no irregularities could likewise be found. The courts adopted decisions *lege artis,* and mostly the decisions were upheld by the *Reichsgericht* as the instance of appellation.

The problem of consular jurisdiction, this paper posits, therefore lies outside the field of law. It is a common phenomenon, especially in criminal law where there has indeed been a dubious or immoral act, that the public forms a certain opinion about the outcome of a case and reacts with great misunderstanding when the decision, even though perfectly reasonable from a legal standpoint, fails to reflect this opinion. The reaction of Tatsui Baba is a good example and, of course, it is particularly easy to assume corruption or racism if the case was decided by a foreign court. Furthermore, exterritoriality created open spaces where it was unnecessary to comply with the local behavioural standards.[81] In other words, there was no sanction for rude conduct. This behaviour might be unimportant legally, but it discredits the system nonetheless.

78 See Fritz Padel, *Die Konsulargerichtsbarkeit in Aegypten und in Der Türkei: Ihre Entwicklung und augenblicklicher Stand unter besonderer Berücksichtigung Deutschlands* (Berlin, 1929), CV at the end.

79 Richard Chang, "The Chishima Case," *The Journal of Asian Studies* 34, n° 3 (1975): 593–595.

80 Berchtold, *Recht und Gerechtigkeit in der Konsulargerichtsbarkeit*, 280.

81 For examples, see Harald Fuess, "Selbstregulierung einer Fremdenkolonie: Deutsche Konsulargerichtsbarkeit in Japan Und Korea, 1861–1913," *Zeitschrift für Japanisches Recht* 18, n° 36 (2013): 103–105; Keiichi Yamanaka, "Der Jagdzwischenfall des Prinzen Heinrich von Preußen während seines Japanbesuches im Jahre 1880: Exterritorialität und strafrechtliche Verhaltensnorm," in *Festschrift für Rudolf Rengier zum 70. Geburtstag*, eds. Bernd Hecker, Bettina Weißer and Christian Brand (Munich: C.H. Beck, 2018), 515–517.

5 Conclusion

Consular jurisdiction ultimately had to fail because few saw value in it. Consular jurisdiction – as a form of comprehensive civil and criminal jurisdiction on foreign soil – stood contrary to fundamental principles of (European) international law. Even for Western jurists, this form of jurisdiction could only be an interim solution until a certain degree of "civilisation" was reached. Additionally, Western jurists found plenty of deficits in the system, which could only have been solved if all states would have reformed the system mutually. It is no wonder, therefore, that Eastern lawyers already found enough arguments in Western literature to argue convincingly that consular jurisdiction had to be abolished in its entirety.

Nevertheless, a clear geographical distinction must be made. In the Ottoman Empire, consular jurisdiction fitted within the Muslim state philosophy. It seems plausible, therefore, that a fundamental objection to the system would be lacking in the works of Ottoman lawyers who wrote in European languages. Conversely, Chinese and Japanese jurists did not hold back on their criticism. However, there was nothing particularly "Japanese" or "Chinese" in the nature of their argumentation. The authors criticised the system using established arguments based on Western law doctrines.

As a result, consular jurisdiction was a curious subject in nineteenth-century legal thinking due to its variety of legal problems and particularities. It was seen as a cruel institution and thus produced little nostalgia in the legal world following its abolition.

Bibliography

Al-Ġazzī, Kāmil Ibn-Ḥusain. *Kitāb Nahr Ad̲-dahab Fī Tārīḫ Ḥalab*. Aleppo: al-Maṭbaʿa al-Mārūniyya, 1923.

Ali, Majid Hassan. "Genocidal Campaigns During the Ottoman Era: The Firman of Mir-I-Kura against the Yazidi Religious Minority in 1832–1834." *Genocide Studies International* 13, n° 2 (2019): 77–91.

Ali, Moulavi Cheragh. *A Critical Exposition of the Popular "Jihad."* Calcutta: Thacker, Spink and Co., 1885.

Alloul, Houssine, Edhem Eldem, and Henk de Smaele, eds. *To Kill a Sultan: A Transnational History of the Attempt on Abdülhamid II. (1905)*. London: Palgrave Macmillan, 2018.

Al-Qāsimī, Ǧamāl ad-Dīn. *Tafsīr Al-Qāsimī Al-Musammā Maḥāsin at-Taʾwīl*. Kairo: Dār Iḥyāʾ al-Kutub al-ʿArabīya, 1970.

Althammer, Beate. "Verfassungsstaat und bürgerliches Recht: Die Stellung von Fremden im Europa des langen 19. Jahrhunderts (1789–1914)." In *Fremd und Rechtlos? Zugehörigkeitsrechte Fremder von der Antike bis zur Gegenwart. Ein Handbuch*, edited by Altay Coşkun and Lutz Raphael. Cologne: Böhlau, 2014.

Antonopoulos, Stamatios. *Über die Exterritorialität der Ausländer in der Türkei mit Rücksicht in Civil- und Strafprozessen*. Berlin: Hermann Bahr, 1895.

Ashirova, Aygul. "Die politische Ideologie der Jungtürken: Osmanismus oder Panturkismus." *Forum für osteuropäische Ideen- und Zeitgeschichte* 13, n° 1 (2009): 65–75.

Baba, Tatsui. *The Treaty Between Japan and England*. London: Trübner, 1876.

Berchtold, Johannes. *Recht und Gerechtigkeit in der Konsulargerichtsbarkeit: Britische Exterritorialität im Osmanischen Reich 1825–1914*. Munich: Oldenbourg, 2009.

Berchtold, Johannes. "Schattenboxen: Rezension zu Turan Kayaoğlu, Legal Imperialsim. Sovereignty and Extraterritoriality in Japan, the Ottoman Empire, and China, New York: 2010." *Rechtsgeschichte* 18 (2011): 216–218.

Borel, Franz Franzewitsch. *De l'origine et des fonctions des consuls*. Saint Petersburg: A. Pluchart, 1807.

Brauer, Arthur von. *Deutsche Justizgesetze in Ihrer Anwendung auf die amtliche Tätigkeit der Konsuln und diplomatischen Agenten und die Konsulargerichtsbarkeit*. Berlin: Carl Heymann, 1879.

Brücklmeier, Eduard. *Die geschichtliche Entwicklung der Konsulargerichtsbarkeit und ihre Rechtsgestaltung für Deutschland im Anschluß an den Weltkrieg*. Leipzig: Mäser, 1927.

Bulmerincq, August von. *Das Völkerrecht*. Freiburg im Breisgau: Mohr, 1889.

Caleb, Raphael. *Die Konsulargerichtsbarkeit in Bulgarien*. Strasbourg: C. & J. Goeller, 1903.

Chang, Richard. "The Chishima Case." *The Journal of Asian Studies* 34, n° 3 (1975): 593–612.

Chang, Richard. "A British Trial in Japan. Regina V. Archibald King (1875)." *Journal for Asian History* 10, n° 2 (1976): 134–150.

Chang, Richard. *The Justice of the Western Consular Courts in Nineteenth-Century Japan*. Westport, Conn.: Greenwood Press, 1984.

Chen, Li. "Law, Empire, and Historiography of Modern Sino-Western Relations: A Case Study of the "Lady Hughes" Controversy in 1784." *Law and History Review* 27, n° 1 (2009): 1–53.

Clercq, Alexandre de, and Charles de Vallat. *Guide pratique des consulats*. Paris: Guillaumin, 1851.

Collin, Peter. "Europäische Entwicklungslinien gerichtlicher und Außergerichtlicher Konfliktlösung im 19. und 20. Jahrhundert." In *Konfliktlösung im 19. und 20. Jahrhundert*, edited by Peter Collin, 1–40. Wiesbaden: Springer, 2021.

Curtis, William Eleroy. *The United States and Foreign Powers*. Meadville: Flood and Vincent, 1892.

Denière, Guillaume. *La juridiction consulaire de Paris 1563–1792*. Paris: Henri Plon, 1872.

Falter, Karl. *Konsulargerichtsbarkeit in Strafsachen*. Erlangen: Hilz, 1909.

Fang, Wu Ting-Fang. "Chinese Jurisprudence." *The American Law Review* 35 (1901): 343–363.

Féraud-Giraud, Louis Joseph Delphin. *De la juridiction française dans les Échelles du Levant et de Barbarie*. Paris: A. Durand, 1859.

Féraud-Giraud, Louis Joseph Delphin. *De la juridiction française dans les Échelles du Levant et du Barbarie: Étude sur la condition légale des étrangers dans les Pays hors Chrétienté*. 2nd ed. Paris: A. Durand, 1866.

Frisch, Hans von. *Der völkerrechtliche Begriff der Exterritorialität*. Brünn: Alfred Hölder, 1917.

Fuess, Harald. "Selbstregulierung einer Fremdenkolonie: Deutsche Konsulargerichtsbarkeit in Japan und Korea, 1861–1913." *Zeitschrift für Japanisches Recht* 18, n° 36 (2013): 53–94.

Gatteschi, Domenico. *Manuale di diritto pubblico e privato Ottomano*. Alexandria: Tipografia della posta Europea, 1865.

Genevois, Ernest. *Histoire critique de la juridiction consulaire*. Paris: A. Durand, 1866.

Genton, Stanislas. *Les capitulations*. Lyon: Imprimerie du Salut Public, 1873.

Gescher, Alfred. *Loose Blätter: Erinnerungen aus meinem Leben*. Münster: C.J. Fahle, 1926.

Goes, Karl. "Das Reichsgesetz über die Konsulargerichtsbarkeit vom 10. Juli 1879: Unter Berücksichtigung seiner Anwendung in den deutschen Schutzgebieten." In *Annalen des Deutschen Reichs für Gesetzgebung, Verwaltung und Statistik: Staatswissenschaftliche Zeitschrift und Materaliensammlung*, edited by Georg Hirth and Max von Seydel, 493–572. Munich, Leipzig: W. Hirth, 1897.

Gottschalk, Johannes. *Die Exterritorialität der Gesandten*. Berlin: Gustav Schade, 1878.

Gundermann, Georg. *Die völkerrechtlichen Grundlagen der Konsulargerichtsbarkeit*. Berlin: Juristische Verlagsbuchhandlung Dr. jur. Frensdorf, 1913.

Hall, William. *A Treatise on International Law*. Oxford: Clarendon Press, 1884.

Hatoyama, Kazuo. "The Civil Code of Japan Compared with the French Civil Code." *The Yale Law Review* 11, n° 6 (1902): 296–303.

Heffter, August Wilhelm. *Das europäische Völkerrecht der Gegenwart*. 3rd ed. Berlin: E.H. Schroeder, 1855.

Hernanz Sanchez, Francisca. *Das Kollision-, Zuständigkeits- und Anerkennungsrecht der internationalen Ehescheidung in Spanien*. Berlin: Duncker & Humblot, 1987.

Hinckley, Frank Erastus. *American Consular Jurisdiction in the Orient*. Washington: W.H. Lowdermilk and Company, 1906.

Hornby, Edmund. *An Autobiography*. Boston: Houghzon Mifflin Company, 1928.

Hübler, Bernhard. *Die Magistraturen des völkerrechtlichen Verkehrs*. Berlin: Puttkammer & Mühlbrecht, 1900.

Jacobovits, Jacob Simon. *Die Consulate als Gerichtsbarkeiten im Osmanischen Reiche*. Vienna: Wilhelm Braumüller, 1865.

Jellinek, Georg. *Allgemeine Staatslehre*. 2. Auflage. Berlin: O. Haering, 1905.

Kaneko, Kentaro. "Les institutions judiciaires du Japon." *Revue de droit international et législation comparée* 25 (1893): 338–356.

Kayaoğlu, Turan. *Legal Imperialism: Sovereignty and Extraterritoriality in Japan, the Ottoman Empire, and China*. New York: Cambridge University Press, 2010.

Koo, Vi Kyuin Wellington. *The Status of Aliens in China*. London: Longmans, Green & Co., 1912.

Kuneralp, Sinan, and Emre Öktem, eds. *Chambre des conseillers légistes de la Sublime Porte: rapports, avis et consulations sur la condition juridique des ressortissants étrangers, le statut des communautés non musulmanes et les relations internationales de l'Empire Ottoman (1864–1912)*. Istanbul: Aygaz, 2012.

Kurkin, Claudia. *Extraterritorialität: Eine Kategorie des transnationalen Rechts*. Tübingen: Mohr Siebeck, 2021.

Lee, Daniel. *The Right of Sovereignty: Jean Bodin on the Sovereign State and the Law of Nations*. Oxford: Oxford University Press, 2021.

Lippmann, Karl. *Die Konsularjurisdiktion im Orient: ihre historische Entwicklung von den frühesten Zeiten bis zur Gegenwart*. Leipzig: Von Veit & Comp., 1898.

Liszt, Franz von. *Das Völkerrecht*. 2nd ed. Berlin: O. Haering, 1902.

Mah, Wing. "Foreign Jurisdiction in China." *The American Journal of International Law* 18, n° 4 (1924): 676–695.

Manz, Volker. *Fremde und Gemeinwohl: Integration und Ausgrenzung in Spanien im Übergang vom Ancien Régime zum frühen Nationalstaat*. Stuttgart: Franz Steiner, 2006.

Martens, Friedrich. *Das Consularwesen und die Consularjurisdiction im Orient*. Berlin: Weidmannsche Buchhandlung, 1874.

Martens, Friedrich. "Premier rapport de M. de Martens." *Annuaire de l'institut de droit international* 6 (1883): 223–229.

Martens, Georg Friedrich, and Charles-Henri Vergé. *Précis du droit des gens moderne de l'Europe*. Paris: Guillaumin et Cie, 1838.

Matsudaira, Yorikadzu. *Die völkerrechtlichen Verträge des Kaisertums Japan in wirthschaftlicher, rechtlicher und politischer Bedeutung*. Stuttgart: Deutsche Verlags-Anstalt, 1890.

Miruss, A. *Das europäische Gesandtschaftsrecht*. Leipzig: Wilhelm Engelmann, 1847.

Müller, Georg Paul. *Die Stellung des Reichsgerichts zur völkerrechtlichen Lehre von der Exterritorialität*. Stettin: Fischer & Schmidt, 1904.

Noradounghian, Gabriel Effendi. "Le traité turco-belge de 1838: La compétence en matière pénale des autorités ottomanes envers les étrangers." *Revue de droit international et législation comparée* 38, 2nd series 8 (1906): 119–135.

Nubar Pascha, Boghos. *Mémoires de Nubar Pascha: Introduction et notes de Mirrit Boutros Ghali.* Beirut: Librairie du Liban, 1983.

Orlando, Feliciano. *Della commissione mista e della competenza sulle domande riconvenionali in Levante.* Constantinople: Besantino, 1847.

Padel, Fritz. „Die Konsulargerichtsbarkeit in Aegypten und in der Türkei: Ihre Entwicklung und augenblicklicher Stand unter besonderer Berücksichtigung Deutschlands." PhD diss., Schlesische Friedrich-Wilhelms-Universität zu Breslau, 1929.

Pélissié du Rausas, Gérard. *Le régime des capitulations dans l'Empire Ottoman.* Paris: Arthur Rousseau, 1902.

Philimore, Robert. *Commentaries upon International Law.* London: William G. Benning, 1855.

Piggot, Francis Taylor. *Exterritoriality: The Law Relating to Consular Jurisdiction and to Residence on Oriental Countries.* London: William Clowes & Sons, 1892.

Polden, Patrick, and Michael Lobban. "The Education of Lawyers." In *The Oxford History of the Laws of England,* edited by William Cornish, Stuart Anderson, Raymond Cocks, Micheal Lobban and Patrick Polden, 1175–1222. Oxford: Oxford University Press, 2010.

Politis, Nikolaos. "Les capitulations et la justice répressive ottomane à propos de l'affaire Joris." *Revue de droit international privé et de droit pénal international* (1906): 660–683.

Reder, Hans. *Das deutsche Konsularwesen in Aegypten.* Würzburg: Richard Mayr, 1931.

Repgen, Tilman. "Eine kurze Geschichte der Fakultät anstelle eines Vorworts." In *100 Jahre Rechtswissenschaft an der Universität Hamburg,* edited by Tilman Repgen, Florian Jeßberger and Markus Kotzur, 1–17. Tübingen: Mohr Siebeck, 2019.

Rolin, Albéric. "L'affaire Joris: Étude sur la Capitulation." *Revue de droit international et législation comparée* (1906): 363–382.

Rustem Effendi, and Seid Bey. *Réponse a quelques journaux aux affaires De Turquie.* Brussels: F. Michel, 1853.

Salem, E. R. "Étrangers devant les tribunaux consulaires et nationaux en Turquie." *Clunet* 18, n° 5 (1891): 393–425.

Savigny, Friedrich Carl von. *System des heutigen Römischen Rechts.* Berlin: De Gruyter, 1849.

Senga, Tsurutaro. *Gestaltung und Kritik der heutigen Konsulargerichtsbarkeit in Japan.* Berlin: R. L. Prager, 1897.

Sheng, Wu Chiu. *La juridiction consulaire en Chine.* Toulouse: Imprimerie régionale, 1936.

Steck, Johann von. *Essai sur les Consuls*. Berlin: Friedrich Nicolovius, 1790.

Story, Joseph. *Commentaries on the Conflict of Laws*. Boston: Billard, Gray, 1834.

Strisower, Leo. *Konsular-Gerichtsbarkeit*. Vienna: Alfred Hölder, 1895.

Tao, Chang Chung. *Les traités inégaux de la Chine et l'attitude des puissances*. Paris: Librairie des Sciences Politiques et Sociales, 1929.

Tsukioka Yoshitoshi, Englishman raping a wine shopkeeper's daughter (Yūbin Hōchi shinbun, roppyaku yonjū gogō). Woodblock print on paper, 35.9 x 23.8 cm. Part of Postal Hōchi Newspaper no. 645. Image (c) The Metropolitan Museum of Art

Twiss, Travers. *The Law of Nations: On the Rights and Duties of Nations in Time of Peace*. Oxford, London: Oxford University Press, 1861.

van den Boogert, Mauritis. *The Capitulations and the Ottoman Legal System: Qadis, Consuls and Beraltlis in the 18th Century*. Leiden: Brill, 2005.

Vorwerk, A. F. *Konsulargerichtsbarkeit*. Berlin: Guttentag'sche Sammlung Deutscher Reichsgesetze, 1908.

Weiser, Walther. *Die deutsche Konsulargerichtsbarkeit oder die Tätigkeit der deutschen Konsulargerichte in bürgerlichen Rechtsstreitigkeiten*. Dessau: Puttkammer & Mühlbrecht, 1912.

Wheaton, Henry. *Elements of International Law*. London: B. Fellows, 1836.

Wheaton, Henry, and Richard Henry Dana. *Elements of International Law*. 8th ed. London: Sampson Low, 1866.

Yamanaka, Keiichi. "Der Jagdzwischenfall Des Prinzen Heinrich Von Preußen Während Seines Japanbesuches Im Jahre 1880: Exterritorialität Und Strafrechtliche Verhaltensnorm." In *Festschrift für Rudolf Rengier*, edited by Bernd Hecker, Bettina Weißer and Christian Brand, 159–177. Munich: C.H. Beck, 2018.

Yu-Hao, Tseng. *The Termination of Unequal Treaties in International Law*. Shanghai: The Commercial Press, 1933.

Zorn, Philipp. "Das deutsche Gesandtschafts-, Konsular- und Seerecht." *Annalen des Deutschen Reichs* 15 (1882): 81–484.

14

Nationalizing Consular Jurisdiction in the Nineteenth-Century Middle East and North Africa

Jessica M. Marglin

1 Introduction

The origins of extraterritoriality in the nineteenth century reach back to the Capitulations (*imtiyāzāt* in Arabic, *ʿahdnâme* in Ottoman): a series of unilateral concessions first granted by Ottoman sultans to Italian city-states in the medieval period, and gradually expanded to other states in Europe and the Americas.[1] The Capitulations allowed foreigners and locals with consular protection a number of advantages while in the Ottoman Empire: they were exempt from most local taxes and enjoyed beneficial rates on customs duties; they could rely on their consular officials to intervene on their behalf with government officials; they were partly under the jurisdiction of consular courts. At the beginning of the seventeenth century, the rulers of Ottoman North Africa – that is, the semi-autonomous provinces of Algiers, Tunis, and Tripoli – began signing their own Capitulations with European states.[2] In the following century, the Sultans of Morocco did the same.[3]

1 J. Wansbrough, H. Inalcik, A. K. S. Lambton, and G. Baer, "Imtiyāzāt," in *Encyclopedia of Islam Two*, edited by P. Bearman, T. Bianquis, C. E. Bosworth, E. van Donzel and W. P. Heinrichs (Leiden: Brill, 2003): 3: 1178–1189; Pauline Guéna, Ian F. Hathaway, Güneş Işiksel, Ana Sekulic, and Tommaso Stefini, "The 'Ahdnâme 'Revisited': Some New Approaches and Perspectives on a Much-Discussed Ottoman Institution," *Turcica*, 53 (2023): 1–9 (and other articles in this special issue). The term "capitulations" is derived from the treaties being organized into chapters, or "capituli." See also, Jacques Lafon, "Les capitulations ottomanes: un droit paracolonial ?" *Droits: Revue française de théorie, de philosophie et de culture juridiques* 28 (1999); Edhem Eldem, "Capitulations and Western Trade," in *The Cambridge History of Turkey*, ed. Suraiya Faroqhi (Cambridge: Cambridge University Press, 2006), 289–290; Fariba Zarinebaf, *Mediterranean Encounters: Trade and Pluralism in Early Modern Galata* (Berkeley, CA: University of California Press, 2018), chap. 3. On the medieval origins, see Zarinebaf, *Mediterranean Encounters*, 96–105.

2 See, e.g., Ignaz De Testa, *Recueil des traités de la Porte Ottomane avec les puissances étrangères*, vol. 1 (Paris: Amyot, 1864), 321.

3 Mohammed Kenbib, *Les protégés: contribution à l'histoire contemporaine du Maroc* (Rabat: Faculté des lettres et des sciences humaines, 1996).

HTTPS://DOI.ORG/10.1163/9789004755192-016

Yet the extraterritoriality of the nineteenth century was quite distinct from the privileges afforded to foreigners and their protégés in the early modern period. Extraterritoriality was not merely an intensification of the early modern Capitulations, but distinctive in kind.[4] The very term "extraterritorial" suggests its nineteenth-century context: a territorial law applied outside (extra-) a territory only makes sense in a world in which territorialism was taken for granted. Although jurists theorized territorial sovereignty long before, recent scholarship argues that territorialism became a firm foundation of international law over the course of the nineteenth century.[5] In this chapter, I argue

4 Maurits H. van den Boogert, *The Capitulations and the Ottoman Legal System; Qadis, Consuls, and Beratlıs in the 18th Century* (Leiden: Brill, 2005), 9–11. One important – though hardly determinative – indication that extraterritoriality is best used only to describe the nineteenth-century form of consular protection is the history of the term itself. Although the Latin equivalent was used as early as the sixteenth century, "extraterritoriality" – as well as its synonym "exterritoriality" – only became widespread in the late eighteenth century. The word seems to appear in French (as "exterritorialité") in the French translation of Georg Friedrich von Martens from 1789: Georg Friedrich de Martens, *Précis du droit des gens moderne de l'Europe fondé sur les traités et l'usage* (Gottingen: Jean Chret. Dieterich, 1789), 276–277. And in English in the translation from 1795: regarding the "exterritorial" status of diplomats (here called "ministers,") see Georg Friedrich von Martens, *Summary of the law of nations, founded on the treaties and customs of the modern nations of Europe: With a list of the principal treaties, concluded since the year 1748 down to the present time, indicating the works in which they are to be found* trans. William Cobbett (Philadelphia: Thomas Bradford, 1795), 228–229. While Latin texts did use the term *extra territorium*, it becomes far more common after Martens, as indicated by the database "The Making of Modern Law: Foreign, Comparative, and International Law" (https://www.gale.com/primary-sources/making-of-modern-law); by the *Oxford English Dictionary*; and by a google ngram (which shows its frequency skyrocketing after the 1880s).

5 Charles Maier, "Consigning the Twentieth Century to History: Alternative Narratives for the Modern Era," *American Historical Review* 105, n° 3 (2000); Jürgen Osterhammel, *The Transformation of the World: A Global History of the Nineteenth Century*, trans. Patrick Camiller (Princeton, NJ: Princeton University Press, 2014), 107–113; Christopher Casey, *Nationals Abroad: Globalization, Individual Rights, and the Making of Modern International Law* (Cambridge: Cambridge University Press, 2020), 26–28. Lauren Benton warns against assuming a "smooth and steady progression toward territorial sovereignty": Lauren Benton, *A Search for Sovereignty: Law and Geography in European Empires, 1400–1900* (Cambridge: Cambridge University Press, 2010), 30. See also Lauren Benton, Adam Clulow, and Bain Attwood, eds., *Protection and Empire: A Global History* (Cambridge: Cambridge University Press, 2018); Richard T. Ford, "Law's Territory (A History of Jurisdiction)," *Michigan Law Review* 97, n° 4 (1999); Gilles Havard, "'Les forcer à devenir Cytoyens': État, Sauvages et citoyenneté en Nouvelle-France (XVIIe–XVIIIe siècle)," *Annales. Histoire, Sciences Sociales* 64, n° 5 (2009): esp. 1009–1011; Lauren Benton and Lisa Ford, *Rage for Order: The British Empire and the Origins of International Law, 1800–1850* (Cambridge, MA: Harvard University Press, 2016), chap. 4. Territorialism was not, however, invented out of whole cloth in the nineteenth century; on Ottoman territorialism in the eighteenth century, see Palmira Brummett,

that it was only in the first decades of the nineteenth century that consular courts began applying their national law. This nationalization of consular courts was necessary for the projection of extraterritorial jurisdiction.

In arguing for extraterritoriality as a nineteenth-century phenomenon, I suggest revising the way most scholars have treated the subject.[6] Some historians have identified turning points that altered the nature of the capitulations before 1800 – for instance, the French Capitulations of 1740 considerably expanded the privileges accorded to foreigners.[7] Nonetheless, even these scholars see these changes – whether in the mid-eighteenth century or the early nineteenth – as a matter of gradual development driven by politics. As the international balance of power shifted, extraterritoriality got out of hand; European states began to use violence to impose less favorable conditions on Muslim-ruled polities.[8] When historians have noted changes to extraterritoriality in the nineteenth century, they have largely focused on its novel neo-imperial dimension.[9] But the substance of extraterritoriality is assumed to have remained largely unchanged.

Mapping the Ottomans: Sovereignty, Territory, and Identity in the Early Modern Mediterranean (Cambridge: Cambridge University Press, 2015); Michael Talbot, "Separating the Waters from the Sea: The Place of Islands in Ottoman Maritime Territoriality During the Eighteenth Century," *Princeton Papers: Interdisciplinary Journal of Middle East Studies* 18 (2017).

6 An exception is Turan Kayaoğlu, *Legal Imperialism: Sovereignty and Extraterritoriality in Japan, the Ottoman Empire, and China* (Cambridge: Cambridge University Press, 2010).

7 Lafon, "Les capitulations," 167–175; Alexander H. De Groot, "The Historical Development of the Capitulatory Regime in the Ottoman Middle East from the Fifteenth to the Nineteenth Centuries," *Oriente Moderno* 83, n° 3 (2003): 599; Eldem, "Capitulations and Western Trade," 319–321. Britain signed a similarly permanent treaty with the Ottoman Empire in 1838: David Todd, "Beneath Sovereignty: Extraterritoriality and Imperial Internationalism in Nineteenth-Century Egypt," *Law and History Review* 36, n° 1 (2018): 111 (although Todd wrongly claims that France only acquired permanent capitulatory rights two months after Britain).

8 Lafon, "Les capitulations," 167–175; Wansbrough *et al.*, "Imtiyāzāt," in *Encyclopedia of Islam*, eds. P. Bearman *et al.* (Leiden: Brill, 2003); De Groot, "Historical Development," 599; James McDougall, "A World No Longer Shared: Losing the *Droit de Cité* in Nineteenth Century Algiers," *Journal of the Economic and Social History of the Orient* 60, n° 1–2 (2017): 23–25; Christian Windler, "Towards the Empire of a 'Civilizing Nation': The French Revolution and its Impact on Relations with the Ottoman Regencies in the Maghreb," in *International Law and Empire: Historical Explorations*, eds. Martti Koskenniemi, Walter Rech, and Manuel Jiménez Fonseca (Oxford: Oxford University Press, 2017), 212–215; Kate Miles, "'Uneven Empires': Extraterritoriality and the Early Trading Companies," in *The Extraterritoriality of Law: History, Theory, Politics*, eds. Daniel S. Margolies *et al.* (London: Routledge, 2019).

9 See, e.g., 'Abd al-Wahhāb Ibn Manṣūr, *Mushkilat al-ḥimāya al-qunṣuliyya bi-'l-Maghrib* (Rabat: al-Maṭba'a al-mālikīya, 1985); Salahi R. Sonyel, "The Protégé System in the Ottoman Empire," *Journal of Islamic Studies* 2, n° 1 (1991); Kenbib, *Les protégés*; Lafon, "Les capitulations."; Feroz Ahmad, "Ottoman Perceptions of the Capitulations, 1800–1914," *Journal of*

In what follows, I argue that the substance of consular jurisdiction transformed after the Napoleonic wars. Consuls certainly had judicial functions in the early modern period, but this rarely involved applying national law and most adjudication seems to have taken the form of arbitration. Only after 1815 – as a reaction to the explosion of foreign subjects in the Middle East and North Africa, as well as a reflection of the changing balance of power – did Western states begin specifying that their consuls should apply their national law abroad.

2 Consular Jurisdiction in the Early Modern World

During the early modern period, the jurisdiction of consuls had very little to do with projecting the jurisdiction of a particular state to nationals outside of its territory. On the one hand, consulates afforded jurisdiction to many who were not members of the state they represented. On the other, the laws applied were only rarely those of the state concerned.

The very first Ottoman Capitulation to France gave French consular officials the right to represent Europeans who had not negotiated their own privileges – which at first included all Europeans except for Venetians. Over the course of the seventeenth century, more and more European states signed their own treaties with the Ottomans and the French no longer had the exclusive right to protect Europeans lacking their own Capitulation. "Merchant strangers" (European merchants without their own ambassador in Istanbul) could choose their protecting country; this meant that into the nineteenth century, consulates served many Europeans who were not members of the nation they represented.[10]

Studies of the French consulate in Tunis show that in the seventeenth century, many non-Frenchmen used the French consular chancellery and adjudicated cases before the French consul. These included not only other Europeans lacking consular representation – like Maltese – but also local Jews

Islamic Studies 11 (2000); Wansbrough *et al.*, "Imtiyāzāt." Even scholars who are more attentive to the legal history of extraterritoriality – rather than its political history – tend to emphasize continuity between the early modern and modern Capitulations: see, e.g., Mariya Tait Slys, *Exporting Legality: The Rise and Fall of Extraterritorial Jurisdiction in the Ottoman Empire and China* (Geneva: Graduate Institute Publications, 2014), chap. 3; Sarah Abrevaya Stein, *Extraterritorial Dreams: Jews, Citizenship, and the Calamitous Twentieth Century* (Chicago: The University of Chicago Press, 2016), 13–15.

10 Van den Boogert, *Capitulations*, 37; Lafon, "Les capitulations," 158–160, 75.

and Muslims, subjects of the Beys of Tunis.[11] By the early nineteenth century the majority of those using the French chancellery in Tunis were indeed French. This was part of a gradual "process of 'nationalization' that penetrated consular institutions in Europe and the Mediterranean" by which the personnel and the clients of consulates became increasingly nationalized.[12]

Ottoman capitulations also gave French consuls the right to protect Catholic religious in the Ottoman Empire – priests, monks, and nuns, regardless of their nationality.[13] Ottoman authorities and the consuls of other European states debated the precise contours of French protection over Catholic religious. Starting in the eighteenth century, Ottoman authorities granted official recognition to local Catholic communities (such as Melkites, a Greek Catholic church, in 1724, and Armenian Catholics in 1740). Should Catholic religious from local Ottoman Christian communities fall under French protection? What about the role of other Catholic states like Spain?[14] Despite conflicts over these questions, the basic idea that the French had some jurisdiction over non-French Catholic religious was uncontested.

Nor did early modern European jurisdiction abroad involve a prolongation of national law. Many cases involving foreign nationals and protégés in early modern consulates were settled by arbitration. Arbitration councils were frequently mixed, involving "Muslims and non-Muslims, Ottoman subjects and Westerners."[15] Even in the absence of arbitration, Maurits van den Boogert has observed that in the eighteenth century, references to national laws were rare

11 Arnaud Bartolomei and Anne Brogini, "De la réglementation aux pratiques marchandes: l'enregistrement des actes dans les chancelleries consulaires françaises (XVIIe–XIXe siècles)," in *De l'utilité commerciale des consuls: L'institution consulaire et les marchands dans le monde méditerranéen (XVIIe–XXe siècle)*, eds. Arnaud Bartolomei *et al.* (Rome: École française de Rome, 2017).

12 Bartolomei and Brogini, "De la réglementation aux pratiques marchandes," § 19; see also Mathieu Grenet, "Recrutement et service dans les petits consulats français de Méditerranée orientale aux XVIIe et XVIIIe siècles," *Cahiers de la Mediterranée* 103 (2021).

13 Gérard Pélissié du Rausas, *Le régime des capitulations dans l'Empire Ottoman*, 2 vols. (Paris: Arthur Rousseau, 1902–1905), 42–56.

14 Lafon, "Les capitulations," 170–171; Jacques Lafon, "La protection des lieux saints: Un conflit franco-espagnol (1868)," in *Itinéraires de l'histoire du droit à la diplomatie culturelle et à l'histoire coloniale*, ed. Jacques Lafon (Paris: Éditions de la Sorbonne, 2021).

15 Van den Boogert, *Capitulations*, 305. See also Todd, "Beneath Sovereignty," 112; Guillaume Calafat, "La juridiction des consuls français en Méditerranée: litiges marchands, arbitrages et circulations des procès (Livourne et Tunis au XVIIe siècle)," in *De l'utilité commerciale des consuls; L'institution consulaire et les marchands dans le monde méditerranéen (XVIIe–XXe siècle)*, eds. Arnaud Bartolomei *et al.* (Rome: École française de Rome, 2017).

among the British and Dutch consular records he examined.[16] I have found the same in French archives.[17] If there was anything that generally characterized European consular practices in the early modern period, it was conformity to "Levantine" practices – a set of legal customs broadly accepted by European consular officials, though not necessarily codified.[18]

British consular courts offer the most obvious example. In Ottoman territory, the Levant Company had the authority to appoint its own consuls and to make its own laws; these consuls exercised jurisdiction in lieu of consuls appointed by the Crown.[19] Yet the extent of this jurisdiction remained unclear. According to some jurists, British consuls not only lacked criminal jurisdiction, but even civil jurisdiction over British subjects; whatever civil jurisdiction they exercised was purely voluntary.[20] Others claimed that Levant Company–appointed consuls had jurisdiction over intra-British civil affairs, though not over matters concerning other Europeans.[21] Moreover, the content of the laws applied by these British consuls remained quite vague:

> The … Levant Company's bye-laws related chiefly to the commercial concerns of that body, and contained but few instructions as to the judicial functions of their consuls. Obliged, however, to exercise those functions with hardly any other rules to guide them than what natural

16 Van den Boogert, *Capitulations*, 259.

17 For instance, the correspondence of the French ambassador in Constantinople with the French Ministre de la Marine (the Minister of Foreign Affairs during the ancien régime) during the first half of the eighteenth century contains exceedingly few references to French or any other national law as it applies to a legal case in the Ottoman Empire. See, e.g., the dispute over an abandoned ship in 1733, in which the French ambassador Louis Sauveur, Marquis de Villeneuve, asked for guidance concerning whether English law or the French naval ordonnance of 1681 should apply: Villeneuve to Maurepas, April 16, 1733, Archives Nationales de France (hereafter AN), AE/B/I/407. References to French laws generally concern the administration of French merchants and sailors in the Levant.

18 Van den Boogert, *Capitulations*, 259; see also Ellen Nye, "'A Bank of Trust': Legal Practices of Ottoman Finance Between Empires," *Journal of Early Modern History* 27, n° 6 (2023); Tijl Vanneste, *Intra-European Litigation in Eighteenth-Century Izmir: The Role of the Merchants' Style* (Leiden: Brill, 2021).

19 Martti Koskenniemi, "Introduction: International Law and Empire; Aspects and Approaches," in *International Law and Empire: Historical Explorations*, eds. Martti Koskenniemi, Walter Rech, and Manuel Jiménez Fonseca (Oxford: Oxford University Press, 2017), 12; Miles, "'Uneven Empires'," 90–91; see also Despina Vlami, *Trading with the Ottomans: The Levant Company in the Middle East* (London: I. B. Tauris, 2015), 2.

20 John Austin and George C. Lews to Lord Genely, August 1, 1837, FO/97/407, The British National Archives, London (here after BNA).

21 Report from Messrs. Freshfield and Kaye, solicitors to the Levant company, June 8, 1812, in "Papers relating to consular jurisdiction in the Levant: Extract from report of the select committee on consular establishment, 1835," BNA, FO/97/407.

> equity suggested, as the laws of England were found in many cases inapplicable to local exigencies, they were under the necessity of creating for themselves the peculiar kind of procedure which is at present observed, assimilating it as much as possible to that followed by their colleagues [i.e. other consuls].[22]

The limited jurisdiction exercised by British consuls was "not sanctioned by any superior authority" and thus did not have "any obligatory effect."[23] For this reason, consuls not only made up their law more or less on the fly, largely emulating the practice of other consulates; they also allowed British subjects involved in lawsuits "to deviate from the course in practice, the result of which has been to introduce vagueness and uncertainty in the progress of suits."[24] The Levant Company was interested in trade, not jurisdiction; to the extent that its officers did exercise jurisdiction over British subjects, they did so largely according to "what natural equity suggested" rather than the "laws of England."

Early modern France was at the forefront of state centralization. Yet it was not until shortly before the French Revolution that comprehensive laws concerning the administration of consular jurisdiction were passed at the national level. Before the sixteenth century, consuls abroad represented cities, not states. Marseille was by far the most important city when it came to Mediterranean trade; it took half a century after its incorporation into the kingdom of France before royal authorities attempted to take over the prerogative of appointing consuls. Even when the French crown appointed a consul in Alexandria in 1532 – the first in the Middle East and North Africa – his post was contested by the municipal authorities of Marseille, who had their own man in the position. The French-appointed consul finally prevailed four years later.[25] Yet throughout the early modern period, Marseille and its Chamber of Commerce retained significant authority over the French "nations" in the Mediterranean; only those Frenchmen with authorization from the Marseille Ch-

22 Report of consul in Smyrna (R. W. Brant) "on the Practice observed in Judicial Proceedings in the Consular Court at that place," May 30, 1835, in "Papers relating to consular jurisdiction in the Levant," BNA, FO/97/407.

23 Ibid.

24 Ibid. See also John P. Spagnolo, "Portents of Empire in Britain's Ottoman Extraterriotiral Jurisdiction," *Middle Eastern Studies* 27, n° 2 (1991): 258–259.

25 Géraud Poumarède, "Naissance d'une institution royale: les consuls de la nation française en Levant et en Barbarie aux XVIe et XVIIe siècles," *Annuaire-Bulletin de la société de l'histoire de France* (2001): 67–69.

amber of Commerce were permitted to reside in the "Levant and the Barbary States."[26]

Even once French consulates came under the authority of the central state, their judicial functions were hardly seen as an extension of territorial law. French consulates had no formal jurisdiction over criminal matters meriting corporal punishment; the suspect was to be sent back to France and judged in Provence.[27] In many civil cases, French officials in the Ottoman Empire frequently preferred to avoid making rulings themselves and either deferred to officials, lawyers, or courts in France.[28] Nor would it have been possible for consulates to apply a unified "French law" under the *ancien régime*; law in pre-Napoleonic France rested in part on local customs (especially in the north).[29] Seventeenth-century legislation regarding consular jurisdiction made no effort to impose uniformity on the substantive laws applied in consulates abroad. The first comprehensive decree regulating the navy from 1681 included a short section outlining the rules for the establishment and responsibilities of consuls. Article 12 noted that the jurisdiction of consuls should conform to the "usages and capitulations made with the local sovereigns."[30]

In 1778, the crown passed decrees demanding conformity among the jurisdiction exercised by French consulates. The edict "regulating the judicial and police functions exercised by French consuls abroad" attempted to lay out

---

26 Jörg Ulbert, "Identifier pour contrôler," *Mélanges de la Casa de Velázquez* 51, n° 1 (March 2021): § 48–49, https://doi.org/https://doi.org/10.4000/mcv.14474. From 1766 to 1777, the Chamber issued only thirty-five such permits per year. See also Pélissié du Rausas, *Capitulations dans l'Empire Ottoman*, 1: 40–42, 399.

27 Van den Boogert, *Capitulations*, 39.

28 See, e.g., Ferriol to Pontchartrain, March 9, 1709, AN.AE/B/I/386; des Alleurs to Pontchartrain, June 5, 1713, AN.AE/B/I/388; des Alleurs to Pontchartrain, October 15, 1714, AN.AE/B/I/388.

29 See esp. Jean Hilaire, *Introduction historique au droit commercial* (Paris: Presses universitaires de France, 1986), 66–82. Commercial cases were regulated in part by the Ordonnance du commerce of 1673 (Isambert, Decrusy, and Taillandier, eds., *Recueil général des anciennes lois françaises, depuis l'an 420 jusqu'à la révolution de 1789: janvier 1672 – mai 1686*, vol. 19 (Paris: Belin-Leprieur, 1829), 91–107.), but customs, usages (in the sense of mercantile practice, for instance), and roman law were also part of the legal mosaic; for these insights, I am grateful to Guillaume Calafat. See also Nathan Perl-Rosenthal, *Citizen Sailors: Becoming American in the Age of Revolution* (Cambridge, MA: Harvard University Press, 2015), 41.

30 Isambert, Decrusy, and Taillandier, *Recueil général des anciennes lois françaises, 1672–1686*, 295; see pp. 282–366 for the full text of the law. For a summary of the judicial functions of consuls in the ancien régime, see Yvan Debbasch, *La nation française en Tunisie (1577–1835)* (Paris: Éditions Sirey, 1957), 222–226; Anne Mézin, *Les consuls de France au siècle des lumières (1715–1792)* (Paris: Ministère des affaires étrangéres, 1998), 37–39.

"rules that are easy to follow, and according to which [the consuls] will adjudicate in different consulates, in a uniform manner."[31] These rules, however, were strictly procedural; the substantive contents of the law according to which consuls should rule remained vague. A decree from 1781 regarding the organization of French consulates in the Levant and the Barbary states outlined a series of special rules governing French nationals in the Middle East and North Africa: they were prohibited from gambling, sending textiles that "could transmit plague," or "go[ing] before the local authorities" without the permission of consular representatives.[32] But this legislation was silent regarding the substantive laws consular courts should use to adjudicate civil and criminal cases.

A related matter is that consular jurisdiction in the early modern Middle East and North Africa differed little from that in Europe and the Americas. Consuls posted in Christian states exercised jurisdiction over their co-nationals in ways that largely mirrored the extent of consular jurisdiction in the Middle East and North Africa. In his 1826 treatise on the institution of French consulates, Laget de Podío, a lawyer from Marseille, begins his chapter on the jurisdiction of French consuls abroad by explaining that "Consuls were instituted in order to … adjudicate in disputes that arise among them."[33] French subjects were expressly prohibited from bringing their fellow French subjects before a foreign court, whether or not they were in France.[34] The jurisdictional

---

31 Jourdan, Isambert, and Decrusy, eds., *Recueil général des anciennes lois françaises, depuis l'an 420 jusqu'à la révolution de 1789: du 10 mai 1777 au 31 décembre 1778* (Paris: Belin-Leprieur, 1826), 333–334.

32 Jourdan, Isambert, and Decrusy, eds., *Recueil général des anciennes lois françaises, depuis l'an 420 jusqu'à la révolution de 1789: du 31 décembre 1778 au 3 mars 1781* (Paris: Belin-Leprieur, 1826), 427–488, quotes at 464 and 466.

33 "Les consuls ont été institués pour protéger le commerce et la navigation des sujets de Sa Majesté dans les pays étrangers, pour prononcer sur les différends qui peuvent s'élever entre eux, et pour fournir au Gouvernement les documens [sic] qui doivent le mettre à portée d'assurer la prospérité du commerce extérieur." Lagét de Podio, *De la juridiction des consuls de France à l'égard de l'étranger et des devoirs et obligations qu'ont à remplir ces fonctionnaires* (Paris: C. J. Trouvé, 1826), 1.

34 See the decree of 1778 concerning the judicial authority of consuls: "Faisons très-expresses inhibitions et défenses à nos sujets voyageant … ou faisant le commerce en pays étrangers, d'y traduire, pour quelque cause que ce puisse être, nos autres sujets devant les juges ou autres officiers des puissances étrangères, à peine de 1500 livres d'amende." Article 2: Jourdan, Isambert, and Decrusy, *Recueil général des anciennes lois françaises, 1777–1778*, 334.

dimensions of consuls' responsibilities were absolutely central to their functioning even in Europe.[35]

This does not mean that the extent of jurisdiction was identical within and outside of Europe. Normative sources from the seventeenth century note that consuls in North Africa and the Middle East had greater jurisdiction than those in "Christendom."[36] And both jurists and non-jurists debated whether consuls were judges (exercising justice in the name of the state) or merely arbiters (adjudicating cases in which the parties voluntarily agreed to abide by their ruling). Despite disagreements, most jurists agreed that consuls in North Africa and the Middle East had powers closer to those of judges, while those in Europe were more like arbiters.[37] As late as 1844, when de Podío published the second edition of his treatise, he explained that consuls everywhere have "the right to adjudicate all disputes, of whatever nature, between Frenchmen – merchants, sailors, and others – in the jurisdiction of their consulates – their cases being prohibited from being brought before any foreign authority."[38]

A major difference between intra-Christian treaties and those with Middle Eastern and North African states concerns the possibility of extending consular protection to locals associated with consulates or foreign merchants. The Ottoman Capitulation granted to France in 1604 was the first to specify the privileges granted to Ottoman subjects working as interpreters (dragomans) for French consulates.[39] Although the relevant article only discussed taxes,

---

35 Calafat, "Les juridictions du consul: une institution au service des marchands et du commerce ? Introduction" in *De l'utilité commerciale des consuls. L'in- stitution consulaire et les marchands dans le monde méditerranéen (xviie–xxe siècle)*, edited by Arnaud Bartolomei, Guillaume Calafat, Mathieu Grenet et Jörg Ulbert, (Rome: École française de Rome, 2017), 143–153. Jörg Ulbert, "Introduction. La fonction consulaire à l'époque moderne: définition, état des connaissances et perspectives de recherche," in *La fonction consulaire à l'époque moderne: L'affirmation d'une institution économique et politique (1500–1800)*, eds. Jörg Ulbert and Gérard Le Bouëdec (Rennes: Presses universitaires de Rennes, 2006).

36 See esp. Calafat, "Les juridictions du consul: Introduction"; Calafat, "La juridiction des consuls français."

37 Calafat, "La juridiction des consuls français." For instance, the Tuscan authorities did not recognize the judicial authority of the French consul. Nonetheless, the consuls there often acted not only like arbiters, but even like judges (§ 11).

38 Lagét de Podio, *De la juridiction des consuls de France à l'égard de l'étranger et des devoirs et obligations qu'ont à remplir ces fonctionnaires*, 2nd ed., vol. 1 (Marseille: Chez l'auteur, 1844), 236.

39 Van den Boogert, *Capitulations*, 65–66. Treaties between France and the Bey of Tunis did not discuss the rights of protégés until that of 1802 (article 7: De Testa, *Recueil des traités, VI*, 1, 399.); see also Mehdi Jerad, "Enjeux marchands et intérêts de pouvoir autour de la juridiction contentieuse des consuls de France à Tunis (1827–1836)," in *De l'utilité commerciale des consuls. L'institution consulaire et les marchands dans le monde méditerra-*

subsequent correspondence made clear that protégés theoretically benefited from other advantages such as falling under the jurisdiction of consular courts for matters involving other Europeans or other protégés.[40] Eventually, Ottoman subjects working with European merchants – including warehousemen and brokers – also acquired patents of consular protection. Those Ottomans with protection were known as *beratlılar* (s. *beratlı*), after the *berat*, or patent issued to them by the Sublime Porte.

The trend to further differentiate the privileges afforded foreigners in Europe from those afforded foreigners and protégés in the Middle East and North Africa only increased in the nineteenth century as the power of consuls in Europe and the Americas waned.[41]

3 The Nationalization of Consular Jurisdiction

In the first decades of the nineteenth century, European states began to demand that consular courts apply uniform national laws. These reforms were undertaken partly in response to legal developments in Europe (such as the Napoleonic Code), and party due to the growing numbers of subjects claiming extraterritorial privileges after 1815. The nationalization of laws applied to Europeans and their protégés in the Middle East and North Africa was an important step in making consular courts *extra*-territorial – in the sense of applying a jurisdiction normally reserved for the territory of a state beyond its borders.

Much of the evolution towards extraterritoriality had its roots in a radical change in the balance of power between the Ottoman Empire and Christian states. This began in the mid-eighteenth century, most importantly with a series of Russian victories over the Ottomans. Starting with the treaty of Küçük Kaynarca in 1774, the Russians annexed a number of formerly Ottoman territories, including the Crimea (in 1783) and most of the Caucasus (in 1829). In 1798, Napoleon occupied Egypt, only to be booted out with British help. And in 1830, France's occupation of Algeria both threatened the territorial integrity of the Ottoman Empire and demonstrated European military superiority to neighboring Morocco and Tunisia. Increasingly, military might was also used to secure the expansion of privileges granted to foreigners and their protégés.

---

néen (*XVII*[e]*–XX*[e] *siècle*), eds. Arnaud Bartolomei *et al.* (Rome: École française de Rome, 2017), § 25.

40 Van den Boogert, *Capitulations*, 112–114.

41 Ulbert, "Introduction," § 10.

At the same time, the number of people who benefited from foreign protection grew exponentially. The community of foreigners and protégés in the early modern period was quite small: in the eighteenth century, they were at most in the hundreds in North Africa, and probably no more than a few thousand for the entire Ottoman Empire.[42] After the Napoleonic Wars, the number of individuals with foreign protection began to increase dramatically. This was due to two factors: migration from Southern Europe, which exploded in the second half of the nineteenth century;[43] and European colonization in the Mediterranean, which produced colonial subjects entitled to the protection of their colonizers – especially Algerians claiming French protection and Ionians and Maltese claiming British protection.[44]

It was during these turbulent decades that consular courts came to be thought of as extraterritorial in the sense of applying the law of the state they represented outside its territory. This change began in France; after the promulgation of the Napoleonic Code, French consuls began to cite its articles in their rulings – suggesting a move towards applying national law in consular courts.[45] In 1851, Alexandre Jehan Henry de Clercq and Charles de Vallat, two French diplomats, published the first comprehensive guide for French consular officials. They explained that consuls were expected to enumerate the

42 See Anne Mézin, *État des Français au Levant et en Barbarie (1756–1832); inventaire détaillé de l'article AE/B/III/290* (Archives Nationales de France, 2020): https://www.siv.archives-nationales.culture.gouv.fr/siv/rechercheconsultation/consultation/ir/consultationIR.action?irId=FRAN_IR_058432. See also Patrick Boulanger, "Les appointements des consuls de France à Alger au XVIIIe siècle," in *La fonction consulaire à l'époque moderne: L'affirmation d'une institution économique et politique (1500–1800)*, eds. Jörg Ulbert and Gérard Le Bouëdec (Rennes: Presses universitaires de Rennes, 2006), § 11. Membership in the Levant Company peaked in the 1670s at 400 (for the entire Ottoman Empire), but declined to less than forty by 1753: Ralph Davis, *Aleppo and Devonshire Square: English Traders in the Levant in the Eighteenth Century* (London: Macmillan, 1967), 61. On the Ottoman Empire, see van den Boogert, *Capitulations*, 90. See also Eldem, "Capitulations and Western Trade," 309.

43 Will Hanley, *Identifying with Nationality: Europeans, Ottomans, and Egyptians in Alexandria* (New York: Columbia University Press, 2017), 100, 78; Julia Clancy-Smith, *Mediterraneans: North Africa and Europe in an Age of Migration, c. 1800–1900* (Berkeley: University of California Press, 2011).

44 C. R. Pennell, "The Origins of the Foreign Jurisdiction Act and the Extension of British Sovereignty," *Historical Research* 83 (2010); Jessica M. Marglin, "The Crémieux Decree Seen from Afar," *The Journal of North African Studies* 28, n° 3 (2023); Salma Hargal, "De la sujétion française à la nationalité ottomane: Le statut des Algériens à l'époque d'Abdulhamid II (1876–1908)," *Turcica* 55 (2024), 163–201.

45 See, e.g., Armand Charles Comte de Guilleminot to MAE, January 30, 1830, Constantinople, 90CCC/84, Centre des Archives Diplomatiques, La Courneuve, France.

specific French laws on which their rulings were based.[46] The extent to which these rules were observed is hard to gauge as most consulates did not begin keeping systematic judicial records until later in the century.[47] In 1862, the French Ministry of Foreign Affairs issued a circular insisting that consul-judges conform to the legal requirements in writing their sentences, since up to that point their "rulings were written in a very perfunctory manner, and do not describe how the trial proceeded."[48] Nonetheless, by mid-century, consular courts were conceived of as French courts applying French law.

In 1825, the British Foreign Office assumed the administration of consulates from the Levant Company. The Foreign Office soon began working to nationalize the judicial functioning of consulates as a direct reaction to the proliferation of British nationals in the Mediterranean. After 1815, Maltese and Ionians – both islands colonized during the Napoleonic Wars – became British subjects, and thus fell under British consular protection. British consuls suddenly found themselves in charge of large communities of Maltese and Ionians, who "inundated the Ports and some of the interior Districts of Turkey with a lawless and dissolute class of persons, who are guilty of many excesses" – including fraud, failure to pay debts, theft, and murder.[49] Legally, however, the consuls' hands were tied. The Levant Company had not possessed any authority to adjudicate criminal cases.[50] Those Ionians and Maltese accused of crimes against Ottoman subjects could be prosecuted in Ottoman courts (with their consuls or dragomans present). But European subjects who committed crimes against other Europeans were prosecuted in their respective consular courts (according to the principle of *actor sequitur forum rei*, that is, jurisdiction following that of the defendant). Without criminal jurisdiction over their subjects in the

46 Alexandre J. H. de Clercq and Charles de Vallat, *Guide pratique des consulats: Publié sous les auspices du ministère des affaires étrangères* (Paris: Guillaumin, 1851), 706, 40, 48. Even after these rules were put in place, however, French courts recognized the special circumstances that applied to consular courts, and that certain "exemptions" to the strict letter of French law "resulting from local customs" applied: Paul Dislère and R. De Mouy, *Droits et devoirs des Français dans les pays d'Orient et d'Extrême-Orient* (Paris: Paul Dupont, 1893), 228–229.

47 In Morocco, for instance, the French embassy in Tangier kept no detailed records of legal procedures or rulings before the 1880s, nor did sentences before this period regularly cite French law: see Centre des Archives Diplomatiques de Nantes (France: hereafter CADN), Tanger F1. This is also true for other states: the first records of American consular courts are from the 1860s: see Lebanon, Civil Record Book, v. 41, RG 84, NARA.

48 Dislère and De Mouy, *Droits et devoirs des Français*, 241.

49 W. F. Strangways to Colonial Office, June 7, 1837, BNA, FO/97/407.

50 "Memorandum respecting the Foreign Jurisdiction Bill, now before Parliament," August 12, 1843, BNA, FO/97/407.

Middle East and North Africa, British consuls were in a bind. Consuls could agree to give up British subjects strongly suspected of violent crime to Ottoman authorities. But this meant ceding the jurisdictional privileges afforded in the Capitulations, which consuls feared would become a "Pretext for Encroachments" on British privileges.[51] Growing concern over crimes committed by Maltese and Ionians from Istanbul to Tunis spurred authorities back in Britain to act.[52]

In 1843, Parliament introduced a one-page Foreign Jurisdiction Bill.[53] This bill advanced the legal fiction that the Queen's jurisdiction abroad should be exercised "as if Her Majesty had acquired such power or jurisdiction by the cession or conquest of territory."[54] The bill was an eloquent attestation to the newfound power of territorialism; it reflected the beginning of *extra*-territoriality – the idea that the monarch's sovereignty extended to her subjects abroad much as it encompassed those within her territory. A year later, the British government issued the First Ottoman Order in Council, a brief document specifying that "any act coming under Her Majesty's jurisdiction" in the "dominions of the Sublime Ottoman Porte" would be subject to the laws of "Her Majesty's dominions."[55]

Over the course of the nineteenth century, newer states passed similar regulations concerning how their national laws were to be applied abroad. The United States government passed a law regulating American consular jurisdic-

---

51 W. F. Strangways to Colonial Office, June 7, 1837, BNA, FO/97/407.

52 Pennell, "Foreign Jurisdiction Act," 479–482.

53 Ibid., 482–484.

54 *A Complete Collection of the Treaties and Conventions, and Reciprocal Regulations, at Present Subsisting Between Great Britian and Foreign Powers, and of the Laws, Decrees, and Orders in Council, Concerning the Same*, ed. Lewis Hertslet, vol. 6 (London: Henry Butterworth and James Bigg and Son, 1845), 842. On this, see also Spagnolo, "Portents of Empire"; Julia Stephens, "An Uncertain Inheritance: The Imperial Travels of Legal Migrants, from British India to Ottoman Iraq," *Law and History Review* 32 (2014): 758.

55 Hertslet, *Treaties and Conventions, v. 6*, 844. In 1857, just after Britain rammed through a new treaty with the Sultan of Morocco (one that was far more favorable to British commercial interests), the Foreign Office promulgated an Order in Council for Morocco (*A Complete Collection of the Treaties and Conventions, and Reciprocal Regulations, at Present Subsisting Between Great Britian and Foreign Powers, and of the Laws, Decrees, and Orders in Council, Concerning the Same*, ed. Lewis Hertslet, vol. 10 [London: Butterworths, 1859], 923–948). Although the Order in Council for Morocco did not explicitly require consuls to rule according to British law, it allowed British subjects to bring civil and criminal suits to the British court in Gibraltar (articles 28 and 30, 935–936), which suggests an expectation that British law would apply. Nonetheless, the Order in Council did allow for consuls to "establish rules of practice to be observed in proceedings before him" (article 32, p. 936).

tion in 1848. This act specified that "Jurisdiction in both criminal and civil matters shall, in all cases, be exercised and enforced in conformity with the laws of the United States."[56] Belgium (independent since 1830) passed a law regulating consular jurisdiction in 1851. The law noted that in countries outside of "Christendom," disputes among Europeans in which Belgian subjects were the defendants "should be adjudicated according to Belgian law."[57] Italy passed an extensive "Legge consolare" in November of 1865, hardly six months after it published the first Italian civil code. This law specified that consuls exercising jurisdictional functions should apply the laws of Italy.[58] Germany published a similar law in 1879.[59]

4 Conclusion

In early modern consulates, law stemmed from a combination of "Levantine" and local customs; the territorial law of the country represented by a given consulate was a relatively rare benchmark by which consuls adjudicated. Only in the nineteenth century did consular courts become *extra*-territorial in the sense of applying the laws of the territory they represented. This does not mean that nineteenth-century consular courts consistently and expertly adjudicated according to their national laws. As in the early modern period, the legal disputes of foreigners were very often adjudicated by local (Ottoman or Moroccan) legal institutions – either because this was stipulated in the relevant treaties, or because the individuals involved opted for local law.[60] But starting in the 1830s, government officials began to build the administrative scaffolding on which to hang national law in their consulates; in theory, at least, consular officials became agents of extraterritoriality. The 108 years between 1815 (when the Treaty of Vienna ended the Napoleonic Wars) and 1923 (the signing of the Treaty of Lausanne, which formally ended extraterritorial privileges in Turkey) might be described as the extraterritorial century.

56 Frank E. Hinckley, *American Consular Jurisdiction in the Orient* (Washington D.C.: W. H. Lowdermilk, 1906), 42–63, quote at 43.

57 "Seront jugées conformément aux lois belges," *Moniteur Belge*, 7 January 1852, 58.

58 Anonymous, *Legge consolare, promulgata con reale decreto 28 gennaio 1866* (Milano: Edoardo Sonzogno, 1866), 22–23, 31–32.

59 Pélissié du Rausas, *Capitulations dans l'Empire Ottoman*, 2: 41.

60 See, e.g., van den Boogert, *Capitulations*; Jessica M. Marglin, *Across Legal Lines: Jews and Muslims in Modern Morocco* (New Haven: Yale University Press, 2016), chap. 6.

Bibliography

Ahmad, Feroz. "Ottoman Perceptions of the Capitulations, 1800–1914." *Journal of Islamic Studies* 11 (2000): 1–20.

Anonymous. *Legge Consolare, Promulgata Con Reale Decreto 28 Gennaio 1866*. Milan: Dell'editore Edoardo Sonzogno, 1866.

Bartolomei, Arnaud, and Anne Brogini. "De la réglementation aux pratiques marchandes: l'enregistrement des actes dans les chancelleries consulaires françaises (XVIIe–XIXe siècles)." In *De l'utilité commerciale des consuls: L'institution consulaire et les marchands dans le monde méditerranéen (XVIIe–XXe siècle)*, edited by Arnaud Bartolomei, Guillaume Calafat, Matthieu Grenet and Jörg Ulbert, 173–198. Rome: École française de Rome, 2017.

Benton, Lauren. *A Search for Sovereignty: Law and Geography in European Empires, 1400–1900*. Cambridge: Cambridge University Press, 2010.

Benton, Lauren, Adam Clulow, and Bain Attwood, eds. *Protection and Empire: A Global History*. Cambridge: Cambridge University Press, 2018.

Benton, Lauren, and Lisa Ford. *Rage for Order: The British Empire and the Origins of International Law, 1800–1850*. Cambridge, MA: Harvard University Press, 2016.

Boulanger, Patrick. "Les appointements des consuls de France à Alger au XVIIIe siècle." In *La fonction consulaire à l'époque moderne: L'affirmation d'une institution économique et politique (1500–1700)*, edited by Jörg Ulbert and Gérard Le Bouëdec, 123–145. Rennes : Presses universitaires de Rennes, 2006.

Calafat, Guillaume. "La juridiction des consuls français en Méditerranée: litiges marchands, arbitrages et circulations des procès (Livourne et Tunis au XVIIe siècle)." In *De l'utilité commerciale des consuls: L'institution consulaire et les marchands dans le monde méditerranéen (XVIIe–XXe siècle)*, edited by Arnaud Bartolomei, Guillaume Calafat, Matthieu Grenet and Jörg Ulbert, 155–172. Rome: École française de Rome, 2017.

Calafat, Guillaume. "Les juridictions du consul: une institution au service des marchands et du commerce ? Introduction." In *De l'utilité commerciale des consuls. L'institution consulaire et les marchands dans le monde méditerranéen (XVIIe–XXe siècle)*, edited by Arnaud Bartolomei, Guillaume Calafat, Mathieu Grenet et Jörg Ulbert, 143–153. Rome: École française de Rome, 2017.

Casey, Christopher. *Nationals Abroad: Globalization, Individual Rights, and the Making of Modern International Law*. Cambridge: Cambridge University Press, 2020.

Clancy-Smith, Julia. *Mediterraneans: North Africa and Europe in an Age of Migration, C. 1800–1900*. Berkeley: University of California Press, 2011.

Clercq, Alexandre de, and Charles de Vallat. *Guide pratique des consulats*. Paris: Guillaumin et Cie, 1851.

Davis, Ralph. *Aleppo and Devonshire Square: English Traders in the Levant in the Eighteenth Century*. London: Macmillan, 1967.

De Groot, Alexander H. "The Historical Development of the Capitulatory Regime in the Ottoman Middle East from the Fifteenth to the Nineteenth Centuries." *Oriente Moderno* 83, n° 3 (2003): 575–604.

Debbasch, Yvan. *La nation française en Tunisie (1577–1835)*. Paris: Sirey, 1957.

Dislère, Paul, and R. De Mouy. *Droits et devoirs des Français dans les pays d'Orient et d'extrême-Orient*. Paris: Paul Dupont, 1893.

Eldem, Edhem. "Capitulations and Western Trade." In *The Cambridge History of Turkey*, edited by Suraiya Faroqhi, 281–335. Cambridge: Cambridge University Press, 2006.

Ford, Richard T. "Law's Territory (a History of Jurisdiction)." *Michigan Law Review* 97, n° 4 (1999): 843–930.

Grenet, Mathieu. "Recrutement et service dans les petits consulats français de Méditerranée Orientale aux XVIIe et XVIIIe siècles." *Cahiers de la Mediterranée* 103 (2021): 213–237.

Guéna, Pauline, Ian F. Hathaway, Güneş Işiksel, Ana Sekulic, and Tommaso Stefini. "The 'Ahdnâme 'Revisited': Some New Approaches and Perspectives on a Much-Discussed Ottoman Institution." *Turcica* 53 (2023): 1–9.

Hanley, Will. *Identifying with Nationality: Europeans, Ottomans, and Egyptians in Alexandria*. New York: Columbia University Press, 2017.

Hargal, Salma. "De la sujétion fraçaise à la nationalité ottomane: Le statut des Algériens à l'époque d'Abdulhamid II (1876–1908)." *Turcica* 55 (2024), 163–201.

Havard, Gilles. "'Les forcer à devenir cytoyens': État, sauvages et citoyenneté en Nouvelle-France (XVIIe–XVIIIe siècle)." *Annales. Histoire, Sciences Sociales* 64, n° 5 (2009): 985–1018.

Hertslet, Lewis, ed. *A Complete Collection of the Treaties and Conventions, and Reciprocal Regulations, at Present Subsisting between Great Britian and Foreign Powers, and of the Laws, Decrees, and Orders in Council, Concerning the Same*. London: Henry Butterworth and James Bigg and Son, 1845–1859.

Hilaire, Jean. *Introduction historique au droit commercial*. Paris: Presses universitaires de France, 1986.

Hinckley, Frank E. *American Consular Jurisdiction in the Orient*. Washington, DC: W. H. Lowdermilk, 1906.

Ibn Manṣūr, ʿAbd al-Wahhāb. *Mushkilat al-Ḥimāya al-Qunṣuliyya bi-l-Maghrib*. Rabat: al-Maṭbaʿa al-mālikīya, 1985.

Isambert, Decrusy, and Taillandier, eds. *Recueil général des anciennes lois françaises, depuis l'an 420 jusqu'à la Révolution de 1789: Janvier 1672 – Mai 1686*. Paris: Belin-Leprieur, 1829.

Jerad, Mehdi. "Enjeux marchands et intérêts de pouvoir autour de la juridiction contentieuse des consuls de France à Tunis (1827–1836)." In *De l'utilité commerciale des consuls: L'institution consulaire et les marchands dans le monde méditerranéen* (*XVII*e*–XX*e *siècle*), edited by Arnaud Bartolomei, Guillaume Calafat, Matthieu Grenet and Jörg Ulbert, 223–240. Rome: École française de Rome, 2017.

Kayaoğlu, Turan. *Legal Imperialism: Sovereignty and Extraterritoriality in Japan, the Ottoman Empire, and China*. Cambridge: Cambridge University Press, 2010.

Kenbib, Mohammed. *Les protégés: Contribution à l'histoire contemporaine du Maroc*. Rabat: Faculté des lettres et des sciences humaines, 1996.

Koskenniemi, Martti. "Introduction: International Law and Empire – Aspects and Approaches." In *International Law and Empire: Historical Explorations*, edited by Martti Koskenniemi, Walter Rech and Manuel Jiménez Fonseca, 1–18. Oxford: Oxford University Press, 2017.

Lafon, Jacques. "La protection des Lieux Saints: Un conflit franco-espagnol (1868)." In *Itinéraires de l'histoire du droit à la diplomatie culturelle et à l'histoire coloniale*, edited by Jacques Lafon, 45–62. Paris: Éditions de la Sorbonne, 2021.

Lafon, Jacques. "Les Capitulations Ottomanes: Un Droit Paracolonial ?" *Droits: Revue française de théorie, de philosophie et de culture juridiques* 28 (1999): 155–180.

Maier, Charles. "Consigning the Twentieth Century to History: Alternative Narratives for the Modern Era." *American Historical Review* 105, n° 3 (2000): 807–831.

Marglin, Jessica M. *Across Legal Lines: Jews and Muslims in Modern Morocco*. New Haven: Yale University Press, 2016.

Marglin, Jessica M. "The Crémieux Decree Seen from Afar." *The Journal of North African Studies* 28, n° 3 (2023): 540–562.

Martens, Charles de. *Guide diplomatique*. Leipzig: F. A. Brockhaus, 1832.

Martens, Georg Friedrich de. *Précis du droit des gens moderne de l'Europe fondé sur les traités et l'usage*. Göttingen: Jean Chret. Dieterich, 1789.

Martens, Georg Friedrich von. *Summary of the Law of Nations, Founded on the Treaties and Customs of the Modern Nations of Europe: With a List of the Principal Treaties, Concluded since the Year 1748 down to the Present Time, Indicating the Works in Which They Are to Be Found*. Philadelphia: Thomas Bradford, 1795.

McDougall, James. "A World No Longer Shared: Losing the *Droit De Cité* in Nineteenth Century Algiers." *Journal of the Economic and Social History of the Orient* 60, n° 1–2 (2017): 18–49.

Mézin, Anne. *Les consuls de France au Siècle des Lumières (1715–1792)*. Paris: Ministère des Affaires étrangéres, 1998.

Miles, Kate. "'Uneven Empires': Extraterritoriality and the Early Trading Companies." In *The Extraterritoriality of Law: History, Theory, Politics*, edited by Daniel S. Margolies, Umut Özsu, Maïa Pal and Ntina Tzouvala, 87–103. London: Routledge, 2019.

Nye, Ellen. "'A Bank of Trust': Legal Practices of Ottoman Finance between Empires." *Journal of Early Modern History* (27, n 6 (2023): 502-25.

Osterhammel, Jürgen. *The Transformation of the World: A Global History of the Nineteenth Century*. Translated by Patrick Camiller. Princeton, NJ: Princeton University Press, 2014.

Pélissié du Rausas, Gérard. *Le régime des capitulations dans l'Empire Ottoman*. Paris: Arthur Rousseau, 1902–1905.

Pennell, C. R. "The Origins of the Foreign Jurisdiction Act and the Extension of British Sovereignty." *Historical Research* 83 (2010): 465–485.

Perl-Rosenthal, Nathan. *Citizen Sailors: Becoming American in the Age of Revolution*. Cambridge, MA: Harvard University Press, 2015.

Podio, Lagét de. *De la juridiction des consuls de France à l'égard de l'étranger et des devoirs et obligations qu'ont à remplir ces fonctionnaires*. Marseille: Chez l'auteur, 1844.

Podio, Lagét de. *De la juridiction des consuls de France à l'égard de l'étranger et des devoirs et obligations qu'ont à remplir ces fonctionnaires*. Paris: C. J. Trouvé, 1826.

Poumarède, Géraud. "Naissance d'une institution royale: Les consuls de la nation française en Levant et en Barbarie aux XVIe et XVIIe siècles." *Annuaire-Bulletin de la société de l'histoire de France* (2001): 65–128.

Sonyel, Salahi R. "The Protégé System in the Ottoman Empire." *Journal of Islamic Studies* 2, n° 1 (1991): 56–66.

Spagnolo, John P. "Portents of Empire in Britain's Ottoman Extraterritorial Jurisdiction." *Middle Eastern Studies* 27, n° 2 (1991): 256–282.

Stein, Sarah Abrevaya. *Extraterritorial Dreams: Jews, Citizenship, and the Calamitous Twentieth Century*. Chicago: The University of Chicago Press, 2016.

Stephens, Julia. "An Uncertain Inheritance: The Imperial Travels of Legal Migrants, from British India to Ottoman Iraq." *Law and History Review* 32 (2014): 749–772.

Tait Slys, Mariya. *Exporting Legality: The Rise and Fall of Extraterritorial Jurisdiction in the Ottoman Empire and China*. Geneva: Graduate Institute Publications, 2014.

Testa, Ignaz de. *Recueil des traités de la Porte Ottomane avec les puissances étrangères*. Paris: Amyot, 1864.

Todd, David. "Beneath Sovereignty: Extraterritoriality and Imperial Internationalism in Nineteenth-Century Egypt." *Law and History Review* 36, n° 1 (2018): 105–137.

Ulbert, Jörg. "Identifier pour contrôler. La monarchie française et l'identification de ses ressortissants expatriés (XVIIe–XVIIIe siècle, Empire ottoman – Espagne)." *Mélanges de la Casa de Velázquez* 51, n° 1 (2021): 39–71.

Ulbert, Jörg. "Introduction. La fonction consulaire à l'époque moderne: définition, état des connaissances et perspectives de recherche." In *La fonction consulaire à l'époque moderne: L'affirmation d'une institution économique et politique (1500–1800)*, edited by Jörg Ulbert and Gérard Le Bouëdec, 9–20. Rennes : Presses universitaires de Rennes, 2006.

Van den Boogert, Maurits H. *The Capitulations and the Ottoman Legal System: Qadis, Consuls, and Beratlıs in the 18th Century*. Leiden: Brill, 2005.

Vanneste, Tijl. *Intra-European Litigation in Eighteenth-Century Izmir: The Role of the Merchants' Style*. Leiden: Brill, 2021.

Vlami, Despina. *Trading with the Ottomans: The Levant Company in the Middle East*. London: I. B. Tauris, 2015.

Wansbrough, J., H. Inalcik, A. K. S. Lambton, and G. Baer. "Imtiyāzāt." In *Encyclopedia of Islam Two*, edited by P. Bearman, T. Bianquis, C. E. Bosworth, E. van Donzel and W. P. Heinrichs, v. 3, 1178–1189. Leiden: Brill, 2003.

Windler, Christian. "Towards the Empire of a 'Civilizing Nation': the French Revolution and Its Impact on Relations with the Ottoman Regencies in the Maghreb." In *International Law and Empire: Historical Explorations*, edited by Martti Koskenniemi, Walter Rech and Manuel Jiménez Fonseca, 201–244. Oxford: Oxford University Press, 2017.

Zarinebaf, Fariba. *Mediterranean Encounters: Trade and Pluralism in Early Modern Galata*. Berkeley, CA: University of California Press, 2018.

PART 3

Asia and Africa

15

Trade, Law, and Empire

The French Canton Consulate, 1776–1786

Juliette Françoise

1 Introduction

The history of the Western consular jurisdiction in China usually starts in the second half of the nineteenth century and covers the forced opening of treaty ports following the Opium Wars (1839–1842 and 1856–1860) for the commercial interests of the free trade proponents of Western powers.[1] However, the history of Western presence in China started a century and a half earlier with Europeans' rising ambition to develop direct maritime trade with China. At that time, the institutional conditions were rather different. In the eighteenth century, Sino-European encounters and commercial exchanges were, indeed, embedded in the Canton system and the East India companies' monopoly in Asia. Strangely enough, in the second half of the eighteenth century, the French Crown maintained, for a brief period of ten years, a consul in Canton which officially held exclusive jurisdictional and judicial authority over the local French mercantile community.[2] This early mark of European extraterritoriality in China nudges us to rethink what extraterritoriality really meant in terms of jurisdictional and judicial practices and trans-imperial interactions.[3] By studying the administrative, diplomatic, and judicial records of the first French consulate at Canton which provide a state-centered and Eurocentric perspective, this micro case study historicizes and re-situates politics of trade and institutional change in relation to China's trade and early modern Euro-

1 On Western consular jurisdiction in China in the nineteenth century, see Pär Kristoffer Cassel, *Grounds of Judgment: Extraterritoriality and Imperial Power in Nineteenth-Century China and Japan* (Oxford: Oxford University Press, 2012). For a subtle analysis of the origins of U.S. legal imperialism in China, see Teemu Ruskola, "Canton Is Not Boston: The Invention of American Imperial Sovereignty," *American Quarterly* 57, n° 3 (2005): 859–884.

2 See also Henri Cordier, "Le Consulat de France à Canton au XVIIIe Siècle," *T'oung Pao* 9, n° 1 (1908): 47–96.

3 For a discussion on the concept of extraterritoriality in the early modern period, see Maïa Pal, *Jurisdictional Accumulation: An Early Modern History of Law, Empires, and Capital* (Cambridge: Cambridge University Press, 2020), 25–47.

 | HTTPS://DOI.ORG/10.1163/9789004755192-017

pean overseas empires' formation.[4] In particular, I look at the process of establishment of the Canton consulate to demonstrate that the French Crown's imperial strategy aimed to ensure the good conduct of the nation's China trade since it was a key stake in inter-European imperial competition. In that sense, the French diplomatic agenda did not revolve much around China but rather the other European powers. Further, the Canton consulate case illustrates how trade and law were two intertwined components of early modern European overseas empires' formation. Legal history, the global history of commodity trade flows, and the history of early modern European empires enable us to situate this micro-analysis of a short-lived institution located in a specific site into bigger historiographical questions about trans-imperial encounters and global empires' formation in the early modern period.[5] This historical inquiry starts with two simple questions: Why did the French Crown establish a consulate in Canton in the late eighteenth century and how did this jurisdictional court operate in practice? The answers, I argue, lay at the crossroads of long-distance trade, law, and empire.

The suspension of the French East India Company's monopoly in 1769 induced not only a new regime of private trade, as all French nationals were allowed to engage in commercial ventures in Asia, but also a new form of administration in the former Company's settlements, trading posts and factories. In Canton, where the former Company maintained a factory, a consulate was created in 1776. As Maia Pal states, "Consular representation belonged to port cities or places of importance for trade."[6] Indeed, the French Crown's imperial geography depicted Canton as a localized site of strategic importance because of its global trading connections. More precisely, Canton was a place to be and to be seen as all the other European trading nations were on-site. In the regime of "private" or "open" or "free" trade, the State's protection of the nation's China trade meant first maintaining direct maritime trade liaisons not only between China and French metropolitan ports but at the scale of the empire. The Crown also looked to control the French mercantile community

4 The First French Canton consulate records are part of the series COL C1/11–16, Correspondance à l'arrivée d'Extrême Orient, Premier empire colonial, Fonds ministériels, Archives nationales d'outre-mer, Aix-en-Provence (hereafter cited as COL C1/ ANOM). Some documents are also kept in series 8MD/16–19, Mémoires et documents, Asie, Centre des archives diplomatiques de La Courneuve, Paris (hereafter cited as 8MD/ CADLC).

5 On early modern global empires' formation and law, see Lauren Benton, *A Search for Sovereignty: Law and Geography in European Empires, 1400–1900* (Cambridge: Cambridge University Press, 2009).

6 Pal, *Jurisdictional Accumulation*, 198.

in Canton. Thus, the consulate appeared as a key institutional apparatus as it conveyed far-reaching jurisdictional, judicial, and police authority over French subjects. To understand this, the Canton consulate has to be re-situated within the nation-specific history of the French consular service. The distinctive feature of the consulate, in comparison to the previous forms of administration the Canton factory experienced, was precisely its judicial functions. During its ten years of existence, this court operated only as a commercial court, offering an arbitration platform for inter-French commercial disputes arising not only in Canton but at the scale of the French empire. The Canton consulate was thus a piece of the French imperial legal order in formation as legal cases connected it to other French jurisdictions.[7] This network of legal entrepôts provided not only legal services to French subjects abroad but also the enforcement of legal guarantees attached to commercial contracts. However, as we will see, the Canton consul rather failed to do so in its judicial practice. Indeed, the consulate appears as a pretty weak institution because it lacked the means to effectively enforce law and police, especially in the context of the American War of Independence (1776–1783) which disrupted maritime liaisons. The legal and spatial ambiguities of the Canton consulate's jurisdiction also undermined the consul's powers in front of the Chinese and Portuguese authorities. By depicting this micro case study as a matter of intra-empire legal ordering and inter-European competition for long-distance commodity trade, I illustrate how trade and law operated in the overseas peripheries of empires.

2 Re-situate: The Global Trading Hub of Canton

In an internal memorandum written in 1785, the French Secretary of State of the Navy and the Colonies observed about Canton that "the city is the *rendez-vous* of all trading nations."[8] The removal of the imperial restriction on maritime trade by the Qing government a century earlier boosted European trading incursions in Southern China ports, the most-favored being Canton, a place of a long tradition of maritime trading activities.[9] The first French vessel,

7 On the concept of "legal entrepôts," see Laurie M. Wood, *Archipelago of Justice: Law in France's Early Modern Empire* (New Haven, CT: Yale University Press, 2020), 3–8.

8 Internal memorandum on Canton, 11 August 1785, fol. 174, 8MD/18, CADLC.

9 Louis Dermigny, *La Chine et l'Occident: le commerce à Canton au XVIIIe siècle, 1719–1833*, 3 vols. (Paris: SEVPEN, 1964); John L. Cranmer-Byng and John E. Wills Jr., "Trade and Diplomacy with Maritime Europe, 1644–c. 1800," in *China and Maritime Europe*, 1500–1800, ed. John E. Wills Jr. (Cambridge: Cambridge University Press, 2011), 183–254.

the *Amphitrite*, reached Canton in 1698.[10] By the late eighteenth century, Canton had become a global trading hub, where European East India companies and private traders came to exchange luxury Chinese goods demanded on their domestic markets like porcelain, silk, picture painters, drugs, and tea against European woolen textiles, North American furs, Asian spices and opium, and, mostly, Spanish American silver coins.[11] This import and export channel which connected Inland China's production centers and markets to global long-distance commodity trade networks, benefited from a strategic location in the Pearl River Delta upstream of Portuguese Macao.

The exclusive position Canton acquired during the eighteenth century as the only official maritime entry port in China resulted from the Qing government's politics to regulate maritime trade, ensure taxes and customs collection, and confine foreigners' presence to the maritime coastal border of China.[12] The unique arrangement they designed, known as the Canton trade and customs system, first relied on the semi-monopoly of the *hong* merchants who were specially licensed by the imperial court merchants to collect taxes and customs, negotiate commercial contracts with European merchants, and act as their guarantors. As a spatial arrangement, the Canton system deployed itself over the Canton-Macao environment. In 1757, the Qing court decided to confine all foreign trade to Canton and constructed a highly restricted contact zone to control the mobility of men and goods.[13] The transshipment of import and export goods was spatially organized so ships with some saleable cargo entering the Pearl River Delta had to anchor downriver at Whampoa Island and only captains and officers were allowed to go to Canton to monitor the movement of cargo and to negotiate commercial deals with Chinese mer-

---

10 For an exhaustive study of the Sino-French trade, see Susan E. Schopp, *Sino-French Trade at Canton, 1698–1842* (Hong Kong: Hong Kong University, 2020).

11 Maxine Berg et al., eds., *Goods from the East, 1600–1800. Trading Eurasia* (London: Palgrave Macmillan, 2015); Maxine Berg, "Sea Otters and Iron: A Global Microhistory of Value and Exchange at Nootka Sound, 1774–1792," *Past & Present* 242, Supplement n ° 14 (November 2019): 50–82; Manuel Perez-Garcia and Lei Jin, "The Economic 'Micro-Cosmos' of Canton as a Global Entrepôt: Overseas Trade, Consumption and the Canton System from the Kangxi to Qianlong Eras (1683–1795)," *Atlantic Studies* 19, n° 3 (2022): 384–403. Concerning global silver flows, see Dennis O. Flynn and Arturo Giráldez. "Born with a 'Silver Spoon': The Origin of World Trade in 1571," *Journal of World History* 6, n° 2 (1995): 201–221.

12 On the Canton system, see Paul A. van Dyke, *The Canton Trade: Life and Enterprise on the China Coast, 1700–1845* (Hong Kong: Hong Kong University Press, 2005).

13 For an analysis of the Canton system as a contact zone see John M. Carroll, "The Canton System: Conflict And Accommodation in the Contact Zone," *Journal of the Royal Asiatic Society Hong Kong Branch* 50 (2010): 51–66.

chants.[14] In the city port of Canton, during the trading season, foreign presence was spatially restricted to specific quarters outside the city wall and access to the city and the interior of the country was strictly forbidden. European nations rented factories, also called *hang,* to *hong* merchants which served as nations' house for residence and storage.[15] At the end of the trading season, after the departure of the vessels, foreigners were forbidden to stay in the factories and had to leave for Portuguese Macao to "winter." The Portuguese indeed enjoyed a permanent lease on the island, granted by the Ming dynasty against an annual rent in 1557.[16] The Canto-Macao environment, as a coherent maritime space, thus encompassed Chinese and Portuguese jurisdictional spaces. This ambiguous overlapping jurisdictional organization created some loopholes that the French Crown, as we will see, exploited to advance its imperial strategy.

In this global entrepôt at the fringes of the Chinese Empire, European nations were only tolerated for half a year, a concrete annual reminder of their precarious position in China. The Chinese government's strict policies which circumvented their economic activities and social life in Canton, accompanied by widespread corruption and extraction practices from the authorities, generated a shared sense of insecurity among Europeans.[17] They did not enjoy trading privileges or legal immunity in China as they did in the Ottoman Empire for instance. Yet, if foreigners were subjected to Chinese jurisdiction, in practice, they enjoyed some informal extraterritoriality.[18] Canton's local authorities, the Viceroy of the Guangdong province, the Governor of Canton, and the maritime customs superintendent, indeed expected foreign communities to resolve disputes among themselves and discipline and punish their nationals. They usually acknowledged the representative of each trading community and the authority he held over its compatriots, "but not as consuls or ambassadors with legal immunity and acting on behalf of an equal sovereign state or government with a formal diplomatic relationship with China."[19] The French were well aware of the European nations' legally ambiguous status in

14 Perez-Garcia and Jin, "The Economic 'Micro-Cosmos'," 384–403.

15 On life in the foreign quarters of Canton in the eighteenth century, see the Swedish case studied by Lisa Hellman, *This House Is Not a Home: European Everyday Life in Canton and Macao 1730–1830* (Leiden: Brill, 2019).

16 G. B. Souza, *The Survival of Empire: Portuguese Trade and Society in China and the South China Sea 1630–1754* (Cambridge: Cambridge University Press, 1986), 194–212.

17 Li Chen, *Chinese Law in Imperial Eyes: Sovereignty, Justice, and Transcultural Politics* (New York: Columbia University Press, 2016), 17–20.

18 Carroll, "The Canton System," 51–66.

19 Li Chen, *Chinese Law in Imperial Eyes,* 19.

China, where they were permitted to trade "rather as a favor than for the sake of any real right, they [the European nations] have no permission from the government which would ensure their residency and their rights, they are only seen as strangers that the law tolerates."[20] Indeed, the Chinese traditional international order functioned on different conceptions of how foreign trade and diplomacy related to one another than the European law of nations. In the Sinocentric tribute system, foreign trade was officially only taking place alongside tributary missions and embassies or as frontier trade, in specific frontier sites and for key commodities.[21] It is debated how European maritime trade fit into this framework.[22] Indeed, some European nations conducted successful embassies to the Qing court during the sixteenth and seventeenth centuries, like the Portuguese and the Dutch, while the 1793 British embassy led by Lord Macartney famously failed to obtain formal diplomatic recognition and other legal and economic privileges.[23] The French never really sought official diplomatic contact. According to John Wills, "From the 1680s on, European trade in Chinese ports was tacitly disassociated from the rules for tribute embassies."[24] For Takeshi Hamashita, European maritime trade was "mutual trade" as it took place at Chinese borders and involved Chinese merchants licensed by the Imperial court.[25] What it is to take is that Sino-European encounters in Canton had no formal diplomatic component therefore no recognition was to be sought. The informal practice of extraterritoriality did not mean that foreigners were not submitted to Chinese law, nor did it undermine Chinese sovereignty. Europeans' responses to the Canton system and their legally ambiguous status varied depending on each nation's balance of power not only against China but also against the other European powers on-site. Europeans globally demonstrated compliance to keep trade running and adapted their tactics to

20 Letter from the Royal Council at Canton to the Navy Secretary of State, 31 December 1772, fol. 42, COL C1/12, ANOM.

21 On the Tribute system, see Takeshi Hamashita, "The Tribute Trade System and Modern Asia," trans. Neil Burton and Christian Daniels, in *China, East Asia and the Global Economy: Regional and Historical Perspectives*, eds. Mark Selden and Linda Grove (London: Routledge, 2008), 12–26; Shangsheng Chen, "The Chinese Tributary System and Traditional International Order in East Asia During the Ming and Qing Dynasties from the Sixteenth to Nineteenth Century," *Journal of Chinese Humanities* 5, n° 2 (2020): 171–199.

22 For the traditional approach, see J. K. Fairbank, "Tributary Trade and China's Relations with the West," *The Far Eastern Quarterly* 1, n° 2 (1942): 129–149.

23 Cranmer-Byng and Wills Jr., "Trade and Diplomacy," 183–254; James L. Hevia, *Cherishing Men from Afar: Qing Guest Ritual and the Macartney Embassy of 1793* (Durham: Duke University Press, 1995).

24 Cranmer-Byng and Wills Jr., "Trade and Diplomacy," 252.

25 Hamashita, "The Tribute Trade System and Modern Asia," 12–26.

the changing environment of the Canton trade. The French case is particularly appealing as France adopted rather radically different tactics than the British, avoiding clashes with the Chinese authorities and exploiting all the leeway it could to protect the nation's China trade.

3 A Change in the French Politics of Trade in Asia

In 1769, in the aftermath of the Seven Years War (1756–1763), the overindebted French East India Company was suspended and its trade monopoly with Asia was suppressed. This sub-sovereign corporate body of the French Crown enjoyed both sovereign prerogatives and trading rights in Asian territories where French subjects were established.[26] This decision which was first a matter of domestic politics affected French positions in Asia on two main levels. First, it introduced a new regime of trade as all French subjects were now allowed to participate in commercial ventures in Asia. This *parenthèse* of "free" or "open" or "private" trade, until the reinstatement of the Company's monopoly in 1785, witnessed the rise of private shipping and a reorganization of French global trading networks.[27] Merchants and shipowners from the Atlantic ports, already engaged in the Atlantic colonial trade, expanded their networks in the Indian Ocean, just like those involved in the Levantine trade from Marseille. At the same time, the French Mascarene Islands, located at the entrance of the Indian Ocean, repositioned themselves as a French maritime entrepôt and port of call along the *route des Indes* while their merchants and shipowners expanded their participation in country trade. These merchant communities were the ones taking advantage of the opening of the nations' China trade. However, during the decade of existence of the French consulate, French private trade faced economic difficulties notably related to France's involvement in the American War of Independence from 1778 onward, which disrupted maritime liaisons.

The new politics of trade in Asia also induced new regimes of administration in the former Company's settlements, trading posts, and factories as they came under the direct rule of the State. In Canton, the French Crown had to rethink and redesign the institutional conditions of the nation's China trade. Following the suspension of the French East India Company, the Company's

26 Philippe Haudrère, *La compagnie française des Indes au XVIIIème siècle (1719–1795)* (Paris: Librairie de l'Inde, 1989); Philip J. Stern, *The Company-State: Corporate Sovereignty and the Early Modern Foundations of the British Empire in India* (Oxford: Oxford University Press, 2011).

27 Dermigny, *La Chine et l'Occident,* vol. 2, 857.

Council at Canton was erected as a Royal Council by the King in 1771.[28] Indeed, while recognizing that "the functions of this comptoir have little to do with trade,"[29] the Navy Secretary of State acknowledged that the nation needed some sort of official representative to "present the nation, oversee the police, and promote French nationals to the Chinese government."[30] However, this arrangement appeared rather precarious and unsatisfactory: personal rivalries among the council's members who were former Company agents now acting as private commission agents and supercargoes for French merchants and shipowners, and abuses of authority threatened not only the conduct of the shipping operations but also the credit of the French nation in Canton.[31]

In 1776, the Navy Secretary of State suggested giving a new "utility" to the Canton factory if another form of administration was to be established, that is "to render justice to French subjects."[32] According to him, it would allow to "give trade the protection that it needs."[33] His draft memorandum summarized the guiding principle of the French imperial strategy in Canton. For the Crown, the nation's China trade was a stake in inter-European imperial competition. As commerce and the State's interests were not bound together as under the Company monopoly, the protection of the nation's trade was now resolving around ensuring the good conduct of French private trading ventures in China.[34] The Crown needed an official agent to ensure public order among the French mercantile community in Canton to mitigate any disruption that could alter the state of affairs. Furthermore, French subjects would need expertise in the conduct of affairs in Canton as well as some protection from both the Chinese authorities and the other European nations. Hence, the first and only ever officially appointed consul, Pierre-Charles-François Vauquelin was a former supercargo who worked twenty-four years for the French East India Company and made several voyages to China.[35] When he died in 1782, he was automatically replaced by the consulate's chancellor, Philippe Vieillard, who acted as vice-consul until the suppression of the consulate in 1786.

28 Schopp, *Sino-French Trade at Canton*, 101–104.

29 Deliberation of the Royal Council at Canton, 4 March 1771, fol. 109–110, COL C1/11, ANOM.

30 Letter from the Navy Secretary of State to the Royal Council at Canton, 6 December 1771, fol. 10, COL C1/12, ANOM.

31 Schopp, *Sino-French Trade at Canton*, 101–104.

32 Draft memorandum, fol. 30, COL C1/12, ANOM.

33 Ibid.

34 On imperial languages and regimes of protection, see Lauren Benton, Adam Clulow, and Bain Attwood, eds. *Protection and Empire: A Global History* (Cambridge: Cambridge University Press, 2017).

35 Dermigny, *La Chine et l'Occident*, vol. 2, 867; Schopp, *Sino-French Trade at Canton*, 130–131.

4 A French Legal Entrepôt in China

This new relationship between the Crown and commerce was institutionalized in the form of a consulate. The choice of this European-born institution although seen as deeply strange from Canton, was not anodyne in the French context. In the early modern period, France enjoyed a unique consular network of medieval origin across Europe and the Mediterranean.[36] The consul was originally the representative, judge, and solicitor of a merchants' community from one city established in another city, either elected by the merchants themselves or appointed by the municipal power of their city of origin. The French Crown progressively took control of the consular network established by cities of Southern France in foreign Mediterranean port cities and, by the end of the seventeenth century, consuls were commissioned agents appointed by the Navy Secretary of State.[37] This long-term institutional evolution resulted in the dual nature of the French consulate in the eighteenth century: it was both a royal administrative and a judicial framework that allowed to regulate the nation's trade, provide protection for the King's subjects but also rule over them abroad, and, finally, ensure the nation's interests by carrying out a representative, diplomatic function. In Canton, the consul should therefore be regarded as a person sent by the King. Furthermore, the creation of the Canton consulate participated in the expansion of the French consular network to the East beyond its traditional Mediterranean anchorage into the Indian Ocean in the eighteenth century. A consulate briefly existed in Basra under the jurisdiction of the French East India Company in the 1720s and one opened in Surat in 1774.[38] Canton was considered the last *échelle* (trading post) of the Levant.[39]

The jurisdictional powers of the Canton consul involved adjudicating, policing, and offering notarial services to French nationals residing or passing by Canton such as civil registry, and the production or authentication of legal acts and contracts. The two key textual sources that define the consul's prerogatives and legitimize its authority, describe its judicial functions and how

---

36 Pal, *Jurisdictional Accumulation*, 194–235.

37 Géraud Poumarède, "Naissance d'une institution royale: les consuls de la nation française en Levant et en Barbarie aux XVIe et XVIIe siècles," *Annuaire-Bulletin de La Société de l'histoire de France* (2001): 65–128; Anne Mézin, "La fonction consulaire dans la France d'Ancien Régime: origine, principes, prerogatives," in *La fonction consulaire à l'époque moderne*, eds. Jörg Ulbert and Gérard Le Bouëdec (Rennes: Presses universitaires de Rennes, 2006), 37–49.

38 The archives of the Surat consulate are kept at the Centre des archives diplomatiques de La Courneuve.

39 Draft memorandum, fol. 30, COL C1/12, ANOM.

he should render justice. The ordonnance of 1776 for the establishment of a consul of the French nation at Canton states that the consul's judicial authority involves both civil and criminal matters: "judgments will be provisionally enforced in civil matters by giving security, and definitively and without appeal in criminal matters when no afflictive penalty is involved, all provide that they are rendered in front of two notables of the nation."[40] The King's instructions to the consul of the French nation at Canton clarify the consul's judicial practice. In litigation, he must first seek an amicable agreement between parties, therefore act as an arbitrator, and, otherwise, render "good justice, summarily, and without any fees." Importance is given to the formalities: "Civil and criminal procedures must have the requisite formalities and the evidence of the offence established legally so that higher courts can rule definitively on the trial." Regarding litigation involving "French, people of the country and other countries," if a private amicable agreement cannot be reached, the consul will act as a mediator, encouraging both parties to take arbitrators.[41] Furthermore, French subjects were forbidden to reach out to a local judge for any dispute among them. The consular jurisdiction was, therefore, extraterritoriality not only as the French Crown asserted its authority beyond its territorial realm but also as it assumed a separation from local jurisdiction.[42] However, this

40 Draft of the ordonnance pour l'établissement d'un consul de la nation française à Canton, fol. 31–37, COL C1/12, ANOM.

41 Draft of the Mémoire du roi pour servir d'instructions au sieur Thimothé, consul de la nation française à Canton, fol. 7, COL C1/13, ANOM.

42 Grotius' original idea of extraterritoriality in the case of diplomats included a positive and a negative component, the two sides of the same coin being the application of home law and the prohibition of the application of foreign law. The applicability of the concept of extraterritoriality to refer not to ambassadors but to consuls whose diplomatic status and immunity privileges were rather imprecise in early modern non-European contexts is much debated. In this volume, for example, Jessica Marglin argues that one cannot speak of extraterritoriality as long as the consuls acted as arbitrators. Speaking of extraterritoriality in the case of the French consulate in Canton in the late eighteenth century may seem even more adventurous as there was no official diplomatic contact or recognition such as a treaty between China and France that would grant jurisdictional and immunity privileges to the French representative in China. However, two elements support the idea that the French consul's jurisdiction in Canton contained at least some 'positive' extraterritoriality. On one side, the French Crown insisted that French nationals residing in Canton should only reach out to the consul's court and that intra-French legal affairs should be adjudicated according to French law, thus ideally isolating the French community from other legal systems of reference and authority. On the other side, in practice, despite prescribing the consul's justice to not contravene local laws and customs, French subjects were subjected first and foremost to French law in their daily civil and commercial matters as Chinese law was only enforced in criminal cases involving murder. Rather than counting and adding up all the components required to fit the

exemption was limited. Indeed, in 1779, the Navy Secretary of State, in a letter to the consul, nuanced the almighty power of French law over French subjects in China as he urged the consul, in his judicial practice, not to "contravene the laws and customs of the country you live in."[43] The exercise of the consul's judicial functions should thus demonstrate certain adaptability to the Chinese legal environment. Additionally, the exercise of the consul's judicial functions met, in practice, many obstructions both in criminal and commercial matters from French subjects, the Chinese authorities, and other foreign nations, revealing not only the discrepancy between the textual assertion of judicial authority and its practice but also the weak position of the French consul at Canton.

During its ten years of existence, the consular court did not adjudicate any criminal case despite the described ongoing violent atmosphere in Canton. This absence rather reveals the lack of means and authority of the French consul. Indeed, the one case of insults and threats of physical violence uttered by three French sailors against their captain in 1783, the consul dismissed it to be "perfectly judged in the Isle of France" where the sailors had boarded.[44] In the one murder case involving a French deserter sailor, a Portuguese, and a Chinese, in 1780, the French consul had no voice, as we will see. The consular justice then uniquely operated as a commercial court for settling inter-French commercial disputes. Despite private trade in Asia being historically conducted by international multicultural business partnerships, no mixed cases were brought to the consul.[45] The consular court rather functioned as an inter-French judicial platform that investigated litigation about intra-imperial maritime ventures. Ironically, this key function of the Canton consulate as a commercial court appeared clearly when it was suppressed in 1786. As the Navy Secretary of State summarized it, "The establishment of the new East India Company renders the Canton consulate without object."[46] The consul was replaced by a royal agent and an interpreter, as a way to maintain a state's

---

perfect extraterritoriality theorized by European jurists, this paper examines the historical reality of the slow, loose, and fragmented penetration and operation of foreign (French) law in China in the late eighteenth century. See the dissenting opinion of Jessica Marglin in this volume.

43 Draft of a letter from the Navy Secretary of State to Vauquelin, 12 July 1779, fol. 86, COL C1/13, ANOM.

44 Copy of the consul's sentence against three sailors, 30 November 1783, fol. 20, COL C1/14, ANOM.

45 On Asian trading networks, see François Gipouloux, *La Méditerranée asiatique, villes portuaires et réseaux marchands en Chine, au Japon et en Asie du Sud-Est, XVIe–XXIe siècle* (Paris: CNRS, 2009).

46 Internal memorandum on Canton, 11 August 1785, fol. 174, 8MD/18, CADLC.

representative in Canton but the full apparatus of the consulate was not needed anymore. The consular institution was indeed deeply attached to private trade.

5 An Arbitration Platform for Inter-French Commercial Disputes

The consul's justice offered an arbitration platform to settle commercial disputes arising not only within the French mercantile community in Canton but also between French merchants, shipowners, supercargoes, and captains across the empire. In fact, the Canton consulate mostly functioned as the antichamber of judicial courts in France and in the other overseas settlements.[47] It was a piece of the French imperial legal order in formation as it was connected, through cases, to the Paris judge-consuls, the Marseille Admiralty, the French consul in Cadiz, and the *Conseil supérieur* of the Isle of France (Mauritius).[48] All parties involved sought rapid justice to not contravene the trading operations as a judicial procedure conveyed delays, tensions, and mistrust within the French mercantile community. Time was key also because of the Canton trade's specific temporality. Foreign merchants only had a five to six-month window from July to January for the trading season. By then, vessels left for Pondicherry, the Mascarenes, and Europe with the monsoon and French merchants residing in Canton had to leave for Macao. All affairs, including judicial ones, had to be settled before.

All the kinds of French men having some business in the nation's China trade appear in the Canton consulate's judicial archives: captains, surgeons, supercargoes, commissioners, and consignees. They all came to China seeking a quickly made fortune. They were all doing some private business at the margin of the nation's China trade, mainly investing in the Manilla trade and Southeast Asia maritime ventures. However, the consular archives offer only rare glimpses of these activities as the only two cases brought upon the consular court concerned the nation's China trade. The first case reveals that it was mostly a *commerce de commission.* French supercargoes in Canton were in fact commissioners and, together with the consignees they employed, they received ships sent by metropolitan merchants and shipowners against a commission. Their business in Canton was to store the goods, sell and buy,

47 For the concept of the "anti chamber," see Arnaud Bartolomei, in *this volume*.

48 On the first French empire's global network of legal entrepôts, see Wood, *Archipelago of Justice*.

provide liquidity, and outfit the ship for their return to France.[49] The firm taking most of the commission deals in Canton in the 1770s was the *maison de commerce* Vigny du Timeur and Co. whose two main associates were Charles Henri de Vigny de Gravelles and Pierre André Montigny du Timeur. For the 1776–1779 expedition, they received two ships, the *Duc de Fitz-James* and the *Pondichéry*, chartered by Saint-Malo's shipowners. They employed a group of consignees in Canton as they both had left by that time and acted as forwarding agents from France. In October 1777, a group of four of these consignees, Gilles Dominique René Sebire de Lompré, Yacinte Delourme, Edmond Eugène Tobin, and François Terrien, reached out to the consul to arbitrate on a matter opposing them to another consignee Paul-François Costar.[50] Newly arrived in Canton, he claimed to have been given all powers over the business of the Vigny du Timeur and Co. firm in Canton by Charles Henri de Vigny, therefore destroying all powers of the other consignees. What was at stake was not only the two ships' management but also the share of the commission between the consignees. After a four-day procedure involving four contradictory *procurations* (proxy) and eighteen written evidence, the arbitral sentence of the consular assembly proposed joint management of the cargoes and a split of the commission between all the consignees. Paul-François Costar first rejected the sentence but then came back on his decision yet too late as it had already been recorded in the chancellery. An amicable private agreement was finally reached twelve days later, in order to no longer obstruct the conduct of the trade with more delays and to secure the interests and trust of the shipowners in France. Indeed, as "the nation's China trade was almost entirely in the hands of the men in litigation," the affair generated, according to the consul, "a bad faith destructive of the true spirit of commerce."[51]

The consul faced similar challenges to his authority in a just as tortuous second case involving the consulate's surgeon, Julien Paris, and Honoré Blancard, the captain of the *Dalliram*, a ship chartered in Marseille in 1777 and arrived in Canton in the fall of 1778. Julien Paris reached out to the consul as he held a *procuration* from Louis Boucher, an inhabitant of the Isle of France,

49 Dermigny, *La Chine et l'Occident*, vol. 2, 840–879; Susan E. Schopp, "French Private Trade at Canton, 1698–1833," in *The Private Side of the Canton Trade, 1700–1840. Beyond the Companies*, eds. by Paul A. van Dyke and Susan E. Schopp (Hong Kong: Hong Kong University Press, 2018), 43–63.

50 Procedure of Sebire, Delourme, Terrien, Tobin & Costar, Bourgogne and le Déan, fol. 49–69, COL C1/13, ANOM.

51 Letter from Vauquelin to the Navy Secretary of State, 16 January 1778, fol. 38–42, COL C1/13, ANOM.

himself *procureur* (attorney) of two Parisian merchants, and Pierre Mauchossé François Nogent de Saulgy, the latter being involved in the Mascarene colonial trade.[52] He sought the enforcement of two sentences rendered by the judges-consuls of Paris in 1777 against Bertrand d'Airolles, accused of fraudulent bankruptcy and condemned to pay two protested bills of exchange to the Parisian merchants. Julien Paris claimed that Bertrand d'Airolles – who illegally boarded the *Dalliram* in Cadiz, was seen in the Isle of France where he was known as Maillard, and later disappeared – was the shipowner of the *Dalliram*. Therefore, the two debts should be repaid on his share of the cargo. Honoré Blancard's interrogation complicated the affair as he revealed that Bertrand d'Airolles who had died in Batavia a year before, had indeed illegally boarded the *Dalliram* in Cadiz but to replace Maillard Son, whose father Nicolas Maillard from Nancy was the shipowner. Bertrand d'Airolles was therefore only a supercargo. As Julien Paris refused any conciliation and requested a judgment, the consul conducted a procedure assisted by four judges interrogating eight crew members. The consular sentence, rendered one month and eleven days after Julien Paris' first request, required both parties to deposit a sum of money at the consulate's chancellery as collateral security while seeking a final judgment in Europe. This rather odd and hardly enforceable sentence reveals the lack of clarity the procedure had brought to the affair. Whether Bertrand d'Airolles used a false identity or assumed someone else's identity remained unclear. As pointed out by Julien Paris who rejected the sentence, the consul and judges avoided settling the affair. In this second case, the Canton consulate operated as the anti-chamber of a metropolitan jurisdiction, the Paris judges-consuls. But it rather failed to enforce the legal guarantees attached to commercial contracts and the sentences rendered by this other French court.[53]

During these procedures, the consul's justice faced diverse forms of obstruction from all the parties involved. However, despite the consular justice's lack of means and apparent weaknesses, French law was in action in China, and the consul's dual position as the judge of the nation and the Crown's representative was never refuted.

52 Procedure for the 1778, fol. 99–113, COL C1/13, ANOM.

53 On the legal underpinnings attached to bills of exchange in early modern European international trade, see Veronica Aoki Santarosa, "Financing Long-Distance Trade: The Joint Liability Rule and Bills of Exchange in Eighteenth-Century France," *The Journal of Economic History* 75, n° 3 (2015): 690–719.

6 An Imaginary Jurisdictional Space?

For French merchants and supercargoes who had experience in China, the creation of a consulate in Canton was rather odd. In a country where commercial and legal customs were so different and the law of nations unknown, a consul was "the most useless thing" for the former East India Company's supercargoes Jean-Baptiste Trollier, who refused the consul's position the Navy Secretary of State offered him in 1776.[54] Nevertheless, the creation of the French consulate was not intended to challenge the customary practices of extraterritoriality foreign merchant communities enjoyed in Canton. The French Crown did not even seek the official recognition of the consulate by the local authorities. The King's instructions detail the consul's ritualized process of entry into service during which he claimed his authority and privileges and was recognized by the different parties. Those parties include "all the King's subjects" and "the other European factories' chiefs."[55] Nothing is written regarding the Qing government in Beijing, nor the Viceroy of Guangdong province, or the Canton Governor. The Canton consulate appears, therefore, as a bizarre jurisdiction with no official existence on the Chinese side, that is the supposed host country, and no legal contractual foundations, like a treaty. This void contrasts with the French consulates in European cities and Mediterranean trading posts, which were approved by either the local municipal powers or the sovereign state thanks to diplomatic treaties like the Ottoman capitulations.[56] On the other side, the French Crown provided to the Canton consulate all the legislative and administrative sources of legitimacy as to any other of its overseas consulates, erecting it as a judicial court for French nationals. By doing so, the French Crown simply ignored China's sovereignty. This odd imperial strategy aimed at maintaining the *status quo* and the internal autonomy the French already enjoyed under the Company in order to keep the direct commercial maritime liaison with Canton running to compete with other European maritime powers.

Indeed, the creation of the Canton consulate rather appears as a piece of France's inter-European imperial strategy. This European-born institution was well-known to other European nations as it was part of their shared and familiar repertoire of international laws and institutions.[57] Therefore, the Canton

54 Copy of a letter from Trollier to Michel, 18 March 1776, fol. 11–12, COL C1/13, ANOM.

55 Draft of the Mémoire du roi pour servir d'instruction au sieur Thimothé, consul de la nation française à Canton, fol. 7, COL C1/13, ANOM.

56 Niels Steensgaard, "Consuls and Nations in the Levant from 1570 to 1650," *Scandinavian Economic History Review* 15, n° 1–2 (1967): 13–55.

57 Benton, *A Search for Sovereignty*, 7.

consulate must be re-situated into the European system of international relations and the inter-European powers' imperial game which stretched into their overseas peripheries. The French Crown did, indeed, seek official recognition of the Canton consulate from the other nations residing permanently in China like the British and the Dutch. The consul also acted as the representative and the protector of the King's subjects and the nation's interests. Repeated violent encounters between French and British crews and several British offences to the French flag nurtured strong diplomatic interactions with the English East India Company's Council during the American War of Independence. Despite the French consul himself acknowledging the growing unfavorable balance of power against the British which led him to even lower the French flag down from 1781 onward, neither his position as the representative of the French Crown nor his authority over French subjects was contested by the British.[58]

The situation was different with Portuguese Macao's authorities and highlights the complex spatial jurisdictional entanglement the creation of the French consulate induced. Indeed, the spatial scope of consular jurisdiction as defined by the ordonnance of 1776 was not so transparent but rather geographically imprecise as it stretched out to "Canton and its dependencies like Wampou, Macau, and others."[59] Notwithstanding, Macao was a Portuguese settlement leased by the Chinese authorities in 1557, governed by a municipal council and military commanded by a governor who was the permanent representative of the Viceroy of the *Estado da India.*[60] In establishing the Canton consulate, the French Crown thereby created an extraterritorial jurisdiction encompassing two different, already overlapping, jurisdictional spaces. Once again, what mattered was the conduct of trade. China's trade spread over the Canton-Macao axis in the Pearl River Delta and its spatial and temporal organization tied together the two port cities. Canton without Macao made little sense. The creation of a French consul in Canton and its dependencies not expressly in Macao and without seeking official permission from Macao's local Portuguese authorities as the host country, generated repeated difficulties with them. The French consul was several times threatened to be denied entry into the city of Macao at the end of the trading season by the municipal Council. The Portuguese argued that Goa had strictly instructed them to refuse entry into the city to individuals not affiliated with a trading company.

58 Letter from Vauquelin to the Navy Secretary of State, 8 January 1781, fol. 132, COL C1/13, ANOM.

59 Draft of the Mémoire du roi pour servir d'instruction au sieur Thimothé, consul de la nation française à Canton, fol. 7, COL C1/13, ANOM. On the boundaries and transparency of the scope of imperial jurisdiction, see Benton, *A Search for Sovereignty*, 2–39.

60 Souza, *The Survival of Empire,* 12–29.

The French were considered as such since the French consul had not been granted the King's *lettre de provision* (notification of appointment) for Macao. In these affairs, the French consul reached out to a higher imperial authority, the Viceroy of Goa, and obtained satisfaction and some official, but late and distant, recognition of his position.[61]

The legal and spatial ambiguities of the Canton consulate's jurisdiction disclose themselves in one case of homicide committed a few years before the famous Lady Hughes affair of 1784.[62] In 1780, a French deserter sailor, named Louis, killed a Portuguese man in a Chinese man's house in Canton. The French consul had no voice in the affair. Initially, the French deserter sailor was supposed to be turned over to Macao's municipal Council to be judged, but the Governor of Canton claimed his privileged authority to have the French sailor Louis punished on the Emperor's land. He was condemned to death and executed.[63] In this clash of jurisdictions, due to the gravity of the crime, the failure of Europeans to police their compatriots, and the potential general disruption it could induce in a confined and tense place as Canton, the Chinese authorities reasserted the primacy of Chinese laws on both the Portuguese Macao's jurisdiction and the informal extraterritoriality foreign communities usually enjoyed in Canton.[64] The consul's failure to assume one of his key prerogatives, that is to ensure French subjects' protection, demonstrated that in most important jurisdictional and judicial cases, power, privileges, and rights mattered.

7 Conclusion

In sum, despite the concrete weaknesses of the French consul's position in China which undermined his attempts to exercise his police and judicial functions in mixed cases involving either the Chinese, the British, or the Portuguese, the French Crown did manage to create an imperial jurisdictional space that fitted its ambition in a flagged strategic site. The consular court

61 See the French consul's correspondence with Macao's Governor and with the Viceroy of the *Estado da India* in 1779 (COL C1/13, ANOM) and 1784 (8MD/18, CADLC).

62 Li Chen, "Law, Empire, and Historiography of Modern Sino-Western Relations: A Case Study of the Lady Hughes Controversy in 1784," *Law and History Review* 27, n° 1 (2009): 1–54.

63 Letter from Vauquelin to the Navy Secretary of State, 6 January 1781, fol. 138, COL C1/13, ANOM.

64 For the local Chinese authorities' perspective on the Lady Hughes affair, see the copy of the Canton's Governor public notice, 12 January 1785, fol. 55, COL C1/15, ANOM.

operated as an inter-French arbitration platform that investigated litigation about intra-imperial maritime ventures and, therefore, it was part of the French imperial legal order in formation. Further, under the imperial eyes of European nations, the Canton consulate's jurisdiction was not an imaginary space. The French Crown's imperial strategy targeted not only the nation's internal matters, especially the regulation of the nation's China trade, but also intra-European competition for empire. However, it was not all about rivalries but also collaboration. Indeed, the European empires' mutual recognition of their representatives, agents, institutions, legal norms, procedures, and practices in different geographical and political settings was key to their formation, operation, and expansion overseas. Mutually recognizing each other's overseas jurisdictions was one way to assert imperial sovereignty. The French consulate in Canton was one piece among many emphasizing China's trade's strategic economic interest to European powers in the late eighteenth century.

Acknowledgement

The author thanks Lisa Hellman for her helpful comments on a draft version of this paper.

Bibliography

Benton, Lauren. *A Search for Sovereignty: Law and Geography in European Empires, 1400–1900*. Cambridge: Cambridge University Press, 2009.

Benton, Lauren, Adam Clulow, and Bain Attwood, eds. *Protection and Empire: A Global History*. Cambridge: Cambridge University Press, 2017.

Berg, Maxine, Felicia Gottmann, Hanna Godacs, and Chris Nierstrasz, eds. *Goods from the East, 1600–1800: Trading Eurasia*. London: Palgrave Macmillan, 2015.

Carroll, John M. "The Canton System: Conflict And Accommodation In The Contact Zone." *Journal of the Royal Asiatic Society Hong Kong Branch*. 50 (2010): 51–66.

Cassel, Pär Kristoffer. *Grounds of Judgment: Extraterritoriality and Imperial Power in Nineteenth-Century China and Japan*. Oxford: Oxford University Press, 2012.

Chen, Li. "Law, Empire, and Historiography of Modern Sino-Western Relations: A Case Study of the Lady Hughes Controversy in 1784." *Law and History Review*. 27, n° 1 (2009): 1–54.

Chen, Li. *Chinese Law in Imperial Eyes: Sovereignty, Justice, and Transcultural Politics*. New York: Columbia University Press, 2016.

Chen, Shangsheng. "The Chinese Tributary System and Traditional International Order in East Asia during the Ming and Qing Dynasties from the Sixteenth to Nineteenth Century." *Journal of Chinese Humanities* 5, n° 2 (2020): 171–199.

Cordier, Henri. "Le consulat de France à Canton au XVIIIe siècle." *T'oung Pao* 9, n° 1 (1908): 47–96.

Cranmer-Byng, John L. and John E. Wills Jr. "Trade and Diplomacy with Maritime Europe, 1644–C. 1800." In *China and Maritime Europe, 1500–1800*, edited by John E. Wills Jr., 183–254. Cambridge: Cambridge University Press, 2011.

Dermigny, Louis. *La Chine et l'Occident: le commerce à Canton au XVIIIe siècle, 1719–1833*. Paris: SEVPEN, 1964.

Fairbank, J. K. "Tributary Trade and China's Relations with the West." *The Far Eastern Quarterly* 1, n° 2 (1942): 129–149.

Flynn, Dennis O., and Arturo Giráldez. "Born with a 'Silver Spoon': The Origin of World Trade in 1571." *Journal of World History* 6, n° 2 (1995): 201–221.

Gipouloux, François. *La Méditerranée asiatique, villes portuaires et réseaux marchands en Chine, au Japon et en Asie du Sud-Est, XVIe–XXIe siècle*. Paris: CNRS Éditions, 2009.

Hamashita, Takeshi. "The Tribute Trade System and Modern Asia." Translated by Neil Burton and Christian Daniels. In *China, East Asia and the Global Economy: Regional and Historical Perspectives*, edited by Mark Selden and Linda Grove, 12–26. London: Routledge, 2008.

Haudrère, Philippe. *La compagnie française des Indes au XVIIIème siècle (1719–1795)*. Paris: Librairie de l'Inde, 1989.

Hellman, Lisa. *This House Is not a Home: European Everyday Life in Canton and Macao 1730–1830*. Leiden: Brill, 2019.

Hevia, James L. *Cherishing Men from Afar: Qing Guest Ritual and the Macartney Embassy of 1793*. Durham: Duke University Press, 1995.

Mézin, Anne. "La fonction consulaire dans la France d'Ancien Régime: origine, principes, prerogatives." In *La fonction consulaire à l'époque moderne*, edited by Jörg Ulbert and Gérard Le Bouëdec, 37–49. Rennes: Presses universitaires de Rennes, 2006.

Pal, Maïa. *Jurisdictional Accumulation: An Early Modern History of Law, Empires, and Capital*. Cambridge: Cambridge University Press, 2020.

Perez-Garcia, Manuel, and Lei Jin. "The Economic 'Micro-Cosmos' of Canton as a Global Entrepôt: Overseas Trade, Consumption and the Canton System from the Kangxi to Qianlong Eras (1683–1795)." *Atlantic Studies* 19, n° 3 (2022): 384–403.

Poumarède, Géraud. "Naissance d'une institution royale: les consuls de la nation française en Levant et en Barbarie aux XVIe et XVIIe siècles." *Annuaire-Bulletin de La Société de l'histoire de France* (2001): 65–128.

Ruskola, Teemu. "Canton Is Not Boston: The Invention of American Imperial Sovereignty." *American Quarterly* 57, n° 3 (2005): 859–884.

Santarosa, Veronica Aoki. "Financing Long-Distance Trade: The Joint Liability Rule and Bills of Exchange in Eighteenth-Century France." *The Journal of Economic History* 75, n° 3 (2015): 690–719.

Schopp, Susan E. "French Private Trade at Canton, 1698–1833." In *The Private Side of the Canton Trade, 1700–1840. Beyond the Companies*, edited by Paul A. Van Dyke and Susan E. Schopp, 43–63. Hong Kong: Hong Kong University Press, 2018.

Schopp, Susan E. *Sino-French Trade at Canton, 1698–1842*. Hong Kong: Hong Kong University, 2020.

Souza, G. B. *The Survival of Empire: Portuguese Trade and Society in China and the South China Sea 1630–1754*. Cambridge: Cambridge University Press, 1986.

Steensgaard, Niels. "Consuls and Nations in the Levant from 1570 to 1650." *Scandinavian Economic History Review* 15, n° 1–2 (1967): 13–55.

Stern, Philip J. *The Company-State: Corporate Sovereignty and the Early Modern Foundations of the British Empire in India*. Oxford: Oxford University Press, 2011.

Van Dyke, Paul A. *The Canton Trade: Life and Enterprise on the China Coast, 1700–1845*. Hong Kong: Hong Kong University Press, 2005.

Van Dyke, Paul A. . *Merchants of Canton and Macao: Politics and Strategies in Eighteenth-Century Chinese Trade*. Hong Kong: Hong Kong University Press, 2011.

Wood, Laurie M. *Archipelago of Justice: Law in France's Early Modern Empire*. New Haven, CT: Yale University Press, 2020.

16

Une juridiction consulaire territoriale en Chine ?

Sacha Gauthier Olssy

1 Introduction

Les fonctions attribuées au consul évoluent au fil du temps et diffèrent selon les régions dans lesquelles elles s'exercent[1]. À partir du XIXe siècle, les consuls des nations occidentales officient sur les cinq continents mais leurs prérogatives ne sont pas identiques en tout lieu[2]. Dans les pays dit de Chrétienté, dans les pays européens et en Amérique, les prérogatives juridictionnelles des consuls sont restreintes, la loi territoriale s'applique à tous les résidents, même étrangers. Ailleurs, les consuls possèdent des prérogatives judiciaires plus étendues, au motif qu'il y a une trop grande différence entre le droit occidental et le droit autochtone[3]. En Chine, les pouvoirs juridictionnels du consul sont particulièrement étendus en raison de l'extraterritorialité dont bénéficient les Occidentaux. Ces derniers sont soustraits à la loi territoriale et ne sont justiciables que des tribunaux consulaires pour tout délit ou crime qu'ils commettraient. De plus, dans certaines villes chinoises, comme à Shanghai ou à Tianjin, la juridiction consulaire s'exerce dans les concessions. Ces dernières sont des territoires appartenant à la Chine mais louées à des puissances étrangères et assignées à la résidence des étrangers. La concession de Shanghai est créée en 1848, suivie de celle de Tianjin en 1860, avant d'être toutes deux rétrocédées à la Chine en 1945. L'évolution de la nature de ces concessions donne aux prérogatives juridictionnelles consulaires une singulière évolution.

La « confusion du droit qui s'applique aux territoires concessionnaires a été soulignée par les juristes français et chinois de l'entre-deux-guerres qui s'éton-

---

1 Jörg Ulbert, « Introduction. La fonction consulaire à l'époque moderne : définition, état des connaissances et perspectives de recherche », *La fonction consulaire à l'époque moderne : affirmation d'une institution économique et politique* (1500–1800), éd. Jörg Ulbert et Gérard Le Bouëdec (Rennes : Presses universitaires de Rennes, 2006), 10.

2 Julien Pillaut, *Manuel de droit consulaire (matières spéciales) : affaires maritimes, police sanitaire, intervention des consuls dans l'administration de la justice, pouvoirs de police en pays de juridiction, concessions en Chine, groupement des Français résidents à l'étranger* (Paris : Berger-Levrault, 1912).

3 Marcel Baudez, « La condition juridique des étrangers en Chine » (thèse de doctorat de droit, Université de Paris, 1913).

naient de l'absence de travaux rigoureux et exhaustifs sur cette question[4] », affirme l'historien Pierre Singaravélou. Nous examinerons par conséquent la juridiction consulaire dans la concession française de Tianjin entre 1900 et 1943. Pour ce faire, il faut faire appel à plusieurs types de sources. Tout d'abord nous nous intéresserons à la législation consulaire et au traité de Whampoa afin de dresser le cadre légal de la juridiction consulaire. Le deuxième type de source que nous avons étudié est la littérature juridique théorique. Cette dernière comprend deux corpus : d'une part les thèses de droit contemporaines de la juridiction, et d'autre part le mémorandum présenté par la délégation chinoise à la conférence de paix à Versailles en 1919. Le premier corpus est constitué de thèses de droit écrites par des juristes français ou des juristes chinois ayant fait leurs études de droit en France[5]. Comme notre recherche est initialement circonscrite à la juridiction française dans la concession nationale de Tianjin, nous avons choisi de n'étudier que les productions universitaires composées en français. Le second corpus, quant à lui, est formé du mémorandum présenté par la délégation chinoise à la conférence de la Paix en 1919. Ces deux corpus offrent l'avantage d'être complémentaires car ils présentent deux points de vue différents sur la juridiction consulaire. En effet, ces thèses reflètent la vision des juristes occidentaux ou occidentalisés. Le mémorandum, lui, incarne l'opinion des Chinois. Enfin, le troisième type de sources que nous avons mobilisé est fondé par les enquêtes judiciaires présentes dans les archives du poste consulaire français de Tianjin. Ces textes nous permettent de présenter le caractère illégal que peut revêtir la juridiction consulaire dans les concessions étrangères, la singularité qu'elle constitue, et les difficultés qu'elle cause dans le traitement des affaires.

Dans cette présente contribution nous montrerons, à la faveur d'un évènement particulier, que la pratique de la juridiction consulaire en Chine outrepasse le cadre légal dans lequel elle doit s'exercer. Par la suite, nous nous interrogerons sur les difficultés tant théoriques que pratiques posées par cette singularité juridictionnelle ainsi que sur les problèmes qu'elles posent pour le respect de la souveraineté territoriale de la Chine. Enfin, nous évoquerons la façon dont les sources juridiques contemporaines perçoivent ces difficultés.

---

4 Pierre Singaravélou, « Dix empire dans un mouchoir de poche. Le territoire de Tientsin à l'épreuve du phénomène concessionnaire (années 1860–1920) », *Territoires impériaux : histoire spatiale du fait colonial*, éd. Hélène Blais *et al.* (Paris : Éditions de la Sorbonne, 2012).

5 Outre les cinq références que nous avons consultées, il existe de nombreux autres travaux sur le sujet, voir par exemple : Michael Hansson, « Les tribunaux mixtes en Égypte », *Nordisk Tidsskrift for International Ret* 5, n° 1 (1934) ; Salvatore Messina, « Les tribunaux mixtes et les rapports interjuridictionnels en Égypte », *Recueil des cours de l'Académie de Droit international de La Haye* 41 (1932).

2 La juridiction consulaire dans les concessions, une aberration du point de vue de la doctrine juridique

Afin de mieux comprendre la nature et les principes de la juridiction consulaire, le manuel de droit consulaire, publié par Julien Pillaut en 1912, est primordial[6]. Ce manuel est spécialisé dans l'intervention des consuls dans l'administration de la justice et confère l'avantage d'être contemporain des faits que nous étudions. Louis Renault, professeur de droit à Paris et jurisconsulte du ministre des Affaires étrangères, remarque dans sa préface que les consuls quoiqu'ils

> soient investis par leur nomination de toute l'autorité que les ordonnances ont attaché à cette charge, cependant, comme ils ont à la remplir sur un territoire étranger, et en vertu d'un acte émané du souverain territorial, l'exercice de cette autorité est plus ou moins restreint. Ainsi donc la conduite des consuls est régie par les prescriptions de leur législation nationale (au sens large) dont l'application doit se concilier avec les exigences de la législation territoriale[7].

Renault insiste donc bien sur le fait que la juridiction consulaire ne peut être exercée qu'en accord avec le souverain territorial. Ce principe est important pour la pratique de la juridiction consulaire que nous aborderons par la suite.

Ensuite, l'ouvrage insiste sur un point essentiel : la juridiction ne peut s'appliquer en principe que sur ce qui est national. Il ne s'étend donc que sur les Français ou les protégés français. L'auteur rappelle aussi que la juridiction consulaire remonte à l'article 12 du titre I, livre IX, de l'ordonnance de 1681 qui confère la juridiction tant en matière civile que criminelle aux consuls qui devront se conformer « aux usages et aux capitulations faites avec les souverains des lieux de leur établissement »[8]. Une fois de plus nous voyons que le droit consulaire est sans équivoque, la juridiction consulaire émane autant de la législation consulaire en vigueur que des capitulations ou traités signés par le souverain territorial.

La première guerre de l'opium qui oppose le Royaume-Uni et la Chine se solde en 1842 par le traité de Nankin. Cet instrument permet l'ouverture de la Chine au commerce étranger et soustrait les Britanniques à la loi territoriale et aux tribunaux locaux pour les rendre justiciables de leur tribunal consulaire.

---

6 Pillaut, *Manuel de droit consulaire*, 6.

7 Ibid., 6.

8 Ibid., 180.

Le traité de Whampoa (1844), signé entre la Chine et la France, prévoit, par les articles 25, 27 et 28, la même chose pour les Français. Ces articles affirment que le tribunal consulaire français est compétent pour :

- Les affaires civiles et pénales entre Français.
- Les affaires civiles et pénales entre Français et étrangers (à l'exclusion des Chinois) lorsque le défendeur dans les affaires civiles ou l'accusé dans les affaires pénales est français.
- Dans les affaires pénales entre Français et Chinois lorsque l'accusé est français.
- Lorsque les affaires civiles entre Français et Chinois, la juridiction est mixte.

Ainsi, l'extraterritorialité dont jouissent les Français en Chine est conforme au caractère personnel de la juridiction consulaire telle qu'elle est prônée par les manuels de droit consulaire.

Or la juridiction que nous étudions s'exerce dans un contexte particulier. En effet, les consuls pratiquent leur juridiction dans une concession. Les concessions étrangères de Tianjin constituent un cas particulier dans l'étude de la pratique de la juridiction consulaire. Ce sont des territoires sous souveraineté chinoise. Ils sont loués à une puissance étrangère et assignés à la résidence des ressortissants de cette puissance afin de leur permettre de s'établir et de pratiquer le commerce sur le territoire chinois. La première concession étrangère est celle des Britanniques à Shanghai créée en 1841. Elle est suivie par celle des Français dans la même ville. En 1860 sont fondées les concessions française, britannique et états-unienne de Tianjin. En 1895, c'est la concession allemande qui est constituée, suivie en 1898 de la concession nippone. Enfin, c'est la révolte des boxeurs en 1900 qui permet aux Russes, aux Italiens, aux Belges et aux Austro-Hongrois d'établir leurs propres concessions. Ainsi de 1900 à 1918, il n'y a pas moins de huit concessions nationales dans la ville de Tianjin, ce qui est un cas unique dans l'histoire. En 1918, suite à leur défaite, les Allemands et les Autrichiens perdent leurs concessions en Chine.

Afin de mieux comprendre l'influence que les concessions exercent sur la juridiction consulaire, il est nécessaire de remonter à leurs origines. Leur création en Chine résulte de deux phénomènes distincts. Le premier, énoncé par le juriste français de l'entre-deux-guerres, Jean Escarra, rappelle que « l'établissement, dans un pays donné, de communautés étrangères plus ou moins importantes conservant une certaine autonomie politique et administrative »[9], n'est en rien inédit. En effet, les concessions sont le fruit de l'évolution des *fondachi*,

9 Jean Escarra, « Le régime des concessions étrangères en Chine », *Recueil des cours de l'Académie de La Haye* 27 (1929).

ces quartiers séparés des villes de l'empire byzantin au Moyen-Âge destinés à la résidence des commerçants génois qui ne sont pas libres de circuler hors de leurs quartiers en dehors de dates prescrites. Ainsi, les *fondachi* et les concessions étrangères crées en Chine en 1842 sont identiques. Les commerçants génois bénéficient dans les *fondachi* d'une autonomie administrative et juridictionnelle à l'instar des étrangers dans les concessions en Chine. De plus, les Génois jouissent de la personnalité des lois qui constitue l'origine de l'extraterritorialité dont bénéficient les Français en Chine[10]. Cependant, Jean Escarra précise que les *fondachi* « n'eurent pas à l'origine le caractère d'une faveur »[11]. Effectivement, les *fondachi* sont désirés par les autorités byzantines qui, confrontées au nombre croissant d'étrangers dans leurs villes, perçoivent d'un bon œil le rassemblement des étrangers dans des quartiers non fortifiés qui présentent l'avantage de faciliter la surveillance des étrangers et la répression de ces derniers en cas de rébellion. Les *fondachi* présentent également des avantages pour les Génois. Ils permettent la conservation de leur autonomie politique et judiciaire. La juridiction génoise possède par ailleurs d'importantes similitudes avec la juridiction consulaire en Chine. En matière civile, les Génois sont soumis à leur magistrat à l'instar des Français en Chine. Dans les affaires mixtes entre Génois et Byzantins, le magistrat génois est compétent lorsque le défendeur ou l'accusé est Génois. Lorsqu'au XVe siècle, les Turcs envahissent les cités byzantines où sont présents les *fondachi*, la personnalité des lois est reconnue. Cette dernière est un système juridique dans lequel les lois applicables diffèrent selon l'origine nationale ou religieuse des individus. Ce système ouvre la voie aux capitulations. L'extraterritorialité stipulée par le traité de Nankin, et dont la caractéristique est la personnalité juridictionnelle, est l'héritière de cette disposition du droit présente dans l'Empire byzantin puis ottoman.

Le second phénomène dont résulte la création des concessions en Chine est la tradition tributaire chinoise. En effet, comme l'explique Françoise Mengin, la Chine se considère au XIXe siècle comme le cœur de la civilisation[12]. Le système tributaire chinois vise la perpétuation de la civilisation en séparant la population chinoise civilisée des barbares. Ces derniers sont appelés à se siniser au contact de la population chinoise ou à être « circonscrits aux confins

10 Sur l'origine et l'évolution des *fondachi* voir : Olivia Remie Constable, *Housing the Stranger in the Mediterranean World. Lodging, Trade, and Travel in Late Antiquity and the Middle Ages* (Cambridge : Cambridge University Press, 2004).

11 Escarra, « Le régime de concessions », 98.

12 Françoise Mengin, « Legs coloniaux et formation de l'État dans le monde chinois », *Legs colonial et gouvernance contemporaine*, éd. Jean-François Bayart *et al.*, vol. 1 (Paris : FASOPO, 2005), 269.

de l'Empire afin de ne pas entrer en contact avec la population chinoise »[13]. C'est cette volonté de confiner les étrangers aux confins de l'empire céleste qui pousse le gouvernement chinois à restreindre le commerce avec les Européens à Canton au XVIIIe siècle. C'est cet objectif de séparer la population chinoise de la population « barbare » qui a conduit le gouvernement chinois à signer en Asie centrale un accord avec le Kokand au Turkestan en 1835. Cet accord, signé sept ans avant les accords de Nankin, a pour but de circonscrire les étrangers à la périphérie de l'empire en faisant des concessions commerciales locales et en leur accordant le privilège d'extraterritorialité. L'accord signé entre le Kokand et la Chine est important car il a servi d'exemple aux traités de Nankin, de Whampoa et à ceux qui ont suivi. À l'instar des capitulations dans l'Empire ottoman, les concessions et l'extraterritorialité dont jouissent les Européens en Chine n'ont pas été imposées par les Européens aux Chinois par le biais des traités. Ils ont été désirés par les Européens et les Chinois. C'est à la faveur d'un événement survenu fortuitement bien après la rédaction des traités que les concessions et l'extraterritorialité dont jouissent les Occidentaux ont été instrumentalisés par les ces derniers afin d'amplifier leurs mainmises sur la Chine.

Les concessions étrangères en Chine, sont dans l'esprit des traités, des territoires sous souveraineté chinoise. Ils sont assignés à la résidence des étrangers à l'instar des *fondachi* dans l'empire byzantin. Toutefois, le juriste chinois francophone de l'entre-deux-guerres Chan Chung Sing, montre que la *land regulation*, le premier règlement de la concession britannique de Shanghai du 29 novembre 1845, élaborée de concert par les consuls britanniques, français et états-uniens, attribue « certains pouvoirs administratifs et municipaux à l'assemblée des locataires étrangers ou à ses délégués, sous la surveillance du corps consulaire »[14]. Cependant, Chan Chung Sing précise que ces pouvoirs administratifs et municipaux sont délégués par les autorités chinoises à la communauté étrangère. La *land regulation*, qui est la réglementation municipale établie par les consuls, est par ailleurs approuvée par les autorités chinoises[15]. En somme, les pouvoirs administratifs et municipaux sont délégués par les autorités chinoises et sont « semblables à un syndicat de propriétaires, pour la bonne gestion de ses intérêts communs »[16]. Sur ce point, la *land regulation* est conforme à l'esprit des traités en matière de concession. Cependant, ce

13 Ibid., 269.

14 Chan Chung Sing, « Les Concessions en Chine » (thèse de droit, Université de Paris, 1925), 24.

15 Ibid., 24.

16 Ibid.

n'est pas le cas de son article 15. En effet, comme le souligne Chan Chung Sing, cet article « interdisait aux propriétaires indigènes de la Concession de vendre ou de louer leur terre ou maison à d'autres Chinois, et l'article 16 défendait aux étrangers de vendre ou de louer aux Chinois sur la Concession »[17]. Cet article porte atteinte à la souveraineté territoriale de la Chine. L'article 25 du traité de Whampoa permet l'installation d'étrangers dans certains quartiers de villes chinoises, dont Shanghai. Il ne dispose pas que ces quartiers doivent leur être spécialement réservés. Cependant, les Chinois, rapporte Chan Chung Sing, ne protestent pas contre cette violation des traités « pour le motif que ce fut leur désir même de séparer les indigènes et les étrangers »[18], en raison de la tradition tributaire que nous venons de présenter. Les consuls ont une interprétation extensive des traités qui consiste à considérer que les concessions étrangères échappent totalement à la souveraineté chinoise. Ce procédé se généralise bien vite. En effet, concomitamment à la création de la concession française de Tianjin en 1861 se déroule en Chine la révolte des Taiping. Cette dernière a une importance capitale dans l'évolution territoriale des concessions en Chine.

La révolte des Taiping est une guerre civile qui a lieu en Chine de 1851 à 1864. Le juriste Chan Chung Sing explique dans sa thèse de droit publiée en 1925 que la révolte des Taiping est un évènement crucial pour l'évolution des concessions étrangères car elle provoque un afflux de réfugiés dans les concessions. Effectivement, bien qu'interdits de résidence par la *land regulation* des concessions de Shanghai promulguée en 1845, Chan Chung Sing démontre que les Chinois sont acceptés en masse dans les concessions en raison de la manne financière qu'ils représentent pour les propriétaires fonciers des concessions. Les Chinois deviennent dès lors si nombreux qu'ils constituent très rapidement la majorité des résidents des concessions. À cela s'ajoute que les magistrats chinois, fidèles à la dynastie mandchoue qui règne en Chine depuis 1644, quittent la ville de Shanghai. Désormais, ce sont les puissances étrangères qui administrent les concessions. Tous les résidents des concessions sont à présent soumis à la juridiction consulaire, même les Chinois, et ce même en matière pénale. Lorsque les Mandchous mettent un terme à la révolte des Taiping en 1865, « l'idée d'une juridiction territoriale n'abandonnait pas l'esprit des autorités étrangères », précise le juriste français Jean Escarra[19].

Ainsi, depuis 1865, le consul de France à Shanghai juge seul légalement les affaires civiles ou pénales entre Français. Conformément aux traités de

17 Ibid., 32.
18 Ibid.
19 Escarra, « Le Régime de concessions », 98.

Whampoa de 1844, le consul de France conjointement avec le *taotai*, magistrat chinois, juge également les affaires commerciales mixtes entre Français et Chinois. Cependant, le consul de France juge aussi seul les affaires entre Chinois survenues dans la concession à l'instar des délits, ou contraventions de police. Il joue également un rôle d'arbitre dans les affaires civiles entre Chinois sur le territoire de la concession de Shanghai. De plus, les affaires pénales n'impliquant que des Chinois dans les concessions relèvent de la juridiction chinoise, mais cette dernière ne peut procéder à des arrestations dans la concession française sans mandats « écrits visés par le consul »[20].

Ces nouvelles procédures judiciaires démontrent la dimension territoriale prise par la juridiction consulaire sur les concessions, une évolution que ne prévoyaient ni législation consulaire, ni les traités de Whampoa et de Tianjin (lesquels précisent le caractère personnel de la juridiction consulaire). Or, cette territorialisation de la juridiction consulaire française prive les magistrats chinois de l'exercice de la juridiction sur leurs propres nationaux dans le territoire des concessions et viole donc explicitement la souveraineté territoriale chinoise. Les Chinois tentent bien en 1867 d'y remédier en proposant un projet de loi allant dans ce sens, mais c'est en vain. Finalement un accord verbal est trouvé entre le *taotai* et le consul : désormais, toutes les affaires concernant les Chinois qui résident dans la concession sont du ressort de la cour mixte franco-chinoise, y compris les affaires exclusivement chinoises. Dans ce cas de figure, c'est le juge chinois qui est compétent et qui statue selon la loi chinoise, mais l'assesseur français siège à ses côtés et intervient lorsque la sentence lui paraît être en contradiction avec l'équité. Lors de conflit entre le juge chinois et l'assesseur, le cas est jugé par le *taotai* et le consul. Même en matière pénale, les Chinois résidant dans la concession sont justiciables de la cour mixte de la concession française mais seulement pour les affaires de peu d'importance. Ainsi si la peine encourue ne comporte pas de sanctions plus sévères que la bastonnade, la cangue, l'amende ou la prison, l'affaire est du ressort de la cour mixte. Il n'en demeure pas moins que la souveraineté chinoise sur les concessions est bafouée. Ce cas de figure n'a pas cours uniquement dans la concession française de Shanghai mais dans toutes les concessions étrangères, qu'elles soient nationales ou internationales, qu'elles se situent à Shanghai ou Tianjin. En outre, ce processus de territorialisation juridictionnelle consulaire tend à rendre justiciable tous les résidents des concessions étrangères du tribunal consulaire de la nation à laquelle appartient la concession. La territorialisation juridictionnelle se heurte donc au caractère personnel des autres juridictions consulaires.

20 Ibid.

3 Les difficultés pratiques soulevées par la juridiction consulaire dans les concessions

En effet, aucune nation ne souhaite abandonner la juridiction consulaire sur ses nationaux. Seuls les magistrats chinois voient leur juridiction sur leurs nationaux présents dans les concessions étrangères leur échapper, au profit de la juridiction consulaire de la nation à laquelle appartient la concession. Cela entraîne une hybridation juridictionnelle entre le caractère personnel de la juridiction consulaire, dont bénéficient les accusés ou les défendeurs, et la territorialisation juridictionnelle consulaire de la nation à laquelle appartient la concession, seule à même de mener une enquête sur le territoire de la concession. Cette hybridation juridictionnelle est par exemple perceptible dans une affaire judiciaire ayant eu lieu à Tianjin[21]. Elle concerne un Français, nommé Lespaze et accusé d'avoir tiré sur un Chinois dans la concession britannique tôt dans la matinée du 31 mars 1930. Cette affaire est donc mixte. Si la juridiction consulaire eût été conforme aux traités et au caractère personnel de l'extraterritorialité dont bénéficient les Français en Chine, le consul français aurait pu interroger les témoins et instruire l'affaire avant de la juger seul au tribunal consulaire français puisque l'accusé est français. Or, en raison de la territorialisation juridictionnelle consulaire dans les concessions étrangères en Chine, les faits s'étant déroulés dans la concession britannique, c'est la police municipale britannique qui s'empare de l'enquête et interroge elle-même les témoins et la victime, pourtant tous chinois. Seul l'accusé français, Lespaze, est interrogé par le consul de France en raison de la personnalité de l'extraterritorialité dont jouissent les Français en Chine. La police britannique transmet par la suite le dossier d'instruction au tribunal consulaire de France de Tianjin, seul compétent pour juger les Français en Chine. De plus, c'est le consul britannique qui cite à comparaître devant le tribunal consulaire français les témoins et la victime chinois, confisquant ainsi la juridiction des magistrats chinois sur leurs propres nationaux.

Cette affaire est intéressante à plus d'un titre. Tout d'abord, elle révèle l'hybridation juridictionnelle consulaire, qui mélange le caractère personnel de la juridiction consulaire et la territorialisation juridictionnelle à l'œuvre dans les concessions. Puis elle illustre le morcellement juridictionnel qui en résulte. En effet, comme il s'agit d'une affaire judiciaire mixte franco-chinoise dans laquelle seul un Français est accusé, l'enquête judiciaire ne devrait être menée que par le consul de France pour être conforme au caractère person-

21 Dossier « Affaire Lespaze », 1927–1946, Centre des Archives diplomatiques de Nantes, fonds 691/PO, article 201.

nel de la juridiction consulaire et aux traités. Or en raison de la territorialisation juridictionnelle consulaire à l'œuvre dans les concessions, c'est la police municipale britannique qui mène l'enquête car le méfait a eu lieu sur le territoire de la concession britannique. Toutefois, cette territorialisation juridictionnelle consulaire de la police britannique ne peut aboutir puisque l'accusé est français et qu'il ne peut donc pas être interrogé ou jugé par le consul britannique. Ensuite, cette affaire montre la violation de souveraineté territoriale chinoise engendrée par la territorialisation juridictionnelle consulaire dans les concessions qui empêche les magistrats chinois d'exercer leurs juridictions sur leurs nationaux. Enfin, cette affaire montre les difficultés qu'engendrent ce morcellement juridictionnel dans une ville qui compte jusqu'à huit concessions nationales entre 1900 et 1914. À ce propos, une autre affaire illustre les complications que pouvait causer l'exercice de la juridiction consulaire dans des affaires impliquant plusieurs concessions étrangères. Nous allons l'exposer à partir des dépositions des différents témoins convoqués et du rapport que la police britannique a envoyé au chef de la police française[22].

Le 11 décembre 1937 au soir, l'inspecteur de police britannique Botham, accompagné par le sous-inspecteur de la police chinoise Meng, se rendent dans un district sous juridiction chinoise où se situe un Country Club. Ce dernier est une société privée proposant la pratique de plusieurs activités sportives et dont l'adhésion est sélective. L'inspecteur britannique est compétent car le cercle sportif où s'est déroulé un incident, appartient à un de ses nationaux. Le sous-inspecteur chinois est aussi compétent puisque le club est situé dans le district chinois. Ils ont été appelés car les fils du téléphone ont été coupés. Après une inspection des lieux et après avoir interrogé le personnel du club, les deux policiers soupçonnent que les fils ont été coupés en vue d'enlever la nièce de l'ambassadeur de Belgique en Chine, mademoiselle Thion. L'inspecteur britannique a une piste lorsqu'il apprend que la voiture d'un dénommé Ferrer, de nationalité française, a percuté la clôture d'une citoyenne chinoise, résidente dans la concession britannique. La police britannique découvre aussi que la voiture avait été louée avec chauffeur par Ferrer pour une durée d'une semaine sous un autre nom (J. Pier and Co). Le chauffeur, un citoyen chinois, indique aux policiers que le samedi 11 décembre à 9 heures il a conduit la voiture au n° 14 Tyne road. Il dit également aux policiers avoir accompagné Ferrer et les trois Russes dans différents lieux, dont un immeuble situé dans la concession britannique et un appartement situé dans la concession italienne. Dès lors, la police britannique perquisitionne au n° 14 Tyne road et découvre

22 Dossier « Affaire Ferrer », 1927–1946, Centre des Archives diplomatiques de Nantes, fonds 691/PO, article 200.

que trois Russes y vivent dans un petit appartement. Les éléments découverts lors de cette intervention confirment l'hypothèse initiale d'une tentative d'enlèvement. Sur les lieux, la police britannique interpelle également un Russe dénommé Marcos. Les deux autres sont arrêtés deux jours plus tard et amenés à la station de police dans la concession britannique. Ces citoyens russes sont justiciables des tribunaux chinois depuis que l'Union soviétique, par l'article 12 du traité de 1924, a abandonné son privilège d'extraterritorialité en Chine. C'est au poste de police chinois qu'ils auraient donc dû être conduits. L'enquête révèle alors que le dénommé Marcos louait également une chambre dans la concession italienne. En vertu de la territorialité juridictionnelle, c'est donc la police italienne qui perquisitionne cette chambre. En revanche l'interrogatoire des trois Soviétiques est mené par la police britannique, qui bafoue au passage la souveraineté chinoise. Marcos déclare alors travailler pour Ferrer et avoue avoir préparé un enlèvement. Les deux autres Russes auditionnés passent également aux aveux et confirment sa déposition. Le lendemain des témoins de nationalités différentes sont entendus et interrogés à l'initiative de la police britannique. Tous confirment la version livrée par Marcos. Dès lors, la police britannique souhaite procéder à l'arrestation et à l'audition de Ferrer. Mais, bien que ce dernier réside dans la concession britannique, il est citoyen français. Il ne peut donc être arrêté que par la police française et poursuivi que par le tribunal consulaire français. La police britannique transmet donc l'affaire au consulat général de France de Tianjin. Le chef de la police française arrête Ferrer et, le 14 décembre 1937, fouille, en présence de l'inspecteur britannique en charge de l'enquête, les locaux de la société J. Pier and Co. ainsi que la résidence de Ferrer, tous deux situés dans la concession britannique. Ainsi la présence de la police française est nécessaire puisque le locataire de l'appartement, Ferrer, est français. Toutefois, la présence de la police britannique est également nécessaire puisque l'appartement perquisitionné se situe dans la concession britannique. À partir de ce jour, il y a un morcellement de l'instruction. La police britannique continue son enquête tandis que les auditions de Ferrer, pourtant suspect principal dans cette affaire, ainsi que les poursuites judiciaires à son encontre sont menées par le consul de France faisant office de juge d'instruction. Toute avancée dans l'enquête menée par la police britannique est donc instantanément communiquée au consul de France afin que ce dernier confronte Ferrer aux nouveaux éléments. Les résultats des interrogatoires sont ensuite communiqués à la police britannique à chaque fois qu'il semble susceptible de présenter un intérêt pour l'enquête.

À l'instar de celle de Lespaze, l'affaire Ferrer illustre la territorialisation juridictionnelle dans les concessions étrangères en Chine. Elle permet également de comprendre les difficultés qu'engendre le morcellement juridictionnel.

Ainsi, il n'y a pas moins de quatre juridictions impliquées dans la résolution de l'affaire : La juridiction française parce que le principal suspect est français ; la police britannique parce que le *Country Club* appartient à un ressortissant britannique et qu'un appartement perquisitionné se trouve dans la concession britannique ; la police italienne parce qu'un autre appartement perquisitionné se trouve dans la concession italienne ; et, enfin, la juridiction chinoise puisque les trois Soviétiques sont justiciables des tribunaux chinois. Mais cette affaire montre aussi qu'en dépit de ces difficultés, le système parvient à fonctionner. L'affaire a pu être résolue et les suspects sont jugés par leurs tribunaux respectifs grâce à une coopération relativement harmonieuse entre toutes les juridictions.

4 L'impossible réforme de la juridiction consulaire dans les concessions

Ces différentes difficultés, nées de l'exercice de la justice consulaire dans les concessions chinoises n'échappent pas à l'attention des juristes contemporains qui se penchent à de nombreuses reprises dans leurs études. En effet, si les juristes de l'époque saisissent la particularité de la juridiction consulaire dans les concessions, tous n'en font pas la même analyse ni ne proposent les mêmes solutions pour remédier aux difficultés soulevées.

Le premier juriste dont nous avons consulté les travaux est Jean Perrinjacquet qui publie sa thèse de droit en 1904[23]. Il affirme que les concessions sont des colonies en raison du processus de territorialisation à l'œuvre dans cette première. Cette analyse erronée démontre le flou juridique qui demeure au sujet de la nature des concessions en ce début de XXe siècle.

Les autres juristes, à savoir Marcel Baudez[24], Yong Tchang Kiang[25] et Chan Chung Sing[26], arrivent tous à la même conclusion : l'originalité de la juridiction consulaire réside dans le processus de territorialisation. Tous ces juristes sont également en accord sur les problèmes que pose ce processus de territorialisation. Effectivement, ils considèrent qu'il pose des problèmes théoriques insolubles tels que l'impossibilité pour la police judiciaire d'une concession de

23 Jean Perrinjacquet, « Des cessions temporaires de territoire : étude du droit international » (thèse de droit, Université de Bordeaux, 1904).

24 Baudez, « La condition juridique ».

25 Yong-Tchang Kiang, « De la juridiction consulaire en Chine » (thèse de droit, Université de Paris, 1922).

26 Sing, « Les Concessions en Chine ».

perquisitionner le domicile d'un étranger sans l'accord de son consul[27], l'absence de moyen juridique coercitif d'un consul pour contraindre un étranger dans une enquête judiciaire[28] ou encore, les demandes reconventionnelles[29].

Une demande reconventionnelle est, en procédure civile, le qualificatif donné à une demande incidente par laquelle le défendeur lors d'un litige se porte lui-même demandeur contre le requérant[30]. Cette demande a donc ceci de particulier qu'elle n'introduit pas de nouvelle instance puisque, par définition, celle-ci est déjà pendante. Elle se greffe à titre d'incident sur un procès déjà en cours. C'est ce que dispose l'article 63 du code de procédure civile. Toutefois, selon cet article, les deux demandes doivent être instruites au cours du même procès pour éliminer le risque toujours possible de décision contradictoire ou difficilement compatible.

Or ces demandes reconventionnelles sont impossibles à réaliser dans le cadre d'un procès civil mixte entre étrangers en raison de la règle *actor sequitur forum rei*. Cette règle désigne le tribunal consulaire de l'accusé comme compétent. Donc le consul qui juge l'affaire principale sur laquelle se greffe la demande incidente n'a de juridiction que sur ses nationaux. Il ne devrait donc pas, selon les traités, être compétent pour juger une demande reconventionnelle dans laquelle le défendeur devient demandeur et le demandeur devient défendeur. Ainsi, les demandes reconventionnelles ne peuvent s'appliquer dans les procès mixtes entre étrangers, et il y a alors deux procès distincts dans deux tribunaux consulaires différents.

Cependant, aucun de ces problèmes théoriques dont se plaignent les juristes étudiés n'en sont dans la pratique. En effet, dans le cas des demandes reconventionnelles, une solution est trouvée. Le tribunal consulaire qui juge la première affaire attend avant d'exécuter sa sentence que le verdict du second tribunal consulaire soit rendu afin de réaliser une compensation entre les sommes à payer par l'une et l'autre partie[31]. Pour ce qui est des affaires pénales, ni l'impossibilité pour la police judiciaire d'une concession de perquisitionner le domicile d'un étranger sans l'accord de son consul, ni l'absence de moyen coercitif d'un consul pour contraindre un étranger à témoigner dans une enquête judiciaire n'ont empêché les enquêtes judiciaires d'aboutir.

S'il est vrai que cette hybridation juridictionnelle consulaire à l'œuvre dans les concessions provoque un morcellement juridictionnel qui complique et

27 Baudez, « La condition juridique », 212.
28 Kiang, « De la juridiction consulaire en Chine », 88.
29 Baudez, « La condition juridique », 67.
30 Pierre Callé, *Code de procédure civile* (Paris : Dalloz, 2019), 166.
31 Baudez, « La condition juridique », 68.

ralentit les enquêtes, elle n'empêche toutefois nullement les consuls de rendre la justice dans les concessions étrangères. En effet, à notre connaissance, dans les affaires judiciaires comme dans les thèses de droit soutenues dans l'entre-deux-guerres que nous avons étudiées, aucune enquête n'est demeurée inaboutie en raison de l'hybridation juridictionnelle consulaire. Ainsi, dans l'exemple que constitue l'affaire Lespaze, le morcellement de la juridiction entre la juridiction territoriale britannique et l'extraterritorialité dont bénéficie l'accusé n'obstrue pas la résolution de l'affaire. Et, en ayant étudié une dizaine d'affaires judiciaires s'étant déroulées dans les concessions étrangères de Tianjin entre 1900 et 1943, nous sommes en droit de penser qu'aucune affaire judiciaire n'a été non solutionnée en raison du morcellement juridictionnel. Le seul réel problème juridique que pose donc dans la pratique la territorialisation juridictionnelle consulaire dans les concessions étrangères en Chine est la violation de la souveraineté territoriale de la Chine.

Ainsi, ce qui est décrié par les juristes n'est pas l'inefficience supposée de la juridiction consulaire, la justice étant tout de même rendue en dépit du morcellement juridictionnel, mais le cas *sui generis* qu'elle représente. L'application du droit consulaire ne convient pas aux juristes qui préféreraient des solutions juridiques plus conventionnelles, avec une seule juridiction compétente sur le territoire chinois quelle que soit la nationalité des prévenus. Cependant, tous les juristes étudiés sont en désaccord quant à la juridiction unique qui doit être mise en place.

D'une part, Marcel Baudez, licencié en droit élève-interprète à Tianjin de 1907 à 1910, propose dans sa thèse de droit intitulée *La condition juridique des étrangers en Chine*[32], publiée en 1913, d'instaurer en Chine des tribunaux mixtes semblables à ceux présents en Égypte depuis la réforme de 1875. Ces tribunaux pourraient ainsi résoudre les problèmes posés par le processus de territorialisation juridictionnelle tout en préservant voire en consolidant la prééminence de la juridiction consulaire en Chine[33].

D'autre part, il y a la solution de la juridiction unique chinoise. Dans un mémorandum présenté à la conférence de la Paix en 1919[34], la délégation chinoise demande la fin du processus de territorialisation juridictionnelle dans l'attente d'être en mesure d'abolir également la juridiction consulaire elle-même. Cette revendication est faite au nom du respect de la souveraineté

32 Ibid., 68.

33 David Todd, « Beneath Sovereignty : Extraterritoriality and Imperial Internationalism in Nineteenth-Century Egypt », *Law and History Review* 36, n° 1 (2018) : 115–137.

34 « Questions à résoudre soumises par la Chine à la Conférence de la Paix », Délégation chinoise à la Conférence de la Paix, 1919, consulté sur Gallica, dernière modification le 10/02/2010, url : https://gallica.bnf.fr/ark:/12148/bpt6k5803758g.texteImage#.

chinoise et de l'application stricte du traité de Whampoa qui, rappelons-le, ne permet que l'instauration de la juridiction consulaire personnelle en Chine. Cependant, ce désidérata demeure lettre morte. Il est repris par la délégation chinoise lors de la conférence de Washington de 1922, toujours en vain[35]. Deux juristes chinois francophones ayant effectué leurs études de droit en France, Yong-Tchank Kiang et Chan Chung Sing, revendiquent à leur tour l'abolition du processus de territorialisation juridictionnelle qui viole la souveraineté chinoise, à nouveau sans succès[36].

Enfin il est intéressant de noter que ce souhait d'abolition de la juridiction consulaire, exprimée tant lors des conférences de la paix de Washington que dans les thèses de droit soutenues par les juristes chinois, repose sur un argumentaire structuré en deux axes. Le premier démontre que l'occidentalisation du droit chinois, débutée au XX e siècle, rend caduques si ce n'est contre-productives les juridictions consulaires. Le second axe tend à démontrer que les juridictions consulaires sont en inadéquation avec les principes mêmes du droit occidental, et qu'elles outrepassent le cadre légal dans lequel elles doivent pourtant être pratiquées. Ainsi, les juristes et les délégations chinoises dénoncent la partialité des consuls dont les missions sont à la fois de protéger leurs nationaux et de rendre la justice. Ces mêmes acteurs soulignent également le cumul des charges administratives et juridictionnelles des consuls. Or, ce dernier reproche qu'adressent les juristes chinois à la juridiction consulaire est celui dont se sont servis les Occidentaux pour justifier l'introduction des pouvoirs juridictionnels en Chine. En effet, dans sa thèse, Marcel Baudez affirme que les tribunaux consulaires en Chine est nécessaire car la justice n'est pas rendue par des juges spécialisés mais par des fonctionnaires « également chargés de remplir l'ensemble des autres tâches de l'administration civile »[37], ce qui est également le cas des consuls. De plus, les juristes et délégations chinoises mettent en avant l'illégalité de la juridiction exercée par les consuls dans les concessions, qui, en se territorialisant, outrepasse son cadre légal définie par les traités de Nankin et de Whampoa. Ainsi, ironiquement, c'est en s'appuyant sur l'occidentalisation du droit chinois et l'illégalité revêtue par la justice consulaire dans les concessions que les juristes et délégations chinoises demandent l'abolition de l'extraterritorialité en Chine.

---

35 Nicolas Vaicboudt, « La conférence de Washington, 1921–1922 : L'idéal d'un nouveau congrès de Vienne pour le XX e siècle », *Bulletin de l'Institut Pierre Renouvin* 42, n° 2 (2015) : 125.

36 Yong-Tchang Kiang, « De la juridiction consulaire » ; Sing, « Les Concessions en Chine ».

37 Baudez, « La condition juridique », 2.

Soulignons, pour conclure, que les manuels de droit consulaire et les traités de Nankin et de Whampoa confèrent à l'instance juridictionnelle consulaire en Chine un caractère exclusivement personnel. Pourtant, à la faveur de la révolte des Taiping, les consuls ont tenté de territorialiser leurs juridictions dans leurs concessions, bafouant ainsi la souveraineté chinoise. Toutefois, cette territorialisation juridictionnelle n'a pu aboutir car elle s'est heurtée à la personnalité des autres juridictions consulaires, aboutissant ainsi à la formation d'une juridiction hybride dans les concessions. Bien que causant des difficultés dans la pratique juridictionnelle (morcellement juridictionnel, ralentissement des procédures), cette hybridation n'a pas, à notre connaissance, empêché les juridictions consulaires de rendre la justice dans les concessions. Ces difficultés causées par l'hybridation juridictionnelle n'ont pas échappé aux juristes contemporains qui ont profité de ce cas *sui generis* pour proposer soit la mise en place d'une juridiction consulaire mixte semblable à celle qui existait en Égypte à la même période, soit l'abolition de la juridiction consulaire. Cette hybridation juridictionnelle en Chine révèle le rapport de force entre les nations occidentales et la Chine. Cela conduit le juriste chinois francophone Chan Chun Sing[38] à énoncer lucidement que cette hybridation juridictionnelle ne saurait être durable et que les concessions étrangères en Chine seront soit converties en colonies ou en condominiums soit supprimées et rétrocédées, « tout dépendra de la puissance future de la Chine »[39]. Cette hybridation juridictionnelle a cependant été conservée jusqu'à l'abolition définitive de la juridiction consulaire en Chine en 1943 et la rétrocession des concessions étrangères deux ans plus tard, en 1945.

Bibliographie

Baudez, Marcel. « La condition juridique des étrangers en Chine ». PhD diss., Université de Paris, 1913.

Callé, Pierre. *Code de procédure civile*. Paris : Dalloz, 2019.

Constable, Olivia Remie. *Housing the Stranger in the Mediterranean World : Lodging, Trade, and Travel in Late Antiquity and the Middle Ages*. Cambridge : Cambridge University Press, 2004.

Escarra, Jean. « Le régime des concessions étrangères en Chine ». *Recueil des cours de l'Académie de La Haye* 27 (1929) : 5–140.

38 Sing, *Les Concessions en Chine*.

39 Ibid., 120.

Hansson, Michael. « Les tribunaux mixtes en Égypte ». *Nordisk Tidsskrift for International Ret* 5, n° 1 (1934) : 104–122.

Kiang, Yong-Tchang. « De la juridiction consulaire en Chine ». PhD diss., Université de Paris, 1922.

Mengin, Françoise. « Legs coloniaux et formation de l'état dans le monde chinois ». Dans *Legs colonial et gouvernance contemporaine*, édité par Jean-François Bayart, Richard Banégas, Romain Bertrand, Béatrice Hibou, Françoise Mengin et Julien Meimon, 264–342. Paris : FASOPO, 2005.

Messina, Salvatore. « Les tribunaux mixtes et les rapports interjuridictionnels en Égypte ». *Recueil des cours de l'Académie de Droit international de La Haye* 41 (1932) : 363–500.

Perrinjacquet, Jean. « Des cessions temporaires de territoire : étude du droit international ». PhD diss., Université de Bordeaux, 1904.

Pillaut, Julien. *Manuel de droit consulaire (matières spéciales) : affaires maritimes, police sanitaire, intervention des consuls dans l'administration de la justice, pouvoirs de police en pays de juridiction, concessions en Chine, groupement des Français résidents à l'étranger*. Paris : Berger-Levrault, 1912.

Sing, Chan Chung. « Les concessions en Chine ». PhD diss., Université de Paris, 1925.

Singaravélou, Pierre. « Dix Empires Dans Un Mouchoir de Poche. Le Territoire de Tientsin À L'Épreuve Du Phénomène Concessionnaire (Années 1860–1920) », Dans *Territoires impériaux : histoire spatiale du fait colonial*, édité par Hélène Blais, Florence Deprest et Pierre Singaravélou, 271–296. Paris : Éditions de la Sorbonne, 2012.

Todd, David. « Beneath Sovereignty : Extraterritoriality and Imperial Internationalism in Nineteenth-Century Egypt », *Law and History Review* 36, n° 1 (2018) : 105–137.

Ulbert, Jörg. « Introduction : La Fonction Consulaire À L'Époque Moderne : Définition, État Des Connaissances Et Perspectives de Recherche ». Dans *La fonction consulaire à l'époque moderne : affirmation d'une institution économique et politique (1500–1800)*, édité par Jörg Ulbert et Gérard Le Bouëdec, 9–20. Rennes : Presses universitaires de Rennes, 2006.

Vaicboudt, Nicolas. « La conférence de Washington, 1921–1922 : L'idéal d'un nouveau congrès de Vienne pour le XX e siècle ». *Bulletin de l'Institut Pierre Renouvin* 42, n° 2 (2015) : 115–128.

17

The End of Extraterritoriality

Thomas Gidney

1 Introduction

The application of extraterritoriality, once a simple guarantor of the rights of small communities of European merchants in the Ottoman Empire began to embody in the nineteenth century a normative hierarchy between the "Civilised" West, and yet-to-be-civilised "East." Following the forcible "opening" of China (1842), Japan (1853), and Siam (1855), Asian states signed duplicate capitulatory treaties with Western states, granting them tariff control, territorial concessions, tax exemptions, and extraterritorial privileges. Implemented as a transitional measure, extraterritoriality protected the Western nationals from the "barbarity" of local laws until a time in which a new legal system could be implemented upon Western lines.[1]

This had profound implications for a state's international bearing, with states subject to such treaties, with Western jurists deeming them as uncivilised or "semi-civilised." States subject to these capitulatory impositions thus existed in a form of purgatory outside of Western "international society," compromising their sovereign equality with Western states until having been deemed to harmonise their legal and diplomatic norms with those of the West.[2] Nationalist movements within states subject to the capitulations increasingly agitated against what they deemed to be "unequal treaties," seeing them as compromising their sovereignty and equality with Western states.[3]

By the end of the First World War, the connection between extraterritoriality and exclusion from Western international society was becoming increas-

1 This argument is best typified in Gong's work but can be found in other similar works Gerrit W. Gong, *The Standard of "Civilization" in International Society* (New York: Clarendon Press, 1984); Brett Bowden, *The Empire of Civilization: The Evolution of an Imperial Idea* (Chicago: University of Chicago Press, 2009).

2 Also called the "expansion thesis": *The Expansion of International Society*, eds. Hedley Bull and Adam Watson (Oxford: Oxford University Press, 1985); Bowden, *The Empire of Civilization*; Gong, *The Standard of "Civilization."*

3 Chiang Kai Shek proclaimed that China had secured its freedom and equality among nations through the end of America's capitulations: telegram from Chiang Kai Shek to President Roosevelt, 13 October 1942, FO 115/3514, TNA.

ingly tenuous. By 1919, many states that were subject to unequal treaties with the West had become active and recognised members of the modern system of international organisations, becoming prominent members of the newly founded League of Nations and its ancillary institutions. The League introduced a common set of rules, procedures, and institutions that all its participants could be considered to be operating within the norms and protocols of Western international society.[4]

Furthermore, these international bodies provided a platform through which states subject to extraterritoriality could voice their indignities and push for its abrogation. Nonetheless, as non-Western states took their seats in Geneva as nominal equals to their Western counterparts, they quickly learnt that the League of Nations was no panacea and that their capitulatory arrangements would remain, often for years, and, in the case of China, decades. The relationship between the continuation of extraterritoriality and the exclusion from international society has thus been questioned by some historians, who see non-European states as active participants within international society, certainly by the twentieth century, but often unequal participants within it.[5]

Extraterritoriality persisted despite the participation of non-Western states in international society, yet the Interwar era (1919–1939) witnessed the effective end of extraterritorial justice. Why Western powers decided to renounce their capitulatory privileges remains an important debate. Under the system laid out by the Western treaty regime, states subject to capitulations would need to prove sufficient harmonisation in legal norms before being deemed "ready" to subject foreigners to local laws. In the English school's "civilisational" approach, legal reform was often complimented by significant societal changes and attempts to replicate the standards set by the West. However, as the West's standards evolved in parallel, it meant that non-Western states were in a state of perpetual catch-up with the West.[6]

The political calculations of Western states also played a considerable role in the decision to abrogate their capitulatory regimes. Japan, the first state to abrogate its "unequal" treaties in the 1890s, did so in a period of early imperial expansion against China and Korea, making it seem increasingly difficult to enforce unequal treaties there, whilst also opening Japan up as a useful part-

4 Bull and Watson, *The Expansion*, 1.

5 Edward Keene, "The Standard of 'Civilisation,' the Expansion Thesis and the 19th-Century International Social Space," *Millennium* 42, n° 3 (June 2014): 651–673.

6 Turan Kayaoğlu, "Westphalian Eurocentrism in International Relations Theory," *International Studies Review* 12, n° 2 (2010): 196.

ner in the Pacific, as later embodied in the 1902 Anglo-Japanese alliance. But Japan had equally rapidly adopted Western legal and to some extent, societal norms, in the years prior to the renunciation of extraterritoriality. By 1919, Japan had forged a path for other states to follow suit, whilst simultaneously joining the West in imposing its own capitulatory treaties on its neighbours.[7]

In the wake of the First World War, despite the global membership of the League of Nations, there was no multilateral moment, no conference or resolution that ended the capitulatory system. Instead, the extraterritorial treaty system was removed one by one, either through unilateral negotiations with a powerful Western state such as Britain or the United States, or through wider forums and conferences where the supplicant state appeared alone, in front of many Western nations, asking to equalise their relationship. Nonetheless, the capitulatory system would largely come to an end through the Interwar period, yet the practice's seemingly abrupt end hides the political nature of its demise, and how in some cases it evolved. An examination of these negotiations reveals significant inferences on what motivated the end of extraterritorial treaty rights, illuminating how international norms develop, morph, or go extinct.

2 Unrequited Expectations: The First World War and the League of Nations

Many Asian states subject to extraterritorial capitulatory treaties participated on the Allied side in the First World War, with China and Siam entering the conflict in a limited capacity in 1917. Others, such as Persia, attempted to remain neutral, but came under British occupation, whilst Egypt, nominally an Ottoman province, had been under indirect British rule since 1882. The Ottoman Empire unilaterally severed its capitulatory treaties with all powers including its future German and Austrian allies on 1 October 1914. This prompted a unanimous protest from both the Allies and Central Powers despite being at war.[8]

By the end of the conflict, neither participation with, nor fighting against the Allies would play a role in the nullification of extraterritoriality. China, Persia, and Siam would participate in the Paris Peace Conference and become

7 Shogo Suzuki, *Civilization and Empire: China and Japan's Encounter with European International Society* (London: Routledge, 2009), 180.

8 Ambassador Morgenthau to the Secretary of State, 10 September 1914, File n° 711.673/34, *Papers relating the foreign relations of the United States, 1914*, ed. Joseph V. Fuller (Washington: United States Government Printing Office, 1922), doc. 1838.

founding member-states of the League of Nations, where they aimed to renegotiate their unequal treaties. The Siamese Delegation met U.S. President Wilson at the Peace Conference in 1919, who stated that treaty revisions on extraterritoriality would be carried out multilaterally at the League, which the United States would ultimately fail to join.[9] However, no such assurances were made by the European delegations. Perhaps the only multilateral gain for Asian states at the Peace Conference was the abolition of extraterritoriality for German and Austrian nationals, symbolically breaching the notion that Europeans could not be subject to local laws.[10]

Accession to the League was often held as a badge of modernity, and entry into Western international society as sovereign equals. Moreover, the League offered a significant multilateral platform through which to challenge unequal treaties. However, Asian states showed a lack of solidarity and did not negotiate as a bloc against extraterritoriality. Japan, now one of the "Great Powers," did not want to relinquish its extraterritorial rights in China, whilst Chinese nationalists claimed that the decision of the Peace Conference to grant the former German concession of Shandong to Japan was motivated by a desire for Japan to participate at the League.[11] Siam often pursued a less confrontational approach, abstaining from voting on Japan's proposal for racial equality, whilst it had no formal recognition of China, having abandoned the Chinese tributary system in the nineteenth century.[12] Conversely, the Chinese delegation, as it worked to revise the capitulations, did so with the expectation that it was one of the Great powers and above small states like Siam, and deserved a seat on the Council of the League.[13] The "Great Powers" however, were more likely to close ranks. Whilst the U.S. ultimately agreed to an end of extraterritoriality with Siam in 1920, which was vigorously resisted by Britain and France, all the Powers collaborated to maintain their treaty rights in China.[14]

The League provided a useful political tool for the "Big Four" – Britain, the U.S., France and Italy – and were able to effectively rebuff Chinese demands to redress their unequal treaties, stating that the decision should be made multi-

---

9 Stefan Hell, *Siam and the League of Nations: Modernisation, Sovereignty and Multilateral Diplomacy, 1920–1940* (Bangkok: River Books, 2010), 37.

10 Wesley R. Fishel, *The End of Extraterritoriality in China* (Berkeley, Los Angeles: University of California Press, 1952), 199. Although in many cases, Allied states offered German and Austrian citizens to come under their jurisdiction in countries subject to extraterritoriality.

11 Hung Ti Chu, "China and the League of Nations," 1937, UNOG Library.

12 Hell, *Siam and the League of Nations*, 45.

13 Alison Adcock Kaufman, "In Pursuit of Equality and Respect: China's Diplomacy and the League of Nations," *Modern China* 40, n° 6 (2014): 630.

14 Hell, *Siam and the League of Nations*, 37.

laterally at the League.[15] However, the U.S. Senate's ultimate decision not to join the League made it a less effective venue to secure the abolition of the capitulations. Instead, negotiations would have to be carried outside of the League. The 1921 Washington Naval Conference, called by the United States, was arranged primarily to disarm, and reduce the size of navies that had blossomed in size during the War. Nonetheless, an often-overlooked part of the Conference was held on the status of China, and the continuation of capitulatory and extraterritorial treaties which continued to benefit a growing population of Western residents in different concessionary territories in China. Riddled with warlordism and managed by a weak state, the Republic of China had little political weight in these talks. Unconvinced by China's repeated demands, the question was deferred to a group of Western experts that would examine whether China was suitably prepared to dissolve its capitulatory regime and whether Chinese law was sufficiently developed to try Westerners.[16]

3 Egypt and Turkey and the Lausanne Conference

Whilst China, Siam and Persia attempted to use their newfound international gravitas at the League to appeal to the West to revise their treaties, civil unrest in Egypt and the rise of militant Turkish nationalism were challenging European capitulatory treaties. British officials feared that Egyptians were being inspired by the actions of Mustafa Kemal's Turkish Republican troops, who defied the Treaty of Sèvres, whilst their military success threatened Allied-occupied Constantinople. The results of the "Chanak" crisis revealed the lack of unity among the Allies, who resorted to negotiation rather than enforcing the Sèvres Treaty militarily. The Conference for the eventual recognition of Turkish statehood began in November 1922 at Lausanne in Switzerland, with the future of extraterritorial rights being one of the most contentious issues.

Turkey rejected the claim that it should be subject to the same capitulations that its Ottoman forebear had abrogated in 1914, which had been reimposed after the War in the Treaty of Sèvres. At Lausanne, Turkish negotiators insisted that the capitulations both symbolically infringed on Turkish sovereignty, but also absolved foreign residents from paying taxes, hampering the

15 Yongjin Zhang, "China's Entry into International Society: Beyond the Standard of 'Civilization'," *Review of International Studies* 17, n° 1 (January 1991): 13 (https://doi.org/10.1017/S026021050011229X).

16 Frank B. Kellogg, "Resolutions regarding extraterritoriality in China, adopted by the Washington Conference on the limitation of armament at the fourth plenary session," 10 December 1921, R1248/17/48718, League of Nations Archive.

nation's finances. Among the Allies, it was the British through their representative, Lord Curzon, that dominated much of the conference, and were not prepared to abandon extraterritoriality without special protections. Allied negotiators feared subjecting their nationals to continued Islamic legal practice, as well as Turkish judges they deemed untrained in Western methods, stating that "confidence is a thing which cannot be imposed, but must be inspired."[17]

To alleviate these fears, the Allies suggested that the inaugurated Permanent Court of International Justice in The Hague to appoint Turkish judges overseeing cases involving foreign nationals.[18] This was a clear infringement on Turkish sovereignty and was rejected. Yet Allied negotiators would not back down until the Turkish negotiators conceded some guarantees for their citizens. So fraught were the negotiations that the Lausanne talks were called off in February 1923, with Curzon departing Lausanne the same day. To resolve the impasse, negotiators needed to find a way of "substituting" the capitulations in favour of an "other scheme consistent with Turkish independent sovereignty whilst guaranteeing necessary protection for foreigners."[19] The attempted compromise was the abrogation of the capitulations in favour of Mixed Arbitral Tribunals, consisting of both foreign and Turkish justices where adjudicating cases involving citizens of Allied states. These courts, which were already in operation in defeated Austria and Germany, somewhat blunted the civilisational element of extraterritorial justice, whilst somewhat alleviating Western fears over the competency of the Turkish judiciary. Nonetheless, the Turks refused the use Mixed Arbitral Tribunals, seeing them as an imposition on their sovereignty, with the West settling for assurances that Turkey would modernise its legal system.[20]

Mixed tribunals were an evolution of the extraterritorial system of consular courts, featuring a judge of the defendant's nationality on the panel.[21] Mixed courts, already had a long history within China, as well as the autonomous Ottoman province of Egypt, which operated mixed courts for civil suits, but retained consular courts for most criminal cases involving foreigners. These mixed courts had come around from negotiations between the Egyptian mon-

---

17 Commission on the Regime of Foreigners. Draft Minutes of the Second Meeting, 28 December 1922, RG 43, A1 115, Box 1, NARA.

18 Ibid.

19 British Delegation, Telegram to Sir Eyre Crowe, 3 December 1922, FO 839/36, TNA.

20 Zülâl Muslu, "The Mixed Arbitral Tribunals and Turkey: Negotiating the International Identity of the Young Republic Under the Sèvres Syndrome," in *The Mixed Arbitral Tribunals, 1919–1939*, eds. Hélène Ruiz Fabri and Michel Erpelding (Baden-Baden: Nomos, 2023).

21 Ibid., 45.

archy and the foreign powers. With the outbreak of the War, Britain formally placed Egypt under a Protectorate and aimed to either replace consular courts with a more centralised system of Mixed Courts or do away with the courts altogether in an anglicised system of national courts in a similar fashion to how law operated within Britain's colonies.[22]

The case was relatively unique in which a colonial suzerain attempted to centralise extraterritorial powers within its protectorate and was met with a backlash from the capitulatory powers. The mixed courts and consular system had been popular with other powers, who saw it as protection of their rights against British domination in Egypt.[23] From the outset, there was resistance to the move, particularly among some in the U.S. who saw this as injecting a "virus" on American public opinion, and an "emasculation" of American rights.[24] Furthermore, renouncing Consular courts threatened retaliation by France in its Moroccan Protectorate.[25] These plans were put on the backfoot, when Britain's control of Egypt began to slip following a civil uprising against British rule led by the nationalist "Wafd" Party. Following two years of widespread resistance to the British Protectorate, Britain declared Egypt to be an independent state in 1921, albeit one subject to controls on its international personality and defence pending an alliance with Britain.

No longer the official governing power, judicial reform and ending the capitulations was now an aim of the Egyptian Government rather than the British. The primary power it had to convince was Britain, and negotiations about reforming the judicial system were connected to a larger array of demands before Britain relinquished its stranglehold on Egypt's foreign policy. The Wafd Party had always placed a premium on foreign support for the cause of full Egyptian independence, and pursuing the abrogation of the capitulations risked losing international support. Under the more "moderate" Premiership of Sarwat Pasha, the Egyptian Government attempted to repeal Consular courts in 1927, to little avail.[26] Only following a breakthrough in talks following

22 The Ambassador in Great Britain (Davis) to the Secretary of State, 19 July 1920, *Papers Relating to the Foreign Relations of the United States*, ed. Joseph V. Fuller, vol. 2, *1920* (Washington: United States Government Printing Office, 1943), doc. 185; Nathan J. Brown, "The Precarious Life and Slow Death of the Mixed Courts of Egypt," *International Journal of Middle East Studies* 25, n° 1 (February 1993): 40–41.

23 Michel Erpelding, "Mixed Courts of Egypt," in *Max Planck Encyclopedia of International Procedural Law*, ed. Hélène Ruiz Fabri (Oxford: Oxford University Press, 2020), https://opil.ouplaw.com/display/10.1093/law-mpeipro/e2711.013.2711/law-mpeipro-e2711.

24 Pierre to Baldwin, 17 November 1917, FO 141/620/8, TNA; Letter to Joseph E. Ransdell, 30 November 1917, FO 141/620/8, TNA.

25 Telegram from Lord Derby to Lord Curzon, 13 May 1919, FO 608/212, TNA.

26 Jasper Yeates Brinton, *The Mixed Courts of Egypt* (New Haven: Yale University Press, 1930), 343–346.

the Italian invasion of Abyssinia in 1935 did talks lead to the 1936 Anglo-Egyptian Treaty, which was soon followed by Egypt's accession to the League of Nations, and the abolition of its capitulations at Montreux in 1937.[27] The transition period of 12 years was long, but with Britain supporting Egypt, other Western powers offered no resistance, and the Mixed Courts of Egypt closed their doors in 1949.[28]

4 The Different Approaches of Siam and Persia

The Turkish nationalist movement had shaken the global system of extraterritoriality by aggressively challenging the West and negotiating from a position of strength. By the end of the 1920s, Siam and Persia would have both secured an end to their capitulatory treaties. The U.S. revision of its treaty regime with Siam became a useful negotiating chip to bring to the British and French who were reluctant to protect their larger number of subjects and their more extensive investments in Siam. However, even the U.S. apparent abrogation had conditions, with a five-year system of evocation in which U.S. defendants could continue to be tried in consular courts, whilst the U.S. refused to abandon its low tariffs until other European states had also agreed.[29]

Whilst the Chinese delegation had used their position at the League to push for treaty revision, the Siamese used their multilateral platform more indirectly. Siamese delegates argued that the League's efforts to quash the trade in opium and human trafficking were hampered by the continuation of the unequal treaties, which they also argued were anathema to the League's ideal of the sovereign equality of its member states. The meagre 3% tariff on foreign goods imposed by these treaties meant the Siamese state was dependent on revenues from opium, whilst extraterritoriality made it difficult to enforce new laws to curb human and drug trafficking by foreigners.[30]

Siam and Persia had very different negotiating positions towards abrogating their unequal treaties. Having secured the end of U.S. capitulations, Siam employed American legal advisor Francis B. Sayre to launch a charm offensive

27 *"An Anomaly among Anomalies": Colonial Membership of the League of Nations*, ed. Thomas Gidney (Geneva: Graduate Institute of International and Development Studies, 2021).

28 Brown, "The Precarious Life," 48.

29 Francis Bowes Sayre, "The Passing of Extraterritoriality in Siam," *American Journal of International Law* 22, n° 1 (January 1928): 81–82.

30 Hell, *Siam and the League of Nations*, 93–99.

around Europe in 1925 to convince European leaders to revise their treaties.[31] Britain feared that abrogating its rights in Siam would set a precedent at the upcoming commission on extraterritoriality with China, but relented, marking a turning point as the biggest European power operating in Siam.[32] By 1926, Siam had abrogated most of its extraterritorial treaties along a similar line to those drafted in the 1920 Treaty with the U.S. Persia followed suit, buoyed by the example of Turkey, and resistant to Japan's request to extend extraterritoriality into Persia, Persia declared that it would unilaterally end the capitulations the following year. This came on the heels of significant developments to Persia's legal code, and the domestically controversial phasing out of Sharia courts. With the collapse of the Russian Empire, Britain held the most significant interests in Persia, and wanted to protect the interests of its subjects operating in the petroleum industry.[33] The French were insistent on appointing foreign judges to Persian courts, threatening to raise Persia's unilateral repeal of extraterritoriality at the League, whilst Britain proposed introducing foreign advisors to tutor the Persian judiciary, a move that was roundly rejected by the Persian Government.[34] Nonetheless, the British were keen to keep the modernising Persian monarch Reza Shah as a viable partner, and acquiesced to the demand "without regard to the probable imperfection of Persian judiciary reforms."[35]

The race of colonial subjects soon became a bargaining chip in negotiations over extraterritoriality. Britain's response to Persia's unilateral abrogation was to see if the repeal of extraterritoriality could potentially be limited to its Indian subjects.[36] This, ultimately, was not accepted. The separation of legal standards among Asian and European subjects had also been used in Siam by France and Britain in 1907 and 1909. Whilst discriminatory, the Siamese themselves sought greater jurisdiction over the growing number of Burmese and

31 Sayre, "The Passing of Extraterritoriality in Siam," 85–87; Gong, *The Standard of "Civilization,"* 236.

32 Hell, *Siam and the League of Nations*, 95.

33 Michael Zirinsky, "Riza Shah's Abrogation of Capitulations, 1927–1928," in *The Making of Modern Iran: State and Society Under Riza Shah, 1921–1941*, ed. Stephanie Cronin (London: Routledge, 2003), 84–102.

34 Sir R. Clive to Sir Austen Chamberlain, 30 July 1927, CO 732/27/6, TNA; Zirinsky, "Riza Shah's Abrogation," 95–96.

35 The Minister in Persia (Philip) to the Secretary of State, 17 January 1928, *Papers Relating to the Foreign Relations of the United States*, ed. Joseph V. Fuller, vol. 3, *1928* (Washington: United States Government Printing Office, 1943), doc. 575.

36 Sir R. Clive, Decypher from Persia, 22 October 1927, CO 732/27/6, TNA.

Indochinese migrants who had previously been exempt from Siamese law, rather than the smaller number of European residents.[37] The ebb of extraterritoriality was thus initially marked more by whom it was applied to rather than its abolition.

5 China: The Long Path to Abrogation

As Turkey and Siam successfully negotiated the repeal of their "unequal treaties," an increasingly anarchic China struggled to convince the Western powers to revise the capitulations. Chinese delegates had attempted to invoke Article 19 of the League of Nations on the revision of treaties deemed either inapplicable or a threat to the "peace of the world," yet the League's Tenth Assembly deemed that the League could only advise on the revision of such treaties.[38] The Commission appointed in Washington to judge China's "readiness" to repeal extraterritoriality postponed its investigation for four years due to the growing political instability in China which culminated in the murder and kidnapping of foreign nationals following a train jacking by a Chinese warlord.[39] Perhaps the only diplomatic victory to date for China had been the USSR's formal renunciation of its capitulatory rights in 1924, a point that many Chinese diplomats used to pressure the foreign powers.[40] When they finally convened in Beijing in 1926, the instability in China meant that the Commission was initially confined to the beleaguered capital.[41] Despite these setbacks, the report was congenial towards China's bid to remove extraterritoriality, acknowledging the upsurge in nationalist sentiment and the desire to

37 Francis Bowes Sayre, "The Passing of Extraterritoriality in Siam," *American Journal of International Law* 22, n° 1 (January 1928): 73–80.

38 Hung Ti Chu, "China and the League of Nations," 7.

39 The Minister in China (Schurman) to the Secretary of State, 13 September 1923, *Papers Relating to the Foreign Relations of the United States*, ed. Joseph V. Fuller, vol. 1, *1923* (Washington: United States Government Printing Office, 1938), doc. 568; this was called the Lincheng incident, Bruce A. Elleman, "The End of Extraterritoriality in China: The Case of the Soviet Union, 1917–1960," *Republican China* 21, n° 2 (1995): 69–70.

40 Many Soviet citizens continued to claim diplomatic immunity following the end of Soviet extraterritoriality in China: Elleman, "The End of Extraterritoriality."

41 The American Commissioner on Extraterritorial Jurisdiction in China (Strawn) to the Secretary of State', 16 April 1926, *Papers Relating to the Foreign Relations of the United States*, ed. Joseph V. Fuller, vol. 1, *1926* (Washington: United States Government Printing Office, 1941), doc. 751.

regain full sovereignty. Yet they could not recommend the immediate abrogation of extraterritoriality.[42]

The report acknowledged the reform of China's legal code and court system which had begun under the Qing dynasty and was continued under the Chinese Republic, yet the report was concerned more about China's tumultuous political situation.[43] Furthermore, the Commission believed that the military acted with impunity, and had during the process of the Commission arbitrarily executed a High Court judge and several notable newspaper editors in Beijing alone. The Commission concluded that until the rights of foreigners could be guaranteed by an extension of the modernised court systems already implemented in major urban areas, and could guarantee the security of foreigners from the arbitrary actions of the army, only then could extraterritoriality be repealed.[44]

The U.S. Secretary of State, Frank B. Kellogg reiterated the U.S. commitment to abrogating the capitulations in the future.[45] The inexorable global decline of extraterritoriality in the 1920s had left China behind, much to the anger of its new nationalist government. The Commission on Extraterritoriality had operated in Beijing, the Capital of the internationally recognised Beiyang Government, but in the months following its publication, it was beset by its rival government in Nanjing led by General Chiang Kai Shek. The "Northern Expedition," led by the nationalist Kuomintang sought to reunify China, ending the Beiyang Government and the warlordism that dominated northern China. By December 1928, China had been nominally reunified under the Kuomintang, with Chiang Kai Shek at the Government's head, although China remained riddled with factionalism.

International recognition passed swiftly to the new Government in Nanjing, with promising signals from the Western powers to negotiate an end to the capitulations. A new treaty with the United States in 1929 would render China back its tariff autonomy, which had been removed in 1903 following the Boxer Rebellion.[46] Throughout 1929, secondary European powers such as Belgium, Italy, Denmark, Portugal and Spain all concluded new agreements with

42 Report of the Commission on Extraterritoriality in China, 16 September 1926, Hathi Trust, https://hdl.handle.net/2027/uc1.$b47432?urlappend=%3Bseq=124.

43 Kayaoğlu, "Westphalian Eurocentrism," 163–164.

44 Report of the Commission on Extraterritoriality in China, 16 September 1926, Hathi Trust.

45 Alma Blabon et al. versus the United States (United States Court of Claims, 3 June 1959), RG 59/A1 5387, NARA.

46 Harold S. Quigley, "Recognition of Nationalist China by the United States," *Current History (1916–1940)* 28, n° 6 (1928): 1060–1064.

China to end their extraterritorial rights, but only on the condition that the Great Powers that had commissioned the Washington Conference report on extraterritoriality also signed. This marked a continuation of the policy of the previous Beiyang Government, which had sought to "divide and conquer" the Western powers following the publication of the 1926 report on extraterritoriality by pursuing the removal of the capitulations of the weakest Western powers.[47] However, Britain, France, Japan, and the United States, pushed back against the Kuomintang's demands, acknowledging their aspirations to the end of extraterritoriality, but stating that despite the declaration of China's unification, large parts of China continued to evade the rule of the central government.

Not dissimilar to the conclusions of the 1926 Report, the Western powers stated that they remained more concerned with China's political situation rather than the state of China's laws. On 30 December 1929, the Nationalist Government declared that 1930 would be the year that China would reclaim its sovereignty and that the process of unilaterally abolishing extraterritoriality would commence on 1 January.[48] The unilateral action against the capitulatory powers backfired. Whereas the Beiyang Government's "salami tactics" of picking off the weaker European powers had seen relative success, the unilateral declaration pushed the Great Powers into greater cooperation.[49]

The United States and Britain, the main negotiating powers, resisted ending their extraterritorial privileges but also prepared an organised retreat. The British negotiator, Miles Lampson, was ordered to retain criminal extraterritoriality, sacrificing civil cases. Moreover, negotiations centred on surrendering certain jurisdictions, with the British ready to release Canton, Hankow, and Tientsin, rather than releasing the most significant international settlement at Shanghai.[50] These settlements combined represented 90% of the Western citizens living in China, but Shanghai's International Settlement was the most significant. The U.S. negotiating position intended to place safeguards in the draft treaty that would absolve Shanghai and Tientsin from the abrogation of extraterritoriality for a decade, a decision that the British resisted.[51]

The instability in China became a particularly difficult negotiating point. The Western Powers argued that they could not abandon consular justice if

47 Fishel, *The End of Extraterritoriality*, 129.

48 Quincy Wright, "The End of Extraterritoriality in China," *The American Journal of International Law* 37, n° 2 (1943): 286–289.

49 Fishel, *The End of Extraterritoriality*, 165, 170.

50 Substance of Instructions Sent to Miles Lampson, 7 March 1931, FO 115/3397/239/1, TNA.

51 Fishel, *The End of Extraterritoriality*, 183; Foreign Office, Memorandum F5330/34/10, 5 October 1931, FO 115/3397/239/1, TNA.

there were no guarantees that China's new legal codes could be enforced. This issue was compounded by the fragility of the new Nationalist Government, with the Powers reluctant to surrender their privileges to a regime that could potentially fold at any moment. Conversely, the Kuomintang had staked a considerable amount of political capital on restoring China's sovereignty by abolishing the capitulations before the Party Conference in May 1931.[52] This coincided with the rapid introduction of five new modern legal codes that were implemented between 1928 and 1931.[53] Attempts to negotiate the Chinese ultimatum were thus fraught and culminated in an extension of the deadline to early 1931 to submit a revision of the existing treaties.

Western concerns about the new Nationalist Government's stability were vindicated when a faction of the Kuomintang in Guangzhou challenged Chiang's new provisional constitution, leading to a breakaway rump state. The lead negotiator for the Chinese in Washington DC, Dr Wu, resigned, aligning himself with the Guangzhou regime.[54] British and American negotiators, now working increasingly in tandem, continued to stall negotiations throughout the summer of 1931. However, the Japanese invasion of Manchuria following the Mukden incident in September put a halt to negotiations over extraterritoriality. By the end of the year, the Chinese Government also accepted that talks over the future of extraterritoriality would be temporarily suspended.[55]

China's war with Japan effectively nullified negotiations with the Western powers, but the resulting conflicts itself did much to effectively end the practice of extraterritoriality. The British now openly negotiated with the United States to stop the negotiations with China, doubting whether the central government would survive the Japanese invasion.[56] Japanese Manchuria, now a puppet state of Japan called Manchukuo, extended extraterritorial rights to Westerners living within it. However, Western states' refusal to recognise Manchukuo under the U.S. "Stimson Doctrine" and the League of Nations resolution of non-recognition meant that extraterritorial rights in Manchukuo were only guaranteed for Japanese nationals, and were applied to other foreign nationals on an ad hoc basis.[57] By 1937, the Japanese had abrogated extraterritoriality in

52 Substance of Instructions Sent to Miles Lampson, 7 March 1931, FO 115/3397/239/1, TNA.

53 Kayaoğlu, "Westphalian Eurocentrism," 178.

54 Fishel, *The End of Extraterritoriality*, 184.

55 Ibid., 186–187.

56 Extraterritoriality China, 28 December 1931, FO 115/3397/239/1, TNA; Cabinet 92 (31), 16 December 1931, 9, CAB 23/69/21, TNA.

57 Fishel, *The End of Extraterritoriality*, 189–190.

Manchukuo, including for its own nationals, following extensive changes to the legal system and insurance that the judiciary was sympathetic to Japan.[58]

This principle of Western non-recognition of Japanese conquests, coupled with Japan's growing expansion into China throughout the 1930s led to a *de facto* termination of extraterritorial privileges across much of China. By 1935, the Japanese declared that extraterritorial privileges would be removed in Manchuria for states refusing to recognise Manchukuo, an act which they carried out in 1937, despite protestation from the United States, which continued to operate its Consular courts after the abrogation.[59] The outbreak of Japan's full scale invasion of China in 1937 was to quickly envelope major cities with large expatriate communities, with Beijing and Tientsin (Tianjin) falling to Japanese forces within a month, followed soon by Shanghai. Extraterritorial privileges were now retained not to protect foreigners from Chinese laws, but from the Japanese armed forces, with foreign powers being allowed to garrison troops in their concessions under the Boxer Protocol.[60]

Japan's conquered territory in China were placed under a new Chinese puppet government in Beijing, which the foreign powers again refused to recognise. However, with the vast majority of expatriates residing in areas under Japanese occupation, Japan pressured Western states to recognise its new puppet government, in exchange for retaining their extraterritorial rights.[61] This pressure intensified following the fall of France to Nazi Germany in the summer of 1940, and the Japanese occupation of French possessions in Asia.[62] On 18 July 1940, a month following France's defeat, the new British Prime Minister, Winston Churchill, raised the issue of extraterritoriality in Parliament, declaring Britain's intention to relinquish its extraterritorial privileges in China following an end to the War.[63] This was seconded the day after by U.S. Secretary of State Sumner Welles.[64]

The accelerating significance of abolishing the privileges during the conflict, contrary to policy since 1931, had been twofold. In March 1940, Japan established yet another Chinese puppet state, this time for territories conquered in the Chinese heartland, led by an ex-Chinese nationalist, Wang Jing-

58 Thomas David DuBois, "Inauthentic Sovereignty: Law and Legal Institutions in Manchukuo," *The Journal of Asian Studies* 69, n° 3 (August 2010): 764.

59 Fishel, *The End of Extraterritoriality*, 191.

60 Watt, *How War Came: The Immediate Origins of the Second World War, 1938–1939*, 356–59 Ibid., 196–197.

61 Ibid., 203–205.

62 Ibid., 205–206.

63 Transit of War Material to China (Hansard, 18 July 1940), cc399–401.

64 Fishel, *The End of Extraterritoriality*, 207.

wei from occupied Nanking. The use of Asian puppet governments played into Japanese propaganda that it was constructing an "East-Asian Co-Prosperity Sphere" under the slogan "Asia for the Asiatics." Despite the fallacious nature of the Co-Prosperity Sphere, the continued existence of extraterritorial rights for Westerners provided useful material for Japanese propagandists that highlighted the inability and subservience of Kuomintang to the Western Allies.[65] Following Japan's attack on Pearl Harbour as well as European colonial possessions in Asia in December 1941, most of the Western expatriate community in China came under Japanese occupation.

The entry of the U.S. and Britain into the War in Asia changed the calculus towards revising the capitulations. Initially the British Foreign Office saw a move to abolish extraterritoriality when British influence in East Asia had been effectively wiped out as a sign of weakness.[66] Yet the fact that extraterritoriality was now *de facto* extinguished and the unpopularity of attempting to reimplement it once the conflict was over eased the idea of abrogating it.[67] A decade prior, Britain and the U.S. had worked together to slow negotiations with China, now they became competitors, fearing that one would abrogate before the other.[68] Britain approached the United States in April 1942 to rekindle discussions on abrogating extraterritoriality in China but with the hope of retaining privileges in Shanghai.[69] The United States decided to coincide the announcement with the anniversary of the founding of the Republic of China on 10 October 1942. The decision to surrender extraterritorial rights was received warmly by Chiang Kai Shek, who wrote to Roosevelt, stating that China was finally "an independent and democratic nation," which had gained "equality among the United Nations."[70]

Britain and the U.S. formally abrogated their extraterritorial rights on 11 January 1943, which was quickly mocked by Wang Jingwei's puppet regime, claiming that it was an empty gesture, and that Japan had done more to

65 Special To The New York Times, 'ASSERTS JAPANESE WOULD CHAIN CHINA', *The New York Times*, 12 January 1942. Alma Blabon et al. versus the United States (United States Court of Claims, 3 June 1959), RG 59/A1 5387, NARA.

66 Viscount Halifax to All Consular Posts in the Continental United States, 9 October 1942, FO 115/3514, TNA.

67 Turan Kayaoğlu, *Legal Imperialism: Sovereignty and Extraterritoriality in Japan, the Ottoman Empire, and China*, reprint edition (Cambridge: Cambridge University Press, 2014), 183–184.

68 Alma Blabon et al. versus the United States (United States Court of Claims, 3 June 1959), RG 59/A1 5387, NARA.

69 Fishel, *The End of Extraterritoriality*, 209.

70 Telegram from Chiang Kai Shek to President Roosevelt, 13 October 1942, FO 115/3514, TNA.

advance the abolition of extraterritoriality through attacking the West rather than negotiating with it like the Kuomintang. Nevertheless, the decision precipitated a reaction from the Axis powers, with Japan racing to sign the abrogation of its extraterritorial rights within Wang Jingwei's puppet regime two days before the Allied signing. Italy followed suit on 14 January as did Vichy France on 23 February, with both officially returning their legation areas to the Chinese puppet regime in Nanking.[71] By the end of the Second World War, the remaining minor European states yet to repeal their capitulatory treaties with China did so, marking a symbolic end to the era of extraterritoriality.

6 Conclusion

The continuation of extraterritoriality in China into the 1940s marked it as a seeming exception to rapidly changing legal norms around its practice. By the late 1920s, extraterritoriality had been effectively repealed in many jurisdictions, revealing that a normative shift had taken place after the First World War, with states subject to such treaties feeling emboldened to challenge their capitulations. Western jurists and negotiators too, often admitted that they felt the system of extraterritoriality was antiquated, and yet chose to perpetuate it further.[72]

Nonetheless, it can be difficult to disaggregate whether political factors, conformity to Western legal standards, or a paradigm shift towards capitulatory regimes were the primary cause for the rapid end of extraterritoriality. In every presented case, extraterritoriality was only repealed following the introduction of new Westernised legal codes. Only the Ottoman Empire attempted to unilaterally repudiate the capitulations without having fully reformed its legal system, and, would see the capitulations reintroduced after the First World War. Yet in the aftermath of the Great War, it was evident in the case of Turkey and Persia, both of which were able to force an end to their capitulatory treaties, that the Western powers continued to have considerable doubts about the new legal codes but accepted the demise of extraterritoriality for political expediency.

---

71 Fishel, *The End of Extraterritoriality*, 213–214.

72 Here the British Consul admitted sympathising with Persia's attempt to rectify its position as a "semi-civilised" state: Consul-General Bristow to Sir R. Clive, 26 May 1927, CO 732/27/6, TNA. This is evident in the case of Siam in Wolcott Homer Pitkins, *Siam's Case for Revision of Obsolete Treaty Obligations Admittedly Inapplicable to Present Conditions.* (New York : s.n., 1919), http://archive.org/details/siamscaseforrevioopitk.

But it was China which marked the epitome of the political nature, rather than the conformity of Western legal norms, as the basis for ending extraterritoriality. The abrogation of 1943 was essentially a war measure following the *de facto* demise of extraterritoriality following Japanese occupation. From the outset of China's attempts to renegotiate its treaties in Paris in 1919, the negotiations and reflections of the Committee to assess China's "readiness" to try foreigners, rested more on the Chinese state's capacity to enforce the law within its territories, rather than the form of the legal system and the content of its laws. However, the focus on state capacity was a double edge, that being the ability of the state to negotiate with the Western powers. Each successive Chinese Government faced significant internal challenges, with the collapse of the 1928 Beiyang Government, and Japan's repeated wars with China thwarting attempts to renegotiate with the Western powers.

Regardless of its legal reforms and the state of its internal stability, China was well represented at the League of Nations, spending a considerable amount of time as a non-permanent member of the Council.[73] For China and other states subjected to unequal treaties, their membership was a statement of their integration into Western international society, but due to the continuation of extraterritoriality, as second-class citizens within it. The League had little direct bearing on challenging extraterritoriality multilaterally. Yet League membership challenged the "normative hierarchy" that extraterritoriality had previously inferred, provided a regular channel of diplomatic communication, and on occasion clashed with extraterritoriality when it hampered international resolutions.

Despite the League's global nature, Western states continued to closely operate when it came to guarding their capitulatory privileges. This is particularly evident in the case of Britain and the United States in China, or Britain and France in Siam. Moreover, Western states often served to check other Western states if they considered abrogating extraterritoriality, such as the resistance to Britain's attempts to end consular jurisdiction in Egypt. In this regard, extraterritoriality became a self-reinforcing practice as Western states resisted attempts to abolish it. Finally, the Interwar years did not mark an outright end of extraterritoriality but often its evolution. Extraterritorialities supposedly transitional nature often transitioned to Mixed Courts rather than seeing an outright end to extraterritoriality. Nonetheless, these cases were outliers and not representative of what had once been a global norm. Extraterritorial courts continued to linger in places such as the international zone

73 Kayaoğlu, *Legal Imperialism*, 159.

of Tangier, or the Gulf states until the 1970s, the vestiges of normative hierarchy that had once spanned the globe.[74]

Acknowledgement

The open access publication of this book chapter has been published with the support of the Swiss National Science Foundation.

Bibliography

Baharna, H. Al, ed. *British Extra Territorial Jurisdiction in the Gulf 1913–1971: An Analysis of the System of British Courts in the Territories of the British Protected.* Slough: Archive Editions, 1998.

Bowden, Brett. *The Empire of Civilization: The Evolution of an Imperial Idea.* Chicago: Chicago University Press, 2009.

Brinton, Jasper Yeates. *The Mixed Courts of Egypt.* New Haven, CT: Yale University Press, 1930.

Brown, Nathan J. "The Precarious Life and Slow Death of the Mixed Courts of Egypt." *International Journal of Middle East Studies* 25, n° 1 (1933): 33–52.

Bull, Hedley, and Adam Watson, eds. *The Expansion of International Society.* Oxford: Oxford University Press, 1985.

DuBois, Bruce A. "The End of Extraterritoriality in China: The Case of the Soviet Union, 1917–1960." *Republican China* 21, n° 2 (1995); 65–89.

Erpelding, Michel. "Mixed Courts of Egypt." *Max Planck Encyclopedia of International Procedural Law,* edited by Hélène Ruiz Fabri. Oxford: Oxford University Press, 2020. https://opil.ouplaw.com/display/10.1093/law–mpeipro/e2711.013.2711/law–mpeipro–e2711.

Fishel, Wesley R. *The End of Extraterritoriality in China.* Berkeley, CA: University of California Press, 1952.

Gidney, Thomas, ed. *"An Anomaly among Anomalies": Colonial Membership of the League of Nations.* Geneva: Graduate Institute of International and Development Studies, 2021.

Gong, Gerrit W. *The Standard of "Civilization" in International Society.* Oxford: Clarendon Press, 1984.

74 *British Extra Territorial Jurisdiction in the Gulf 1913–1971: An Analysis of the System of British Courts in the Territories of the British Protected ... Era,* ed. H. Al Baharna (Slough: Archive Editions Ltd, 1998).

Hell, Stefan. *Siam and the League of Nations: Modernisation, Sovereignty and Multilateral Diplomacy, 1920–1940*. London: River Books, 2010.

Kaufmann, Alison Adcock. "In Pursuit of Equality and Respect: China's Diplomacy and the League of Nations." *Modern China* 40, n° 6 (2014): 606–638.

Kayaoğlu, Turan. "Westphalian Eurocentrism in International Relations Theory." *International Studies Review* 12, n° 2 (2010): 193–217.

Kayaoğlu, Turan. *Legal Imperialism: Sovereignty and Extraterritoriality in Japan, the Ottoman Empire, and China*. Cambridge: Cambridge University Press, 2014.

Keene, Edward. "The Standard of 'Civilisation', the Expansion Thesis and the 19th-Century International Social Space." *Millennium* 42, n° 3 (2014): 651–673.

Muslu, Zülâl. "The Mixed Arbitral Tribunals and Turkey: Negotiating the International Identity of the Young Republic under the Sèvres Syndrome." In *The Mixed Arbitral Tribunals, 1919–1939*, edited by Hélène Ruiz Fabri and Michel Erpelding, 65–89. Baden-Baden: Nomos, 2023.

Pitkins, Wolcott Homer. *Siam's Case for Revision of Obsolete Treaty Obligations Admittedly Inapplicable to Present Conditions*. New York: [s.n.], 1919.

Quigley, Harold S. "Recognition of Nationalist China by the United States." *Current History (1960–1940)* 28, n° 6 (1928): 70–88.

Sayre, Francis Bowes. "The Passing of Extraterritoriality in Siam." *American Journal of International Law* 22, n° 1 (1928): 70–88.

Suzuki, Shogo. *Civilization and Empire: China and Japan's Encounter with European International Society*. London: Routledge, 2009.

Wright, Quincy. "The End of Extraterritoriality in China." *The American Journal of International Law* 37, n° 2 (1943): 286–289.

Watt, Donald Cameron. How War Came. The Immediate Origins of the Second World War, 1938–1939. Pantheon Books, 1989.

Zhang, Yongjin. "China's Entry into International Society: Beyond the Standard of 'Civilization'." *Review of International Studies* 17, n° 1 (1991): 3–16.

Zirinsky, Michael. "Riza Shah's Abrogation of Capitulations, 1927–1928." In *The Making of Modern Iran: State and Society under Riza Shah, 1921–1941*, edited by Stephanie Cronin, 81–98. London: Routledge, 2003.

Index

Entries are generally in English, unless they are technical terms or proper names. Bold numbers refer to a French text

Common Nouns

Proper Nouns

Places

www.ingramcontent.com/pod-product-compliance
Lightning Source LLC
Chambersburg PA
CBHW071334230926
51849CB00002B/395
* 9 7 8 9 0 0 4 7 5 5 1 8 5 *